*Cambridge Studies in Social Anthropology*

*General Editor:* Jack Goody

# 49

## THE BUDDHIST SAINTS OF THE FOREST
## AND THE CULT OF AMULETS

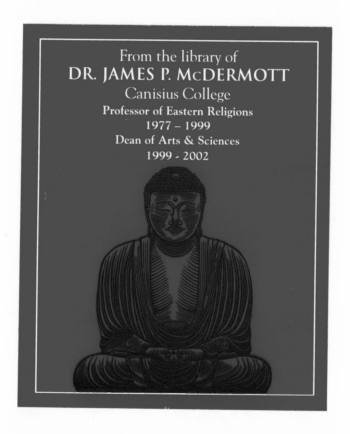

*For other titles in this series turn to page* 415

# The Buddhist saints of the forest and the cult of amulets

## A STUDY IN CHARISMA, HAGIOGRAPHY, SECTARIANISM, AND MILLENNIAL BUDDHISM

## STANLEY JEYARAJA TAMBIAH

*Professor of Anthropology*
*Harvard University*

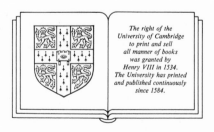

The right of the
University of Cambridge
to print and sell
all manner of books
was granted by
Henry VIII in 1534.
The University has printed
and published continuously
since 1584.

## CAMBRIDGE UNIVERSITY PRESS

*Cambridge*

*London   New York   New Rochelle*

*Melbourne   Sydney*

Published by the Press Syndicate of the University of Cambridge
The Pitt Building, Trumpington Street, Cambridge CB2 1RP
32 East 57th Street, New York, NY 10022, USA
296 Beaconsfield Parade, Middle Park, Melbourne 3206, Australia

First published 1984

Printed in the United States of America

*Library of Congress Cataloging in Publication Data*
Tambiah, Stanley Jeyaraja, 1929–
The Buddhist saints of the forest and the cult of amulets.
(Cambridge studies in social anthropology; no. 49)
Includes index.
I. Buddhism – Thailand. 2. Buddhist monks – Thailand.
3. Buddhist cults – Thailand. I. Title. II. Series.
BQ554.T347  1984  294.3′657′09593  83 – 15113
ISBN 0 521 25984 3 hard covers
ISBN 0 521 27787 6 paperback

The wealth kings get from society
Is a transitory thing.
But the ascetics of the forest
Yield us an imperishable tithe from their austerities.

*Śakuntalā*

It is where the talk is of marrying, or of giving in marriage, that reference is made to such things as that. For whoever, Ambattha, are in bondage to the notions of birth or of lineage, or to the pride of social position, or of connection by marriage, they are far from the best wisdom of righteousness. It is only by having got rid of all such bondage that one can realize for himself that supreme perfection in wisdom and conduct.

*Ambattha Sutta*

Then the Blessed One spake, and said: ''Know, Vāsettha, that (from time to time) a Tathāgata is born into the world, a fully Enlightened One, blessed and worthy, abounding in wisdom and goodness, happy, with knowledge of the world, unsurpassed as a guide to erring mortals, a teacher of gods and men, a Blessed Buddha. He, by himself, thoroughly understands, and sees, as it were, face to face this universe – the world below with all its spirits and, the worlds above, of Māra and Brāhma – and all creatures, Samaṇas and Brāhmans, gods and men, and he then makes his knowledge known to others. The truth doth he proclaim both in its letter and in its spirit, lovely in its origin, lovely in its progress, lovely in its continuation: the higher life doth he make known in all its purity and in all its perfectness.''

*Tevijja Sutta*

# Contents

# Contents

## Part III
### The cult of amulets:
### the objectification and transmission of charisma

## Part IV
### Conceptual and theoretical clarifications

# Acknowledgments

The bulk of the material on which this book is based was collected during field research conducted in Thailand in 1978–9. The book also contains information collected on previous field trips, principally in 1971 and 1974.

First and foremost, I must thank the National Science Foundation of the United States for giving me for the period 1978–81 a generous grant to carry out a research project entitled "Concepts and Manifestations of Power, Authority, and Causation in Urban Thailand." The objectives of this research were: to investigate Thai cultural conceptions concerning "power," "authority," "merit," "charisma," and "causation"; to locate the persons who are credited with these capacities and propensities (such as monks, politicians, administrators, businessmen, physicians, healers, mediums, and athletes) and to find out how they are alleged to have acquired them; and finally to extract the underlying pattern of ideas in traditional fields of "knowledge" and "practice" in such areas as medicine, meditation, ritual healing, astrology, and statecraft and to assess how they fit in contemporary Thailand with modern (Western) ideas and practices.

A rich harvest of information, including written materials, was obtained. Although the present book makes use of only a portion of it, it has at the same time engaged me in textual studies and library research in the United States after my return from Thailand. I hope in future years to report on other aspects of the researches that have so far not been committed to writing.

I am greatly indebted to my wife, Mary Wynne, who helped me in both field and library research, and to my field assistants in Thailand, Thanin Vijayangkura, Somchai Shinatrakool, and Kosol Meekun. Thanin in particular was my indispensable and constant companion in Bangkok on our visits to monasteries, slums, bazaars, government offices, schools of traditional medicine, cult centers and shrines, meditation hermitages, and the consulting rooms of astrologers.

As usual, many of my Thai friends known from past visits gave me their time and cooperation. Let me mention just a few: Dr. Chancha Suvannathat, Director of the Behavioral Science Research Institute at Sri Nakharinwirot University, for

# Acknowledgments

giving me office space and other facilities and help in recruiting assistants; the late Tahwon Koedkietpong, who did some translations for me from Thai into English; Sumitr Pitiphat, whose generosity, knowledge, hospitality, and friendship were enjoyed by all the members of my family; Sathienpong Wannapok, an old friend, who some years ago accompanied me to North and Northeast Thailand and instructed me; and, finally, Sulak Srivarak, Somdet Phra Rajavaramuni, and Dr. Akin Rabibhadana.

The analysis and writing of this book have taken some four years, and I am grateful to the John Simon Guggenheim Memorial Foundation for awarding me a fellowship that freed me from teaching duties in the spring term of 1982 and thereby enabled me to complete this book. I thank Professor Karl Lamberg-Karlovsky, Director of the Peabody Museum at Harvard, for bearing the costs of photographs and figures prepared by his staff. I also thank many secretaries in the Department of Anthropology at Harvard for patiently decoding my scrawl and typing the manuscript, especially Carol Kouffman, Donia Carey, Beryl Noble, and Jane Trahan.

It is with great pleasure that I acknowledge the expert editorial assistance given by Dan Rosenberg and Alan Trevithick; the critical linguistic assistance given by Michael Rhum, who standardized the transcription of words in Sanskrit, Pali, and Thai; and the translation of certain pieces of writing from French into English by Debbie Tooker.

I owe a large debt to Professor C. F. Keyes, who gave a close reading to my first draft and offered many useful suggestions for its improvement.

While admitting to the benefits I have received from these scholars, I must also relieve them of any blame for errors of fact and interpretation contained in this book.

I thank my family – Mary Wynne, Jonathan, and Matthew – for tolerating my seclusions and absences while working on this book.

The Thai people regularly perform a rite called *waj khrū* (paying respect to one's teacher). On this occasion, I should like to acknowledge all that I owe to my first teacher in Sri Lanka, Professor Bryce Ryan, who subsequently also taught me at Cornell University. In the early fifties Professor Ryan introduced the disciplines of sociology and anthropology to the University of Ceylon and taught me (and several others) in a "deracinated" condition that the study of one's own people and traditions in the villages of Asia is a most absorbing voyage of discovery. I dedicate this book to him as my teacher, friend, and sponsor.

# Note on transcription

In this book, Pali and Sanskrit terms are romanized according to the generally accepted system. Thai terms are romanized according to a system based on the "general system" published by the Siam Society in its *Journal* of July 1935 (Vol. 28, pt. 1). The main modifications are: the use of *au* for *ǫ* (except for *ǫi*, which is written *oi*, and in certain place names, such as Nakhon for Nakhāun); the use of *ue* for *u'*; and the use of the macron to indicate long vowels. Due to the exigencies of typesetting, long vowels written as digraphs have two macrons as follows: *āū, ūē, āē,* and *ōē*. Efforts have been made to keep spelling as consistent as possible, but the spelling of place and personal names does not always conform to this system due to the vagaries of the printed sources used. The spelling of personal names, of course, follows the individual's preference wherever known.

# 1

## Introduction and manifesto

Although it stands by itself and is an autonomous whole, this book should also be regarded as complementary to my previous effort, *World Conqueror and World Renouncer: A Study of Buddhism and Polity in Thailand against a Historical Background.*[1] At various points it intersects with themes and issues developed in the earlier one: These intersections are indicated in footnotes. Together this book and its predecessor should fuse into a larger cumulative whole.

*World Conqueror and World Renouncer* was essentially a discussion of the dialectical relations between the Buddhist *saṅgha* (order of monks) and the Thai polity, whose apex was kingship, during the nineteenth and twentieth centuries. The Thai polity was a member of the larger family of Theravāda Buddhist polities of South and Southeast Asia. These polities shared certain presuppositions and values regarding their constitution, of which the most prominent was a symbiosis and mutuality between the *saṅgha* as an order of monks dedicated to the vocation of liberation and the king as a righteous ruler whose obligation was to protect and secure the religion of the Buddha as the special treasure of his people. The importance of this overarching principle that characterized these Buddhist polities prompted me to outline in the first part of *World Conqueror and World Renouncer*, so as to serve as a doctrinal and historical backdrop, the normative ideas developed and/or embedded in early Buddhism concerning kingship, society, and polity, the relations between the *bhikkhu* (monk) and laity, and the constitution of monastic communities and their relations to the larger sociopolitical context. By "early Buddhism" I did not mean Buddhism at its very beginning or during the life of Buddha – even the experts know too little about this time of origins – but Buddhism as it had crystallized by the time the Pali canon – or at least most of it – had been composed.

Early Buddhism as demarcated by Max Weber was roughly the time immediately anterior to the reign of Emperor Aśoka, and I am happy to accept this periodization. My reading of the canonical texts of early Buddhism convinced me that, although most of them have to do with the monk's vocation (as one

I

would expect of a literature composed by monks primarily for monks), yet they contained seminal and fateful value statements and characterizations of ideal Buddhist kingship, and of the relation between kingship and *Dhamma* (morality/ duty) and the social order, in *contradistinction* to the Brahmanical theory of society and kingship; the relation between *Dhamma* and *artha* (instrumental politico-economic action); and the relation between *brāhman* and *kṣatriya* ruler. These embryonic but germinal ideas were realized in the Aśokan era and came to fruition at that time. Aśoka was by no means a historical accident or the agent who for the first time gave a political dimension to Buddhism, as was postulated by Weber. Moreover, in the eyes of Buddhists over the centuries, ever since the Aśokan era, a certain ideological mold regarding kingship and *saṅgha*, religion and polity, had set and acted as a persisting and perduring influence on the Buddhist polities of South and Southeast Asia. The theme of continuities and transformations, investigated from a classical point of reference and departure in early Buddhism, as stated above, seemed to be a meaningful way to study the trajectory of Southeast Asian Buddhist kingdoms, their tensions, and their dynamics.

The patterns I established in *World Conqueror and World Renouncer* with regard to the relations between *saṅgha* and polity were incomplete in one respect. There, I mostly dealt with the collaborations and ruptures between the king and that part of the *saṅgha* which we may in shorthand call the official monastic establishment; that is, the town-and-village-dwelling monastic communities insofar as they became a part of a looser or tighter ecclesiastical hierarchy, whose leaders were concentrated in the political capitals and who by and large buttressed and legitimated kingship. Phases of "purification" and "revival" of religion, as well as of "decline" of the ordination "lineages" of monks, were treated as part of the dialectical relations between king and political authority, on the one side, and the *saṅgha*, internally subdivided on sectarian lines, on the other.

The incompleteness of this story consists in not highlighting or focusing on a number of polarities: between town-and-village-dwelling monks and forest-dwelling monks; between the vocation of scholarship and books and that of meditation; and between a (more) ascetic and reclusive mode of life and a (more) active laity-oriented life, which tended in various combinations to divide, if not bifurcate, the *saṅgha*. Throughout the history of the Buddhist polities of Sri Lanka, Burma, and Thailand, one grand division of the *saṅgha* – that between monastic fraternities and/or communities labeled as forest dwellers on the one hand and as town/village dwellers on the other hand – has persisted and has affected the pattern and the course of the relations between polity and *saṅgha*. In fact, the relation between polity and *saṅgha* could be construed as having been *triadic* – one side being the dynamic relation between king and the "establishment" *saṅgha*, the second side being the relation between the king and the "forest-dwelling" monastic communities, and the third side being the internal

2

# Introduction and manifesto

dialogue between the town-dwelling and forest-dwelling emphases within the *saṅgha* itself, with their attendant consequences such as disputes about the correct disciplinary rules, the espousal of ascetic practices, the degree of dedication to meditation as opposed to scholarship, and so on. The relation between political authority and the internally segmented *saṅgha* could thus be profitably regarded as a center–periphery dialectic exhibiting a variety of pulsations and oscillations.

As a social anthropologist whose main fieldwork in Thailand was focused on contemporary Thai society, what caught my attention in the early and late seventies, and became the starting point for the investigation that developed into this book, was the great veneration that many Thai in Bangkok – of different social status and educational levels, both high and low, male and female, affluent and poor, powerful and weak – had for a certain number of famous forest monks, recently dead or living, who were acclaimed as saints (*arahants*). They were meditation masters credited with extraordinary wisdom, love, and charismatic powers. These saints, who had lived and worked in humble circumstances on the periphery of Thai society and territory, received the adulation and prostrations of the urbanites of the country's capital, which was the hub of the Thai polity and society and the central arena where power and wealth were won and lost. Concurrently with the acclamation of the saints, I noted two other enthusiasms that were at first sight difficult to reconcile: an increased participation by the laity in Buddhist meditation, a pursuit traditionally relegated to monks, and an intensification of the cult of amulets, a traditional preoccupation now reaching the pitch of fetishistic obsession among those same fevered urbanites. The amulets held in the highest esteem and to which were attributed the greatest efficacy were – apart from certain famous antique and vintage rarities – those blessed by the famous forest saints of modern times. Both the saints and the amulets were common subjects in the popular Thai literature of magazines, books, and newspapers.

In the course of tracing the connections between the charisma and the hagiography of present-day saints, the increasing lay interest in meditation, and the classification and efficacy of amulets, I have branched out in many directions. As in my previous book, one of the paths, or rather a grand highway, on which I travel is both doctrinal and historical. The path of the *arahant*, his vocation and his discipline, his efforts and the fruits of his achievements, are the subject of course of much canonical and commentarial literature. Buddhaghosa's *Visuddhimagga* (the path of purification), composed around the fifth century A.D., serves as a landmark and a beacon of illumination. Furthermore, since Sri Lanka, Burma, and Thailand have had a long tradition of forest-monk communities, I situate my description of present-day Thai forest monks in a broader historical landscape. The historical portions are not so much concerned with telling a chronological story as with discovering certain structural patterns and tendencies that crystallize in various circumstances and social contexts.

3

# Introduction and manifesto

The book is divided into four parts. Part I sketches the classical Buddhist doctrinal concepts of the *arahant*, his path of purification, and his position in a Buddhist hierarchy of beings. It also provides some idea of the known historical accounts of the forest-monk traditions in Sri Lanka, Burma, and Thailand, and extracts from them some ideas to guide the subsequent treatment of Thai phenomena.

Part II, the central portion of the book, deals with the line of famous Thai forest monks in recent times: their biographies; the hermitages they have founded; and the pattern of relations between the meditation master and his ordained disciples, and between the master, as saint or holy man, and the laity. These substantive issues are approached by probing Buddhist hagiography.

One of the most famous forest saints of Thailand, Acharn Mun, is the subject of a well-known biography by one of his disciples, Acharn Maha Boowa. I present a summary of this biography and discuss it as a masterly exercise in Buddhist hagiography. My exegesis of the multiple implications and facets of this piece of hagiography is guided by the view that to do justice to the task a simultaneous study had to be undertaken of the saint and his life as the *subject* of the biography and of the biographer himself as disciple and as the *author* of a work, whose shape was influenced by the larger sectarian circumstances in which he found himself and by the propagandist objective which impelled his writing. The analysis of the dialectic between biography and biographer is at the same time a grappling with the relation between text and context and the weaving of a single totality of meaning.

I have employed the notion of *indexical symbol* to tackle the study of text and context, semantics and pragmatics, meaning that refers back to classical constructs and forward to uses in the present. The concept of *indexical symbol* was first proposed by Burks, who derived it by combining two of the terms in Charles Peirce's threefold classification of signs (symbol, icon, and index). Jakobson labeled the same concept *shifter*, following Jespersen.[2] The main point about *indexical symbols* or *shifters* is that they have a duplex structure, because they combine two roles – they are symbols that are associated with the represented object by a conventional semantic rule, and they are simultaneously also indexes in existential, pragmatic relation to the objects they represent. The dual meanings point in two directions at once – in the semantic direction of cultural presuppositions and conventional understandings and in the pragmatic direction of the social and interpersonal context of action, the line-up of the participants and the processes by which they establish or infer meanings.

Let me illustrate the way in which I have used the notion of *indexical symbol* with regard to the biography of a modern saint, Acharn Mun, as a text. The traditional accounts of the lives of Buddha himself, and of other famous Buddhist saints, have as models to some degree influenced the actual life of our Thai saint as well as the retrospective account of his disciple. At this level of exegesis, a

4

passing glance at the conventions of the Christian hagiography of medieval saints is also informative.

The scrutiny of present-day pragmatics and indexical uses to which hagiographies are put takes me into the sectarian affiliations of the biographer (and his teacher, the saint) and into the sectarian rivalries and differences between Thailand's two major monastic sects, the Thammayut and Mahānikāi, the distinct styles of meditation they sponsored, and their patrons and political connections in the capital. In other words, this pathway of interpretation takes us into the interplay of religion and politics within which the biography has a place. Moreover, the scrutiny of sectarianism in its manifold aspects allows us to see how the seemingly antithetical interests of the laity in practicing meditation and in possessing amulets become reconcilable, if not actually congruent, activities.

In sum, I have employed the notion of *indexical symbol* to comprehend synbolic and semantic meanings, on the one hand, and indexical, existential, and pragmatic meanings on the other hand, as riding on the same form and melding into an amalgam.

Part III of the book is concerned with the cult of amulets and the objectification and transmission of charisma. Sacralized amulets in the form of small images of the Buddha or famous saints, or of medallions struck with the faces and busts of the same, and amulets of other shapes and representations, are an old phenomenon in Thailand. There are classical and medieval classifications and systems of names for this fecund variety of sacred objects – relics, statues, images, *stupa* monuments, etc. – and complex explanations of their roles and uses. These explanations range from their pious consideration as "reminders" to their awed treatment as sacra radiating fiery energy and protective or fertilizing powers. In fact, one finds on pursuing this question that the beliefs and attitudes surrounding amulets are virtually of the same kind as those surrounding famous Buddha statues. I have therefore been tempted to devote one chapter to the myths of origin and the travels of two famous Buddha images – the Siṅhala Buddha and the Emerald Buddha Jewel – which are credited with supranormal powers and which have acted as the palladia of several kingdoms and principalities in Thailand and Laos. In the course of such forays, I hope I have contributed something to answering the puzzling question: What is the orientation of Buddhists to Buddha images, relics, and other sacra? In any case, the answer has to be more complex than the simpleminded proposition that the Buddhists "cognitively" know that the Buddha does not exist but "affectively" feel his presence. And, once again, treating these objects as *indexical symbols* and *indexical icons*[3] enables us to appreciate their semantic and pragmatic meanings and values as an amalgam.

I present a certain amount of ethnography on the manufacture of amulets, the rituals of sacralization they undergo, and the methods by which their powers are activated. These preliminaries bring us to the role of modern Thai saints, forest monks, and meditation masters in the sacralization of amulets and to the uses to which the lay sponsors and possessors of these amulets put them in the life-affirming activities of this world – in the manipulations of politics, commerce, and love, and in the pursuit of both altruistic and selfish goals.

Part IV is devoted to conceptual and theoretical clarifications on the basis of preceding substantive accounts. The first issue is millennial Buddhism, to which we are led by considering the cosmographic and cultic features of the hermitages of some contemporary meditation masters that are spectacularly lodged on the slopes and crests of cosmic mountains and by charting the pilgrim's progress to such a hermitage. The esoteric, cultic, and mystical features of these hermitages composed of circles of disciples and lay devotees show unmistakable similarities to esoteric and "messianic" associations in Burma, and they all raise the question of the possible link between them and the militant and violent millennial insurrections that have been recorded as sporadically exploding in Burma and Thailand during the past couple of centuries.

The facts pertaining to the cult of the amulets, and to the role of Buddhist holy men in the conferment of potency on them, also lead along a second path, this time to general anthropological and sociological theory. The Weberian conception of "charisma" as a gift of grace, as a form of authority that was spontaneous and resistant toward discipline and regulation, does not square at all with the supranormal powers and "charisma" of the Buddhist saints achieved without divine intervention by the undergoing of an ascetic and contemplative regime. This confrontation leads me to propose a typology of charisma that takes into account the proposals of Shils and Eisenstadt.

Penetrating as was his treatment of charisma as an interpersonal phenomenon, Weber was blind to the transfer of charisma to objects, and the sedimentation of power in objects, which mediated social relationships. This was probably because he would have seen amulets, sacra, regalia, and relics as belonging to the "magical religion" of the masses, a fare for which he had no stomach. The question of objectification of charisma or the sedimentation of powers in amulets is more rewardingly treated within the scope of the Maussian theory of the gift and the Marxian conception of the fetishism of commodities. It is hoped that the attempts to place the cult of amulets within the general scope of the fetishism of objects, and the Buddhist conception of the saints' acquisition of special powers within the general scope of theory of charisma, are examples of a fruitful traffic between Indology and anthropology. The Indology consists in viewing these phenomena in their particularity, clothed in their distinctive linguistic and cultural dress, and situated in a long civilizational tradition; the anthropology consists in taking the next step of bringing these phenomena, discerned in their own cultural and historical terms, within the scope of a more general and comparative sociological apperception.

6

# Introduction and manifesto

The book aspires to illustrate several passages – from history to anthropology, from text to context, and from Indology to anthropology. And the author nails to his mast this statement on perspective: I have in my previous writings and in this book as well been influenced by the view that to confine the study of "religion" to the doctrinal beliefs and philosophical constructs is, as Wilfred Cantwell Smith[4] has argued, an unfortunate rationalist Enlightenment legacy that both unduly narrows and pauperizes the phenomenon. For me, Buddhism is a shorthand expression for a total social phenomenon, civilizational in breadth and depth, which encompasses the lives of Buddhist monks and laymen, and which cannot be disaggregated in a facile way into its religious, political, and economic realms as these are currently understood in the West. I am mindful and influenced in this respect by the views of Louis Dumont on Indian society as a hierarchical totality.

I have found that those who espouse the narrow-minded view of religion, as stated above, also frequently have a linear view of the development of Buddhism, from a pure, pristine, philosophical, salvation-search-oriented beginning, un-stained and unsullied by the character and concerns of the social milieu in which it arose, to the later states of ever-widening popularization and vulgarization and deviation from the initial purity, in which are at play all the human passions and this-worldly concerns of the masses. This posture can be baptized as "the Pali Text Society mentality" – although there are extraordinary individuals who be-longed to this society who did not merit this opprobrium – which is not only portrayed by some Western scholars of a puritanical bent but also by some Sri Lankan scholars who have not emancipated themselves from the presuppositions of that "reformist Buddhism" inspired and propagandized by Theosophists with such vintage names as Olcott and Blavatsky and imbibed by the rising middle classes of the southwestern littoral of Sri Lanka.

The proponents of the elitist thesis of the vulgarization of high religious tenets by the masses in whom dark passions of the id surge in an anti-Buddhist rage come in various guises – but the worst are those who propose a historical thesis without practicing history. Unsullied Buddhist principles were formulated in early Buddhism in India; then, after an imaginary leap in time and space, we see distortions and deviations in popular religiosity in Burma or some such outlying region.

In my previous writings, and again in this book, I have tried to demonstrate that the philosophical abstractions of the canonical *suttas* and the elite scholar monks are often reiterated by the patterns of ideas embedded in myths and popular rites; that even the early Buddhism of the Pali canon and of classical commentary cannot be fully understood unless we see it as an interwoven tapestry of biographical, philosophical, mythological, and cosmological strands, so mas-terfully revealed by Paul Mus and his associates; and that if there was develop-ment in Buddhism over time it was informed by both continuities and transforma-tions, the latter being not merely the gross handiwork of the masses but wrought

7

by all parties, elite monks and ordinary monks, kings and court circles, urban merchants and traders, and peasant farmers and artisans, all responsive to their existential conditions and aspirations.

I am in sympathy with the indictment by Peter Brown (in his recent *The Cult of the Saints*)[5] of what he calls the "two-tiered" model of modern scholarship on the religious and ecclesiastical history of late antiquity and the early Middle Ages:

The views of the potentially enlightened few are thought of as being subject to continuous upward pressure from habitual ways of thinking current among "the vulgar" . . . When applied to the nature of religious change in late antiquity the "two-tiered" model encourages the historian to assume that a change in the piety of late-antique men, of the kind associated with the rise of the cult of saints, must have been the result of the capitulation by the enlightened elites of the Christian church to modes of thought previously current only among the "vulgar." The result has been a tendency to explain much of the cultural and religious history of the late antiquity in terms of drastic landslips in the relation between the elites and the masses . . . Applied in this manner, the "two-tiered" model appears to have invented more dramatic turning points in the history of the early church than it has ever explained.

# PART I

## THE *ARAHANT* AND THE PATH OF MEDITATION

# 2

# The Buddhist conception of the *arahant*

The *arhat* (Skt) or *arahant* (Pali) has been glossed in several ways: literally "able, worthy," a person who has reached the goal;[1] "worthy of worship";[2] "one who is entirely free from all evil desire";[3] "the perfected saint";[4] "saint worthy of the respect of all";[5] and so on.

It is part of the received wisdom that pristine Buddhism, possibly a Kṣatriya-sponsored protest against Brahmanical claims of superiority on the basis of divinely ordained birth status and ritual functions, and against Brahmanical purity preoccupations in social intercourse, declared that one is a *brāhmaṇa* by birth, and allowed open recruitment to the order of *bhikkhus* from all ranks and *varṇa* status orders.

Though this pristine Buddhism repudiated the Brahmanical assignment of differently evaluated *Dhammas* (moralities) and vocations for the hierarchized status orders and proclaimed a single liberation quest for all human beings, it nevertheless accepted an inequality of spiritual achievement among human beings and their consequent ranking on the basis of *karmic* action in past lives and in the present.

On this ladder of achievement, the perfected saints are not only placed at the top but minutely differentiated from one another according to their merits. An apt example is "the jewel discourse" (*Ratanasuttam*) of the *Khuddakapātha*, a Theravāda canonical text.[6] For the most part employing binary categories that are asymmetrically evaluated, it proceeds from the inferior to the higher mode of existence, at each level the superior category being the ground for the distinction at the next level. The discourse takes the seven jewels or treasures (*ratanam*) of the *cakkavatti* (universal ruler), as enumerated in the *Mahāsuddassana Sutta*, as a point of departure in order to generate its own hierarchical scheme in which lay persons and renouncers of different achievements and attributes are placed.[7]

The jewel, we are told, is twofold – that "with consciousness and without consciousness." The wheel and gem jewels, gold and silver and so on, are of the second kind: "not bound up with faculties." That endowed with consciousness is a continuum "beginning with the elephant-jewel and ending with the counsellor-jewel." [The divide here is between animals (*tiracchana*) and human beings (*manussa*).] Of the two, the jewel with consciousness is counted foremost, because those without consciousness are used for the decoration of those with consciousness.

Human beings are twofold, consisting of the woman (*itthi*) and the man (*purisa*). And man is accounted foremost "because the woman jewel performs service for the man jewel." The man jewel in turn divides into the house-dwelling (*agārika*) and homeless (*anagārika*) types, and the homeless is accounted foremost because "although a wheel turning monarch is the foremost of the house-living jewels, nevertheless by his paying homage . . . to the homeless jewel, and by his waiting on him and reverencing him he eventually reaches heavenly and human excellence till in the end he reaches the excellence of extinction."

The homeless jewel divides into the ordinary man (*puthujjana*) and the noble one (*ariya*), and then later again into the initiate who is in need of further instruction (*sekkha*) and the adept who does not (*asekha*, i.e., the *arahant*). An adept is also twofold as the "bare-insight-worker" and the "one whose vehicle is quiet." The latter also differentiates into one who has reached "the disciple's perfection" and possesses pure insight and one who has not. Among the perfected disciples, the "hermit enlightened one" (*paccekabuddha*) is accounted superior, but it is "the fully enlightened Buddha" (*sammāsambuddha*) who is accounted the foremost. "Thus no jewel is ever the equal of a Perfect One in any way at all."

Another text, the *Niddesa* (I. *Mahāniddesa* and II. *Cullaniddesa*) provides a list of six ranked *munis*: the *muni* who remains in the house (*āgāramuni*), the *muni* who has left the house (*anāgāramuni*), the *muni* who needs further instruction (*sekhamuni*), the *muni* who does not (*āsekhamuni*), the *paccekamuni*, and the *munimuni*. The *muni* who does not need further instruction is equated with the *arahant,* the *paccekamuni* with the *paccekabuddha*, and the *munimuni* with the *sammāsambuddha*.[8]

That the Jewel Discourse's ranking was not merely academic is attested to by the great Siṅhala chronicle, the *Mahāvaṁsa*, which states that at the consecration of the Lohapāsāda (the Brazen Palace) in Anuradhapura those *bhikkhus* who were "simple folk" (*puthujjanā*) stood on the first story of the building; the "Masters of the Tipiṭaka" (the canon) on the second; those who attained to the first three stages of salvation on the third, fourth, and fifth; and the *arahants* on the highest story.[9]

The *Majjhima Nikāya* attributes to the Buddha a discourse in which he gives a descending scale according to the levels of achievement along the path of salvation and corresponding rebirth chances of several categories of monks, with

# The Buddhist conception of the *arahant*

a concluding allusion to the laymen's reward of being born in heaven.[10] The highest are "those monks who are perfected ones, the cankers destroyed . . . who are freed by perfect knowledge – the track of these cannot be discerned."[11] Next are "those monks in whom the five fetters binding the lower (shore) are got rid of . . . they are attainers of utter *nibbāna*, not liable to return to this world." They are followed by "those monks in whom the three fetters are got rid of, in whom attachment, aversion and confusion are reduced, all these are once-returners who, having come back to this world once will make an end of anguish." The fourth category are monks "in whom the three fetters are got rid of, all these are stream-attainers . . ." The lowest are "those monks who are striving for the *dhamma*, striving for faith and bound for awakening." Finally, ". . . all those who have enough faith in me, enough affection, are bound as though for heaven."

*The Questions of King Milinda*, written in Northern India at the beginning of the Christian Era,[12] has been described by Rhys Davids as "a book of standard authority" which "occupies a unique position, second only to the Pali Piṭakas (and perhaps also to the celebrated work of Buddhaghosa, the 'Path of Purity')." Buddhaghosa, the doyen of Buddhist commentators, mentions the book and cites it as an authority no less than four times in his commentaries. It is therefore interesting that this book, whose aim is clearly didactic, whose popularity and influence are still evident in the Buddhist countries of Southeast Asia, whose coverage of issues is wide ranging, should have devoted a fair amount of attention to the characteristics and achievements of the *arahant*.

It enumerates "seven classes of minds" to illustrate the differential achievements of those engaged in the salvation quest. In an ascending series, the first class is composed of minds untrained in the management of the body or of conduct or of thought. These minds are slow-witted and act slowly because of the "intricate entanglements of wrong dispositions." Each mind is like the slow and heavy movements of a giant bamboo with its overgrown and interlaced vegetation and entangled branches.

The second class consists of those who have attained to right views and have grasped the doctrine of the Master. They are known as *sotāpanno*, the stream-enterers, whose thinking powers have surmounted the three lower stages and/or fetters of delusion, self-doubt, and dependence on rites and ceremonies and outward morality. Each mind is like the movement of a giant bamboo that has a "clean trunk as far as the third knot, but above that has its branches intricately entangled."

The third class is composed of the *sakadāgāmins*, the disciples who will return only once to this world, and then attain *arahantship* before passing away. In these disciples lust, ill-will, and delusion are reduced to a minimum; their minds are like a giant bamboo that has a clean trunk as far as the fifth knot.

Next come the *anāgāmins*, those who will not return again to this world but will attain *arahantship* in heaven. They have gotten rid of the five lower fetters and their minds are brought quickly into play with regard to the ten stages; their minds are like a giant bamboo that has a clean trunk as far as the tenth knot.

From these the fifth class is to be distinguished. It is composed of *arahants* whose stains have been washed away, in whom the four great evils of lust, becoming, delusion, and ignorance have ceased, whose craving for future lives has been broken to pieces, who have reached the higher insight (*pattapaṭisambhidā*), and whose hearts are purified. An *arahant*'s mind is like the movement of a giant bamboo "which has been pruned of the branches arising out of all its knots" and whose smooth trunk is no more encumbered "with the jungly growth of vegetation."

The sixth class is composed of *paccekabuddhas,* who are Buddhas for themselves alone, "dependent on themselves alone, wanting no teacher, dwellers alone like the solitary horn of the rhinoceros, who so far as their own higher life is concerned, have pure hearts free from stain." But these heroes are like crossers of shallow brooks who stand hesitant and afraid in front of a mighty ocean, deep and wide and ever-moving.

The immensity of the ocean is the image of the complete Buddhas (*sammāsambuddha*), whose minds are purified in every respect, whose mastery of knowledge and insight knows no limit, and from whose well-burnished, dartlike minds nothing is hid. And it is through reflection that the inexhaustible knowledge of the Tathāgata is exercised in relation to any task that presents itself.

It can be said that *The Questions* suggests that since the attainment of complete buddhahood is exceptional, and that of *paccekabuddhahood* rare, it is the *arahant* who is held up as the exemplary model for the Buddhist converts to renunciation. In Part II, *The Questions* continues further its characterization of the *arahant*, by first comparing the *arahant*'s condition with that of the lay householder, and then reminding us that the saint is nevertheless human in some of his frailties.

Although a layman, enjoying the pleasures of sense and dwelling with his family, can reach the excellent condition of *arahantship*, yet it is "the recluse who is the lord and master of the fruit of renunciation" and who can accomplish his aim without delay because he is "content with little, joyful in heart, detached from the world, apart from society, earnest in zest, without a home, without a dwelling place, righteous in conduct, in action without guide, skilled in duty and in the achievements . . ." (pp. 57–9).

Moreover, a layman entering the condition of *arahantship* is subject to two conditions: "either that very day he enters the Order, or he dies away, far beyond that day he cannot last." When King Milinda then asks what is to become of a layman who could not on that day find a teacher or preceptor to ordain him, Nāgasena replies in a vein which subtly declares the improbability of the layman's achievement: Since no one can ordain himself as a member of the *saṅgha*, the layman must die just as nourishing food will nevertheless "through indigestion, take away the life of one whose stomach is unequal to it" (pp. 96–7).

Indeed, still later in the exposition, Nāgasena states unequivocally that there is no realization of *arahantship* in one single life without a previous keeping of the *bhikkhu's* vows and that "only on the utmost zeal and the most devout practice of righteousness, and with the aid of a suitable teacher, is the realization of Arahatship attained" (p. 254).

Extraordinary and disciplined adepts they may be, yet *arahants* are subject to all too human limitations and foibles. They suffer from bodily pain but not from mental. They have no mastery over ten qualities that inhere in the body and accompany it from existence to existence: "cold and heat, hunger and thirst, the necessity of voiding excreta, fatigue and sleepiness, old age, disease and death." Nevertheless, the *arahant* is master of mental pain: The mind of the *arahant* is "well practised, tame, brought into subjection. . . . When affected with feelings of pain, he grasps firmly the idea of the impermanence of all things," and ties his mind "to the post of contemplation."

Again, an *arahant* may be guilty of offenses pertaining to disciplinary rules of the Order – such as not fully observing the required etiquette in his dealings with women, imagining the wrong time for the midday meal to be the right time, forgetting to fulfill an invitation he has accepted, mistaking food that has not been left over for leftover food, constructing his cell according to the wrong dimensions – but the *arahant* does not breach "the ordinary moral law"; he does not commit the ten modes of evil action such as "killing, theft, unchastity, lying, slander, harsh language, frivolous talk, covetousness, malice and false doctrine."

As with the heroes of other complex religions, and perhaps precisely because he receives such stress in Theravāda Buddhism, the *arahant* as a perfected monk does not present a transparently clear or consistent image. The archetypal examples of the *arahant* ideal are of course the immediate disciples of the Buddha. They exemplify the theme so strongly stressed in the canonical texts: that their virtues are the result of a disciplined quest by men and women who depended on their human faculties alone. But these same early texts also intimate that the salvation quest could be practiced, and the grasp of the knowledge of salvation could be achieved, in more than one rigidly charted way.

Tradition has it that three disciples of the Buddha had specialized in different aspects of the doctrine and made different contributions to the codification of the scriptures at the First Council: Ananda recited the *Suttas* (sermons or discourses), Upāli the *Vinaya* (monastic disciplinary rules), and Sāriputta the *Abhidhamma* (classical philosophy and commentary). But, for our purposes, a better example is provided by two famous pupils of the Buddha who are coupled from the very beginning, are referred to as the right-hand and left-hand disciples of the Buddha, and are so presented in statuary, murals, and bas-reliefs standing on either side of the Master. They were companion seekers of truth as young Brahmins, and together approached the Buddha to solicit ordination.[13] Moggallāna, the left-hand disciple, became famous for his intense immersion in meditation and for perfecting mystic powers (*iddhi*), which accrue from its practice. Pictures and murals of his feats using supranormal powers for defending the Buddhist faith are frequently found. Sāriputta, the right-hand disciple, is celebrated for his wisdom and mastery of the *abhidhamma* commentaries. We note that, though paired, the preferred valuation, represented by the right hand, is accorded to the man of knowledge. Nevertheless, it is perhaps even more significant that the right- and left-hand traditions stemming from the same Master and divided between those two famous disciples crystallize into two vocations open to monks in institutionalized Buddhism: the vocation of books (*ganthadhura*) and the vocation of meditation (*vipassanādhura*), the concentration on "learning" (*pariyatti*) and the concentration on "practice" (*pratipatti, paṭipatti*).

But this duality tends to evoke another celebrated differentiation between the village dwellers (*gāmavāsin*) and the forest dwellers (*āraññavāsin*). Forest dwelling emphasizes living apart from society and having minimal transactions with laity, while village/town dwelling implies regular interaction, as for instance ensues from teaching laymen the doctrine, performing rites for them, and providing a "field of merit" (*puññakkhetta*) in which laymen may cultivate merit. [14] These two tendencies are associated with two other close disciples of the Buddha – Ānanda, who is linked with a more "worldly" stance, and Revata, the younger brother of Sāriputta, who evoked admiration on account of his hermit's existence.

But this distinction again carries further connotations whereby forest dwelling tends to be identified with the practice of meditation and also sometimes with the adoption of certain ascetic practices (*dhūtaṅga*). Hence the coining of another pair of labels, the ascetics (*paṁsukulikā*) versus the preachers (*dhammakathikā*). As one recent writer has put it, all the first terms in the dichotomies presented designate "the domesticated Sangha: preachers, village-dwellers, and literary specialists," while the latter terms tend to define "a cluster associated with reform: disciplinary fundamentalism, living apart from society, and meditation." [15]

There is, finally, another contrast that fits into this context of discussion – stress on monastic leadership only by seniority versus stress on the claims of charisma. This contrast is represented on the one hand by Kautanya, the first disciple converted by the Buddha, and Mahākassapa (Mahā Kāśyapa) who, though lacking in seniority, was elected patriarch of the Order at the First Council. Ferguson perceptively concludes that: "All these opposing roles reflect real sociological dimensions and strains within the modern monkhood, and thus the arahats can be seen as important symbols of rival but equally orthodox paths to Theravāda Buddhist ends." [16] I may add that such stresses and strains also characterize Northern Buddhism in contrast to Southern: For example, the *Aśokāvadāna* makes quite clear that while the Northern branch of Kashmir and Northwest India held Ānanda, the dispenser of loving-kindness (*mettā*) to be their patriarch, the Southern Indian branch upheld the claims of Kāśyapa, who exemplified strict adherence to the *Vinaya* disciplinary rules. It is congruent therefore that Mahāyāna Buddhism elaborated the ideal of *bodhisattva* and Theravāda the ideal of the *arahant*.

Kāśyapa emerges as an exceptional monk who combined two salient values and emphases that lesser monks would find difficult.[17] He is pictured as both a recluse who kept aloof from the congregations of monks and a watchdog of the community's discipline who remonstrated with offenders. He was a forest dweller who was elected convener of the First Council and codifier of the *Dhamma* after the Buddha's death. He is honored in the Pali tradition as the foremost among those who observed the ascetic acts of purification (*dhūtaṅga*), and it is said that he habitually vowed to observe all thirteen *dhūtaṅga* concurrently. The Buddha honored him by exchanging robes with him. He is said to have possessed the seven physical marks of a Great Man (*mahā-puruṣa*), and he has been immortalized by the mission allotted to him, of awaiting the advent of Maitreya Buddha in order to hand over the robe of Gautama Buddha.

Now the central figure in this book is a contemporary *bhikkhu* who manifests some of the problematic features in the profiles of Kāśyapa and Moggallāna, features that might be seen by historical institutionalized religious interests as difficult to manage and regulate. He is that type of *bhikkhu* who is a forest dweller and distinguishes himself from the establishment *saṅgha* by conspicuously adhering to certain ascetic practices and single-mindedly engaging in meditation. He is credited with mystical powers and becomes the focus of lay followings that are spontaneous and fervent, and as such his hermitage and congregation differ in organization and spirit from the ordinary village or town monastic complex (*wat*).

But such monks in ordinary times are the target of the deprecations, suspicions, and enmity of the established *saṅgha* and the civil administrations – for they tend to escape the net of bureaucratic control and supervision. In fact, the problematic features of the reclusive and ascetic can be discerned in early Buddhism itself, indeed in the time of Buddha himself.

It is said that since some of the early disciples who entered upon the religious life preferred to be recluses, the Buddha permitted them to do so after they had been ordained or had at least some instruction; but they were obliged to remain in contact with the order by periodically participating with other monks in the *uposatha*[18] celebrations. Mahākassapa himself used this reclusive option. And this sanctioning of forest dwelling is said to be the precursor for the founding of the *āraññavāsī* as a separate sect (*nikāya*) in Sri Lanka.

More vexed is the question of ascetic practices and mortification of the flesh (*tapas*). The Buddha himself gained the knowledge of the Middle Path which leads to insight, wisdom, and Nirvāna by rejecting both the life given to sensual pleasures, which is degrading, ignoble, and profitless, and the life given to mortifications, which is painful, ignoble, and profitless.[19] There is the famous encounter between the naked ascetic and the Buddha which is taken as the occasion for denigrating the extant mystic lore surrounding the efficacy of austerities. The practice of austerities is cast in a ludicrous light when this adept of self-torture enumerates twenty-two methods of self-mortification in respect of food and thirteen in respect of clothing from which the ascetic may make his choice. Besides, he castigates his body in other ways – for example: by being a "plucker-out-of-hair and beard," thereby destroying pride in mere beauty of appearance; a "croucher-down-on-the-heels," moving about painfully by jumps; a "bed-of-thorns-man"; or one who is "clad-in-dust" (he smears his body with oil and, standing where dust clouds blow, lets dust and dirt stick to his body).[20]

Nevertheless, self-mortification is a persisting idea and practice in the religious life of India. The individual who subjects himself to an ascetic regime has always in Hindu and Buddhist societies attracted the admiration of the laity. Moreover, asceticism has been always associated with the acquisition of special powers – even those of controlling nature and of coercing the deities. Although the Buddha is said to have rejected austere asceticism, he does not appear to have denied the efficacy of a controlled, ascetic mode of life, if not for all his disciples, at least for those disciples who were inclined in that direction.

The Buddha's steering of the middle course implied the acceptance of different options and paths (within limits of course) that different *bhikkhu* may follow. In fact, with regard to the ascetic practices the *Vinaya* has a not entirely consistent story to tell. Typically the rules are pronounced by the Buddha occasion by occasion when it is brought to his attention that the newly recruited monks gave offense through their unseemly behavior. The *Mahāvagga*[21] reports the case of a *bhikkhu* who embraced the religious life for his belly's sake and for the commodious life that seemed available to the Buddha's disciples. The Buddha prescribed as a corrective that at the *upasampadā* (higher ordination ceremony) the four "resources" or foundations of monastic life (*nissaya*) should be communicated to the candidate:[22]

"The religious life has morsels of food given in alms for its resource: Thus you must endeavor to live all your life." Meals given by lay patrons by invitations and on ceremonial days are extra allowances.

"The religious life has the robe made of rags taken from a dust heap for its resource." Linen, cotton, silk, woolen, and other garments are extra allowances.

"The religious life has dwelling at the foot of a tree for its resource." *Vihāras*, storied dwellings, caves, and other habitations are extra allowances.

"The religious life has decomposing (cow's) urine as medicine for its resource." Ghee, butter, oil, honey, and molasses are extra allowances.

In these sayings, we have perhaps an affirmation of the pristine ideal of the life of a renouncer, when he was an ascetical peripatetic wanderer, and a simultaneous acceptance of the comforts of settled monastic life in villages and towns, which was a later development.

In the *Cullavagga*[23] we have again a famous setting of the norm when a contending disciple proposes to render the disciplinary rules more stringent in five points. Devadatta, the Buddha's kinsman and schismatic challenger, wishing to stir up a division in the *saṅgha*, accompanied by his friends, proposed to the Buddha that he lay down the following restrictive practices as more appropriate for the quelling of passions and as more conducive to arousing the admiration of the lay public. He proposed that the *bhikkhu* should be permanent dwellers in the woods: Whoever went to the vicinity of a village would thereby commit an offense. They should, their lives long, beg for alms and be disallowed from accepting invitations. They should dwell under the trees and not sleep under a roof.[24] They should, finally, abstain from eating fish.

The Buddha's evenhanded judgment was "No, Devadatta. Whosoever wishes to do so, let him dwell in the woods; whosoever wishes to do so, let him dwell in the neighborhood of a village. Whosoever wishes to do so, let him accept invitations from the laity. Whosoever wishes to do so, let him dress in rags; whosoever wishes to do so, let him receive gifts of robes from laymen. Sleeping under trees has been allowed by me, Devadatta, for eight months in the year; and the eating of the fish that is pure in the three points – to wit, that the eater has not seen, or heard, or suspected that it has been caught for that purpose" (*Cullavagga,* VII, 3, 15).

Although Devadatta's rebellion was defeated by Sāriputta and Moggallāna, who brought the 500 dissidents back to the fold, and although Devadatta died in rage bleeding from the mouth, yet it is relevant to note that his show of greater austerity did win over for a time a number of (insightless) ordained *bhikkhu* and lay supporters in the city of Rājagaha, which is a token of the popular admiration for those who mortify their flesh.

Of the perfected and liberated seekers, it is clear that the *paccekabuddha* is the quintessential lonely, wandering, forest-dwelling ascetic. Mahāyāna Buddhism would have little to do with any enlightened being who was not able or concerned to teach others the truth; and though Theravāda has something to say about him, he is nevertheless a puzzling being whose incompleteness is thrown into relief by comparison with the Buddha himself. Kloppenborg cites from the Sutta-Nipāta Commentary[25] these comparisons: The perfect buddha is born only into families of khattiyas (warriors) or brahmans, while the *paccekabuddha* may be born in the families of householders as well. Perfect buddhas are not born in the world period of devolution, they are born in the world period of evolution. *Paccekabuddhas* are born when no perfect buddhas are found or in the time of the birth of a buddha. It is only in times in which no perfect buddhas are manifest that it is possible to attain to the status of a *paccekabuddha*. Though possessed of the knowledge of self-enlightenment, *paccekabuddhas* lack omniscience, which belongs only to a perfected buddha. However they are possessed of supernatural powers, can reach high levels of meditation, and can stimulate others to take up a religious life by indirect instigation and example.

The concept of the *paccekabuddha* provides a context for exploring a strand in Buddhism that may be contrapuntal to the path of learning and village dwelling that became the dominant tradition in the institutionalized *saṅgha* and at times solidified into scholastic dogmatism. Indeed, the regime of personal spiritual development, crystallized as meditative exercises and mystic experiences, came in time to be linked with one strong and marked depiction of that kind of *arahant* who led the reclusive, ascetic, meditative life.

*The Questions of King Milinda* describes certain wondrous powers accessible to the *arahant*, powers deployed for good causes and that fire popular expectations. An *arahant*, while still alive, may out of pity for gods and men make the resolve that such and such wonders may take place at this *cetiya* (the mound erected over his ashes). Then, by reason of his resolve, wonders happen there.[26]

There are the magisterial reminders by the Buddha that false claims to the possession of mystical powers is a grave *pārājika* offense that warrants expulsion of the monk from the order[27] and that mystical powers (*iddhi*), which become available to the meditator when he reaches certain levels of mental concentration, should not seduce him from the higher aim of salvation.[28] And although Buddhist literature throughout the ages has shown an ambivalence toward the pursuit and use of supranormal powers, yet there has never been any doubt as to the Buddha's possession of them. A story in the *Dhammapada Commentary*[29] illustrates these themes. Once the Buddha was asked "Have you not laid down a precept forbidding the performance of miracles?" after he had accepted a challenge to a contest of supranormal powers with some heretics. "I have not," replied the Buddha, "laid down a precept for myself; the precept was intended only to apply to my disciples." He then performed the famous twin feat of Śrāvastī (to which we shall refer later).

Indeed, that these wondrous powers are available to the *arahants* is affirmed in the canonical *Sammana-Phala Sutta* and in the *Mahāparinibbāna Sutta*,[30] the quintessential *sutta* of the entire canon and a vital text to all Buddhist schools, preserved for us in six different versions.[31] To the *bhikkhu* disciples, particularly to his beloved Ānanda, the Buddha reveals that the acquisition of the mystical power of *iddhi*, by which the body can perform actions superior to the ordinary limitations of matter, is one of the fruits of meditation and mental training supported by upright conduct. The Buddha informs Ānanda that he had "developed, practised, accumulated, and ascended the very heights of the four paths of *Iddhi*" and that it was within his capacity to exercise it and prolong his life for the rest of the *kalpa* that had yet to run.

The same claim and promise is periodically reaffirmed in classical commentaries and popular exegeses. We shall take up this theme when we examine some portions of Buddhaghosa's *Visuddhimagga*, but here let me cite as evidence of the persistence of these beliefs Spence Hardy's *A Manual of Buddhism, in its Modern Development*, which expresses what the Siṅhalese characterization of the *arahant* was in the mid-nineteenth century (1853) as gleaned from popular Siṅhalese texts. These texts eclectically synthesize Buddhist notions from several sources and from different times. On the one hand, the *arahants* unmistakably

## The Buddhist conception of the *arahant*

partake of humanity; have bodily frailties; and have burned away their desire, usually after a very laborious exercise of discipline; on the other hand, their achievements afford them supranormal powers.

### Saints in early Buddhism

Lamotte, in a magisterial review of sources,[32] clearly shows that already in early Buddhism a tradition of writing the "biographies" (*avadāna*) of famous *arahants* had begun, and that together with this hagiographical tradition there developed an embryonic cult of the saints, which is attested to as much by evidence from Hīnayāna as Mahāyāna branches of early Buddhism.[33]

It is true, says Lamotte, that the Buddha included the question of whether or not a saint exists after death among the "reserved points" (*avyākr̥tavastu*) and that he asserted that when the body of the saint is broken and its life gone out, "gods and men will no longer see him." But, continues Lamotte, in a vein that is refreshing and an object lesson to many an ahistorical and asociological idealizer of early Buddhism, there was a gap between theory and practice. The Buddha had presented himself as a spiritual master, "he who shows the way," and his disciples made of him "a god superior to the gods." He had confined the divinities to the cycle of transmigration and had reduced them to the level of inferiors, yet his disciples remained loyal to their ancestral and class cults. Nothing could keep the Buddhists from also having their saints, from writing their history, and even from immortalizing a certain number of them. Nothing could keep the communities from preserving the memory of the doctors of the Law whose authority they had known and who had made them famous.

An enumeration of the Buddha's disciples is given in the *Etadaggavagga* of the Pali canonical *Aṅguttaranikāya* and of the *Ekottarāgama*: The chapter lists forty-two *bhikkhu* (monks), thirteen *bhikkhunī* (nuns), ten *upāsaka* (pious laymen), and ten *upāsikā* (pious laywomen), and nominates Ājñāta-Kauṇḍinīya as the first of the members of the order; Sāriputta, the first of the great sages; Mahā-Moggallāna, the first among those who possess supranormal powers; Mahākassapa, the first among those who practice strict discipline; and Ānanda, the first of the scholars; etc.

Now, in the commentaries assigned to this chapter, one finds biographies, some more detailed than others, of these disciples. It is of special interest for us to note that the *Manorathapūraṇī*, which was compiled in the fifth century A.D. by Buddhaghosa as a commentary on the *Aṅguttaranikāya*, contains seventy-five biographies.

Perhaps quite a different point emphasizing the early saints as a collectivity of both men and women is made in the *Thera-* and *Therī-gāthā*, the eighth and ninth books of the *Khuddakanikāya*. These 107 poems in Pali, by anonymous composers, make the ancient saints – both men and women – their mouthpiece. The

21

saints celebrate in these poems the beauty of their ideal – the renunciation of desire, the extinction of passions, the overcoming of suffering, and the peace of *Nibbāna*.[34]

Another relevant text is the *Apadāna*, the twelfth book of the *Khuddakanikāya*. It is a composition in verse in which 550 *thera* and 40 *therī* tell of some of their previous lives and of their final ascension to the state of *arahant*. Lamotte remarks that "the influence of the popular and lay milieu" is evidenced by the fact that these saints attribute their sainthood, not so much directly to their following the path, but to their acts of piety in their previous existences when they offered flowers, water, fruits, and fans to the previous Buddhas. The latter in exchange "predict" their future attainment.

A composition in Sanskrit similar to, but not identical with, the *Apadāna* is the *Pañcaśatasthavirāvadāna*, "Exploits of the Five Hundred Ancients." These saints relate the "fabric of their acts" (*karmaploti*) that led to sainthood, in the presence of the Master, when he summoned 500 of them by air to the edge of Lake Anvatapta a little while before he attained nirvāna. The antiquity of this text is suggested by the fact that this collection of *avadāna* was the object of a Chinese translation executed in 303 B.C. by Dharmaraksa under the title of *Fo-Wo-po-ti-tseu-tseu-chouo-pen-k'i-king*.

The rich postcanonical literature on the early disciples and saints selectively focused on a few from among the potentially large numbers. The most celebrated in central Asia and China more or less is the group called the "ten great disciples," comprising in order Śāriputra, Mahā-Maudgalyāyana, Mahā-Kāśyapa, Subhūti, Pūrna-Maitrāyanīputra, Aniruddha, Mahā-Kātyāyana, Upāli, Rāhula, and Ānanda. They figure as an iconographic group notably in the caves of Touen-houang and are mentioned in Chinese texts that date from around 320 B.C. to the twelfth century A.D.

A matter of some hagiological interest is how in early and later classical Buddhism the "nonexistence" of *arahant* after their death was squared with their perduring "presence" in the world for the benefit of humankind. The tradition holds, says Lamotte, that many *arahant* inhabiting mountain peaks, streams, springs, and ravines, having decided that they had accomplished "what they had to do," decided after the death of Buddha to follow him into *nibbāna*.[35] It was with great difficulty that Mahā-Kāśyapa persuaded 500 *arahant* to remain alive in order to participate in the Council of Rajagṛha and compile the Buddha's teachings. And these too in time passed away.

But the Sanskrit texts show how exceptions were made on behalf of those *arahant* for whom *nibbāna* will be delayed so long as the Law remains on earth. There was the expectation imposed on Mahā-Kāśyapa, as the trustee of the Buddha's robe, that he must again put that robe on the Buddha of the future, Maitreya. Dressed in *pāṁsukūla,* rag-robes of the Blessed, and buried in the womb of Mount Kukkuṭapāda, Kāśyapa is immersed in meditative *nirodhasamā patti,*[36] but he will awake with the coming of Maitreya to accomplish his mission.

22

# The Buddhist conception of the *arahant*

Another *arahant*, Piṇḍola Bhāradvāja, the apostle of Kauśambī, equally must remain on earth as long as the Good Law existed. In punishment for his faults, particularly, his "greediness and his imprudent miracles," he was banished from Jambudvīpa, but he continued to fulfill his duties in foreign lands and to readily appear to all who called him. Two others who may be cited here are the disciple Kuṇḍopodhānīya, who destroyed the treasures of the King Śuṅga Puṣyamitra, who persecuted Buddhism and massacred the religious; and Rāhula, the Buddha's son, who was especially qualified to be heir and continuator of his father.[37]

Thus the idea arose that some *arahant*, for either or both of these reasons – as punishment for an old fault or in anticipation of a future mission – lived a prolonged life that allowed them to engage in a specified activity that furthered Buddhism. They were first of all considered to be the protectors of the Law (at the side of certain deities[38]), and to perform this role they will stay here below without entering into *nibbāna*. They will be witnesses to the faith at the time of "false religion" and of persecutions. They will make the image or presence of the Buddha, and of famous monks, appear; they will speak to the winds, turn dreams into reality, and, when the Maitreya Buddha descends to this world, they will be finally authorized to enter *nibbāna*.

In time, there was a proliferation of the lists of these saints – first numbered at four, these *arahant* protectors of the Law were later raised to eight, sixteen, and then eighteen.[39] There were of course further elaborations. Mahāyāna Buddhism would, for instance, replace the sixteen *arahant*-protectors with sixteen lay *bodhisattva* of Indian origin; led by Bhadrapāla, they preceded the multitude of *bodhisattva* coming from the Buddha's fields in foreign regions, who have at their head Maitreya, Mañjuśrī, Avalokiteśvara, and so on. "We are here," comments Lamotte, "at the point of intersection of the Small and Great Vehicles. One can see how the *arahant* credited with prolonged lives invented by the Hinayanists have opened the way for countless and depersonalized *bodhisattvas* honoured by the Mahāyāna."

With regard to the hagiography of the saints in early Buddhism, we may extract from the foregoing account some stereotyped themes that we may expect to recur in the hagiographies composed later and pertaining to later local saints, even in foreign lands. The saints' attainment is prefigured by a vow taken in a previous life, and this vow is validated by a "prediction" on the part of the Gotama Buddha or one of his predecessors. The saint is destined to a prolonged life of activity in this world, and this long presence is featured as a retribution for some evil *karmic* acts in the past. The individuality of the saint in question emerges in some personal quirks and in the particularity of the task assigned him in the protection of the religion. It seems to me that these notions of a saint's intention being implemented as a long-term project extending over several lives, his cumulative merit of good deeds before his final effort, his committing an evil act that condemns him to a long period of life on earth, also hold a mirror to every lay Buddhist who venerates him. For they hold for each layman as well the

23

possibility of his ascent to *arahantship* at some future time if he committed himself here and now to travel the path. Thus are saint and layman, ordained renouncer and worldly householder – though distinctly divided here and now – united in a Buddhist hierarchy of beings in which the lowest can ascend to the highest over the cycle of rebirths.

## The cult of the saints in modern times

Now of what relevance are these classical Buddhist saints for the life of Southeast Asian Buddhists of our time? Charles Duroiselle, in a report he wrote in 1923 as the superintendent of the Archaeological Survey,[40] had this to say about the popular saints in Burma. He began with the observation that while Mahāyāna was par excellence the religion of *bodhisattvas* and saints, Theravāda Buddhism, because of its austere doctrine stressing the attainment of *arahantship* through the absolution of all passions, did not encourage the saints "which was the reason saint worship has made so little headway in Burma." However, after making the usual derogatory noises of the purist "reform Buddhist" intellectual, and hinting that the corruption stems from early Mahāyāna influence that was anterior to the eleventh century, he concedes that saint worship exists in Burma, usually among the less enlightened, and was characterized by rites, ceremonies, and prayers to saints for whom shrines were constructed. The worshipers "perform all these rites for the obtention of worldly advantages and particular favours."

The saints Duroiselle lists as possessing "power, in the present, of granting to their devotees that which they ask for on the performance of certain rites" are Shin Upagok (Upagutta thera), Shin Thīwali (Sīvali thera), Shin Aṅgulimālā (thera), and Shin Peindola (Piṇḍola thera). Shin Upagok, says Duroiselle, is "the greatest in Burma among the Buddhist saints to whom a particular cult is rendered." The popular tradition carries back the belief in Upagutta to the time of the great Aśoka himself in the third century B.C.[41] It appears that Aśoka, enthused by the extraordinary superhuman power of Upagutta, had an image in his likeness fashioned and made offerings to it; soon after that the custom spread over Burma. "The saint is represented sitting cross-legged with the soles of his feet upwards; he holds his begging bowl in his left hand, while his right hand is held as if in the act of taking the food it contains; his head is slightly raised upwards over his right shoulder, expecting the sun to appear among the clouds." Upagok (Upagutta) is associated in Burma and Thailand with rain making and with protection against the ravages of Māra, and I have documented elsewhere rites addressed to him in a village in Northeast Thailand.[42]

The worship of Shin Thīwali, says Duroiselle (now less burdened by his sense of Theravāda orthodoxy), "though not accompanied by so much eclat and festivities as that of Shin Upagok, is, however, very widespread in Burma. . . . In the time of the Buddha, the thera Sīvali was among those saints who were famous each for a particular gift. The gift of Sīvali, which was the result of a good deed performed in a former existence, was that of all the monks it was he who received the most offerings, of every conceivable kind from the laity. This explains why now the Burmese worship him: the worship of him who received the most offerings and gifts among the monks naturally brings on to his worshiper no small a share of that extraordinary virtue." So it is believed that those who repeatedly recite before his shrine some ten stanzas "receive unexpectedly many presents from friends and relations: they enjoy perfect immunity from dangers and disease; wherever they stay or go, they are beloved by all; in all mundane affairs their words carry great weight; they have no dream but those that are auspicious, bad dreams being averted from them."

"The statuettes of Shin Thīwali represent him as a monk carrying all the requisites of his state, with fan and staff. He is most often placed in a small shrine heavily gilt . . . " We may add to this account the observation that Sīvali is the subject of numerous amulets that circulate in Burma and North Thailand. Shin Thīwali, interestingly, did suffer from the results of a cruel act committed by him and his mother in a past life:[43] His mother carried him for seven years and labored for seven days before she delivered him.

Shin Angulimāla is no other than the notorious robber and murderer whose conversion by the Buddha is told in vivid terms at many places in the canonical and later works. Pregnant women, especially those in difficult labor, have recourse to him. This taker of lives becoming a protector of births is attributed to his seeing a woman in labor and his going to Buddha and telling him with compassion and pity what he had seen. The Buddha ordered him to return to her and make this testimony: "My dear, I do not remember from the moment I became one of the Āryan family (i.e., the order of the monks) having willfully deprived of life any creature." On hearing this statement, the woman was released from her agony. (Angulimāla has the same significance in Thailand, and a special *paritta* chant is named after him.)

Shin Peindola was considered to be a great curer of diseases, and some of his images show him to be holding medicinal fruit. At the time of his writing, Duroiselle found Peindola to be of little importance in Burma and given less veneration than the preceding three.

## The question of latter-day saints

The question of whether *arahants* can arise in our present time is an intriguing one on which monks and laity are likely to give divergent views. In Sri Lanka, it is said that Maliyadeva was the last *arahant*; he is mentioned in the *Mahāvaṃsa* as an *arahant* who lived in the time of King Dutugamunu, the Siṅhala hero of the second century A.D. Gombrich reports that monks who can be characterized as "traditional," and who hold that Buddhism as a historical phenomenon (*śāsanē*) will last only 5,000 years, believe that the "*sāsanē* has already declined so far that it is no longer possible for men to attain *nirvāna*." This opinion was, he reports, "very prevalent among the laity." However, others said that "there *may* still be human *arhats*, but it is unlikely and/or undiscoverable." The general tenor of Gombrich's reporting is that Sri Lankans today find it hard to believe that a contemporary can or has become an *arahant*.[44]

If this information is correct,[45] then the Burmese and Thai peoples seem to be different in their receptivity to the idea of the appearance of *arahants* in their midst at all times, past and present. J. P. Ferguson has correctly observed that Theravāda Buddhism has overwhelmingly stressed the centrality of the *arahant*, the fully perfected monk, and that "in Burma today the *arahant* remains a vital symbol of the religion as found in both contemporary texts and rituals." He also affirms that the same is true of Thailand: "The *arahat* ideal . . . exists as the ultimate model for any living monk, and the more saintly the monk, the more likely he will be assigned miraculous powers by his supporters . . . The excitement generated by the hope that the (*arahat*) ideal will again be manifest in the real is at the heart of the religion."[46]

A contemporary Thai monk meditation teacher and the head of a famous forest hermitage in the Northeast has written a biography of a monk whom he, and many Thai both monks and laity, have acclaimed as an *arahant*. We shall deal at length with the biography later, but let me remark here that, in this biography, the author, after a discussion of the concept of *arahant*, reports that his acclaimed teacher had once told his disciples that "there were many *arahants* who had passed away in Thailand, for example, three in the cave of Chiengdao in the northern province of Chiengmai, two in the caves near the town of Lopburi, one in the Khao Yai mountain in the vicinity of Nakhon Nayok in the Northeast, and another in the monastery of Thart Luang near the Northern town of Lampang."

Now how did our biographer explicate the *arahant* conception? An *arahant*, he tells us, is "a wonderful and supreme person, both to himself and to the three realities of existence. It is very difficult for one of them to appear in the world. An *arahant* is next only to the Buddha in superiority."

*Arahants*, we are further told, can be divided into four types.[47] The lowest is an *arahant* who has achieved the "full-final attainment" and is subject to no more rebirths, but he possesses none of the additional attainments. The second has achieved the minimum requirement stated above, and also enjoys the threefold knowledge of recollection of past lives, clairvoyance concerning the births and deaths of other beings, and insight. The next higher type is blessed, in addition to insight, with the sixfold psychical feats of levitation, claraudience, mind reading, recollection of past lives, and clairvoyance. There is finally the highest type of *arahant* who, in addition to the foregoing, is endowed with four kinds of "fluency of discernment," namely the giving of explanations with regard to causes and to results, fluency in the use of language, and in the methods and techniques of application; he is not only one who has attained salvation but also able to be a supreme teacher.

*Arahants* are believed to have passed away (*parinibbāna*), says our Thai author, in certain distinctive ways. "Some passed away while sitting cross-legged, others while lying on their right sides, and still others while walking or standing. In most cases, however, they seemed to have passed away while lying on their right sides or while sitting cross-legged. . . ." They bid farewell to the mundane world in a serene manner "showing no suffering or restlessness, such as can generally be seen in the cases of ordinary people."[48]

Such currently held notions and expectations are a crucial context for our ensuing study of a certain number of forest monks in Thailand who have combined ascetic practices (*dhūtaṅga*) with the regimen of meditation and have established forest hermitages themselves. In popular conception, some of them have been or are considered to be *arahants*, and they are in the limelight as holy men of charisma. They are persons of near national reputations, at least among the Buddhists.

But my exposition has to begin with a classical paradigm formulated several centuries ago – in a text called the *Vissuddhimagga* – which, as an impeccably orthodox *Theravāda* exegesis of doctrine and practices, has something very complex and more to tell us about the *arahant*. And what it does tell about him has profound implications for our understanding of the popularly acclaimed saints of contemporary Southeast Asia.

# 3

# The Path of Purification

## The ascetic practices

The *Visuddhimagga*, the classical Theravāda treatise on meditation, states in detail the techniques to be employed during meditation, the levels of meditative experience that are achieved, and the pitfalls and triumphs that await the practitioner. This classic has been a principal guide for Buddhist meditators down the ages and constitutes a major point of reference in our study of present-day Thai meditation masters and forest saints.

The *Visuddhimagga*, the work composed by Buddhaghosa in the fifth century A.D., contains a summary and interpretation of the basic teachings of the Buddha contained in the Pali *Tipiṭaka* rendered according to the "*abhidhamma* method." Ñāṇamoli[1] calls it "the principal non-canonical authority of the Theravāda"; it is at the same time "a detailed manual for meditation masters" and a "work of reference." It was composed during the epoch of renascence in Pali studies after a period of decline in literary activity in the early centuries in Ceylon and South India. This period of decline corresponded with the ascendance of Sanskrit composition in Indian Buddhism. By A.D. 400, the time was ripe for a Pali recension of the Siṅhalese commentaries, and Buddhaghosa, coming to Ceylon from India, was apparently the instrument of this Pali renascence.[2]

The legend concerning the test imposed on Buddhaghosa by the Siṅhalese Elders and the manner in which the *Visuddhimagga* was composed indicate its doctrines and teachings are genuinely pristine and have been transmitted without corruption and that the *saṅgha's* ordination lineage has had an unsullied continuity through time. The legend reported in the ancient Siṅhalese chronicle of the Great Monastery, the *Mahāvamsa*,[3] and in the popular Burmese novel *Buddhaghosuppatti*, probably composed in the fifteenth century,[4] states that when Buddhaghosa requested the Siṅhalese Elders to give him all the texts so that he might compose the commentaries, he was given two stanzas to comment upon so as to test his scholarship and orthodoxy. Using those stanzas as his "text," he summarized the Piṭakas and the Siṅhalese commentary in the work called *Visuddhimagga*. In order to test the author's skill, the god Sakka stole the manuscript, forcing Buddhaghosa to write another version, and he stole that again and made Buddhaghosa rewrite a third version. Then Sakka returned the missing two texts, and when all three were compared they were found to be identical in every respect—there being no differences in the chapters, or the order in which the material was arranged, or even in the phrases and syllables of the canonical texts cited. I interpret this tale as not only attesting Buddhaghosa's accuracy, but also, by extension, as proclaiming the unsullied clarity of the Siṅhalese religious documents, preserved and transmitted by an orthodox *saṅgha*, which can admit only a single unambiguous translation at the hands of an exemplary translator. (Indeed, such an ideal is partly at least the inspiration for the number of recensions of the Pali *Tipiṭaka* sponsored by famous kings during periods of purification and revival of religion.) It is fitting, therefore, that after his death Buddhaghosa was reborn in the *Tusita* heaven surrounded by divine nymphs in a golden mansion seven leagues broad.

## The contents of the *Visuddhimagga*

The *Visuddhimagga* as an overall composition brilliantly demonstrates the central Buddhist tenet that knowledge and wisdom are joined with practice and that the practice of the meditative exercises provides the experience and understanding of the doctrinal tenets. Knowledge in the abstract cannot be divorced from and secured apart from practice as disciplined conduct.

There is a tripartite ordering to the *Visuddhimagga*. There is first of all the elucidation of how to systematically cultivate *sīla*, usually translated as "virtue"; next follows the description of the procedures by which *samadhi*, concentration, is cultivated. Finally, there are the instructions for the cultivation of *prajñā* (or *paññā*),[5] insight or understanding. There is not so much a linear as a dynamic relationship between the three objectives.

It has to be understood from the outset that the *Visuddhimagga's* objective is to show the path that leads to purity, and as such it is *primarily* addressed to *bhikkhu* and not laymen,[6] to seekers who have gone forth from home into homelessness. Purification is to be understood as attaining to *nibbāna*, which is "devoid of stains."

The *Visuddhimagga* begins with a verse taken from the canon:[7]

> When the wise man, established well in Virtue (*Sīla*),
> Develops Consciousness (*Samādhi*) and Understanding (*Paññā*),
> Then as a bhikkhu ardent and sagacious
> He succeeds in disentangling this tangle.

Buddhaghosa's originality lay in grouping under these three labels taken from canonical usage the eight elements that make up the Noble Eightfold Path that was expounded as the last of the Four Noble Truths by the Buddha in his very first sermon, the *Dhammacakkappavattana-sutta* (Setting in motion the wheel of truth), which he delivered after he attained enlightenment. Many would hold that the heart of the Buddha's teaching lies in this sermon and that it is therefore appropriate that Buddhaghosa's great work takes it as a point of departure.[8]

Buddhaghosa gives a number of preliminary glosses on what the triad of virtue, concentration, and understanding signifies. For example, we are told that purification "from the defilement of misconduct" is the fruit of virtue, purification "from the defilement of craving" is the fruit of concentration, and purification "from the defilement of false views" is the fruit of understanding. Or again, virtue is the avoidance of "devotion to indulgence of self desires," while concentration surmounts sense-desires, and understanding is the means for "surmounting all becoming."

That the three types of activity stand in a hierarchical relation is clearly expressed in their correlation with "the four paths" leading to, or – better still – the four stations or levels of achievement terminating in, enlightenment: the path of stream entry, the path of once-return, the path of nonreturn, and the path of *arahantship*. Here is the correlation: "Likewise the reason for the states of Stream-entry and Once-return is shown by Virtue; that for the state of Non-return, by Concentration; that for Arahantship by Understanding. For the Stream-enterer is called Perfected in the 'kinds of virtue'; and likewise the Once-returner. But the Non-returner is called 'Perfected in concentration'. And the Arahant is called 'Perfected in understanding.'"[9]

In the rest of this chapter, we shall further elucidate the character of and relation between *sīla, samādhi,* and *prajñā,* but let it be clearly understood that certain portions and themes of the *Visuddhimagga* will be selectively focused upon because of their relevance for the present-day activities of the ascetic forest monks of Thailand. In other words, my presentation of the classical work is selective; at the same time, I maintain that there is nothing in it that distorts the contents of the text.

The last line of the verse cited earlier says that the *bhikkhu* who has achieved the three accomplishments "succeeds in disentangling this tangle" as a "network of craving," which consists of an "inner tangle" that arises from one's own craving and an "outer tangle" that arises from another person's. Buddhaghosa recognizes both internal and external bases for consciousness and extends the analysis by invoking the suggestive metaphor of a bamboo grove (already exploited by *The Questions of King Milinda*) for representing the *entangling and interfacing of the cravings of human beings*. This doctrinal commentary is premised on the recognition of an I–thou duality, of individual consciousness being a product of the interaction of internal and external experiences, of the human condition as an interweaving of beings, from which entanglement liberation is sought. In other words, this quest of negation is not premised on an atomistic view of society, nor does it imply that individual liberation is attainable without an awareness of the larger social condition and its interconnections.

*Bhikkhu* Ñāṇamoli makes a comment that intergrades with this realization. When the Buddhist ascetic goes into seclusion and, first and foremost, practices virtue by "restraining his sense doors," he does not leave the world; rather, "he retreats from the clamour of society to the woods and rocks, he takes his world with him, as though withdrawing to his laboratory, in order to better analyze it."[10]

And at the end of his secluded quest, the ascetic is envisaged by the *Visuddhimagga* as being acclaimed by the world, indeed the cosmos, for his victory resonates through it. The text says that four kinds of benefits accrue from "developing understanding," namely, "removal of the various defilements, experience of the taste of the Noble Fruit, the attainment of cessation, and achievement of the worthiness to receive gifts . . . " (p. 819). The last mentioned is of particular interest to those of us interested in institutionalized Buddhism: Such a person who has developed understanding, says the *Visuddhimagga* in its concluding pages, is "fit for the gifts of the world with its deities, fit for its reverential salutation, and an incomparable field of merit for the world" (p. 833).

## The practice of virtue (*sīla*)

The practice of virtue implies the "restraint of the faculties," and there are several restraints enumerated, such as restraint by the rules of the *saṅgha* (the Pāṭimokkha), restraint by mindfulness (which guards the eye faculty), restraint by energy (by which sense desires when they arise are not allowed to endure), restraint by practicing right livelihood, and so on. Such "nontransgressions" give meaning to virtue as coolness (*sītala*).

It is clear that the practice of virtue is an undertaking addressed to both laymen and monks, though most of the admonitions are addressed to the latter's code of conduct. Buddhaghosa tells the householder that there are five benefits deriving from the perfecting of virtue: He comes "into a large fortune as a consequence of diligence"; his "fair name is spread abroad"; he enters without fear or hesitation "an assembly, whether of khattiyas (warrior nobles) or brahmans or householders or ascetics"; he "dies unconfused," and after death he "reappears in a happy destiny." Buddhaghosa clearly specifies the laity's practice of virtue as their avoiding wrong livelihood and their observing the five precepts as a permanent undertaking, the eight precepts on *uposatha* days, and the ten precepts whenever possible. The benefits accruing to the *bhikkhu* from practicing virtue include his being dear to his fellows "in the life of purity and loved by them" and being "held in respect and honoured by them."[11]

The training precepts for *bhikkhu* are of course more numerous, and expectably the *Visuddhimagga* discourses with meticulous and forensic eloquence on the propriety expected of the *bhikkhu* (and novices) in their conduct toward one another and toward the public. The transgressions toward fellow members of the *sangha* include "jostling elder *bhikkhu*" while standing or sitting or when bathing, sitting in front of them or on a high seat in their presence, walking on a high walk while they walk on a low walk, waving arms while talking, and so on.

The controlled behavior of the *bhikkhu* in demeanor, dress, gestures, and eating is beautifully discussed in this passage, which gives us some sense of the modulated and genteel, even finicky, manners inculcated in men who are at the same time ascetic renouncers positively contaminating themselves with the contemplation of decay and the stench of death and appropriating the rags of the charnel house for their patched-up robes. (Incidentally, the appearance and manners emphasized for a *bhikkhu* sharply contrast with the matted hair, long nails, and ash-encrusted, half-naked body of the stereotype *sannyāsi* of Hinduism.):

Furthermore, a *bhikkhu* is respectful, deferential, possessed of conscience and shame, wears his inner robe properly, wears his upper robe properly, his manner inspires confidence whether in moving forwards or backwards, looking ahead or aside, bending or stretching, his eyes are downcast, he has (a good) deportment, he guards the doors of his sense faculties, knows the right measure in eating, is devoted to wakefulness, possessed of mindfulness and full-awareness, wants little, is contented, is strenuous, is a careful observer of good behavior, and treats the teachers with great respect. This is called (proper) conduct.[12]

The *bhikkhu* is not taken in by externals, neither the "signs" nor the "particulars," he "apprehends only what is really there," such as the ephemeral decaying body that dwells in a woman, laden with jewelry, perfumed and made up, who passes by.[13]

There are delicious exposures of the schemes by which *bhikkhu*, seemingly refusing gifts from laymen on the grounds of their fewness of wishes and needs, actually entice them into showering upon them fine robes by the cartloads. The *bhikkhu* who falsely accepts "out of compassion for the donor" is remorselessly condemned thus: "Such grimacing, grimacery, scheming, schemery, schemedness, is known as the instance of scheming called rejection of requisites"(p. 26).

The *Visuddhimagga* relates many stories of Buddhist saints as illustrations of *bhikkhu* who have fulfilled "the restraint of the faculties." A famous instance is provided by the Elder Cittagutta. He lived in the Great Cave at Kuraṇḍaka, on whose wall there was a marvelous painting on the theme of the renunciation of the buddhas; but over a period of sixty years the monk had been oblivious of the painting because he had never lifted up his eyes, nor for that matter had he seen the great ironwood tree that grew at the entrance to his cave.

The story of the Elder Mahā-mitta is about a reward that results from practicing virtue, in this case in the form of an efficacious result in the mundane world.

In this story, we see a glimmering of the phenomenon that this book tries to describe as a salient issue in Thailand today: the mystical power of the *bhikkhu* who has successfully closed his sense doors and by virtue of that can shower benefits upon those who are slaves of their senses. The Elder Mahā-mitta's mother was suffering from a poisoned tumor, and she asked her daughter who was a nun (*bhikkhunī*) to seek out her brother and ask him to provide some medicine. Mahā-mitta declared that he knew of or possessed no medicine save this: "Since I went forth I have not broken (my virtue of restraint of) the sense faculties by looking at the bodily form of the opposite sex with lustful mind. By this declaration of truth may my mother get well. Go and tell the lay devotee and rub her body." The old woman's tumor shrank away like a lump of froth (p. 40).

## The ascetic practices

The *Visuddhimagga* devotes its second chapter to what are called *dhūtaṅga*, which can be translated as "ascetic practices."[14] These practices are conventionally considered optional today as far as regular *bhikkhu* are concerned. They in fact smack of austerities and have become the hallmark in Thailand of wandering monks who dwell in forests, caves, and wild places and are dedicated to the practice of meditation in seclusion. The Thai expression "*dōēn thudong*" conveys the sense of walking (and wandering) ascetics.

The meditating monk should undertake the ascetic practices, recommends the *Visuddhimagga*, "For when his virtue is thus washed clean of stains by the waters of such special qualities as fewness of wishes, contentment, effacement, seclusion, dispersal, energy, and modest needs, it will become quite purified; and his vows will succeed as well" (p. 59).

The manual enumerates thirteen kinds of ascetic practices:

1. *The refuse-rag-wearer's practice:* The *bhikkhu* collects refuse cloth for robes. *Pāṁsukūla* means "refuse" in the sense of its being found in such a place as a street, charnel ground, or midden, or in the sense of its being in a vile state.
2. *The triple-robe-wearer's practice:* The *bhikkhu* has the habit of wearing the triple robe (*ti-cīvāra*), namely the cloak of patches, the upper garment, and the inner clothing.
3. *The alms-food-eater's practice:* The *bhikkhu's* vow is to gather and eat the lumps (*piṇḍa*) of alms food offered by others. (The word *bhikkhu* is derived from *bhikkhā*, meaning alms.)
4. *The house-to-house-seeker's practice:* The *bhikkhu* wanders from house to house collecting food; he is a "gapless wanderer" (*sapadāna-cārin*) in the sense that he walks from house to house, to all houses, indifferently and without distinction, begging from everyone and showing no preference.
5. *The one-sessioner's practice:* The *bhikkhu* eats only one meal a day in one uninterrupted session.

6. *The bowl-food-eater's practice:* The *bhikkhu* receives and eats the alms mixed together in one bowl, and he refuses other vessels.

7. *The later-food-refuser's practice:* The *bhikkhu* refuses extra food (or further helpings) offered him after his only meal has been concluded.

8. *The forest-dweller's practice:* The *bhikkhu* adopts the habit of dwelling in the forest.

9. *The tree-root-dweller's practice:* The *bhikkhu* dwells at the root of a tree.

10. *The open-air-dweller's practice.*

11. *The charnel-ground-dweller's practice.*

12. *The any-bed-user's practice:* The *bhikkhu* sleeps on any place that is allotted to him when he is in a community of monks, and in that sense he is an "as-distributed user."

13. *The sitter's practice:* The *bhikkhu* refuses to lie down and when resting adopts the sitting posture. (The sitter can get up in any of the three watches of the night and walk up and down, for lying down is the only posture disallowed.)

These are "the practices of a *bhikkhu* who is ascetic because he has shaken off defilement by undertaking one or another of them" (p. 80). We thus note that the ascetic monk need not choose to practice all of them. Of course, the recommendations regarding dwellings (8–10 above) imply alternative locations that a monk cannot adopt simultaneously but can adopt at different times in his wanderings. Moreover, some *bhikkhu* may undertake these vows intermittently whenever they wished to retire to a stricter mode of life for brief periods.

It is noteworthy that the *Visuddhimagga* interprets the ascetic practices in a flexible manner, so as not only to suit individual circumstances, but also to legitimate the practices of village- and town-dwelling monks. Thus while it is recommended that a *bhikkhu* undertake these practices in the presence of the Buddha or one of his principal disciples or, in a decreasing scale of achievements, anyone from a "nonreturner" to an ordinary *bhikkhu*, yet, even in the absence of the last, a *bhikkhu* might undertake the ascetic practices by himself.

Again, the major rules themselves were defined as capable of three grades of conformity – strict, medium, and mild. Take the first rule, the "refuse-rag-wearer's practice": Here the minimum requirement is that this ascetic practice is broken if the *dhūtaṅga bhikkhu* accepts a robe directly from the hands of a householder. But the commentary tells us that apart from the refuse cloth picked up (such as that collected from the charnel ground and rubbish heap or that used for cleaning childbirth stains or that gnawed by cattle), an ascetic is also permitted to take the cloth "dropped at the door of a shop" or thrown on the street by those who seek merit, or left at "the king's consecration place." These concessions can readily serve as a decorum within which normal merit-making donations can take place. Furthermore, we are told that it is permitted for a *bhikkhu* who has taken this vow to receive a robe placed at his feet by another *bhikkhu*. The commentary concludes with this definition of the limits: There are those kinds of refuse-rag-wearers, "the strict, the medium, and the mild." One who takes from the charnel ground is strict; one who picks up a robe placed in his way is medium; one who takes a robe placed at his feet by another *bhikkhu* is mild (p. 64).

Again, "the alms-food-eater's practice" is capable of three gradations. The strict practitioner will go to the door of a house to have his bowl filled or accepts alms brought to a refectory and given there; the medium practitioner may sit at a place and wait for his bowl to be filled; the mild one may consent beforehand to receive food on the following two days. But note that the moral is drawn that the latter two practitioners "miss the joy of an independent life," thereby underscoring the massively important fact that a wandering ascetic's independence hinges on his not being bound to others by durable bonds. Thus the benefit for the strict practitioner is that "he is always a stranger among families and is like the moon; he abandons avarice about families; he is compassionate and impartial; he avoids the dangers in being supported by a family."

It is the same point of observing impartiality as well as avoiding the temptation of greed and gratification of the senses that is driven home in respect of "the house-to-house-seeker's practice." Where a monk has regularly received nothing from a house or a street, he may go past it on his almsround, but wherever he has received anything at all it is not allowed subsequently to go past it and leave it out. Nor must he on his almsround miss a village or settlement that lies in his path; but having sought alms there, and if he has not received sufficient food, he may go to the next village in correct sequence. The "greedy alms round" is one in which the monk goes "only to the house where good alms food is given," and he who behaves in this manner breaks his vow.

Vows 5, 6, and 7, are closely linked and are intended to curtail greed for food and indulgence of the taste buds. The three grades of the one-sessioner's practice (5) are defined thus: The strict observer will not accept any more helpings once he has indicated that he wants no more by placing his hands over the bowl; the medium allows his bowl to be replenished as long as all the food in his bowl has not been consumed; the mild may continue to eat as long as he does not get up from his seat. The later-food-refuser's practice (7) is simply an elaboration of this, carrying further the niceties of curbing food intake.

The bowl-food-eater's practice (6) is of particular importance because it takes the *bhikkhu* one step further in his "closing his sense doors." While a layman's palate and culinary art consist in distinguishing dishes and elaborating recipes, an ascetic erases these distinctions between dishes and assaults his sense of taste by mixing different kinds of food in the same bowl and eating all at once. As the *Visuddhimagga* puts it, the benefit is that the "craving for variety of tastes is eliminated." (No wonder this ascetic practice is cause for much admiring comment among Thai laity who relish their food.)

There are, however, limits to this mixing of foods. The manual allows for curry made with cured fish to be eaten separately from rice gruel, for mixing these can be "repulsive." But the manual is relentless in grading the modes of eating: The "strict" eater mixes and breaks up the rice lumps, fish, meat, etc., *before* he starts to eat the food, the "medium" eater is allowed to break the food only with one hand *while* eating (hence he is called "hand ascetic"), while the "mild" eater (the "bowl ascetic") is allowed to break up food with his hand and his teeth *while* he is eating.

Vows 8, 9, 10, and 11, relating to the dwelling place of the ascetic, state positively and dramatically the difference between a layman's and an ascetic's mode of life. Of the places appropriate for an ascetic – the forest, tree root, open air, and charnel ground – it is the forest that best represents the opposite or negation of village life. The forest-dweller's vow is phrased in one of two ways, which illustrates our point: "I refuse an abode in a village" or "I undertake the forest-dweller's practice."

A village is defined as any human settlement from one cottage to many; even a caravan in continuous existence for more than four months counts as a village. A village's precincts or boundaries are meticulously defined, thereby throwing light on the ascetic's preoccupation with disentangling himself from the bamboo clump of lay life: If the village is walled, its precincts cover the area encompassed by a stone's throw from the wall; if it is not walled, its limits extend to a distance of two successive throws from the precincts of the last border house, the precincts of this house being established by the distance covered by a woman throwing water from a basin standing at the door!

The *Visuddhimagga* gives two citations from canonical sources that suggest an intriguing interpretation. The *Vinaya* is cited as declaring: "Except the village and its precincts, all is forest," and a confirmation is provided from the *Abhidhamma* (*Vibhaṅga*), which says: "Having gone out of the boundary post, all that is forest." We note here that the delimitation does not contrast village with forest, in a dichotomous opposition, but says the forest is everything beyond the village, encircling (and perhaps even encompassing) the latter, which is a bounded core.

Be that as it may, it is stipulated that a forest-dwelling ascetic visiting a village abode must leave it "in order to meet the dawn in the forest"; if a forest-dweller's preceptor is ill and cannot receive what he needs from the village, the preceptor should be taken to a village abode and attended to there, but the forest dweller should normally in these circumstances observe the dawn stipulation, unless his preceptor's illness has worsened and requires his presence. The dawn rule is of course not broken if a forest monk goes to a village, and "hears the *Dhamma*" (e.g., listens to a sermon or participates in a *uposatha* rite) there, and meets the dawn in the village.

As with the other vows discussed already, the forest-dweller's vow also has three ranges of observance (excluding the exceptional circumstances described above): "Herein, one who is strict must always meet the dawn in the forest. The medium is allowed to live in a village for the four months of the Rains. And the mild one, for the winter months too."

The vows to live by a tree root (i.e., under the shade of a tree) or to follow the open-dweller's practice underscore their rejection of the layman's mode of dwelling by phrasing one form of the vow as "I refuse a roof." The benefit is that "the impediment of dwellings is severed." Once again, the permitted range in observing this vow is defined thus: The strict ascetic makes a tent of his robe right out in the open and lives under it; the medium is permitted to dwell near a tree, rock, or house, so long as he does not seek shelter under them; the mild observer is allowed to shelter under a rock overhang without a drip ledge cut in it, a hut made of branches or cloth stiffened with paste, or a shelter left by fieldwatchers.

Of these roofless and/or extra-village habitations, the charnel ground is certainly the site that unremittingly and remorselessly brings home to the *bhikkhu* the immediacy of the body's subjection to decay and the illusion of the sense of self as an enduring entity. The cremation ground affords the opportunity to be mindful of death, to vanquish fear and dread, and to observe the very *process* of decaying and of becoming, a true antidote to the fallacies of reification. Thus the *Visuddhimagga,* with its usual attention to concrete details, tells the *bhikkhu* that he should walk up and down the charnel ground looking at the pyre with half an eye and that he should take note of all the objects he sees during the day so that they will not assume frightening shapes for him at night. Moreover, *by no means denying the phenomenal reality of ghosts and spirits,* the manual advises that the ascetic "should not take such foods as sesame flour, pease pudding, fish, meat, milk, oil, sugar, etc., which are liked by non-human beings" and that even if such beings "wander about screeching, he must not hit them with anything."

Finally, in the list of ascetic practices, the last vow of the sitter's practice seems particularly onerous: The meditating ascetic takes the vow not to lie down to sleep, but to rest sitting up, so as not to indulge the pleasures of lying prone, lolling, or entering a state of torpor. The relief relates to whether a backrest, cloth band, or binding strap is allowed.[15]

In sum, then, the *dhūtaṅga* practices project in sharp relief the differences between the *bhikkhu*'s ascetic regime and the lay householder's mode of life. The rules that the ascetic observe no social distinctions between houses as "the gapless wanderer," that he live without a roof over his head as a forest dweller, that he possess the bare minimum of clothes and not amass possessions, tell us not only that he is removed from lay society, but also that he can ensure his neutrality, impartiality, and ultimately his universal compassion by avoiding durable relations and reciprocities with the laity.

Moreover, while the *bhikkhu* strives for an ascetic life experience by controlling his senses and wishes and limiting his social intercourse and physical movement, he at the same time erases the layman's cognitive and affective maps by crossing the latter's boundaries of social and physical spaces, culinary distinctions, and pure–impure categorizations. The ascetic who closes his sense doors while the layman's are open is also a *breaker* of conventions, a dissolver of man-made cultural categories by which he orders and reifies the world into a durable reality. Thus it is a necessary corollary of his resolution not to reify that the ascetic is a mindful observer and contemplator of *process*, of growth and decay and dissolution; and what better subject is there for this than the human body and what better viewing ground than a place of cremation?

# 4

# The stages and rewards of Buddhist meditation

The main objective of this chapter is to develop and interpret the *Visuddhimagga's* treatment of mystical or supramundane powers (*iddhi*) that are alleged to become available to the adept practicing concentration (*samādhi*) meditation and to suggest, on the one hand, that the detailed treatment of this subject by Buddhaghosa is integral rather than secondary to his mapping the path of meditation and, on the other hand, that this map of mental consciousness and mental processes internal to the meditator parallels and is homologous with the map of the external cosmos and its processes of degeneration and regeneration.

As Conze has aptly said: "Meditational practices constitute the very core of the Buddhist approach to life. . . . As prayer in Christianity, so meditation is here the very heartbeat of the religion."[1]

The single most important text on meditation in the Pali canon is the *Satipaṭṭhānasutta*. The chief textbook on the subject for the Theravāda School, written from the standpoint of the Mahāvihāra fraternity, is Buddhaghosa's *Visuddhimagga*, which is without peer in any other Buddhist school; a second work is Upatissa's *Path to Liberation*,[2] also written in Sri Lanka but this time from the perspective of the Abhayagirivādin sect. Lastly, we must mention *The Manual of a Mystic*,[3] a Siṅhalese handbook of probably the sixteenth to eighteenth centuries, which deals with the *jhāna* levels of absorption in *samādhi* concentration and may have been a product of the influence of Siamese monks.

The ultimate aim of Buddhist meditation is enlightenment, but *nibbāna* is a state that cannot be positively described. So what is rewarding to enter is the path of meditative purification itself, which serves "to promote spiritual development, to diminish the impact of suffering, to calm the mind and to reveal the true facts of existence. Increased gentleness and sympathy are among their by-products . . . and a feeling that death has lost its sting."[4] The poems of the early saints, both male and female (*Thera-gāthā* and *Therī-gāthā*) are blissful, selfless affirmations of the knowledge that there is no eternity about conditioned things.[5]

# The stages and rewards of Buddhist meditation

## The Path of Concentration (*samādhi*)[6]

The *Visuddhimagga* lists forty "subjects of meditation" (*Kammaṭṭhāna*). They consist of the following:

1. Ten devices (*kasiṇas*): four elements – earth, water, fire, and air; four colors – blue, yellow, red, and white; and light and limited space.
2. Ten kinds of foulness of decaying corpses (*asubbhas*), namely the bloated, the livid, the festering, the cut-up, the gnawed, the scattered, the hacked and scattered, the bleeding, the worm infested, and a skeleton.
3. Ten recollections: the chief of these being the trinity – the Buddha (the Enlightened One), the *Dhamma* (the Law), and the *saṅgha* (the community) – which are followed by the recollections of virtue, generosity, the deities, mindfulness of death, the body, breathing, and peace.
4. Four divine abidings or stations of Brahma: loving-kindness, compassion, gladness, and equanimity.
5. Four immaterial and formless states: the base or station of boundless space, of boundless consciousness, of nothingness, of neither perception nor nonperception.
6. One perception of the repulsive and disgusting aspects of food.
7. One definition or analysis of the four elements.

Now the *Visuddhimagga* correlates the choice and efficacy of these meditation subjects with two factors – the temperament and capacity of the meditator, and the level of *jhāna* consciousness that can be attained by meditating on one subject or another.

The Pali sources contain some interesting assertions about characterology, and, in general, three kinds of people are distinguished according to whether they are governed by greed, hate, or delusion. It is worth studying in detail the correlation of subject with temperament:[7] Firstly, the ten kinds of foulness, and mindfulness of the body, make up eleven meditation subjects suitable for one of greedy temperament. The four divine abidings and four color *kasiṇas* are eight subjects suitable for one of deluded temperament or one of intelligent temperament. The remaining *kasiṇas* and immaterial states are suitable for all kinds of temperament; and "any one of the *kasiṇas* should be limited for one of speculative temperament and measureless for one of deluded temperament."

Although there is attention to breathing as a way of bringing about calm, Buddhist meditative traditions have not elaborated or become preoccupied with body relaxation and control over the body's physiological processes, as has happened for instance in Haṭhayoga. Rather, a distinctive Buddhist way of developing mindfulness and detachment is through the contemplation of death, together with the cultivation of the mental states of tranquillity, calm, and compassion.

The *Visuddhimagga* firmly recommends that the beginner should dedicate himself to a teacher and live in dependence on him, for then "he is not

unresponsive to correction, does not go about as he likes, is easy to speak to."[8] The beginner whose resolution to meditate is sincere can solicit the teacher for a meditation subject, for he "who has acquired the penetration of minds" can know the pupil's temperament "by surveying his mental conduct." It is in this context that the text develops the concept of *Kalyāṇamitta*, "the good friend," who is the giver of the meditation subject, guides the pupil through his exercises, comments on and interprets his experiences, and urges him on to greater effort when the pupil too readily mistakes certain lower states of bliss for the final liberation.

Now the forty subjects do not by themselves exhaust the entire range of meditation. They principally cover those practices that relate to the cultivation of "mindfulness" and "concentration." They do not apply to the subject of insight (*vipassanā*) meditation, which confers wisdom and understanding (*paññā*). Such wisdom that leads to enlightenment in the full sense comes only after the *bhikkhu* grasps the true nature of objects and the *dharmic* constituents of the universe, when he comprehends the processual features of the *khandhas* (the five constituents of the personality), the links of "conditioned co-production," and the four noble truths.[9]

The meditative path is described as the cultivation of five cardinal virtues – faith, vigor or energy, mindfulness, concentration, and, finally, wisdom. What is particularly recommended is "balancing faith with understanding, and concentration with energy," a formula that is often diagramed as the mind's chariot being pulled by four horses. Faith is the indispensable starting point and implies an intentional and resolute act of the will to confer trust on the three jewels of the Buddha, the *Dhamma*, and the *saṅgha*. Energy is the driving force behind the religious practice and quest. Mindfulness, or "one-pointedness" of mind, is a necessary virtue, without which an adept cannot progress, because it purifies the mind, defeats attachment, helps to defeat the illusion of the self as a reified entity, and in an incipient manner affords tranquility and insight, which are the complete fruits of the higher levels of concentration and insight meditation, respectively.

The instructions for engaging in meditation on a *kasiṇa* go something like this. The *bhikkhu* should find a monastery favorable to the development of concentration; he should avoid incompatible and hostile *bhikkhu*; wherever possible, he should find "a good friend" as a teacher; he should sit down comfortably[10] in a secluded place and first review the dangers of sense desires; next arouse happiness in recollecting the special qualities of the Buddha, the Dhamma, and the Saṅgha; and then apprehend the *kasiṇa* signs he has chosen. If, for instance, the *kasiṇa*

Figure 1. A mural from Wat Bovonniwet, Bangkok. The upper half depicts the simple huts and meditational exercises of the forest dwelling monks, while the lower half depicts the elaborate architecture of a village/town *wat* and its merit making activities.

chosen is an earthen object, he apprehends with the mind what the eye has apprehended and in this way a counterpart sign that is purer than the object sign is internalized.[11]

Now concentration is of two kinds: access concentration and absorption concentration. In the former, the mind becomes concentrated on the plane of access by the abandonment of hindrances; the counterpart sign arises together with access concentration; from this threshold the mind advances to the absorption plane "by the manifestation of the *jhāna* factors."

The meditator with increasing skill ascends from one *jhāna* level of absorption to another up to the eighth level. For instance, the first *jhāna* is "accompanied by applied and sustained thought with happiness and bliss born of seclusion."[12] The whole body is pervaded by a rapturous bliss and happiness. At the second *jhāna* level, these experiences are accompanied by increasing "singleness of mind" and the disappearance from awareness of the primary object and discursive thought; at the third level, there is an intensification of equanimity in addition to one-pointedness of mind. The "purification" of the mind goes through several levels at which "lower" or "grosser" mental states and perceptions associated with "material states" are transcended and higher spiritual, formless states are reached. From mindfulness at the beginning, the adept reaches "access," which is the threshold of a fuller collectedness, and from there he ascends into ecstasy and one-pointedness in which abstraction becomes complete.

## The Path of Insight

From the standpoint of the *Visuddhimagga*, the mastery of the *jhānas* – the enjoyment of supreme bliss and the acquisition of supramundane powers – is of secondary importance to the cultivation of "discriminating wisdom," *paññā* (Pali) or *prajñā* (Skt). While the deeper absorption levels of *samādhi* are "games" of concentration, the crux of the meditative training is the path that begins with mindfulness, proceeds through insight (*vipassanā*), and concludes in *nibbāna*.

Mindfulness is promoted by restricting attention to a bare noticing of objects and attending to facts of perception as they arise at any of the five sense-doors or in the mind, rather than attaching the mind to these events and abstracting from them cognitive and perceptual patterns. [Previous training in *samādhi*, especially in reaching levels of absorption (*jhāna*), is useful though not necessary, for the beginner can be taught a method of "bare insight" through which mindfulness is attained.][13]

In due course, the normal illusions of continuity and rationality that sustain cognitive and perceptual processes give way to a correct apprehension of the random and discrete units out of which reality is continually being structured. With the emergence of the true realization of these processes, mindfulness matures into insight.

# The stages and rewards of Buddhist meditation

Contemplating mind and its object, previously separate, are now nondualistically conjoined, and in unbroken succession occurs a chain of insights of mind knowing itself, culminating in the state of *nibbāna*.

Let me sketch in a few of these links in this chain.[14] The first realization is that the phenomena contemplated are distinct from the mind contemplating them. They are then seen to arise as effects of their respective causes, regardless of the meditator's own will and self as an abiding entity. This is the experience of *anattā*, literally "not-self," the dissolving of the conception of "I" as a reification: From here, there arises the realization of *anicca* (impermanence); phenomena are seen to arise and pass away in an endless chain, creating in the meditator the sense of disenchantment that what is constantly changing cannot be the source of lasting satisfaction. This state of detachment from one's world of experience enables the understanding that the processes of self and world formation are the source of *dukkha* (suffering).

The next level of consciousness is worth underscoring because we shall find it referred to when we relate the reported meditational experience of some contemporary Thai meditation masters and "perfected saints." The adept experiences the "knowledge of arising and passing away" in that he or she clearly sees the beginning and end of each successive object of contemplation. This clarity of perception gives rise to "ten signs" (*nimitta*), such as: the vision of a brilliant light and other illuminations; the elation of rapturous feelings, including tremor in the limbs and the sensation of levitation; the calm of tranquility and pliability of mind and body; the joy of devotional feelings and faith, which on the one hand employs the Buddhist trinity as the object of meditation and on the other produces a confidence in the virtues of meditation that in turn generates the desire to urge friends and relatives to practice it; and, finally, sublime feelings of happiness suffusing the whole body, an unprecedented bliss that is sustained and motivates the meditator to tell others of this extraordinary experience. These five signs are accompanied by the remaining signs: by an intensified experience of previous mental victories such as quick and clear perception, strong mindfulness, equanimity, and finally, a subtle attachment to the illuminations and sublime raptures mentioned above.

But this level of consciousness is a *pseudo-nirvāṇa* (a "mistaking of what is not the Path for the Path"), and the *Visuddhimagga* labels the signs just described "The Ten Corruptions of Insight." The meditator, elated by the emergence of these signs, becomes attached to them and falsely imagines that he has attained enlightenment and finished the task of meditation. When the meditator realizes by himself or through advice from his teacher that these signs pertain to a station along the way rather than his final destination, he weans himself from attachment to them and begins a detached contemplation of them.

From this point on, the meditator ascends to the summit. His perception of objects becomes clearer and rapid, and the world reality is seen to be in a constant state of dissolution. The previous state of joy is followed by fear and dread which grips the mind, and all mental formations are seen to be dreadful. The meditator wishes to escape from them, and he experiences great pain in his body and mind, which appear as hostages to suffering.

This pain is made to cease by applying the practice of contemplation to it. Contemplation, now quick, effortless, and indefatigable, gives instantaneous knowledge of "not self," "impermanence," and "suffering," and the meditator transcends both delight in, and dread of, mental objects and abandons them all.

The final leap is made to *nibbāna*, when all formations are seen as limited, circumscribed, devoid of desirability, or alien. *Nibbāna* is the state of "signless liberation" (*animitta-vimokkha*), in which there is "no occurrence and no-information" of phenomena. Ego consciousness is abandoned for good. *Nibbāna* destroys the defiling aspects of self-hatred, greed, ignorance, and in this respect the fruit of the Path of Insight is superior to the Path of Concentration, for the latter only succeeds in suppressing, not destroying, these defilements.

There are four levels of, or stations in, the realization of *nibbāna* – which we have already alluded to in our previous discussion of *arahantship*. The four levels of achievement in an ascending series are "stream enterer," "once-returner," "nonreturner," and a "fully realized" *arahant* best exemplified in the perfected Buddha.

There is a state apart from *nibbāna* that is called *nirodha* (cessation). If in *nibbāna* awareness is focused on the cessation of consciousness, in *nirodha* awareness ceases altogether so long as the meditator is in that state. *Nirodha* is accessible only to a nonreturner or an *arahant*, who has also mastered the practice of *vipassanā* and is able to reach the highest *jhāna* absorption level of "neither-perception-nor-nonperception." The state of *nirodha* can last up to seven days,[15] and the meditator should set a time limit before he embarks on meditation leading to it. In returning to normal consciousness, he traverses the *jhānas* in reverse order – progressively awareness is resumed, the body functions normally again, and the mind reactivates discursive thought and sense perception.

## The middle ranges of meditation

Although the pursuit of concentration and insight are described as two separate paths, they nevertheless can intersect or come into conjunction at various points. Moreover, the feelings of bliss, equanimity, and supramundane powers that arise at the third and especially the fourth levels of concentration absorption are clearly parallel to the ten signs of rapturous feelings and brilliant visions and experience of body levitation that characterize in the Path of Insight the level of "knowledge of arising and passing away. " But just as, ideally, the enjoyment of *iddhi* powers in concentration have to be left behind, so must the raptures of false-*nibbāna*, which are labeled the ten corruptions. Yet these same levels of attainment are the most fruitful and exciting to the world of ordinary human beings caught up in suffering and the round of existence.

For in a live socio-religious context, while meditation masters are likely to claim to be well on the way to the top, they are unlikely to make the ultimate and immodest claim of having reached *nibbāna* itself. In any case, that master who has made the leap into perfect *arahantship* is unlikely to be conscious of the world itself and is very near to passing away (*parinibbāna*) from human existence.

It is the masters who have reached the middle ranges of both paths – who enjoy rapturous bliss and feel compassion for humanity *(mettā)* and equanimity, who have access to supramundane powers and also feel the compelling urge to preach their positive message to their friends, disciples, and relatives and to use their virtuous powers for the benefit of humanity – it is these masters and proto-saints who are the foci of cults and lay followings. And, in due course, the most saintly of them will also be seen to withdraw into the state of *nirodha* for days at a time and then to pass away in austere majesty.

## The acquisition of *iddhi* powers

It would be a mistake to consider the *iddhi* powers that become available in the process of *samādhi* as a weird "magical" effect and/or a "miraculous" phenomenon in the sense of their character being abnormal or contrary to the Buddhist understanding of mental processes. The *iddhi* are not bizarre results of the suspension of laws of mind and world process, but by-products of their mastery. This "rational" basis of *iddhi* powers is part and parcel of the gloss provided by Buddhaghosa himself, a gloss that sounds close to *instrumental action* – traditionally defined in the West as the appropriateness of means for achieving chosen ends.

While Bhikkhu Ñāṇamoli, the translator of *Visuddhimagga* into English, translates *iddhi* as "supranormal power," he provides us with this decisive evidence. The Pali term *iddhi-vidhā* literally means "kinds of success." In terms of Buddhaghosa's gloss, *iddhi* means success "in the sense of production, in the sense of obtainment" (p. 414). What is produced or obtained is called successful, and in this sense the metamorphosis of lust is a success, as is the satisfactory practice of renunciation. We are further informed that success, by another method of glossing, is "a term for the effectiveness of means; for effectiveness of the means succeeds with the production of the result intended . . . "(p. 414). It is this efficacy of means in relation to an end that is the kernel of the phenomenon of *iddhi*, a feature that has been ill-understood in conventional discussions of the subject.

The *Visuddhimagga*, when it discusses *iddhi*, is of course primarily concerned with that kind of "success" and "efficacy" generated in the meditative process of the *samādhi* kind. But it is not irrelevant to note that for Buddhaghosa the rubric *iddhi* includes other kinds of manifestations of success as well, which are quite different from those generated by meditation.[16] The neutral criterion of a means-and-ends relation encompasses the same rubric of *iddhi*.

### "HAVING BEEN ONE, HE BECOMES MANY"

Let us take the first *iddhi* power deriving from *samādhi* and grasp its mechanics. The above heading is really the first among an inventory of successes to which the meditator "directs his mind":

Having been one, he becomes many; having been many he becomes one. . . . He appears and vanishes. He goes unhindered through walls, through enclosures, through mountains, as though in open space. He dives in and out of earth as though in water. He goes on unbroken water as though on earth. Seated cross-legged he travels in space like a winged bird. With his hand he touches and strokes the moon and sun so mighty and powerful. He wields bodily mastery even as far as the Brahma World.[17]

The adept does these things by first making his meditative passage through the first four *jhānas* (he traverses the plane of seclusion, through equanimity and bliss, to the plane of neither pain nor pleasure). The first three planes are the *accessory planes* in which the body becomes "light, malleable" after the adept steeps himself in "blissful and light perception," and the fourth plane is the natural plane for obtaining *iddhi* powers. "Emerging from the basic *jhāna*," the adept "resolves" to accomplish the required transformation.

There is a double transformation achieved. Through the experiencing of bliss and the attainment of equanimity, and thereafter "the perception of lightness," the adept is liberated from the hindrances that stand in the way of "applied thought." This results in transforming the material body of the adept into an ethereal body: "his physical body too becomes light as a tuft of cotton," and he creates a path in space by means of the earth *kasiṇa* and goes on foot, or by means of the air *kasiṇa* he travels by air like a tuft of cotton (p. 442). Thus the adept achieves a mind-made transformation upon himself, and this transformation of mind and body is meant to be in line with the Buddhist theory of the arising and dissolving of *Dhamma* states and formations. But the adept simultaneously by resolve effects a second transformation upon the outer world also: Focusing on the appropriate *kasiṇa* as the subject of meditation – for example, earth, water, air, or fire – he changes the land into water and dives in and out of it, or the sea to land and walks on it, or the space to earth and treads in it, and so on.

There are many fine points, hair-splitting distinctions, and ingenious mechanisms of transformations in which the reader is likely to get lost. For example, the transformation in which the adept changes his "appearance" or produces the appearance of another object (e.g., the apparition of an elephant in the sky) is distinguished from the process that results in a "mind-made body"; this latter is the method by which the meditator creates from "this body another body possessing visible form, mind-made,'' like a reed being drawn from its sheath, a sword from its scabbard, or a snake from its slough. It is this second *iddhi* that enables the adept to see a visible object with a divine eye, or to hear a far-away sound with a divine ear element, or to converse with Brahma or visit the Brahma heavens ''while remaining here.'' No bodily power as such is involved in these successes, for they are mind-created.

We should finally note that, at least in the *Visuddhimagga*, there is no denunciation of these supranormal powers as evil or sinful. On the contrary, it sees them as fruits of concentration. However, they are at the same time hindrances to full insight and are irrelevant to the path of insight meditation that leads to full understanding of suffering and deliverance from it. The *Visuddhimagga* does say that the training of the mind to the point at which *iddhi* can be performed is extremely difficult and ''only one in a hundred or a thousand can do it.'' But of course the buddhas and saints do not have to subject themselves to the mental exercises every time they wish to exercise *iddhi* powers.[18]

### OTHER *IDDHI* FEATS

The process of effecting these feats becomes somewhat clearer, for instance, in the description of ''the divine ear element'' and ''the recollection of past lives,'' for the underlying principle is projection from near to far, from immediate experience to more distant ones, from material and gross sensations to ethereal and divine ones.

When the divine ear element is developed, the adept ''hears both kinds of sounds, the divine and the human, those that are far as well as near,''[19] far off even in another world-sphere. How is the divine ear aroused? The *bhikkhu* entering the *jhāna* levels of consciousness first directs his attention to the gross sounds normally within range of hearing and then gradually extends his attention to more and more subtle sounds in all directions. These sounds become more and more evident as the ascent is made upward to reach the absorption consciousness of the fourth *jhāna*. Then arises the divine ear element whose area of hearing extends from that of a single finger-breadth to the limit of the world-sphere and beyond.

The technique recommended for a *bhikkhu* who wants to develop the faculty of recollecting past lives is as follows. The beginner goes into solitary retreat on his return from his almsround and his meal thereafter; he attains the fourth *jhāna*, emerges, and adverts to his most recent act of sitting down, then the next proximate act, and the next proximate and so on, in a regress backward in time through a whole night, and a day, and then through years to his own rebirth that began this existence of his; and he moves further backward to recall the mentality-materiality (*nāma-rūpa*) occurring at the moment of death in his preceding existence, and so on through the chain of rebirths.

Logically, of course, the recollection of one's past lives leads to the recollec-

47

tion ultimately of the many aeons and cycles of world destruction and regeneration of our pulsating cosmos. Thus from the trajectory of a single person's existence is developed the network and tangle of the cosmos both in space and time: "He recollects his manifold past lives, that is to say, one birth, two births, . . . a hundred births, . . . a hundred thousand births, many aeons of world contractions and expansions . . ." (p. 451).

The *Visuddhimagga* documents with its usual meticulousness the differential capacities of different adepts – other sectarians, ordinary disciples, great disciples, *paccekabuddhas*, and buddhas – in remembering the number of past aeons, in descending upon any place they choose backward and forward along the chains, and in the intensity and vividness of remembrance of the details of past events. The buddhas at the summit of the hierarchy of adepts can remember aeons without limit, can descend in time "with the lion's descent wherever they want," and can see the past with the intensity and clarity of "the glorious Autumn sun's dusk with its thousand rays."

The two chapters on the "direct knowledge" that produces *iddhi* powers are sumptuously illustrated with examples of the feats performed by the Buddha and his disciples. Indeed, the Buddha figures as the chief exponent of *iddhi*. A famous example is the twin feat whereby the Blessed One resolved that the citizens of Sāvathi should see the inhabitants of Sāketa across a vast distance that separated the two towns and whereby also "he split the earth in two and showed Avīci (Hell), and he parted the sky in two and showed the Brahma World" (p. 428).

There is again the extraordinary feat by which the Buddha lifted his feet and placed them on the summits of Mount Sineru and Mount Yugandhara and, taking his residence during the rainy season retreat on the Red Marble Terrace, delivered his exposition of the Abhiddhamma to the "deities of ten thousand world spheres" (p. 428). Then follows one of the incidents known so well by the multitude of Buddhists past and present, and celebrated in a colorful, expectant, and pious ritual all over Thailand: After his preaching to the gods was over, the Blessed One informed Sakka of his intention to return to the human world, and in response the gods built "three flights of stairs, one of gold, one of silver and one of crystal," so that the Buddha could descend flanked by the deities.[20]

Among the Buddha's disciples, it is, as we have indicated earlier, Mahā-Moggallāna who is credited with extraordinary *iddhi* powers, and the *Visuddhimagga* regales us with his feats, second only to the Buddha's. Since he is a quintessential perfected saint who through meditation acquired such powers and is a model for emulation by many adepts, we should give an example or two of his feats.

At the time of the "twin miracle" described above, an assembly gathered "that was twelve leagues across" and said that they would not disperse until they had seen the Blessed One. People asked first the Elder Anuruddha to find out where the Blessed One was, and he with his divine eye saw where the Buddha had taken up his residence for the rains. They then asked the venerable Mahā-

## The stages and rewards of Buddhist meditation

Moggallāna to pay homage to the Buddha and carry their message to him. "In the midst of the assembly the Elder dived into the earth. Then, cleaving Mount Sineru, he emerged at the Perfect One's feet. . . ." When he delivered the message of the people of Jambudvīpa, the Buddha asked Moggallāna where his "elder brother, the general of the Dhamma," Anuruddha, was. Being told that he was at the city of Saṅkassa, the Buddha told Moggallāna to return and inform the people that he would descend the next day to the said city for the Mahāpavāraṇā ceremony. This is how then the marvelous descent of the Buddha, flanked by the gods, took place, after he had experienced the "revelation of the worlds" (*loka-vivaraṇa*) when, standing on the summit of Sineru, he surveyed the thousands of world-spheres, looked right down to Avīci and up to the realm of the Highest Gods. In passing, we should note the important point that the two disciples, Anuruddha, the "general of the *Dhamma*," and Moggallāna, the possessor of *iddhi* powers, are pointedly paired, ranked by the people and the Buddha, and shown to act in a complementary fashion.

Perhaps the most dramatic of Mahā-Moggallāna's feats is his encounter with the royal *Nāga*, Nandopananda. Because the *nāga* had no confidence in the Three Jewels, the Buddha asked Moggallāna to cure him of his wrong view. The *nāga* incensed at the spectacle of "bald-headed monks" led by the Buddha proceeding above to the divine world of the Thirty-three scattering "dirt off their feet on our heads," "spread his hood over the realm of the Thirty-three and made everything there invisible" (p. 436). Mahā-Moggallāna, proclaiming that he would tame the *nāga*, himself assumed the form of a huge royal *Nāga*, and "surrounded Nandopananda fourteen times with his coils and raised his hood above the other's head, and he squeezed him against Sineru." Then followed other trials of strength: the *nāga* blew a blast at the monk, but he *attained the fourth jhāna* and was untouched and unharmed. Finally, the subdued *nāga*, assuming the form of a young Brahman, took his refuge with the Buddha.

### The meditative states and Buddhist cosmology

A feature that has been insufficiently appreciated in the commentaries on the *Visuddhimagga* is that the topography of the meditative states and levels reached by the inner consciousness of the meditator is remarkably similar to – homologous with – the Buddhist cosmology of the various *lokas* (worlds) that compose the cosmos and their pattern of interrelation. This correspondence is not merely a matter of interpretive reading on my part. Indeed, the *Visuddhimagga* itself, after having discussed the *iddhi* powers as manifestations of "direct knowledge" in Chapters 13 and 14, makes the transition in the latter chapter from the capacities of the adept to recall past lives and to see with the "divine eye" the "passing and reappearance of things," to the description of the periodic creation and dissolution of the cosmos and its worlds in cycles of aeons of time.

49

# The *arahant* and the Path of Meditation

The hierarchy of levels on the *samādhi* path is first of all formulated as an ascent from *material states* of consciousness to *formless states* of consciousness. The material states begin at the lowest "access" state of concentration, then proceed to the first *jhāna* level, and from there in succession through feelings of bliss to the fourth *jhāna* level of equanimity and one-pointedness of mind and the cessation of breathing. The formless states begin at the fifth *jhāna* level of consciousness of infinite space (together with equanimity and one-pointedness), proceed through successive levels of objectless infinite consciousness, and conclude with the eighth and final *jhāna* state of neither-perception-nor-nonperception. In this ascent, we should note that the critical transition is from the fourth *jhāna* level of materiality to the fifth *jhāna* state of formlessness, and it is no accident at all that the supranormal *iddhi* powers *are attained only after the meditator has reached the critical fourth level*.

Now what is the correspondence between this meditative scheme and map of consciousness and the cosmology of world formations and dissolutions? Because not every reader will have the appetite for the complex arithmetic of the cosmic scheme, let me give the bare details necessary to make my point.[21]

First of all, the cosmic scheme postulates three broad levels of worlds, the *kāma loka, rūpa brahma loka,* and *arūpa brahma loka:*

(1) The *kāma loka* of sense and form, of bodily form and sensual feelings, is the lowest. It is internally differentiated into 11 *lokas* thus: At the bottom is the world of hells situated in the bowels of the earth; next come the 4 *lokas* inhabited by humans, animals, and ghosts; on top of this are located 6 *deva loka* or heavenly worlds. The *deva loka* are internally differentiated into 6 ascending worlds, which include the abode of the four *lokapāla* (guardians); the next higher *Tāvatiṁsa,* which is the abode on the top of Mount Meru of Sakka or Indra; and the *Tusita,* where the next expected buddha, Maitreya, dwells waiting to be born.

(2) The next cosmic level is made up of the *rūpa brahma lokas*, the worlds of form only, in which dwell certain *brahma* beings. It is internally divided into 16 superimposed worlds, and what we need to keep in mind is the location therein of certain worlds mentioned in the *Visuddhimagga* and that will be mentioned shortly. The Ābhassara is the sixth level, the Subhakiṇha is the ninth level, and the Vehapphala is the tenth level.

(3) The third and highest level is the *arūpa brahma lokas*, the worlds of formlessness, the abode of the quintessential *brahma* beings. These are divided into 4 ascending levels. (The breaking out of the last level implies the leaving behind of the cosmos and entering the state of void.)

According to the cyclical theory of world formation and dissolution described in the *Visuddhimagga*, there is periodic destruction of the cosmos by water, fire, and air. There is in the instance of destruction by fire the successive appearance of seven scorching suns, which cause drought and first burn the *kāma* world. The fire rises to the summit of Mount Meru, the realm of the four *lokapāla*, and of the

Thirty-three, ruled over by Indra, and "so it goes right on up to the plane of the first *jhāna*," and "when it has burnt three lower Brahma Worlds, it stops there at the Ābhassara World."

This fire is followed by a rain, and the water level of the cosmos rises up and then subsides, and as it sinks the lower (Brahma) world emerges first, and then the four upper divine worlds of the sensual sphere (*kāma loka*) come into view. When the water level sinks to the level of the earth, strong winds hold it stationary. Beings are reborn first in the (*arūpa*) Brahma world of Ābhassara and then progressively get grosser and more sinful as they descend through the various levels to the earthly level of full materialization. This creation story has been set out in the *Aggañña Suttanta* and has already been a topic of comment in my previous book.[22]

Now the world can also be destroyed by the action of water and by the action of air, each agent carrying destruction to a *higher jhāna* level than that attained by fire. While destruction by fire stopped at the first *jhāna* level, "the waters take possession of the earth up to the place of the second *jhāna*," and when they have dissolved the three Brahma worlds there, they stop at the Subhakiṇha world; then when regeneration takes place "beings falling from the Subhakiṇha Brahma world are reborn in the places beginning with the Ābhassara World." Similarly, the wind destroys the cosmos up to the third *jhāna* level and stops at the Vehapphala Brahma world, until regeneration of life takes place again. We thus note that the process of regeneration of life at the beginning of each cosmic cycle is from above to below, from spirituality downward into increasing materiality. This is the precise inverse of the meditational process, which ascends from material states into the ethereal spiritual formless states. We may also note that the destruction of the cosmos by fire, water, and wind stops at the limits of material states covering *jhāna* levels 1 through 3, and does not reach up to the fourth *jhāna* level, which in the topography of meditation is the critical level of take off into equanimity, one-pointedness of mind, and the formless *arūpa* states of consciousness.

Again, the *Visuddhimagga* formulates a direct correspondence between the occurrence of mental defilements in human beings and living creatures, such as greed (*rāga*), hate (*dosa*), and delusion (*moha*), and the destruction of the world by the elements: When greed is conspicuous, the world is destroyed by fire; when hate by water; and when delusion by wind. And of course these same mental defilements are the ones destroyed by the meditative discipline.

To sum up: For our purposes, to follow the logic of the *Visuddhimagga*'s scheme of world formations and dissolutions and its correspondence to the levels of human consciousness in *samādhi* meditation, we should appreciate that the triad of cosmic levels reduces at a more basic level to the dyadic opposition between material states and formless states, and that the middle level of worlds characterized by form only (*rūpa brahma loka*) is an intermediate zone. It is from this intermediate zone that in the cosmological scheme the regeneration (and therefore materialization) of life begins after each destruction and spreads downward in increasingly grosser forms. In the meditative scheme, it is from the same zone that begins the opposite process of the meditator's leap from material levels of consciousness into the higher formless states of transcendence.

# 5

## The forest-monk tradition in Southeast Asia

### A historical backdrop

The classical and well-entrenched duality within the *saṅgha* between those monks labeled forest dwellers (*āraññavāsī/vanavāsī*) and village or town dwellers (*gāmavāsī/nagaravāsī*) is frequently seen as corresponding (though not always perfectly) to another division between monks devoted to the vocation of meditation (*vipassanādhura*) or "practice" (*patipatti*) and the vocation of books (*ganthadhura*) or learning (*pariyatti*). While these dualities or oppositions may seem sharply defined and mutually exclusive, it is important to realize that ideally the *bhikkhu* should combine both vocations and that in actuality one vocation does not necessarily exclude the other. Moreover, the oppositions are not necessarily homologous and need not therefore create consistent profiles; thus in Thailand, as elsewhere, town-dwelling monks and urban monasteries have promoted meditation, and there have been forest-monk communities that have produced well-known scholars. Nor have forest dwellers and town dwellers, or those dedicated to learning and those to meditation, necessarily constituted separate sects. Burma provides us with examples of mainstream "orthodox" sects or fraternities spawning groups or sections that hive off and dedicate themselves to "purer" *Vinaya* practices or more appropriate vocational paths, however they are defined. For Sri Lanka, a famous example is Välvita Sara-ṇaṁkara, who initiated a reform movement within the dominant Siyam Nikāya with the aim of learning and observing the *Vinaya* rules. Correspondingly, as instantiated by the history of the *Thammayut* sect in Thailand, a reform-oriented sect that begins in opposition to the establishment may itself in the course of time develop the full spectrum of activities and orientations manifested by the latter.

Finally, there is still another source of ambiguity that spoils any simple dichotomization. Orthodoxy is frequently seen as conformity with the disciplinary rules defined in the canonical *Vinaya* code. And conformity with the *Vinaya* rules does not require the observance of *dhūtaṅga* (ascetic) practices, which are

53

doctrinally optional. Burma provides evidence of fraternities that rebelled against the receipt of land gifts and other endowments and the life of "luxury" they might afford; but these fraternities did not thereby adopt the "ascetic" (*dhūtaṅga*) practices. However, there have been pious persons, both monastic and lay, who have deemed the *dhūtaṅga* practices to be the quintessential expression of the renouncer's code, and regarded the *tapassi* (hermit or ascetic) and the *Paṁsukū-likas*, a special case of the ascetic monks, as striving to fulfill the ideal norms of early Buddhism. In Thailand today the hallmark of the forest monk is that he observes a certain number of these ascetic practices.

Whatever the divergent strands and tensions in early Buddhism,[1] it is certainly the case that by and large "learning" and "practice" came to be seen by institutionalized Buddhism as not only different vocations but also that the former was the preferred basis of regular *saṅgha* life. Yet, as we shall repeatedly point out, the tradition of "practice" conflated with "forest dwelling" and "meditation" has frequently, if not always, been regarded in its formal status as a legitimate branch or half of the *saṅgha*, with the village- and town-dwelling monks being regarded the "favored" branch enjoying official titles and regular royal and lay support.

According to Rahula, by the first century B.C. the basis of the *sāsana* in Sri Lanka (Anurādhapura) was declared to be learning and the vocation of books rather than the vocation of practice. The writing of the *tipiṭaka* scriptures around the first century B.C., and of the great chronicles Dipavaṁsa and Mahāvaṁsa in the subsequent centuries, was an affirmation of the direction taken.[2] Similarly, Rahula informs us that by the sixth century A.D. Sri Lankan Buddhism had decisively rejected the ascetic hermit (*tapassi*) in favor of the village- and town-dwelling monks. Concordant with these preferences was the coming down on the side of *Dhamma-dāna* (the monk's duty to reciprocate the layman's material gifts with spiritual gifts) rather than on the side of *mutta-muttaka* (the monk's acceptance of gifts without any obligation to return) as the desirable relation between monk and layman. The *saṅgha* comes to be called a "merit field" (*puññak-khetta*) where a layman sows seeds of merit and reaps a good harvest in the next world.[3]

## Medieval and modern Sri Lanka

It is possible that Rahula underrated the persisting presence and intermittent impact of the ascetic monastic communities in the early Buddhism of Sri Lanka and that he may have given a much too simple picture of the village-dwelling and town-dwelling vocations as creating a bifurcation of the *saṅgha* into two separate sects or groups. It is quite clear that, at least for the early medieval periods – the ninth through thirteenth centuries – the ascetic traditions figured in somewhat complex ways in the interrelations between *saṅgha* and polity. Let us follow the story as told by Gunawardana[4] for this period which spans the last stages of the Siṅhala Kingdom centered in Anurādhapura and its subsequent shift to Polonnaruva as the capital, whence during the twelfth and thirteenth centuries it contributed so vitally to the religious and political developments in Burmese Pagan and Thai Sukhothai.

It seems that the ascetic communities of the time were known by two labels taken from two ascetic practices recommended in texts such as the *Visuddhimagga* and the *Vimuttimagga*.[5] The *Paṁsukūlikas* took their name from the tradition of using discarded rags for their robes, whereas the *Āraññikas* took theirs from the practice of contemplative life and meditation in the seclusion of the forest. To get some glimpse of the way the monks who assumed these labels were distributed on the ground, we must consider at least three variables. Firstly, the ascetic groupings in question might have intersected with, or had their representation within, the three major *nikāyas* (sects/fraternities) into which the Siṅhala *saṅgha* was then alleged to have been divided. These were: the Mahāvihāra (Great Monastery) Nikāya, which appears to have been both in Anurādhapura and Polonnaruva the dominant sect for much of the time and which in any case has left behind the vast majority of the chronicles and texts from which the history of the times is reconstructed; the Abhayagiri Nikāya, which was a big presence as well and which was more open to doctrinal and commentarial schools outside the "orthodox" Theravādin tradition espoused by the former; and the Jetavana Nikāya, which was a breakaway group from the Abhayagiri, but which, being smaller in size, seems to have vacillated in its alliances with the other two in the ups and downs of factional rivalries.

Secondly, the Paṁsukūlika and Āraññika communities were distributed throughout the kingdom – some living in the environs or peripheries of the capital, the others in the interior spread over a wide area. There is also some evidence that their architectural forms and layout might have differed from those of the monasteries in the capital. Thirdly, as already suggested by Buddhaghosa in his elucidation of them in the *Visuddhimagga*, the ascetic practices were capable of flexible interpretation according to "strict," "moderate," or "soft" standards. Thus a variability in the practices of different communities bearing an ascetic label must be taken to be a normal condition.

## THE PAṀSUKŪLIKAS

Though the Paṁsukūlikas were known in Sri Lanka from at least the second century B.C., they came into prominence in the seventh to the tenth centuries. Some of the monasteries belonging to this "sect" were in the vicinity of the capital, and others are known to have existed in the provinces and in the Matale, Mahiyangana, Ritigala, and other regions.

The Paṁsukūlikas of the Abhayagiri monastery affiliation are known to have left it to form a school or fraternity (*gaṇa*) of their own in A.D. 872 during the

## The *arahant* and the Path of Meditation

reign of Sena II.[6] But, on the other hand, the Paṁsukūlika grouping at the Mahāvihāra remained within the fold right into the tenth century.

In due course, the Paṁsukūlikas by their very vocational practices attracted royal liberality and donations of the sort one associates with the town-dwelling monks affiliated with the capital. Several kings, including Aggabodhi V and VII and Mahinda IV, are on record as having given them special foods, garments, gold, and arable land together with equipment, slaves, and attendants.

The Paṁsukūlikas, along with the monks of many other monasteries of Polonnaruva, left for Ruhuana in protest against the confiscation of monastic property by Vikrama Bāhu I (1111–1132) and thereafter have not appeared in the historical records of Sri Lanka.

### THE ĀRAÑÑIKAS

The Siṁhala chronicles do not mention the Āraññikas before the tenth century, and references to them in other sources are rare. They too enjoyed the patronage of kings and queens, who not only built forest hermitages for them but also sent them medicaments and choice foods.

A remarkable feature is that "while there are several references to the Āraññika monks of the Mahāvihāra *nikāya*, there is no such information on those affiliated with the Abhayagiri and Jetavana nikāyas."[7] But, once again, although signifying a special vocational emphasis within the predominant *nikāya* of the times, Āraññika establishments also show evidence of distinctive achievements that set them apart from the usual monastic communities.

The Āraññikas seemed to have flourished even in times when the main establishments at the capital underwent hard times and reverses. Dimbulāgala was a famous Āraññika settlement, situated some ten miles southeast of Polonnaruva. It was known in the twelfth century to have had about 500 monks. It attracted many pilgrims as a repository of the corporeal relics of the Buddha; it may also well have been a center for the practice of meditation;[8] and it produced some of the leading scholars and hierarchs among the *saṅgha* of the twelfth and thirteenth centuries.[9]

By and large, the Āraññikas seemed to have lived in the "forest," whether this is interpreted as the peripheries of towns and villages or the deep interior, and they devoted themselves to both philosophical contemplation and scholarly endeavors. In fact, some of the renowned teachers and commentators of the period belonged to them, thus demonstrating that the vocations of meditation and learning can be combined in the best institutions.

In any case, what is of special interest to us is that their prestige was at its climax precisely at that period of medieval history when both kingship and *sāsana* were revitalized and achieved a final flowering, especially during the reign of Parākrama Bāhu I (1153), in whose time took place a historic reform and "purification" of the *saṅgha*.[10] This reform consisted of the expulsion or punishment of "deviant" monks, the reconciliation of the eight independent fraternities into which the *saṅgha* had fragmented, and appointment of a *mahāsāmī* as the head of the *saṅgha*. It is remarkable that this attempt at forging an ecclesiastical unity and hierarchy was achieved by Parākrama Bāhu with the collaboration of a monk named Mahākassapa, a scholar and master of the Vinaya, who presided over the synod and came not from one of the main monasteries inside the capital but from the historic forest-dwellers' (*āraññika*) monastery of Udumbaragiri, located some ten miles from it and probably belonging to the Mahāvihāra Nikāya.

It is vital to note – I reiterate a point I have made in my book *World Conqueror and Renouncer* – that both the Galvihāra inscription and the *Cūḷavaṃsa* chronicle compare the roles of Parākrama Bāhu and the Mahākassapa with those played by Emperor Aśoka and Mogalliputta Tissa in the Third Council.

We have seen, then, that the forest-dwelling monks, dedicated to a more or less ascetic and meditative life in the forest, though removed from the day-to-day religio-political life of the capital, could, by their very distancing – which earned them a popular reputation and acclaim as following the ideal religious life of a *bhikkhu* – periodically enter the arena at the capital to help purify and set things in order.[11] The active participation of monks of the Āraññika sect in this *saṅgha* reform marked their significant position in the *sāsana* as a whole.

Now, it is of capital importance that a subsequent *saṅgha* reform, of which the one discussed above was the precursor – namely, that recorded in the Dambadēni Katikāvata, which was codified during the reign of Parākrama Bāhu II – was transported together with Siṅhala Buddhism to the early Thai kingdoms of Sukhodaya and Lān Nā, and thereby provided the organizational structure for the *saṅgha* for Southeast Asian Buddhism. In this constitutional charter we find the formal recognition of the *saṅgha* as divided into two sections in which the forest dwellers are one. The *katikāvata* recognized that the *sāsana* was divided between the *gāmavāsins* on the one hand and the *āraññavāsins* on the other, each section to be headed by a *mahāsthavira*, a title given to a monk of twenty-five years' standing. Both sections with their own heads were placed under the overall headship of the *mahāsāmi*, the head of the *saṅgha*. And the provision that should the post of the *mahāsāmi* fall vacant, the successor should be appointed from among the two *mahāsthavira* leaves us in no doubt that a monk of *āraññika* affiliation could at that time become the head of the *saṅgha* hierarchy and the entire community of monks of the island.[12]

It is relevant now to refer to another critical revival and unification in Sri Lanka sponsored in the Kandyan Kingdom in the eighteenth century. It included the elevation of the two main monasteries in the capital, namely Malwatte and Asgiriya, to preeminent positions such that they were given jurisdiction over all the monasteries on the island. Thus a dual reorganization was introduced, with each division or chapter being headed by a supreme chief monk (*mahā-nāyaka*) and assisted by two deputies (*anu-nāyakas*) and a committee of chief monks *(nāyakas)*. Exclusive powers were given each division to admit novices to higher ordination at the capital, and various sacred sites and monasteries and endowments throughout the kingdom were assigned to the two divisions, which were "formally" assigned the northern and southern regions. What is of interest to us is that Asgiriya is said to have originated as a forest-dwelling (*araññavāsī*) fraternity, whereas Malwatte belonged to the village-dwelling (*gāmavāsī*) tradition. By the middle of the eighteenth century, this distinction had apparently lost its original significance, most of the Asgiriya monks being in fact village dwelling. Thus the two chapters in time became parallel structures. Nevertheless, we should bear in mind the persisting nature of the partition of the *saṅgha* and the use of the two labels; I shall shortly show how the dichotomy still operates meaningfully in the Kandyan ritual of state called the *perahera*.

Although in the late eighteenth century the Asgiriya and Malwatte chapters showed no substantive differentiation in their orientations, they yet were divided as opposed factions, Asgiriya supporting the king and his Nayakkar kinsmen (of South Indian origins) and Malwatte, including the *saṅgharāja*, V älvita Saraṇaṁkara, siding with the opposition.[13]

There is some evidence of an interest in meditation on the part of Saraṇaṁkara in the mid-eighteenth century, to which we shall advert later, but let me now take the story of the forest-monk traditions in Sri Lanka to modern times.

A rich documentation of the Sri Lankan forest monks of the nineteenth and, in greater detail, twentieth centuries is provided by Michael Carrithers in a work that is in press, and of whose content I can only give some brief indications.[14] Carrithers develops his general principles by means of documenting detailed biographies of eight leading forest dwellers. It transpires that Sri Lanka manifests a spectrum of tendencies among the various monks who have followed forest-monk practices.

In 1972, Carrithers made a count of approximately 150 forest-monk hermitages in Sri Lanka, which were all "less than 100 years old, and all but a handful . . . less than 20 years old." Most of these hermitages were founded or inspired by a few leading figures, most of whom were still alive. This seems to imply that the earlier ascetic and meditative tradition had declined during the colonial times and that they were revived in recent times, thus representing a feature of what Heinz Bechert has called "Buddhist modernism."[15] Carrithers's evidence suggests that, although there may have been an overall decline, yet the forest-monk-*cum*-meditative tradition had not disappeared; in fact, his evidence could have prompted him to take a stronger view of continuity than he has actually taken.

The Island Hermitage located just off the southwest coast of Sri Lanka was founded around 1911 and has been largely occupied by European monks. These monks have combined strict disciplinary practices with meditation and have achieved a remarkable reputation for scholarship. The founder of the hermitage

## The forest-monk tradition in Southeast Asia

was Nyanatiloka, and another famous member was Nyanaponika. When Carrithers visited it, it had fourteen *kutis* individually occupied.

For us, what is more interesting is Carrithers's treatment of what he calls "folk asceticism," from which derives many of the forest-monk hermitages founded and populated by Sinhalese monks. Many of these local monks interestingly had hived off from the established sects, like the Siyām Nikāya, to start stricter fraternities in the spirit of reform. Reform itself, true to the pattern of purification recurrently staged in Theravāda Buddhist countries, takes the canonical texts and the classical *Visuddhimagga* as a point of reference.[16]

Paññānanda is identified as a mid-nineteenth-century figure who founded the oldest continually occupied hermitages extant in Sri Lanka, namely, Batuvila and Kirinda. He was born in 1817 in Tangalle in the South, and in his time arose the Low Country reform movements that founded the Amarapura fraternities and subsequently the Rāmañña Nikāya, in the founding of which Paññānanda actually participated.

Paññānanda designated his hermitage at Kirinda as *tāpasārāma* and referred to himself and his disciples as *tāpasa* monks; Paññānanda practiced at one time or other all the *dhūtaṅga* (ascetic) practices. Now it is clear that Paññānanda's interpretation of hermitage life was fully informed by the *Vinaya* texts, the *Visuddhimagga*, and also that it was rooted in the Jātaka tradition. And his regime combined meditation with active preaching and teaching (rather than scholarship). This combination of activities was not thought to be contradictory, and in fact, as we shall see in our account of recent forest monks in Thailand, it indicates an entrenched pattern.

Now, I want to use the example of Paññānanda to make two points of more than a parochial Sri Lankan import. Firstly, Carrithers cites a biography of the monk, which was in turn based on an earlier biography.[17] These biographies, called appropriately *caritaya*, recount besides other things Paññānanda's encounters with wild animals (a leopard and a snake) and with deities and report a dream foretelling his destiny. I submit that these are "conventional" incidents reported in many of the lives of famous Southeast Asian forest monks and that this biographical tradition in Sri Lanka is part of a larger Theravāda tradition.

Secondly, Carrithers reports that Paññānanda had a number of teachers, of whom one was a forest-dwelling monk named Sumangala, with whom he studied meditation for a while, and whose ascetic powers are still spoken of. I submit again that such facts suggest that there was a continuing tradition, sparse perhaps but not exactly moribund, that cannot be attributed to that kind of Buddhist modernism associated with the Theosophists and with Anagārika Dharmpāla.

An important strand in the contemporary forest-monk phenomenon is a serious and disciplined movement among Sinhalese monks started by Kadavädduve Jinavaṃsa and his collaborator, Ñāṇārāma. Jinavaṃsa was born in 1907 near Matara, and his group of hermit monks were called Śrī Kalyāṇi Yogāśrāma

## The *arahant* and the Path of Meditation

Saṁsthāva.[18] The affiliations of this movement were with the reformist Rāmañña Nikāya. Jinavaṁsa was a Pali scholar and essayist who advocated a reform of monastic practices. His associate Ñāṇārāma was the skilled meditation adept and teacher; he can be said to have "recreated" a meditation tradition out of the principles and precepts set out in the *Visuddhimagga*, the heritage bequeathed by Paññānanda, and the stimulation provided by Burmese influences.

Jinavaṁsa was able to establish his hermitages with lay support and for the express purpose of training pupils in meditation. That the ablest forest monk imbued with a teaching mission and endowed with entrepreneurial skills is capable of establishing institutional networks is attested by the fact that "The tenth anniversary in 1961 saw the *samsthava* fully constituted with 100 monks and 40 hermitages or meditation temples. . . . It enjoyed more internal cohesion than any of the circumambient village Sangha" (Carrithers).[19]

I cannot refrain from including an incident that attests to the excitable piety of the laity who crave for exemplary saints. In 1973, rumors spread in Colombo that a monk from Ñāṇārāma's teaching hermitage had attained the status of *sotāpanna* (stream enterer). Pious laity were getting ready for their lavish dona-tions to the hero. From the point of view of the hero's teacher, the status in question was a sober description of his pupil's progress in meditation and in the understanding of Buddhist truths.

The final band in the Sri Lankan spectrum is occupied by the Tāpasa Movement, a spectacularly visible and correspondingly volatile and short-lived movement in the early 1950s. Carrithers dubs them "folk ascetics," for their conduct was based on more "folk ideas than on canonical commentarial versions of the meditative life."[20]

The first Buddhist *tāpasa* monk of modern times was Subodhānanda, who in 1898 renounced his ordination and left a Siyam Nikāya temple near Colombo. He subsequently took the robes again as a self-ordained ascetic, a *tāpasayā*. The concept and the role are based not on the canonical texts, in which self-ordination is not countenanced, but on Jātaka tales of how the Buddha left home to ordain himself. Though earlier in his ascetic career Subodhānanda was subject to the taunt of *theyyasaṁvāsaka*, meaning "coresident monk by theft" (a label culled from one of the stories in the canonical *Vinaya* texts), by the end of his life in 1948 his movement had gained a certain respect; he left behind three well-established temples and a couple of vocal pupils. Subodhānanda actually wrote a pamphlet in support of a new group of monks who, in the heady revivalistic atmosphere of the years after independence in 1948 and the imminent celebra-tion of the 2500th anniversary of Buddhism, founded forest-monk communities within the fold of the recognized ordination traditions.

It is these slogans and precedents that stimulated certain young men in the early fifties to self-ordain themselves as ascetics and to publicize their renuncia-tory gestures. The best known of these was Tāpasa Himi, who at the age of 18, inspired by the example of another monk who had left the established *saṅgha* and reordained himself, shaved his head, donned a robe, and squatted in a cemetery near his home.

Thereafter Himi and his followers – all young, innocent of formal religious training, and responsive to the histrionics of happenings – took to residing in cemeteries, to sitting cross-legged under trees, and to walking in single file "measuring their steps." They laced these with a caustic preaching style directed at the religious establishment.

News of the young ascetics spread, and they became popular preachers. Within two years, Himi's reputation had grown, and so had the number of lay pupils and the scale of lay support. At the peak of their reputation, Himi and seventeen disciples went to the old capital of Kandy and occupied a hilltop. The laity mobbed them and showered them with gifts, and the number of hermits increased to thirty-five within two days. They then daringly occupied the Temple of the Tooth, and this signaled their fall; they had pushed the religious establishment too far, and the police dislodged them. An invitation to go to Burma did not materialize, and soon afterward the movement was subject to harassment and abuse by the police and the public, which now turned against them. Himi escaped to India for a year; the other *tāpasayā* disbanded or became regular monks.

I must record – especially as proof of the Siṅhala Buddhist public's responsiveness to millennial hopes and the appearance of the rare *arahant* among them – that, at the height of the effervescence, rumors spread that Tāpasa Himi had supranormal powers, that he could fly, that he was seen in the moon, that he could speak ten languages. Some even assimilated him to the saints of ancient Sri Lanka, others to the *bōdhisattva* of the Jātaka stories. He even received the ambiguous title of *Väbada Budu* (the first term being his village; the second could refer to the Buddha himself or be simply used as an honorific).

This short-lived movement is instructive. Negatively, it demonstrates that a movement based on self-ordination and whose members have little "professional" training in monastic discipline are condemned not to take institutional root. Positively, it demonstrates that this ascetic protest by youths and the enthusiastic, though short-lived, lay support it enjoyed are "religious" phenomena embedded in politico-economic issues. Apart from the reform of the *saṅgha* attitudes of the time, this was a period of increasing literacy of youth unaccompanied by increasing employment opportunities; furthermore, the fact that the larger part of the lay support was from the ranks of the lower and poorer castes[21] suggests that this was a time when the gap between egalitarian democratic ideals and the realities of the traditional hierarchy was keenly felt.

## Burma

Mendelson tells us a complex story of the Burmese forest-monks of the *arahanta* tradition and the diverse contexts in which they appeared. They have acted as

# The *arahant* and the Path of Meditation

reformists and breakaway groups, they have formed special groupings within a larger fraternity, and they have achieved the status of a separate sect reproducing the spectrum of activities of the established sects. "The forest monks, much like hermits, did not necessarily cease to belong to a mother community which might well be of the village kind. Later in time, forest monks began to appear in forest communities, devoting themselves no longer to meditation alone but indulging also in cultural and educational activities, as did town and village monks; in short, they seem to have been treated in some places as separate sects."[22]

Paññasāmi, the author of *Sāsanavaṁsa*, belonged to that branch of the *saṅgha* that had pro-Siṅhala orientations, and he identified himself with the Upper Burma *arahanta* tradition. He clearly was intolerant of "abuses" in the parent community that stemmed from the receipt of land endowments and taxes and favored those who left for the forest in protest.

Paññasāmi gave this account of an early split in the Burmese *saṅgha*. There was a dispute in the thirteenth century over the management of fields and lands dedicated to seven monasteries built by King Uzana II. Three monks left for the "forest" and took up residence in a mountain meditation monastery and cave. "Those Elders [who left] were called those who walked alone. But the remaining monks were called village-dwellers who walked with many. From that time onwards there were two separate groups [of monks]: forest dwellers and village dwellers. There was also a class of the Order known as monks who were recipients of the taxes on fields and lands dedicated to the monastery."[23]

This kind of origin story is repeated by another Burmese chronicle, the *Thathana Linkara Sadan*, which says that after a dispute about land arrangements at the Campaka Monastery, two monks who were also brothers, Thatanadara and Parakkama, left to become "lone forest dwellers." One brother went east and the other west, and they set up two abbeys, the West Parakkama and East Parakkama. In this account, however, the monks who departed are identified as the *arahanta* line and the orthodox monks who remained as the Ānanda (Sri Lanka) line.[24]

Mendelson rejects any simplistic identification in Burma of the "forest monks" as the Maramma (Upper Burma) Saṅgha and the "village monks" as the Sīhala (Sri Lanka) Saṅgha.[25] He proposes the alternative view – which accords with the Sri Lanka facts that we have reviewed – that the chroniclers of the established Sīhala Saṅgha traced their lineages through those monks in either forest or village communities whom they considered orthodox in behavior and criticized unorthodox behavior wherever it occurred, even among the forest dwellers. The forest-monks whom Paññasāmi, for example, admired were those who did not accumulate land endowments but who meditated or rigorously observed the *Vinaya* rules. "Too much materialism in the Saṅgha triggers both internal monastic reformers and lay purification movements, and the forest monks Paññasāmi favors are more likely to be the reformers than the reformed."[26]

Gifts to monasteries, sacred sites, pagodas, or famous Buddha statues comprised lands as well as slaves to look after and work them. Such property interests inevitably led to disputes and lawsuits between monks themselves, monks and laity, and even monks and kings. And during Pagan times there were periodic attempts by kings to reclaim or confiscate religious lands that had grown too large or belonged to monasteries out of favor.[27] When we add to this the sporadic instances of far-flung, village-based autonomous monastic communities becoming too lax in the observance of *Vinaya* rules, we see good reasons not only for reformist monks to break away to live the pure life but also for genuinely ascetic forest communities to be called upon periodically to help clean the stables.

There has been a continuity in the Burmese pattern of reformist thrusts from within the *saṅgha*. During the nineteenth century, reformist monks tended to see themselves as "lone forest dwellers" of the *arahanta* tradition which was strengthened and vitalized by infusions of Siṅhalese orthodoxy through the medium of successive "pilgrims" sent to Sri Lanka for reordination.

It is neither in Sri Lanka nor in Thailand but in Burma that we find the best evidence in the last 130 years of reformist and forest-monk traditions being elaborated in the face of royal attempts at "purification" as well as "domestication" of the *saṅgha*. This is best illustrated by the creation of major sectarian movements during the reign of King Mindon (1853–78). He attempted to create a unified *saṅgha* hierarchy as well as purify the religion by convening the Fifth Buddhist Council in order to produce a recension of the Pali canon. The Thudhamma, which constituted the dominant establishment, collaborated with the king, but an impressive number of "puritanical sects" – whom Mendelson calls the "Mindon sects" – stood aside. The main noncooperating sects were the Shwegyin in Upper Burma and the Dwaya in Lower Burma. (The Shwegyin sect will be subject to a close scrutiny shortly.) There were also smaller fraternities of similar orientations, such as the Weluwun and the Pakokku. But this period of flux – King Mindon was after all the last great Burmese king before the fall of Upper Burma to the British – also gave rise to more radical and extremist groups known by the label *paramat*. (A notable instance was the Hnyetwin, which has continued to this day.) Finally, at the edges of this politico-religious turmoil emerged the *gaings*, the volatile movements and cults that developed around the *weikzas* – charismatic monks, ex-monks, and holy men, reputed to possess supranormal powers associated with alchemy, meditation, astrology, amulets, medicine, and other esoteric arts. This full spectrum of religious institutions, and the fissiparousness that formed it, have continued into modern times. The *gaings* focused on *weikzas* are a fuzzy and intriguing phenomenon best considered later in this book in relation to millennial Buddhism after we have given a full account of the contemporary meditation masters of North and Northeast Thailand and when we are in a position to see in their proper perspective a variety of holy men.

The Shwegyin sect merits an extended statement on account of the range of dialectical tensions it manifested in its relation to the Burmese political authorities[28] on the eve of Burma's colonial submission. The history of the Shwegyin goes back to the reign of King Pagan (1846–53), during which the head monk appointed by him expelled from the capital and from all important monastic centers the Shangalegyun Sayadaw for his advocacy of a strict *Vinaya* discipline based on reformist forest-monk notions. The banished monk and his sister founded a remote forest monastery near a village south of Shwebo, and they had a young disciple, the Shwegyin Sayadaw, who later became the founder of the sect in question.

This was a period of crisis in Burmese history. A beleaguered kingship threatened and shamed by the British conquest of the maritime provinces diverted its efforts to the purification of the religion, and correspondingly the *sangha* too "leaned toward more self-denial, greater self-discipline, and a zeal for purification as a counterbalance to diminished kingship."[29] King Mindon in some respects resembled his counterpart in Thailand, King Mongkut, in that he had spent some time in the monasteries himself; and he was the agent of the Shwegyin sect's return to royal favor. Mindon in fact backed two horses at the same time. While supporting the officially appointed head of the *sangha* (who had been his father's favorite) and the Thudhamma Council of officially honored elder monks who administered Buddhist disciplinary law, Mindon also deliberately honored the forest monks, approved of their practices such as eschewing the use of sandals and umbrellas, and asked them to draw up a new set of monastic rules to be presented for approval by the council. Moreover, aside from the monastery he had built in 1855 for the Shangalegyun Sayadaw, Mindon in the teeth of the opposition of the town monks backed his protégé monk's successor, the Shwegyin Sayadaw, and built for him five monasteries near Mandalay Hill, soon after the completion of the capital city of Mandalay in 1859.

But the collision between the head of the *sangha* and the Shwegyin Sayadaw came to an impasse, and in a historic decision Mindon not only gave royal approval to the Shwegyin Sayadaw to leave the capital for the forest but also gave him and his followers a separate status as a sect no longer under the authority of the Thudhamma Council. Thereafter, in the remaining years of King Mindon's reign the Shwegyin sect had its cake and ate it too, or, rather, managed the extraordinary feats of keeping its independence while enjoying royal patronage and munificence and of oscillating between administrative responsibilities and withdrawal from them. The Shwegyin acted as a moral counselor to the king, who faithfully supported the five Shwegyin monasteries so that their thousand or more students were fed by royal grants and did not have to go on daily alms rounds. Moreover, after the death of the head of the *sangha*, Mindon gave the Shwegyin Sayadaw the responsibility to act as *Thathanapyu* in the Alon area, up the Chindwin River. Undismayed by the Sayadaw's refusal of an honorary title in 1871, Mindon escalated his favors and offered the Sayadaw twelve monasteries, including the famous Mahawithudarama Taik, which became the seat of the sect's leader. The sect developed rapidly, and the donations were redistributed among the disciples.

But if the sect seemed near domestication, its next step signaled its withdrawal into reclusive life. When Mindon convened his famous Fifth Buddhist Council to purify the scriptures and to unify the *sangha*, the Shwegyin Sayadaw took no part in it, retired four years later from all his official *thathanapyu* duties, and spent longer and longer periods of time away from the capital at forest retreats.

Mindon's successor, King Thibaw, attempted to solve the sectarian problem by nominating *both* the Shewgyin Sayadaw and the Taungdaw Sayadaw as joint heads of the *sangha*. The former refused the office but helped administer for a time nine ecclesiastical departments in Upper Burma. During this time, the Shwegyin sect's missionary monks were sent, with royal backing, to key centers. Nevertheless, despite Thibaw's backing, which even exceeded that of his father, the Shwegyin returned to forest life in 1884 in the face of his increasing misgivings regarding the society at large. Surely enough, the next year the Burmese monarchy came to an end.

The Shwegyin's attitudes and achievements are as intriguing as they are impressive, and they have left an enduring mark upon his sect. At a time of colonial intrusion, challenges from Christianity, and political turmoil, he demonstrated that it is by a distancing from royal patronage and from the laity – while accepting their bounty – that the forest-monks could preserve their integrity, as well as build up their organizational network. While proud of its royalist origins, the sect had not been overwhelmed by power, wealth, and honors. "At the same time at [the Shwegyin's] death he left behind an organization held together by respect for him, for other teachers, an acceptance of hierarchical authority, and a countrywide network of reformist monasteries looking to Mandalay for leadership."[30]

The twentieth-century posture of the Shwegyin sect has been a withdrawal into its forest-monk life of discipline and scholarly contemplation combined with an internal concern to improve its organizational structure by means of consolidation and centralization. After some experimentation, in 1927 a reliance on aged leaders was abandoned, and six monks were appointed to oversee day-to-day affairs. At the same time, district-level positions, which were previously locally determined, were brought under central control.

The years during and after World War II were a time of nationalist politics and volatile experiments. But while the establishment Thudhamma monks joined political organizations, the leadership of the Shwegyin sect disapproved of participation in nationalist politics. The result was an even more emphatic separation of its members from the attitudes and activities of the Thudhamma majority. The sect's leader, Sankin Sayadaw, was a dedicated forest-monk, who specialized in *vipassanā* meditation and remained uninvolved in political movements. And the sect as a whole has continued to maintain its traditional profile – of involvement with meditation as a vital activity combined with an even more pronounced emphasis upon scholarship and teaching. If it is an independent sect within a nonunified Burmese *sangha*, it is yet conservative and more comfortable with hierarchy than with loose autonomy for its member groupings. And its greatest strength lies in Upper Burma.

## Thailand

A remarkable theme in the ideology of the early Thai kingdoms established in Sukhodaya and Chiengmai was that the carriers of the brand of Siṅhala pure Pali Buddhism that they received and treasured were monks of the forest-dwelling tradition. The intercourse between Sri Lanka and Thailand began with King Rāmkhamhāēng inviting to Sukhodaya a high priest from Nagara Śrī Dharmarāja who was preaching the Siṅhalese Theravāda doctrine. It climaxed in the fifteenth century, when a mission of monks from Lān Nā (Chiengmai) went to Sri Lanka to be reordained. On their return, they founded the Siṅhala sect, sponsored the revival of the Theravāda doctrine and Pali Literature, and energetically built temples. This fertile encounter with Sri Lanka was "objectified" in the Thai collective consciousness in the form of a statue called the Phra Sihing (the Siṅhala Buddha/the Lion Buddha) and the mythology associated with it; this will be the subject of a later chapter.

The nascent Sukhodayan stage of state formation was fittingly supported by the reformist and evangelical Buddhism of the forest monks. The religious vitalization first in Sukhodaya in North-central Thailand, and subsequently in the northern Lān Nā polities of the Chiengmai region, was closely associated with the Siṅhala sect of forest-dwelling monks (*araññavāsī*) under the leadership of the monk Sumana and his associate Anomadassi.

To Rāmkhamhāēng's grandson, King Līthai (Dharmarāja), is credited the mid-fourteenth-century inscription at Wat Sī Čām, which says: "When the Somdet Phra Mahāsāmī (Sumana the monk) came from Sīhaḷa (Sri Lanka) he brought a body of laymen with him and, in his faith, brought also two precious relics of the Buddha." Another inscription at the Monastery of the Mango Grove commemorates the arrival of the monk Sumana in 1362, his installation at this monastery, and his ordination of King Līthai himself as a monk.

Sumana, in fact, exemplifies the integral link between the forest-monk traditions of Sri Lanka, Burma, and Thailand in the fourteenth century. Sumana's brand of forest-monk Buddhism can be linked via Martaban in Burma to the famous Udumbaragiri forest monastery in Sri Lanka of the Polonnaruva period. Sumana and his associate Anomadassi went to Martaban to study Siṅhala Buddhism from a monk named Anumati, who in turn had traveled to Sri Lanka to be ordained there, and returned with eleven others to Burma in 1331 to found the Udumbaragiri forest-dwelling order.[31] In 1369, Sumana and his followers went north to North Thailand (Lānnā) to the Chiengmai region and thence began a new chapter of the Siṅhala forest monks' participation in the legitimation, crystallization, and, finally, political expansion of the Thai dynasty under the rule of the *cakkavatti* kings, Tilokarāja and his grandson Phra Mūeang Kāeo (1495–1528).

The Thai dynasty was founded at Chiengmai by King Mangrāi at the end of the thirteenth century and was finally subjugated by the Burmese in 1578. In between, there was an epoch of lively politics and proselytizing Buddhism. (A period of 200 years had to elapse before North Thailand was again to be brought under Thai suzerainty by King Taksin.) The Buddhism of the monks of the North before the Thai takeover was of a Mon-Lāva variety and in time came to be identified as the order of town dwellers (*nagaravāsī*), in contrast to Sumana's forest dwellers. The latter were invited to come north by the seventh king of the Thai dynasty, King Kūēnā (1367–88). Sumana brought with him a Buddha relic and the *Tipiṭaka* canon, the twin symbols of popular cult and sacred learning, and pointedly chose to live just outside the historic city of Lamphūn. A chronicle, *Tamnān Mūlasāsanā Wat Sūan Dāūk*, reports that Sumana informed the king when asked to choose a site: "All men of wisdom, beginning with the Omniscient Lord Buddha, whenever they came to a market town to lead the townspeople and villagers to salvation, have been accustomed since ancient times to settle at a measured distance of five hundred bow lengths from the gatepost of the town."[32]

Swearer and Premchit[33] discern in the North Thai chronicles three phases in the nexus between Buddhism and dynastic politics in Chiengmai during a 150-year period:

1. King Kūēnā (1367–88) enshrines the relic brought by Sumana at Wat Sūan Dāūk, which becomes the center of Sumana's forest order, confers the title of *rājaguru* on him, and even endows the order with revenue-producing lands. In this first phase, then, Sumana and his Udumbaragiri order enable the newly founded Thai dynasty (as new ethnic overlords) to gain eventual dominance over the indigenous ruling elements who traced their affiliations to Ādittarāja of Haribhuñjaya (Lamphūn).

2. In the reign of Sām Fāng Kāēn (1411–42), however, sectarian religious controversy breaks out, and the order of Sumana's successors, now the establishment, with Wat Sūan Dāūk as their center, is challenged by a newly arrived Siṅhala order from Ayudhyā, which first establishes itself in centers like Lamphūn outside the capital, and criticizes the order of Sumana for accepting money and owning rice lands; in addition, it espouses a *Vinaya* discipline different from it.[34] It would seem that this new Siṅhala order is also of a forest-dwelling variety confronting another of their kind with the usual reformist critique. The political outcome of this rivalry is the deposition of Sām Fāng Kāēn and the usurpation of the throne by his tenth son, Tilokarāja, who, it is presumed, attains to the throne in part because of his championing of the newly arrived Siṅhala order.

3. Tilokarāja's remarkable extension of the territories of his kingdom, west into the Shan States of Upper Burma and east toward Lūang Phrabāng, goes hand in hand with his sponsorship of the (new) Siṅhala order, which becomes the dominant order not only in the capital of Chiengmai but also in the major

## The *arahant* and the Path of Meditation

Northern towns, with monks of other affiliations reordaining themselves into it. The two leading monks of the Siṅhala order are honored with titles and residences: The king builds for Ñāṇagambhīra a royal chapel in Chiengmai, while Mahāsāmī Medhaṁkara, appointed *rājaguru*, ordains the king as a monk for a while and is the recipient of a *prāsād* built for him at Wat Čēdī Lūang (Monastery of the Royal Dagoba). Another monastery, Wat Pā Daēng (Monastery of the Red Forest), remodeled and expanded, becomes the center of the order in the capital. Tilokarāja, by virtue of his political and religious acts, not only assumes the title of *cakkavatti*, but is also acknowledged as the reincarnated Aśoka of North Thailand.

The Northern polity and Buddhist civilization of Lānnā reaches its climactic flowering during the reign of Tilokarāja's grandson, Phra Mūeang Kāēo (1495–1528). Of particular significance is the level of Pali scholarship and literary composition reached, as attested by the historical chronicle, the *Jinakāla-mālī* (1517); the great commentary, *Maṅgalatthadīpanī*; and other works, such as the *Phra Buddha Sihing* chronicle, which we shall cite later.

It is, however, important to remember that even during the reigns of these two famous kings, the Siṅhala order was by no means the only one. The *Jinakālamālī* tells us that at the consecration of a new *uposatha* hall at Wat Čēdī Čet Yāūt, monks from three *nikāyas* from all the main towns were present, and they are identified as the Sīhaḷa, Nagara (the pre-Thai order), and the Pupphārāma (the Sumana–Suan Dāūk order).

On the basis of our survey of developments in Sukhodaya and Lānnā, we can make some general statements regarding the role of the Siṅhala forest-monks – who are by no means a unitary community – in Thailand during medieval times. The turn of events in both Thai polities shows that the Siṅhala order by and large chose to collaborate purposefully with the ruling powers, and thereby took a stance that in many respects was markedly different from the troubled, equivocal, and distancing stance taken by the Shwegyin forest-dwelling sect in Burma during King Mindon's reign and after.

The Siṅhala communities publicized their forest-dweller label by taking up their monastic residence on the outskirts of the capital and other towns and distinguished themselves by their skill in meditative absorption, strict discipline, and knowledge of the Pali scriptures. At the same time, they forged a close legitimating alliance with the rulers of the burgeoning Thai polities and became the chroniclers that treated the fortunes of religion and kingship as closely bonded themes.

By no means the sole member of the *saṅgha*, the Siṅhala order made its impact in the classical Thai polities in contrast to the local branches of town-dwelling monks. Prince Damrong has described the co-presence of the forest- and town-dwelling monks in this way:

From stone inscriptions at Sukhothai [Sukhodaya] and Chiengmai, it appears that monks of the Ceylonese sect lived in monasteries outside the towns . . . For both at Sukhothai and

# The forest-monk tradition in Southeast Asia

Chiengmai, all the big monasteries which were the landmarks of the cities, such as the Monastery of the Great Relic and the Monastery of the Royal Dagoba, were all built in the towns. There were also smaller monasteries built closely together about four kilometres outside the towns. These monasteries were regarded as important for the Ceylonese [Siṅhala] sect. They included the Mango Grove Monastery where the Supreme Patriarch of Sukhothai resided, and the Red Forest Monastery, residence of the Patriarch of Chiengmai. This kind of monastery was built in a place far enough from the houses, but close enough to the towns for the monks to walk to the towns to collect alms in the morning.[35]

The logic of newly founded political dynasties' and/or kingdoms' zealous support of ascetic forest-monk fraternities may lie in the fact that they are an effective counterweight to already established village- and town-dwelling monasteries and other localized and propertied cults and temples.[36] Newly emergent kings may wish to challenge the established cultic and/or monastic complexes that are not their creatures by sponsoring new ordination lineages of forest monks, whose ascetic, "pure" practices can attract lay attention and support. The sponsorship is then part and parcel of the "purification" and "revival" of the religion, which is a reiterated theme in the chronicles.

But it is also evident that these forest-monks labored outside established capitals and towns. Starting as little-endowed fraternities, and locating themselves on forest edges on the frontiers of advancing settlements, the forest-monks could act as elite carriers of literate civilization and could serve as foci for the collective religious activities and moral sentiments of frontier settlements. It is an alliance of this sort, a paired relationship between the founding kings with *cakkavatti* expansionist ambitions and the ascetically vigorous forest-monks at the moving edge of human habitation, that provides us with one plausible key for understanding the dynamism behind the "Buddhist polity" in southeast Asia, a dynamism that replicated the ruler–monk coalition in the expanding territories and also domesticated the local cults and incorporated them within a Buddhist hierarchy and cosmos.

Thai traditions relating to the role of various kinds of holy men – besides monks, other persons in question were known by such names as *rūēsī* (*ṛṣi*), *chīphākhāo*, and *khrū-bā-āčǎn* – in the founding of new settlements in North Thailand are both intriguing and shadowy.[37] Charnvit attributes to monastic establishments an active role in colonizing frontier regions and expanding territories of kingdoms; he explains the advantages accruing to the lay colonists serving the monks in these terms:

Settlement in a new center of Buddhist religion or attachment to a Buddhist temple, according to old practice of the Menam Basin, were grounds for exemption from corvée labour. Those who became *khā-phra* or temple slaves were no longer eligible to be drafted for corvée labour by any ruler. They worked only for a temple and its monks, and the service required by the Buddhist order was considerably less strenuous than that demanded by kings or rulers . . . As for the ruler who authorised new settlement of this kind, he supported it because it provided him with a way of expanding his realm and heightening his prestige largely by concentrating and increasing his pool of manpower . . . Buddhist temples had become a binding force which tied a population together and this was one of the basic concerns of rulers in the area.[38]

Once established, the temple with its monastic inmates and its cohort of attached slaves could in turn attract new colonists settling on their own account and also favored officials of the king whose servants were given corvée exemption.

About the activities of forest-monk communities in the medieval Ayudhyān era, and especially the discipline and technique of meditation they followed, we know little. But there is some evidence of an entrenched meditative tradition in Thailand extending back at least to the Ayudhyā period. This evidence comes via the *Manual of a Mystic*,[39] a Siṅhalese handbook devoted to the treatment of the *jhāna* levels of absorption associated with the *samādhi* form of concentration meditation. Although much of the *Manual*'s treatment of *samādhi* tallies with some of the contents of the *Visuddhimagga*, there are portions that do not, and that may have been incorporated from Yoga methods and/or developed in later times from Buddhist canonical materials.[40]

D. B. Jayatilaka, who was instrumental in getting made a copy of the original, surmised that the original Siṅhalese text was written during the remarkable Buddhist renaissance and revival in Sri Lanka in the middle of the eighteenth century, to which Siamese *bhikkhu* contributed impressively.[41] Of particular importance were the two missions sent to Siam in 1743 and 1750. A moving spirit in the reform at that time was the Saṅgharāja Saraṇaṁkara[42] and his disciples, whose works contain ample evidence as to the existence of *jhāna* practice in Sri Lanka in the eighteenth century. Mrs. C. A. F. Rhys Davids does not find implausible the suggestion that the Siamese monks who came over to Sri Lanka about, or shortly before, this period had a hand in the revival and encouragement of *samādhi* meditation on that island. Such an occurrence fits into the well-known pattern of periodic exchanges between the polities of Sri Lanka, Rammaṇa and Pagan (Burma), and Chiengmai and Sukhodaya (Thailand) by which they revitalized one another's religious traditions and institutions.

The fate of the forest-monk (*āraññavāsī*) tradition in Thailand during the last 130 years or so is not simple to recount: On the one hand, there have been attempts from the time of Mongkut onward, since the 1840s, to encompass some of its aspirations within the Thammayut movement. On the other hand the bureaucratization thrust from Bangkok, especially at the turn of the twentieth century with the objective of forming a hierarchized national *saṅgha*, has tended to obliterate it as a formal division of the *saṅgha*. These two developments will concern us in later chapters.

Although we have no detailed, reliable evidence on the place of forest monks in the *saṅgha* organization during Ayudhyān and early Bangkok times, it is interesting that during King Mongkut's time there were four great divisions (*khana*) of the *saṅgha*: the northern (left) and southern (right) divisions, whose members were the town-dwelling scholar monks (*ganthadhura*); the central division, which was composed of the forest-dwelling monks (*vipassanādhura*); and, lastly, the newly constituted Thammayutika group, which all through Mongkut's reign was administered as part of the one Mahānikāi order and gained the status of an independent sect (*nikāya*) only in King Chulalongkorn's reign.[43] The four divisions were administered by four ecclesiastical officials appointed by the king from the heads of royal monasteries.

The *Sangha* Act of 1902, passed in King Chulalongkorn's reign, seems not to have accorded the forest-monks a formal administrative recognition. The act changed the previous central division of the forest-monks into a central geographical division of the Mahānikāi sect; thereafter, until today, the forest-monks have not enjoyed a separate administrative recognition in either the Mahānikāi or Thammayut sects, which constitute the two major divisions of the Thai *sangha*.

It is, however, interesting that right through the nineteenth century the development and expansion of the capital city of Bangkok (and Thonburī on the other side of the Čao Phrayā River) reflected a pattern of town-dwelling monasteries in the center of the city and of forest-monk establishments at the city's edge.

O'Connor[44] has observed that in the early reigns of the Čakkrī dynasty, say the first three monarchs, the major royal *wat* as well as the highest-ranking monks were located either within the city walls or on the Thonburī shore. Since by royal policy the Chinese settled downriver outside the southeastern wall, and Westerners chose to congregate further south along the river, it was in the area north of the city, dotted with dispersed Thai settlements, that many of the new *wat* were established. A good example is the Bāngkhunphrom-Thēwēt area immediately north of the city: By the fifth reign, there were nine *wat* there, and a new one was added during it.

A noteworthy feature about these new *wat* developing on the northern edge of the city, its frontiers so to say, was that they specialized in two complementary activities – the conduct of cremations and mortuary rites, for by custom cremations were forbidden within the city walls; and the practice of meditation.[45] Because we have already seen in the *Visuddhimagga* that decomposing corpses and charnel grounds were appropriate objects of and locations for certain modes of meditation, the relation between officiating at mortuary rites and practicing meditation could have been integral. Compared with the established royal *wat* within the city walls and on the Thonburī shore, which concentrated on Pali learning and were attuned to the monarch's political aims of unification of the country, these new *wat* were more like forest hermitages, attracting wandering meditation monks (*phra thudong*), who founded monastic residences, taught meditation, distributed their charisma by blessing amulets, and then moved on. Examples of such forest-monk institutions were Wat Mai Bāngkhunphrom, Wat In, and Wat Sangwēt. A meditation teacher and forest-monk, famous for his psychic powers and for his sacralization of images and amulets, who at the same time was held in veneration by the Bangkok religious and royal establishments was Somdet To, whom we shall celebrate later when we deal with the cult of amulets. The forest-order communities established at the edge of Bangkok in the nineteenth century were recognized by and incorporated into the overall *saṅgha* hierarchy, but at the same time they kept their distance from the capital.

## Paradigms

From our foregoing historical survey of forest-monk traditions, I wish to extract two schematic "maps" that might serve both to orient and to interpret some of the ethnography on Thailand that I shall present in this book.

### TRIADIC RELATIONS

There is a triadic relationship between the king or ruler and the "establishment" *saṅgha* of primarily village- and town-dwelling monks on the one side and forest-dwelling "ascetic" or "contemplative" monks on the other. This triad is the result of the interplay of two variables. (See Figure 2.) On the one hand, the *saṅgha* has always from early or classical times manifested two modalities or "vocations" that ideally should be "combined" but frequently in practice got polarized. This polarization also usually had a politico-spatial expression in the form of the location of monastic communities at the "center" (i.e., the political capital and satellite-town centers) and at the "periphery."

The center–periphery grid divided again into two contrasts. There was firstly the "center" defined as the limits of the capital or town. Frequently, the capital was bounded by the city walls, within which again was the bounded space of the palace and relic shrine (Mahādhātu) or chapel holding the palladium. The capital's penumbra or margins consisted of "woods" or sparsely populated

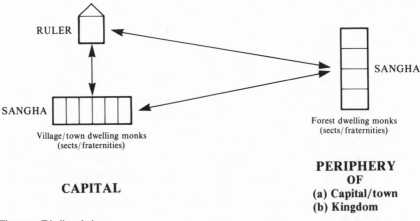

Figure 2. Triadic relations

"gardens." Then, secondly, there was the center of the kingdom or *mūeang* and its outermost periphery of border regions, deep interior, and satellite principalities.

Now the triadic configuration is the product of the interaction of the ruler of the kingdom at large (and in earlier times additionally the lesser rulers of the satellite provinces and chiefdoms *(mūeang)* and tributary principalities)[46] with the bifurcated *sangha*. Because the ruler was located at the capital or town, there was always a primary alignment between him and the town-dwelling monks. But this established *sangha* itself fragmented for various reasons into sects, which competed for political patronage and became embroiled in notoriously volatile palace politics. Moreover, the sects also varied in the rigor of their adherence to the disciplinary rules. The periphery of contemplative or ascetic breakaway or radical monastic communities were a counterweight to those tendencies and might be periodically called upon by the political authorities and the laity to help "purify" the *sangha*. The forest communities, in turn, once they were well-established and the recipients of lay generosity and donations, might develop a spectrum of diversified activities and in due course take the shape of the establishment monasteries.

Although I have presented these triadic relations as dynamically oscillating between modalities in terms of the historical ebb and flow of politics, this oscillation was captured and asserted as a synchronic pattern in the rituals of various classical Buddhist polities. Let us take examples from Sri Lanka and Sukhodaya to illustrate this coding.

1. I have earlier referred to the three large monastic fraternities *(nikāya)* of the Anurādhapura period in Sri Lanka as being the Mahāvihāra, the Abhayagiri, and the Jetavana, each of which had its parent monastery at or near the capital city. In actual fact the "heterodox" rival to the "orthodox" Mahāvihāra was the Abhayagiri vihāra, which was formally labeled a "forest monastery." It was placed north of the citadel (while the other two were to its south) and furthest removed from it. Interestingly, the Abhayagiri vihāra had a special relation to the Buddha's tooth relic. Fa-Hian, who visited the island in the fifth century A.D., described the elaborate and popular annual festival held in honor of the tooth relic.[47] It was taken in procession from the shrine in the center of the city where it normally resided,[48] to the Abhayagiri monastery outside the capital where it resided for three months. At the end of this period it returned to the city. [Fa-Hian reports that the outward procession was staged in the middle of the third month, and my guess is that this was the beginning of the *vassa* (rains) season when monks go into a three-month retreat. The tooth relic thus annually went into seclusion and returned to the city with intensified potency.] Fa-Hian reported that as a result of the rites performed the kingdom suffered "neither from famine, calamity nor revolution."[49]

2. A parallel statement is made in the tooth relic festival and the *perahera* procession staged in the Kandyan Kingdom since the eighteenth century. We have earlier mentioned that the two main fraternities or chapters of the Mahānikāya

sect had their central monasteries in the environs of the capital of Kandy. The Malwatte monastery was (and is) located to the south of the palace complex, and the Asgiriya monastery, formally identified as a "forest hermitage," was (and is) situated to the north (or more accurately northeast) of the palace complex on the forest periphery or fringe of the city. The tooth relic itself was housed in the Palace of the Tooth Relic (*Daladā Māligāva*), which was part of the palace complex itself. The custodianship of the tooth relic was vested in the king and the chief monks of the Malwatta and Asgiriya fraternities. The daily offerings to the relic are conducted by monks from these two monasteries on a rotational basis. As staged today, on each night of the Asala festival,[50] which occurs in the month of July–August [that is, near the end of the traditional Buddhist rains-retreat (*vassa*)], the tooth relic together with the "weapons" of the four major guardian deities of the kingdom circumambulate the city at night and return to the Daladā Māligāva. On all these nights the chief official of this shrine, the Diyawadana Nilame, ceremonially carries the "relic basket" (*karanduva*). But on the final night of the festival take place certain sequences[51] whose ritual import is discernible only in terms of the triadic structure I have postulated. After the grandest and most spectacular circumambulation of the final night, the procession adjourns for an hour or so, assembles all over again, and proceeds to the Asgiriya "forest" monastery, where it arrives at about 2.00 a.m. The relic basket is conducted in ceremony to the shrine, there called the *Gedigē* Vihāre, which architecturally resembles the Palace of the Tooth Relic in the city center. Unlike on previous occasions, it is now the chief monk (*mahānāyaka*) of the Asgiriya monastery or his representative, rather than the Diyawadana Nilame, who carries the basket inside, and the golden and jewelled ornaments wrapped around the relic basket are checked against a list, the checking being witnessed by the Diyawadana Nilame and the Asgiriya monks concurrently. Then the relic basket, now housed in the shrine room, receives offerings of flowers and food behind closed doors. Then the doors are opened again for a while so that the public can worship it. The relic resides at the monastery until the early afternoon (2:00 p.m.), when it is taken on its final "day procession" (*Daval Perahera*).

The reformation of the *perahera* for the final "day procession" takes place as follows. Having accompanied and left the tooth relic at Asgiriya monastery, the rest of the main procession, with the gods in attendance, proceeds to the river to perform the "water-cutting" ceremony, which ensures rains and prosperity, and then returns to the Asgiriya to join up with the relic for the final circumambulation of the city.

3. Let us now invoke a parallel statement from the classical Sukhodaya Kingdom. The layout of the capital clearly showed the triadic structure. In the center of the city stood side by side the king's palace to the east and the shrine (and monastery) where the Buddha relics were enshrined (Wat Mahādhātu). In the city resided the *nagaravāsī* (town-dwelling monks), and outside it, on the western fringe, was situated the Mango Grove where resided the Sīhala forest-

dwelling sect. The chronicles (*Jinakālamālī* and *Mūlasāsana*) tell the story of the establishment of the Sīhaḷa sect in Rammaṇadesa (at Pan located near Martaban). The leader of this forest-dwelling sect bore the title of Mahāsāmi, invested upon him by the Siṅhala king. Two Thai monks, Anomadassi and Sumana, went to Pan to be reordained by the Mahāsāmi, and Sumana returned to Sukhodaya at the request of King Lōē Thai (1299–1346) to found the order of Sīhaḷa monks there.

It is his successor, Lī Thai (1347–74), who dramatized the theme that concerns us. He received in his capital the eminent Mahāsāmi from Pan and settled him in the Mango Grove on the capital's fringe; the reception was in royal style, in that the king and his officials escorted the monk from the east gate of the city to the west gate and out to the Mango Grove, along the principal street, the Rājamarga, which had awnings along the whole length in order to protect the dignitary from the sun and rugs on the path so that his feet would not touch the ground.

The king matched this event by himself, at the end of the rainy season retreat, seeking ordination for a brief period at the hands of the *mahāsāmi*. Griswold describes the king's inscriptions relating to the event thus: "Donning the yellow robe, he raised his hands in salute to the statue, to the copy of the Tipiṭaka which was kept in the palace, and to the Mahāsāmi Sangharāja, pronouncing his resolution to attain Buddhahood, whereupon the earth quaked. The king was then ordained *samanera*, and proceeded on foot all the way to the Mango Grove. There . . . he received, the *upasampada* as a *bhikkhu* the next day."[52] Not long afterward, the king led a successful military campaign.

4. Although we do not see such mutualities and oscillations being staged in the Bangkok epoch since 1782, yet we see a similar pattern in certain features of the rituals devoted to the palladium of the kingdom, the Emerald Buddha, housed in the shrine (Wat Phra Kāēo) standing in the grounds of the Grand Palace.[53] The Emerald Buddha was brought from Vientienne by the founder of the Čakkrī dynasty, Rama I. Following earlier traditions, the Emerald Buddha's clothes and adornments were changed twice a year, the king himself acting as the chief officiant. At the beginning of the rainy season, the Buddha was fitted with monastic garb, and at the beginning of the following cool season it was decked in full royal regalia. (This oscillation was modified in the third reign when the image was given a third royal outfit for the dry season.) And in Bangkok the changing of the palladium's clothes from the monastic to the royal style was a time for the chanting of the great story (*mahāchāt*) of *Vessantara Jātaka* which, as is well known, portrays first the virtuous king's great acts of giving away his rain-giving elephant and wealth and children, followed by his banishment to the forest and his subsequent rehabilitation and return to the full splendor of kingship.

## PENTADIC RELATIONS

I must now hasten to correct a "deficiency" in my sketch of the triadic relations in Figure 2 and the spelling out of its significance. The scheme is partial in that it gives no separate place to the people at large, the laity, whose dynamic and lively relations with the *saṅgha*, both in its town-and-village-dwelling and its forest-dwelling manifestations, cannot be subsumed in the expression "ruler and polity." But the historical facts we have examined so far are largely inadequate in this respect, for the chronicles and inscriptions are records of dynastic and royal history.

The fullest representation of the situation has to be minimally pentadic by virtue of inclusion of the "people." It has been mapped in Figure 3, which at this stage can only serve programmatically but will come alive in what is to follow in my description and interpretation of recent events in Thailand. I hope to describe in due course how the laity that is differentiated on multiple dimensions participates in my narrative in their various capacities: as royals, nobles, and commoners; as urban and rural dwellers; as urban officials, bankers and merchants, and laboring folk; as people of the capital and of the provinces; and so on. If we take the forest-monks as the point of reference, Figure 3 highlights the fact that despite their primary impulsion to remove themselves from worldly entanglements and preoccupations as much as possible, yet they are constantly besieged and tempted on two sides.

The laity in general – the village and town householders (the political powers and merchants included) – pursue them because they wish to partake of their supranormal powers (*iddhi, aphinihān*), which they are credited with on account of their meditational exercises and ascetic lives. The cult of the amulets and charms that these holy men are requested to bless is a major basis for the religious followings that build around their charisma.

The rulers themselves and their political machinery have always buttressed their legitimacy, and indeed fulfilled their role, by supporting the *saṅgha* and being supported in turn. In the past, there were two critical moments – one when kingdoms were being first established, expanded, and consolidated, the other

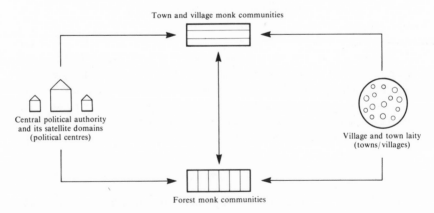

Figure 3. Pentadic relations

when they were in deep turmoil and near disintegration – when the forest-monks appeared to have rendered invaluable services to monarchy. There is an inner logic to what at first sight is an unlikely conjunction between the imperial ruler and the ascetic renouncer: Each may pursue his objective with integrity and yet buttress the other.

We have already remarked that the forest-monks were effective groundbreakers, colonizing and civilizing the forest frontiers and attracting settlements around them. However their better documented role historically is their acting as a vitalizing force and as a countervailing agent to the religious establishment during periods of religious purification and cultural renaissance. In normal times, of course, the ruler and his political satellites, the supportive *sangha* at the capital, have both symbolized and realized the Buddhist values associated with *cakkavatti* (king of kings), *bodhisattva* (buddha to be), the *Dhamma* realm in which the religion flourished, and the exemplary center. Yet there were times often enough when things have gone awry at this centered-*maṇḍala*, wracked, even decimated, by dissension, wars, epidemics, droughts, rebellions, and other misfortunes. There was all the more a need to recharge and fortify monarchical legitimacy and creative powers by tapping the purity and charisma of the untarnished forest ascetics. Their very distance from everyday mundane affairs, their disinterest in ephemeral gains, and their alleged capacity to act in detachment in the spirit of cosmic love (*mettā*) guaranteed their ability to replenish and revitalize the realm, whenever the center could not hold. But even here there is no iron law or necessity to enter the fray and set the realm aright, as the Shwegyin sect of Burma has demonstrated. There may be times when the only way the forest-monk communities can preserve their integrity is to set a distance from polity and society at large. But this again is not necessarily an enduring stance, for in the final reckoning the Buddhist *sangha* cannot exist apart from society.

# PART II

## THE HAGIOGRAPHY OF A BUDDHIST SAINT: TEXT AND CONTEXT; THE POLITICS OF SECTARIANISM

# 6

*᷍᷍᷍᷍᷍*

# The biography of a modern saint

Phra Acharn Mun was born in Northeast Thailand in 1870 and died in 1949, in his eightieth year by the Thai way of reckoning (see Figure 4). He is regarded in Thailand today as having been not only a great meditation master and exemplary monk, but also a great teacher (*acharn*)[1] who trained a number of illustrious disciples, who were famous in the recent past or are famous today. Indeed, Mun is regarded by numerous pious Buddhists as an *arahant* (perfected saint) in the classical sense.

One of the saint's disciples, who is himself a meditation master and teacher at a Northeastern forest hermitage, Phra Acharn Maha Boowa, wrote a long biography of the saint.[2] It was first written and published in Thai in serialized form in a religious journal called *Sā Sapdā* (Glorious Week) and was subsequently published as a book in 1971 under royal patronage. Because of the popularity and significance of the subject matter, the biography has been recently translated into English by Siri Buddhasukh, an ex-monk of the Thammayut sect, to which belongs the biographer and also belonged the saint. Buddhasukh now works for the World Federation of Buddhists, whose headquarters are in Bangkok, and also teaches at the Mahāmakut Monks' University, which too is a venture of the Thammayut sect.

Siri's translated biography was published in 1976.[3] A thousand copies were printed and distributed free in the Thai tradition of "merit making": Distribution of books containing religious material at cremations and commemorations is the Thai custom, especially among the affluent.

While we shall take up later in detail the significance of this biography, I have said here enough to intimate to the reader that the biography that I am about to summarize is not some bizarre, unusual document chosen for its "fantastic" qualities, but is the creation of a much respected famous monk, who enjoys prestige within the Thammayut sect – which is powerful and has royal connections – and within the *sangha* as a whole. Its publication in *World Federation of*

# The hagiography of a Buddhist saint

Figure 4. The meditation master and saint, Acharn Mun.

*Buddhists Review* and its distribution by agencies connected with the *saṅgha* attest to its acceptability to the establishment and to the exemplary role of the saint whose story is told.

## Early efforts

Mun was born on Thursday, January 20, 1870, in the commune (*tambon*) of Khambong, Khongčīam District, Ubon Rātchathānī Province. His father was Nai Kamduang KanKaw and his mother was Nang Chan. He had eight brothers and sisters, only two of whom were alive when he died. "He was the eldest, of small stature and fair complexion. He was, from childhood, agile and full of vigor, intelligent and resourceful" (p.1.).

At 15 he was ordained as a novice in the village monastery of Khambong, and although he disrobed two years later, his life there had a profound effect on him. "Later, at the age of twenty-two, the call of the chaste life seemed irresistible," and his parents sponsored his ordination at Wat Liab in the provincial capital of Ubon in 1896. After his ordination, he went to practice *vipassanā* (insight meditation) with Phra Acharn Sao Kantasilo of Wat Liab; Sao is the only known teacher of the Master and we know very little about him.

### The prophetic dream

In the course of his meditation practice, which was not then bearing much fruit, he had one night a dream. He walked out of the village into a dense, almost impenetrable jungle, but managed to go through it and to emerge "to find a meadow stretching on before him to the horizon." He labored on and came to a felled log (*chāt*), which was rotting; he climbed and walked on it, contemplating that it was no longer capable of growth. This Thai name for a particular tree (*chāt*) sounds the same as the Thai abbreviation *chāt* of the Pali word *jāti*, which means "birth" [biographer's footnote]. The meadow extending to the horizon in all directions reminded the dreamer of the infinity of deaths and rebirths "succeeding one another like a snake eating its own tail." Then a great white horse approached him, he mounted it, and it carried him over the vast terrain. On the way he saw a beautiful silvery-white glass case with the Pali canon – Tipiṭaka – inside, and the horse disappeared after fulfilling its mission. "This spot was at the end of the vast open land. From there could be seen a steaming, uninhabited jungle made impassable with thorny, twisted bushes." But before opening the case to have a look at the scriptures inside, he woke up.

This prophetic dream "gave him the assurance that he would be able to achieve his goal within this lifetime" provided he did not slack in his efforts. From then on, he committed himself to rigorous meditation practice (controlling every movement with the mental recitation of *buddho*) and to the strict observance of *dhūtaṅga* (ascetic) practices. These were: wearing rag robes; refusing robes directly offered him by a donor; going out for almsfood, except on the days he decided to fast; eating only food that was put into the almsbowl during his almsround; having only one meal a day; eating from the almsbowl only; possessing only the three robes that he wore (and a bathing cloth); and dwelling in forest areas, under trees in valleys, within caves or under cliffs (except for brief periods when he was invited into a town). He also occasionally observed the other remaining ascetic practices (p.3). Now, the *dhūtaṅga* ascetic observances and the vipassanā meditation are represented by the biographer as "external" and "internal" practices by which the "defilements" are eradicated so as to make possible the goal of Deliverance.

In due course, when Mun was firmly established in his contemplative activity, he interpreted the full meaning of his dream as follows. The life of the householder is the forest of suffering and danger, and the ascetic and meditative life carried him through that forest into the open meadow of unobstructed view. "The great white horse, then, was the mode of rigorous practice which would take him to Deliverance and to the intricately designed Tipiṭaka case. However, due to his own imperfections he was not able to open the Tipiṭaka case and was therefore not to be well-versed in the academic side of the Doctrine. . . . His accumulation of merit (*pāramī*) in the past was not enough, so he said, and that was why he was given only a chance to look at the outside of the Tipiṭaka case. . . . '' Although the Master claimed not to possess the highest scholarly fluency and discernment, yet as the biographer points out, he was in actual fact an incomparable teacher of meditation and instructor in *Dhamma*.[4]

At Wat Liab, it took three months of frenzied and aimless search before the most congenial method of meditation was discovered. The young neophyte first began his meditation sittings by contemplating the corpse and had images appear before him of bloated and festering bodies being torn to pieces by vultures, dogs, and crows; these were followed by quick changes of visions – of climbing and walking on mountains and so on. But such volatile and distracting experiences brought no peace and balance of mind. He then decided to refrain from concentrating on external objects and events and focused his attention on his own body. Having spent some time in walking meditation (*caṅkamana*), he turned to sitting meditation using his body (its nature and its processes) as the central theme and reached the condition of *one-pointedness* of mind. This introspective method of meditation became his favored technique, which he later modified as he engaged in more advanced practices and efforts.

The Master would later tell his disciples that at this time, toward the close of the last century and the turn of the next, there was little interest in Thailand in the practice of meditation and mind development, especially in the mode of life of the *dhūtaṅga* monk. Such monks apparently provoked feelings of apprehension and fear among the rural folk, especially among women and children. Their strictly controlled behavior and avoidance of unnecessary contact with laymen; their wearing of yellowish-brown robes dyed with gum extracted from the wood of the Jackfruit tree; their carrying a large umbrella (*klot*) slung over one shoulder, the almsbowl over the other, and a water kettle hanging on the side; and their custom of walking in a single file – all these features inspired awe as much as respect. But in due course their deportment and conduct won the support of the population of dispersed villages, near which they took up residence, and on whose alms they depended for their food.

It is customary for *dhūtaṅga* monks to wander forth at the end of the three-month rains retreat each year, seeking secluded places in remote regions. Acharn

# The biography of a modern saint

Mun made it a rule "to head for mountains and forests with a group of houses or a small village nearby in which he might go for his alms-food. He spent more time in the Northeastern region than in any other part of the country, since this region abounds in mountains and forests near such towns as Nakhorn Panon, Sakol Nakhorn, Udorn Thani, Nongkai, Loey and Lonsak" (p. 8). He also spent much time in the Kingdom of Laos in such towns as Thā Khāek, Vientienne, and Lūang Phrabāng, which too are located amid great forests and high mountains. Because he was bent on the eradication of defilements, Mun preferred *living alone and moving constantly* as a homeless seeker. On these wanderings, he dedicated himself to incessant contemplative exercises: The body was mentally dissected and all its movements and acts – whether they be going out on an almsround, the sewing and dying of robes, or the eating of a meal – were subject to continuous monitoring by mindfulness. Long sleep was an enemy, leading to laziness and indulgence; walking meditation was a good antidote. And the quantity of food accepted and manner of eating were exemplary for one whose objective was Deliverance. No food was accepted after going on the almsround; food brought back was sorted and the amount chosen for eating was *mixed together* so as not to indulge the sense of taste. Before consuming it, its *repulsiveness* was contemplated. "Throughout the whole process of eating, every mouthful, every movement, was to be safeguarded by continual mindfulness of its repulsiveness." Such a way of eating makes a *bhikkhu* "the rightful owner of that food which has been obtained by others' sweat and hard labor." The only meal of the day thus over, the inner struggle would actively begin again on the meditation walk cleared from the jungle.

We now approach a theme that is constantly reiterated by Buddhists even in, indeed especially in, relation to the meditative and contemplative quest. Although Acharn Mun was indeed making progress, and occasionally enjoyed the bliss resulting from his meditation, yet he also encountered problems that he could not solve himself and that led him into blind alleys. *This was because he lacked a competent teacher,* and such a lack "confirmed the truth of the importance of a *kalyāṇamitta* (a good friend or a competent teacher) to an aspirant in mind-development.... Lack of a *kalyāṇamitta*, on the other hand, causes both delays and dangers and is a serious drawback for all aspirants" (p. 11). Thus in such assertions we meet with one of the important dualities concerning the *dhūtaṅga* monk: On the one hand, he is committed to a secluded, wandering life of loneliness; on the other hand, he is very conscious of being disciplined and guided by a Master around whom cluster similar-minded disciples.

Although at the beginning Mun had a meditation master, Phra Acharn Sao, the latter apparently found Mun's mind so fleeting and volatile that he confessed that Mun should monitor his own mental experiences and solve his own problems. Though somewhat of an adept at sitting meditation, as exemplified by his experience of levitation (one classical index of the possession of *iddhi*), yet because of his tranquil and serene nature Acharn Sao preferred not to be venturesome and experimental in his meditation exercises. Moreover, Acharn Sao is said to have made a resolution to become a *paccekabuddha* (a "silent" Buddha who pursues his own salvation), and this resolve showed that he was not much interested in teaching others, a resolve that accorded with his not being resourceful in the art of teaching. There was a stage when both Sao and Mun were intimate, accompanied each other, and had common followings of monks and lay disciples.

Acharn Mun's biographer describes in vivid terms the propensities of Mun's volatile and restless mind, which had to be brought under control by strict, disciplined methods, and then draws the conclusion that the Master's trial was made onerous by the lack of a competent teacher, and that how privileged the Master's pupils themselves were in having a supreme teacher to guide them. We are told that in its uncontrolled moments Mun's mind experienced a panorama of forms and shapes: "Sometimes it darted into the heaven realms, admiring the joys and glories to be found there, for hours. At other times it plunged into the hell realms, touring them and taking pity on the beings suffering there the fruits of their former deeds" (p. 14).[5] Acharn Mun broke the wild stallion of his mind by cultivating mindfulness and by developing stringent training methods for himself; this knowlege he was able to impart later to his disciples: "He often told this to his disciples to remind them of the advantages they enjoyed through his counsel and his company" (p. 15).

### The first long pilgrimage and the adventures at the Sarika Cave in the Great Mountains of Nakhon Nayok

From Ubon, Acharn Mun journeyed to the border town of Nakhon Phanom and then crossed over to the forests and mountains of Thā Khāek in the Kingdom of Laos. At this stage of the story, the biographer introduces us to a new theme, which we shall encounter again and again in the hagiology of the forest saints. It relates to their encounter with wild beasts and their fearless and serene taming of them by the power of the *Dhamma* words and of meditation. The foremost of these wild beasts is the tiger. And that by tradition the tiger is the wild beast *par excellence* made innocuous by the *dhūtaṅga* monk is evidenced for us by the murals in the chapel at Wat Bowonniwet that were painted in the last century. Other beasts similarly pacified are wild elephants, wild monkey troupes, poisonous snakes (*nāga*), and the like.

The Thā Khāek mountains are described as abounding with ferocious tigers, mostly man-eaters, who attacked the local forest peoples (who are incidentally represented as having "no more intelligence than children" and as "heartless" and lacking in concern for others). Although the local inhabitants lived in fear of these marauding beasts, Acharn Mun was not molested by a single tiger; "only their tracks were to be seen or their roars heard at night." He had no fear of them

86

at all and was later to describe these dangerous trips as mere commonplace happenings.

Having wandered through the Northeastern villages, Acharn Mun journeyed down to the central part of Thailand and spent a rains retreat at Wat Pathoowan in Bangkok, where he regularly went for instruction and advice from the abbot of Wat Boromnivas, Phra Upali Gunupamacariya.[6] After the rains retreat, he journeyed up to the town of Lopburi and stayed at various caves in the vicinity "developing meditation and insight." He subsequently sought out a distant place of solitude in the Sarika Cave of the famous Khao Yai (the Great Mountains) near the Northeastern border town of Nakhon Nayok.

His arrival at the cave began with a dramatic encounter. The villagers would not take him up to the cave because many previous *bhikkhu* who visited the cave had been stricken with disease; and some four of them had been killed by it. The cave was possessed by a Great Demon with terrible powers and jealous of his rights; he had successfully punished any and every *bhikkhu* intruder.

Acharn Mun was undaunted and looked upon his stay at the cave as a testing ground for developing his mindfulness. On the fourth night, he was stricken with a stomachache, which had troubled him before, but never with such seriousness. He was unable to digest food and he passed blood. The herbal medicine given him by the villagers did not relieve him. He therefore decided to stop taking conventional medicine and to resort to the therapeutic effect of the *Dhamma* alone, no matter what happened to his body. He told himself, "Let this body die here in this cave if the power of the dharma cannot cure this illness. I have progressed far enough to be fairly certain of the Path, Fruition and Nirvana." He then began his meditation and abandoned attachment to life. "Mindfulness and wisdom together with faith and exertion then hammered on the mind which does not die but which is always death-stricken." The battle raged from dusk to midnight, and the mind realized the nature of the aggregates, and their formations, including this gripping pain, and "the illness totally disappeared and the mind withdrew into absolute, unshakable one-pointedness."

When afterward his mind "emerged to a less profound and more responsive level called upacara, there seemed to be a light radiating from his body," and it revealed a tall black man about ten meters high. Acharn Mun thus was finally confronted with the apparition of the club-wielding demon owner of the cave, and there followed a dialogue of threats from the demon and nonviolent moral persuasions on the part of the monk. The demon was first made to concede that its powers were limited – that it could not match the Buddha, who had the "power beyond karma," the power of eradicating from his own mind the desire to dominate and to harm others. Then the monk admonished the demon about the destructiveness of its power and its acts and pointed out that his own vocation as *bhikkhu* was to follow the Path of Righteousness for his *own benefit as well as that of others*. The demon was spellbound and subdued; it admitted that from the very beginning it had seen a light radiating from the monk that had paralyzed its aggressive intentions. The demon declared that it was really chief of tree spirits and promised to act as the monk's guardian as long as he lived in the cave; it went further and declared itself to be a lay devotee of the Triple Gem of Buddhism, adopted the monk as its teacher, and finally brought the entire retinue of its followers to pay homage to the monk.

During the dialogue, the monk's mind "withdrew into the unshakable state of *appana-samādhi*"; entering meditation, it reached new heights of bliss and peace and new understandings of the truth. Soon afterward, the monk's digestion improved, and his stomach disorder disappeared for good.

Acharn Mun is said to have undergone certain special mental and spiritual experiences while he was at the Sarika Cave. One night, for instance, he was strongly overcome by the feeling of *samvega*, a mental awareness of the weariness and illusory nature of man's present circumstances, coupled with pity and compassion for human beings suffering from ignorance, self-delusion, and vanity.

Occasionally at night "arahant disciples of the Buddha would give him sermons while he was sitting in meditation"; they would instruct him on the necessity for unfluctuating mindfulness, for destroying and not accumulating mental defilements, and for nourishing the mind, because "supreme in the world is mind," the priceless treasure. "A recluse," the *arahants* instructed, "taking delight in moral practice, meditation, mindfulness, wisdom, and exertion is sure to become a samana in the real sense of the term, either at present or in the near future." The venerable monk later told his own disciples that listening to the sermons of the *arahants* was like listening to the instructions of the Buddha himself. It was in this cave that he reached the path of the nonreturner (*anāgāmī*).[7]

One night, following upon many successive nights of meditative experience, he was "strangely overcome by loving-kindness and compassion for his fellow *bhikkhus*." He was now certain that he was not groping in the dark anymore and "that the Absolute Cessation of Suffering was not far away." Moved by compassion for his disciples and wishing to have them share his experience and attainment, he decided to leave the cave of his trials and triumph and return to the monasteries of the Northeastern provinces. The terrestrial angels and their chief, whom he had previously converted, sorrowfully came to say goodbye, and he gave them moral instruction.

Let us conclude the cave episode by returning to the theme of the *dhūtaṅga* monk and wild animals. Acharn Mun related to his disciples several adventures with them, and two themes recur in these tales. Firstly, the meditating monk pacifies the animals, and even wins their protection, by the practice of compassion (*mettā*), which flows from the monk and envelops the animal. Secondly, a monk like him achieves the capacity to communicate with the animals, not merely through being able to interpret their noises, but also because an *arahant* is versed in "the language of the mind, which is supreme to all the languages in the Three Worlds" and enables him to give extensive assistance to all beings, visible and invisible, animal and man (p. 191).[8] Thus the transcending of the world of sense and form also enables the acquisition of a wordless higher language that encompasses all lower tongues and media of communication.

These truths are illustrated, for instance, by the Acharn's encounter with a monkey troop – the suspicious chattering monkey-leader was becalmed by the monk's loving-kindness, and the monkeys roamed about near him until their curiosity was satisfied. "It is generally seen that wherever forest bhikkhus stay, there the forest beasts will assemble in large groups, both the large and the small," concludes the author in a way reminding us of the life of another saint in a different religious tradition, Saint Francis of Assisi.[9]

The amusing monkeys are of course a diversion compared with the fearsome tigers. Once, in a secluded part of Laos, a large tiger visited Acharn Mun and a companion monk, Phra Sitha, while they were meditating in nearby locations. The tiger approached and watched Acharn Mun at a distance while he was engaged in nightly meditation and did not threaten him. One night the tiger crept and sat near where Phra Sitha was engaged in walking meditation, and when the monk, feeling compassion for it, suggested to it that it could better spend its time finding food, the tiger gave out an ear-splitting roar in objection – he preferred to stay and guard the monk. Later, on waking up in the early hours of the morning, the monk found that the tiger had disappeared.

I would like to suggest that the encounters between *dhūtaṅga* monk and tiger, and the preoccupation of the *dhūtaṅga* monks with such beasts, has a moral significance that emerges from their dialectical relationship. Both are in a sense wanderers of the forest, one however by *nature*, and the other by a supreme moral *choice* by which he leaves the lay society behind. The tiger is wild and ferocious and an apt representation of the sensual, "ignorant," *kammic* dimensions of life; the meditating monk, by comparison, controls his sensory attachments by mental control and reflects compassion (*mettā*). The tiger is also the wild beast inside man steeped in desire and defilements. The critical feature of this encounter is that the monk not only subdues the tiger by the nonviolent power of his *Dhamma* and *mettā*; he also demonstrates thereby that he has incorporated, subordinated, and encompassed within him the powers of the wild beast.[10]

There is still another dimension. The Acharn considered that the wilder the place abounding with ferocious tigers the better it was for mind development. Because the tiger aroused fear in all its aspects in the *bhikkhu*, it forced him to engage in walking meditation deep into the night. The *bhikkhu*'s battle was "between fear and dharma," and the tigers helped to implant *Dhamma* in the mind. The prospect of being devoured by tigers "drove the mind to *dharma*." "Knowing that it is helpless, such a mind will fix itself on a theme of meditation or recitation until it is absorbed in dharma" (pp. 66–7), and thus was fear in tiger form superseded and eradicated.

This issue of wild animals tempts me to break the story in order to indulge in a digression. Carrithers, in his study of forest monks in Sri Lanka,[11] describes the attitudes toward and encounters with wild beasts on the part of Siṅhalese forest monks but is not stimulated to integrate this information into his overall interpretive scheme. This is perhaps because he tends to view such phenomena as part of "folk asceticism," whereas their occurrence in Burma and Thailand as well persuade one that they are an integral part of entrenched and widespread Southeast Asian forest-monk traditions, more civilizational than parochial in nature.

The following is an example provided by Carrithers. At Kumbirigala forest hermitage in the south of the island, Ānandasiri and his pupils spend much time in silence alone in the forest and value their contact with wild animals. Carrithers remarks that it is in the attitudes that Ānandasiri and his disciples cultivate toward these animals that *paññā* (wisdom) – understood as both *vipassanā* (insight) and *mettā* (loving-kindness) – is more clearly manifest. Ānandasiri emphasizes that the forest with its animals is a priceless hermitage, for the animals make the monks understand the origins and nature of fears and that in turn leads to anticipations of *dukkha* (pain and suffering), and that in turn leads to stilling and overcoming. At Kumbirigala, Carrithers continues, the expectation of meeting an animal is ever present in the minds of the monks, and when they meet an animal "they neither run away, nor approach but address it in kind but clear terms."

I find that the *Manual of a Mystic*[12] has several apt passages on the therapeutic value of wild animals for the eradication of fear under captions such as "Insight into what is to be feared" and "Insight and evil." "The insight into evil," says the *Manual*, "is the name given to that by which a Yogi realizes the evil nature of all conditions; to him all aggregates appear like a forest haunted by dangerous wild beasts; like lions, tigers and so forth; like a land haunted by evil water-sprites; like an enemy with drawn sword armed, or food with poison mixed, or like a blazing house" (p. 131). We might recall that the *Manual* discovered in Sri Lanka is believed to have been based on the teachings of Siamese monks who visited the island in the eighteenth century.

Before I continue with Acharn Mun's remarkable career, let me pause briefly to provide a map with which to follow the rest of the story. Acharn Mun's peripatetic journeys from now on can be divided into three broad phases. (1) He made one long stay in the Northeast (I shall call this his second visit), traveling to various places; (2) he went north deep into the Chiengmai Mountains; and (3) he finally returned again to the Northeast, where he died in 1949.

Acharn Mun's sojourn at the Sarika Cave marked his attaining to a certain level of achievement in his meditation, and his departure from the cave marked his wanting to convey to his disciples the lessons he had learned. In this account of his second visit to the Northeast, the underlying pattern consists in his achievement of certain spiritual conquests accompanied by greater psychic powers.

Paralleling this progressive personal achievement is his gathering of increasing numbers of disciples wherever he went, his concern with teaching them, and his overseeing of the forest-monk communities so that they were organized appropriately for the dedicated pursuit of meditation. This phase is then followed by the Acharn's trip to Chiengmai, where in a cave of the northern mountains – in an ordeal paralleling his first victory in Sarika Cave – he made the final progress from nonreturner to fully enlightened *arahant*. From this eminence, he descended again for his last visit to, and teaching tour in, the Northeast, where he finally died in 1949. His mortuary rites and the extraordinary events that occurred at that time constitute the last chapter in this saint's life.

## The second visit to the Northeast

Acharn Mun's second visit to the Northeast entailed traveling to many towns, teaching and encouraging people, both monks and laymen. He traveled back and forth in Thailand between Nakhon Rātchasīmā, Sīsakēt, Ubon Rātchathānī, Nakhon Phanom, Sakon Nakhon, Udon, Nong Khāi, Lōēi, Lomsak, and Phetchabūn; he also visited Laos several times, particularly Vientiane and Thā Khāēk. But of course in between these towns werē deep forests and sparsely populated villages, and much time was spent oscillating between forest life and brief urban visits. In areas south and southwest of the town of Sakon Nakhon "there were vast forests and great mountains, and it was here he preferred to stay longest for the purpose of eradicating defilements" (p. 50).[13]

Seeing that the Master was peripatetic and his following fluid, it becomes essential to describe the pattern of life of these fluctuating and dispersed communities of *dhūtaṅga* monks and the network of relationships that linked them. Wherever Acharn Mun stayed there was always a large gathering of followers, both *bhikkhu* and novices on the one hand and lay disciples on the other, who gathered around him. Considering the lay devotees as the outermost penumbra, let us leave them aside at this point and focus on the ordained religious who gathered around the Master as his immediate circle.

"There were sometimes sixty or seventy bhikkhus and samaneras in the place where he was staying," not counting those living in separate groups some distance away and coming to him frequently for instruction. There was no "administrative" hierarchy set up; it was assumed that each participant was seriously devoted to meditation and aware of the ascetic practices to be followed. The *bhikkhu* and novices spent most of the time by themselves in seclusion. They only assembled to receive instruction from the Master or at mealtimes. "Except at these times all would be engaged day and night in walking or sitting meditation at their respective places of retreat."

Acharn Mun apparently followed a rigorous and taxing routine of meditation, which served as a model to all his disciples. After the morning almsround, followed by the day's only meal, he would begin his walking meditation, which would last until noon. After a brief rest, he would begin his sitting meditation, which would continue for one and a half hours. Then he would resume his walking meditation. At four o'clock, he would sweep and tidy up the area around the place he was staying (whether it be a monastic residence or a jungle platform). Then he would bathe and practice walking meditation until about 8 or 9 o'clock in the evening, when he would resume his sitting meditation. Generally, he went to sleep at 11 o'clock and rose at 3 a.m. to resume meditation until the almsround. If sermons had to be given to celestial or other supernatural beings late at night, he would adjust his sleeping hours to accommodate them.

One of the central events in the disciples' routine was their assembling at the place where the Master was staying for their fortnightly recitation of the *Pāṭimokkha* (code of monastic discipline). This recitation was usually followed by the Master's instruction to the assembly in the form of a sermon and his answering questions put to him afterward.

"During the instruction hours, only the Venerable Acharn's voice would be heard, the other bhikkhus and samaneras assembled there, no matter how many, sitting in complete silence." Each listener sat "spellbound" drinking "the nectar of his sermons," which apparently lasted several hours and were considered "practical lessons for the development of both meditation and wisdom" (p. 49).

The actual living conditions in the jungle were spartan in the extreme. The beds of the disciples were usually small raised platforms made of pieces of split bamboo, two meters long and one or one and a half meters wide, raised about fifty centimeters above the ground. Each platform would be about thirty to forty meters away from the next one; the distance might be greater if the forest space was vast. The trees and bushes between the platforms were left as they were, and tracks for walking meditation were cleared by lay devotees, one track for each *bhikkhu*. A track would be anywhere from ten to twenty meters long.

If no raised platforms were built, the *dhūtaṅga* monks slept on the ground on beds of leaves or straw. The monsoon rains, particularly during the months of December and January, caused severe discomfort. If the monks had not built makeshift shelters or found some caves, the only roof over their heads was the umbrella (*klot*) with a mosquito net hung over it. The monk's outer robe was used as the blanket or raincover. It is no surprise then that these monks, exposed to inclement weather, rains, and cold in the higher forested altitudes, were frequently victims of chronic and debilitating malaria. Malaria with its high fevers and deliriums became another "suffering" to be endured on the path to liberation and must have curiously intersected with the monks' meditation experiences and altered states of consciousness.

These monks depended for their food on the impoverished households of the jungle villages near which they pitched their umbrellas. They went forth every day in single file, and their observance of the *dhūtaṅga* rules in regard to having a single meal a day, eating the food all mixed up in the almsbowl without the aid of other containers, and refusing food subsequent to the almsround, appears to have been exemplary and watchfully enforced by the Master. Believing that staying in the wilds provided opportunities for contemplation of both external things and inner development, the Master led his disciples and made them live "under trees, in forests, on mountains, in caves, under precipices or in cemeteries" – in places ordinary householders regard as wild and fearful. Because I have already in the previous section given descriptions of some of the meditative experiences of the Master and his encounters with wild beasts and supernatural agents, I shall merely summarize in this section other such experiences so as to minimize repetition.

I should make the preliminary point that for the Master and his disciples (as indeed for Buddhaghosa in the fifth century) the reality of beings on other planes of existence was accepted, whether they be ghosts, demons, gods, or angels. However, in true classical tradition, traceable to the canonical version of what the Buddha himself said, Acharn Mun's reply to questions about the existence of such entities is that they are irrelevant to his own pursuit and that the fear of such spirits is a product of one's own worries and imagination. Such preoccupations will disappear if people's minds did not reach out to grasp them.

One of the important forms of instruction adopted by the Master, outside the formal sermon, was the discussion in the evenings (from seven onward) with disciples about their individual meditative experiences – for it was recognized that, because of different levels of achievement, aptitudes, and mental tendencies, the meditative experiences and visions could differ, as could the meditative supports and techniques chosen. A number of disciples appear to have experienced visitation by gods and demons, and the journey to heavens and hells was achieved by those who had reached the appropriate *samādhi* level.

At this time, a remarkable feature of the activities of the Master was the fact that "terrestrial angels" listened to the instructions that he gave his disciples at night; moreover, "celestial angels" would arrive late at night, circumambulate the Master three times, "keeping him always to their right," and then seat themselves and politely request him to instruct them on some aspect of the *Dhamma* that interested them. They appreciated his sermons very much, and, having uttered *sādhu* (it is well), they circumambulated him and departed. Frequently, the celestial angels informed the Master of their coming in advance; the Master would sit waiting for them in deep meditation and would emerge from the third level of concentration (*appanā*) to the second level of access concentration (*upacāra*). "The dialogue between the Venerable Acharn and these beings was carried on directly through mind, there being no language barrier as in the society of man and animals" (p. 61). Compared with humans, the angels showed a capacity for quicker understanding of the teachings and a greater respect for their teacher.

We are told that at this period of time the Master brought peace and bliss wherever he went and stayed. It is said that three times during the day he "radiated loving-kindness" with maximum intensity – in the afternoon during his sitting meditation, before going to sleep, and after waking up. "In his comprehensive radiation of loving-kindness, he would first balance his mind and radiate its force to traverse the worlds in all planes, upward, downward, and horizontally without any interruption. The radiance of his mind at that time was indescribably bright, being limitless and unobstructed, and far brighter than hundreds or thousands of suns" (p. 63).

One of the events associated with his radiation of loving-kindness was his eradication of smallpox in a village in Laos called Ban Tham: The stricken villagers begged him to be their refuge. He assembled them, persuaded them to accept the Triple Gem as their refuge, and taught them certain inner practices on their behalf. There were no more deaths after this, and the infection disappeared.

This dramatic example is one of many documented by the biographer in which the Master is represented as a kind of missionary taking the rudiments of Buddhist commitment and ritual to the northeastern villages, which were infested with spirit beliefs and spirit cults. (There are in fact exaggerated claims made of totally uprooting the old beliefs and practices and supplanting them with the Buddhist Triple Gem; but this should not make us lose sight of the fact that these *dhūtaṅga* monks did, during the periods they took up residence among the forest folk, teach them some Buddhist precepts and engage them in Buddhist rites of giving alms and taking the five precepts and so on.)[14] The Master and his circle of followers are described as spending numerous rains retreats in isolated villages and making their conversions and conquests. These villages lay on the circuitous forest paths between the major towns of the Northeast–Ubon, Nongkhai, Sakon Nakhon, Nakhon Phanom, and so on.

While staying on the side of a mountain, west of the historic city of Lūang Phra Bāng in Laos, the Master had nightly visits from the *nāga*-king and his retinue of servants who lived under the mountain; they were delighted by the *Dhamma* preached to them. Another set of encounters between the Master and a *nāga*-king took place when the Master spent some three years in the village of Sarm Phong in Nakhon Phanom province: The serpent that lived somewhere on the Songkhram River attended the Master's *wan phra* (sabbath) sermons to his disciples and also came to visit him late at night during his meditation sittings.

The Master also had remarkable powers of clairvoyance by which he was able to read the thoughts or know the acts of his disciples, a power feared by those of his disciples who had infringed rules or engaged in mental impurities or disobeyed him and who would in due course be firmly reprimanded. For all disciples an occasion for "injurious sense impressions arousing lust" (*visabhāga*) was when they went into a village for almsfood and encountered girls and women (especially those who dressed themselves carelessly). The fear of women (with misogynist resonances) seems to have been a common preoccupation. Human sounds, especially the voices of females, were considered inimical to meditation concentration, and the welfare, safety, and restraint of female devotees and white-robed "nuns" (*māē chī*)[15] in forest hermitages were considered a burden to the meditation masters.

At this stage of his career – during the course of his second visit to the Northeast – the Acharn had reached the intermediate level of meditation and wisdom, which characterizes the third grade of the Noble Disciple, the nonreturner (*anāgāmī*). He had achieved the complete mindfulness of the body, and his mind trod the middle path between the poles of taking delight in emotions or feeling repelled by them. A nonreturner of this stature is entitled to be reborn in the fifth plane of the Brahma realm. This intermediate level of achievement easily enabled the Master to communicate with beings from other planes of existence and also to disaggregate his mind from the body and tour the celestial heavens and unhappy hells. The Acharn had the attestation of the angel leader that the radiance of his loving-kindness enveloped both the earth and the sky, and that "while giving instructions to his bhikkhus and samaneras, his voice thundered in all directions... and could be heard from a great distance" (p. 95). The comparison here of course is to the deafening roars of the tigers, which reverberated in the mountains like a terrifying symphony (p. 94).[16] The Acharn was also aware of the dangers of that subtle and habit-forming effect of meditation that ensues from reaching the "unshakable level" (*appanā*), when the mind becomes self-satisfied and seduced by the bliss of resting within the cocoon of seclusion and complacency and does not wish to make further progress in the path of wisdom. The Acharn told his disciples that he remained at the level of a nonreturner for a long time, because he had no teacher to give him further counsel and because he had to "pioneer the wilderness," undergoing painful ordeals and much effort. The biographer writes that twice he was moved to tears while listening to how his teacher "had courageously laboured under affliction" and that he felt "awed by the profundity of the dharma he had realized."

At this stage, the Acharn felt that his inner development was not yet complete because there was one more level to develop before "full-final Attainment could be reached." He had spent some four or five years in the villages like Sarm Phong, Huay Sai, Kham jee-ee, Nongsoong, and Khoke Klarng in the Nakhon Phanom Province because of their mountainous terrain, and his nearness to villagers, tigers, and celestial beings. He had also spent much time instructing his monk and novice disciples. He knew that he had to make one more leap in his inner development to reach complete attainment and that this could be accomplished by total seclusion and lonely vigil. Before he could set out on a journey to achieve this, he had to make arrangements for the care of his mother, who had lived with him these past six years and whom he had initiated as a "nun." He decided to return to his home village in Ubon Province to leave her there, and with this purpose in mind he and his pupils left for that province. On their way, they spent the rains retreat in the village of Nong Khorn in Amnāt District, where the Master instructed the ordained and lay disciples.

In the ensuing dry season, the Acharn took his mother to her home village by slow stages. He stayed in this village a suitable amount of time, instructing his mother,[17] kinsmen, and lay devotees, "delighting them all with his sermons and instruction." Then he took leave of his mother, and made his way *alone* on a true *dhūtaṅga* journey "like a lone bull wandering in the wilds" (p. 104), stopping wherever he wished to refresh himself or meditate and to appreciate with "rapturous delight" the mountain scenery. He carried on his shoulder his umbrella and almsbowl. Inside the bowl were stored robes that were not being worn, a water filter, needles, thread, and other requisites. A water bottle was carried by hand. Whenever possible, at the end of a day's journey he stopped at the edge of an isolated village, where he would beg for alms the next morning.

He thus made his way through the Dong Phya Yen Forest to the capital city of Bangkok to spend the rains retreat at Wat Pathoomwan and to discourse with his friend, the titled abbot of Wat Boromnivas, Phra Upali Gunupamacariya. Together, they left by train at the end of the retreat for the northern capital city of Chiengmai. This leads us to the next phase in Acharn Mun's career: He was to stay in the wilds of Chiengmai for eleven years (1929–40), during which time he achieved full *arahantship*.

Before we write of the events in Chiengmai, we should record one incident that took place during his stay in Ubol, for it attests to the Master's strict adherence to the Renouncer's rejections of this-worldly entanglement of a certain sort, namely, "community development" as championed by the modern missionary monk (*dhammadūta*) movement, and the enlisting of famous forest monks today to bless national undertakings.

Apparently, the Acharn one night had a dream that distressed him – he was walking with his disciples, a number of whom were as usual "orderly and respectful, beautiful and impressive," when suddenly some disciples passed by, "shamelessly" overtaking him, and others carrying wooden pincers tightly gripped his chest, making it difficult for him to breathe. The Master felt that this incident presaged evil conduct by some of his disciples, over whom he decided to maintain close surveillance. And the dream became a reality when one day two monks – one of whom was a disciple living elsewhere – arrived, accompanied by the governor of the province and other officials, and sought the Master's cooperation in asking people to contribute money toward the construction of two or three schools for children. The Master rejected this request because, as the biographer says, "being involved in construction work and asking for money from the people" were things the Master would never do, because "he was a bhikkhu" (p. 101).

## In Chiengmai for eleven years

At Chiengmai railway station, the titled monk from Bangkok, who was well known to all the townspeople from governor to businessmen, was welcomed by a number of laymen. And the Meditation Master, Acharn Mun, who was not known to such a public, accompanied his eminence to Wat Čēdī Lūang, the principal *wat* of the Thammayut sect in this city.

A large number of the pious assembled to listen to a sermon by the famed Bangkok monk, Phra Upali, but he instead invited his companion to speak. Acharn Mun gave an impressive sermon, "delighting all his listeners," and at its conclusion retired to his hut. Then Phra Upali took the opportunity to praise the wise words of the ascetic monk, giving the sermon the name "dawn of deliverance" (*muttodaya*).[18] He praised his achievements in mind development (*kammaṭṭhāna bhikkhu*) and then went on to announce his belief that Acharn Mun was a noble disciple who had attained the level of a "nonreturner" (*anāgāmī*).

Having stayed in Chiengmai city for a time, Acharn Mun took his leave and, wandering alone, sought the seclusion of forests and mountains. He spent a great deal of time in the mountain areas of Māe Rim and Chīang Dāo during both rainy and dry seasons. He had previously suspended the achievement of the supreme victory by choosing to help others; now he was making a last intensified effort; it was "a showdown resulting in either death or achievement." And in this effort for the final goal his loving-kindness for other beings had to cease for the time being.

The Acharn was later to describe to his pupils the ordeals of this last struggle, which left them "awe-struck and breathless." His body and mind were healthy and buoyant; his mind frolicked like a large fish in the ocean and manifested the powers of a trained but spirited horse; his mindfulness and wisdom had reached the *Dhammacakka* (the Wheel of *Dhamma*) level, spontaneous and uninterrupted. The last battle between *Dhamma* and defilements was enjoined, and his task was to realize the truth of the conditionality of all physical, mental, and psychic phenomena. One afternoon he sat on the top of a large, flat rock under the leafy branches of a lone tree, by the side of a mountain "near a remote hill-tribe village, and until late into the night he contemplated the Law of Dependent Origination"[19] both in its serial and reverse order, forward and backward, and with the great weapons of mindfulness and wisdom, the Acharn dethroned "the powerful and crafty monarch of the Three Realms," namely Ignorance.

Although his feelings of loving-kindness toward others were momentarily in abeyance, the Acharn in the middle of his victory remembered with gratitude the Buddha and that his Path was intended for all, that many other disciples of the Buddha had realized the same truth. And he made the decision "to bring the Buddha's message once again to those who would listen to it in earnest and with respect." For the remainder of the night, the Master was moved to tears by the feeling of *samvega* for his past ignorance, which brought him untold suffering. He was later to describe his journey to his disciples as "The Path Through the threshold of Death."

At dawn, he extended his thanks to the tree under which he had meditated; and although he had no need to seek food because of his experience of bliss, yet because he felt loving-kindness for the hill-tribesmen who had given him alms before, he went as usual to beg for food.

During that same night of vigil and deliverance, terrestrial and celestial angels joined in a wholehearted appreciation of the Acharn's attainment, which it is said "thundered over the realms of consciousness" and made the worlds "tremble with awe and wonder" (but human beings steeped in their pleasures may not have been aware of this cosmic tremor). The angels requested a sermon, but because the Master was still engrossed in the supreme truth, he asked them to defer their wish. On the following night they came again and praised him for the light that penetrated and made transparent all the realms and gave bliss to all beings enveloped by it.[20]

From the somewhat diffuse account in the biography, one infers that the Acharn meditated in deep solitude, probably on or near the Chīang Dāo mountain, until he reached his deliverance, but that soon after his disciples began to collect around him, he was now ready again to spread his message, wandering with them and retreating into meditation whenever necessary. Among the disciples named are Phra Thet from Nongkhāi and Phra Sarn and Phra Khao from Wat Tham Klong Plane in Udon, who are well known meditation teachers in their own right in recent times. They were, however, directed to find their own secluded places to meditate, meeting him for guidance. It is recorded that the Master was stringent with his disciples of this time, urging them to show self-sacrifice and courage and to be reconciled to death if that should become necessary as a result of their exertions. His teaching in Chiengmai was "absolute, unbending and admitted no leniency," especially after the profound experience of his attainment. And because of the special psychic abilities he had developed he was able to reprimand or console, as fit, those of his disciples who deviated from the path. There are instances cited of his giving "the Lion's roar" in anger when disciples silently questioned his instructions or had deviant thoughts. He would say: "Sure you are not perfect, you are under the guidance of a teacher and need training and development." As the biographer puts it: "The Venerable Acharn was a model of both external practice . . . and . . . inward abilities of clairvoyance, clairaudience and telepathy," which he showed in relation to different orders of beings, as the following examples show.

On the nights following the Acharn's attainment, there were a number of buddhas attended by several *arahant* disciples – their number varying with the achievement of each buddha – who paid him visits in appreciation of his deliverance and instructed him on various matters. The Tathāgata's *Dhamma,* they said, is like a remedy for illness, but until sentient beings "whirling helplessly in the tempestuous wind of their own sufferings" take notice of the *Dhamma* and put it into practice, no one can offer them any help.

The buddhas also told the Acharn that the Tathāgata he saw was "none other *than absolute purity of mind*" and that they had come to him only in the *sammati* (assumed, mundane, relative) form. To which Acharn asked the critical question:

# The biography of a modern saint

"I have no doubt in the Buddha and the *arahant* disciples, but how, after your complete passing away without remainder (*anupādisesa-nibbāna*) are you still able to come in such a form?" In reply, the Buddha said that for one who has attained to absolute purity and is without form such a temporary assumed form is necessary in order to make contact with someone like the Acharn who has attained to absolute purity but who still exists in a mundane form. The absolute deliverance is void of signs and manifestations, but in order for it to be made known a mundane form is necessary and therefore assumed.[21]

The encounter with the buddhas and *arahants* had still another implication. From the way that they conducted themselves – walked, sat, meditated, paid obeisance, and conversed – the Acharn learned two things:

1. He saw what the traditional modes of dress, sitting, walking, meditating (both while walking and sitting), and so on were in early Buddhism. Because, as we know from sectarian disputes, such details of monastic discipline are an important preoccupation of the *saṅgha* in Southeast Asia, we may infer that the Acharn's sense of the continuity and legitimacy of the present-day *saṅgha*'s customs in such matters was confirmed.
2. The Acharn wondered about this seeming lack of order among the Buddha's disciples, "who were renowned for their orderliness and discipline," but soon realized that the traditional hierarchy based on the seniority of ordination was but a "relative truth," which was subsumed and of no importance at the higher level of achievement based on the *Dhamma* of deliverance. Absolute purity implies absolute equality among those who have been delivered, from the buddhas down to the *arahants* (and even to the *sāmaṇeras* who had been delivered). But even among this democracy of equally delivered, when an occasion arose for paying conventional respect, then a graduated seating order was observed in which the buddha was seated in front and the *sāmaṇeras* were seated behind the monks. And irrespective of level of attainment, seniority in ordination was respected in this context.

The foregoing section is double-edged. On the one hand, it asserts the equality among those monks and novices who have reached deliverance irrespective of their statuses as observed in the worldly *saṅgha*; on the other, the principle of seniority of ordination, which is a classical rule observed among the *theravādin* elders, is affirmed as ordering respect relationships. All in all, this affirmation by the *dhūtaṅga* monk of organizational principles that allegedly refer to early Buddhism has leveling implications for the official *saṅgha* hierarchy of today with its "bureaucratic" titles and competencies, insignia and accoutrements.

Soon after his enlightenment, Acharn Mun had an encounter with his "wife from former lives," which will evoke for the buddhologist a comparison with the Buddha's relations over numerous former lives with his wife Yasodharā, whom he in his final life deserted at night as she lay sleeping with the newly born prince, Rāhula. The Acharn and his wife of former lives had together made a resolution to become buddhas in the future,[22] and now he had outstripped her; she complained that she had no one to counsel her now that he was delivered from this ocean of suffering. In reply, the Acharn cited the example of the Buddha, who reached the goal first but, showing loving-kindness toward his wife, returned to help her progress on the same path. He promised to do the same for his own wife. He recommended that she take rebirth on the plane of existence appropriate to her "disillusionment" as well as her merits, and she took birth in the celestial realm called *Tāvatiṁsa* and then decorously returned to his presence to listen to his instruction. This dialogue between the Acharn and his former spouse took place over several hours while the Acharn was in deep and continuous meditation from 8 o'clock the previous evening until 5 o'clock the succeeding morning.

During this post-enlightenment period in the mountains of Chiengmai, the following deeds and accomplishments are accredited to Acharn Mun:

1. He showed his ability for mind reading, his subjects being his own disciples. He was aware, without seeing or hearing about the incident, that a monk-disciple had fallen in love with a tribal girl and commented that however hard he might try to resist the carnal desire, he would not be able to resist it because of the action of his *karma*. The prediction was proved right, in spite of the removal of the monk to another village. A monk, whose previous history as a boxer was unknown, joined the Acharn's circle; the Acharn by his clairvoyance not only knew this, but also that the monk thoughtlessly carried with his possessions some photographs of himself as a boxer.

2. The Acharn also showed he had powers of clairaudience. One of the hill-tribe communities among whom he and a companion lived for a time suspected them of being tigers disguised as men. The Acharn not only knew at a distance the discussions between the headmen and the tribesmen, but also subsequently converted them to the mindful recitation of *buddho* and convinced them of the wonderful results that followed from following some basic Buddhist precepts. There are recorded other instances of the hill tribes "bathing in the radiance of his instruction."

3. He also gave instruction "to such invisible beings as ghosts, demons, terrestrial and celestial angels and the higher angels called Brahma"; apparently, there were more celestial beings inhabiting the forests of Chiengmai than those of the Northeast, and it is claimed that at this time he gave more assistance to the angels than to any other order of beings. Furthermore, one night, while he was staying in a village of the Muser (Lahu) tribe, a group of angels visited him from Germany[23] and requested a sermon on the subject of Victory; they made repeated visits thereafter to pay him homage and listen to him. Perhaps the crowning achievement in this respect was the frequent visits made by the deity Sakka (Indra) and his angel followers – to them he gave sermons, following their preference, on loving-kindness pitched at the "unlimited, all-embracing and impersonal" level of *appamāṇa brahmavihāra*.

4. The Acharn recounted the many occasions on which the hungry ghosts (*preta*), of whom there were countless numbers, swarmed round him to beg for his assistance; many of them had died so long ago that there were no living relatives who could make merit on their behalf and dedicate the fruits to them.

5. The Acharn once had a remarkable vision concerning three elephants while he was meditating on a mountain deep in the forest. A large elephant approached him, he mounted it, and he was followed by two other elephants on which were seated two young *bhikkhu*. The Master led the procession out of the three worlds and reached a cave, which he entered, but not the two *bhikkhu*. He bade them farewell, saying that

this was the last moment when his appearance in the mundane world would be absolutely severed from rebirth and he would never again return to it.

The Acharn himself interpreted this dream as signifying that "at his passing away there would be two young *bhikkhu* blessed with the same attainments as himself" (p. 174); however, he did not identify them. At another level of interpretation, he said, the dream stated that meditation and insight are helpful instruments to an *arahant* until the last moment of his life for the subduing of suffering. A buddhologist might speculate that this dream might be related to the sculptural and iconographic tradition of having two disciples, Sāriputta and Moggallāna, flanking the seated Buddha.

### Return to the Northeast

All in all, during his stay in Chiengmai there were not many *dhūtaṅga* disciples under his training, for he stayed in the wilds most of the time. In 1940, upon the persistent urging of a titled monk, the abbot of an important *wat* in the Northeastern town of Udon (Chaokhun Dhammacedi of Wat Bōdhi Somphorn), Acharn Mun agreed to return to the Northeast. He and those of his disciples willing to accompany him to Udon left the forest, went to Wat Čēdī Lūang of Chiengmai city, and were there met by a delegation from Udon. Before leaving, the Acharn gave a memorable three-hour sermon on Vesākha Day (on which the Buddha was born, reached enlightenment, and passed away).

The train first took the party to Bangkok – there being no direct train to Udon from Chiengmai – where Acharn Mun took up residence at Wat Boromnivat. At Bangkok, many people came to see and question him. Some of the pronouncements he made were these: Morality has always something to do with the mind, which is the producer of both good and evil; mind control encompasses the 227 *Vinaya* precepts and must come first before word control and deed control. It is not possible "to separate the characteristics of morality from the person who observes it, not even from the blissful results of its observance." It is because they merge together that one cannot separate morality and its results and treat them like commercial goods; it is because there is no attachment in morality, such as can be found in the person who is attached to his property, that morality can produce true bliss and security.

When asked by an Elder how did the Acharn solve doubts and find answers to questions in the solitude of the wilds when the Elder himself, surrounded by books and scholars in Bangkok, was frequently at his wits' end, the Acharn replied that his mind is never dissociated from the *Dhamma*, which is its preoccupation day and night; that it is in the mind that all problems and defilements occur; and that it is with one's mind that one dissolves them, for the Buddha has said "one is the master of oneself" (*attā hi attano nātho*). This is why the Acharn said he prefers to come to grips with all problems through self-help in the seclusion of the wilds. The Elder, greatly impressed, summed up by making a distinction between "the dharma in the Scriptures" (about the authenticity of which over time one cannot be sure) and "the dharma of the mind," these two *Dhammas* being "on different levels, producing different tastes" (p. 209). However, the Acharn affirmed that just as during the time of the Buddha the disciples went to him for instruction and clarification of doubts, he too would not hesitate to go to the Buddha if he was alive today: His own efforts had been difficult and long for lack of a competent teacher, but lacking one, the only alternative is to grope oneself through steadfastness of aim and dedication of effort.

While in Bangkok, the Acharn refused all invitations for meals in lay devotees' homes because they would have interfered with his daily routine. From Bangkok, he and his party traveled to Khorāt, the first Northeastern town on the way to Udon, where they stopped for a while at Wat Sālavan, a forest monastery. He declared here to a lay questioner that the Four Noble Truths were completely within his mind, that a person's most valuable and incomparable treasure was his mind. He also affirmed that "the mind that is dharma" was able "to bestow peace and bliss upon others" and that as long as there was breath in his body so long would he serve others "for their own sakes."

On finally reaching Udon Thānī, the Acharn made his first stay at Wat Bodhi Somporn, where Choakhun Dhammacedi, who was instrumental in persuading the Acharn to return from Chiengmai, presided. "There he was reverently welcomed by a great number of people from the various districts of Udorn Thani and also from the towns of Nongkhāi and Sakon Nakhon."

The Acharn then chose to spend his first rains retreat at Wat Nonenivet, chosen with Chaokhun Dhammacedi's advice and consent. While there, Dhammacedi, his enthusiastic benefactor and admirer – for he too had some interest in meditation – "regularly led groups of lay devotees, consisting of government officials, businessmen and common people," to see Acharn Mun and receive instruction from him every Wan Phra.[24]

There was also a constant stream of his former disciples, both monks and laity, who came to see him after his prolonged absence and to renew their learning from him. In fact, during this rains retreat he conducted a program of intensive teaching and instruction, which it would be profitable for us to review. The biographer makes a point of informing us that the timetable of instruction and practice that the Acharn implemented at this later stage and final return to the Northeast was different from that observed at earlier phases.

The *bhikkhus* and *sāmaṇera* living at Wat Nonenivet were expected to devote all their time to inner development. Nighttime was set apart for instructing the monk-disciples, and "he would begin his instruction with morality and then move to meditation, wisdom and deliverance."

He often stressed the importance of the observance of morality; failure to develop it breeds lack of shame and leads to violation of other *Vinaya* prohibitions; its observance is rewarded with inner *bhikkhuhood* and its combination with meditative exertions for the sake of insight leads to the Path of Fruition and the purging of the mind of defilements. This is the meaning of the Thai word *phra* (Pali: *vara*); it stands for a monk "excellent" in behavior, wisdom, and insight.

After the time set for instruction was over, any disciple with doubts or problems relating to the process of his mind development could usually approach him for individual questioning. He thus took pains to render selfless service to others.

At this period of time, even with creeping old age and enfeeblement of body, he still kept to a taxing schedule. He slept for four hours at the most. After waking in the early morning, he practiced both sitting and walking meditation in that order. Then he went out on his almsround and ate his only meal of the day. After this, he did walking meditation until noon, rested awhile, and engaged in sitting and walking meditation until 4 p.m. Sweeping the dwelling area and a bath came next, followed by several hours of walking meditation and recitation, concluding with several hours of sitting meditation before going to sleep. On special occasions, he might continue his sitting meditation throughout the night without any sleep. During the rains retreat, of course, part of the night was devoted to instruction, as said before.

The Acharn stayed for two rains retreats in the town of Udon (spending the intervening dry season in the forest village of Nong Nan Khem because, in spite of his age, he still liked to wander alone), and then on the invitation of a pious lay disciple, Khun Mae Noom Juvanon, he went to Sakon Nakhon and took up his residence at Wat Suddhavas. After receiving many visits from his devotees, he moved again from the town to the forest hermitage in the village of Namone, where he energetically directed ordained disciples. The routine observed at this forest hermitage is as follows. The disciples were expected to practice meditation assiduously either inside their humble individual huts or on their meditation walks. At four o'clock in the afternoon they came together to sweep the open area of the hermitage compound, fill the water jars, and then bathe. Even at these times they were self-controlled, practicing mindfulness and not engaging in idle conversation. After this joint duty, they would retire to their own places for more exertion. The two set periods when they came together again was for their morning meal in the hall and for their intermittent evening instruction. Mindfulness was observed on the almsround, and there was no chatting during the meal.

We are told of the time when the master and disciples lived for five years at a forest hermitage in Nong Phue (see below in this chapter). On their almsrounds, the disciples walked to the village in a single long line. There were benches or long seats prepared for them by the villagers, on which they would sit to recite the *anumodanā* passages of acknowledgment and blessing after they had received the food. Then they returned in the same way.

The meal itself was an occasion for contemplative practice. Before eating together in one place, the disciples were urged to contemplate the nature of the food mixed up within their almsbowls and the purpose for eating it; while eating, self-restraint was observed, and in chewing care was taken not to make any noise that might cause annoyance to others. "After eating, the place was wiped and cleaned, alms-bowls were washed and then dried for a few moments in the sun before being returned to their proper places" (p. 225).[25]

The orienting conception behind such controlled practice is well expressed by the biographer: "Mindfulness is to be developed to control every moment and movement of exertion, until it finally becomes *mahāsati* (great-mindfulness) which then produces *mahāpaññā* (the great wisdom)" (p. 225).

The *Dhamma* instruction in the evening was held every six or seven days, but in the meantime any practitioner who faced an obstacle could approach the Master for advice. The general picture was one of individual monks or novices applying their utmost effort in their own dwellings or walks; on moonlit nights they could be seen treading their tracks and on dark nights the lanterns told the same tale.

For his nightly recitation by himself, the Master usually chose from the scriptures such long discourses as the *Dhammacakkappavattana Sutta*[26] and the *Mahāsamaya Sutta*. On some occasions, however, he would translate these *suttas* for his disciples, his focus being on the "practical" implications of the words rather than their etymological meanings. Although he had little academic training, he had an extraordinary capacity for translating the Pali texts.

From the village of Namone, the Acharn moved on to the village of Ban Koke, about two kilometers away. At both these places the number of disciples staying with him was quite small, about ten or eleven in all, in accordance with the small number of living places available. It was in Ban Koke that the biographer himself, Acharn Maha Boowa, was first admitted as a novice-disciple.[27]

During the rains retreat at Ban Koke, the Master conducted his instruction every six or seven days for about two hours or so each time, sometimes extending it to three or four, and the listeners absorbed in his teaching "experienced no stiffness of body or fatigue." They felt, says the biographer, reflecting his own neophyte experience, that they were reliving the time when the Buddha taught his disciples, that in fact the venerable Master "was delivering the dharma which was to him the Absolute Present."

The biographer also notes that sometimes during the period of these rains retreats the Acharn "would recall experiences of his former lives for his disciples, whereas at other times he would tell them of the early states of his exertions in this life, which included the phenomena and insights resulting from meditation and contemplation," and carry the story through to "the critical moment when achievement was about to be won and he was to leave the quagmire forever" (p. 232). (We may note here that the Master in recalling his former lives manifests the capacity that the Buddha himself showed in the *Jātakas,* and also the powers of *iddhi* described in the *Visuddhimagga.*)

From Ban Koke, at the end of the rains retreat, the Master returned briefly to Namone village, but then moved again to a village deep in the forest (Ban Huey

Khan) and from there to a deserted monastery on the hillside at Nasinuan village. Here he stayed for several months and was stricken with fever for several days "until he cured it, as usual, by the therapeutic effect of the dharma" (p. 231). In 1942, he went to the town of Ubol to attend the funeral rites of his meditation teacher and co-practitioner – Acharn Sao – and then returned to Namone village (Sakon Nakhon Province) to spend another rains retreat there.

He had thus altogether spent some three retreats in these villages of Tong Khobe District; then he was invited by the devotees of the village of Nong Phue to "uplift their spirit" by coming to stay with them. He accepted and set out on foot on a journey that took some three or four nights. A few days later he was stricken with malaria, which intermittently affected him with fever for several months.

Despite these reverses, the forest hermitage of Nong Phue, and the wider district in which it was located, became a center for *dhūtaṅga* monks. This happened for good reasons. The village of Nong Phue is situated in the middle of the valley, surrounded by forests and mountains. The valley is fairly wide and suitable for farming at various places; the surrounding numerous mountains and vast forest offered numerous secluded places for a great number of *dhūtaṅga* monks all year round, in both the rainy and dry seasons. The forest hermitage was on a direct but ascending path from the district town of Nong Phue that was about 20 kilometers long, and there were other longer, winding (but easier) paths to it. Motor transport was possible between towns, and plenty of the laity, including businessmen and government officials, and also monks from these towns, thronged to the hermitage to see him.

Despite the distance and the dangers of malaria and physical discomfort, many monks and novices sought out the Master to become his direct disciples. Thus during the rains retreat the hermitage of Nong Phue itself housed some twenty to thirty disciples; but more found accommodation in nearby villages in groups of two to ten. On Wan Phra days, especially when the Pāṭimokkha recitations were done fortnightly, there would be twenty to thirty disciples from outside coming to attend, the numbers swelling even more if other monks from nearby *wat* joined them. Outside the rains retreat, if the Master stayed there, the number congregating from outside could reach fifty to sixty or more.

Not only was the scale of attendance on the days of Pāṭimokkha recitation larger, but the mode of instruction also was intensified: It was more oratorical, more "strong and stirring," more extensive and profound than usual.

The limelight now must be accorded to the ascetic monks dotted and dispersed in all those forested mountains, who would come down and return in a steady stream, traveling great distances to listen to the Master's instruction on Pāṭi-mokkha days and receiving advice with regard to their problems.

These ascetic meditators would stay either alone or two together in secluded places separated from one another by six kilometers or more (even up to thirty). They would walk the forest trails, stopping for water or food at hamlet settlements, arrive at the Master's hermitage, stay overnight, and return to their solitude and self-dependence, replenished. Despite their physical separation and only occasional meeting with him, these disciples had a strong link with their teacher who was their radial center.

They had a powerful sense of their defilements and a fierce battle raged inside them for their eradication. The Acharn's stirring instructions helped the monks to extinguish the defilements or at least to make them beat a hasty retreat for a while. This is why, although it is true that *bhikkhu* are expected to eradicate the defilements mainly by themselves, yet they were substantially helped by the Acharn's guidance and were therefore attracted to their teacher "perhaps to an unusual extent in the eyes of the others." This is also why *dhūtaṅga* monks who stayed and practiced in remote, secluded areas walked long distances to consult the Acharn whenever they were faced with problems they could not solve. An Acharn comes to know each disciple's achievements and limitations and the obstacles that block his way, and a disciple in turn also discerns the level of development of his Acharn when he relates his inner experiences to his Acharn for advice and explanation. There are also times when a disciple is deluded into thinking he has reached his final attainment, and a knowing Acharn will correct this false belief and direct him toward higher effort.

The ascetic practices verging on self-mortification practiced by the Master and recommended to these disciples are aptly summarized thus: "There were a variety of practices for self-discipline which they undertook and which included: not sleeping; reducing food intake or eating no food at all for a length of time appropriate to the endurance of the body; all night walking or sitting meditation; sitting meditation in a dangerous place, such as the mouth of a cave where a tiger was dwelling, on a tiger's pathway, in a cemetery where corpses are newly buried or burnt, or even at the edge of a high precipice. In all these instances, the purpose was the same: to tame the unruly mind by forcing it to face whatever it was afraid of..." (p. 238), to draw it back within itself instead of allowing it to dwell upon whatever external is feared, to convince it of its own power, and to develop the qualities of courage, poise, and peace. "Let what you are afraid of be your trainer and your teacher" was the advice by which he cured a pupil's fear of tigers. In the same way, the Acharn taught the disciples who were victims of malaria to use the therapeutic effect of *dharma* to cure themselves; illness faced and survived by exercising the courage of mindfulness and wisdom makes it possible to face not only future illness but the critical moment of death itself.

The Acharn stayed in the village of Nong Phue for five years; he was now seventy-five, and he did not often go out to secluded places as had been his habit before. There was not much communication with invisible beings either; his attention was largely devoted to his disciples. The regime was the same as documented earlier, but the biographer describing these last years writes warmly of the informal discussions at night between pupils and the Master, when the pupils from places near and far would relate and exchange the unique experiences they had and the strange problems they had encountered, whether these were about inner *Dhamma* realization or communication with invisible beings. The variety of experiences related to the different levels of attainment of the disciples; and the Master capped them with his own.

## The fatal illness and the mortuary rites

In his seventy-ninth year,[28] during the hot month of March in 1949, the Acharn fell ill. The Acharn already knew that this was to be his last illness and announced the fact to his disciples, telling them that there was no remedy to cure it. From then on he showed irritation when offered medicine. The countdown had begun, he said, and the law of flux was now proving itself on his body.

News of his final illness soon spread rapidly, and people, both lay and or-dained, disciples and devotees, swarmed to Nong Phue, walking some 25 to 30 kil-ometers off the highways between the towns of Udon and Sakon Nakhon to reach the forest village. The aged were transported in bullock carts. He continued to instruct his monks and novices, though not as regularly as before, and gave audience to as many importunate lay devotees as he could. And in spite of his weakening body, he kept the *dhūtaṅga* practices: He regularly begged for food, the distance he walked diminishing with the progress of the illness, from full distance to the village, to halfway, then to the gateway of the hermitage, and finally to the meeting hall, where the lay donors met him and filled his bowl. When he was no longer able to walk, he still ate in his bowl and only once a day. The monks and novices mounted night watches.

The Master's deterioration continued through the rains retreat, and when this period was over, more and more disciples thronged from all directions eager to pay their respects to him. He insisted that he did not want to die in this remote village, because on his account many local animals would have to be killed to feed the multitudes, there being no meat market nearby. It would be ironic if his death would be the cause of death to animals to whom he had always extended loving-kindness. He therefore directed his disciples to transport him to the town of Sakon Nakhon. The villagers, who wanted him to die in their humble settlement and, though poor, were keen to make and finance the arrangements for the cremation, were disappointed but obeyed.

The Master was carried on a stretcher some 24 kilometers to Wat Bahn Poo in the nearest district of Phannā Nikom. Hundreds of weeping, grief-stricken disciples and devotees followed the stretcher. The journey took a whole day. The plan was to give the dying saint a rest and then take him to the town of Sakon Nakhon. He was placed in a small meeting hall, and hundreds of people swarmed to see him, for it is the people's belief that one has to be blessed with merit to be able to see and recognize an *arahant*, and catching a glimpse of him or, better still, paying respects to him, would give them the assurance that their lives had not been wasted.

The Master's condition worsened, and he urged his disciples to take him to his destination without delay. The disciples delayed ten days to give him rest but, unable to resist the Master's words to the effect that his suffering body was a burden and he did not want his life prolonged, they acquiesced. A close lay disciple, Mrs. Noon Chuvanon, brought a car borrowed from the Highway Department and personally invited him to leave for Sakon Nakhon. The car reached Wat Suddhāvas in the town at noon, and he slept till midnight and woke up in a final flickering of life. Three lines of the religious were seated by his side – his old friend and admirer, Chaokhun Dhammacedi of Udon, sat closest to him at the head of the first line; the second line was composed of his past pupils who were themselves now Teachers (Acharns); and finally his current disciples made up the third line.

The Master lay on his right side in the Lion's posture,[29] but a pupil eased him halfway onto his back in order not to tire him; in this position, he passed away at 2:23 a.m. The biographer records that many, including himself, thought that their Master "had attained to parinirvāṇa" (p. 279). The next day, the senior *bhikkhu* and government officials in town came to pay their last respects, and it was decided to broadcast over the radio that the *arahant*'s cremation ceremony would be staged three months later in the third lunar month of B.E. 2493 (1950), so as to give time to all disciples and devotees living in various parts of the country to attend, if they wished to.

Throughout this long interval of three months "there were no crimes of violence, stealing, quarrelling, or drinking bouts. Those who had lost valuables were able to later recover them by reporting to the authorities in the monastery area..." (p. 276).

It was estimated that some 10,000 people attended his cremation at Wat Suddhāvas. "The forested area on the outskirts of Wat Suddhāvas bloomed with the white umbrellas of the forest monks who had come"; altogether, some 2,000 monks and novices clustered inside Wat Suddhāvas and nearby monasteries. "Booths and sheds of all shapes and sizes had been erected all over the area and food and drink were served freely to all" (p. 275). Loudspeakers blared instructions and accounts of the ongoing enactments.

Devotees piled up a small mountain of offerings, consisting of sacks of rice and robes numerous enough to fill a factory warehouse. Food was cooked in gigantic pots by laymen, and *dhūtaṅga* monks and novices in groups of thirty to sixty were fed in monks' dwellings, sheds, fields, and other available sites.

The cremation ceremony itself lasted "three nights and four days." The time for cremation had been set for midnight (of the thirteenth day of the waxing moon of the third lunar month of Magha), and at the appointed time before the eyes of the patiently assembled massive crowd a "miracle" happened: "The summer sky was bright and clear but it suddenly became overcast by a small cloud which hovered over only the cremation area. Just as the fire was lit and the flames leaped towards the coffin, the area was suddenly cooled by a drizzle which lasted about fifteen minutes before the cloud disappeared, leaving the moonlit sky as bright and clear as before'' (p. 227).

The body was consumed by the pyre of burning sandalwood (specially brought from Laos), and the ashes collected the next morning were distributed to ''the bhikkhu delegates from the various towns who attended the ceremony so that they could be enshrined in places to be specially built''; lay disciples from various towns also received portions.[30] As soon as the formal distribution was over, others present rushed to the remains of the pyre and gathered all the dust and cinders that remained. They regarded the dust and ashes as a treasure, which they pressed ''to their bosoms with a triumphant smile.'' On the very place where the cremation pyre stood was later built the convocation hall of Wat Suddhāvas.

The Acharn's ashes in due course became relics. Those who had been fortunate enough to receive the ashes had enshrined them in their homes and venerated them there. For four years nothing extraordinary happened. Then one day a certain pious lady, Mrs. Khamanāmool, went to Wat Suddhāvas, where Acharn Mun had been cremated. After she made offerings to the monks, she received from the abbot some ashes from a burnt bone from the upper part of the Acharn's body. She took the ashes home in an urn and on opening it found to her wonderment that the ashes ''had all become relics'' – they had turned into ''smooth and glossy grains, sandlike in appearance, resembling relics of the Buddha and some other arahant disciples in ancient times'' (p. 280). She then rushed to the hotel she owned and opened an urn there where she had kept some of the Acharn's ashes that she had previously received, and she found that those ashes too had become relics. Altogether now she was the proud owner of 344 relic grains. People thronged to her house to see the holy objects and, being a generous person, Mrs. Khamanāmool distributed some of the grains to various persons, the biographer himself being fortunate to receive grains on two occasions.

Over the years, similar incidents were reported regarding the ashes in the keeping of other devotees. Other wondrous events took place, too: Sometimes two grains of the relics became three, ''symbolic of the Triple Gem,'' and sometimes two grains merged and became one. The Master's hair, which was shaved once a fortnight, was also found to have been transformed into relics in places where disciples had thought to enshrine it.

''Why do the ashes of arahants become relics?'' asks the biographer. The body of an *arahant* and a worldling, he goes on to explain, have the same ingredients, with this difference: The mind of an *arahant* has been absolutely purified, whereas that of the worldling contains defilements. ''Body matter is then transformed in accordance with the condition and nature of the mind.'' A purified mind can therefore purify the physical body in much the same way as a defiled mind can defile the body (p. 283). The process of body purification takes a long time; if an *arahant* lives long enough after his attainment, there is an opportunity for the body to eliminate its "toxic ingredients" by virtue of the mind's regular withdrawal into the most profound depths of concentration and hence the likelihood of his ashes turning into relics after his death. Noble Disciples can be divided into two groups, according to their history of attainment: The *daṇḍā-bhiññā* is one who, having reached the level of Non-Returner, takes a long time before achieving *arahantship*; the *khippābhiññā* is one whose attainment is "sudden," taking little time, and he does not live long after his attainment. It is the former whose prolonged and many meditative exercises have a chance to purify the body, and Acharn Mun is a quintessential example of such a Noble Disciple.

The venerable Master has passed away, but there is still a link between him and his disciples, who are prone to have visions during their meditation. He appears in their visions and, as he did when he was alive, gives them whatever instruction or advice is necessary to overcome an obstacle, "much the same way as the arahant disciples had appeared and instructed him" (p. 302). "An experience such as this on the part of some disciples, and those [experiences] of the Venerable Acharn himself in listening to sermons given by the Buddha and arahant disciples may be likened to the Buddha giving sermons to his mother Queen Maya in the Tavatimsa heaven by means of a vision" (p. 302).

Today the Master's "elder disciples, through his training and guidance, have been firmly established in the dharma and have now become Acharns in their own right, leading people along the Right Path. All have large numbers of disciples in various parts of the country. And there are still other disciples who are millionaires in the dharma, but who prefer a solitary, secluded life" (p. 303).

# 7

# The Buddha's life as paradigm

### Recent biographies of monks

Before we attempt a detailed interpretation of the biography of Acharn Mun, we should explore what sort of tradition of writing biographies of monks exists in Sri Lanka, Burma, and Thailand. This inquiry is called for because our biographer Maha Boowa himself states in his preface that "the method of presentation here follows that of the ancient compilers who recorded the biographies of some Noble disciples in various texts in the hope that they may be encouraging examples for posterity." In Sri Lanka and Thailand, as in Burma, there are numerous popular biographies of the Buddha[1] and famous *arahants*.[2] Many of these stories of *arahants* are adaptations of old stories transferred to new subjects. But the biographies are not necessarily confined to these heroic figures alone.

That a lively tradition of composing biographies of monks developed in Sri Lanka, primarily in the nineteenth and twentieth centuries, is attested by Malalgoda's study, which uses to advantage this genre of local Siṅhala literature. Malalgoda cites at least ten sources that carry the word *caritaya* (or *caritam* or *cariyava*) in their titles: Of these, one is an edited reprint of an eighteenth-century work, five were published between 1901 and 1913, and the rest later. Furthermore, biographical information on monks is also available in Siṅhala publications that describe the genealogy and history of the various sects and fraternities that developed in Sri Lanka in the nineteenth century. An interesting addition to this list is a biography of a monk called Miripanna Dhammaratana, a famous Siṅhala poet, published in 1868 in English.[3]

Although some of these biographies were about forest-monks,[4] most of Malalgoda's biographies are concerned with famous reformist or activist monks during the years 1700–1900. I shall select two instances. One subject was Välvita Saraṇaṁkara, the reformer and leader of the "pious ones," of whom I have written earlier. Another was Hikkaduve Sumaṅgala (1826–1911), a scholar monk of the "low country" who belonged to the Siyām Nikāya and who opened in 1873 the Vidyodaya College in Colombo for the education of monks at a time when the main educational establishments at Kandy were at a low ebb.

Although the vast majority of these biographies were composed and published at the turn of the century and later, more generally as a result of the spirit of religious revival and fervor and more specifically as a result of spreading literacy and the introduction of printing presses (the first publications printed in Siṅhalese were done by the Christian missionaries in the nineteenth century), yet the caritaya-type biographical genre goes back to earlier times. For instance, the more recent biographical accounts of saṅgharāja Saraṇaṁkara rely largely on two accounts of his life composed in 1779 and circa 1780, the first in prose, the second in verse.[5] Thus, apart from the tradition of oral accounts of the lives of famous monks, biography as a literary composition seems to have existed before the nineteenth century.

In the case of Thailand – if we accept the authority of Keyes – it appears that the written biographies of Buddhist saints and other well-known monks were produced "after the beginning of the twentieth century, that is, after a radical change had occurred in Thai literature, stimulated by Western influences and especially by the introduction of printing." However, Keyes holds that oral biographies of monks and other individuals have long existed and that "the written biographies of 19th century monks draw upon such oral accounts."[6] In contemporary Thailand, there are to be found a multitude of printed biographies of the lives of monks. As Keyes puts it, it is only necessary to have been an abbot of a local monastery to merit a biography, but there are certain others who command greater attention. "Some biographies of famous monks have been written because the subject has gained a reputation as a high-ranking official or even patriarch of the Thai Sangha; others are of monks who are renowned for their 'magical' (saksit) powers; and still others are of those who have gained fame for their theological discourses. Only a very few are of those recognized as saints, and to this very limited class belong the biographies of Khrūbā Sīwichai and Ācān Man."[7]

Krūbā Sīwichai, a venerated monk of Northern Thailand, is the subject of many biographies, ranging from popular pamphlets and articles in magazines to palm-leaf texts.[8] These literary sources and their contents – which chart his life, ascetic practices, charismatic powers, religious works, and political challenges – are dealt with in Chapter 21. The center of attention here, however, is the life of Acharn Mun, which, according to his biographer, Maha Boowa, was written according to a Buddhist hagiographical style. It seems to me that to fully grasp the implications of Acharn Mun's biography, as of other acclaimed Buddhist saints, we might begin with the contours of the received life of the Buddha himself.

# The Buddha's life as a paradigm

## The life of the Buddha

The Buddhist notion of "biography" is conveyed by words like *carita, caritam,* and *avadāna.* The biography of the Buddha, fragmentary in the canonical Pali literature, but elaborated and mythologized in subsequent times by all Buddhist schools, is an integral part of the dogma and doctrine referred to as the *Dhamma.* The *Vinaya* rules are stated in the context of events that took place during the Buddha's itinerant teaching mission in the company of disciples. (The *Skandhaka* documents these rules, which, in the Pali scriptures, are divided into *Mahāvagga* and *Cullavagga.*)[9] The Buddha's discourses in the *Suttapiṭaka* are similarly personalized and contextualized, as indeed are the Jātaka accounts of the Buddha's former lives strung on a long chain of rebirths. In Buddhist postcanonical literature, a quintessential "first-ever" biography in the *caritam* mode is the poetic *Buddhacarita,* composed by Aśvaghoṣa.[10] Many versions of Aśvaghoṣa's text have been discovered in India, Tibet, China, and elsewhere. According to Northern traditions, Aśvaghoṣa was the twelfth Buddhist patriarch, and Chinese sources say he was a contemporary of Kaniṣka, who ruled in Kaśmīr in the early centuries of the Christian Era. Kaniṣka is alleged to have carried him off from Pāṭaliputra when he attacked that imperial city. In the Council of Sarvāstivādin elders that Kaniṣka is said to have convened, Aśvaghoṣa acted as vice-president.

The *Buddhacarita* is a poetical account of the Buddha's life, and some scholars hold that Aśvaghoṣa imitated the style of Kālidāsa's *Raghuvaṁśa,* his work showing, however, elaborations and devices of a later stage in the development of the Sanskrit language. What is of particular interest to us is that his work relates the story of the Buddha's early life.[11] It thus starts with Suddhodana and Māyā reigning in Kapilavastu, the Buddha entering Māyā's womb, his birth in Lumbini Park, and Asita's disclosure of the career awaiting him.

The childhood of the Buddha, his sporting with the young women in the palace, and the birth of his son Rāhula are described. The centerpiece is the three trips he made as a youth from the palace to the park outside the city and his meeting with the three apparitions of sickness, old age, and death. Celebrated is the description of the women of the city craning from the upper roofs of their mansions to have a glimpse of the handsome prince as he returns from these trips. His restlessness and aversion to palace life culminate with his departure on his horse Kaṇṭhaka, accompanied by his horsekeeper Chandaka. Another celebrated description is that of the sleeping palace women in careless postures and with distorted facial expressions; it is accompanied by a reflection on the nature of women and men's lust for them. Thus the composition elaborates on the decisive incidents in the Buddha's life that led to his heroic renunciation, and its sensuous poetry has moral overtones and a didactic purpose.

The original *avadānas* were stories or legends of the historical Buddha (and of previous buddhas) and of his followers, usually concerning their previous lives.

(However, in time, a story of a previous life of the Buddha was given the special label of *jātaka*.) Compared with the concept of *vaṃśa*, which implied some kind of succession of kings or teachers, the *avadāna* seems to have referred to "a great action having decisive consequences,"[12] or, as another gloss would have it, "illustrious actions, heroic deeds, or a narrative of such actions and deeds."[13] The *Vinaya* texts of many Buddhist schools incorporated *avadānas* of the Buddha, and their inclusion served a larger dogmatic purpose. Whatever *avadāna* was related – whether it be a prophecy of the Buddha or some act of an *arahant* – it was used to highlight a point of discipline or a moral precept. Besides the *carita* or *avadāna* legends of heroic deeds pertaining to the Buddha and the saints, perhaps the best-known text of this genre in Buddhist literature is the *Aśokā-vadāna*,[14] which deals with the illustrious actions of Emperor Aśoka.

## Frames of analysis

In order to attempt an ample interpretation of the biography of Acharn Mun, it is necessary to develop several different "frames of analysis," frames that are not disjunctive or separate but cumulatively produce the amplitude we seek. Firstly, we must have some idea of the basic design of the biography of the Buddha. To gain an understanding of this, it will be necessary to distinguish the biography of the Buddha in its earlier form from its later form (or forms),[15] when it was elaborated substantively and also woven into regional and local traditions. We should also try to uncover the Buddhist "historiographic vision" that is embodied in some representative chronicles like the *Mahāvaṃsa* and *Jinakālamālī*, which fuse in a single temporal schema the Buddha's life with the acts of the *saṅgha* and these again with the political history of kings and kingdoms.

Secondly, we have to grasp the main ordering principles behind traditional Buddhist saintly biography, whose protagonists were the *arahants*, even the buddhas. They were the exemplary disciples who followed in the Master's path. This exploration will be enhanced by taking a sideglance at medieval Christian hagiography to establish similarities and differences and by taking one or more classical examples of Buddhist masterpieces of saintly lives and comparing them with our own text concerning Acharn Mun. The latter exercise should help us in deciding in what ways our text is "stereotyped" and follows a classical paradigm and in what ways it is "particularized" and "individualized," thereby reflecting many contextual circumstances concerning not only the subject but also the author of the biography. We might then be able to evaluate in what sense and to what degree our text might be rated a "masterpiece." A "masterpiece," it seems to me, is a felicitous conjunction of a masterly life and a masterly biographer.

Thus, thirdly, we have to bring to life the biographer himself: As far as possible, we should trace his own career as a disciple of the master and a witness to his feats; trace the circumstances in which he came to compose the biography;

trace the "propagandist" and indoctrinating purposes that might have motivated his writing; and trace the political, religious, and social dimensions of the events in which he participated. As Reynolds and Capps point out, "sacred biographies" are extraordinary documents because "they recount the process through which a . . . religious ideal is established and, at the same time, participate in that process."[16] While the previously stated two frames are the province of the historian, the anthropologist could make a distinct contribution to the third: Through his firsthand study of the contemporary events, he should be able to illuminate the context of composition, which is at best meagerly available with regard to chronicles and texts composed in early times.

The rest of this chapter will deal with the first frame of analysis. The second and third frames will be separately tackled in the succeeding chapters.

## Earlier and later Buddhist biographical and historiographical traditions

Various scholars have in one way or another seen the need to demarcate the contents of an earlier Buddhist oral and literary tradition from a later more elaborated and embellished one. Thus Warder, for instance, distinguishes between a "primary historiography" and a "secondary historiography," the first referring to more or less a contemporary and direct record of events as exemplified by the more or less circumstantial accounts of the activities of the Buddha.

Later, we have successive biographies of the Buddha such as the *Mahāvastu, Nidānakathā, Śākyamunibuddhacarita, Lalitavistara*, and Aśvaghoṣa's *Buddhacarita*, in which the narrative is more or less transformed into a legend: the events are not such as we would expect in a circumstantial historical narrative, but fit into certain patterns. . . . In fact all actions are supposed to be conditioned by past events according to the Buddhist doctrine of moral causality. Just as action is related to past events, so it is pregnant with its future consequences. This patterning naturally led secondary Buddhist historians to select, distort and imagine events in such a way as to improve the ethical picture of history presented.[17]

Although a firm distinction cannot be imposed between earlier and later accounts – for it is clear that the canonical texts, written some time after the Buddha's death, already show tendentious patterning and mythologizing of the Buddha's life and teaching – yet it is clear that the Pali *Tipiṭaka* texts, particularly the earlier sections, have a more circumstantial flavor. If we must choose an example, we might say that Oldenberg's account of the Buddha's life[18] is accurately based on material dispersed in the canonical Pali texts of the Theravāda School. Oldenberg asserts (and other biographers like Thomas and Rhys Davids would agree with him) that "a biography of Buddha has not come down to us from ancient times, from the age of the Pali texts, and we can safely say, no such biography was in existence then."[19] Nevertheless, there are of course unconnected fragments of the Buddha's life story embedded in the *sutta* discourses, a particularly prominent one being the *Mahāparinibbāna Sutta*; in the *Vinaya* (especially the *Mahāvagga* and *Cullavagga* sections of the *Skandhaka*); and in other texts. A biography put together from such canonical Pali sources has, as Oldenberg's account reveals to us, very little to say about the Buddha's family origins, his childhood and marriage, and a great deal to say about: the events concerning his enlightenment; his teaching career, which includes both the philosophical truths he preached and the events connected with the founding of a community of monks and the rules by which they were to live; and, finally, his death and cremation rites. In fact, this is the kind of selective emphasis that rings true and is what we ought to expect, if we accept that the centerpiece of the early Buddhist story of its founder and saint is not his personalized early life but his self-effacing achievement of enlightenment and the transmission of that experience to his disciples. We shall in due course compare the central differences in the achievements of early Buddhist and early Christian saints.

### Frauwallner's thesis

If we accept that the *Vinaya* texts contain the largest amount of details of the Buddha's biography and extend the inquiry to the *Vinaya* texts of some six schools[20] presently available to us (of which the Pali version is only one), then what might one learn about the early biographical accounts of the Buddha? This is a question posed by Frauwallner, which he answers in a brilliant, if polemical, manner. All the *Vinayas* were divided into two parts: the *Vibhaṅga*, which is a commentary on the ancient confession rules of *Prātimokṣa*, and the *Skandhaka*, which is an exposition of the monastic rules. It has been indicated by more than one scholar that the *Vinaya* of the Pali school, which begins quite abruptly, is closely connected with regard to its contents with the *Mahāparinibbāna Sutta* of the *Dīghanikāya*, of which it is a continuation. Frauwallner affirms as a fact Finot's surmise that the *Mahāparinibbāna Sutta* and the account of the councils originally formed one continuous narrative, "which told in the manner of a chronicle the last days of the Buddha, his death and the beginnings of the Buddhist Church."[21] The story of the Buddha's death and the account of the two earliest councils, according to Frauwallner's reconstruction, formed a narrative that was a fixed component of the *Vinaya* placed at the end of the *Skandhaka*. The *Skandhaka* in the *Vinaya* of the Pali school begins with the Buddha's illumination and includes his first sermon delivered at Benares and the first conversions, concluding with those of Śāriputra and Maudgalyāyana. The *Vinaya* of the Dharmaguptakas and Mahīśāsaka begins earlier, and describes the Buddha's lineage. The biography is even more complete in the *Vinaya* of the Mūlasarvāstivādin, in that the tale is carried still earlier to the origin of humankind. In the face of this, Frauwallner suggests that there has been a "crumbling away" from an earlier connected story that contained accounts of the Buddha's early career, his illumination, his conversions of disciples as a teacher, his laying down the *Vinaya* rules, and his death followed by the councils. Thus the core of the *Skandhaka*, consisting of the exposition of the monastic rules, was enclosed by a biography of the Buddha – on one side from his birth to the beginning of his teaching activities, and on the other side from his death to the two councils.

This reconstruction is given greater plausibility by the fact that the *Skandhaka* gives the monastic rules in the form of episodes narrating the events that gave occasion to the laying down of individual rules. Moreover, the narrative is interspersed with legends. This adds strength to the thesis of a great unity to the literary work, which consciously framed the monastic rules within the imposing plan of a biography of the Buddha. This earliest work must have been composed in the old home of Buddhism, whose centers were Rājagṛha, Śrāvastī, and Kauśāmbī; it was composed after the Vaiśālī Council but before the schisms and Aśoka, say between 100 and 160 years after the passing away of the Buddha.

Frauwallner has an answer to the puzzling fact that a number of the biographies of the Buddha that relate his life from his birth stop short suddenly at the beginning of his teaching activity. The best-known examples are the *Nidānakathā* – at the beginning of the *Jātaka* collection of the Pali school, the *Lalitavistara*, and the *Mahāvastu*. They have come into being, Frauwallner says, "through the incomplete biographies of the Buddha at the beginning of the *Skandhaka* being cut loose and becoming independent."[22] The very fact that some Buddhist schools possessing different *Vinayas* also possess these incomplete biographies that stop suddenly is proof of their being disconnected from the beginning of the *Skandhaka*. After being thus cut loose, the early biography of the Buddha was further elaborated and embellished by various schools.[23]

Now, although the Finot–Frauwallner thesis has not gone uncontested,[24] I wish to highlight a pattern that can be said to be noncontroversial. Whether there was an old *Skandhaka* text that combined the Buddha's biography with the *Vinaya*, as Frauwallner would have it, or whether the complete biographical accounts (including that contained in the *Vinaya* of the Mūlasarvāstivādin) were a long time in formation with cross-fertilization between the different Buddhist communities (as Lamotte would have it) is not material to my theme, which focuses on the fact that all Buddhist schools in their established state and in their canonical and noncanonical texts (particularly of the *vaṁsa* and *avadāna* kinds) have either through parallel developments or through mutual influence fashioned a remarkable view of the "historical" unfolding of Buddhism. I write particularly from the standpoint of Southeast Asia.

The point of origin in these accounts is a charismatic figure, the Buddha, who by virtue of his resolve to be enlightened belongs to the line of former buddhas, and who by virtue of descent is part of the lineage of former *cakkavattis* starting with Mahāsammata. This Buddha in his last life achieved illumination, taught the doctrine to the disciples, and founded a monastic order.

After his death, the preservation and maintenance of the doctrinal knowledge and relics of the Master passed from an individual *mahāpuruṣa* (great man) to a *collective* fraternity of monks, the *saṅgha*. We thus get the transition from a "biography" to a "monastic history." The story of the councils, of schisms, and of codifications of disciplinary rules is the story of the early Buddhist order; if there is a line of patriarchs of this early "church," it is relatively unimportant compared to the Vedic line of teachers or the Christian line of apostolic successors.

With the alleged Third Council, held under the auspices of Mogalliputta Tissa and Emperor Aśoka, we reach the third phase of Buddhist historiography: the missions of Aśoka, the transplantation of Buddhism to Southeast Asia, where now the *saṅgha*'s and the doctrine's fate is embedded within a Buddhist polity capped by a Buddhist kingship, the *dhammadīpa* of Lanka providing the model and point of reference for the kingdoms in Burma, Thailand, and so on. Thus, "Buddhism as early monastic history" makes the passage in this third stage to "Buddhism in polity." No doubt subsequent "periodizations" are possible in this Buddhist account of Buddhism's history, but what I wish to stress here is the dynamism of this world view.

A "history" that begins with a great man, is transformed into an order of monks as the continuers of the tradition, and then expands into a *saṅgha* and *sāsana* within a polity, is of course "objectively" a cooked and tendentious account. But it is precisely because that historical vision contains a magnificent plan of unfolding; a set of moral criteria by which to evaluate the acts of kings and monks; and a framework for describing a succession of kings (*vaṃsa*), together with a succession of monastic lineages and saintly *theras* (elders) that the Buddhist scholar monks of Lanka, Burma, and Thailand wrote the kind of continuous historical chronicles that are so conspicuously sparse, if not lacking, in India. There, the priestly accounts of authenticating religious knowledge and privilege in terms of a line of Brahman teachers had no way of leading to and joining up with the *vaṃsa* accounts of royal dynastic succession. And the early destruction of Buddhism and its decline in the face of a Brahmanical restoration did not allow the emergence in India of an unfolding historical vision that materialized in Southeast Asia.

In passing, we may note that, on the one hand, the Buddhist account of the progression from charismatic religious leader and his cultic following, through "church" formation, to "world religion," is remarkably close to Max Weber's preferential (and tendentious) scheme for discussing the origin and development of major religious movements. On the other hand, the manner in which Buddhist historiography begins with biography, assimilates it to the acts of a monastic community, and assimilates that in turn to the dynastic history of a national polity is a remarkable exercise in how three "structural" types of accounts are transformed from one into the other, thereby giving us an object lesson in periodization, chronological sequencing, and totalization that is not surpassed by Lévi Strauss's last chapter in *The Savage Mind*.

# The Buddha's life as a paradigm

## The integration of the Buddha's biography
## in two chronicles

Let me now advance a reason why the "biography" of the Buddha – his *caritam* as an account of his acts – is an integral part not only of the *Dhamma* as doctrine but also of all Buddhist "historical" chronicles, which are variously called *vaṁsa*,[25] *tamnān* (Thai), *avadāna*, and so on.

The primary answer lies in a comparison between the sources of authority in the Vedic and Brahmanical sacred knowledge on one hand, and the Buddhist on the other. The Vedic tree of knowledge is rooted in divine acts of creation of the universe and in divine revelations of sacred knowledge necessary to maintain the universe. But Vedic sacred knowledge, principally that pertaining to sacrifice and ritual, was revealed to individual first teachers and *ṛṣis*, and it is a line of such teachers transmitting that knowledge over time who gave authority to that knowledge. The Vedic texts do not speak for themselves; it is the propounder that speaks for them.

But a revolutionary feature of Buddhism is that the doctrinal knowledge, embodied in the *Dhamma*, stems from the Buddha, who as a human being strove for and attained the wisdom of enlightenment by his own efforts. He is the sole authority for the canon; in theory, subsequent teachers can comment and expand, but they cannot reveal new knowledge. It is the *saṅgha* that through periodic councils collectively preserves the canon and removes from it impurities and schismatic tendencies that have entered it. Hence the central importance of the councils – invented and real – that punctuate the continued transmission of the Buddhist canonical knowledge. Given the Buddhist source of scriptures and their subsequent line of transmission, it becomes imperative that the Buddha's sermons and precepts given in the course of a lifetime, especially during his long career as teacher after enlightenment, be aggregated and put together as a unified biography that is simultaneously a codified dogma. Moreover, if the chronicle histories have as their principal theme the manner in which the *sāsana* (religion) has been maintained through various vicissitudes, then they must always begin with the career of the Buddha himself, which combined in one amalgam the *Dhamma* he preached, the disciplinary rules he prescribed, and the cycle of rebirths he underwent.

Let us take two examples, the Siṅhalese *Mahāvaṁsa* and the Thai *Jinakālamālī*, and see how the Buddha's biography forms a necessary prelude to their religio-political tales.

1. The *Mahāvaṁsa*[26] thus begins with Gotama, our Conqueror, resolving, on seeing in olden times the Buddha Dīpaṁkara, to become a buddha so that he may release the world from evil. Indeed, Gotama offers homage in succession to twenty-four preceding *sambuddhas*, and having received from them the prophecy of his future buddhahood, he strived for and achieved the highest enlightenment

and thus "delivered the world from suffering." Then follows a brief but graphic recollection of the Buddha's sitting at the foot of a *bodhi* tree at Uruvela (Bodh Gayā) in the Magadha country, his mastery of his senses and deliverance after seven weeks of tarrying there, and his subsequent going to Benares to give his first sermon, which set rolling the wheel of the law.

In the ninth month, the Buddha set forth for the isle of Lanka to win it for the faith. He first visited Mahiyangana, the site of a future *stupa*, struck terror into the *yakkhas* (autochthonous demons), and banished them to another island. (After the Buddha's death, a disciple of the Thera Sāriputta would bring the Conqueror's collarbone and enshrine it at this *stupa*.)

This is followed by a listing of the Buddha's royal lineage. It begins with Mahāsammata, the great sage and first king in the Buddhist story of creation, lists the descendants of Mahāsammata, and terminates with the Buddha's parents: "The son of the great king Suddhodana and of Māyā was our conqueror."[27] Thus once again we see that the Gotama's resolve to become a Buddha, which had continued through his previous lives, is conjoined with his royal lineage, which destined him to be a world conqueror (*cakkavatti*). The Buddha's antecedents consist of two lines or *vaṁsas*, which meet in him – the line of buddhas, preceding him at enormous intervals of time (*Buddhavaṁsa*), and the line of kings and universal monarchs extending from Mahāsammata (*Rājavaṁsa*).

This biography of the Buddha then changes into a history of the early *saṅgha* and of the codification of both the *Dhamma* doctrines and the *Vinaya* rules of discipline. Early *saṅgha* history is formulated in terms of the Three Councils, the first at which the codification of the *tipiṭaka* ("three baskets") took place; the second, when the first schism took place; and the third, convened by Emperor Aśoka and the elder Mogalliputta Tissa, which provided the stimulus for the sending of the Buddhist missions, one of which came to Lanka. From this point on, the *Mahāvaṁsa* introduces the Siṅhalese colonizers of the island, and from there is well on its way to its major theme: How Lanka was converted to Buddhism and fulfilled the prophecy that it would be the special haven of Buddhism, and how this *sāsana* maintained itself through the vicissitudes of many a kingly reign.

2. The *Jinakālamālī*, which we have already used copiously, has again to be scrutinized in regard to this question of the treatment, firstly of the Buddha's biography, secondly of the early history of the Buddhist *saṅgha*, and then of the implantation of Buddhism in Sri Lanka, as a necessary prelude to relating the story of Buddhism in Thailand. It is no mean fact that of the 186 pages of the English translation, 96 are devoted to this prelude, and that of these 96, 55 are devoted to the Buddha's biography.

We want to pay some attention to the *Jinakālamālī*'s account of the Buddha's biography, because it is an example of a popular Thai account that either directly or indirectly has been a model for later Thai accounts not only of the Buddha's life but also of the lives of *arahants*. To what extent Acharn Mun's biography

# The Buddha's life as a paradigm

follows the tradition set in the *Jinakālamālī* is a relevant consideration for us. In terms of Thai literary traditions, the *Jinakālamālī* belongs to a genre called *tamnān*, which roughly means story, legend, or myth and is "frequently used for documents dealing with the history of Buddhism or of particular Buddhist monuments."[28] "The main theme of *tamnān* history," says Kasetsiri, confirming what we have said of other classical Buddhist *vaṁsa* texts, "is clearly religion and it is the Gotama Buddha who is the moving force in it. Its purpose is to describe the development of Buddhism. Kings and kingdoms come into the picture insofar as their actions contribute to promoting Buddhism."[29] There was a crop of *tamnān*-type chronicles in the Chiengmai region of North Thailand in the fifteenth and sixteenth centuries, the best known, besides the *Jinakālamālī*, being: *Tamnān Mūnlasātsanā (Mūlasāsanā)*, written before the 1420s; the *Nidāna Bra Buddhasihiṅga* (the chronicle of the Siṅhalese Buddha, which we have referred to earlier), written in the early fifteenth century; and the *Cāmadevīvaṁsa*, composed in 1570. All of them were written by Buddhist monks, and all except the *Mūnlasātsanā* were written in Pali.

Compared with the Siṅhalese *Mahāvaṁsa*, the *Jinakālamālī* presents a more lengthy account of the Buddha's life and concentrates on slightly different features of that life.[30] The *Jinakāla* text is divided into "the epochs of the Conqueror," which reveal "the succession of the Dispensation commencing with the aspiration of our teacher, the Exalted One Gotama," to reach enlightenment.

In much greater detail than the *Mahāvaṁsa*, the *Jinakāla* relates stories of how the aspirant to enlightenment came to make his resolve in his previous lives; this "account of the mental resolve" is followed by "the account of the distant antecedent," which repeats the same resolves, but this time in relation to the names of the twenty-four immediately preceding buddhas, whose genealogy begins with Dīpaṁkara and concludes with Kassapa.

This prelude of numerous mental resolves made during a long chain of rebirths is followed by the enumeration of the Buddha's kingly genealogy, beginning with Mahāsammata and concluding with Suddhodana. This once again is given in much greater detail than in the *Mahāvaṁsa*.

The stage is now set for the biography of the historical Buddha and the events of his last life ("the account of the intermediate antecedent"). It is announced in Tusita heaven that the "omniscient and enlightened one" will appear in the world. The place and clan of his birth, and his parents, are chosen. Queen Mahāmāyā dreams of the "lordly white elephant" entering her right side, and ten months later Prince Siddhattha is born with thirty-two auspicious marks upon him. An account is given of the prince's chariot drives to the pleasure park and his successive meetings with an old man, a sick man, a corpse, and a *bhikkhu* renouncer. Then follow the prince's "great renunciation" of his householder's life; his ascetic striving, culminating in his routing of Mara and his hosts; and his realizing the knowledge of omniscience and the attributes of enlightenment.

Now comes "the account of the proximate antecedent." The first important event is his preaching his first discourse at Benares to his first five disciples and his setting in motion the wheel of the *Dhamma*. Subsequently at Uruvela the Buddha subdues and converts *nāga*-kings, entertains visits from Sakka and other deities, and makes a visit to the island of Lanka. Then there is a listing of various events in the Buddha's itinerant teaching career: his admission into ordination of Mahāmoggallāna and Sāriputta, and hundreds of other monks, who all reach *arahantship*; his successive residence in the cities of Uruvela, Rajagaha, and finally Kapilavatthu – his birthplace and his father Suddhodana's capital. He spends the annual rains retreats in different places, such as the Bamboo Grove, the cities of Vesāli and Kosambi, and so on. He performs various miraculous acts, which attest to his supramundane powers – for example, he subdues the two *nāga*-kings Cūḷodara and Mahodara and he enacts "the miracle of the double manifestation" of his person: He places his feet at the summits of Yugandhara Peak and Mount Sineru, takes three strides across the heavens, sits amid the deities, and preaches to his mother.[31] Toward the latter part of his life, he has more or less two permanent abodes, the Jetavana Grove and the Pubbarāma Monastery, the first endowed by the rich merchant Anāthapiṇḍika, and the second by Migāra.

The passing of his two chief disciples, Mahāmoggallāna and Sāriputta, is the prelude to the Buddha's own death. But note that, while lying on his couch of final passing away in the sala grove in the land of the Mallas of Kusinārā, the Buddha tells Sakka, the king of the deities: "Great King, Prince Vijaya, son of King Sīhabāhu, attended by the company of 700 men, has gone to the Island of Laṅkā today; my Dispensation will become established there in the future; do protect him together with his followers as well, and the Island of Laṅkā" (p. 51). At the same time he makes other predictions, two notable ones being that the great King Aśoka will establish the great *bodhi* tree in Lanka, and that the relic of his right collarbone will be enshrined in the Thūpārāma dagoba in Lanka.

The next logical topic is the distribution of the Buddha's relics after his cremation. The relics apportioned by the Mallas of Kusinārā and the various recipients are listed. It is to be noted that the relics listed consisted not only of the Buddha's bodily relics (bones), and his teeth, hair, and topknot, but also his staff, robe, water jar, belt, bathing cloth, coverlet, footprint, rug used as a seat, razor, and needle case.

This concludes the biography of the Buddha. The subsequent contents of the *Jinakāla* up to the point when the chronicle begins to deal with happenings in Thailand may be outlined. First, we have brief accounts of the Three Councils ("the epochs of the recitals"). Then we have the story of the establishment of Buddhism in Lanka by Mahinda during the time of King Devānampiya Tissa. It is to be noted that the establishment of the dispensation is described in terms of the implantation of the *bodhi* tree and the arrival of the bodily relics of the Buddha, that is, the acquisition of sacred objects that embody various powers and emit the rays of the truth of enlightenment. Finally, there are accounts of a succession of Siṅhalese kings, including Duṭṭhagāmaṇī (the hero of the *Mahā-vaṁsa* chronicle), the holding of the Fourth Council, and the arrival of the tooth relic from Kaliṅga. We at last come to Thailand, which receives its dispensation in turn from Lanka: The *Jinakāla* begins its chronicle of Thai events with the founding of the city and kingdom of Haripuñjaya, whose first ruler was the Princess Cāmadevī, who came from the city of Lāva (Lopburī).

# 8

# The ordering principles behind Buddhist saintly biography

From the time of early Buddhism to the present, biographies of famous Buddhist monks have been written, and some of these monks have been acclaimed as *arahants*. In general, three features have distinguished this genre of Buddhist literature. Firstly, they have followed a certain stereotype and are more noted for imitative repetition than creative innovation. Secondly, the biography served a moral, didactic purpose – the story of a saint was told not for its own sake but to edify and chasten the reader and listener. Thirdly, the expectations of a saint consist not only in his living in the most exemplary and pious fashion, but also in his performing miraculous feats, in his blessing the unfortunate and making them prosper, in his healing the sick in mind and body, in his astrological foretelling of the future, and in his giving varied signs and expressions of his holiness and compassion (*mettā*). Considered as a literary device and work of art, a hagiographical work is not complete without anecdotes of supramundane and transcendental powers, for without such signs of achievement a saint is not a saint, merely a virtuous man.

Now we should not credit these features only to Buddhist hagiography. Much the same could be said with few modifications of medieval Christian biographies (and perhaps analogies can be found in other religious traditions as well). For instance, biography formed an important part of the literature of medieval England, and the biographies of the Latin saints achieved maturity in form and expression. But it could be said that the biographies written from the time of Bede to the time of Sir Thomas More (say between A.D. 700 and 1500) followed fixed Latin models and therefore rarely evidenced developments or modifications in the practice of writing. This was so because they were devotional biographies, whose heroes were ideal figures rather than individuals and of whom certain edifying and awe-inspiring feats were expected as signs of the divine favor they enjoyed. These biographies reflected the corporate Christian spirit and faith of the Middle Ages and, whatever the substantive differences between the doctrines and

## Principles behind Buddhist saintly biography

dogma of Buddhism and Christianity, there were certain common impulsions flowing from the corporate spirit of these religions that produced certain common features in the hagiographical style. In this respect, perhaps medieval Christian hagiography differs more from modern Western biography than it does from traditional Buddhist hagiography.

As Stauffer[1] perceptively remarks of the Western tradition:

> There is one difference immediate and arresting between the medieval conception of biography and our own. We consider the biographer not as one who generalizes, but as one who individualizes. . . . He seeks, and has sought since Boswell, not the ideal, but the characteristic. This eagerness for particulars would not have been easily understood by the early biographers. During the Middle Ages the office or position, rather than the individual, frequently attracts the biographers, so that Bede writes his *Historia Abbatum*, or Matthew Paris his *Vitae Viginti trium Abbatum S. Albani*, or Gervase of Canterbury his *Actus Pontificum Cantuariensis Ecclesiae*. The tendency towards generalized biography is most marked in the development of saints' lives. In this particular literary type, the standard becomes strictly formalized. In the common popular biographies the saints lose their individual characters to merge in a single ideal figure.

Like the Buddhist notion of illustrious or heroic acts that build up a *carita* or *avadāna* as collections of deeds, the medieval Christian biography was built up of sacred deeds. Stauffer continues: "The figure of a saint is drawn by means of a mosaic of small anecdotes of action. For this reason, *Acta Sanctorum* becomes a fitting title for the collections. The life of a saint, to the orthodox medieval writer, could not be described by presenting his personal appearance, his thoughts, his peculiar bent of mind, the development of his opinions, his debt to society or his influence upon history. The life of a saint was a collection of his deeds."[2]

"The saint is not individualized . . . The necessary centering upon his holiness, which give these lives admirable unity, makes characterization impossible . . . Because of the limitations of its theme, duplication and reiteration of anecdotes is inevitable." And just as it happens with the Buddhist hagiography, so in the early Christian lives many incidents are transferred from the acts of the prophets, the apostles and the Saviour. "In succeeding biographies earlier miracles are borrowed wholesale, until in the collections of the twelfth, the thirteenth, and later centuries, when conscientious hagiography was rapidly falling into decay, the memorial to a local saint is often a perfunctory patchwork of *mirabilia* plagiarized from a dozen sources."[3]

There are of course creative exceptions to this stereotype, both in the medieval Christian and Buddhist traditions. But before we outline the contours of some of the masterpieces, it is necessary to establish a fundamental difference in the devotional objectives of Christian and Buddhist hagiographical accounts of saints.

The difference lies in this: The early Christian saint was a *martyr*, while the Buddhist saint was a *renouncer*. To us today the word martyr suggests a "sufferer," but early Christianity understood him or her to be a "witness." Tertullian at the end of the second and the beginning of the third centuries used the term *martyr* not only for those who had already given their lives for the faith but for those who, having borne witness, were awaiting death, and even for those who, having confessed Christ, escaped the final penalty.[4]

The story of the apostles is, of course, a story of martyrdoms, as is that of many of their successors. The stories of martyrs play a large part in the work of the first historian of the church, Eusebius Pamphili, bishop of Caesaria, whose ten books comprising his *Ecclesiastical History* were written in the first quarter of the fourth century. His favorite term for martyrs was "the athletes of religion," and "glorious" was his favorite adjective.

As Helen White points out, this martyrology was related to the impulsions and needs of early Christianity, such as the persuasiveness of its extraordinary story about Jesus, its spread, and its witnesses under persecution. At the very beginning of the religion, the problem of its truth was of paramount importance, and "the evidence of its actual witness its best solution." But in later times, especially when in the third and early fourth centuries persecutions fell upon the Christians, the problem of truth was not so absorbing as before. The martyr, in the face of the trauma of persecution, appeared heroic. His taking punishment without losing faith was seen as a "miracle," wonderful to those who heard the awesome account. "His assurance, his confidence not in himself but in his faith, the very integrity of his resolution, are like a fresh revelation to his fellows." His suffering was taken to be a participation in the sacrifice of Christ and as a revelation. "It seems only logical, therefore, that one of the earliest and most influential of hagiographic genres to develop was the address of consolation and encouragement to the faithful in time of persecution."[5] Especially moving is the story if written by a martyr himself awaiting death, as for instance Ignatius of Antioch (circa 110); martyrdom then became the chalice of salvation and the baptism of blood, which effected the remission of sins. As Peter Brown has remarked, the pious independence of the martyrs who had refused to sacrifice and conform with Roman paganism was an object lesson. "The cult of the martyrs was the only form of popular devotion in the Early Church; and, in Africa, the accounts of how 'these prize fighters of the Lord' had snubbed raging governors were read from the altars on innumerable anniversaries."[6]

Now the Buddhist analogue of the Christian martyr is the Renouncer saint (*arahant*). He too undergoes a profound suffering – both bodily and mental, through observing ascetic practices and taxing meditative exercises and by detaching himself from the lure of desires and attachments. His heroic act of "renunciation" is aimed at attaining *liberation*, and his feat attests to the truth of the Buddha's message and its realizability.

This difference between the two religions' saints also affects the particulars of the popular cults that spring up to commemorate and honor them and to seek their grace and favor in their afterlives. The quintessential Christian martyr's blood has been shed and his body tortured and mangled with weapons or burned and reduced to bones and ashes. The battered remnants – his bloodied clothes, pieces of the cross, fragments of bone and ash, the murderous weapons – all these become relics that bear direct evidence of the sacrificial death and also carry some part of the martyr's saintly virtue. The commemorative cult and anniversary festivals focus attention on the tomb of the martyr, and during the proceedings the passion of his death and the legend of his life are recited. Finally, the martyr as canonized saint becomes a patron to his clients, who plead for favors and benefits through his intercession with God.

As Peter Brown puts it in another work, a hallmark of the Christian hagio-graphies is that "the martyrs, precisely because they had died as human beings, enjoyed close intimacy with God. Their intimacy with God was the *sine qua non* of their ability to intercede for and so to protect their fellow mortals. The martyr was the friend of God."[7]

The cult of the Buddhist saint too forms around his bodily relics, such as the bone, hair, tooth, ashes, and "reminders" associated with him (e.g., the almsbowl and *bodhi* tree), but these relics and objects are not witnesses to his bloody death but to his asceticism and compassion. In the end, a cult emerges focused on *stūpas* and monuments, in which are embedded the relics, and he too is beseeched to grant favors, not as intercessor or friend of any deity but as wielder of supramundane powers won by his own salvation effort, unaided by a god.

Just as there is a communion of saints in the universal church of Christ, so is there a communion of Buddhist saints who as his band of disciples have followed the Buddha into liberation. And thus this established hagiography of the collectivity of saints becomes a basis for cavalier plagiarism precisely because of its permanent meaningfulness and dependability.

But if Christian martyrology and Buddhist hagiography tend to take stereo-typed forms for all the reasons I have mentioned, still we must confront the vital masterpieces that are in their finest chapters absorbed with the individual. In the midst of the formulaic episodes and miraculous apparitions, these books present enough details about the particular saint as a living man or woman acting in a place and at a time in the company of other credible persons. Such achievements contribute to the sincerity and emotional appeal of the entire masterpiece, which fuses *memorabilia* with *mirabilia*. It might be that these best pieces of hagiology are created in the historical context of an expanding vital religion infused with missionary aspirations and led by bold preachers, revered recluses, and magnificent prelates of the established church. At such times, heroic figures and their apt biographers appear together and illuminate the ethic and ethos of their larger communities.

If Bede's *Saint Cuthbert* or Bishop Adam of Eynsham's *Magna Vita Sancti Hugonis* are considered the flowers of the hagiology of the medieval English church, then one could perhaps point to the biography of the Tibetan saint,

Milarepa,[8] composed in the Tibet of the eleventh or twelfth century, and the biography of Acharn Mun, the contemporary Thai piece, as flowers of the Buddhist hagiological tradition.

## Why is the biography of Acharn Mun a masterpiece?

Acharn Maha Boowa met his teacher late in the Master's career, and he recounts the oral accounts that he has heard from others before he records his own experience with the Master – a framework that perhaps explains some of the repetitions and redundant features of his biography. Acharn Mun's biography, despite its prolixity and repetitions, is a masterpiece in that working within a hagiographical tradition the author introduces vivid incidents and concrete details that help to particularize and individualize the saint. The Master's peripatetic wanderings are mapped in a way that conveys his wanderlust as an expression of Buddhist detachment. His encounters with wild animals are dramatized such that a traditional theme associated with the quest of the *dhūtaṅga* monk is made to convey the dialectic between spiritual conquest and animal desires. His recalling and interpretation of meditation experiences are awe inspiring and gripping and transform the oft-cited stages of a meditation into a mystical journey. His personal quirks, his ''fierceness'' as a teacher, his piercing understanding of his pupils' weaknesses – these give flesh and blood to the stereotyped ''teacher-pupil relationship'' that inevitably crops up in studies of the *saṅgha*.

But to be a masterpiece, the individual life and career described must also convince us that it addresses and illuminates a collective crisis, and achieves important societal ideals, such that the protagonist is acclaimed a hero or saint. How does the Acharn Mun biography, or rather his hagiography, relate to a Thai national crisis or live up to Thai expectations of a hero? Let me give brief notice of the ideas and themes I hope to develop in succeeding chapters. For the Thai people today – as in the past – the *authenticity* of a *bhikkhu*'s life as a renouncer, a renouncer who has transcended worldly attachments and is at the same time capable of universal compassion – is a vital expectation. And today there is a crisis relating to the established *saṅgha*, the institutionalized monastic communities and centers of worship, which have long enjoyed the patronage and protection of the government and whose authenticity is in question at the same time as the *legitimacy* of the political authorities is in question in the face of internal domestic tensions and external political threats.

The forest-dwelling *dhūtaṅga* monk has always been a questioner of the institutionalized, study-and-rite-oriented, sedentary village- and city-dwelling monk. His path is alternative to, though fraught with problems for, monastic communities that intend to live by the *Vinaya* rules.

Now in the case of Acharn Mun, it is clear that he rejected the career of the run-of-the-mill village- or town-dwelling monk and took the path of a lonely meditating and wandering ascetic. The biography as such gives us little information on the course of his personal crisis that led to his rejection of orthodoxy, but one sees something of the radicalism of his gesture in his telling his disciples later that at the time he became a *dhūtaṅga* monk, the tradition, though known, was ill-regarded by the people at large who were apprehensive about its ascetic and peripatetic mode of life.

His career thereafter cumulatively spirals in a heroic mode. He wanders alone without a master to teach him, and he singly struggles his way to deliverance. His brief sojourns near jungle villages, and in remote *wat*, portray an interaction that reminds one of the *parfaits* in the remote Pyrenees Mountains of medieval fourteenth-century southern France, whom Ladurie has vividly described in *Montaillou*.[9] The "heretical" *parfaits,* leading simple lives, eating fish and no meat, moving from village to village, entering into free moralistic dialogue with the unlettered peasant, voicing the alleged Cathar heresy, stood in sharp contrast to the remote, institutionalized, hierarchical, wealthy, grabbing Catholic church and its priests; the *parfaits* were readily recognizable as authentic "saints" by their simplicity and their exposure to the danger of the church's Inquisition. The *dhūtaṅga* monk of Acharn Mun's time was not a heretic, but he was not liked by the established *saṅgha* hierarchy either. Eating rough food once a day, clothed in rags, and preaching *Dhamma* to the peasants forgotten by government officers and titled monks alike, he was a *virtuoso* whose authenticity was transparent, and his achievement of supranormal capacities plausible, to those among whom he moved.

This was the starting point for Acharn Mun's acclamation by wider and wider circles, until the reverberation was heard in the national center, which then became a patron in turn. But this incorporation of the periphery into the central establishment and authorities is itself related, as we shall see, to a collective crisis, political, moral, and religious, and attempts to cope with it.

The biography of Acharn Mun rates as a masterpiece for still another authentic reason. An earlier collection of legends composed in India as the Buddha's biography later became both elaborated and particularized in the Tibetan, Chinese, Siṅhalese, and other societies where Buddhism diffused, took root, and was indigenized.

Both the elaboration and particularization (or parochialization) of a core paradigmatic source take place by means of lengthening the plots and adding circumstantial details to the incidents, such that the double feat is achieved of enabling both the local oral specialists and authors to exercise their creative gifts and the local audiences to be convinced that the religious truths recounted had become manifest among themselves, and not in faraway places. Just as the sacred geography of Jambudvīpa was recreated in Burma or Thailand, so were the sacred events, like the illumination of the Buddha under the *bodhi* tree, or his *parinibbāna* with the attendant mortuary rites of a *cakkavatti*, made real by grafting local ritual and custom onto the canonical versions.

129

## The hagiography of a Buddhist saint

An enchanting and entrancing illustration of these processes and achievements is provided by Bigandet's *The Life or Legend of Gaudama, The Buddha of the Burmese*, a text that reports legends of the Buddha as "derived from the perusal of the religious books of the Burmans, and from frequent conversations on religion, during several years, with the best informed among the laity and the religious . . ."[10] Take Chapter 5 of Volume I, which relates the story of the Buddha's illumination: Two elaborations (among others) relate to the miraculous appearance of a throne "superior in perfection to all that art could produce," upon which the Buddha sits to meditate in the cross-legged position. The throne on which he sits has a double meaning: On the one hand, as his preceding five dreams of universal sovereignty and his battle with Māra make clear, it is the seat of the ruler of the universe; on the other hand, as the Buddha's subsequent meditations and deeds make clear, it is this throne that he leaves behind to become the transcending and encompassing knower and wielder of cosmic truth.

That the Buddha is first made to claim the virtues of a *cakkavatti* ruler before he realizes the knowledge of the Four Great Truths that dispel ignorance and give him the powers to recall his former existence and survey all beings now in existence, is conveyed in this scene: Māra asked the Buddha: "How do you dare to pretend to the possession of this throne? . . ." The Buddha replied: "My witnesses are not like yours, men or any living beings. The earth itself will give testimony to me. For, without alluding even to those offerings I have made during previous existences, I will but mention the forty-seven great ones I made whilst I lived as Prince Wethandra (Vessantara) . . ." In this Burmese version, then, the Buddha's awesome acts of donation as a righteous ruler in his last life but one are recalled.[11]

The suspense of the all-too-understandable doubts of the deities as to whether the Buddha wishes to, and is able to, give up the throne is conveyed thus:

There he stood, his eyes fixedly riveted on the throne, without a single wink, during seven consecutive days, given up to the most intense and undisturbed meditation. The Nats, observing this extraordinary posture, imagined that he regretted the throne he had just vacated, and that he wanted to repossess himself of it. They concluded that, such being the case, Prince Theiddat had not as yet obtained the Buddhaship. When the period of seven days was over, Buddha, who knew the innermost thoughts of the Nats, resolved to put an end to their incredulous thinking respecting his person. . . . he raised himself high up in the air, and, to their astonished regards, he wrought at once more than a thousand wonders, which had the immediate effect of silencing all their doubts.[12]

While the above Burmese legends elaborate in no uncertain terms the *cakkavatti*-Buddha relation that is more cryptically stated in the canonical *suttas*, the Burmese version of the *parinibbāna* of the Buddha[13] enriches and contemporizes the classical story with local Burmese customs.[14] And the story is elaborated far beyond the limits of the canonical *Mahāparinibbāna Sutta* to include the story of Kassapa (the leader of the *saṅgha* after the Buddha) persuading King Ajātasattu to collect all the distributed relics (save the one at Ramagama destined to go to

Sri Lanka) and to bury them in eight *chedi* so as to await the time of the appearance of "the great and renowned monarch under the name of Athoka (Aśoka)," who would spread the relics all over the island of Jambudvīpa. This retrospectively invented prophecy that is woven into the life of the Buddha to legitimate future history is presented with "realistic" – even if exaggerated – detail culled from Burmese traditions of burying relics and treasure in their sacred monuments.[15]

Similar considerations can be applied to the biography of Acharn Mun, who as an *arahant*, even a Buddha, is described as having lived a life that reproduced *some* of the legendary events in the Buddha's career. For obvious reasons, it is the *parinibbāna* of the Buddha that is imitated most widely in describing the death scenes and mortuary rites of the Buddhist saints. In the case of the Acharn Mun story, we saw how precedents set by the Buddha's life and death – for example, his foreknowledge of death, his dying lying on the right side, the falling of rain at his cremation rite, the distribution of relics, are woven with Thai customs and rites relating to the mortuary rites of great persons, both monks and laity (especially royalty). Examples are the dressing and storing of the body for three months, the festival-like assembly of large collections of monks and laity, the burning of the corpse at the Mount Meru of a famous *wat*, the keeping of ashes and relics of the dead in urns, and so on.

Another example of enriched texture through localization might be taken from the description given in Acharn Mun's biography of the manner in which he and his disciples implemented the *dhūtaṅga* practices set out in the *Visuddhimagga*. The begging for food in villages while walking in single file with eyes cast down; the sites chosen for meditative vigils, including caves and edges of precipices on spectacular forested mountains; the spacing of disciples' shelters and meditation walks; the pattern of instructional relationship between master and pupils – all are examples of the traditions developed by Thai (and Burmese) forest monks, traditions that are an amalgam of classical precedents and parochial elaboration that make the account authentic and ethnographic.

# 9

# The disciples of the Master

Before I embark on the third complex frame of analysis that will complete my interpretation of the biography, I want to again introduce the concept of *indexical symbol* as a useful device for comprehending how all the layers of meaning and significance, both "semantic" and "pragmatic," ride simultaneously on the same "form" (the biography) and thus constitute a single *totality* of meaning.

The main point about *indexical symbols*, as I have already stated in Chapter 1, is that they have a duplex structure, because they combine two roles – they are symbols that are associated with the represented object by a conventional semantic rule, and they are simultaneously also indexes in existential pragmatic relation with the objects they represent. This duality thus points in two directions at once – toward the semantic direction of cultural presuppositions, paradigms, and conventional understandings; and toward the pragmatic and interpersonal context of the activity in question, the lineup of the participants and the processes by which they establish meaning, and create, affirm, or legitimate their positions and privileges.

Let me relate these conceptual and analytical statements to this book. The biography of Acharn Mun is an *indexical symbol* in the sense that on the one hand the saint's life is symbolically and semantically related to the classical conventional hagiographies of the Buddha and exemplary Buddhist saints (the theme of the preceding two chapters), and on the other hand the composition is indexically and pragmatically related to the purposes and objectives of the disciple-author, the context in which he composed it, and its distribution to and reception by the public, who are its readers and audience. This latter exegesis is the task of this and the succeeding two chapters.

# The disciples of the Master

## The disciples of Acharn Mun

Our biographer, Acharn Maha Boowa, is one among a group of disciples who in one way or another claim to be of the same "ordination lineage" as the Master, or to have been associated with him for a length of time. These disciples are the foremost and most prominent "forest teachers" in contemporary Thailand, and their legitimacy and authenticity rests to an important degree on the claim of association with the Master. One writer who made a tour of the Northeast provinces in 1969, visiting as many meditation teachers as he could, remarked that all those he visited and named "were disciples or close associates" of Acharn Mun, who "during his travels across Northern and Northeastern Thailand . . . gained many disciples, who likewise have become ahjahns [*acharns*] and are best noted for their meditation practices and resultant accomplishments."[1] Again, a second source, who composed another guide to meditation *wat* in Thailand, confirms this assertion: "Northeast Thailand has probably the greatest proliferation of meditation temples in the country. Most of these forest temples run in the tradition of the great teacher, Acharn Mun."[2]

The following is a list of the disciples or associates of Acharn Mun who had established their own forest hermitages and were recognized as meditation teachers in the mid-seventies:

| Name | Forest hermitage |
|---|---|
| 1. Acharn Maha Boowa (age 56 in 1978) | Wat Pā Bān Tāt, Udon Province |
| 2. Acharn Chā (age 54 in 1978) | Wat Pā Pong, Ubon Province |
| 3. Acharn Fun[3] (age 70 in 1978) | Wat Baan Na Huang Chang, Sakon Nakhon Province |
| 4. Acharn Pen (age 40+ in 1978) | Wat Doi Thammachedi, Sakon Nakhon |
| 5. Acharn Lee | Wat Prachanikom, Roiet Province |
| 6. Acharn Thēt | Wat Hinmākpeng, Nongkhāi Province |
| 7. Acharn Khao | Wat Tham Klongplane, Udon Province |
| 8. Lūang Phāū Būa | Wat Pā Nong Sāēng, Udon Province |
| 9. Acharn On | ? Udon Province |
| 10. Acharn Kamdee | ? Lōēi Province |
| 11. Acharn Chawp | ? Lōēi Province |
| 12. Acharn Sing Tong[4] | Wat Pan Kāēowit, Sakon Nakhon Province |
| 13. Lūang Pū Wāēn[5] | ? Chiengmai Province |

There are three features that should be highlighted in the relation between the Master and his disciples.

1. The first we have already remarked on is that the Master himself had no teacher and made the pilgrim's progress through his own experiments and endeavors, while the disciples stress their relation to the Master as their teacher in meditation.

2. The second feature represents a distinct transformation. A striking characteristic of the Master was that he was truly peripatetic throughout his life. His life is a story of constant traveling, two periods of reclusive isolation followed by peripatetic tours, especially in the Northeast. And even in the immediate years

preceding his death, he "settled" in Sakon Nakhon Province only to move restlessly from *wat* to *wat*, from settled areas deeper into the sparsely inhabited forests and mountains. Nong Phue, set in a valley surrounded by mountains and forest, where he finally died, was fittingly in accord with his tastes.

By comparison, all the Master's disciples, who are now teachers in turn, have established their own hermitages, which have become their stable centers, more or less, where their teaching is conducted. Many of them in addition have founded certain branch monasteries or "daughter houses" in parts more remote from their main centers, so that disciples can retreat there for more intensive and reclusive practice of meditation. Moreover, the first generation of the Master's disciples have by now trained their own disciples, who have themselves hived off from their teachers and founded their own teaching hermitages. Thus the most famous meditation masters of today have two kinds of satellite hermitages revolving around them – the branch hermitages they have themselves founded and those established by their disciples grown to maturity.

Thus, at first sight, there seems to be a transformation from the initial state when a peripatetic Master perpetually traveled, halting, sojourning, and teaching for a while at each place he chose to stop, to the more "institutionalized" second stage portrayed by the disciples, who have tended to found and reside in stable centers, while at the same time establishing directly or indirectly satellite hermitages. But a close scrutiny of the Master's own travels will show that this transformation, though real, is not a disjunctive shift. For the paradoxical achievement of Acharn Mun was that, while being a homeless peripatetic wanderer virtually throughout his life, he managed to create cells of disciples at the various nodal points of his journeys. Because his wanderings covered much territory, these cells were many.

Let us recall certain features of his life. He was for much of the time accompanied by a small coterie of disciples when he took up temporary residence near some remote hamlet or settlement. During the rains retreats, he took up residence in some rural *wat* and intensively trained disciples; some disciples resided with him in these small *wat*, and others residing in nearby *wat* came to him for instruction. Thus, although Acharn Mun cannot be said to have founded *wat* or hermitages, he ennobled many of the temples he stayed at – converting the resident monks and novices and initiating others who became newly ordained, inspired by his teachings, to the meditative vocation. Thus all the meditation masters we previously listed at some time or other studied with him as his disciples, but most of them cannot be said to have studied with the Master at the same time. There is scarcely any organized linkage between these ex-pupils today, each of whom is now the center of his own system of satellite hermitages and network of pupils, whose relationship in turn to their masters becomes tenuous and attenuated as they hive off. I shall describe this feature shortly; here let me note the fact that the Master himself was the active creator of a sprawling and dispersed network of *wat* and hermitages where resided cells of pupils he trained, and in this kind of network it is the relations of the pupils to a common master, or rather the memory of their association with him and their receiving the religious practice from him, that constitutes the central bond and the tradition that is transmitted through time.

Let us also recall the significance of the acts and attitudes of the humble villagers who materially supported the Master and his disciples. Even ascetic solitary wanderers are, by virtue of the rules of the *Vinaya*, dependent for their food, medicine, and robes on laymen and have always had contact with laity. But these contacts with the rural folk are limited to soliciting alms and to occasional preaching and moral instruction. Nevertheless, it is these same rural folk who not only show their deep respect but also, believing in their supranormal powers and saintly virtue, circulate and retell stories about them; the news that a saint is among them spreads from village to village. Such stories and claims are of course ratified and substantiated by the Master's disciples. Thus the two circles of followers surrounding the Master – the inner circle, constituted of his ordained disciples, and the outer circle, a penumbra of rural lay supporters – must be seen to act dialectically and cumulatively in the recognition of a forest-monk as a saint and in the spread of his reputation. It is through such processes that a *dhūtaṅga* teacher is first and foremost created at the grass-roots level, before he is appropriated by the metropolitan center and the country as a whole.

3. The third feature of the relation between the Master and his disciples consists in a certain differentiation, or even polarization, that occurs in their religious specialization and which was not a notable cleavage in the Master.

It could be said that in the spectrum of activities, capacities, and reputations associated with the Master there were two poles, the "rationalist" and the "tantric." The "rationalist" pole was represented by the "purist virtuoso" who is dedicated to practicing meditation, contemplating the philosophical truths of dependent-origination, and cultivating the wisdom of *nibbānic* truth. One might say, echoing Max Weber's words, that the rationalist path portrays the extraordinary metaphysical achievement of Buddhism that unites "the *virtuoso*-like self-redemption by man's own effort with universal accessibility of salvation" with "contemplation as the path to salvation with an inner-worldly vocational ethic."[6] In this aspect, the virtuoso thinks of the attentions and demands of the laity as intrusions to be escaped from, devalues the cult of images and amulets, deemphasizes merit-making rites, and wishes his hermitage not to be a place of social gathering by the laity.

The "tantric" pole was represented by the same virtuoso in his mental state of tranquility, compassion, and loving-kindness; bearing a cosmic love for people at large, he wanted to convey to them some part of his mystic experience and psychic conquests. To echo Max Weber again, the tantric path, representing the cultivation of "a cosmistic brotherliness," shows one way out of the man-made cage of estrangement and alienation from fellow men and dependence on the inexorable power of material goods. In this aspect, the virtuoso as a man of charisma of achieved powers may wish to give all beings a taste of calm bliss and relief from their impermanent physical and mental sufferings. Given this sympathy, the man of illumination is under pressure from the laity to transfer his virtues through ritual action.

Now the Master, Acharn Mun, was no crude dispenser of charms or amulets,[7] no master of ceremonies but, though a purist, rationalist practitioner of meditation, also affirmed his mystical experiences and visions, which were attested by his disciples. He was also very much driven to be a preacher who instructed not only his cells of disciples but also, occasionally, vast gatherings of laymen. He was acclaimed as an *arahant* in his lifetime, and this reputation rested as much on his ascetic life and orthodox practices as upon his tantric experiences and claims of supranormal feats.

It is thus to be expected that what was a single spectrum of divergent tendencies in the Master might become polarized orientations in the disciples. I shall describe the orientations and hermitages of two different disciples of the Master to illustrate this polarization.

### Acharn Chā: the vocation of self-redemption by contemplation

Acharn Chā, a forest teacher of the Northeastern tradition, fifty-four years old in 1978, trod the path of the wandering ascetic that Acharn Mun did. Although of Mahānikāi affiliation, he by his own account actually spent a short but enlightening period of time with the Master.[8]

Acharn Chā's primary hermitage is Wat Pā Pong: Founded around 1959, it is situated in Warrin District, Ubon Province, in a forest. The nearest village is about a fifteen-minute walk away. There is a forbidding notice – a very unusual thing to see in Thailand – posted at the entrance, which says: "No running or shouting; no liquor allowed; talk quietly; if you have no business please stay out." Let me first describe Acharn Chā's chief and branch hermitages before underscoring his strict regime.

Sunno Bhikkhu[9] reports that in 1978 there were some forty to eighty monks (and novices) and forty to sixty nuns at Wat Pā Pong. We may take note of the large number of resident nuns, a sure sign of the hermitage's fame as a place of meditation. Another sign of Acharn Chā's reputation as a meditation master is the number of Western pupils who seek him out; by 1979 some two dozen had already lived and studied with him.[10] Acharn Chā is described by many as running a disciplined hermitage, which in due course became one of the best known and most liberally supported *wat* in Ubon Province, attracting both urban and rural pious laymen.

The main preaching hall and dining room are large "functional" structures. The numerous individual monks' huts are scattered and spaced so as to be obscured from each other's view.[11]

# The disciples of the Master

The monks go for alms each day and eat one meal a day in their bowls, following orthodox *dhūtaṅga* practice. Outside their communal sittings and chores, socializing and gossip among monks is not encouraged. The monks and novices usually wake around 3 a.m., individually engage in a one-hour meditation practice, and then conduct a collective morning chanting for half an hour. Around 6 a.m., they go on their almsround to the village, and by 9 a.m. they conclude their sole meal.

Thereafter, the inmates are left to themselves to engage in meditation or study. They congregate in the afternoon at around 3 p.m. to do chores like sweeping the meeting hall and refectory, cleaning the compound, and filling the water jars.

Night time is again a period of communal practice. There is a collective meditation sitting from 6 to 7 p.m., followed by an hour's chanting[12] and reading, the *Vinaya piṭaka* on the monks' disciplinary rules being a favorite text. Acharn Chā may every few days give a discourse after the chanting is concluded. In theory, any individual disciple can approach the Master to discuss his progress. Outside of the regularized daily program, individuals can and do engage in solitary meditation according to their preference.

Acharn Chā's success and organizational abilities are manifested in the number of branch hermitages he has founded. Sunno Bhikkhu reports that in 1978 "in and around Ubol Province, Acharn Chaa had about ten branch temples of various sizes, each with one of his own disciples as teachers."[13] One was on an island, another in the mountains, and the rest on the edges of villages. These branch hermitages are intended to provide the Acharn and his disciples opportunities to practice meditation away from the demands of the city and of the numerous lay visitors. Kornfield may be reporting[14] a further stage in the establishment of an ever-widening network when he says that Acharn Chā's disciples have started their own teaching centers and that they were "teaching in more than thirty mountain and forest branch temples throughout northeast Thailand." This extraordinary "institution building" by Acharn Chā induces the surmise that it may be an accompaniment and by-product of the rationalist meditator's devotion to establishing and inculcating a systematic meditation technology.[15] [Once again we are faced with the duality that we saw in the Master (Acharn Mun) himself: A dedication to the meditation path necessarily involves the teaching of the hard-won wisdom to others.]

The most famous of Acharn Chā's branch hermitages is Wat Khao-namtok-tham-sāēng-phet, which translates as the "Wat of the Mountain Water-fall and Cave of Diamond Light." This hermitage, which normally has a small number of assiduous meditators,[15] among whom are included most of the Acharn's Western disciples, is situated some 15 kilometers outside the district town of Arunat Charoen in Ubon Province and, true to its fanciful name, is sited on a mountainside dotted with numerous caves amid lush vegetation. One should note, however, that even this remote hermitage is by no means outside the reach of pious laymen. Burns reports[16] that, when he visited this hermitage together with Acharn Chā, in

137

the morning "some well-to-do lay supporters" of the Acharn arrived to make an offering of food for the meal of the day, and that subsequently he (Burns) was given a ride in a car to a nearby town by these visitors.

Acharn Chā's orthodox, even "purist," tendencies are evident in many ways. He has the reputation of running his hermitages in a manner that is even stricter than that of most Thammayut *wat*, which proclaim themselves to be more "orthodox" than their Mahānikāi counterparts. Acharn Chā has asserted that the Mahānikāi and Thammayut sects are phenomena of Thai tradition and history and that, as long as one observes the discipline, it is not important to which sect a monk belongs. He has expressed anti-establishment views against the mainstream *saṅgha*: that Buddha images and sacralized water have no inherent power; that ghosts and deities have existence only in our minds; that monasteries should not be the venues of festivals, fairs, games, and idle gossip; and that meditation and direct contemplative experience are more important than the study of books. The *Dhamma* of the Buddha is not found in books.

Sunno Bhikkhu reports Acharn Chā's meditation teaching as emphasizing "mindfulness in all postures, watching defilements in the mind and letting go of them. Mindfulness of breathing is taught to establish enough concentration to examine the five aggregates in the light of impermanence, suffering and voidness of self. One is cautioned not to try to gain anything from meditation." One recognizes here an orthodoxy consonant with the prescriptions of the *Visuddhimagga* and with that purist side of it, which urges the adept to go beyond seeking conscious satisfactions and supranormal powers.

### The compassionate illuminate and the Path of Bliss: the hermitage of Acharn Fun

Acharn Fun died in 1978 at the age of about seventy. Older than Acharn Mun's disciples of the generation of Acharn Chā and Acharn Maha Boowa, Acharn Fun's age indicates that he must have trodden for some time the path of the solitary wanderer before he met the Master. I mention this because the Northeastern tradition of the *dhūtaṅga* monk has always carried with it certain tantric associations and charismatic attributes.

Acharn Fun established his hermitage some ten kilometers off a main highway in the district of Pannanikom in Sakon Nakhon Province. The *wat* is reported in 1978 to have had twenty-five to forty monks and novices. In its daily routine and in the mode of instruction followed by the Acharn, this forest hermitage was similar to others in that: The monks went on daily almsrounds and ate from their bowls; during the day they were left to themselves, except for the afternoon chores; and they had group meditation sittings in the evenings, during which frequently the Acharn gave discourses.

# The disciples of the Master

The meditation system that the Acharn taught bore the stamp of Acharn Mun's teachings. Acharn Fun emphasized concentration meditation, using a repeated *mantra* and mindfulness of breathing to establish one-pointedness of mind. Then there is a shift to the meditation of the body, which leads to the contemplation of impermanence, suffering, *anattā*, and the Four Noble Truths. But within this stereotyped format, there is a possibility for variable emphasis, and Acharn Fun appears to have tried to lead his disciples to the experience of tranquil bliss and happiness.

Burns witnessed the worship on a full-moon night at the hermitage attended by the residents as well as visiting laymen. Many devotees arrived in the morning to present food for the morning meal and then stayed on. Many others arrived in the afternoon. The proceedings began at 8 p.m. with the arrival of the Acharn among the assembled monks, novices, and laity. The usual routine on such an occasion is as follows. A half-hour recitation of chants is followed by a discourse, for example, on the doctrine of *anattā* (no-self), which is comprehended by examining the components of the body and mind. Then all assume the lotus position and Acharn Fun's "insight practice" consists in an attempt to induce a state of bliss – Burns describes the proceedings as a "hypnotic trance" – by the Acharn's intoning of words and instructions to the following effect: "See your body from head to toe; examine each facet with a clear mind . . . Happy, happy, and calm . . . There is no worry or concern, just happy and calm . . ." After effecting an entry into meditation, there is silent meditation for about twenty minutes. Discourses alternate with meditation sittings for a couple of hours. It is clear from this account that, while the monks may daily follow the meditative path, the Acharn's accent when he dispenses meditation to the lay public is on creating a calm and happy mood in line with lay interest.

When Burns left the hermitage, the Acharn gave him "a metal charm," which bore his image and the instruction that should he have a stomach upset he should dip the charm into a glass of water and drink the liquid. Indeed, Acharn Fun's fame in Thailand was associated with the cult of the amulets blessed and distributed by him, in which activity he was joined by many other forest teachers whose mystical visions, loving-kindness (*mettā*) and ritual blessings, and supranormal powers will be described in Chapters 18 and 19.

## Acharn Maha Boowa: disciple and biographer of the Master

We have illustrated how a duality present in the Master could become more sharply polarized in his pupils as the rational-contemplative and tantric-ritualistic modalities. But of course it is still possible for a disciple to depict both sides of the Master. It seems to me that Acharn Maha Boowa, ardent disciple and biographer of the Master, is an apt subject for the probing of this proposition.

# The hagiography of a Buddhist saint

Some of Acharn Maha Boowa's sermons and teachings principally concerning the meditative regime are printed in the *Review* of the World Federation of Buddhists;[17] another source is Kornfield,[18] whose documentation of the Acharn's teachings are probably based on his writings as well as his spoken remarks. (I include as an appendix to Chapter 10 an oral account given me by a Western student of Maha Boowa of his understanding of his mentor's teachings on meditation.)

After matching Acharn Maha Boowa's formal and abstract teachings with the contents of the hagiography of his own teacher, Mun, one cannot but come to the conclusion that he (as indeed many other forest-monk teachers) discourses in a "double mode," one being abstract, philosophical, and discursive and the other being mystical, visionary, and cosmological. On the one hand, the disciplinary regime he imposes on himself and his disciples is, as we shall see in our description of his hermitage, orthodox and exemplary. Also, his technical discourses on meditation cannot once again be faulted in the sense that they reflect the "correct" views, as expressed for instance in the classical text, *Visuddhimagga*, which we have previously analyzed. In other words, Acharn Maha Boowa is capable of expounding, and frequently does so, in "rational" philosophical terms the Buddha's "dependent-origination" doctrine, or the "meditative path" as dedicated to liberation, which students of Buddhism, particularly Western scholars (like Kornfield) can readily pick up and assimilate to their understanding of Theravāda Buddhism. But Acharn Maha Boowa is also, as we have recognized from his biography and can infer from his addresses in the Lao-Thai dialect, a superb propagandist and preacher and a witness to the virtues and powers of his own Master. We have seen how with almost "tantric" ardor and abandon he describes in a "cosmological mode" the meditation experiences of his Master (and himself) and enumerates with unflagging enthusiasm the supranormal feats and conquests of his Master, without the slightest doubt or skepticism regarding his attaining *arahant*, nay even buddha, status. Indeed, Maha Boowa has written the biography in a mode that many earlier hagiographers have followed in describing the career of the Buddha and his disciple-saints, a mode that postulates a correspondence between the internal experiences of the hero as microcosm and the external formations of the cosmos as macrocosm, between the hero's levels of consciousness, which he traverses up and down, and the cycles of cosmic materialization and disintegration – in short, a mode suited to describe and celebrate the powers of the Buddhist virtuoso as a man of charismatic powers.

Maha Boowa's biography is thus firmly grounded in popular Thai religiosity, which awaits the emergence of the *arahant* (saint) or the *khrūbā* (respected teacher) in their midst, and acclaims them ardently. These men have been not simple "negators" of, or "escapers" from the world in any simple or extreme sense. Rather, they have led millennial or reform movements; or have as active "missionaries" "colonized" frontier regions and helped bring them under the king's umbrella; or have suffused their love and their piety to the people around them, giving them an exemplary ethic around which they could consolidate and integrate in "vicarious oblation," to borrow a phrase from Ernst Troeltsch.

# 10

# The biographer as exemplary
# forest-monk, meditator, and teacher

Our biographer, Acharn Maha Boowa, is a well-known teacher in the forest-ascetic tradition of Northeast Thailand and is the abbot of Wat Pā Bān Tāt, a forest hermitage that stands on the edge of the village on some 100 acres of forest land about 12 kilometers south of the town of Udon in Northeast Thailand. Jack Kornfield describes it as an exemplary hermitage: "Much of (its) learning, as in the other Thai-Lao forest monasteries, is through the disciplined, strict, and extremely simple way of life. One simple meal a day, small cottages, well water for bathing, alms round at sun-up, long periods of silence, and some isolation all contribute to a life that requires little worldly thought. The forest monastery then, as well as being a facility for intensive meditation, is also a very special educational environment."[1]

I made a visit to Wat Pā Bān Tāt in 1971, and I shall report information and impressions gathered that will give us some idea of the organizational structure and routine of a forest hermitage that is alleged to follow strictly in Acharn Mun's tradition. From an extended account (supplemented by the other brief accounts of hermitages already given), we can discern the distinctive features of a forest hermitage and how it compares with the regular Thai *wat*.

Let me begin with the observation that Maha Boowa's hermitage had by the early seventies attracted about a dozen Western disciples who had been ordained as monks and had devoted themselves for varying periods of time to the practice of meditation. One of my chief informants at the hermitage was Phra Paññāvaḍḍho, such a Western convert, who was the first foreigner to be ordained in Thailand, some sixteen years previously (calculating from October 1971, the time of my visit). Son of a mining engineer who had worked in Mysore State in India, Paññāvaḍḍho was born in India and lived there until he was eight. He himself had been trained as an electrical engineer. On a visit to Thailand he had been ordained, then returned to England. There he had met another English monk (Kapilavathu) at Hampstead, teamed up with him, and returned to Thailand. He said that he decided to renounce lay life when he realized the pointlessness of a life that would require him to be an engineer until his retirement, after which he would have some five more aimless years to live. He joined the hermitage in 1962 and had resided there continuously for the past nine years.

## Acharn Maha Boowa's biography

Because Maha Boowa in the biography of his Master underscores his discipleship with him and "lineal" descent from him, it comes as no surprise that Maha Boowa's own life is a "reproduction" of essential features of the Master's career, while also showing certain differences. Maha Boowa in fact was born in the village of Bān Tāt, the very village on whose edge the forest hermitage was founded. His early career is much like his Master's in its peripatetic stage; but his later career is unlike his Master's, in that like all other disciples he has founded a permanent hermitage as a center for instruction. There is thus a dramatic shift in his life from the earlier to the later phase.

Ordained novice as a young boy at Wat Bodhisamporn in Udon, Maha Boowa resided and studied there until he was ordained a *bhikkhu*. He had engaged in Pali studies and had passed a couple of the lower examinations, but he was interested in practicing meditation. His abbot recommended he contact Acharn Mun, who was then in Nakhon Sawan.

For some nine years Maha Boowa was closely attached to Acharn Mun – he would receive instruction from him, spend periods of time meditating in the forest, and return to the Master for questions and clarifications. He walked in *thudong* style through several of the faraway provinces, never staying long in a place, nor accepting long-standing pupils. After this peripatetic tour, he returned to his village and mother. Like the Master, Maha Boowa has a special relationship with his mother, and his filial attachment to her and solicitude for her is much in evidence.

Maha Boowa pitched his umbrella and mosquito net in the forest adjoining his natal village and went on his almsrounds. The villagers, recognizing his piety and ascetic virtues, came to him for *Dhamma* instruction and invited him to found a *wat*. He consented, it is said, partly to instruct his fellow villagers and partly to take care of his mother. This happened around 1955.

Two villagers donated the land for the hermitage, and the villagers built a *sālā* (hall) with rough boards and *kuti* (cubicles) with split bamboo walls and grass roofs. Maha Boowa at the same time began to accept pupils and to visit other *wat* to give instructional sermons. Maha Boowa is said to have described the change in his life in the words "the tiger inside him has been killed," and therefore "the villagers can now relax." In due course the buildings were improved – besides the refurbished *sālā*, a wash house with water-storage facilities was built, and the impermanent *kuti* gave way to wooden structures. The villagers provided the wood from the forest, but the monks and novices themselves built these later structures.

### Acharn Boowa's hermitage

In 1971, the hermitage was composed of the following: Besides the abbot, Maha Boowa, who was now fifty-eight, there were eleven resident monks, seven of whom were Thai; the remaining four were from Britain, the United States, and Canada. Five of the Thai disciples were of Northeastern origin. (See Table 10.1 for details.)

There were in October 1971 only two resident novices, both eighteen years of age and of Northeastern origin; two more novices were expected to take up residence.[2] The hermitage had no resident temple boys (*dekwat*), but some village boys, relatives of the abbot, came in the mornings for a couple of hours – to serve food to the monks, fetch water, and so on.

It was emphasized to me that an important feature of the monastic life in this hermitage was that monks and novices are, outside their meditational exercises in isolation, expected to engage in the physical labor of not only the daily cleaning of the buildings and compound but also of constructing, repairing, and maintaining the buildings. The monks are forbidden to dig the ground and cut trees – this work the novices (and lay helpers) do. Once the trees are felled, a monk can work on the wood. In matters of eating food and drinking beverages, once again the disciplinary rules are observed. The novices (and visiting laity) serve these items to the monks, who are allowed to drink only water on their own. We note from these facts that for Wat Pā Bān Tāt, unlike the mainstream village and town *wat*, the novices are a minor category who are there to serve the monks and may otherwise be trained in meditational exercises; it is the monks, whose main occupation is meditation, who constitute the main category of inmates.

The "nuns," more correctly the *māē chī*, were at this time only two in number, one of them being the abbot's mother. It is important to appreciate the "peripheral" position assigned these women, who at the same time continue the traditional female role of cooks and providers of food to the monks. Since the food that is daily collected from villagers on the alms round is usually "rough" and sometimes insufficient in quantity, the two nuns run a kitchen and cook a pot of meat and vegetables to supplement it. The money for this food is taken from hermitage funds.

The physical and spatial layout of the hermitage is such that there is, first of all, a marked separation of the kitchen area and nuns' quarters from the monastic buildings. Next, there is a separation within the latter, of the *sālā* and wash house (which are the "communal" structures that are easily accessible from the

Table 10.1. *Monks residing in hermitage*

| Monks in order of seniority | Nationality | Approximate age | No. of lents (*phansa*) completed | Other comments |
|---|---|---|---|---|
| 1 | Thai | 46 | 25 | |
| 2 | Thai | 49 | 18–20 | Had been married. |
| 3 | Thai | 32 | 12 | |
| 4 | Thai | 30 | 8 | |
| 5 | Thai | 30 | 8 | |
| 6 | British | 46 | 9 + 7 | First nine years spent as a monk of Mahānikai sect, and was reordained into the Thammayut sect. |
| 7 | Canadian | 35 | 7 | Was on a world cruise and met a foreign monk, Khantipālo, who converted him. |
| 8 | Thai | 28 | 4–5 | |
| 9 | U.S.A. | 23 | 3 | |
| 10 | British | 45 | 2–3 | Unmarried; previously an accountant and company manager. |
| 11 | Thai | 20 | | Recently ordained, was novice before. |

gateway) from the individual *kuti*, which are dispersed in the forest and hidden among trees, each having an adjoining meditation walk.

The nuns, including the abbot's mother, are ordinarily expected to keep their physical distance from the monks' space, including the *sālā*, which serves as the preaching hall. They, like the other laity, come to the *sālā* on *wanphra* and other days of public worship.

It might be said that an administrative organization is practically nonexistent. Organizational arrangements that one comes to associate with regular *wat* – such as a *wat* committee (*kammakān*), normally composed of the abbot, some monks, and lay members, which handles *wat* finances and organizes *wat* fairs and celebrations, etc. – is lacking. There is no lay accountant (*waiyāwatcakāūn*) and no fund or foundation (*mūnnithi*). The abbot apparently turned over all donations and money gifts to his mother for safekeeping, and she made payments as instructed by the abbot. Thus we begin to see that the forest hermitage, although it may impose strict disciplinary rules on the inmates and may stimulate and provide the right conditions for a systematic "rationalized" pursuit of meditation and contemplation, manifests little institutionalization with regard to a hierarchy of offices or administrative committees. The hermitage actually revolves around a single personage – the Acharn – who is the radial meeting point of multiple dyadic and personalistic teacher–disciple and saintly monk–lay donor relations. This feature will become clearer when we examine later the teacher–disciple relations.

# The hagiography of a Buddhist saint

First let us examine the relation of the hermitage and its inmates with the lay householders. It is the villagers of Bān Tāt who daily give food to the monks on their almsrounds and are the original hosts for the hermitage, giving as we have seen the land for it and putting up the first buildings. The villagers thus have a warm relationship with the hermitage, and apart from their attendance on days of worship they may come individually to consult the abbot. In fact, one monk informant claimed that the villagers regard the abbot as their "informal head" and consult him about village prospects and problems. Laymen singly or in groups may, and do, visit individual monks and novices.

The abbot and his monks do perform rites for the laymen in the village and in Udon town. Merit-making ceremonies at home such as house blessing are conducted, but these are not frequent. More frequent are funerary rites, which are conducted in as simple a manner as is possible. On the day of cremation at the house of the deceased, during the actual cremation, and during the nights preceding and following the cremation, the usual *bangsukūn* and *paritta* chants are recited.

The most important occasion when laity assemble in the hermitage itself is during the fortnightly recitation of the *pāṭimokkha* confessional, if this also coincides with the *wanphra* sabbath. Lay donors arrive in the morning bringing food. At 5 p.m. the monks recite the confessional by themselves; afterward the abbot gives a discourse to the monks and laity. Laymen also come to the hermitage on other *wanphra*, and the abbot usually addresses them. Calendrical festivals like Mākha Būchā and Visākha Būchā are not automatically celebrated, but are staged only at the request of the local villagers. After a circumambulating candle procession, a discourse is given by the abbot.

Reviewing these transactions, one could say that although the abbot has certainly not isolated the hermitage from the laity, and indeed has not rejected for himself and his disciples the performance of merit-making rites for the laity, yet if the rites he performs are compared with those usually conducted by the regular *wat*, it is clear that he has tried to keep them simple and spare. Informal conversations with laymen are considered to be more productive than doing rites for them. This downplaying of ritualistic chanting is in fact carried over into the daily routine of monks and novices. Every village and town *wat* in the country conducts morning and evening chants (*sūat mon chāo, sūat mon yen*) for its ordained residents, but this forest hermitage does not have these sessions, for its emphasis is on "living quietly and concentrating on mindfulness." It was claimed by an informant that communal chanting brings no benefit to those living in a meditation *wat*; in the urban monasteries, collective chanting does contribute to the calm of the monks living among noises and intrusions.

Let us now review the daily routine of the disciples. They wake up around 4:30 a.m. or even earlier, and many of them meditate until about 5:30 a.m. Then, before going on the almsround to the village, all in single file, they have to clean their cottages and the communal hall. By 7 a.m. they will return to the hermitage and eat together their morning meal – the only meal of the day, following *dhūtaṅga* tradition. All the food received in bowls is placed in vessels, each monk or novice retaining in his bowl the quantity of rice he wishes to eat. Sitting on the central platform in the *sālā* they share the food and then wash the dishes and plates. Some of the food eaten may have been cooked by the two nuns and brought to them; alternatively, if there is much food collected a portion may be sent to them.

After the meal the religious are left to themselves until about 12:30 p.m., when they might meet near the wash house to have a drink. They are then left free until 3:30 or 4 p.m. During these intervals no meeting or gossiping is encouraged, and all the disciples are to be found in their cottages, or on the walks, meditating or following their own pursuits.

The inmates meet then around 4 p.m. to engage in the compulsory tasks of sweeping all the pathways, taking water to all the *kuti* and the lavatories, and once again cleaning the *sālā*. Then they all bathe. If they have worked hard at some physical task in the afternoon, they may be given a drink of cocoa or milk in the evening, before they retire around 9 p.m. This daily schedule emphasizes coming together for the communal meal and communal tasks and separating for isolation to follow the vocation of an ascetic monk. Within this ordering of daily time, individuals may follow their particular interests. For instance, a particularly dedicated adept, or someone following a special, intensified program, may wake up at 2 a.m. and meditate until morning, or even meditate right through the night and only take an afternoon nap. In the same way, some adepts may fast occasionally or even for extended periods of time lasting from a week to two weeks. A Western monk fasted through the rains retreat in five-day intervals. (A case of a monk who fasted for 30 days and then got up and went on the regular almsround was mentioned to me.) Phra Paññāvaḍḍho said that he practices meditation for three or four hours a day, two hours before going to sleep, wakes at midnight to meditate for another two hours, then sleeps until 4:30 a.m. It appeared that for all the inmates nighttime and early morning were preferred for meditation; during the day chores had to be done and there were other distractions.

This flexibility and voluntariness, this fashioning of one's regime within the formal disciplinary limits and rules, is matched by the Acharn's mode of instruction. Following his own Master's precedent, Maha Boowa does give discourses and sermons to all his assembled disciples, but the pupils are encouraged to practice on their own in their own dwellings. The abbot is said to assess the temperament and aptitude of each pupil and to relate dyadically to him, suggesting techniques and methods suited to each (as proposed by the *Visuddhimagga* itself). He may be stern toward some and more lenient toward others. Each pupil is encouraged to discuss his experiences and progress with the Acharn. But these consultations, just like the Acharn's collective discourses, are not regularized or prepared. The sermons are *ex tempore* and the consultations ad hoc. Especially at the beginning of the meditative vocation, initiation and instruction by a master is necessary, because there are technical matters involved and dangers to be avoided.[3] If, during the course of a sitting, a strange or upsetting experience is encountered, the Acharn is consulted. It is thought that each pupil, as he becomes more and more adept in his exercises, will be able to progressively monitor and examine his experiences and assess the levels and stages he has reached. The fact that certain standard signs and manifestations are associated with various levels is supposed to allow the adept to compare present experiences with past ones. A disciple is not expected to boast to others, especially laymen, about the level he has obtained.[4]

And as was the case with Acharn Mun and his disciples, disciples come and go. About two or three monks at a time, more often the Thai monks, leave the hermitage; their place is taken by others. Some leave to resume lay life or to reside in a city *wat*, but others may take the radical step of going to a remote mountain cave to meditate by themselves for a long stretch of time. Some are unsuccessful and return, and some persist and launch their own peripatetic careers. It was estimated that in the seven years preceding 1971 some fifteen to twenty monks had thus gone away to remote places. In the Udon region two hermitages were founded by Maha Boowa's pupils.[5]

One thing stands out about the disciplinary practices and interests of the members of this hermitage. There is scarcely any emphasis on the reading of books or the study of texts (*ganthadhurà*). In this entire hermitage, only two persons have any kind of "scholarly" orientation. The Acharn himself has a measure of competence in reading Pali texts; moreover, he writes compositions in Thai. The other is the British monk Phra Paññāvaḍḍho, who said that he has been learning Pali and has attempted to translate some texts into English. No one else can read Pali.

The entire emphasis, then, is on practice (*paṭipatti*) and not study (*pariyatti*).[6] Very definitely, it is a disciple's practice of meditation that is stressed over and above the reading of books or the memorization of chants. Monks and disciples of the forest hermitages do not prepare themselves for the official *saṅgha*'s academic examinations on the *Dhamma* and Pali studies.

What kind of advice and orientation to the *bhikkhu*'s path does Acharn Maha Boowa impart to his disciples? Because Maha Boowa is an able pamphleteer and preacher, his views are recorded in writing. Before referring to these, let me report what some of the disciples themselves told me, because they are spontaneous statements laced with homespun metaphors made in the informal context of their own hermitage:

• A disciple should be *mindful* of everything he does – whether he is sweeping the floor or picking up a cup. He must keep his mind in the present and seek after wisdom (*paññā*). He must comprehend the laws of *karma* as evidenced in everyday acts: If you place a pot in the middle of the floor, it will get knocked down. External circumstances have internal repercussions and correspondences.

• One should do things with *effort*; one should not be slack or lazy but do everything expediently and thoroughly. Such effort overcomes natural sloth and trains one in achieving mindfulness; this is the concept of *samādhi*.

• One should *keep one's eyes open*. By this is meant seeing things not superficially but right through to their true condition. One then sees *dukkha* (sorrow) as the true condition of this world. One sees a slum or shanty town, one turns away in disgust, and the *citta* (mind) does not hanker after the world. The same feelings are evoked by affluent places. The jungle also evokes the same understanding. The animals, though they possess nothing except what they have on themselves, are discontented just like humans; they, however, are ridden by "fear," which is not man's natural condition. Or if you observe the vegetation, you see how it grows and decays. All these observations lead to wisdom.

• The methods of *samādhi* (concentration) and *paññā* (insight) are interrelated. Usually, *samādhi* precedes *paññā*; some persons may already possess *paññā* but must develop continuous concentration fully to use it. It is important to realize that if one enters into *samādhi*, one should still retain control of one's mental processes and be able to break the meditation at will and return to a normal state. This is quite different from a spirit medium in a state of trance.

• As regards the starting techniques for entering the meditative state, the Acharn recommends several – one is the repetition of a formula like "Buddho" to develop initial calm; another is the technique of breathing in and out and fixing one's attention on breathing (*ānāpānasati*); a third is the contemplation of the body as a whole, of its thirty-two parts, and repulsive and unpleasant things. The first two techniques derive from *samādhi*, but the Acharn does not mind which techniques are adopted.

• There are four postures for meditation, such as sitting, standing, walking, and lying down. The Acharn himself prefers the walking and sitting methods, but he allows his disciples to choose according to their preference. Walking and sitting are the two most frequently adopted in the hermitage.

It is quite clear from these excerpts that Acharn Maha Boowa's instructions are quite "orthodox" and in line with the exposition given in the *Visuddhimagga*. Certain of Maha Boowa's translated essays,[7] and excerpts of his views as reported in Kornfield,[8] are more formal and more sophisticated statements of the wisdom and practices he has sought to inculcate among his disciples and which he makes it a point to associate with his own Master, Acharn Mun. I have summarized the contents in Kornfield in an appendix to this chapter so that the reader can appreciate both sides of the intellect of this teacher – its sure knowledge of the classical textual formulations and its skill in expounding them with imaginative metaphors and indigenous idioms.

Let me conclude this sociological account of the forest hermitage on a comparative note. Because Phra Paññāvaddho was a Westerner, born, bred, and educated in a context inflected by Christianity, I asked him to tell me how Buddhist contemplative monasticism differed from the monastic institutions of early Christianity. He made these telling comments:

# The hagiography of a Buddhist saint

1. A Christian monastery "has four walls and a gate"; by comparison, this hermitage is open: people can wander in and out without formality.

2. A Christian monastery is more rigidly organized; it has more rules and regulations. Although a Buddhist monastery also has its own disciplinary rules, it allows more "freedom" to the individual member, who is allowed to and expected to work out his own method and regime according to his own inclinations and temperament.

3. The Christian monastery thinks of itself more as a community and a collective unit than does a Buddhist. For a *bhikkhu*, the monastery is a "convenience" rather than a primary focus of affiliation.

4. In a forest hermitage like Wat Pā Bān Tāt, physical work is engaged in, not for its own sake, but because it needs to be done. The monks here do more physical labor than those who reside in the regular village and urban *wat*, because for one thing they can do a better job than lay workers, but, more importantly, because lay workers coming from outside disturb the tranquillity of the place.

I may round off these acute comments by reminding the reader of certain other comparative features. An integral feature of the Benedictine Rule (A.D. 529) is that the monk submit himself to the vow of obedience to God and to the authority of his abbot. There is no such submission or renunciation of individual will on the part of the Buddhist *bhikkhu*. A second integral feature of the Benedictine Order was the conception of the monastery as a "separate family of renunciation," as a self-supporting cell, whose members devote themselves to work and prayer, "*laborare et orare*." The Benedictine Rule elevated toil and signified a moral attitude to work that was systematized as a part of the regimen of monastic life and helped to make the monastery a self-sufficient economic unit (and later a wealthy corporation). A correlated feature was "the rule of stability," which Benedict said would remove from the monks the need to go abroad, a temptation gravely harmful to their souls. The Thai monk knows little of that attachment to the monastery where he has been first ordained – he can move from *wat* to *wat*, teacher to teacher, in pursuit of his own vocation and path.[9]

# Appendix

## *The instructions of Acharn Maha Boowa*

I summarize here some of the main teachings of Acharn Maha Boowa about the objectives and techniques of meditation, the experiences that it may generate, and the dialectical relation between concentration and wisdom for the achievement of *nirvāna*. These teachings, which are reported by Kornfield,[10] supplement those that are already summarized by me in the biography of Acharn Mun in Chapter 6. Here, Acharn Maha Boowa as a teacher adopts a dogmatic and pedagogical prose; there, he wrote as an adoring disciple in the language of extolling hagiography.

*Morality (sīla).* Morality sets a limit to the "outgoing exuberance" in a person's activities of body and speech. The practice of morality enables a person to live in a "cool" way with a happy and easy heart. Moral behavior can be natural to a person and does not have to be asked for as precepts from a monk or a person in an official capacity.

*Concentration.* All types of meditation are for controlling the "outgoing exuberance of the heart" (*čai*). The Thai consider *čai* to be the seat of the emotions and also an entity that has a capacity for "attachments." Concentration, which means calmness or stability of heart, is that which opposes the "outgoing exuberance." The heart does not want to take the medicine of meditation, by which *Dhamma* is brought into the heart as its guardian.

The Buddha enumerated forty supports of meditation, which vary with the different temperaments of people. The three supports favored by Maha Boowa are the contemplation of the thirty-two parts of the body; contemplation of the Buddha, the *Dhamma*, and the *sangha*; and awareness of breathing in and out. When one finds the type of meditation that suits one's character, one should begin with a preparatory repetition of a word so that "the sound captivates the heart."

In describing the use of the breath as the objective support of the heart, Maha Boowa says that through it mindfulness should be established; as one feels the breath at every moment one senses that it becomes progressively finer "until finally it becomes apparent that the finest and most subtle breath and the heart have converged and become one." When one has attained the most subtle level of breathing he will be bright, cool, calm, happy, and reach a nondual state of absorption and of knowledge of the heart alone.

During the practice of a given type of meditation, the characteristics of that form of meditation (e.g., the body parts) may appear; one should pay close attention to them and fix them in one's heart and then contemplate their unpleasant and loathsome aspects as rotting and decayed, as breaking down into their elements. Thus one eliminates delusion, which gives rise to sexual craving, which is one of the "outgoing exuberances" of the heart.

All methods of meditation lead to the same goal – peace and happiness; in other words, to *nibbāna*. One should therefore not get bogged down with concern with methods other than the one one has chosen, nor should one become preoccupied with the right order of practicing virtue, concentration, and wisdom; the defilements of passion, hate, and delusion are not arranged in persons the same way, and it is of no consequence in which order they arise in one.

*Wisdom develops concentration*

"The true purpose of meditation practice is to bring calm in the heart." If one cannot attain calm by lulling the heart with a preparatory method, one must employ wisdom to sever the root cause of distraction and to subdue it by stratagem and intimidation. There are some persons who have to train their heart to attain concentration by using wisdom; in this case "wisdom develops concentration"; and when concentration develops, it in turn develops wisdom. The results that come from training in both these ways – "concentration develops wisdom" and vice versa – are the attainment of deep calm and wisdom. Maha Boowa gives a sophisticated explanation of how learning may interfere with the practice of meditation:

A person who wants to train his heart to become skillful and to know what is behind the deluding tricks of the defilements, must not be attached to study and learning in Buddhism to such an extent that it gives rise to defilements. But also he must not abandon study and learning; for to do this goes beyond the teaching of the Buddha.

In other words when one is practicing meditation for the purpose of developing concentration, one must not let the heart grasp at what it has learned by study, for it will be led into thoughts of the past and future. One must instead make the heart keep to the present, which means that one's only concern must be just that aspect of Dharma which one is developing.

When there is some question or point of doubt in connection with one's heart which one is unable to resolve, one may then check it by study and learning after one has finished meditation practice. But it is wrong to check one's practice all the time with what one has learned by study, for this will be mere intellectual knowledge and not knowledge which comes from development in meditation.

### Developing concentration

In this section, Acharn Maha Boowa expands the stages in developing concentration, particularly access concentration followed by absorptive concentration.

In access concentration, sometimes an image *nimitta* (of oneself as a corpse or some other corpse, etc.) may appear, and a clever disciple will take it as his "learning sign" for developing deeper concentration. One must see in the learning signs the characteristics of impermanence, suffering, and nonself. When one has become skilled at concentration, "one may let the heart go out and follow the sign and find out what is taking place" – this will be of value in understanding the events of the past and future.

There are, however, types of people for whom signs do not appear, no matter how long the heart remains in a concentrated state. These are the types of whom one may say "wisdom develops concentration." In any case, wisdom and concentration are a "Dharma pair" that go together and cannot be separated. But basically it is concentration of all types that aids and supports the development of wisdom.

There is one obstacle that concentration may engender. In practicing it, the adept may become attached to the state of calm and happiness it evokes, and may want to remain in its repose without advancing further to develop wisdom. "This is becoming addicted to concentration and being unable to withdraw from it in order to go further."

*Wisdom.* In this final section, Maha Boowa expounds the goal of wisdom. Having reached sufficient calm in meditation, one trains himself to investigate the parts of the body with wisdom and to realize that delusion and attachment to beings and functions, and separation from them – all these are about and within this body of ours. Infatuations of love and hate are infatuations within this body; not wanting death is anxiety about this body. Beings are inundated by defilements until they are unable to extricate themselves, and the body is the cause of them all.

When the heart views the body in the foregoing way, with wisdom, it becomes wearied both of one's own body and the bodies of other people and animals. The heart, in using the spyglass of wisdom to go sightseeing in the "city of the body," can see one's own "body city," and then that of all other people and animals, quite clearly; it sees that all components of this city are divided into the three aspects of impermanence, suffering, and nonself, and into the four elements of earth, water, air, and fire.

Next, Maha Boowa discusses the deep insight that arises in connection with "the Dharma of mind" (*nāma*), that is, the mental constituents of the five aggregates, feelings (*vedanā*), perceptions (*saññā*), mental formations (*saṅkhāra*), consciousness (*viññāṇa*). "These four mental Dharmas are the activities of the heart, they come from the heart and are its deceivers, which can hide and obscure the truth."

Investigation of the four mental *Dhammas* with wisdom – whether singly or together – leads to the understanding of how they change all the time, how they appear, remain for a time, and die away and cease. Being without a self, these impermanent things are also impersonal. "Internally, externally, everywhere throughout every realm, they proclaim with one voice that they are impermanent . . . . that they are always independent and free, and that whoever out of delusion becomes attached to them only meets with suffering, depression, and sorrow . . . ."

These *Dhammas* in nature are in themselves entirely free from any defilements or evil ways, but they come to be associated with them because of the heart, which is under the power of ignorance. "Because of the power of seizing and grasping, this 'ignorant heart' wanders through birth, old age, sickness, and death, going round and round in this way through each and every life, regardless of whether it is higher or lower, good or evil, through all the three realms of becoming." The heart begins to stain and color everything in the universe in a false manner, thus altering the natural state.

As soon as ignorance has been destroyed from the heart due to the superior power of "path knowledge" (i.e., the Noble Eightfold Path), which is the weapon of wisdom, *nibbāna* will be revealed to the one who acts truly, knows truly, and sees truly. Because now the heart is in a state of *Dhamma* and impartiality, one can say "that the heart and all the Dharmas in the universe are mutually in a state of complete peace and calm by virtue of the perfect truth."

# 11

# Sectarianism and the sponsorship
of meditation

### The royal road to Bangkok

The following criticisms and explanations of the phenomenon of forest teachers
being acclaimed as *arahant* (saints), of the cult of amulets associated with them,
comes from one of the best scholar monks in Thailand, who some years ago
disrobed to become a layman. His criticisms have to be understood in the context
of two considerations: He belonged to the Mahānikāi sect, and his sympathies
were naturally with it with regard to its rivalry with the Thammayut sect; and he
was a scholar monk who not only was most orthodox and correct in his observance
of disciplinary rules, but also had a deep understanding of the philosophical and
doctrinal principles of the Theravāda version of the Buddha's teachings.

This commentator, Mr. X, was contemptuous of the fact that a writer by the
name of Sittachetavanna had claimed that there were a number of *arahant* –
maybe about 100 – in Thailand today; Mr. X had written a scathing riposte to this
claim, in which he pointed out that the *arahant* of olden days never *pluksēk*
(chanted powerful words) as the modern ones do. (The commentator was referring
here to the sacralization of amulets.)

Mr. X held up Acharn Chā of Ubon as an exemplary forest-monk and
meditation teacher who did not engage in the low art of *saiyasāt* ("magic"). I
have already given an account of Acharn Chā as a forest-monk teacher of the
Mahānikāi sect and reported that he is acclaimed by many persons in Thailand as
an exemplary teacher of meditation (see Chapter 9).

Mr. X's pungent criticism, most decidedly not a majority view, provides us
with a useful point of entry for discussing the contextual features of Maha
Boowa's composition. He criticized Acharn Maha Boowa for writing an exaggerated biography of Acharn Mun and for calling him an *arahant* and crediting
him with supranormal powers. He then referred cryptically to some central

# Sectarianism and the sponsorship of meditation

features of *saṅgha* politics in these words, which can serve us as a starting point for exegesis: "Seeing the success of Phra Phimolatham's [the abbot of Wat Mahathad] program of popularising *Vipassanā* meditation throughout the country, Wat Bovonniwet engaged in the counter-campaign of popularising and celebrating the achievements of the provincial forest meditation teachers like Acharn Mun, Acharn Fun, Lūang Pū Wāen, and Acharn Maha Boowa, who are all of the Thammayut sect. When Maha Boowa, a foremost propagandist, comes to Bangkok he resides at Wat Bovonniwet. So the King's (and the Royal Family's) showing interest in and having dealings with such forest monks as Lūang Pū Wāen and Acharn Fun in recent times has something to do with the Thammayut sect's sponsorship of these so-called provincial 'saints.'"

These remarks suggestively raise issues of sectarian rivalry within the Thai *saṅgha*, and of the propagation and popularization of meditation and the cult of the saints being in some part linked with that rivalry. They further imply that the sects and their leaders have important connections with high politics, including the royal family, and that royal sponsorship and the attendant bringing of certain forest-monks into national prominence have a great deal to do with the logic of center–periphery relations in contemporary Thailand.

## The biographer's Bangkok connections

The fact is well known that Acharn Maha Boowa occasionally visits Bangkok. On these visits, he resides at the central Thammayut monastery of Wat Bovonniwet and conducts some teaching sessions in meditation. (Although Maha Boowa has been the most frequent visitor, other forest teachers like Acharn Fun and Acharn Wan of Sakon Nakhon are known to have visited and preached at Wat Bovonniwet.)

Acharn Maha Boowa's association with Wat Bovonniwet and his personal connection with the abbot of this *wat*, Somdet Phra Yansangvorn (formerly Phra Sasanosophon), are critical for understanding the support the forest-monk hermitages in the distant peripheral provinces of the Northeast have received from the country's ecclesiastical and political center. The abbot of Wat Bovonniwet is himself a teacher of meditation and conducts lessons with the help of two or three assistant monks. He has not received training in meditation as such; he has not been to Burma; he has taught himself with the aid of books. And although an enthusiast, he is not counted as a great meditation adept. Yet he has an important elite following among educated Thai of royalist inclinations and among Western neophytes. He is unique among the Thai teachers in holding meditation classes once a week in English for both monks and laymen. Not only do many Western monks get ordained at this prestigious *wat*, but they also start their tutelage under this abbot. Moreover, by the 1970s it had become a convention that all foreign

155

monks wishing to study meditation in Acharn Maha Boowa's forest hermitage of Wat Paa Baan That had to spend about a year in Bangkok at Wat Bovonniwet preparing themselves. Of course, only those ordained into the Thammayut sect would prepare themselves in this way. Moreover, the abbot's office at Wat Bovonniwet became a kind of central link and information center for most of the forest hermitages in the Northeast, and foreign monks wishing to spend some time in one of the remote and stunningly beautiful hermitages were advised to make their arrangements through the abbot.

For some years now, Somdet Phra Yangsangvorn has been in charge of the *sangha*'s missionary program abroad, which is concerned with sending Thai monks to other countries, particularly Malaysia in Southeast Asia, and to Western countries, to reside in the increasing number of Thai temples being established there, and to propagate Buddhism among foreigners as well as to serve the needs of Thais living there.

The centrality and the weight of Wat Bovonniwet can be gauged from these indications. The headquarters of the Thammayut sect have been situated at Wat Bovonniwet, and all meetings of the sect have been held here since the time of the princely Supreme Patriarch Wachirayān at the turn of this century. The office is manned by monk-officers, many of whom may reside at other Thammayut *wat* and come to work here. The head of the sect (Čaokhana Yai) has a council or committee (kammakān), which consists of all the Thammayut monks of *phrarāt-chakhana* status and some others elected by them. This committee oversees the work of the regional, provincial, district, etc., levels of organization of the sect.

The Mahāmakuṭa Rājavidyālaya Foundation[1] is an organization of the sect, and it in turn sponsors and finances educational activities, of which the principal one is the Mahāmakut Monks' University, also located on the grounds of Wat Bovonniwet. Founded in 1893 by Prince Wachirayān, this foundation receives money from many Thammayut *wat*, a principal donor being Wat Bovonniwet. Accordingly, it is fit that the abbot of Wat Bovonniwet is the president of the foundation.

A second activity of the foundation is the running of a printing press, which actively prints a number of books and publications in both Thai and English and sells and distributes them through a bookshop. Once again, this enterprise harks back to the time of Wachirayān.

Thus, although Wat Bovonniwet may not be at any one point of time the seat of the head of the sect, or of its principal officers (for this depends on criteria of seniority), it is considered the chief *wat* of the sect on account of the location of the sect's headquarters and of the Mahāmakut University there. And because of these considerations alone, the abbot of Wat Bovonniwet is assured an important place in the *sangha*.

There is another reason of course, which we have at various places mentioned, which has assured this *wat* a prominent place in the country as a whole and in the

## Sectarianism and the sponsorship of meditation

capital in particular. It has not only since Mongkut's time had a succession of princely abbots, but has also been the residence of reigning monarchs, crown princes, and "celestial" (*čao fā*) princes when these have been temporarily ordained as monks and novices.

Let us run through the prominent names in these two lists. Inevitably we must begin again with Mongkut, who has fathered a line of abbots and reigning princes.

Prince Mongkut assumed the abbotship of the *wat* in 1837; it had previously been called Wat Mai and was now named Wat Pavaranivesa (Bovonniwet), meaning "residence of Pavara," which was the title of the deputy king.[2] The *wat* then became at one stroke the seat of the highest-ranking prince of the realm and the center of a new sect. When Mongkut ascended the throne in 1851, Prince Pavaret (the son of the deputy king to Rāma II), who had been groomed by Mongkut, became abbot and had a long run until 1892, during which period he had also served as head of the Thammayut sect and later as supreme patriarch.

The next abbot was Prince Wachirayān (Vajirañāṇavarorasa), son of King Mongkut and half-brother of King Chulalongkorn. He remained in office from 1892 to 1921 and also became successively head of the Thammayut sect in 1906 and supreme patriarch in 1910.

He was followed from 1921 to 1958 by Phra Vajraranavongse, son of a prince of *maūm cao* status and a distant relative of King Mongkut. Expectably, he too was elevated to the supreme patriarchship in 1945.

Here ended the royal lineage of abbots. The present abbot, Somdet Phra Yansangvorn, a commoner and the sixth in line of succession, assumed office in 1961. Both because of the prestige of the office and because of his personal prestige and activities, he has leap-frogged over some more senior monks to gain the title of *somdet* and automatically a place in the Mahāthērasamākhom (the *saṅgha*'s Supreme Council of Elders). And he is credited with having excellent relations with the royal household.

Now let us relate the temporary royal ordinations conducted by this line of abbots. King Mongkut had expressed the desire after his accession to the throne that all his sons who wished to enter the *saṅgha* for a period of time should reside in Wat Bovonniwet or, as second choice, in one of the Thammayut *wat* he had restored or founded. In particular, he had wanted the celestial princes in line for the throne to reside at Wat Bovonniwet. This tradition has been followed to this day.[3] Thus, Crown Prince Vajiravudh resided at the *wat* after his ordination in 1905; his preceptor at the ceremony was abbot Wachirayān. In 1917, Prince Prajathipok (who ascended the throne in 1926) was ordained by the same Wachirayān and resided at the *wat* afterward. The present king, Bhumipol, while a monarch was ordained in 1956 for fifteen days, and again took up residence at the *wat*.[4] (The present abbot of Wat Bovonniwet acted as one of the two *ācariyas* at the ordination and acted as his mentor afterward.) Finally, in November 1978,

157

the present crown prince also followed this tradition (and once again the present abbot of Wat Bovonniwet acted as one of his *ācariyas*, the other being the abbot of Wat Cakkrawat).[5]

It is a matter of great pride to Wat Bovonniwet that this long royal connection has left a permanent trace in the *wat* in the form of two buildings, called Tamnak Panyā and Song Prōt, which are specially reserved for the occupation of the monarchs and celestial princes after their ordinations. Tamnak Panyā was initially a residence standing in the Royal Palace. Rāma III had it moved brick by brick to Wat Bovonniwet so that it could become the residence of Mongkut, who lived in it until he left the *saṅgha*. It has since then served as the obligatory residence of monarchs and celestial princes during their temporary ordinations. In 1890, King Chulalongkorn built a more modern and comfortable residence called Song Prōt (meaning "when taking the ordination"); thereafter, the ordained royals spent the first one or two nights in the Tamnak Panyā before moving into it.[6] Moreover, the grounds of Wat Bovonniwet contain other traces of royalty – such as the umbilical cords of the four children of the present monarch, which lie buried in groves, and the numerous trees planted by the royal family on various occasions.

Partly because of its "exclusiveness," and its being a place of special privilege, Wat Bovonniwet does not compare with Wat Mahāthāt, the largest and most important monastery of the Mahānikāi sect, in the number of its inmates and its openness to the public at large. In November 1978, just before the end of the rains retreat and departure of "temporary" monks, there were in residence at Wat Bovonniwet some 70 "regular" monks, 30 "temporary" monks, 13 novices, and 300 temple boys. In its internal residential division into *khana* sections, in its running its own ecclesiastical school, and in its management of internal affairs through a committee of abbot and titled monks, it is not different from many other Bangkok monasteries. But it is distinctive with regard to its elite lay supporters, who frequently invite the monks for lunches and merit-making ceremonies at their homes. The number of plush cars drawn up near the monastery before the noon meal – cars bringing lay donors to the temple bearing food, or sent to carry monks to lay homes – is a sign of the veneration as well as the prestige enjoyed by this monastery.

Now with these background facts sketched in, let us return to our biographer. It is no unimportant part of the association between the two men that the abbot of Wat Bovonniwet has sponsored the translation into English and publication of some of Maha Boowa's compositions, which were distributed free through the Thammayut sect's press and bookshop (Mahāmakut Press), and through individual monks and laymen. Moreover, some of the Acharn Maha Boowa's expositions on meditation have been published in English in the *Review* of the World Federation of Buddhists.[7]

A word or two about the World Federation of Buddhists (WFB) is in order to complete Acharn Maha Boowa's Bangkok connections. There were in 1978 some seventy-two WFB Regional Centers located throughout the world. Thailand was the host country for the headquarters of the federation. The government of Thailand has built a luxurious building to house the headquarters, and the Department of Religious Affairs provides the budget for its activities. Aside from publishing the review, the headquarters sponsors many Buddhist activities, the most important of which is the holding of weekly meditation classes for monks and laity alike.[8]

I have in an earlier work[9] documented in detail the fact that the Department of Religious Affairs is heavily staffed by educated ex-monks, most of whom were members of the Thammayut sect. Likewise, the most important Thai lay administrators of the WFB Center are men of similar background. Let us take as our example Siri Buddhasukh, who was in 1978 the "Chief of the International Section" of the center and editor of the *Review*. He is particularly appropriate to consider because he is the translator into English of Acharn Maha Boowa's biography of Acharn Mun, the text which I summarized in Chapter 6.

Siri was born in Kalasin Province. Like many other Bangkok monks, he came to the capital as a novice (*sāmaṇera*) in his teens and took up residence in the Thammayut monastery called Wat Boromnivas. He resided there for ten years, during which period he attended the Mahāmakut University for monks run by the Thammayut sect and obtained the B.A. degree. He then disrobed, studied for his B.A. again at Prasarmitr Teachers College, and then spent two years at Benares Hindu University, where he secured an M.A. degree in sociology. At the time I met him in 1978, he was holding two jobs, one at the WFB Center and the other as a lecturer at the Mahāmakut University. The facts I have presented enable us fully to appreciate the connections that Acharn Maha Boowa, a Northeastern forest monk, has established with the religious and lay authorities in Bangkok who actively propagate "religion" (*sāsana*). These connections enable his teachings and writings to get a distribution among both Thai- and English-speaking elite circles.

### The Thammayut order's strength, and the setting
### for sectarian rivalries

Insofar as Maha Boowa's biography of Acharn Mun is "propagandist" in seeking to disseminate the story of a Buddhist saint who was a member of the Thammayut sect, we have to probe into sectarian rivalries in contemporary Thailand. The circumstances surrounding the founding of the Thammayut sect, its distinctive features and stamp, and its orientations and achievements in the nineteenth century have by now been so well documented that I shall only strive to give here a concise and "mnemonical" account of the events arranged so as to illuminate the issues that concern us in the book.[10]

The Thammayut sect was founded by Mongkut when he served as an ordained

159

prince, and it gained formal recognition and autonomy as one of the four components of the national *saṅgha* in the time of the King Chulalongkorn. Mongkut's stated aim in founding the new sect was to improve upon the lax practices of the extant *saṅgha*, that is, the Mahānikāi sect. He pointedly called his grouping Thammayut, "those adhering to the doctrine," in contrast to the established Mahānikāi, whom he dubbed "those adhering to long standing habit." In the manner of most sectarian divisions in the Theravāda tradition, Mongkut adopted certain disciplinary practices concerning the mode of wearing the robes, the ceremony of ordination, the style of chanting, and so on, which were allegedly closer to the pristine practices and therefore in the true lineage of succession extending from the Buddha. In any event, these practices served as diacritical features of the new sect.

But there were other features of his "reformist" movement that bear intriguingly upon our theme of forest-monks. Mongkut did formulate certain rules of conduct for his disciples that were more "ascetic" and in line with the *dhūtaṅga* practices, which the *Visuddhimagga*, let us recall, enumerated only *as optional but not obligatory sīla* (conduct) *for monks*. Although Mahānikāi monks ate two meals a day, Thammayut monks were to eat one a day. Many Mahānikāi monks, especially in the towns, neglected their almsrounds, but Thammayut monks were to eat food placed in their almsbowls. Moreover, unlike Mahānikāi monks, who accepted curries and relishes in separate dishes, the Thammayut brethren were to accept all offerings of food in the same bowl and eat the food with all tastes and dishes mixed.[11]

These ascetic practices of the *āraññavāsī* tradition were not, however, combined by Mongkut with an emphasis on the practice of *samādhi* (concentration) and the cultivation of wisdom through insight meditation. Whereas Mongkut did stress that the exemplary Thammayut monks should combine scholarship with some proficiency in meditation, the latter pursuit did not become a central component in his conception of the monk's vocation. Let us recall his early experience as a monk, when he was faced by the unfortunate results of the *saṅgha*'s de facto separation of *pariyatti*, which was construed as the study of texts (*ganthadhura*), from *paṭipatti*, which was construed as the practice of meditation (*vipassanā-dhura*), as more or less two incompatible specializations. Ordained in 1824, he first resided at Wat Mahāthāt. When the succession to the throne went to his half-brother, he decided to continue as a monk, and moved to Wat Samorai, which was situated at some distance from the capital and as a forest-monk monastery was famous for the teaching of meditation and spiritual exercises rather than for the inculcation of learning. It was because his teachers could not provide the doctrinal and canonical explanations for the meditative practices that he became disenchanted with them and returned to Wat Mahāthāt to study canonical texts. His flair for languages and "scripturalist" orientation combined to make him a Pali scholar in a little time. So the leader of the Thammayut movement became an ecclesiastical examiner and set out to improve monastic education. He turned many of his disciples into able Pali scholars and holders of degrees. This literary explosion was furthered by Mongkut's founding a press for printing and popularizing Pali works.

We thus see in the constitution of the early stages of the Thammayut sect a paradoxical content: Mongkut espoused some of the ascetic practices that were the hallmark of forest-dwelling monks, but he also championed the study of texts and was dedicated to taking the pure religion to the people, as good town-dwelling monks should ideally do. In this case, however, there was a coherent relation between the two emphases: Thammayut monks would be exemplars of disciplined conduct, and they would be the agents who would transform the religion among monks and laity alike. Concordant with this missionizing zest was Mongkut's exhortation that his monks preach extemporaneously and vigorously in the vernacular rather than resort to composed sermons with Pali words incomprehensible to most of the listeners.

Another component of the Thammayut scripturalist and reformist package was its "rationalism" or, as some would describe it, its "demythologizing" stance. The well-known example advanced is Mongkut's rejection of the *Traiphūm*, the regnant cosmological treatise with its mythological description of the cosmos and its workings, its array of "superstitious" beliefs, and its encouragement of "ritualistic" actions, and his desire to bring the *Dhamma* in conformity with the canons of the empirical science, which he learned from Western contact.[12]

These dynamic and fertilizing constituents produced in King Chulalongkorn's time the finest flower of the Thammayut sect in the person of Wachirayān, the princely son of Mongkut, half-brother to the king, the abbot of Wat Bovonniwet, subsequently head of the Thammayut sect, and supreme patriarch of the *saṅgha*. He is perhaps, as an admirer puts it, "without question the most celebrated bhikkhu in the ecclesiastical history of Thailand." Let us briefly recall the developments that stemmed from, on the one hand, his scholarship and his reform of monastic education, and, on the other, his zeal for administrative reform of the *saṅgha* as a whole, which led him to a collaboration with the political authority and participation in its "national" and "centralizing" objectives. Wachirayān is credited with the second wave (after Mongkut) of reforming the education of monks and novices in monastic schools; he substituted written examinations for oral and composed a number of textbooks, many of which are standard texts even today. He founded the university for monks, Mahāmakuṭarājav-idyālaya, in 1893. He was also a prolific writer in Thai and Pali – his translations, commentaries, and sermons, together with his textbooks, found ready publication and distribution through the press owned by the Thammayut order. Wachirayān not only addressed himself to better educating the ordained, he also sought to educate the lay public, and many of his compositions were directed at them.

This emphasis – that monks should enlighten people as active teachers of Buddhism – prepared the way for King Chulalongkorn's enlisting of the princely monk in his program to promote widespread primary education in the provinces.

# The hagiography of a Buddhist saint

Wachirayān, appointed as an "organizer of religion and education of the Buddhist population," committed his scholar monks and rural *wat* to the dissemination of elementary education, a commitment that in turn led to the overhauling of the entire *sangha*'s ecclesiastical administrative structure. A national educational program, created and disseminated from the center, was sought to be implemented through the country's numerous monasteries, which were not tightly interrelated and also practiced local and regional traditions. Wachirayān soon saw the need to unify and bureaucratize the national ecclesiastical *sangha* to achieve its objectives; he took as his model Prince Damrong's plan to reform the provincial administration to create a centralized patrimonial-bureaucratic structure. He collaborated with Prince Damrong, King Chulalongkorn's most effective agent of national integration *cum* royal centralization, in transforming the Thai *sangha* into a national hierarchy more amenable than ever before to control from Bangkok. The *Sangha* Act of 1902 was the end result of these developments.

Another fateful result that was a necessary corollary of this program of national unification and centralization was the "homogenization" of Buddhism. The Thammayut brand of central Thai Buddhism was to be the criterion of pure Buddhism, and regional traditions of Buddhist practice, worship, and identity were to be obliterated in favor of a Bangkok orthodoxy and of central Thai language as against variant languages, such as the Tai Yuan of the North and its associated script.

In the northern capital of Chiengmai, the Thammayut order was introduced by a ranking monk sent by Wachirayān, and in fact a local princely family assisted in changing the affiliation of the important *wat* of Čēdī Lūang to this new order. It was at this *wat* that Acharn Mun, the Meditation Master, once resided briefly during his wanderings and preached (see Chapter 6). To this day, Wat Čēdī Lūang remains the center of Thammayut activities in the province, and in recent times its deputy abbot has maintained strong links with the Thammayut *wat* in Bangkok.[13]

Now, it is this kind of religio-political activism spearheaded by the Thammayut sect's ablest representatives that produced in the early decades of the twentieth century a reaction with millennial resonances from the famous Northern *khrū bā* ("esteemed teacher") of charismatic qualities, Phra Sīwichai, and his monk disciples and lay followers. In Chapter 20, I shall tell the story of this monk who came out of the local Northern tradition of holy men and resisted the tentacles spreading from Bangkok. What Phra Sīwichai challenged and reacted against was precisely the Bangkok-promoted attempt at nationalizing, centralizing, regulating, and homogenizing the *sangha* order and *sāsana*. The Sīwichai defiance of Bangkok was not long-lived; an accommodation was reached and the process of unification has since then proceeded more or less unimpeded.

In the twentieth century, the main agents and devices of the Bangkok-based central authorities in creating a unified national *sangha* have been the royal monasteries of both Thammayut and Mahānikāi affiliation, the system of titled ecclesiastical positions, the monastic schools relating their education to centrally administered examinations, the regulation of ordination into the *saṅgha*, and so on. But the *saṅgha* authorities, among whom those of Thammayut affiliation have been dominant for many past decades, have also attempted to foster in the Northern and Northeastern frontier provinces the forest hermitages at the same time as they have sought to break the local bases of religious prestige and charisma of the divisive and rebellious sort represented by Khrūbā Sīwichai. There is a paradoxical element in this situation, which we have to unravel.

We have already seen how Mongkut's Thammayut movement, while downgrading the earlier forest-monk tradition, also sought to incorporate and encompass it. While Mongkut declared that meditation and ascetic practices uninformed by learning were of little value, he incorporated some of the ascetic (*dhūtaṅga*) practices into the code of "pure" *vinaya* practices he formulated.

Later, during the great era of the upgrading and spread of monastic education under the leadership of Prince Wachirayān of the Thammayut sect, the monks of *araññavāsī* tradition in the border provinces did not participate in this system of education, and since then have neither sat for the clerical examinations (*naktham* and *prayōk*) nor been considered eligible for scholarly or ecclesiastical administrative titles and offices. As I have mentioned before, most "forest hermitages" have had no consecrated precincts and entitlements for the holding of higher ordination (*upasampadā*) in their premises. Thus there is no doubt that they are in an important sense placed "outside" the channels and resources of the official *saṅgha*. This is not to say that they are considered "illegitimate" or "deviant," for all the forest monks today have undergone proper ordination, and the majority of them, as we have seen, are of Thammayut affiliation.

But there are reasons to suppose that precisely because of the benign interest taken in them by the Thammayut sect, these forest hermitages have the probability in due course of changing into full-scale monasteries flying the Thammayut banner and becoming part of the establishment. Ferguson and Ramitanondh have recently hypothesized[14] that "...the Thammayut Sect at the provincial level is possibly an alternative avenue of royal governmental influence over the monkhood in addition to the channels available through the hierarchy and honorary system," and concluded that the forest monks of Acharn Mun are the pioneer ground breakers who will evolve into more traditional Thammayut monasteries in a few decades.

Kirsch has also recently remarked on the penetration of the influence of the Thammayut monks into the Northeastern countryside,[15] where "they are found in 'forest' temples located on the outskirts of provincial centers and rural villages where they follow their ascetic regime and carry out their exemplary role distinct from the village monks of the Mahānikāi." He also noted that "in the countryside where Thammayut monks are found, their strongest lay supporters are drawn from among the group of local leaders, school teachers, storekeepers, and a nascent group of local traders who are also oriented to national concerns and are the innovators and modernizers of village society."

We hope to clarify hypotheses of this nature. From our broader perspective, we see an understandable fallacy in Kirsch's essay. Probably because he did his fieldwork in the Northeast and has had little direct knowledge of the Thammayut monasteries of Bangkok, Kirsch expatiates in general terms on how today "to be a Thammayut monk requires a conscious commitment and a higher level of personal involvement than is necessary for the Mahānikāi monk," and that because the Thammayut monk's role is "so demanding" pious laymen feeling unable to live up to these expectations are forced to live and achieve in the secular world rather than become monks themselves. The truth of the matter is that the asceticism and dedication to the path of liberation that are the hallmark of many of the provincial forest hermitages that I have earlier described is confined to the periphery and is not matched by the great Thammayut monastic foundations of the capital. Aside from such discriminating features concerning the style of the wearing robes, wearing sandals, style of chanting, and so on, the Thammayut and Mahānikāi monasteries of Bangkok show no difference in style and comfort of life. Monks of both sects go on almsrounds optionally and rarely eat from their bowls (let alone mix foods and tastes); monks of both sects show more concern for learning and for officiating at rites and receiving gifts than for meditation and reclusive contemplation. The architecture of their *wat*, with gilded and ornate *bōt* and *wihān*, is similar. The list of similarities can be expanded, but the point I am trying to make is that since the reformist and purist times of Mongkut and Wachirayān, the Thammayut sect has developed an internal differentiation wherein the dominating urban center has settled into the interests and style of life of established mainstream Buddhism, whereas the periphery clings to and endeavors to live up to the ideals of ascetic practices and meditative contemplation. As we shall see, it is the "slackness" of the center and its increasing loss of credibility, and the achievement at the periphery of some of the central values of monastic Buddhism, that provides the scenario for the coming into national prominence lately of the forest saints, and for the intensification of the cult of the amulets.

Today monks and monasteries of the Thammayut order tend to be more committed to the orientations and demands of the ecclesiastical hierarchy than are the majority of the Mahānikāi members. But the margins of difference are not large between the Thammayut monasteries, which are becoming increasingly differentiated, and the Mahānikāi monasteries, whose best members have been imbued with many of the reformist orientations promoted by Wachirayān on a national scale. Nevertheless, there exist some perceptible differences. Most Thammayut *wat* do not hold festive temple fairs and *kathin* ceremonies, and many deplore and ban exuberant and histrionic sermons by preaching monks (*nakthēt*), who draw crowds and their donations. In contrast, many Mahānikāi *wat* are famous for their festive, colorful rites; what they lack in elite lay support they make up for in commoner religiosity. Many Thammayut *wat*, on the other hand, have become more relaxed and worldly in other respects: Astrology flourishes in them, and they are the wealthiest crematoriums of the capital. In Pali scholarship, Mahānikāi can pit its own learned with the best of Thammayut.

One of the lessons of the history of the Thammayut sect in Thailand is that a reformist sect formed in reaction to the traditionalized ritual orientations and interests of *gāmavāsī* mainstream monks cannot enduringly sustain its ascetic aspirations. As it develops and expands, it manifests internal differentiation and cleavages, which reproduce the original split. The Thammayut sect's alliance with political authority, together with its impulsion to reform monastic and lay Buddhist practices, embodied a tension, if not incompatibility, between ascetic living and worldly involvements. On the other side, *gāmavāsī* monastic communities also constantly spawn specialist groups, which pursue meditative and ascetic traditions and may even break away to found forest fraternities. The Mahānikāi sect in Thailand, precisely because it is a diverse collection of monastic communities, has shown these tendencies. It is because of these processes that the division between forest-dwelling (*āraññavāsī*) versus village-dwelling (*gāmavāsī*) which, as noted before, has been present from old times in the *saṅgha* of Sri Lanka, Burma, and Thailand, does not consistently represent the substantive differences that the labels signify. There has always been in these countries a dialectic and even a formal dichotomy with the *saṅgha* between ''the middle way'' of the *gāmavāsī* and the more radical ascetic, reclusive, meditative way of the *āraññavāsī*, but these modalities do not consistently crystallize into groupings of monks that are exclusively one or the other.

The reasons for the leaders of the Thammayut sect's developing mainstream orientations have a great deal to do with their political connections and weight from the time of its founder. By 1851, when Prince Mongkut's service as a monk concluded, he had enlisted, besides Wat Bovonniwet, his seat, five other *wats* in and around the capital to serve as the centers of Thammayut teaching.[16] Although he took no punitive action against the Mahānikāi and was careful not to cause sectarian conflict while he was king, he clearly acted as the royal patron of the sect he founded. It is not surprising that in the first years of his occupation of the throne he founded four new Thammayut monasteries in Bangkok-Thonburī, and appointed as their abbots and other chief functionaries his best disciples from Wat Bovonniwet.[17]

The Thammayut sect's monasteries, although small in number, have had an obvious weight by virtue of their orthodoxy and dynamic performance and the royal support they enjoyed. Although during Mongkut's reign the Thammayut sect was only a branch of the Central division (*khana*) of the *saṅgha*, the other two being the Southern and Northern, yet the connection of the sect with royalty was established beyond doubt. Mongkut's appointment of the prince-abbot of Wat Bovonniwet as the supreme patriarch began the double tradition as far as possible of selecting members of the royal family as supreme patriarchs of the *saṅgha*, and of reserving the patriarch's position to monks of the Thammayut sect. And King Chulalongkorn clearly wished, though he was conscious of his role of patron of the entire *saṅgha* and therefore of both sects, to follow the precedents set by his father with regard to the abbotship of Wat Bovonniwet, the headship of the Thammayut sect, and the patriarchship of the entire *saṅgha*.[18]

In 1910, Prince Wachirayān, abbot of Wat Bovonniwet and head of the Thammayut sect,[19] was appointed supreme patriarch. He held office for twelve years. The next and last patriarch (up to the present) with royal connections was Phra Vajraranavongse, again abbot of Wat Bovonniwet; he was appointed in 1945.

Now there was a conspicuous advantage about the location and the overall organization of the Thammayut monasteries that has in the past, and still does in the present, enabled the sect to be an effective actor in *saṅgha* politics on the national stage. It was a sect with its principal base in the capital, a base that was as narrow as it was influential. Unlike the loosely related and independently founded *wat* of the established Mahānikāi sect, the majority of the Thammayut *wat* were founded either by monarchy or nobility and, in the early decades at least, the abbots and principal monks of these new houses were selected from among the circle of the founder's disciples. Thus the Thammayut sect has always maintained a much tighter network than the Mahānikāi sect with its decentralized structure of numerous and autonomous *wat*; it has also maintained stricter disciplinary standards and a greater unity as a pressure group than the much larger, looser, and discordant Mahānikāi sect.

The sectarian rivalries that surfaced after the promulgation of the 1941 Saṅgha Act and have continued to the present day show the strengths and weaknesses of both sides. This act was intended to liberalize the ecclesiastical organization and bring it in line with the country's political system, which had been democratized after the so-called revolution of 1932. Thus under the provisions of the 1941 act, the *saṅgha*, in imitation of the Assembly of People's Representatives and the cabinet system, would also be administered by an elected Ecclesiastical Assembly and an Ecclesiastical Cabinet under the headship of the supreme patriarch appointed by the king.

This constitution proved to be a recipe for competition between the Mahānikāi and Thammayut sects for the cabinet ministerial and deputy-ministerial posts. The division of spoils was resolved as an equal representation of members of the two sects on the cabinet – a formula that confirmed the political strength of the Thammayut sect, which was (and is) in numbers a minority sect.[20] And as I have described elsewhere,[21] it is in this context of rivalries and tensions that a struggle crystallized between two ambitious monks, Phra Phimolatham, abbot of Wat Mahāthāt and ecclesiastical minister of the interior, and Somdet Phrama-hāwīrawong, abbot of the Wat Makut (of Thammayut affiliation) and ecclesiastical prime minister, in which the latter emerged as the victor and subsequently became the supreme patriarch.

The discord in the *saṅgha* gave the opportunity for Prime Minister Sarit to

## Sectarianism and the sponsorship of meditation

intervene, with fateful consequences. Phra Phimolatham was forcibly disrobed and incarcerated, and the Saṅgha Act of 1963 was promulgated, replacing the previous democratic constitution with an authoritarian one that concentrated power in the office of the supreme patriarch and his advisory Council of Elders (Mahāthērasamākhom). This constitution has in turn generated protests and dissatisfaction among the majority of younger monks particularly of the Mahānikāi sect.

Phra Phimolatham's fate at the hands of the authoritarian Prime Minister Sarit and his military colleagues had a great deal to do with his sponsorship of a program to disseminate and popularize meditation throughout the country among both monks and laity. Phra Phimolatham's propagation of *vipassanā* meditation involved not so much the setting up of forest hermitages populated by monks who had retreated into reclusive contemplation as the enlisting of numerous urban and village *wat* to teach meditation not only to monks and nuns but also, and perhaps more importantly, to pious laymen of all ages and occupations.[22]

In the next section, I shall describe the Phimolatham meditation drive in some detail as illustrating a style of propagation stemming from the Mahānikāi sect. Let the following excerpt serve as an interpretive framework for that description:

We can now surmise why this popular program and the influence wielded by the monk sponsoring it might have been construed as a political threat by Sarit and his military colleagues. It is clear that the program served as a basis for marshaling the support and loyalty of several monks and laymen. Most importantly, that *political* power was grounded theoretically in a monk's *spiritual* excellence and *religious* achievement. This source and basis of power were inaccessible to lay politicians and soldiers whose power rested on the control of physical force. Insofar as there exist mechanisms within the *saṅgha* for generating a collective support in society that can be claimed to be independent of and immune to naked political power, the political authority will seek to curb them. This is indeed why Sarit would and did try to taint Phimolatham's activities as "politically subversive"; and this is indeed why a seemingly religious project for the revitalization of religion could be branded as a "political" attempt to amass power dangerous to the regime.

But when the *saṅgha* lends its religious weight to the championing of a political program that legitimates the political authority and seeks to strengthen it further, then, of course, the political authority is likely to appreciate and reward the *saṅgha*'s spiritual excellence.[23]

This has been the case with the Thammatyūt program, which consisted of monks actively participating in the promotion of community welfare and national development. And it is now the case with the forest meditation teachers, whose radiation of spiritual virtues can be tapped and harnessed to the legitimation of established political power.

# 12

# The Mahānikāi sect's propagation
# of lay meditation

The lay popular religiosity of the seventies as observed in Bangkok showed, among others, two contrapuntal interests and activities. One was the general interest, especially among the middle class and educated urban categories (and among them, especially the elderly and the retired) in the practice of meditation. Instruction was taken from monk, sometimes lay, teachers, and collective sittings were held in the halls of *wat* at set times, especially on *wanphra* and Sundays. In a general sense, this show of interest in meditation has intensified in recent years with the spread of literacy and education, with the translation into the local language of Pali texts, and with the accompanying realization that meditational exercises are not the sole province of the monk. In a sense, then, when increasing numbers of laymen observe the eight or ten precepts on *wanphra*, and congregate at *wat* for meditational sittings, the layman–monk distinction as portraying totally different regimes and styles of life is blurred. Nevertheless, there is a striking contrast between the forest ascetic monk totally devoted to meditation and the search for liberation on the one hand, and on the other hand the educated informed layman practicing occasional meditation to lend him some tranquility and detachment from the cares, stresses, and involvements of a layman's life in the world.

At first sight, the lay interest in meditation seems to contradict the widespread lay interest in the traffic in and possession of amulets, which are believed to possess efficacious life-giving and life-protecting powers that have been transferred to and objectified in them by the world-transcending meditation masters and forest saints. However, this seeming contradiction is softened, once we realize that the urge to possess the objectified charismatic powers of the forest saint springs from the same admiration and respect that informs the lay admiration of the saint's exemplary life. The forest acharns are in a real sense *illuminates*, men who have been touched by the transcendental, men who on that account achieve a pneumatic leadership, and, as inspired teachers, make accessible to the masses some of the philosophical truths and efficacious practices of the Buddhist quest for liberation. This in fact becomes part of their mission: not to be the spiritual leader of the community as a scholar-monk, the student of *abhidhamma*, but as the exemplary illuminate whose social function inevitably is to make accessible to the masses the great mystical virtues, thereby giving their mundane lives an infusion of energy. Viewed from this perspective, the simultaneous interest of the laity in meditational exercises and in the amulets blessed by the forest teachers is not incongruous, though of course many more laity participate in the latter cult than evince interest in meditation. The cult of the amulets itself is embedded in the lay ethic of gift giving (*dāna*) and merit making with respect to the *saṅgha*.

Now, I do not want to give the impression that the tradition of meditation represented by the forest teachers of Northeastern and Northern Thailand is either the main tradition or the oldest tradition of meditation from the point of view of the laity and *saṅgha*. Besides that represented by the forest teachers, there are other traditions, the best known of which is that practiced and disseminated by some of the famous urban monasteries of the capital city and provincial towns. (To be counted with them are some famous village monasteries that are not in the forest-hermitage tradition.) Although it is not an aim of this book to provide a full picture of all the schools and traditions of meditational teaching and practice in Thailand, yet it is necessary to give some sense of the general interest, among sections of the *saṅgha* and laity, in meditation, in order to explain why the forest teachers are in the limelight today.

All the urban and village monasteries of the established *saṅgha* are engaged in the performance of various rites and recitations; most of them devote themselves to "study" in the sense of preparing monks and novices for *naktham* examinations, and some of them also maintain schools for the teaching of Pali. If the general run of *wat* have these as their main orientations, some among them have also shown a special interest in the practice of meditation, firstly for the ordained monks and novices and secondarily for interested laymen.

Thus out of some 25,000 *wat* in Thailand in 1969,[1] only a small fraction either specialize in meditation or teach it. Indeed, while the teaching of *Dhamma* is a recognized activity of most *wat*, the teaching and practice of meditation is a special voluntary activity of an individual monk or a small circle of monks, who attract ordained students from their own and other *wat*, and also lay disciples from the general public. All urban monasteries are divided into residential sections (*khana*), each in the charge of a senior monk (*čaokhana*), and the meditation teacher and his disciples tend to be grouped in a section of their own. The national monastic centers, such as Wat Mahāthāt (of Mahānikāi affiliation) and Wat Bovonniwet (of Thammayut affiliation), may conduct a variety of educational and ritual activities. The propagation of meditation may be only one of these activities and is usually associated with some famous teacher-monk like Phra Thepsiddhimuni at Wat Mahāthāt (who was a pupil of and took over the propagation of meditation from Phra Phimolatham) or the present abbot of Wat Bovonniwet, Somdet Phrasangwan.

# The hagiography of a Buddhist saint

Aside from these national centers, there are some well-known urban monasteries that, while engaged in a spectrum of activities, are primarily known as centers that have specialized in meditation: Well-known examples are Wat Pāknām in Thonburī (which was particularly famous during the time of Čaokhun Maṅgaladebamuni, now dead) and Wat Pleng, also in Thonburī. But because the practice and dissemination of meditation in these urban *wat* is linked to particular masters, who live and teach there, the reputation of these *wat* as meditation centers wanes with their death. A case in point is Wat Rakhang, located in Thonburī. It previously had a resident Burmese monk who had many meditation students, including the two monks (Phra Phimolatham and Phra Thepsiddhimuni) who would later propagate meditation from Wat Mahāthāt on a countrywide scale. But after his death it began to concentrate on *Abhidhamma* studies, which now became the interest of some of its resident scholar-monks.

A scrutiny of the meditational activities of Wat Pāknām and Wat Pleng in the late 1970s – and of Wat Mahāthāt, the largest and most influential monastery of the Mahānikāi sect – indicates that the teaching imparted by the teacher to his disciples is not systematic or intense and that the practice of meditation by the disciples is not particularly absorbing and time consuming.[2] As a matter of fact, as will become clear in our account of the propagation of meditation by Wat Mahāthāt, some of the urban meditation teachers are much more involved with the propagation of meditation to the laity, as part and parcel of a drive to extend and intensify their participation in the Buddhist religion (*sāsana*). The participation sessions (which include sermons and chants) are an integral component of this evangelism. Such popularization also enables the scholar-monk to gain prestige, renown, and access to mass media like radio and television.

## Wat Mahāthāt in the early 1970s as a center of propagation of meditation to the public

Wat Mahāthāt, the largest monastery in the country, had in the early 1970s during the rains retreat some 260 resident monks, 80 novices, and several "temple boys" (*dekwat*) who were attending the secular schools in the capital. On its grounds is situated a monks' university – Mahāčulālongkāun – which is attended by pupils from other *wat* as well.[3] While religious and secular teaching constitutes the most conspicuous activity of the *wat*, it is also the scene of many others, ranging from astrology to meditation.

In the late 1950s and early 1960s, the propagation of meditation was perhaps the *wat*'s most advertised task, and the enthusiast who planned and implemented it with missionary zeal was its abbot, Phra Phimolatham, who also held the powerful position of "minister of the interior" in the *saṅgha*'s Ecclesiastical Cabinet (Khana Sangkhamontrī). Phra Phimolatham's dissemination program was ambitious and countrywide: He was able to stimulate "branch" monasteries

## Mahānikāi sect's propagation of lay meditation

in Bangkok, the Central Plain, and then the Northern and Northeastern provinces to propagate and popularize meditation, not only among the ordained monks and novices but also among the laity. A central tenet in the "Burmese" system of insight meditation he espoused was that laymen could learn and practice it after a fairly brief, intensive period of training. This large meditation drive, which spread like a wave, enlisting lay enthusiasm, had striking religio-political ramifications and consequences, which were described in the preceding chapter, and which are not unrelated to the "politics" of the contemporary highlighting of, and enthusiasm for, the Northeastern forest meditation teachers and their hermitages. Wat Mahāthāt's meditation program in the 1970s was a much-diminished remnant of an earlier, vigorous movement and the present meditation teacher, Phra Thepsiddhimuni, is the successor to Phra Phimolatham. Although less illustrious in that he is neither the abbot nor a member of the Supreme Council of Elders, he however propagates meditation in a manner that owes something to the campaign style of his master and sponsor.

Around 1953–4, the residential section (*khana*) 5 at Wat Mahāthāt became the center of propagation. Many meditation cubicles were built around the *bōt*, and a fund for financing the dissemination of meditation was started. By 1955, the same year in which Phra Phimolatham was victimized by the political authorities, numerous *wat* throughout the country had become satellite propagation centers under the direction of Wat Mahāthāt. One informant, a high-ranking titled monk at the same *wat*, estimated that more than 100 *wat* had participated and that, although both monks and laity were disciples, the laity predominated, because meditation spoke directly to their interest in "calming their minds" to offset the pressures of daily life. My informant recalled some ten *wat* as important points of propagation: Wat Vivekāśrama in the town of Chonburī, south of Bangkok; Wat Jalapradāna, just outside Bangkok in Nonthaburī Province; Wat Mūēang Man in the Northern capital of Chiengmai; Wat Phrabāttākphā in the Northern town of Lamphūn; Wat Nāūbāūlūang in Sanpātāung, also in the North; Wat Thawkot in the Southern capital of Nagara Śrī Dharmarāja; and Wat Pā in Ubon and Wat Phra Narāimahārāt in Khorāt, both located in the Northeast. Within Bangkok city itself a number of *wat* were enlisted, particularly Wat Parināyok and Wat Thungsāthit. It is noteworthy that this incomplete list nevertheless mentions *wat* located in the major regions of the country as well as in the capital city.

In the 1970s, some twenty years after the fall of Phra Phimolatham, a few of these monasteries remained as part of the meditation program propagated from Wat Mahāthāt under the direction of Phra Thepsiddhimuni. Outside Bangkok, three formerly important centers were still conducting meditation teaching for monks, nuns, and the laity – Wat Vivekāśrama, Wat Jalapradāna, and Wat Mūēang Man.[4] Before dealing with Phra Thepsiddhimuni's activities in Bangkok, let me describe the activities of Wat Mūēang Man as a case illustration of the meditative tradition popularized by Phra Phimolatham.

# The hagiography of a Buddhist saint

## An urban meditation *wat* in the Phra Phimolatham tradition

Wat Mūēang Man, situated in the city of Chiengmai, was considered to be one of the best-known centers of meditation instruction established under Phra Phimolatham's inspiration. In October 1971 when I visited it, it was still actively engaged in this activity, and I shall describe the abbot, his teaching techniques, and the organization he had established in some detail to illustrate the pattern of instruction and the foci of interest that were associated with the Phra Phimolatham movement. The sketch should be compared with that given of Acharn Maha Boowa's forest hermitage.

Phrakhrū Phiphat Ganavipāla, the abbot and meditation teacher, was born in Hāut District in Chiengmai Province in 1923 and ordained novice at twelve years of age and monk at twenty-one. As a novice, he was sent to Wat Chaiphrakīat in Chiengmai city. He passed the lowest grade of the *Dhamma* examination (*Naktham trī*) and failed the first Pali examination. He is thus no scholar.

After serving as a monk for two lent seasons, he was recalled to his village *wat* to replace the abbot, who had died, leaving no successor. (At this time, the present regulation that a monk can become abbot only after five years of service had not been passed.) He was the only monk in the *wat*, but there were two novices, and he decided that as soon as the first novice was ordained monk, he would leave him in charge and go into the forest to meditate. He had read some books on meditation, but he had no teacher. And he was in due course able to fulfill his desire: He did go by himself to a cave in Thamthāūng forest – a historic cave that had been previously occupied by forest monks and had portions of scriptures written in Tai Yuan on the walls – and meditated during one rains retreat.

However, word was sent to him from Wat Mūēang Man in the big city, offering him the abbotship. At the same time as he became abbot, he heard about Phra Phimolatham's effort to set up meditation centers throughout the country and that interested monks from various provinces were visiting Wat Mahāthāt to undergo training. So in 1953 he went down to Bangkok for a lent season; on his return to Chiengmai he set up a meditation center, Wat Mūēang Man, which was officially opened by Phra Phimolatham.

Phrakhrū Phiphat then decided to go to Burma for further training in meditation. The connection with Burma had already been made by Phra Phimolatham, who had already invited two Burmese monks (Asapha and Sathimmajotika) to teach meditation in Bangkok. Phrakhrū Phiphat spent two years and seven months in Rangoon studying *vipassanā* meditation with Mahasi Sayadaw and *Dhamma* (*pariyatti*) with U-āchariya.

On his return to Chiengmai, his meditation program got under way with an increased number of disciples. In two successive years (1963–4) he built a new wing in his *wat* with sixteen rooms for resident meditators; the money was given by lay donors. In late October 1971, the inmates of Wat Mūēang Man consisted

## Mahānikāi sect's propagation of lay meditation

of 16 regular monks, 6 "temporary" monks,[5] 43 novices, 11 nuns (*māē chī*), and 19 temple boys. All persons who sought to be ordained in the *wat* as monks or novices were subject to a seven-day meditation course; thereafter, each initiate could decide whether he wanted to continue with meditational training or devote himself to religious studies (*pariyattitham*).

All 8 candidates who presented themselves for ordination before lent and intended to be "temporary monks" were given during the three-month rains retreat one month's intensive training in meditation together with their religious studies. Of the 16 regular monks in the *wat*, 10 were engaged in practicing *vipassanā*, whereas the remaining 6 were *pariyatti* scholars. Only 3 of the 43 novices chose the path of meditation. The rest were students in the monastic school.

There were 11 resident nuns, of whom 2 were engaged in meditation practice. Phrakhrū Phiphat attracted some foreign nuns, who had first to undergo training in meditation before being initiated as nuns. Thai women were also allowed to be initiated. Because "nuns" are a "peripheral" category of *wat* inmates[6] – in that they are normally allocated their living quarters away from the monks' residences in space that is technically associated with the laity (*kharāwāt*) and not the religious and that is also where the monastic kitchen is situated – and yet are, wherever they are found, some of the most assiduous practitioners of meditation, it is appropriate to say a word or two about their "initiation." Before nuns are allowed to reside in a *wat*, they must get the permission of their parents or husbands. The initiation rite (*būat chī*) consists of the candidate first having her head shaved and presenting herself before the abbot dressed in colored lay clothes. She asks to be accepted by reciting a Pali passage, the abbot chants "the three refuges" with the candidate repeating after him, and then he gives her "the eight precepts" that she will always observe. At the conclusion of the rite, she changes into white clothes,[7] which together with her shorn head mark her as a nun.

The abbot claimed that over the years he has had many foreign disciples, from other Asian countries like Sri Lanka and from Australia and England. He also allows monks from other *wat*, and lay disciples, to come to his *wat* for short periods of time. He estimated that in the previous year he had permitted about fifty such persons.

The abbot said that he teaches the Burmese system of meditation: One form consists of "the rising and falling of breathing in a sitting posture" (which of course is a variation on the classical *ānāpānasati*); the other is the walking technique, which he described as consisting of six stages.

At the beginning of the training, the abbot gives his pupils collective instruction on the sitting postures, walking technique, etc. After this, every pupil practices by himself or herself in his or her room. The monks and nuns are housed in separate wings. Each room has a bed, space along one end for use as a meditation walk, and a toilet. Each pupil is expected to report daily, except on *wanphra*, to the abbot and talk about his or her progress: The abbot himself visits each pupil's room for the dialogue. There is only one other occasion when the abbot addresses his pupils as a collectivity. This is on the day of shaving the head before *wanphra*, when the abbot talks on general matters and gives them admonitions. It seems such talks do not exceed an hour and could be shorter. The abbot expects his resident pupils to practice meditation both in the morning and in the evening, preferably soon after rising in the morning and completing ablutions and before going to bed at night.

During the early stages of their practice, the abbot allows his monk-pupils to go on almsrounds. But once they reach higher stages of concentration, he discourages them from going outside for almsrounds, for conducting ritual, or to the market. The advanced pupil may stretch his legs inside the *wat* compound and is fed daily from food cooked in the *wat* kitchen – a special fund for this purpose exists – or from food brought by the laity as offerings on every *wanphra*, on festive days, and when cremation rites are performed in the *wat*.

But when a pupil has been judged by the abbot to have reached the eleventh stage and upward he is allowed to go outside the *wat* freely, for now he is not easily distracted by things and events of the world. This system of regulating the physical movements and social contacts of the disciple according to his progress was, the abbot said, a distinctive feature of the Burmese system of meditation, which was adopted by Phra Phimolatham at Wat Mahāthāt.

When asked whether he permitted his pupils to read books, the abbot said that he permitted no books, not even books on the subject of meditation. Books provide "theoretical knowledge" and consulting them interferes with practice. Like a patient, the pupil should take the medicine that is given him, and there is no need to teach him how to make the medicine or trace the symptoms and course of a disease. The abbot, on further probing on my part, held that a *bhikkhu* who is dedicated to reaching his own salvation and is practicing in solitude does not require the theoretical knowledge of books. But *pariyatti* learning has its uses for monks who want to teach *Dhamma* to other people; it is also useful for the intellectual conceptualization of experience, even meditative experience. He concluded that for a *bhikkhu* dedicated to the practice of *vipassanā*, practice (*paṭipatti*) is more valuable than study (*pariyatti*); the former is gold and the latter silver. For instance, said the abbot, Khrūbā Sīwichai, Northern Thailand's heroic monk in the early decades of this century, who built the road to Doi Sutep, had no learning but he was an adept at meditation.[8] Ideally, of course, the abbot concluded, it is good for a *bhikkhu* to be accomplished in both pursuits.

Although Wat Mūēang Man pursues the traditional activities of a city *wat*, the abbot's special interest in teaching meditation has colored them. I have already referred to the abbot's discouraging of monks immersed in meditation from officiating at merit-making ceremonies in lay homes. Northern Thai *wat* tradition-ally participated in the Bāūk Fai festivals, at which balloons were sent up and a fireworks competition was held by firing rockets with tails. Many monks participated in the making of the rockets, and the launching pads were often made at the edge of *wat* compounds adjoining fields. Abbot Phiphat said that he did not permit monks in his *wat* to participate in *bāūk fai* at New Year and other festivities.[9]

The abbot has not himself founded other meditation centers, but he claimed that some of his disciples have done so. He cited Wat Tamuangon in Sankampāēng District and Wat Thamthāūng in Čāūmthāūng District in Chiengmai Province as examples.

In the light of this sketch, we can highlight some of the similarities and differences between the regular and established village and urban *wat*, which under the inspiration of the Phra Phimolatham drive became centers for meditation instruction,[10] and the forest hermitages, which have been established according to the *dhūtaṅga* tradition of Acharn Mun. Wat Mūēang Man, described here, and Wat Pā Bān Tāt will serve as our main case studies, one exemplifying the city *wat* and the other the forest hermitage.

The city *wat* has the usual distribution of monks, novices, and nuns; only a minority of the novices and some of the monks will be participants in the meditative vocation, whereas the rest will be oriented toward study and the conduct of merit-making rites. The forest hermitage is likely to have more monks than novices, and all the inmates are expected to devote themselves to meditation. The city *wat* has short-term disciples, and is likely to be host to nuns and elderly laymen wishing to subject themselves to brief periods of meditative contemplation; the forest hermitage sees itself more as a community of professionals, which is willing to include the laity in devotional and meditational sittings only on *wanphra* or special festive days. The city *wat* is more interested than the forest hermitage in directly disseminating meditation to the laity as part of the laity's everyday morality and practice, and to make an impact on it as its teacher: The forest hermitage's famous meditation adepts and teachers are likely to be treated by pious laity as exemplary illuminates radiating mystical virtues, although they too become famous for their teachings.

As regards the theory and technology of meditation, although the protagonists and actors themselves assert they are following the "Burmese system" (of Mahasi Sayadaw) and/or the "*dhūtaṅga* tradition" (of Acharn Mun), it is not a distortion to say that these variant traditions recognizably stem from classical Theravāda precedents like the *Satipatthāna Sutta* and the *Visuddhimagga*. It is, however, interesting to note that the Burmese tradition – focused on urban monasteries constrained by the noise, temptations, and turmoil of city life – has sought to confine and regulate the physical movement of its disciples, whereas the forest-monks, keeping social contacts to a minimum, are free to disperse themselves in the surrounding forest. Whereas most inmates of both city *wat* and forest hermitage seem to be conscious of a distinction, and even an incompatibility,

## The hagiography of a Buddhist saint

between study (interpreted as the study of *Dhamma* and Pali) and practice (interpreted as meditational exercises), it is the city *wat* that experiences this contrast more directly and acutely as a split in the interest and activity of its ordained inmates.

### Phra Thepsiddhimuni's activities

We have seen that Phra Thepsiddhimuni took over from Phra Phimolatham at Wat Mahāthāt. Within Bangkok itself, Wat Parināyok and Wat Thungsāthit, important units in the old network, were now parts of Thepsiddhimuni's network, in that he visited them periodically to teach monks and the laity.

Phra Thepsiddhimuni's organization at Wat Mahāthāt for the propagation of meditation was quite modest in 1971. *Khana* 5 continued as the propagation center, of which he was head. There were two assistant teachers of meditation, one an elderly monk 71 years old, and the other 36 years old, both of North Thai origin. They had both studied under Thepsiddhimuni. There were in the *khana* five other monks and four novices (*sāmaṇera*): The latter especially acted as receptionists and ushers for visitors to the meditation center, each serving for two months according to a roster. The reception room had pamphlets in English and Thai on meditation, and two rooms were set apart for meditation practice for the *khana* residents and other individual pupils, both lay and ordained. The novices in *Khana* 5 went on almsrounds each morning; but the big meal of the day before noon was provided daily by pious laymen for all the section members. The novices whom I talked to informed me that their *khana* was considered well-off: Their teacher was famous, and he received ample gifts in kind and money, part of which he dispensed to his protégés. One final point to note is that, although Phra Thepsiddhimuni's organization at Wat Mahāthāt was modest, there were similar modest dissemination units established in the "branch" monasteries. It is this network of centers that helped implement a coordinated program and scheduled the teacher's visits.

A twenty-year-old monk who was a member of Phra Thepsiddhimuni's center at Wat Mahāthāt claimed that the teacher had in all about 300 monks, 50 novices, and 650 laymen (of whom 450 were estimated to be females) as his disciples in the various participating *wat*. Three features should be noted about Wat Mahāthāt's network for the propagation of meditation. Firstly, what I have called "branch" monasteries were not founded by the "missionary" teachers Phimolatham and his successor. They were already in existence and became "associates" in the program under the persuasion of Phimolatham, who was an eminent, prestigious, titled monk. (By comparison, the "branch" monasteries of the forest *acharns* are their own or their disciples' foundations.) Secondly, all these centers of propagation were the regular type of urban monasteries, so different in architecture, numbers of residents, activities, and orientation from the forest hermitages of the Northeastern *acharns*. Thirdly, the member units of the Mahāthāt network all belonged and belong to the Mahānikāi sect, whereas the majority of the forest institutions we are studying are of Thammayut affiliation.

These differences receive an interesting twist from the fact that Phra Phimolatham is himself a Northeasterner from Khon Kāen, and so is his successor, Phra Thepsiddhimuni. I have elsewhere discussed the weighty representation of Northeasterners in the *sangha* and the significance of their presence in the country's capital.[11] Phra Phimolatham learned his system of insight meditation first from a Burmese monk who resided at Wat Rakhang and subsequently from the famous Burmese teacher, Mahasi Sayadaw; he sponsored Phra Thepsiddhimuni's learning of meditation at Wat Rakhang and his subsequent journey to Burma. One of Thepsiddhimuni's teachers in Burma, Asaphathera, was now residing in Thailand at Wat Vivekāśrama in Chonburi. Thepsiddhimuni's status as a celebrity was realized when he went to London to establish the Buddhapadīpa monastery there and installed his student, Phra Sobhuna, as a teacher of meditation.[12]

Phra Thepsiddhimuni is a very busy and active propagandist, but, paradoxically, this show of energy makes it difficult to assess the "effectiveness" of his program. The difficulty arises from the fact that his constituency is both clerical and lay without preference. Moreover, he visits many associate monasteries, delivering sermons and leading meditation sittings for both monks and the laity, and, on top of this, actively broadcasts over the radio and appears in television programs. Such dissipation of his energies may not be conducive to cultivating a systematic meditation regime of the type the forest meditation teachers are able to do in their hermitages. But, on the other hand, his traveling-salesman style may be appropriate for spreading meditation to the laity at large in the fashion of a "popular mysticism," so to say.

Some suggestion of the busy life Thepsiddhimuni leads is conveyed in this schedule of activities that he was reported to be following on a particular *wanphra* by one of his novice assistants. "The *čaokhun* (monks who have titles of *phra rātchakhana* status and above are addressed and referred to by this honorific) will be out all day preaching, lecturing, and teaching meditation. He starts with a radio broadcast in the morning, then teaches meditation at the *Thammawičai* center at Wat Mahāthāt. After lunch, at which he will meet some lay donors, he will again give a sermon and lead a meditation sitting at Wat Chanasongkhrām. From there, he will in succession visit these other *wat* in the city doing the same – Wat Makkasan first, then Wat Parināyok (a branch *wat* where he will also hold dialogues with the resident practitioners and check on their progress), then Wat Prachalabentham. His last stop is at Wat Chansamosaun at Bānglamphū from 8 to 9 p.m. Then he will return here to sleep. He pursues an active program on Sundays, too: He makes the morning broadcast, which is followed by collective meditation sitting at Wat Mahāthāt."

# The hagiography of a Buddhist saint

Let me now reproduce from my field notes some features of two such sessions conducted principally for the laity – one witnessed in 1971 and the other in 1978.

1. On the morning of Sunday, December 12, 1971, I arrived at the Meditation Hall of Wat Mahāthāt. The day's program of meditation sittings and lectures was posted outside: Phra Thepsiddhimuni would teach the practice of *vipassanā* meditation from 9 to 11 a.m. and 1 to 2 p.m.; from 2 to 5 p.m. there were to follow three lectures by other monks, one being on "the wisdom deriving from *vipassanā* meditation," another on "Thammathūt (missionary) work in England," and so on.

I attended part of the meditation sitting. The room was large and had comfortable armchairs; already by 9:15 a.m. there were some 78 persons practicing meditation in the sitting posture. Virtually all of them were elderly (there were a few young women in attendance), and the women predominated, amounting to 59 of the sitters. All the meditators, both men and women, were in Western clothes; they looked like "retired" educated, middle-class folk. In another quarter-hour, the sitters had increased to about 100, with the women conspicuously in the majority.

Then Phra Thepsiddhimuni appeared on the stage. He lit the candles at the Buddha altar and led the congregation in reciting some chants. The sermon followed: It was an impressive performance; it was delivered with a low-voiced, soothing fluency. At its conclusion, the congregation resumed its meditation sitting.

In this example, I want to underscore the fact that the meditation teaching was addressed solely to a lay audience, which was orderly, urban, educated, and of middle-class status, and that this same retired laity of women and men usually comprised most of the worshipers at Wat Mahāthāt during the sabbath (*wanphra*) rites. Many of them could be identified as *upāsaka* and *upāsikā* who during *sabbath* days and during the monks' rains retreat (*vassa*) frequently observed the eight or ten precepts. Lastly, such pious lay practices also fitted in well with the ethic of meritorious gift giving (*dāna*), as illustrated by the facts that inside this same meditation hall was a large blackboard on which were written 282 names of persons who had contributed over 5,000 *baht* ($250) each to the Mahāčulālong-kāūn Monks' University Fund (*mūnnithi*) and that outside it stood another prominent board with the names of 225 donors of over 1,000 *baht* each.

2. When I visited Wat Mahāthāt on a *wanphra* in August 1978, I found that Phra Thepsiddhimuni's collective meditation sittings for the laity were now held in the new auditorium of the *wat*'s monastic school. (This school normally gives instruction in Pali studies to monks and novices, and part of its regular syllabus was instruction in meditation every afternoon by Phra Thepsiddhimuni and his assistants.)

On every *wanphra* and every Sunday afternoon, Phra Thepsiddhimuni and his assistants instruct the laity in meditation practice. On this particular day, at about 2 p.m. there were about 120 persons immersed in the sitting position, of whom some 80 were women. The elderly predominated among men and women. Phra Thepsiddhimuni had already given them a discourse before lunch, and now from 1 to 3 p.m. his chief assistant, Phrakhrū Palatphanom, was leading the congregation in meditation practice, assisted by another monk (who was given the designation of *lekhā*, scribe), and two novices, all members of Phra Thepsiddhimuni's section. While the laity meditated in the hall, the monks gave instructions over the microphone from an office on the side.

I engaged the *lekhā* in conversation. He had reached Prayōk 5 in his Pali studies.[13] I asked him why laymen studied and practiced meditation, and he said that they wished to attain to *nibbāna*; it was not necessary to don the monk's robe to seek this goal. To the question of what powers derive from meditation, he said that it conferred powers such as invisibility and the assumption of multiple forms at will. These powers had both good and bad implications: If experienced, they are good because they confirm what the Buddha said as being true and thereby stimulate faith, but the bad aspect is that meditators who do not experience them will lose faith and be disheartened.

Because I had recently investigated a cult of healing through meditation (in which the meditation master, a layman, sought to heal patients in collective meditation sittings),[14] I asked the *lekhā* whether illnesses can be cured through meditation. He replied that an adept who has reached *arahant* status can obviously effect cures, but he will not want to do so, because he is on the path to *nibbāna*. A genuine *arahant* would attempt to achieve purity of heart and tranquility. If an *arahant* engages in the show of supranormal powers, it would be only in order to promote the religion. When I asked him about the plausibility of the cult master's claims to heal through meditation, he replied that this cult leader in question practices *samādhi* (concentration), which enables the achievement of peace of mind (*čai sangop*) and that *samādhi* could possibly cure disease by suggestion and hypnosis. *Samādhi*, he said, is a "lower" activity and practice than *samathā*, whereas *vipassanā* is quite different and is concerned with breathing techniques and the control of mental formations.[15]

These remarks help us to appreciate how and why many laymen see in meditational exercises – however imperfectly understood and practiced – some kind of therapeutic virtue, some relief from their personal problems, and even a meaningful channel for their efforts. The following examples of teacher–pupil intercourse might help us to see how the laity, in this case young persons, come to engage in meditation.

Whereas collective meditation sittings and worship are conducted in the large meditation hall, small groups of disciples may come to Thepsiddhimuni's residential section (*Khana* 5) for lessons and sittings with one of his teaching assistants. On November 19, 1971, I visited *Khana* 5 at around 9:20 a.m. to find three young women in conversation with a monk. They were his disciples, and, as their teacher, he would not only instruct them but also "examine" them about their meditation experiences and progress.

At the time of my arrival, he was examining them. One woman said that she was fearful of practicing meditation because she was afraid of seeing ghosts (*phī*). To which the teacher replied that the equivalent of *phī* in the Pali language was *phaya* (*bhaya*), which meant "fear"; so ghosts are really one's own mental images of fear. The second disciple confessed that she was able to practice and concentrate for only ten minutes at a time; she was advised to increase the length of her sittings. The third disciple testified that she could now sit for half an hour at a time: Although she felt pain in her legs at first, it soon passed away and she attained to a mental well-being and peace of mind (*čit sangop*).

Then the teacher led them in a brief meditation practice, which lasted about thirty minutes. They all closed their eyes and crossed their legs in the appropriate sitting posture. The teacher told them to breathe in and out, in and out, and when bodily pain was felt, they should mentally say "I am feeling pain" and consciously observe it. . . . The teacher was clearly instructing his pupils in the elementary exercises of meditation.

After the sitting was over, I gathered this information from the three pupils:

1. One was twenty years old, the daughter of a cloth merchant in Bangkok, and a second-year student of English literature at Thammasāt University (which was located only a few hundred yards from Wat Mahāthāt). This was her third meditation class, and now that the university was in vacation she hoped to come regularly, perhaps every afternoon. When asked how she became interested in meditation, she replied that her grandmother used to study meditation in a hermitage near Khorāt and that she herself was a member of her university's philosophical society, which had visited Wat Mahāthāt's meditation center. This visit had stirred her interest.

2. The second disciple was a fourth-year student of English Literature at Thammasāt University. Her father was a police colonel; he was a Buddhist, but her mother was a Protestant Christian. Her two brothers were Buddhist, whereas she and her sister were Christian. This was her third lesson in meditation. She took a course on the philosophy of India this first semester, in which she was introduced to Buddhist philosophy and meditation. She hoped to attend regularly on a long-term basis. She had practiced meditation for an hour the previous day in her dormitory, and she thought she had seen some ghosts; she felt somewhat afraid because she lived in an old palace that had been converted into a dormitory.

3. The third disciple said she was a story writer. She was twenty-two years old and said that she felt mentally confused and had a poor memory. So her mother, who was connected with the *wat*, especially its Abhidhamma Foundation, had advised her to engage in meditation practice. She had so far come daily for the past week; this was, however, her last lesson; she felt that from now on she could practice by herself at home.

Soon after the three young women had concluded their class, a young monk and a novice arrived for instruction. Their biographical details are interesting, for they were only temporary initiates who will revert to lay status soon – and will therefore carry their meditative experience and interest into lay life.

The monk had been ordained only the previous day. He was twenty-eight years old, had received his M.A. degree in agriculture from a university in the Philippines, and had returned to Thailand eighteen days ago. Before starting to work for Esso, he wanted to make merit for his parents by serving as a monk for fifteen days. His father was a colonel in the Thai army, and his parents already knew Phra Thepsiddhimuni. He therefore wanted to be initiated into meditation. He had had his first lesson in meditation last night, and today's was the second. At the end of his lesson before noon, an attractive female "cousin" of his arrived bearing food for his lunch. She too was a graduate of a Philippines university.

The novice was eighteen years old. He was a high school graduate of Saint John's College, Bangkok, and he had been ordained some six days previously. His parents, who are Buddhists, as well as he himself, wished for his ordination. His father was a merchant, a supporter of the *wat*, and had recommended that he take meditation lessons. He did not know whether he wanted to be ordained a monk later on.

## The hierarchy of lay achievements

I have thus far attempted to convey what the practice of meditation might mean to the contemporary urban Thai laity. Lay persons, according to age, education, capacity, and effort reap different rewards and attain different levels of achievement. Doctrinal Buddhism, while imbuing all human actors with *intentionality*, and while making humans the centerpiece of the cosmological scheme by allowing them the capacity for the complete transcendence of substantiality, also asserts as a fundamental principle that humans are born unequal because their present lives reflect the sum of virtues and demerits of past lives. Nevertheless, they are also given the freedom in their present lives to act positively and uplift themselves.

It is fitting that I now call upon Phra Phimolatham, one of Thailand's most famous propagators of meditation to the laity, to expound the implications of the differential capacities and efforts of human beings. These remarks were made to me in the course of an interview:

The practice of meditation should have meaning and significance for monk and layman alike. The layman can find the time to meditate during weekends and holidays. But like sharpening a knife – it is easier to sharpen it in one intensive effort than by sharpening it for a few moments a day – a layman should achieve a level of meditational experience by an initial intensive effort. Once he has achieved this he can be mindful in anything he does – while writing, or working, or even scolding another person. There are five kinds of energy that must be harnessed in a balanced way. *Sati* (consciousness) is the driver of the carriage; the more of it he has the better. The carriage is pulled by two pairs of horses: *Viriya* (effort), the active principle, is balanced by *samādhi* (concentration), which is passive. *Saddhā* (faith) is paired with *paññā* (wisdom). Too much of the wrong kind of learning or wisdom leads to student revolts, and too much faith leads to ignorance.

*Vipassanā* means the same thing as wisdom (*paññā*), that is, seeing things as they are. For a layman, this wisdom has many uses. One who practices meditation will not be led into corruption while doing his job; he will be aware of his true responsibilities and act accordingly. A road will be built in the cause of national economic development because it is useful for traveling, not because it affords an opportunity to line one's pockets.

A layman who is married and practices meditation sees his wife as a wife, a mother as a mother, not confusing them with divine angels (*thēwadā*). . . .

There are three kinds of eyes – human eyes (*maṁsacakkhu*); eyes of deities (*dibbacakkhu*), which see things far away and in darkness; and the wisdom eye (*paññācakkhu*). The last is the vision of *vipassanā*.

One needs merit (*bun*) to be able to practice *vipassanā*. If a man's store of *bun* is great, he can become an adept in seven days; if he has less, then it takes seven months. Some men don't make it at all for lack of merit.

There are different kinds of humans, or, as the Buddha said, four kinds of horses harnessed to a carriage: The horse that knows where to go by the horseman simply pulling at the reins; the horse at which the horseman points the switch and threatens to prod it to make it go; the horse that actually has to be prodded and punished to make it go; and finally the horse that cannot be made to move at all. It is the human of this last kind who cannot be taught *vipassanā*, and such humans constitute the majority of mankind. However, in society an equilibrium is reached because the minority with wisdom can guide and control the majority. There is the saying that the wise are in number like the horns of a buffalo and the ignorant like its hairs.

Or, to put it differently, it is said that there are three groups of human beings: The *uparimakāya* group are the upper part, the neck and head of the body; the *majjhimakāya* are the middle, from neck to waist; and the *heṭṭhimakāya* are the lower, from waist to legs. The three groups must be educated accordingly. All three are necessary. But if we educate them all to be heads, the body will not be able to walk.

Phra Phimolatham's pithy comments echo the assertion of the classical texts with which I began this book (Chapter 2) – that there is a hierarchy of human beings according to their capacities and intentional efforts. The path of purification through meditation, he asserts, however, is not open only to the *bhikkhu*; but it may not be appropriate or suitable for all the laity either. But for those of the laity who find a measure of success in practicing it, the fruits of meditation can elevate and make altruistic their conduct in this world.

# 13

# The center–periphery dialectic
## The Mahāthāt and Bovonniwet sponsorship of meditation compared

The mid-fifties were the climactic years of the countrywide sponsorship of meditation by Wat Mahāthāt. It represented an impulsion generated from the capital, which, as the radial center of the country, attempted to spread a religious renewal to the periphery, to the various provinces that were thought to need a revitalization. We have seen that the monk who was at the center of this missionary drive, Phra Phimolatham, was the abbot of the country's largest *wat*. He was a titled monk holding a high position in the ecclesiastical hierarchy, and he incarnated the prestige of the established *saṅgha* in its self-assured authority and superiority over the *wat* distributed throughout the country. Phra Phimolatham was up to a point a scholar-monk, but not eminently or exclusively; he was an adept teacher and propagator of meditation without being a great meditation "master" or a dedicated ascetic and recluse on the path to *arahantship*. He was rather the urbane, eloquent, powerful cleric of the establishment, especially of the Mahānikāi sect – the largest in the country, the sect with which the great body of the nonaristocratic commoner population was affiliated, a sect of varied achievements and worldly attachments.

It is very much in line with this orientation that Phra Phimolatham's meditation drive was (and still is, under the leadership of Phra Thepsiddhimuni) addressed to both monks and the laity alike; in some respects, the latter has been the more important constituency. And it was for this reason that Prime Minister Sarit, aided and abetted by certain Thammayut-sect authorities, could construe it as more than simply "religious," as threateningly "political," in significance.

The efficacy of Phra Phimolatham's drive derived to an important degree from the fact that it is the rural peasant population of the provinces, of which the Northeastern provinces are prominent, that supply the vast majority of the country's monks, including those in the cities. It is also from the ranks of these monks that virtually all titled monks of the *saṅgha* are recruited today. (In Phra Thepsiddhimuni's hands, the Wat Mahāthāt propagation of meditation today is both more circumspect in the care taken to dissociate it from politics and more limited in its spread among the public.)

It is worthwhile, before remarking on and appreciating the contrasting features of the Wat Bovonniwet patronage of the meditation teaching of the forest-monks, to allude to the missionary movements of the sixties and seventies, which immediately succeeded and replaced the Phimolatham effort. I refer here to the *Thammathūt* program of the *sangha*, in which educated monks from the capital were sent to the provinces to spread the *Dhamma* and at the same time to legitimate and stimulate national and community development; and to the *Thammačārik* program, organized by the Department of Public Welfare and implemented among the hill tribes with the help of the monks. These programs have been already analyzed in detail.[1] Here let me allude to the fact that this program, whose initiator was the director of the Department of Religious Affairs, received the approval and legitimating stamp of the elders of the *sangha*, of whom the most prominent ones were of the Mahānikāi sect; moreover, the Mahačulālongkāūn University, run by the Mahānikāi sect and located at Wat Mahāthāt, became the architect of special projects in which its graduate monks participated. The *Thammathūt* movement had reached a low ebb by the beginning of the 1980s; some of the reasons for this relate to sectarian rivalries and also to fears among lay politicians about the "political role" of monks.

In contrast to Phimolatham's dissemination of meditation from the capital city and the chief urban seat of the Mahānikāi sect, the movement that has gradually formed around the Northeastern forest meditation teachers has spread from the periphery of the country to the center. What the center has done through the agency of Wat Bovinniwet – the most prestigious *wat* of the Thammayut sect, a *wat* of royalist connections, that enjoys the confidence of the generals in power – is to recognize, publicize, and incorporate the exemplary achievements and charisma of the forest teachers in their dispersed hermitages, originally held together by their recognition of a discipleship to the sanctified Master, Mun. What enabled this movement from periphery to center is the link between an able propagandist, hagiographer, and forest teacher, Acharn Maha Boowa, and a titled, prestigious monk located in the capital, who enjoys connections with secular authority and power but is genuinely enthusiastic about the dissemination of meditation to an elite congregation, Somdet Phra Yansangvorn.

Compared with Phra Phimolatham's active propagation of a movement from the center outward, Phra Yansangvorn's role is a more passive one of collaborating in the incorporation and legitimation by the center of achievements that had already been realized in the country's faraway provinces. And it is important to note about the forest meditation masters that their primary effort and objective has been to practice meditation as ascetic recluses, that their teaching mission has been first and foremost to their ordained disciples, and that the circles of lay donors and enthusiasts that formed around them were penumbral. Their functioning as fields of merit for lay donorship, their conducting meditation sessions for lay congregations on sabbath days and festivals, their participation in the cult of the amulets – these are not at the core of the orientations of the forest teachers, but have become by the cumulative logic of popular religiosity the main foci of lay worship. Neither the founding of the network of hermitages by the forest-monks nor the cults of the amulets that have formed around them have been construed by the central political and ecclesiastical authorities of contemporary Thailand as politically problematic or a challenge to their authority; rather, as I shall demonstrate in later chapters, the cult of the amulets consists of the tapping of the charisma of the forest saints by the already established political and financial elites and interest groups for the advancement of their own worldly purposes.

A few words now on the circumstances surrounding the decline of the *Thammathūt* movement.[2] I have already commented on the problematic features of this program when it was functioning at full strength in the early seventies.[3] It seemed then that a result of the monks' engagement in development work would be to draw the *sangha*, especially its ecclesiastical hierarchy, into closer relations with the government hierarchy and officials, both at the central and regional levels. Leaving aside the ill-conceived and ill-fitting nature of Thai monks' "civilizing" role among the hill tribes, it seemed, on the one hand, that precisely because the vast majority of Bangkok monks were of rural origin, the plan to send educated energetic young monks on *Thammathūt* work back to their provinces of origin seemed feasible, despite the probable lack of fit between the village and metropolitan perspectives. But, on the other hand, while monks could effectively perform educational and counseling roles as part of their teaching the *Dhamma*, it was questionable whether they were equipped and appropriate to lead and sponsor community-development projects. I cautioned that one should be realistic about the degree to which monks, whose basic preoccupation is the task of ethical study and practice, had the organization and capacity to shoulder countrywide development plans, and I drew attention to a historical precedent, namely the princely *sangharāja* Wachirayān's cooperation in the 1890s with the political authorities in using the provincial *wat* and monks for the extension of secular elementary education in the provinces. He subsequently withdrew from this collaboration because he realized that the *sangha* was becoming overbureau-cratized and involved with government administrative machinery, the load was too heavy for the monastic system to carry, and the monks were not in the long run the most effective transmitters of secular knowledge. (Suksamran, writing after me, was explicitly vocal about his misgivings about the Thai monks' participation in *Thammathūt* and other missionary programs.)[4]

By 1980, the *Thammathūt* effort in its original form – that is, conceived by the authorities, both ecclesiastical and secular, and using educated young monks from the capital's religious universities[5] – was a spent force. Certain persons were hopeful that provincial monks, themselves conceiving and implementing their own *thammathūt* programs, might continue the work with greater chances of success.

Be that as it may, the decline of the *Thammathūt* project was attributed by some informants to the death of Colonel Pin Mutukan, the director general of the Department of Religious Affairs, and its chief architect and governmental sponsor. He had been the chief fund raiser for the project and had pulled all the relevant strings. After his death, the government made a series of some three or four short-term appointments of officials from other ministries to Colonel Pin's post – officials who had no familiarity with the religious affairs department's previous policies and programs, and who by virtue of the turnover could not give continuity and direction to its activities.[6] This period of confusion coincided with the drying up of funds from two foundations – one German and the other American – that had previously financed the projects, especially those initiated by the monks' universities.

Moreover, it appears that sectarian divisiveness has further weakened the *Thammathūt* program. By 1978, the abbot of Wat Čakkrawat, a high-ranking, titled monk of Mahānikāi affiliation, was put in charge of the training of all missionary monks in the country; but the abbot of Wat Bovonniwet, who is of the Thammayut sect, was put in charge of sending missionary monks to foreign countries, a task in which this *wat* has always played a key role. This division of powers on sectarian lines has contributed to the standstill.

These immediate and proximate causes and effects are linked with wider contextual developments. On the one hand, young intellectuals, including those from university circles – circles not unconnected with the left-wing politics manifested in the students' insurrection of 1973 – had commented adversely on what they considered the authoritarian military government's manipulation and exploitation of the *saṅgha* for its own purposes. In particular, the senior titled monks were criticized for collaboration in national development projects that compromised the purity of the *saṅgha*.

In any event, it was not this criticism, but a governmental backlash against the "political" activism of the educated young monks themselves, that has intensified sectarianism. A Young Monks' Movement (*Yuwa Song*) came into being. It was formed primarily by monks of Mahānikāi affiliation attending Mahāčulālongkāun University located on Wat Mahāthāt grounds. These young monks published a journal and some pamphlets criticizing the effeteness and conservatism of the *saṅgha*'s Council of Elders (*Mahāthērasamākhom*). They wanted a return to the *saṅgha*'s democratic constitution, as outlined in the Saṅgha Act of 1941, and the abandonment of the 1963 Saṅgha Act, which created the present authoritarian rule of ossified elders. Moreover, these monks of Mahānikāi affiliation joined the issue of a more democratic organization of the *saṅgha* with the issue of the complete rehabilitation, including the restoration of his titles, of Phra Phimolatham, who had been defrocked by Prime Minister Sarit in 1963. This clearly reopened old sectarian wounds. Political activism among monks – reminiscent of the late 1930s and early 1940s, after the civilian revolution of 1932 – was manifesting itself, and the secular and ecclesiastical authorities' fears were intensified by the sympathy shown by some young monks for the students' insurrectionary cause[7] and by the participation of some young provincial monks in the protests made at the capital by farmers for the remedy of agrarian grievances.[8] There was thus a conjunction of student revolt, agrarian grievances, labor protests, and political activism among a section of the *sangha*.

The growing demands by the younger generations of monks for the reform of the *sangha*'s ecclesiastical organization in a more democratic and representative direction was not, it was claimed by certain leaders of the young monks, popular with the Thammayut sect. According to the Sangha Act of 1962, the membership of the Mahātherasamākhom (the Council of Elders) was equally divided between the two sects, despite the much larger membership of the Mahānikāi. A return to the 1941 act would imply that in the elected Ecclesiastical Assembly at least the Mahānikāi will have a larger representation and a bigger voice (though the competition between the two sects has previously resulted in an equal division of cabinet positions), a prospect not favored by Thammayut monks. It is for this reason that, according to the same leaders, the Thammayut monks hold that it is improper for monks to discuss and debate issues in the manner of parliamentary politicians. This is a tendentious view because the *Vinaya* recommends that monks meet and conduct their affairs in assembly, in which even a junior monk can accuse a senior monk of a violation of disciplinary rules.

## The resurgence of sectarian rivalries

Although the young monks' action was more a plea for greater democracy and a revitalization of *sangha* leadership than a deliberate revival of sectarian rivalry or an attack on the privileged position of the Thammayut sect, yet we must be attuned to certain resonances and reverberations that disclose sectarian tensions. These tensions are germane to our grasping the logic of the Thammayut sect's promotion of the cult of forest saints.

In a certain sense, it is correct to say that the Mahānikāi sect, to which belong the vast majority of *wat* in the country, and which commands the support of the commoner population, is too fragmented and tolerant of variety to project a sharp image. In comparison, the Thammayut is a smaller, more tightly knit, more tightly organized sect, as witnessed by the manner in which its central committee (Khana Kammakān Khana Thammayut) runs its affairs under the direction of the sect's head (*čaokhana yai*). It is also, as we have seen, royalist and has cultivated royalist and aristocratic support; hence it readily lends itself to being seen as conservative, elitist, and hierarchically minded. The Thammayut monks are referred to by critics as "the palace monks." In any case, ever since their founding and the founder's preoccupations with following the "pure" disciplinary customs, the Thammayut sect has sought to instill in its monks a sense of "refinement" in demeanor and conduct, which, combined with its insistence on "separateness" from the Mahānikāi sect on account of its following the purer and more refined customs, can give rise to resentments against its "snobbery." As one wit remarked to me, "Thammayut is like Chulalongkorn University,[9] while Mahānikāi is like Thammasat University" – a remark that those who know the character of these prestigious secular universities will savor. In a subtle way, it has come about that the core strength of the Thammayut sect lies in the Central Plain surrounding the capital; although there are a certain number of Thammayut *wat* established in the Northeast, yet their weight in the sect's affairs has not been prominent. In contrast, whereas the Mahānikāi is more evenhandedly represented, monks of Northeastern origin have played an influential role in its affairs because the Northeast contributes a major portion of the *saṅgha*'s monks.

One informant, who I have strong reasons for not doubting, went so far as to claim that by preference most of the Thammayut monks are recruited from the Central Plain provinces, such as Suphanburī, Rātburī, and Phetburī, and that some of the best-known Thammayut *wat* in Bangkok, such as Wat Rajabopit, are under pressure from their aristocratic lay supporters, a number of whom are of royal origin and have titles of Māŭm Čao, Māŭm Rātchawong, and Māŭm Lŭang, to recruit monks from the said provinces, where their own strength lies. He went so far as to claim that the aristocrats' preferences for monks according to their origins was in this descending order: Central Plain, the South, the North, and, last, the Northeast. Although there are monasteries in the capital that have primarily Northeasterners, such as Wat Noronat and Wat Boromnivas, or primarily Southerners, such as Wat Rajapathigaram and Wat Rajathiwas, yet their lay supporters in Bangkok are commoners from those same regions now residing in the capital, the most prominent among them being merchants.

A conspicuous difference between the small coterie of Thammayut *wat* and the large collection of Mahānikāi *wat* concerns their wealth. One of the most important sources from which urban monasteries derive money with which to support their activities is the staging of cremation rites.[10] By virtue of their royalist, aristocratic, governmental connections – which are therefore attractive to the *nouveaux riches* and socially mobile – certain Thammayut *wat* in Bangkok enjoy a lucrative patronage. They are accused by the other side of building monumental *phra meru* (crematoria) and gilded halls in order to act as the funerary priests of high-ranking and affluent persons. The facts speak for themselves: Wat Thēpsirin is traditionally the cremation site for royals and aristocrats; Wat Somanāth, the top brass of the army; Wat Phra Sīmahāthāt, the air force; Wat Kreuawan, the navy; Wat Trisothathep, the police; and Wat Thāt Thāŭng, affluent and/or high-ranking civilians. They are all Thammayut *wat*, and much of their money is tended by the sect's opulent Mahāmakuṭa Rājavidyālaya Foundation.

The Thammayut sect's finances were further enhanced by its ownership of the Mahāmakut Press, which prints most of the textbooks used in monastic *pariyatti* schools. Because of its publications, it is sometimes accused of controlling the knowledge imparted to the monks and novices.

There are diverse charges which, whether true or false, fuel the sectarian tensions. It is claimed by some that because of the influence wielded by the Thammayut in the membership of the *sangha*'s Council of Elders (Mahāthērasamākhom) and because of its connections with the palace – the king after all is the secular head of the *sangha*, and high *sangha* appointments are given the seal of approval by him – senior monks of Northeastern origin are in noticeable ways discriminated against in the granting of titles and thereby in appointments to the highest positions in the ecclesiastical hierarchy.[11]

Now we come to the interesting question of how, given this alleged Thammayut distaste for Northeastern representation in its highest ranks, the forest meditation teachers of the Northeast are much in vogue and supported and lauded by the highest circles, both royal and clerical. Seemingly discordant facts must be put together. It is a matter much emphasized in Acharn Maha Boowa's biography of Acharn Mun that he was ordained into the Thammayut sect and that the majority of the forest meditation teachers are of the same tradition. It is emphasized that Acharn Mun, despite one or two exceptions, insisted that his disciples be ordained in the Thammayut way.

It seems to be the case that the Thammayut sect is increasingly represented in the Northeast by the forest meditation hermitages, a pattern reinforced by the connections built between Acharn Maha Boowa and the abbot of Wat Bovonniwet in Bangkok in sending candidates to the hermitages from Bangkok, distributing publications, and so on. The monarchy's own dealings with some of the forest saints, most recently the sponsorship of amulets to be blessed by Lūang Pū Wāēn in the North, gives the final seal of patronage and legitimation. Thus we see how the Northeastern monasteries of the forest meditative tradition have moved into the center of Thammayut religious claims, an incorporation that at the same time does not challenge the sect's authority structure and ecclesiastical offices, because the forest monks (*āraññavāsī*) by tradition are excluded from the *sangha*'s system of titles and offices and are outside the *sangha*'s system of examinations.

Now the Northeast is the stronghold of many important titled monks of the Mahānikāi sect. Indeed, as we have seen, Phra Phimolatham's strength and popularity even to this day are evident in that region, and many of the young monks are of the same origin. Moreover, the Mahānikāi support is most powerfully felt in the traditional urban and village monasteries, not in the forest hermitages. In recent times, the rivalries and tensions between the two sects have found expression in the Northeastern provinces of Khon Kāēn and Lōēi; it is commonly known that the provincial ecclesiastical governor of Lōēi is antipathetic to the Thammayut. I was given this example of the dramatization of the rivalry between the sects when they have *wat* in the same village. In a certain village in Tambon Renu of the province of Nakhon Phanom, the Mahānikāi *wat* stages fairs and collects money for the purpose of constructing more imposing buildings (this is the traditional orientation of established village and urban *wat*), whereas the Thammayut *wat* accents its forest traditions and does not concern itself with the conduct of Sunday schools for village children or even lay education in general, which too are traditional orientations of mainstream *wat*. The different monastic orientations are also reflected among the lay supporters, who, as the rivalry takes on schismatic proportions, find themselves pushed into being exclusive supporters of one or the other *wat*. In these developments it is not the case that the *thudong* meditative monks who are truly dedicated to their vocation are embroiling themselves in "politics"; but once government officials and laity of royalist or other preferences take on the role of supporters and sponsors, then the forest-monks, just like the traditional *gāmavāsī* monks, are open to political manipulation and uses that are extraneous to their interests. And when brokers and mediators between the periphery and center appear within their own ranks, the doors are opened to the inflection by, and intrusion of, the interests of the larger context in which the *saṅgha* is embedded.

By the end of 1976, both Mahānikāi and Thammayut were in a position to accuse each other of soiling their hands and to wash their dirty linen in public. On the one hand, there was the "scandal" associated with Phra Kittivuḍḍho, a titled monk who came out of the Wat Mahāthāt stable, preached a "muscular" Buddhism, and saw no demerit in killing communists (who were branded as enemies of country, religion, and king; "incomplete persons"; and more bestial than human). He trained novices and monks to be activists in a special institution founded by him.[12] On the other hand, ex–Prime Minister Thanom Kittikachorn, who after mishandling the student revolution was deposed from the country with two other ruling military figures, had sneaked back into the country in September 1976 and sought sanctuary in Wat Bovonniwet, whose abbot had agreed to ordain him as a monk – an act that, it was whispered, must of necessity have received royal assent. Events such as these, and the attitudes and sentiments they evoke, volatile and multivalent, tell us that they have a great deal to do with the boundaries that separate *saṅgha* from polity, *bhikkhu* from layman (including the king), and the complementary exchanges between them.

In concluding this part of the book, let me underscore these points. The exegesis of the biography of Acharn Mun as an "indexical symbol" has traversed a long distance, beginning with Buddhist hagiographical conventions and concluding with contemporary sectarian politics. The biography has served us as a vehicle for unveiling important aspects of religion as "a form of life," to use Wittgenstein's phrase, in contemporary Thailand. The interpretive task required a full account of the interplay of religion and politics within which the biography, together with the subject of the biography and its author, has a place.

I have also tried to demonstrate that the separate vocations of meditation and "practice" and of books and "learning" are not in the recent history of Thailand – as in the classical past of Sri Lanka, Burma, and Thailand – clear-cut labels, do not produce consistent profiles, and do not always constitute separate sects. The processes of internal differentiation within the Mahānikāi and Thammayut sects, and within the *sangha* as a whole, have interacted with many features to create a complex story that we have attempted to unravel. These features are: the center–periphery relations between the capital (and the central region of Thailand) and the distant provinces with their ethnic, linguistic, and regional differentiations; and the aspirations and interests of a lay populace, divided into segments such as governing urban elites, urban middle-class and mercantile interests, rural folk, and the like.

In this complex story, the modern-day saints and their followings have served as our focal point. In the next part of the book, I begin describing other dimensions of their activities and the further significances these activities have for Thai society and polity.

# PART III

## THE CULT OF AMULETS:
## THE OBJECTIFICATION AND TRANSMISSION
## OF CHARISMA

# 14

# The cult of images and amulets

## The popularity of amulets in Thailand today

"The tourist," Griswold has remarked in an essay on the Buddha image, "who comes to Bangkok and visits the monasteries . . . will see in every *vihāra* and ordination-hall a Buddha image, nearly always larger than life-size and often colossal, occupying the place of honor; and he will see an indefinite number of lesser ones distributed in halls and galleries – often several hundred of them, and in certain monasteries more than a thousand. Frequently he will see people prostrating themselves before an image, offering flowers and incense, and displaying every sign of fervent devotion. If he goes into the National Museum, he will find that there are more Buddha images than works of any other kind on display. If he goes into a private house, he may find a special room set aside for Buddha images . . . (and) . . . they will receive, from time to time, the same sort of homage as in the monasteries."[1] Griswold might have added that the sense of overwhelming ubiquity of Buddha images in Bangkok is further heightened by their presence by the thousands in shops, particularly the "antique shops," that have mushroomed in recent times, in response to the tourist trade. These shops are stacked with Buddhas in stone, wood, and metal; gilded to heighten their luster or broken to lengthen their age; many genuinely old and probably lifted from sacred historic sites, and as many modern and faked to look like the classical rarities. This onrush of images into the shops is not disassociated from the recent pillage in Cambodia and the massive smuggling out of northern Burma. They too are refugees and hostages, just like many men, women, and children, affected by the recent wars in the region.

This remarkable profusion of Buddha images is not the end of the matter. Griswold continues: "Quantities of votive tablets, of metal or terra cotta, stamped with tiny figures of the Buddha in tens, hundreds, or even more, can be seen in museums and private collections. They are often objects of great beauty; yet in most cases they were made not to be seen at all, but in order to be buried away

195

inside a monument, or perhaps inside the arm or body of some colossal statues. The same may even be true, though less often, of bronze images of considerable size, up to almost a metre in height: a few years ago the left arm of the huge Mangalapabitra image at Ayudhya was found to contain a quantity of such bronzes, apparently many of them made for this particular purpose. . . .''

There is still another use of votive tablets: as amulets – not discussed by Griswold – but which must be regarded as a conspicuous feature of popular religion. These amulets, little represented in museums and antique shops for Western tourists, are displayed in heaps in the open bazaars and traditional markets of Bangkok and all provincial cities. Being objects of small dimension, representing in miniature figures or busts of the Buddha, or famous monks, or even famous kings and princes, they are attached to necklaces and chains and worn around the neck by men and women, or carried on their persons, or carefully kept at home.

The Thai term for what I call amulet is *khrūēang rāng khāŭng khlang*, *khāŭng khlang* meaning an object having sacred or supranormal power; *khrūēang rāng* meaning amulet. Frequently, the phrase is abbreviated to *khrūēang rāng*. Such sacralized objects can be of many sorts: Buddha images, medallions or coins (*rīan*) of persons and emblems with imprints, clay tablets with similar imprints, animal and bird shapes, and so on.[2]

These images, votive tablets, and amulets are treated with respect by Buddhists, who often ''worship'' them with palms pressed together (*wai*) and say apologetic words before touching, moving, or wearing them as the case may be; they also frequently propitiate these objects with offerings or purify them by sprinkling sacralized water. The language appropriate to them is the ''royal vocabulary'' (*rājāśabda*), which is spiced with a lexicon of Sanskrit and Khmer words. Amulets are usually strung on a necklace and worn around the neck. It is a rare Thai who wears a single amulet: Most wear several, not exposed but secreted inside the shirt or blouse. It is also not unusual for people to carry some on their person in some other way and also to keep a number in their homes to be cherished, looked at, and asked for protection or good fortune according to need.

Many amulet wearers would usually, when they put the necklace on in the morning or before leaving the house, say a sacred formula (*gāthā*) to the amulet and then using both hands transfer its virtue and power to their own heads. Moreover, in order to replenish the potency of the amulets, wearers would present them for further sacralization by famous monks or holy men, who would touch them with their hands, say words, and sprinkle them with holy water (*tham hai saksit*, meaning to render powerful).

Practically every Thai, whether of Thai, Chinese, Laotian or some other origin, whether of the Buddhist, Moslem, or some other religious affiliation (except perhaps Christian), would like to own an amulet or wear one. Because the most important type of these amulets bears the image of a Buddha or a

# The cult of images and amulets

famous *bhikkhu*, it is primarily a Thai Buddhist and Chinese clientele that is especially interested in it.

There is a roaring trade in amulets. There is also a vast popular literature – brochures, cheap magazines, glossy illustrated editions for collectors, and weighty books for connoisseurs on how to recognize the genuine article and detect the fake (see Figure 5). Moreover, amulets are an inexhaustible subject for newspaper articles and daily gossip, in which stories of windfall fortunes and miraculous escapes from danger attributed to amulets are told with awe.

The cult of amulets is no mere "superstition" or "idolatry" of the poor or unlettered. If you confronted a prosperous man in the streets of Bangkok – well dressed in suit and tie, or imposing in military uniform – and asked him to open his shirt collar, you would see a number of amulets encased in gold, silver, or bronze hanging on his gold necklace. (In the United States, an analogue might be that if you asked an affluent person to empty his pockets or her purse, you would find a variety and a superfluity of credit cards encased in plastic jackets.)

Businessmen, military men, ordinary folk, the man or woman on the street – all openly talk of their interest in these amulets and readily show them to you, explicating their virtues and history. The scholars, university students, and teachers are more discreet, though no less credulous. Even the most "liberal" or "progressive" of them, espousing "modern science" and holding against superstitions, and even proclaiming left-wing or at least antimilitary sentiments, wear them or keep them at home; some of them may not wear them regularly, but only on those occasions when they feel in need of special protection.

Let me describe the modest necklace of three amulets that was worn in 1979 by a doctoral student in education at Sri Nakharinwirot University under the collar of his shirt. Somchai was in his early thirties, had taught in a secondary school for a few years, and had qualified to enter the graduate program at the university.

1. A copper amulet in the shape of a coin (*rīan*) made to commemorate a birthday of Phra Acharn Fun, a famous forest ascetic monk who resided in Sakon Nakhon Province. The medallion had the bust of a monk on one side and a monk's bowl and pot on the reverse side with the following words: "75 years old on August 20, Wat Udomsomphāūn, Amphōē Mūēang, Sakon Nakhon Province, 2517" (i.e., 1974). This *arahant* monk became so famous for his piety and ascetic life that the King and Queen traveled to the Northeast to attend his mortuary rites. A friend of Somchai's who lives in Udon Province personally received it from the hands of the venerable monk and gave it to Somchai as a present.

2. An antique clay amulet dug up during an excavation in a *wat* in Kamphāēngphet Province. It was called Phra Sīthit (four directions) Ngopnamoi (round shaped oval piece of sugarcane). The amulet showed the Buddha placed in four directions. Somchai received it as a gift from the father of a fellow student who was the education officer of the province.

3. *Phra rāūt* (freed), a Buddha amulet made of metal that comes from Lamphūn in North

197

เหรียญพระมหาพุทธพิมพ์
วัดไชโยวรวิหาร
จ. อ่างทอง

เหรียญหล่อพระพุทธ
วัดพะเนียงแตก
จ. นครปฐม

๑๐

Figure 5. The front and back views of two amulets from a Thai book on amulets called *Kittikhum Phra Thēra Phra Khāčān* by Thanakann Khongsat.

Thailand. It grants freedom and protection from bad things. An old man of Somchai's acquaintance in his hometown of Chonburī in the Central Province gave it to him.

During the course of my stay in Thailand in 1978, Somchai was to add to this necklace another amulet that he himself purchased when he visited a forest hermitage in Khonkāēn Province (Northeast Thailand); the amulet contains the image of another saintly monk credited with virtue and power, Lūang Pū Pāng; it was sacralized by him. Many such amulets are sold today at the hermitage.

This example can be replicated many times, but it is sufficient to make two

# The cult of images and amulets

points. Our subject, born and bred in the Central Province, was wearing amulets that came from spots and sources located in the distant provinces of Thailand (in the Northeast and North in this instance). He was also wearing amulets that have a historical dimension: old amulets dug up at historic temple sites, amulets sacralized by famous monks both dead and living. We can thus visualize the people of Thailand physically located in different parts and following different pursuits carrying on their body or holding in possession amulets that embody the associations and "vital energy" of the past and present (historical heritage) and of diverse persons and places within the kingdom (geographical spread). The amulets are an example of how many contemporary Thai of diverse social and regional origins carry on their persons material signs and mental images of national identity and history.

The questions of what beliefs the wearers and possessors of amulets hold about them, what virtues and powers they attribute to them, and, moreover, how these notions relate to "orthodox" Buddhist doctrine, are complex for the reason – not unfamiliar to students of complex societies – that there are many levels of meaning that attach to the words and acts of persons differentiated by status, context, and circumstance, and that the doctrines of Buddhism – whether early or late, written or oral, canonical or noncanonical – carry ambiguities and multiple implications. Let me make a start by reporting the views on the matter expressed to me by a layman and a monk in 1978.

1. I asked a successful businessman, who said that amulets had power to confer protection and prosperity, as to how they rendered this aid. He remarked that to be successful in business, first of all one has to be honest, diligent, and practice "morality." What the amulets do is to reinforce these virtues, give confidence to the honest man, and lend certainty to his normative commitments. "You have to practice the moral precepts (sīla tham) beforehand, if the amulets are to benefit you. If persons are immoral, the amulets will not help them. And the monk who sacralizes them does not want the amulets to get into the wrong hands. The sacralization of amulets" he continued, "employs Dhamma, and this procedure is not to be equated with saiyasāt, the 'magical art,' which employs mantra (mon) that may be used for good as well as evil purposes."

2. The acting abbot of Wat Thāt Thāūng, an affluent Bangkok wat of Thammayut affiliation where the rich hold their cremation rites, had this to say about the efficacy of amulets: "Originally the Buddha's image was made in remembrance of the Buddha and to remind oneself of his virtues and not to do evil. But at present those who wear the images as amulets believe that they will give them body protection (paungkan tua), and that they will ensure that good action will yield good returns."

When I asked him about the significance of chanting sacred words (sēk khāthā) over the amulets, he replied: "Today all Buddha images have undergone chanting (pluk sēk), and the layman who possesses an image thereby has his belief in its 'goodness' (khwām dī) confirmed and strengthened. The 'goodness' or virtue of the monk who chants is transferred to the image by the action of 'mind waves' so to say."[3]

"The crux of the matter then is that the possessor of the image believes in the virtue and goodness in the *lūang phāū* ["the respected father," a title given to respected elderly monks]. The virtuous monk transfers his goodness to the amulet, which is received by the layman who believes in the monk's attainments.

"Also when a *lūang phāū* dies, amulets bearing his facial image may be minted, and a ceremony held for saying sacred words over them in which nine (or more) monks will do the recitation. This ceremony is called *phithī pluk sēk phra*.

"Such chanting over images and sanctifying them is done only to images of the Buddha and of famous monks, with *one exception*.[4] The king's image may be sanctified by monks in this way, and on such an occasion, the king will select the monks whom he wishes to officiate."[5]

The views of these two informants advert to many matters and issues: to the importance of intentionality and ethical behavior on the part of an amulet possessor, to the amulet being a "reminder" of the Buddha's person and virtues, to the rite of sacralization of the amulet by an elderly and virtuous monk, and so on. Because these views were held by the informants as being concordant with the "Buddha *sāsana*" (Buddhist religion), let us see what earlier texts and formulations have to say about the worship of the Buddha's relics and images and other sacred objects associated with him.

### Relics and images: canonical and noncanonical views

Buddhists everywhere today venerate the Buddha's relics and images. How do their orientations compare with the doctrinal position stressed in many places in the Theravāda canon that the Buddha has reached extinction in the void of *nibbāna* and does not exist anymore? There is no simple clear-cut answer possible because the interpretive positions taken by different commentators, monk and layman alike, are characterized by linguistic stretching, ambiguities, and equivocations.

The *Mahāparinibbāna Sutta*, probably the most quintessential *sutta* in the entire Buddhist canon,[6] presents in quick episodic succession the multiple strands of early Buddhism as a simultaneous totality – the norms the community of *bhikkhu* should observe; the fruits accruing to the meditator; the entrusting to monks of the *Dhamma* as their guide and to laymen of the Buddha's relics, which are enshrined in *dāgaba*; the sanctioning of merit-making pilgrimages to these reliquary monuments; and so on. Furthermore, this canonical text (as do many others) employs royal metaphors for characterizing attributes and powers of the Buddha's doctrine and his relics as they bear on this world. The *dāgaba*, monuments enshrining relics, have become over time "fields of merit," in which the devotee can reap certain harvests.

# The cult of images and amulets

Thus to the hoary and vexing question of how, if the Buddha is extinct, pious Buddhists can make offerings to him and seek aid from him, Nāgasena, at the beginning of the Christian era, gave the answer in *The Questions of King Milinda* that the Blessed One is set entirely free and therefore accepts no gift; nevertheless, acts done to him, notwithstanding his having passed away and not accepting them, are of value and bear fruit. An orthodox answer then was that the Buddha's attainment is symbolized in his images and by his relics, and when men pay homage to them goodness is caused to arise within them because the relics and images act as a field of merit in which men can plough, plant, and produce fruits.[7]

An orthodox gloss on the role of sacred objects is that they act as "reminders" of the Buddha's victories over desire and ignorance and cause inspiration and gladness to arise from such recollection. The Pali word *cetiya* (*čēdī* in Thai) comes from the Sanskrit root *ci*, "to heap up," "to arrange in order," and in this sense is aptly applied to a *stūpa* as a monument. But it also connotes *cit*, "to fix the mind upon something," "to remind," to "instruct," and in this sense is similar to the English word "monument" (from the Latin *monere*, "to advise," i.e., to remind).

In early Indian art, say before the first century A.D., the Buddha was never represented in human forms but only by symbols (although this convention or interdiction did not apply to human beings in attendance). It is surmised by scholars that the Vedic deities too were not anthropomorphically represented in the Vedic period. In any case, the use of the symbols (Coomaraswamy calls it an "aniconic" method) was so elaborate that it constituted by itself "a complete artistic vocabulary and an iconography without icons."[8]

In this early Buddhist art, the Buddha was represented by substitute symbols, which were reminders of the great events in his career: The *bodhi* tree represented his attaining enlightenment under a tree, protected by the serpent Muchalinda; the wheel (*cakra*) his preaching the first sermon, which "set the wheel of the Doctrine" in motion; the *stūpa* his cremation and the enshrining of his relics; the footprints (*pāduka*) his sojourn in the wilderness; and so on. Some of the symbols taken as a set designated the Four Great Events (afterward eight) of the Buddha's life.

The *Kaliṅgabodhi Jātaka* (J., IV, 228), while giving an early Buddhist view against the representation of the Buddha in human form, also provides a discriminating classification of *cetiya* (as cult objects, sacred symbols, reminders). In the introductory part of the story, Ānanda desires to set up in the Jetavana a substitute for the Buddha, so that people may be able to make their offerings of flowers, not only when the Buddha is in residence, but also when he is away preaching elsewhere. To the Buddha's question as to how many kinds of *cetiya* there are, Ānanda replies that there are three – those of the body (*sārīrika*), those of association (*paribhogika*), and those prescribed (*uddesika*). The Buddha rejects the bodily relics on the grounds that they can be venerated only after his passing away, and he rejects the "personalized" symbols because such are "groundless and merely fanciful," that is, they are only artificially, arbitrarily, and by convention referable to the absent being. So he concludes that only a great wisdom tree that has been "associated" with a Buddha is fit to be a *cetiya*, whether the Buddha is still living or is extinguished. Thus, according to this precedent, the associated symbols, such as the *bodhi* tree, the wheel (*cakra*), the footprints, and such entities are declared the most appropriate.

The *Kaliṅgabodhi Jātaka*, or some variant formulation, may well serve as the precedent for a transformed valuation of "reminders" given by a Thai monk, probably Bōdhiraṅsi. He wrote around A.D. 1417 a chronicle about the origins and travels of a famous Buddha image, called the Buddha Sihing,[9] which served as a palladium of Thai kingdoms and principalities, particularly in the fourteenth century. The chronicle was written to celebrate the powers of the image and the eminence of its royal possessors, especially the kings of Laṅ Nā, in whose possession it was at the time the monk wrote the chronicle.

The chronicle, which we shall cite again in the next chapter, begins with the following myth of origin of the statue. When three kings of the island of Sīhaḷa (Sri Lanka) wanted an image cast in the authentic likeness of the Buddha, they consulted some twenty holy men, and a *nāga* claiming to have seen the historical Buddha transformed himself into an apparition of the Buddha. The kings then determined to have the statue cast, depending on the memory of the holy men who had seen the apparition to provide the model. At this point, the chronicle says that the holy men, endowed with the supernatural powers of knowing the past, recalled that the Buddha himself had validated the casting of an image as a meritorious act. He had once told Ānanda, his favorite disciple, that there were three kinds of *cetiya* (reminders), namely *paribhogacetiya, udisacetiya,* and *sārīrikacetiya*. (Notton glosses the first as all that had been used by the Buddha, the second as "all that which has been determined by him," and the third as all that has been left by him.) The Buddha image would be a merit included in the category *udisacetiya*.

The foregoing serves as a useful introduction for understanding a classification of "reminders" into four types given by a modern scholar of Thai art forms:[10] (1) *sarīradhātu* or *dhātucetiya* (bodily relics), (2) *dhammacetiya*, doctrinal reminders, as contained in the canon, originally referring to the *Dhamma* transmitted orally and later including the written canonical texts as well; (3) *paribhogacetiya*, reminders by association, which include objects with which the Buddha has had physical contact, such as his almsbowl and robes, the footprints he has left, the *bodhi* tree under which he reached enlightenment, and, more generally, all the sites associated with his peripatetic career; and (4) *uddesikacetiya*, indicative reminders, which Griswold glosses as "reminders by convention," that is, man-made substitutes, replicas, or icons of *paribhogacetiya*. They are all copies of originals, so to say. Examples are: trees grown from the seeds or cuttings taken from the original *bodhi* tree; replicas of *stūpas* containing the Buddha's bodily relics or footprints; representations of historic sites or of great events associated with the Buddha in painting, sculpture, and architecture; and so on.

We know that from early times these objects were not merely regarded as reminders and fields of merit, but also as repositories of "power." This "power" on close scrutiny is seen to stem from many bases – such as, first of all, the powers possessed and radiated by the Buddha himself by his "presence"; then the powers of the makers and sacralizers of these objects, who had either been in contact with him or had attained heroic proportions themselves as heirs of his doctrine; then the efficacy attributed to the rituals of sacralization themselves; and, lastly, the power of the substance – the metal, gem, wood, or stone – out of which the object was created. In other words, the answers to the following questions – Why are there so many Buddha images in Thailand? Why are small images and tablets of exquisite craftsmanship made if only to bury them inside larger statues? Why do fervent Buddhists perform complex rituals of devotion and propitiation? – call for further amplification.[11]

In actual fact, in both *Mahāyāna* and *Theravāda* traditions, the Buddha image has come to be credited with "radiance" and a "fiery energy." It has also become the focus of an elaborate iconography, such that its sacredness and potency were intensified.

The attribution of "radiance" and "fiery energy" ultimately goes back to the experience of the "enlightenment" of the Buddha, which was climaxed by his realization of the Four Noble Truths. For instance, the account given in the canonical *Vinaya Piṭaka*[12] speaks of the Gotama's mounting of the four *jhānic* meditative trances, which successively gave him the capacities to detach himself from sense objects and passions and to reach "one-pointedness" of mind, calmful bliss, and even-mindedness. The trances led again to the three pure cognitions achieved in three successive watches: "the knowledge of the memory of former becomings," of the qualitative births and rebirths of beings everywhere ("the arising and passing hence of beings"), and, finally, "the destruction of the cankers."

In sculpture, the styles of the seated Buddha in five positions[13] capture the stillness and luminosity of the meditative enlightenment experience, and thereby his cosmic presence. The Buddha images (in the different seated, standing, walking, and lying positions) are overlaid with rich iconographic "reminders," such as the Tree of Life (*Vṛkṣa*), the Earth-Lotus, the Wheel of Law (*Dharma Cakra*), etc., from which also emanate fiery energy (*tejas*), creative life, and the very movements (*saṁsāra*) of the universe itself. In sum, then, the Buddha statue, seen both as symbolizing those powers as well as radiating them, could become a much valued and sought after treasure.

Griswold points out that besides the efficacy of the sacred objects – such as images – as reminders of the doctrine (which can start a mental process that will end by dispelling the fear of demons), we must accept this primary fact: "In the traditional belief, moreover, every Buddha image inherits some fraction of the *teja*, 'fiery energy,' which the Buddha himself possessed in incalculable abundance, and which is conventionally represented by a fiery halo, a flame springing from the top of the head, the gilded surfaces of bronze or stone, and so on."[14] Similarly, the belief that miniatures worn around the neck confer invulnerability can be explained in more than one way. "Some people would say that the *teja* inherent in the image transmits itself to the wearer and makes him immune from harm; others might argue that by reminding the wearer of the Doctrine, and particularly that part of it that counsels constant alertness, it enables him to keep out of harm's way."[15]

Griswold then delivers a striking answer as to why Thai (and other) Buddhists made miniatures in huge quantities to be buried inside stupas and colossal images: "They were a sort of electric charge, suffusing the stupa or the statue with *teja*: even if most of them proved to be inert, or nearly so, on the basis of probability at least a few of them would turn out to be particularly effective. Looked at in another way, they were intended to assure the durability, the invulnerability, of the Reminder that contained them: and even if they failed in that, and the Reminder were ever broken open, they would pour forth in an explosion of fiery energy, *teja*, conferring their benefits as reminders and protectors far and wide upon future generations."[16]

As part of the evidence relating to recent and/or present-day Thai formulations concerning the character of the Buddha's presence in this world, let me cite the case of Thailand's famous meditation master, Acharn Mun, who, in the course of his meditational experiences, saw and spoke to the Buddha and his long-dead *arahant* disciples. Acharn Mun was moved to ask the crucial question: If the Buddha and the *arahants* had completely passed away, how is it that they can manifest themselves in this manner? To which the Buddha is alleged to have said that because Acharn Mun was still in human form, the Buddha, who has attained absolute purity, had to assume a temporary form to make contact with him. "The absolute deliverance," he was told by the Buddha, "is void of signs and manifestations, but in order for it to be made known a mundane form is necessary and therefore assumed." The Buddha's words, said long ago, are partially captured and clothed in the *Dhamma* texts and are vehicles of instruction and remembrance; the Buddha's presence manifest long ago is "indexically" present (to use Charles Peirce's concept) in images and relics and other icons and indices, but they too are vehicles that aid human understanding.

A short step taken from such interpretations could easily lead to a cosmological "doctrine of presence," which has reached its fullest development in the *Mahāyāna* schools of thought and practice, though *Theravāda* exegetics has not ignored the issue. This doctrine would hold that the Buddhahood as absolute purity of mind has no form and sense, having transcended the three realms of *kāma*, *rūpa*, and *arūpa lokas*; but to make its presence felt, Buddhahood has to assume the mundane forms of the cosmos so that beings in it can apprehend the truth. Such a notion of cosmic presence actualized of course illuminates the conceptions behind the architecture of *stūpas* and of monumental edifices such as Borabudur and Angkor Vat, as Paul Mus (1935)[17] has so brilliantly revealed to us. It would seem that when we fully understand the symbolism of Buddhist architecture, myths, rites, and texts as they obtained in the past and obtain today in Southeast Asia, the classic Mahāyāna–Theravāda distinctions become sometimes, if not always, difficult or irrelevant to impose on the complex reality and varying circumstances – either because both traditions have interacted at various times or because they have elaborated similar conceptions.

## The bodies of the Buddha

This issue of the several "bodies" of the Buddha, both in Theravāda and Mahāyāna traditions, is relevant to our understanding of how Buddhists see the Buddha's differentiated "presence" in the cosmos. The Theravāda traditions on this matter are of course not as elaborated and systematized as the Mahāyāna traditions, but are important nevertheless.

The Mahāyāna conceptions of the three bodies of the Buddha (*trikāya*) are well known.[18] (1) The *Dhamma-Kāya*, Body of Law, is the Buddha in *nibbāna* or *nibbāna*-like rapture. The very nature of the Buddha is his enlightenment, his perfect wisdom, and his knowledge of the Law, the absolute Truth. (2) The *Sambhoga-Kāya* is the Buddha's second body, the "body of enjoyment or beatific body." The Buddha, as long as he has not attained *nibbāna*, possesses and enjoys, for his own bliss and for others' welfare, the fruit of his charity as a *bodhisattva*. (3) *Nirmāṇa-Kāya* are buddhas in their aspect as human beings, who are contrivances or phantoms created at random by the real buddhas (see 2 above), who are possessed of beatific bodies and are sovereigns of the celestial worlds, *Tuṣita* heavens, or Paradises (*Sukhāvatīs*). *Nirmāṇa-Kāya* is usefully translated as "transformation body," in the sense that the Buddha transforms himself into multiforms according to the dispositions of the creatures to be saved. This comes close to the notions of *avatārs* and *rūpas* of Hindu deities.

Another formulation has it that the multiple conceptions of buddhahood, as for instance widely prevalent in Tibetan Buddhism, derive from the power of the Buddha to manifest himself at various levels of existence to visit the needs and capacities of different religious practitioners: "Parallel with the three stages of the threefold world, the world of desire, the world of form and the formless world, buddhahood is conceived of conventionally as possessing *Three Bodies*, an *Absolute Body* which corresponds to the formless world, a *Glorious Body* which is manifest in the heavens to meditating sages, and a *Physical Body* which appears on earth usually as a human teacher."[19] These *Three Bodies* may be represented by Buddhas of different names, such as *Boundless Light*, *Powerbolt-Being*, and *Lotus Born*, each typical of the three bodies listed above.

# The cult of amulets

The Theravāda formulation of the Buddha's bodies[20] implicitly begins as we have seen before in the *Mahāparinibbāna Sutta*'s assignment of the custodianship of the *Dhamma* as Law to the *saṅgha*, and the bodily relics and ashes to the laymen. Although, as we have also said before, the notion of *Dhamma-Kāya* as the Body of Law is canonical,[21] the elaboration of the notion of *rūpakāya* (especially identified with the Physical Body, marked with the auspicious signs of the *mahāpurisa*, the great beings destined to be either a buddha or a *cakkavatti*), corresponds to the development of the anthropomorphic images of the Buddha that increasingly supplement, and even on occasion supplant, the relic *stūpas*. Reynolds draws our attention to the notion of "mind-made body" (*mano-mayakāya*) as it appears in Buddhaghosa's *Visuddhimagga* in connection with ascending from grosser mental and physical states to certain *jhānic* states of mind in *samādhi* meditation.[22] He describes how in certain later Theravāda traditions,[23] perhaps influenced by both Yogic and Mahāyāna ideas, attempts were made, on the one hand, to identify *Dhamma-Kāya* with the following of the Path per se (by the practice of morality and meditation), culminating in the realization of *nibbāṇa* and, on the other, to specify the Buddha's personalized attainments and glory in terms of his various bodies extending from the physical body to bodies associated with stages on the Path, culminating in the Emptiness Body.

I am not proposing that the Mahāyāna and Theravāda formulations in their "orthodox" aspects are similar. There are notable differences. The Mahāyāna tendency, first of all, is to fuse a distinction to which Theravāda holds fast: the distinction between the *Dhamma-Kāya* as the body of the *Dhamma* as scriptural teaching, and the multiform body of the Buddha embodying his soteriological attainments. Again, the Mahāyāna thrust has been to postulate the *Sambhoga-Kāya* as the enduring real Buddha, while the human Buddhas are merely random incarnations; in contrast, the Theravāda orthodoxy's starting point is the historical Buddha, human but also *mahāpurisa*, from whom emanated the *Dhamma*, although Buddhahood itself, as a state of enlightenment, is given a supranormal ontological status. This however opens up a small space for partial rapprochement. As de La Valée Poussin points out, no one would say that an *arahant* is not a human, although he is considered to be living his last existence, but according to the earliest Pali canonical records, Gotama categorically declared that an *arahant* could be a *deva*, or a *gandharva*, or a Yakṣa, or a man: "I am not a man . . . Know, O Brahman, that I am a Buddha." Poussin concludes that the nonsuppression of such declarations by the Pali scriptures attests to the antiquity of the schools that held the Buddha to be a hyperphysical or supramundane being (*lokottara*). Moreover, the Siṅhalese account of the Third Council under Aśoka, provided it is reliable, in stating the Thera opposition to the Vetulyavāda docetic theory that the Buddha remained in the Tuṣita heaven, and only sent a phantom of himself to the world, corroborates this argument.

If one stands back from the particularities of the formulations concerning the various "bodies" of the Buddha, and from the ontological and cosmological systems of diverging Buddhist schools, can one meaningfully propose that there are generalities, from the point of view of a semiotic theory of signs and reminders? It is to be expected, given a Buddhist perspective, that the various levels or stations on the salvation Path will in due course be "reified" or crystallized as different "bodies" or "deities." This crystallization can be seen as taking shape, either as a vertical gradient or as a *maṇḍala*, starting from the "signless state" (as the *Visuddhimagga* called it) at the top or the center, and extending to positions imbued with most form and sense (and therefore most grossness and impurity) at the bottom or the periphery. There are "evolutionary" and "devolutionary" implications to this gradient. In an "evolutionary" or unifying sense, each successive upward or centripetal thrust from gross material-ity through spirituality to the state of void both transcends and encompasses the lower or outer state from which the leap is made. Thus the highest or central state of enlightenment is a presence that encompasses all lower states and has the potentiality to affect and transform them. The "devolutionary," descending, or distributive vision starts from the still point of unity; each level of unfolding is also a production of multiple and differentiated forms, whose grossness and impurity increase at the same time as their purity and radiance weaken as they recede from the center.

# 15

# An enumeration of historic and popular amulets

There are, as I have said before, many kinds of amulets and sacralized objects that are the focus of devout attention. There are small Buddha images; there are medallions or coins (*rīan*) with imprints of the seated Buddha, of the figures of famous monks, and of famous kings and deities. There are clay tablets with similar imprints. Finally, there are images of birds, animals, and special human beings (other than those mentioned above).

These amulets comprise a highly diverse congeries in their age and time of making, their markings, the circumstances of their manufacture, and their spatial distribution throughout the country. If there is a single attribute that applies to them all, it is that they are "sedimentations of power," but this scarcely aggregates them into a closed set capable of systematic classification. The Thai do not have a single system of categories that exhaustively label and classify amulets, but they have names for each individual amulet, and some named amulets fall into larger classes.

In this book we are primarily concerned with the amulets that are currently being sacralized by famous forest saints and meditation masters. But because these amulets belong to a larger tradition and universe of amulets, it is necessary to have a fair idea of the major classes or types of amulets that circulate in Thailand, even if this enumeration is incomplete and the classes in part a construct of the author.

I would differentiate four classes of amulets:

1. Amulet representations of famous and historic Buddha images, which have played the roles of palladia of the Thai kingdoms.
2. Amulets that owe their fame to the reputation of famous Buddhist monks, especially of the nineteenth century, who sponsored their making and sacralized them. The most famous of them are called *phra somdet* and *phra kling*.
3. Miscellaneous amulets, a large residual class of representations of gods, humans, animals, birds, and anomalous beings, sacralized by monks and lay experts skilled in *saiyasāt* ("base arts").

208

## An enumeration of historic and popular amulets

4. The contemporary amulets being blessed by the forest-dwelling meditation masters, some of whom are acclaimed as "saints" (*arahants*).

In this chapter, I shall discuss the first three classes, and this discussion will serve as a backdrop to the contemporary amulet cult focused on the forest saints.

### Some important Buddha images and their amulet representation

Several historic *wat* in Thailand, both in Bangkok and in the provinces, contain Buddha statues that are famous not only for their sculptural excellence but also for the benefits they confer on the worshipers. And, naturally, some of the amulets most in demand by the public are minuscule representations of these national treasures. There are several Thai books and catalogs freely sold in the bazaars that describe these statues and amulets and praise their virtues. I shall use one such book purchased at one of the markets (*talāt*) of Bangkok to convey the character of these popular attributions; the book also contains photographs of the statues and describes amulets and the names of the monks who sacralized them.[1]

The book enumerates the following "magnificent" Buddha statues as having special powers (*saksit/anuphāp*), energy (*bāramī*),[2] and protective virtue. They give mental refuge to people, inspire them to have faith, and help them to bring their projects to successful conclusions. To quote the text: "One who regularly worships these important Buddha statues will acquire 'dignity' (*sangāsī*), live well and happily (*yū dī mī suk*), be free of suffering (*phon thuk*), and enjoy prosperity (*carōēn rung rūēang*) both in the present and future, for all time." The following Buddha statues are mentioned:[3]

1. Phra Buddha Jinasīha (Buddha, the Victorious Lion) of Wat Bovonniwet, Bangkok
2. Phra Buddha Jinarāja (Buddha, the Victorious King) of Wat Phra Srīratnamahādhātu, Phitsanulōk, North Thailand
3. Phra Kāēo Morakot (the Emerald Buddha) in the Chapel of the Grand Palace, Bangkok
4. Phra Buddha Trairatnanāyaka of Wat Pananchōēng, Ayudhyā (the old capital)
5. Phra Buddha Sothorn of Wat Sothornwararam, Chachōēngsao, Central Thailand
6. Phra Buddha Benlaem of Wat Phetsamutworawihān, Samutsongkhrām, Central Thailand
7. Phra Buddha Khaotakran of Wat Khaotakran, Phetburī, Central Thailand
8. Phra Buddha Raikhing of Wat Raikhing, Nakhon Pathom, Central Thailand

There are three Buddha images that were found together in Phitsanulōk, an ancient city of the Northern Thai kingdoms. Around them have been woven great legends, and two of them have now found their way to Bangkok. The three images are Buddha Jinasīha and Phra Srī Sāstā (the Great Teacher), which are now installed in Bangkok; and Buddha Jinarāja, which still remains in its original location in Phitsanulōk (although an exact replica was made by the order of King Rāma V and placed in the *bōt* of Wat Benčamabophit in Bangkok widely known as the Marble Temple).

One of the distinguishing marks of all three images is that the four fingers of the hand, apart from the thumb, are made of equal length.[4] The robes are draped in the Siṅhala fashion, hence some argue that they were made sometime after the Siṅhala-type images had come to Thailand, the probable date of making being the mid-fourteenth century. (I shall refer to this question shortly.)

Thai Buddhists hold in great veneration the Jinasīha and Jinarāja images together with the Emerald Buddha (which is a palladium of the country and intimately associated with kingship) and attribute to them great virtues and powers. The legends they have inspired give us valuable insights into Thai ideology fed by religious, political, aesthetic, and nationalist sentiments. They also highlight the proclivity of past kings to capture and transfer to their own capitals the palladia and regalia of other kingdoms to buttress their own legitimacy and to aggregate in their own capitals the powers and potencies embodied in the sacred objects. This by the way gives us one clue as to why Buddhist kings plundered each other's Buddhist temples in seeming violation of the fact that they shared a common religion.

### Buddha Jinarāja and Buddha Jinasīha:
### two historic Northern images

There is a marvelous legend about the casting of the statues, which apparently was committed to writing by King Mongkut himself. It runs as follows:

Somdet Phra Sītham Traipidok, the ruler of the kingdom of Chīang Sāen in the North, wrote to the ruler of Śrī Sajjanālaya and Svargaloka, from where his own wife had come, asking him for the loan of "Brahmin craftsmen" to help him to have some statues cast. The craftsmen of Śrī Sajjanālaya were famous for their skills. Five craftsmen were accordingly sent.[5] King Traipidok merged them with the other craftsmen he had collected from his own kingdom and from Haripuñjaya (Lamphūn), and together they made clay models for three statues. On the auspicious day of "the pouring of the gold," King Traipidok invited monks who lived in the city as well as monks who lived in the forest to come together and chant *parit* in order to ask for the help of the deities. Brahmanical rites were also performed, after which the molten base metal, mixed with gold, was poured into the molds. On breaking the molds it was discovered that Buddha Jinasīha and Phra Śrī Śāstā had turned out well, whereas Buddha Jinarāja was flawed. Several other attempts to cast it failed. Much grieved, King Traipidok and his queen prayed for success, invoking the power of their merit (*bun bāramī*) to come to their aid. Then a man wearing white clothes appeared on the scene and helped to make the mold. He worked industriously and did not speak a word. He worked all day and night without resting, and when the mold was finished the auspicious day was set for pouring the gold. When the metal was poured into the mold, the man in white departed, leaving the city by its northern gate. He

## An enumeration of historic and popular amulets

disappeared at the settlement called *Taphākhāo* (literally "maternal grandfather in white robes"). When the mould was broken open, the statue was found to be flawless and beautiful. King Traipidok is then alleged to have founded a new city of Phitsanulōk, built Wat Śrī Ratnamahādhātu there, and installed the statues in the *vihāra*.

The three statues, thus, continues our source, are beautiful, dignified, and excellent. They are guarded by divine angels (*thēwadā*) and protected by a sky deity (*čao fā*). They all have been much respected and worshiped since ancient times.

As a marginal comment to this legendary account, one should point out that there are several versions of the story of origin of the statues and that in the opinion of experts they were cast sometime between 1257 and 1377 during the Sukhodaya Period, probably during the reigns of either the fifth or sixth kings. The fifth king, Līthai (Mahā Dhammarāja I), is considered by some as the best candidate in relation to the legend concerning the casting. "The legend says that a King came down from the north to attack the city of Srī Sachanalai (Srī Sajjanālaya), and built a town called Phitsanuloke where he ordered the casting of three Buddharupas of miraculous beauty, probably assisted in the task by a deva who came to earth."[6] Līthai is also a popular candidate because of his reputation for devotion to the religion and his sponsorship of monuments.[7] But definite attribution remains uncertain, although the time of their casting is roughly known and should tally with the period when Siṅhalese monks arrived in North Thailand.

To return to our popular account: Citing "the royal annals" as its source, it proudly asserts that many Thai kings of the subsequent Ayudhyā Period made official visits to the city of Phitsanulōk in the course of their royal tours of their kingdom and revered the Jinasīha and Jinarāja images. A veritable parade of illustrious Ayudhyān kings is presented for us.

King Rāmēsūan, while on his way north to attack the kingdom of Chiengmai in 1384, is alleged to have stopped at the historic site to divest himself of his royal clothes and regalia to pay homage to the statues. He sponsored a seven-day celebration.

King Nārāi, the great, is said to have paid homage to the statues in 1660 and to have staged a celebration lasting three days. This example was followed by King Boromkot in 1740, who also staged a three-day entertainment.

We are then given a list of kings and viceroys who had longer connections with the city of Phitsanulōk: King Borom Trailōkanāt, who built a *vihāra* at Wat Cūlāmanī in Phitsanulōk in 1449 and was ordained there as monk for eight months; Somdet Phra Boromrātchamappakun, who in the capacity of great viceroy (*mahā uparāt*)[8] administered Phitsanulōk as a governor from 1505–8; Somdet Phra Mahā Dhammarāja, who again as viceroy ruled over Phitsanulōk from 1429–54; finally, the great king, Nārēsūan, who too when he was viceroy ruled Phitsanulōk Province from 1558–66 before he ascended the throne.

# The cult of amulets

King Rāmēsūan's act of piety on the way to war was subsequently repeated in the eighteenth century at another historic moment, when King Taksin advanced north to stem Phra Čao Fāng's attempt to secede and set up his own kingdom; Taksin made a stop at Phitsanulōk, took off the sash worn across his chest, and offered it to Buddha Jinarāja. On his successful return south, he stopped again, this time to conduct a three-day victory celebration on behalf of the Buddha who had helped him and his army.

Certain events that took place in the Bangkok period under the Čakkrī kings – particularly in the reigns of Rāma III and Rāma IV (Mongkut) – beautifully illustrate the vital powers attributed to these Buddha statues and the importance of the placement of two of them in Bangkok, the capital city founded by a new dynasty.

The *uparāt* (deputy king) during Rama III's reign, who built Wat Mai (which later came to be called Wat Bovonniwēt) in Bangkok, took a particular liking to the Buddha Jinasīha and had it moved down to Bangkok around 1828–9. The bronze image was placed on a specially built raft and floated down the rivers. It was installed in the *bōt* of Wat Mai in the southern wing at the back of the already-existing main image, but in 1838 the princely abbot Mongkut, appreciative of its beauty and history, obtained permission from King Rāma III to move it into the main hall and to make it the presiding image in front of the original one.[9] The final act in this story is the placing in front of the Buddha Jinasīha of three life-sized figures of the three distinguished abbot princes of Wat Bovonniwēt: Krom Lūang Vajirañāṇavaṅsa; Krom Phrayā Pavares Variyalaṅkarṇa; and the most illustrious of them, Krom Phrayā Vajirañāṇavarorasa (Prince Wachirayān). The last two figures were ordered cast by King Vajiravudh (King Rāma VI) in 1916 and 1919 respectively, whereas the first was recently cast at the express wish of the present monarch.[10]

The Phra Śrī Śāstā image arrived in Bangkok even earlier, either in the reign of Rāma II or in the early part of the reign of Rāma III. Its small size facilitated this earlier move by an abbot of a *wat* in Thonburī; subsequently, after it was moved around without a final destination, King Mongkut had it moved to Wat Bovinniwet and placed in a special *vihāra* built for it in 1863. It is this same *vihāra* that has the murals of the thirteen ascetic (*dhūtaṅga*) practices described in the *Visuddhimagga*, and which are emblematic of the forest monks' way of life.

The Buddha Jinarāja, however, still stands in its original *vihāra* in Phitsanulōk, thereby lending sanctity and potency to the territory that was the heart of the Sukhodaya Kingdom, which contemporary Thai regard as representing the quintessence of Thai civilization. This particular view of the continuity of Thai civilization, and of the central place of Sukhodaya in it, is probably a special viewpoint advanced since the mid-nineteenth century, first by King Mongkut and subsequently by King Chulalongkorn and his able ministers, of whom Prince Damrong was the ablest ideologist and propagandist.[11]

## An enumeration of historic and popular amulets

Be that as it may, King Rāma V had an exact replica of the Buddha Jinarāja statue made to be placed in the *bōt* of Wat Benčamabophit (the Marble Temple) in Bangkok, which was built by him, and which even today houses predominantly monks of Northern origin. Thus, in a sense, all three of the great Sukhodaya-style images now reside in Bangkok in *wat* with which the Čakkrī kings have had and still have close connection.

We now come to the topic that is of special interest to us, namely, the amulets that have been made bearing representations of the Buddhas Jinarāja and Jinasīha. Naturally, since Buddha Jinasīha has been installed in Bangkok since the last century it has been a particularly favored subject for medallions. A batch of medallions representing this Buddha was made in 1897 and is popularly regarded as "the grandfather of medallions" (*pū rīan*). The medallions have the shape of a leaf of the *bodhi* tree under which the Buddha attained enlightenment. This batch of medallions was cast to commemorate the return of King Chula-longkorn to Thailand after a tour of Europe. He distributed them to courtiers and officials when he conducted a merit-making ceremony in the palace, at which monks from the royal *wat* chanted and received gifts.[12] More recently, in 1942 Phra Sāsanāsobhana (Phra Cham) of Wat Makutkasat (a famous Thammayut royal *wat* in Bangkok built by King Mongkut) sponsored the making and sacralizing of a batch of medallions containing the figures of both Buddha Jinasīha and Buddha Jinarāja.

But of course it is Buddha Jinarāja still sitting in splendor in the historic northern town of Phitsanulōk that has been most frequently copied by amulet makers. There are many such medallions that were made and are avidly searched for even today by amulet hunters. Some examples are:

1. The batch made and sacralized at Wat Bodhārāma, Nakhon Sawan, Central Thailand, in 1918. Many important senior monks from outside this city, from Bangkok in particular, were invited to participate in the sacralization.[13]
2. Phrakhrū Mo, the abbot of Wat Sām Čīn in Bangkok, sponsored the making of a batch of Buddha Jinarāja amulets; the amulet is popularly referred to as Phra Chin after the black lead (*chin*) that was used to make it.
3. Phra Putlawithinayok (Bun) of Wat Bangklangkeo of Nakhon Pathom, the historic Buddhist center in Central Thailand, sponsored the making of another batch.
4. Finally, Buddha Jinarāja medallions were made at Wat Ban Kai in Rayong Province, Central Thailand, under the leadership of its abbot, Phrakhrū Wichittammamuwat (Wong).

It is significant to note from this list that all the sponsors of the Jinarāja amulets were monks, that these monks were members of the "established" *saṅgha*, that the casting of the amulets and their sacralization took place in *wat*, and that these *wat* were located in various parts of Central Thailand, only one of the locations being the capital city of Bangkok itself.

# The cult of amulets

## The Emerald Buddha jewel

The Emerald Buddha is Thailand's best known and most revered Buddha image. It enjoys this primacy because it is the palladium of the kingdom of Thailand. It became this when the founder of the Čakkrī dynasty, Rama I, placed it in his own chapel royal standing within the compound of the grand palace in Bangkok, where it has been venerated ever since as the patron and guardian, at one and the same time, of the Čakkrī dynasty and the country over which it rules.

The Buddha's tooth relic in Sri Lanka and the Emerald Buddha jewel in Thailand express the conviction that political sovereignty in these countries was incapable of being conceived apart from its affiliation with Buddhism, its sponsorship and protection. I have stated elsewhere that at the highest level the fusion of kingship with *bodhisattvaship* makes the king himself, in certain contexts, a ritual officiant of central importance. The most telling evidence for this is that just as in Sri Lanka the temple where the tooth relic was housed was part of the palace complex, so in Thailand is the Wat Phra Kāēo (which houses the Emerald Buddha) part of the grand-palace complex. Furthermore, the changing of the ornaments and clothes of the Emerald Buddha three times a year is performed by the king in person, just as the Siṅhalese kings of old officiated at daily offerings and at festivals.[14] The parallel is even stronger when we realize that both palladia were associated with rain making and fertility and that, especially in the Thai case, the clothing of the statue in a sparse monk's robe in the wet season (the period of the rains retreat of the monks) and in full regal costume in the succeeding cool season[15] was an apt representation of the oscillatory and complementary relation between the Buddha as renouncer and the *cakkavatti* as world ruler,[16] between the season of rain (and the planting of crops) and the season of harvest and plenty, between the phases of intensified piety in lay life and the phase of life-affirming activities.[17]

These few indications of the current status of the Emerald Buddha in contemporary Thailand would be sufficient for understanding why this image is produced by the hundreds in miniatures to be placed in domestic and other shrines and why it is also a popular subject for amulets that are worn or carried by numerous Thai. In fact, we have barely scratched the surface of its meaning and potency. There are more Thai and Laotian chronicles written about this sacred object than any other, the three main being: the *Ratanabimbavaṁsa*, reckoned to have been written in Sukhodaya some time after 1450; the Jinakālamālī,[18] a text we have already used, written in Chiengmai in the early sixteenth century, which devotes a section to it; and the *Amarakatabuddharūpanidāna*,[19] which appears to have been composed in Vientienne, later than the preceding chronicle, but in the same century.[20]

The two chronicles, the *Amarakata* and the *Jinakālamālī*, more or less agree in their accounts. The *Jinakālamālī* focuses particularly on the circumstances that allowed King Tilokarāja of Chiengmai to get possession of it, and the *Amarakata* continues the story until the Emerald jewel became the possession of the kingdom of Vientienne together with the historic Siṅhala Buddha image (*Phra Sihinga*).[21]

The *Amarakata* is written in three parts. The "first epoch" describes the origin of the emerald jewel, in which the monk Nāgasena features as the instigator; the "second epoch" describes the passage of the jewel from the Pāṭaliputta in India to Sri Lanka, and from there to Pagan, whose King Anuruddha is given a central role. The further travels of the jewel are plotted until the jewel reaches Chiengmai. The "third epoch" describes the events that led to the jewel leaving Chiengmai and going to Lānchāng in Laos and from there to Vientienne. (It remained in Vientienne for 200 years until in 1778 a Thai general, who later replaced King Taksin to become the first Čakkrī king, having defeated this Laotian principality, sent back to the Thai capital of Thonburī the Emerald Buddha and the *Phra Sihinga*.)

### THE POWERS OF THE GEM TREASURE

Both the *Amarakata* and the *Jinakālamālī* provide myths of origin that bring into prominence, as do no other chronicles, the special potency of the image as attributable in large part to the substance from which it is made, in this case a "precious" stone. The year was the five-hundredth after the Buddha's passing away. Nāgasena, residing in the *Tāvatiṁsa* heaven, had been born in this world, and had been King Milinda's adviser and agent of his conversion to Buddhism. This Nāgasena, upon the death of his guru, Dhammarakkhita, decides that an image of the Buddha would make his religion "extremely flourishing" and "very prosperous" in this world and, rejecting gold and silver as substances that would put the statue in jeopardy among wicked people, he reflects thus: "The Buddha, the Doctrine and the Church each represents a gem, so I have to get a precious stone with a very great power in it to make the statue of the Lord."

Lord Indra, in the company of the celestial architect and artificer, Visukamma, descends from heaven, and volunteers to assist Nāgasena in the search. The first choice is the precious stone, the *Maṇijoti* (the resplendent jewel) on Mount Vipulla under the protection of genii Kumbhaṇḍa. But this stone is not available because it has already been reserved for the enjoyment of a future *cakkavatti* (universal monarch). It is thus suggested that Indra take instead another magnificent gem that is in the center of a ring, with 650 precious stones as its retinue; this cluster lies adjacent to the cluster of the *Maṇijoti* jewel, which is surrounded by 1,000 gems.[22] This proffered gem is the *Amarakata* emerald jewel, which Indra accepts.

How are we to figure out the significance of this sequence in which the greater gem is reserved for the *cakkavatti* and the lesser is offered for the Buddha image?[23] The seeming slight can be explained adequately only if we accept that the emerald gem (that is to be shaped as a Buddha) takes its value from its future

215

use. It is destined to be associated with and to be possessed by actual kings, who are lesser representations of the exemplary, absolute, and millennial *mahāpurisa* (great man) of the canonical scriptures.[24] Hence the full force of the fact that the emerald gem, by spatial contiguity with the universal monarch's jewel, partakes of its virtues and potency.

In the classic *Mahāsuddassana Sutta*, it is said that the *cakkavatti*'s gem treasure when raised aloft casts light and enables his fourfold army to "march out of the gloom and darkness of the night." So the emerald gem, too, must possess a similar radiance and illumination. Indeed the stone *qua* emerald has other rich associations.[25] As a possession of the goddess Mani Mekhala, it produces lightning and induces the monsoon rains. Its close association with Indra brings to mind the fact that Indra's own coloration in Thai tradition is emerald green and that in Northern Thailand there flourished the cult of Indrakhila under Buddhist aegis, which guaranteed fertility and prosperity to the kingdom. The cult of the Emerald jewel, showing remarkable similarities in mythology and physical form with the Indrakhila, replaced the latter, and especially in the reign of King Tilok (Tilokarāja) of Chiengmai, the Emerald jewel received the same kind of Buddhist *paritta* recitations by monks that the Indrakhila did.

### FROM GEM TO IMAGE

Returning to the *Amarakata* chronicle, let us take up the story of the fashioning of the image. Indra assigns the task of carving the image to Visukamma, and he takes seven days and nights to fashion Buddha's likeness. Upon completion, Indra and Visukamma bring the image down from heaven to a waiting assembly presided over by Nāgasena for the purpose of consecrating it. Placed in a golden palace given by Indra, serenaded by celestial and human music produced by gongs, drums, cymbals, and trumpets, whose tumultuous sounds fusing into a single sound ascend to the Brahma heaven, surrounded and acclaimed by a vast gathering of monks and men, the image is given its name. Then Nāgasena takes a golden vessel containing a crystal casket, in which are enclosed "seven relics of the Omniscient Lord," and recites this invocation: "May these relics go into this *Buddha* if for the blessing of all men and angels, his image is to last as long as five thousand years."[26] And then into the forehead goes one relic, into the head of the right humerus another one, into the head of the left humerus a third one, two inside the knees, and the last one into the breast.

These details describe a ceremony of consecration of the image, an important aspect of our study of images and amulets. Although the subject is the Buddha himself, it is, however, deities and men who have fashioned the image, given it a name, and embedded relics in it to the accompaniment of recitations and music. The procedures and events we have reviewed so far suggest that the Emerald Buddha has a triple potency stemming from its gemlike nature (its "natural properties" being of course given cultural valuations associated with the *cakkavatti*, with Indra, and so on), its "likeness" to the physical presence of the Buddha, and its incorporation of the Buddha's relics.

We must next indicate an implication already discernible in the consecration ceremony. Nāgasena, the monk, billed as the initiator of the making of the statue and as presiding over the consecration, this Nāgasena who had already been the mentor of King Milinda, is now paired with the king of Pāṭaliputta, who at the head of the population of the kingdom is present at the image's sanctification and to whose care the image is first given. This is the image's first political connection among a series that are to follow, which constitute the central subject matter of all the chronicles.

### THE TRAVELS OF THE EMERALD BUDDHA

By far the most remarkable feature of the Emerald Buddha is its travels from one principality to another, from one king to another, being a pawn among Buddhist kings as well as a moral gauge of their virtuous conduct. Thus, two actions are attributed to it: Wherever it is venerated (and veneration goes with virtuous conduct), there prosperity reigns; but wherever there is kingly misrule and civil turmoil, it abandons that place and moves to a more worthy capital. The chronicle attributes to the monk Nāgasena a prediction at the time of its consecration that made out as if the statue was destined to traverse five Buddhist lands of Southeast Asia – Laṅkādvīpa, Rāmalakka, Dvārāvatī, Chiengmai, and Lān Chāng (which cover territories in present-day Sri Lanka, Burma, Thailand, and Laos) – brilliantly illuminating their religion.

But the circumstances that made it change its residence, as later told in the chronicle, are varied: political misrule; defeat and conquest in warfare; pious revival of religion; transfer through dynastic marriage; theft and secret transfer. Thus, after 300 years of existence under the protection of the king of Pāṭaliputta, it is transferred to secure its safety during a civil war to the southern land of Sri Lanka. After 200 years there, it is solicited together with the Pali scriptures by King Anuruddha of Pagan, but by misadventure it arrives in the Khmer capital of Angkor. Thence, owing to the misdeed of a Khmer king, it is spirited away by a monk to the Thai kingdom of Ayudhyā, from where it moves to the lord of Kamphāēngphet. The lord of ChīangRāi carries it off next and a prince of Chiengmai sends him offerings, begging for it. From Chiengmai, the image moves to Laos in the last phase of the chronicle. In this story of restless travel, a legendary story not entirely lacking in historical veracity, there are some climactic sequences that are understandable once the plot is known.

The first climactic sequence relates to the Pagan king Anuruddha, in whose time the Pali scriptures were taken from Sri Lanka to Pagan. Historically it is probably true that around this time something of this sort happened, and that the Burmese kingship, championing a religious revival, saw its paragon in the Sinhalese form of Buddhism, partly on account of its alleged purity based on its authorship of the Pali canon and partly because it could provide a distinctive legitimation of a new, expanding polity. And we know that the Thai kingdom of Sukhodaya, and subsequently the Lānnā kingdoms like Chiengmai, themselves became sponsors of Siṅhalese Buddhism and had access to it in part via Pagan (see Chapter 5).

According to the chronicles, King Anuruddha, finding the Pagan canonical and commentarial texts deficient, goes to Sri Lanka (riding through the air on his steed) to acquire new copies of the texts. At that time, the Emerald Buddha also was located in Sri Lanka. Anuruddha returns from Sri Lanka to Pagan on his flying steed; one set of the manuscripts is loaded on one boat, another copy of the same set together with the Emerald Buddha are loaded on another. The second boat loses its way on the high seas and drifts to Angkor, where the king gets possession of the two treasures. And, most surprisingly, Anuruddha, flying to Angkor, frightens the Angkor king into parting with the texts by impressive supernatural feats, but forgets to take along with him the Emerald statue!

It looks as if the legend by this fiction is contriving to do two things: to (1) draw into its confines a sacred object located in Angkor and the focus of great veneration[27] and (2) at the same time to identify this object and cult with the practice of Buddhism as sponsored in North Thailand. This contrivance is tendentious, and this tendentiousness can best be understood in terms of the next climactic phase of the story, which takes place in the kingdom of Chiengmai. It is there that Siṅhalese ''pure'' Pali Buddhism and Angkor's guardian cult meet in actuality; or, in the terms of the legend, it is there that the scriptures and image, previously separated, come together again.

From the point of view of monk Ratanapañña, the author of *Jinakālamālī*, the raison d'être of the story of the Emerald jewel is that it was the kingdom of Chiengmai that became heir to the Pali scriptures and the image. There are two implications to this reuniting. Whatever the true facts, the author is suggesting that the Chiengmai polity is the meeting point and coalescence of the two socio-religious traditions of Pagan and Angkor;[28] and it is the destiny of this Thai polity to become the bearer and protector of the pure and complete religion previously splintered and sundered. The hero of this unification and flowering is King Tilok, who installed the image in his capital, making it the object of great veneration, and also sponsored the revision of the Pali canon so as to arrive at its authentic form. King Tilok, we may recall, is alleged to have also sent a mission to Bodhgaya and was a patron of Buddhist art, a high point in Lān Nā sculpture of the lion-style Buddha with *cakkavatti* nuances being attained in his time.

The last phase of the Emerald Buddha, as chronicled in *Amarakata*, illustrates another side of the image's fortunes; if under King Tilok's parasol of dominion, religion and society prosper and the image is the center of an established cult, the subsequent travels of the image in Laos reveal the imperative need among contenders in civil war to carry it in their baggage. We are told that the Siṅhala Buddha accompanies a princess of Chiengmai from Lān Nā to Laos, where she marries King Bodhisāra, the ruler of Lān Chāng. But all hell breaks loose after Bodhisāra dies. His two half-brothers divide up the Laotian kingdom and prepare to fight each other, and his son Jethādhirāja, who succeeds him in Chiengmai, leaves for Laos to restore order, taking good care to transport the Emerald Buddha with him. In Lān Chāng he places the Emerald Buddha side by side with the Siṅhala Buddha, which is already there, thus pairing the two historic palladia. But Jethādhirāja's daily devotion to both images does not assure him the empire he wants. He eventually, somewhat dispirited, makes his way to Vientienne. There he aggregates the images in his Laotian capital, and under their guardianship his kingdom experiences some stability and peace.[29]

## Amulets blessed by famous monks of the past

There are, according to one informant, a political scientist at a Bangkok university, four criteria that determine the power (*saksit*) of amulets. The first is the age of the amulet – the older the better. The second is the name and fame of the monk – the *lūang phāu* or *lūang pū* ("respected father"/"grandfather") – who sacralized it. The third is the proof it has given of its efficacy to owners. The last is the sum of money that was paid to purchase it. The heart of the matter is that the most famous amulets in Thailand today are the Buddha amulets made in batches and sacralized on certain historic occasions by famous monks credited with virtue and loving-kindness (*mettā*), frequently enjoying royal patronage and public respect.

The best-known amulets of the past and those made currently have distinctive shapes and markings. Each type or batch is alleged to have a special identification mark (*tham ni*), usually a distinctive "imperfection," which ensures against fakes. For like any antique market, the market for amulets is literally flooded with fakes. Many experts intently peering through magnifying glasses, and many authoritative books giving pictures and descriptions of amulets, abound in the bazaars of Bangkok and elsewhere.

### THE PHRA SOMDET AMULETS

A famous category of amulets in Thailand are called *phra somdet* amulets. They are small tablets, usually made of white or yellow clay, with a figure of a Buddha sitting in *samādhi* meditation style embossed on them. The pedestal on which he sits may have three, seven, or nine layers, three and nine being the more popular.

Historically, perhaps the most famous amulet maker and sacralizer, as judged by present-day Thai assertions and beliefs, was Lūang Phāu Tō, a forest monk who lived in the period of the fourth and fifth reigns (King Mongkut and King Chulalongkorn) in the latter half of the last century.[30] King Chula in particular is said to have had much belief in his sanctity and to have patronized him. He is said to have taken up residence in many different *wat* in Bangkok, especially during the rains retreat, and to have sacralized these *phra somdet* amulets. The most famous amulets are associated with four Bangkok *wat*:

1. The tablets made at Wat Rakhang show the Buddha seated on a three-layered pedestal ( ▬ ). A variant made at Wat Suthat, also with a three-layered pedestal ( ▬ ), has more yellow in the clay as a result of adding more dried jasmine to it.
2. Amulets made at Wat Ketchaiyo have the Buddha seated on a nine-layered pedestal. The Buddha is also distinguished by his long ears and by an incision on his chest.
3. Another location was Wat Plap; the amulets made there were small and oval shaped; the pedestal has three layers and the lowest in particular is in strong relief.
4. Amulets with seven-layered pedestals were made for Wat Bāngkhunphrom.

The problem of the authenticity of the *phra somdet* amulets is complicated by the fact that more than one batch of the same style tablet may have been made at different times in the same *wat* and sacralized by Lūang Phāu Tō or other monks. (A still further complication is presented by fakes made widely by amulet sellers and hawked as the genuine thing.) Anyway, the *phra somdet* amulet of the first batch (*run*), personally sacralized by Lūang Phāu Tō, is deemed to be an envied collector's piece. It is popular knowledge in Bangkok that a big businessman and millionaire by the name of Pomphan paid 700,000 *baht* (US $35,000) for a single tablet of the first batch. There are annual contests held in Bangkok for judging these Buddha-image amulets (*prakūat phra*), and Pomphan's piece is the uncontested winner in its class. It is rumored that another millionaire offered Pomphan 800,000 *baht* for the amulet but was, not unexpectedly, refused.

## THE PHRA KRING AMULETS

The *phra kring* amulets are another famous category. The *phra kring* are small Buddha images with a hollow inside them containing a small piece of metal so that when they are shaken a tiny ringing sound is created; "*kring*" is the onomatopoeic word that describes the sound. The most famous batch of these *phra kring* amulets was made at Wat Bovonniwet, the central *wat* of the Thammayut sect, with royal connections under its famous princely abbot Pavares. He was made supreme patriarch of the Thai *sangha* and died in 1892 at the age of eighty-four after a long period in office. This abbot is famous for two things: for being the preceptor (*upajjhāya*) to a king and several princes during their ordinations as monks (for brief periods), and even more importantly for the public at large, as the monk who cast and sacralized the amulets that have come to be called after him *Phra Kring Pavares*. The official history of the *wat* reports as follows: "Only a small number of about thirty were recorded as being made, and with their rare beauty and perfection including the high supernatural power which they are believed by later generations to have acquired, these images have turned into priceless objects sought after by collectors all over the country. Wat Bovoranives itself possesses only one perfect specimen of this image in its museum . . ."[31] Hence it is understandable that there are a number of fakes in the country being hawked as the genuine article.

Another famous batch of the *kring* amulets was cast by Wat Suthat, a royal *wat* of the Mahānikāi sect, and thus named *Phra Kring Wat Suthat*. Apparently when first made they were distributed primarily to the nobility. They are much sought after today.

There is one important fact to be noted about these *phra somdet* and *phra kring* amulets. They were made in the last century by charismatic monks whose careers were fulfilled at the capital city, usually as abbot of a *wat* of royal status and as a titled ecclesiastical official; or at its periphery, as a famous meditation teacher in a *wat* belonging to the forest-dwelling tradition. Thus, in a way in the nineteenth century, both the highest-ranking monks within the city walls of Bangkok and on the Thonburī shore, and the monks specializing in meditation and ascetic traditions in *wat* located on the northern edge of the city, were related to the capital city and its centralized monarchy in a center-periphery specialization. One should not underrate the historical processes by which, especially during the reigns of Mongkut and Chulalongkorn, ''sanctity'' became aggregated in the capital. Within the *saṅgha* itself, the new reformist orthodoxy of Pali learning and adherence to *Vinaya* discipline sponsored by the Thammayut sect radiated outward from Bangkok to suffuse and influence the rest of the country.

Let us briefly compare the two monks Prince Pavares and Lūang Phāu Tō, both memorable amulet sacralizers. Prince Pavares derived his charisma from royal antecedents and royal patronage; moreover, he was the abbot of a *wat* made prominent by Mongkut, which since then has acted as the center of the Thammayut sect. In fact Pavares succeeded Mongkut as the second abbot of Wat Bovonniwet in the very year (1851) that Mongkut left the *saṅgha* to ascend the throne.

Lūang Phāu Tō[32] is particularly intriguing to us because, while following the path of a peripatetic forest-dwelling monk whose special powers rested on meditative exercises and *sīla* practices, he also enjoyed good relations with the ecclesiastical and political authorities of the center. Lūang Phāu Tō was a highly revered monk in the fourth and fifth reigns, excelling both as a forest monk and a titled monk. On the one hand he rose to the highest reaches of the Thai *saṅgha*, as signified by the *somdet* title conferred upon him; yet he centered his activities on monasteries at the northern edge of the city – Wat In and Wat Mai Bāngkhunphrom – that specialized in meditation, teaching, and practice.[33]

At both these *wat*, Lūang Phāu Tō built monuments in which he embedded numerous small images (*phrakhrūēang*), which he blessed and charged with mystical powers (*aphinihān*) traditionally associated with meditating forest-monks. In King Chulalongkorn's reign, a disciple of Lūang Phāu Tō, Lūangpū Phu, became the abbot of Wat In, and he too attained fame for his supernatural powers emanating from meditative practices.

# The cult of amulets

As we have noted with regard to the career of Acharn Mun, the exemplary Meditation Master, the hardy *Thudong* monk may found monastic residences and form cells of disciples, but he is a compulsive wanderer. It therefore comes as no surprise that Lūangpū Phu and Somdet Tō would periodically leave Bangkok to wander in the forest.

To this day, Wat In bears evidence of the prestige and special powers of Somdet Tō, who, among other exploits, built a giant outdoor standing Buddha. This statue, principally because of its association with Somdet Tō, and the radiant small images he filled it with, receives from the laity both offerings and requests for protection throughout the year. This continuing popularity of the *wat* comes each year to a climax in its week-long fair, at which generous piety and robust fun mix in agreeable fashion.

Special attention is being drawn to these facts because, while in the nineteenth century – especially in the reigns of King Mongkut and King Chulalongkorn – the capital was not only the political center but also the religious hub, and from these centralities stemmed power and charisma of various sorts that was distributed outward to the society and country at large, the most famous forest-monk monasteries specializing in meditation and ascetic practices were on the periphery of Bangkok. Today, as we shall see, the capital has to go to the periphery of the country, to its faraway provinces, to find "saintly" monks and receive special blessings from their hands. This reversal is a reflection of the crisis in political and moral confidence in Bangkok (1978).

The power of historic sites and centers of political and religious authority to fecundate the present is represented by the scramble for relics, amulets, and antique objects when they surface from archaeological excavations sponsored by the government or from illegal digs. The latter piracy is quite common, and the well-stocked antique shops in Bangkok bear witness to the profitability of the activity. Let me cite one example of how ancient capital cities and historic sites have yielded objects vibrating with living power:

In 1957 in the course of excavation valuable antiques were discovered in the crypt of Wat Rātbūrana, a historic *wat* in the old capital of Ayudhyā. This *wat* was built in the fifteenth century by King Paramarāja II (Čao Sām Phrayā) in memory of his two older brothers (Ai and Yi), who died fighting each other in a succession conflict. The double killing occurred in classical heroic style when the two combatants exchanged blows seated on charging elephants. The surviving brother built the *wat* as an expiation for their bloody acts and in memory of his fallen brothers. Among the valuables found were royal regalia made of gold and precious stones, jewelry, golden images of the Buddha, and some 84,000 small images of the Buddha in different styles. It is the last item that concerns us here, for they are clay amulets, which are much in demand today. I was informed that the government sold a vast number of these amulets to the public and that the proceeds collected helped to finance the building of the Čao Sām Phrayā National Museum in Ayudhyā, which houses the antiques found.

## An enumeration of historic and popular amulets

Another category of Buddha amulets that owe their popularity to their connection with a historical center are the Phra Rūang amulets. Phra Rūang is alleged to have been the name (or title) of the first king of Sukhodaya; the same name has been conferred upon his dynastic successors. These amulets reproduce the form of the Sukhodaya-style Buddha and divide into some three kinds: the Phra Rūang Pōēt Lōk, which "opens the world"; the Phra Rūang Nang Pūēn, which has a bullet impression in the back; and the Phra Rūang Song Pūēn, on which is imprinted a bow and arrow. All these amulets confer invulnerability to injury from bullets and weapons.

### Other amulets

The third class of amulets is residual and is composed of a vast number of highly miscellaneous objects – representations of gods, humans, animals, birds, and anomalous beings who are credited with varied potencies defying exhaustive listing: sexual prowess, success in business, personal charms, sweet talk, physical strength, and so on (see Figure 6). In theory, these objects have been sacralized by the potent words of monks or lay cult masters claiming special powers; in fact, there is no way of knowing who made them and who sacralized them. They are fetishes that cost little and in some cases may be taken to specialists for a new sacralization with chanted words and holy water sprinkling. But as we shall see from the individual descriptions below, apart from the specialist's ritual input many of these objects are representations of animals, birds, or other things whose "natural" properties are metaphorically and metonymically transferred to the owner of the amulet.

For the purpose of description, I shall divide these variegated amulets into two classes: human beings and deities; and animals and birds.

#### HUMAN BEINGS AND DEITIES

1. *Rak yom*.[34] These are two small figures of two brothers carved of wood and put into a bottle containing sandalwood oil. *Rak* means black; *rak* is the older brother carved from a black wood; *yom* is the younger brother made of white wood. The perfumed oil is said to be the food of this pair of brothers, who are alleged to give protection to the person carrying them. Before an owner goes on a trip, he (or she) tells the amulet words to this effect: "*Rak yom* my sons, go with me who am your father (or mother) and protect me from danger." It is also claimed that if a man were to daub some of the oil on a woman, she would fall crazily in love with him.

We may note that the pair of black and white brothers are boys who are supposed to be at the service of the owner. The owner of the amulet seeks to control and employ for his use the strength, energy, compliance, and dependence of immature boys.

Figure 6. An assortment of amulets purchased by the author in Bangkok. Three of them are described in the text:

# An enumeration of historic and popular amulets

2. *Kumān thāūng*. This is also the figure of a small child. If made of wood, he too is kept in a bottle of sandalwood oil; if made of metal, he is worn or carried in the usual way. What is distinctive about *Kumān thāūng* is that he has only one testicle, and in Thai belief such an anomalous person has much strength, power (*saksit*), and sexual prowess. A one-testicled man does not have to be fortified by amulets – for he is a superior athlete. In fact, the Thai expression for such a person is that he has "copper testicle" (*kabān thāūng dāēng*), copper here signifying the burnished strength of the metal. Before an owner of *Kumān thāūng* – as indeed of *rak yom* – eats a meal, he as their "father" and provider should invite them to partake of it.

Incidentally, it is relevant to note that in the popular Thai classic novel *Khun Chāng Khun Phāēn*, Khun Phāēn is described as killing his pregnant wife, extracting the foetus, saying sacred words (*sēk khāthā*) over it, and then using the ghost baby as a *Kumān thāūng*. An amulet seller had this to say of *Kumān thāūng*: "He is the ghost of a dead male child. You can ask him to do things for you. He will take care of your house and he will hit on the head of anyone who enters without permission. You can command him to go and tell a woman that you love her."

3. *Nāng Kwak* means the beckoning woman; the amulet made of metal or clay shows a kneeling woman beckoning with one hand, which is said to represent her calling clients and buyers to shops. It is thus a popular amulet among male and female traders, shop-keepers and peddlers (*phāū khā māē khā*).

An alternative embodiment is a plant, actually called *nāng kwak*, which is grown in front of shops by merchants. It is a plant of the sedge variety and has a lush growth of leaves, an apt representation of plenty. It is fast growing and spreads with ease.

4. *Pit tā hā lāp*, literally meaning "cover eyes and find fortune," consists of a sitting figure who has closed his eyes with his hands. The amulet enables the carrier to attract other persons who will love you and give you gifts. The following story was told me by an amulet seller: There was once a handsome young monk, and people fell in love with him and wanted to offer food and gifts to him. To escape this importunate plenitude, he closed his eyes so that the lay admirers could no more see his face. In spite of this they continued to come and see him and to love him.

5. *Pit tā mahā ut* is a sitting figure who has closed all his orifices – eyes, ears, genitals, and anus – with his hands and feet. This figure who is thus closed up from external intrusion protects the possessor from outside harm. By the same token, its efficacy is double-edged, for if left at home it may close the doors to good fortune entering the house, or if carried by a pregnant woman it may block childbirth. The principle behind the ambivalence may be stated as follows: The closing of the body's orifices results in the conservation of the insides and the prevention of intrusion from outside. According to context, either of these features may be an advantage or a disadvantage.

6. *Phra Ngang* is a metal image of a deity that has a curved phallic-looking horn projection on its head; it is believed to enhance the possessor's sexual powers. The amulet is alleged to come from Cambodia.

7. *Phra Siwali* is a representation of a wandering ascetic (*dōēn Thudong*), an old monk,

carrying umbrella and stick. It is said that a person who possesses and respects it will never starve, because the ascetic traveling alone in the forest was able to subsist by himself.

8. *Jūjaka* is the greedy old *brahman*, who in the well-known *Vessantara Jātaka* (which describes the Buddha's acts of selfless giving in his life previous to his last one), prodded by his young wife, asks Vessantara for the gift of his two sons. An amulet seller explained that one who carries the *Jūjaka* image will have servants and youth to serve him, but since the old *brahman* was an evil person, monks will never sacralize his amulet by chanting. This is left to a lay expert.

9. *Kanhājāli* are the figures of the two sons of Prince Vessantara (Kanhājinā and Jāli); they are joined together and are shown in a kneeling position showing obedience to their father. The implication is that the amulet owner will have control over servants and young subordinates.

ANIMALS AND BIRDS

Let us now describe the animal and bird amulets.

1. *Sālikā khū* are a pair of mynah birds that face each other. This amulet will make people show *mettā* toward you; they will feel close toward you in the fashion of the two birds exchanging mutual looks and amity. The mynah bird is noted for its pleasant sounds, and a popular love charm is called *Sālikā linthāūng* (golden tongue) and enables the possessor to talk sweetly.

2. *Plā ngōēn plā thāūng* means "silver fish, gold fish" and is popular once again with traders and shopkeepers because they are believed to facilitate the sale of goods and confer prosperity. The most usual form of the amulet is a pair of fish, colored gold and silver, which are hung like a mobile over the doorways to shops under which customers must pass.

3. *Sai* is a bamboo fish trap that again is hung in shops (sometimes even taxi drivers have small *sai* dangling above the dashboards of their taxis) and is believed to bring money on the analogy of fish being caught in a trap. (Although it is an inanimate device, it is conveniently included in this section.)

4. *Sīphueng*. This is a set of four amulets placed in a circular plastic box. On a base of beeswax are placed images of a mynah (*sālikā*) bird, of a pair of silver and gold fish, of the beckoning woman (these three have already been described), and a miniature waistband. All these amulets combine to produce good fortune and the ability to charm others through a show of kindness (*mettā*).

The *sālikā* sings mellifluously, and the amulet enables one to become a silver-tongued enticer. This personal charm enables one to persuade others, and persuasion here is not limited to romantic conquests. A trader needs charm to win his buyer with compliant words and deeds and a client needs it to win favors from his patron. The silver and gold fish and the beckoning woman help achieve the same results, especially in commerce.

The beeswax has a similar role to play. It is believed that if you approach a woman or a superior (*phūyai*) with beeswax daubed on your lips, you will be able to persuade them to show kindness toward you. The English phrase "honeyed talk" conveys the idea perfectly.

5. *Singtō* is the representation of a mythical lion, which is very popular in the country. It is not irrelevant that it is the emblem of the Ministry of Interior, the most powerful ministry in the government, which controls local administration, the police force, primary education, and so on. It is also interesting that the two major universities, Thammasāt and Chulalongkorn, sport the lion emblem, in different colors, on their crest. The Thammasāt students refer to themselves as the "red lions" and the Chula students as "black lions."

6. *Sing* is the lion as it is known in its natural form in the forest. The *sing* amulet gives the wearer protection from fanged and dangerous animals.

7. *Sūēa*, the tiger, has the same potency. The popular notion is that when one wears this amulet one "feels hot" (*rāun*) and energized, and thus one is aroused to go out and fight other people. Generally in Thai usage the state of feeling hot in this sense signifies animation and a capacity to do things both physically and intellectually; thus *rāun wichā* means the capacity to talk impressively with others rendered by acquiring knowledge of a subject.

8. *Wūakrathing*, the gaur, a ferocious and strong beast of the wild-buffalo variety, again is a potent symbol for reasons easily perceived. There has in recent years grown up in Thailand a rightist, anticommunist, illiberal, and "neofascist" youth movement that specializes in violence and calls itself the "red gaurs."

9. *Nok Khum* is a bird that traditionally is associated with the protection of houses and buildings against fire and theft.

10. *Khīao mū thūēan* is the boar's tusk used as an amulet. The much sought after but rare tusk is solid right through, not hollow. The boar's tusk is frequently used in exorcism ceremonies; the body of the patient possessed by a spirit (*phī*) is stabbed and scored with the tusk and the spirit is thus forced to leave (*khap lai phī*).[35] The tusk is also seen as granting protection from attack and penetration by spirits.

It is clear that many of these human, deity, animal, and bird amulets are used for the control and manipulation of other persons; a few are used for distinctly nefarious purposes. Although these amulets can be made and sacralized by lay specialists, still some of the most famous makers are said to be certain *lūang phāu* (respected father) monks. In such cases, we are definitely dealing with, from the viewpoint of doctrinal purity, the "degenerate" end of the monk spectrum: If the famous forest-monks at the top are regarded as saints conferring their *mettā* in laudable ways, these other monks at the bottom are definitely looked upon as dabbling in "magical" arts (*saiyasāt*) and laying claim to mystical skills that have little to do with the path of purification and *nirvāṇa* liberation. These are the higher and lower paths within the community of monks.

Some names of elderly monks famous for making certain potent amulets were reported to me. Lūang Phāu Plae of Wat Pikunthong in Bangkok had a reputation for sacralizing amulets of the beckoning woman, the silver and gold fish, and the one-testicled boy; he made golden-tongued mynah bird amulets for evoking love;

animal amulets of lions, tigers, and gaurs to give protection from wild animals, including snake bites; and fire-protection amulets. Lūang Phāū Khane, who resides in Prāčinburī Province, was famous for making the pair of black and white brothers (*rak yom*); Lūang Phāū I, for making the penis amulets (*palat khik*). Lūang Phāū Seng of Wat Kalyānamit (Bangkok) has a wide reputation as a master tattooer, an art that is concerned with imparting protection and good fortune by means of designs and figures painted or tattooed on the body.

## Street machismo and the amulet craze

In the course of my fieldwork in Bangkok in 1978 (as well as during my previous work in the city in 1971 and 1973), I traveled in taxis and buses. I felt that the traffic was so dangerous and the chances of accident and theft so imminent that it was the counsel of caution not to drive a car myself. I daily saw a frightening show of aggressiveness and machismo, especially on the part of taxi drivers, who virtually terrorized other drivers by speeding, weaving in and out, making sudden stops, and violating traffic rules – though not an insignificant number of civilian drivers also participated in this free-for-all. The taxi drivers were by no means the exception; they were the focal examples. It seemed to me that the city's roads were an extraordinary site wherein the ordinary man, the lowly commoner, and recent rural immigrant, sitting in control of an engine on wheels, felt free to show no respect for the status of other motorists and to muscle his way through. Thai society, as we well know, is hidebound by etiquette, respect norms, and *krengčai* modesty; it is patterned on asymmetrical relations between patrons and clients, superiors and inferiors (*phūyai* and *phūnoi*), in the office, factory, home, and army. The streets of Bangkok are one location where anonymity reigns, and status holds no sway (except where the police or royalty are concerned). The Thai can be as aggressive as hell on the roads, and they combine this with a preoccupation with protection from danger and with physical safety. With the gun, a soldier or a thug carries amulets and symbols of good fortune. The show of power by laymen is accompanied by a cannibalizing search for the men of piety and charisma who can confer blessings and immunities upon them.

By 1978, there were other manifestations in the society at large, which were of one piece with this traffic behavior. The urban crime rate was soaring, including rape and violence. Of another order were the student insurrections, which were met with a show of ruthless strength by the armed forces; the mounting insurgency movements in the provinces; and the farmers' demonstrations and labor strikes: All these also signify an unleashing of aggression in the society at large and a questioning of a constituted and conservative authority whose legitimacy is at stake.

The juxtaposition in the same society of contexts of status-bound propriety and self-effacing obedience to authority, on the one hand, with, on the other, spasmodic bursts of violence, retaliation, and rebellion, is gaining increasing salience and is truly coming to a head in the metropolis of Bangkok.

One derives an oblique understanding of the juxtaposition by carefully studying the stylistic aspects and the presentational idiom of traditional Thai murals and paintings, where the highborn and high-ranked heroes and heroines wear stereotyped, frozen, masklike expressions – static, elegant, formal – and express their internal power with minimal, controlled movements, while the lowborn commoners and rambunctious individuals portray dynamic face and limb movements and even excesses of conduct.[36]

There is today a certain transformation in this "feudalistic" concept of the different behavioral styles of the high- and low-status orders. Increasingly, the traditional vertical alignment is being eroded by competition between diverse groups in which persons irrespective of rank or status, soldier and man in the street, official and student, worker and farmer, are expressing both styles of behavior – stylized etiquette and unbuttoned aggression – in different social and political contexts and in their separate ways.

In a sense, then, the Thai craze for and insatiable collection of protective amulets and other fetishes should be viewed in relation to their propensities and preoccupations with the exercise of power, in which violence shows its dark face. That it is men rather than women who obsessively collect amulets is in accord with the fact that it is they who predominantly participate in violent competition for coercive power.

But this is only one facet of contemporary Thai society. Its obsession with amulets, its lavish "merit making," and its insatiable consultation of astrologers and diviners – women are even more avid participants than men in the latter two activities – are a function as much of hopeful aspirations for social mobility; for making money in an expanding, though stilted, urban economy; and for achieving career success through education as they are of authoritarian domination, vast disparities of wealth and power, and uncertainties of international politics.

# 16

## The "likeness" of the image to the original Buddha

### The case of the Siṅhala Buddha

The Buddha images, and other objects that imitate them, are created with power and energy because they have undergone a "life-giving process" that "animates" them. The "life-giving process" is the subject of this and the next chapter; it has two "circuits" linked up in the rites that sacralize the images and transfer potency to them. Griswold has succinctly stated the essence of the whole phenomenon of sacralization as practiced in Thailand:

Usually life and miraculous powers are transfused into new images from an older one – the chief cult image of a monastery which in turn has received them from a still older one, and so on back to one of the original likenesses. To transmit the succession to the images that are about to be cast, a long "sacred cord" is formed into a circuit: attached at its beginning to the cult image, it passes along a line of monks, each one holding it between his fingers; continuing its way, it encircles each of the moulds prepared for the new images; finally it returns to the cult image so as to complete the circuit. One or more of the monks go into meditative trance, producing an invisible charge in the circuit which transmits the life and supernatural qualities of the cult image to the new ones as the metal is poured.[1]

The first circuit consists of joining a newly cast image to an existing sacralized, and probably historic and famous, image by a cord such that the latter's energies and virtues can be transmitted to the former. The underlying logic of this is that there is a line of authenticated images or statues, which represent a line of likeness or similitude leading back ultimately to the original (historical) Buddha himself.

The second circuit relates to the fact that the rite of charging with life is conducted principally by monk-officiants, through whose hands too the sacred cord of transmission passes, and who by chanting and through meditation energize the image. To cite Griswold again: "Important castings, which take place in monastery precincts at an auspicious moment chosen by astrologers, are accompanied by a life-giving rite. The purchasers of routine images, cast without ceremony in the craftman's shop, arrange for them to share in such a rite in a monastery at the first opportunity."[2]

## "Likeness" of the image to the original Buddha

We have developed in the preceding chapter some of the implications of the "orthodox" Theravāda doctrinal position – that the Buddha image made in the "likeness" of the historical Buddha is a "reminder" of his teachings and virtues, of his victories over desire and ignorance. We also noted that, in due course, in both Mahāyāna and Theravāda traditions the Buddha image came to be credited with "radiance" and "fiery energy," an attribution that goes back to the Buddha's experience of "enlightenment."

In Buddhist societies, it is held that in order to inherit some fraction of the infinite virtue and power the Buddha possessed, an image *must* trace its lineage back to one made in the "authentic" likeness of the Master himself. But how can the patron, the one who commissions an image, be certain that the statue he chooses as a model is really in an authentic line of succession? The safest course is to choose as a model a statue that has already proved itself by its unusual, supranormal powers. Because such a proven statue will have already become illustrious, there is every reason to copy a famous one, none at all to copy an obscure one.

An investigation of the ramifications surrounding the pedigree of Buddha statues, and how their authenticity relates to their alleged virtues and powers, has to grapple with issues of these kinds:

1. How is the "likeness" of the image to the original living Buddha reckoned?
2. If successor images are replications of "originals," how does one account for changes in iconography and style?
3. If replications and copies of "originals" can be made, how much of the virtue and powers of the originals do they embody?
4. In turn, if copies of "originals" are possible, then copies (or fakes) can be passed off or substituted for "originals"; what are the circumstances under which such switches become possible, even advantageous, for the owners or sponsors?
5. What is the place of the sponsor and the maker of an image, and its sacralizer, in the assessment of its virtues?
6. What is the weight given to the material of which the image is made (e.g., bronze, stone) and with which it is decorated or overlaid (e.g., gold leaf and jewels) in the reckoning of its virtues?

It is of course not possible to address all the issues here, but let me hang some of them on the peg of the authenticity of the Buddha statue and treat the question of authenticity in relation to a famous Buddha statue, the Phra Sihing or Sinhala Buddha, which was believed to possess supranormal powers, and which conferred legitimacy and powers upon many kings and rulers in Thailand and Laos in the role of palladium of their polities (see Figure 7). I shall first plot the travels of the Sinhala Buddha because they provide the religio-political context for understanding the dialectically related issues of an image's authentic likeness to the Buddha himself and the inevitability of reproductions and copies of "originals."

Two principal sources will be used to discuss the career of the Sinhala Buddha. The first, the *Jinakālamālī* chronicle,[3] was allegedly composed by a monk

Figure 7. The Siṅhala Buddha in the National Museum, Bangkok.

around the second decade of the sixteenth century (1515–16) during the reign of King Tilakapanattu of Chiengmai. It is an unadulterated panegyric that seeks to establish the pure lineage of Northern Thai Buddhism and to represent the Northern kingdoms as Buddhist polities in which kingship and *saṅgha* are closely interwoven and mutually supportive. The centerpieces of the chronicle are King Tilokarāja, who ascended the throne in A.D. 1441, and his grandson, King Tilakapanattu, who began his reign in 1495, during which the chronicle was composed.

The second and earlier source is the *Phra Buddha Sihing* chronicle,[4] whose author was, if the accounts given of the history of Chiengmai are trustworthy, a monk named Bodhiraṅsi, who is also said to have written the famous work *Cāmadevīvaṁsa*. The *Phra Buddha Sihing* was composed in Pali around A.D. 1417.

The travels of the Siṅhala Buddha were truly remarkable as described in the chronicles and as popularly believed in Thailand. Prince Damrong, the great administrator and writer in the reign of King Chulalongkorn in the latter part of the nineteenth century and the beginning of the twentieth, placed the first landing of the statue at Nagara Śrī Dharmarāja, and its subsequent removal to Sukhodaya by King Rāmkhamhāeng, between 1277 and 1317. From there it traveled to these kingdoms and principalities: Ayudhyā in 1378; Kamphāengphet in 1382; Chīangrāi in 1388; Chiengmai in 1407, after the Burmese had taken Ayudhyā; and finally Bangkok in 1795, when Chiengmai came under Siamese (Central Thai) control.

The Siṅhala Buddha has a momentous significance in Thailand, because it (like the Emerald Buddha) is associated in Thai traditions with the first coming of the "pure" Pali Buddhism from Polonnaruva in Sri Lanka to Sukhodaya in Thailand (and Pagan in Burma) in the thirteenth century. In the Thai collective consciousness, the coming of this pure Buddhism and the founding of the first Thai kingdoms are cotemporal and interwoven.

We have already mentioned in Chapter 5 that the religious vitalization first in Sukhodaya in North-central Thailand, and subsequently in the Northern Lān Nā polities in the Chiengmai region, was closely associated with the Siṅhala sect of forest-dwelling monks (*āraññavāsī*), especially under the leadership of the monk Sumana. It should come as no surprise, then, that the authors of the *Jinakālamālī* and *Phra Buddha Sihing* chronicles were members of the Siṅhala fraternity of monks who forged a close legitimating alliance with the burgeoning Thai rulers and their polities. The Siṅhala Buddha itself is in large part an "objective correlative" in Thai consciousness of the historic Northern Thai interaction with the Siṅhala sect of forest dwellers.

## The travels of the Siṅhala Buddha

The Siṅhala Buddha was alleged to have been made in Sri Lanka about 700 years after the passing away of the Buddha. But some 1,800 years ago, it traveled to Thailand. According to the *Jinakālamālī*, the Siṅhalese king allowed the image to be dispatched to Thailand upon receiving a request from King Rāmkhamhāeng of Sukhodaya, who had been informed of the wondrous nature of the Siṅhala image by the king of Nagara Śrī Dharmarāja.

Driven by a severe gale, the ship that carried the image hit a rock and was wrecked. "But the Sinhalese image remained (afloat) on a single plank. The plank drifted along for three days and reached, by the power of the Naga kings, the vicinity of the city of Siridhamma."[5] Guided by a dream, the king of Nagara Śrī Dharmarāja went in a ship looking for it, and rescued the image. He then sent word to Rāmkhamhāeng, who personally came to the city of Nagara Śrī Dharmarāja and conducted the image to Sukhodaya. King Rāmkhamhāeng built a magnificent *thūpa (stūpa*/reliquary monument) at Sajjanalaya, together with an image house resembling a celestial abode, and he dedicated them in the presence of assembled multitudes from the cities of Sajjanālaya, Kamphāengphet, Sukhodaya, and Chaināt.

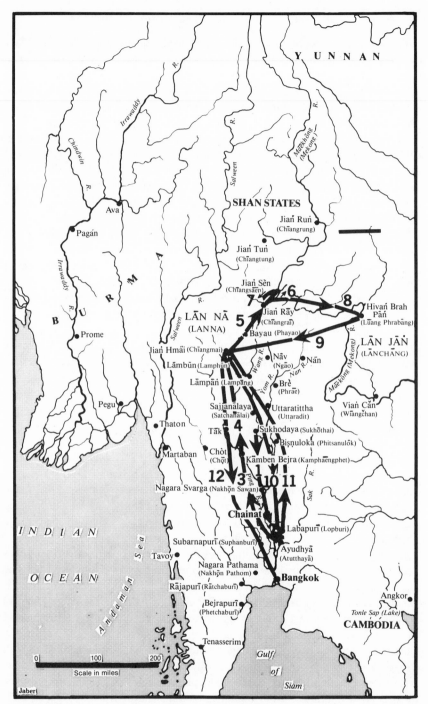

The travels of the Siṅhala Buddha, beginning from Sukhodaya. The arrows indicate the direction of the journeys and the numbers next to the arrows their sequence.

## "Likeness" of the image to the original Buddha

What do we make of this arrival story? We know that Nagara Śrī Dharmarāja, situated in South Thailand, is one of the oldest centers of Buddhism; we are aware that the "upstart" kingdom of Sukhodaya stands to gain by having among its credentials amicable contact with this historical city, which in fact is traditionally viewed as having contact with Siṅhala Buddhism and as being a source for the transmission of that Buddhism to Sukhodaya. Thus, in the legend Nagara Śrī Dharmarāja is the mediator between Siṅhala Buddhism and Sukhodayan religion.

The *Jinakālamālī* next gives this account of the image's fortunes and travels (see map). King Rāmkhamhāeng's successors honored and venerated it, and certain events took place in the reign of King Lideya (Līthai/Luthai), who was widely known as Dhammarāja, "the Righteous Monarch." Rāmādhipati, paramount lord of Kamboja kingdom, whose capital was the city of Ayudhyā, captured the city of Chaināt, but subsequently consented to return it to Līthai Dhammarāja, who then conducted the Siṅhala image to the city of Chaināt and honored it there.

After Līthai's death, the usurper Vattiteja, who had seized the city of Ayudhyā (and the kingdom of Kamboja), succeeded in capturing the city of Chaināt, and took the image away to Ayudhyā and honored it there. The king of Kamphāengphet, desiring to possess this fabulous image, sent his mother to seduce Rāmādhipati with pleasant words, and she managed to get hold of the image and to dispatch it with haste to her son.

Our story then takes us to Mahābrahma, the ruler of Chīangrāi and Chiengmai. (The *P' ra Buddha Sihing* chronicle,[6] taking the ruler of Chīangrāi[7] as the point of reference, relates a myth of origin of the image that I shall reproduce in the next section. At this point, let us stay with the *Jinakālamālī* text.) Mahābrahma heard about the wondrous Siṅhala image from a monk who had come from the South and who whetted his desire for the image by showing a wax model of it that he had made. Equipping an army, Mahābrahma marched to Kamphāengphet to capture the image from King Tipañña, the current possessor of it. In due course, a reconciliation between Tipañña and Mahābrahma was arranged; gifts were exchanged, and Mahābrahma succeeded in persuading Tipañña to part with the image.

King Mahābrahma, "who felt as though anointed with nectar, in due course arrived at the city of Nabbisi (Chiengmai) carrying the Sīhaḷa-image in a golden palanquin and placed the Sīhaḷa-image in the Great Monastery inside the inner city." Soon, however, Mahābrahma moved the image "to the city of Jaṁrāya (Chīangrāi) for the purpose of making another image of bronze, its exact replica," and he consecrated this replica at Pallaṅkandīpaka in Chīangsāen. Bringing the Siṅhala image back to Jaṁrāya, he kept it for a while at the monastery of Mahābuddharūpa and had still another replica, resembling the original in dimensions and appearance, "cast from an alloy of bronze, lead, gold and silver and held a great ceremony in honour of the dedication of the Buddha statue."[8]

# The cult of amulets

In this account of the travels of the Siṅhala Buddha, travels so intimately connected with the imperatives of kingship and kingdom making, a couple of points that emerge at the end should be underscored. We are clearly told that Mahābrahma placed the image in a *wat* situated in the inner city. Because the most important complex in the inner city is, of course, the king's palace, the implication is that the image is housed in a shrine on the palace grounds. In other words, it is a royal palladium. We are also privy to the remarkable fact that Mahābrahma had two replicas of the Siṅhala image cast, which he planted in two major cities in his kingdom; the original itself being in his capital. We see in this act the process of distributing the charisma of the image at different points in the kingdom; but this same act has also resulted in the making of three Siṅhala Buddhas, whose existence would in later times raise the question of authenticity among contesting rivals, all claiming to be the real thing. In fact, some scholars have pointed out that Mahābrahma's casting of the replicas accounts for the presence of at least three present-day images, all claiming to be *Sihingbuddharūpa:* one at Bangkok, another at Wat Phra Sing at Chiengmai, and a third at Nagara Śrī Dharmarāja. There are in fact more pretenders in existence, a matter that may be the despair of art historians but a joy to the social scientist investigating the phenomena of charisma and sovereignty and their fragmentation and aggregation. We shall return to this matter in the section below entitled ''Fact and Fiction.''

## The origin myth of the Siṅhala Buddha

With the record of the travels of the Siṅhala image behind us, let us now scrutinize its origin myth, of which we shall refer here to two versions, the second of which is more important for us.

 1. The *Jinakālamālī* gives this account.[9] Seven-hundred years after the passing away of the Buddha, there lived ''twenty canker-waned Arahants'' on the island of Laṅkā. The Siṅhalese king, wishing to see a likeness of the Buddha, visited the elder of the monastic order and, referring to the tradition that the Buddha had visited the island three times, inquired whether anyone who had seen him then was alive. ''At that very instant, on account of the canker-waned Arahants, the king of the Nāgas appeared before him in the guise of a youth and created a likeness of the Buddha in order to dispel the doubt of the king of the Sīhaḷas. For seven days and nights the king paid homage to the image of the Buddha.'' He then summoned sculptors, had a beeswax model made in the likeness of the apparition, and had an ''alloy of molten tin, gold and silver poured within.'' When the shaping was finished, the image ''became dazzling and resplendent like the living Buddha himself.'' The king venerated the image, and ''his sons, grandsons and greatgrandsons too, in lineal descent, paid homage to the Sīhaḷa-image.''

Let me make a preliminary comment or two before we pass on to the second version of the myth. We note that the canker-waned *arahants* are the intermediar-

ies between king and *nāga* – their spiritual merit enables the unusual manifestation. Secondly, the constant references to seven days and nights in the myths and
legends – seven days and nights for which the apparition of the Buddha lasts, the
same period of time for which kings pay homage to images, and so on – seem to
recall the great "awakening" of the Buddha's enlightenment, when for seven
days and seven nights he remained in abstracted bliss. Might one suggest then,
especially in respect of the reiterated pious ambition of reproducing in images the
Buddha's "likeness," that just as a watch or trance of seven days and nights
concluded for Gotama the attainment of Buddhahood, so the same period com-
pletes for the devotee the contemplation of the Buddha image or the paying of
homage to it? As we shall see, the gap between the ambition to realize the
Buddha's likeness and the impossibility of realizing it in actual fact constitutes a
rich theme for generating events in mytho-history.

2. The second version of the myth – contained in the *P'ra Buddha Sihinga*
chronicle – is not only richer and more complex, but also its first recitation is
described as taking place in a context that allows us to infer the myth's performative significance. The context is that of the enthusiastic espousal of the Buddhism
of the Sinhala sect of forest-dwelling monks, and, even more significantly
perhaps, of the integral role that the newly arrived technology of the casting and
worship of images played in the propagation of the religion.

The background for the recitation of the myth of the Pra Sihing is as follows.
The image had exhibited its miraculous powers in its first place of residence in
Sukhodaya. King Kūēnā of the Lān Nā, desiring to introduce in his kingdom the
forest-dwelling monks who had vitalized religion so much in Sukhodaya, invited
their leader Sumana to come to his kingdom and settled him in Lamphūn.
Sumana requested that the king of Lān Nā have four standing images of the
Buddha cast as an aid to his propagation of religion. This is one of the first
references to the casting of bronze images in Northern Thailand.

As this point of time the Prince of Chīangrāi, the ruler of a nearby principality,
was visited by a monk who showed the prince a wax replica of a very famous
image known as the Sinhala Buddha, which belonged to the ruler of Kamphāēngphet. After relating the many wonders it had performed, the monk told its
antecedents:

Some seven centuries after the Buddha's passing away, three princes of Sri
Lanka wanted an image made in his authentic likeness. While they were consulting some holy men, a benign dragon (*nāga*) appeared, and, saying that he had
known the Sage well, offered to provide a model. He transformed himself into an
apparition of the Buddha, resplendent with the bodily markings of the *mahāpurisa*
(great man) and seated in the attitude of meditation. He had warned the holy men
not to worship the apparition, as that would involve demerit. After allowing them
seven days to study his apparition, he resumed his normal form and went
away. Artists were summoned to make a wax mould from the holy men's
description. Gold, silver, and tin, amounting to sixteen coconut-shell measures,

were collected, and while the molten metal was being poured into the mould, a prince struck in anger an incompetent workman with his stick. This evil deed caused a defect in the casting of the statue's hand. The soothsayers advised that the defect should be left as it was because a later owner would repair it. The monk then related the subsequent career of the image, the details of which we have already considered. Note in this story that once again it is royal persons who yearn for an authentic likeness of the Buddha and holy men (*arahants*) who provide the proper ambience for the miraculous manifestation.[10].

The second version tells us that the image, constituted of precious metals and cast with elaborate preparation, is flawed in the outcome because of an evil deed committed by one of the princes: To my mind this flaw, as a mythic device, creates a tension and a contradiction that impel an unfolding of events. The flaw makes the image an incomplete likeness at a third remove (an incompleteness already implied in its being a recollection of an apparition of the real Buddha); but the flaw has a positive function. It also creates the possibility of a more virtuous king of the future owning the image and making it complete and perfect; however, until that time arrives (this virtuous king will of course always be that royal person currently aspiring to capture it from another), the image will pass from hand to hand, a pawn in a war of unsavory stratagems between rival kings. Indeed, the monk's recitation of the famous image's story incited the prince of Chīangrāi to wage a war with the ruler of Kamphāēngphet to gain the prize by force and induced the besieged ruler to part with an image. Delighted with the miracles it performed, he took it home and had a copy of it made in bronze.

**Fact and fiction**

Keeping in mind the career of the Siṅhala Buddha as related in the chronicles, let us finally ask "what are the 'facts' of the case as may be seen by an archaeologist–art historian?" According to Griswold, the original Buddha image that is claimed to have come from Sri Lanka cannot be identified today, nor for that matter the image the prince of Chīangrāi got from Kamphāēngphet. Currently in Thailand, there are five or six images that are located in different towns, which popular opinion identifies with the original; five of these are in the Lān Nā style of the golden age, while the sixth, located in the southern town of Nagara Śrī Dharmarāja, shows features of the Ayudhyān style. None of them could have been made in Sri Lanka, the mythic place of origin. The connoisseurs of Bangkok claim to have the authentic image in their capital, but such claims do not go uncontested by the inhabitants of the historic cities Chiengmai and Nagara Śrī Dharmarāja.

In any case, the tradition of the Siṅhala Buddha belongs to the era that coincides with the beginning of a school of bronze sculpture in Lān Nā and a

## "Likeness" of the image to the original Buddha

revitalization of Buddhism inspired by, and based on, the Sukhodaya tradition. Hence, Griswold has dubbed the Tai Yuan imitations of Sukhodaya statues as "the style of Sumana," a style that preceded the style of the "Lion" type associated with the renowned reign of King Tilok.

We must conclude this story with the Pra Sihing image, which now resides in the National Museum of Bangkok. It is seated in the attitude of meditation, and Griswold deems it a fine example of the Mixed type of the Lān Nā golden age – a style that was concurrent with the Lion type of Lān Nā. It is likely that it was the "Siṅhala" Buddha the people of Chiengmai were worshiping in the latter part of King Tilok's reign.

How then are we to fit this fact of a later dating of the museum's exhibit, and the hypothesis that the Siṅhala Buddha came into prominence at an earlier period, the period of "the style of Sumana"? The unraveling might start with the proposition that the "original" Siṅhala Buddha, referred to in the chronicle of that name, was a Sukhodaya copy of a Siṅhalese original or else was the copy, at a further remove, made by the prince of Chīangrāi. The chronicle closes with the installation of the image in 1389, but adds a prophecy that it would be taken back to Ceylon in 1457. This prophecy of departure is also a prophecy of the image's return to Chiengmai – in other words, the "reappearance" (as an event in the legend) should imply the creation of a copy at yet one more remove, a figure of the Lān Nā Mixed type, incorporating the iconography of its predecessors in important respects. This creation is probably the National Museum's present exhibit (Figure 7).

The Siṅhala Buddha's fortunes have declined in the past few centuries. It appears that in 1548 the Siṅhala Buddha was taken away to the neighboring kingdom of Lān Chāng. Although a few years later it returned to Chiengmai, the image did not recover its previous prestige – either because another had been substituted at Chiengmai as the palladium or because its capture signified the unpalatable shame that an object so closely associated with Chiengmai's political sovereignty could have been spirited away by a rival. At any rate, when the king of Ayudhyā seized it in 1662, he was informed that its magical powers were exhausted. It returned to Chiengmai in 1767 and was brought to Bangkok in 1795 by the founder of the current ruling Čakkrī Dynasty (Rāma I), where it has remained since. Popular belief in it as a source of miraculous powers was revived in recent years; however, it is in one among many historic images aggregated in Bangkok. There are some that outshine it, particularly the Emerald Buddha jewel, which is the palladium of the kingdom of Thailand today.

But an unexpected change in the fortunes of the Siṅhala Buddha took place in April 1982 during the Rattanakosin bicentennial celebrations. As part of these celebrations, the present king, Rāma IX, conferred the title of Mahā (Great) upon his ancestor and founder of the dynasty. The most spectacular event was the royal barge procession down the Čao Phrayā River: On April 5, the king and the crown prince sailed in the principal barges; a week later, on April 12, the Phra Buddha Sihing (Siṅhala Buddha) – or rather that version of it now in the capital – sailed in the king's barge in a similar procession, substituting for the king's person.

## Continuity through replication

It should be quite evident by now that the chronicle tradition in reporting the legendary histories of famous images loosely interweaves two antithetical themes. But the looseness of the weaving makes it quite evident again that there is little, at best only a halfhearted, effort to efface the contradiction, for what the chronicle conveys, and what matters most to the pious Buddhist, is the continued maintenance of Buddhist religion and civilization, even though the continuity is achieved through the replication and renewal of earlier forms. It is in this sense that we have to evaluate the fact that there are several representations in Thailand of the Siṅhala Buddha, rendered in different styles and at different periods, which all claim to be the original, the original itself enveloped in the mists of myth.

The *Jinakālamālī* itself leads us to the right solution. While reporting the events of the coming of the Siṅhala religious dispensation to North Thailand, it records how a king of Chiengmai, Lakkhapurāgama, marched to Chīangrāi, seized the Siṅhala image from Mahābrahma, took it back to Chiengmai, placed it in the Čēdī Lūang (Great Cetiya), and honored it reverently. Then follow these two verses:

> In Laṅkā, in the city named Siridhamma, in (the city) called Sukhodaya, in Jayanāda and Ayojjhā and in (the city) named Vajirapākāra.
> In Nabbisi and Jaṁrāya, similarly in the islet of Pallaṅkadīpa, was the noble Sīhala-image honored by kings and commoners.[11]

What is being disingenuously reported is that the Siṅhala Buddha representations are in nine locations: one in the parent country of Sri Lanka, the rest in Thailand. Rather than raising the question of authenticity, we are called upon to reflect on the (necessary) multiple incarnations and residences of the "likeness" of the true Buddha, all of them being sacrosanct by virtue of the generations of people who have venerated them.

## The implications for political legitimacy

The mobility of the Siṅhala Buddha is a pointer to many features of the traditional polities in question. The polities were what I have elsewhere called "galactic" in organization:[12] that is, a loose formation composed of a central domain surrounded by vassal states and, at the outer rim, by tributary states, which are all reproductions on a smaller scale of the dominant center: These galactic polities were fluid formations, and the center–satellite relations and patterns changed constantly. One corollary of such instability is that there were no stable dynasties of rulers who succeeded one another according to defined and predictable rules of heirship. If there were "divine" kings, they were continually dethroned by palace rebellions and wars of secession. The "divinity," or claims to righteous or universal kingship, were based on "personal charisma" rather than on institutionalized rules pertaining to the tenure of an "office." Dynasties when formed were shortlived. Factional coalitions and oppositions, rather than constitutional blueprints and strict considerations of division of labor, dictated the galactic distribution of power and administrative organization in terms of replication, duplication, and parallelism.

Individual kings of personal charisma who assumed kingship found, among other things, two more or less enduring *bases* for claiming "legitimacy" and through it stability of power. One was the claim to being a *cakkavatti* or a *dharmarāja* on the basis of personal achievement and commitment to Buddhist norms of kingship. These positions, according to Buddhist norms, are not so much inherited as proven by individual *karma* and meritorious conduct. Though these positions cannot be inherited, those attaining them can claim to be *incarnations* and *avatāras* of archetypal heroes.

A second basis, linked with the foregoing, is the possession of *palladia* and *regalia*, which are enduring sedimentations or objectifications of power and virtue. Possession of them is a guarantee of legitimacy. But these sedimentations of virtue and power will remain with the possessor for as long as he is virtuous and deserving. They cannot be removed from their locations against their consent; and their travels are evidence of their changing hands and their passage from one deserving ruler to another.

For us, anthropologists and historians, the travels of a Buddha statue, such as those of the Siṅhala Buddha (or the Emerald Buddha Jewel), provide us with a chain or "genealogy" of kingdoms and polities that these statues have legitimated and also with a map of a vast political arena in Southeast Asia, made up of a number of principalities – pulsating, changing boundaries and affiliations, and possessing an identity by virtue of commitment to a religio-political ideology on the one hand and by virtue of sharing similar economic, demographic, logistical features on the other.

The *sacra* themselves, in their turn, are seen to derive their powers to affect and transform the world by virtue of their "authenticity," their "likeness" to the original, and their "pedigree" – all of which in the last resort are values generated and conferred upon the objects by the human actors themselves. Thus we are confronted with a dialectic: The Buddha statue as a palladium is a product of the circumstances of its making and the authenticity given it by its makers, sponsors, and patrons. In this sense, history is embedded and objectified in it. It is this very sedimented presence in it that in turn radiates upon and influences human actors and events. This unfolding of events in turn is registered in the object. There are exchanges between sources, agents, and beneficiaries of power. What we have witnessed in the case of Thai kings, monks, and Buddha statues is a dialectic of human actors' relations vis-à-vis one another with the artifacts they make and in which they embody their past.

# 17

~~~

# The process of sacralizing images and amulets

## The transfer of power by monks

We now come to the rituals of sacralization of amulets and the process by which potency and efficacy are transferred by the monks to the amulets. The actual sequence may vary from ceremony to ceremony, as we shall see in the illustrations below, but the underlying mechanisms are the same, in that there is a chanting of sacred words (*sēk khāthā*), the transferring of potency by sitting in meditation (*nang prok*), and the like. Moreover, the sacralization of amulets is essentially similar to the chanting and transference procedures by which Buddha statues are ceremonially installed and "animated" by the "opening of the eyes" (*bōēk phra nēt*). As a matter of fact, it is a common practice that, when a Buddha statue is being sacralized at a *wat*, the laity (and monks) will bring small statues newly purchased or cast, and their favorite amulets, so that they too can undergo the rite. The ritual procedures highlight an important fact about consecrations and installations. The Buddha cannot become immanent in a statue until his "presence" has been activated by monks by their recitations of the *Dhamma* and by the transfer of their spiritual virtues and energies as followers of the Path. Similarly, although amulets in the shape of an animal, bird, human, or deity have certain virtues related to their form and intrinsic nature, it is the monk and lay specialist who importantly charge them with efficacy. This double aspect of installation has to be kept in view. The gods and other suprahuman agents are nonentities without their worshipers and officiants, just as the latter have no identities without their gods and collective representations.

I shall now give a number of descriptions of the sacralization procedures enacted at various stages of the making and installation of Buddha statues and amulets and highlight their salient features.

243

# The cult of amulets

## The making and sacralization of amulets at the shrine of the pillar of the city of Bangkok

The *lak mūeang* is the "pillar of the city" of Bangkok; because it is the foundation pillar of the country's capital city, it is a focal point for the country as a whole. The Bangkok pillar was installed in 1792 at the very beginning of the Čakkrī dynasty. The pillar is placed in the center of a shrine, where also reside the guardian deities of the capital.[1] Hundreds of people flock to the shrine every day to ask for favors from the pillar and the deities and propitiate them with flowers, candlesticks, joss sticks, silk scarves, gold leaf, and food and drink for favors granted. The pillar is personified and referred to as Čao Phāū, which, literally meaning honored father, is the usual reference and address term for a guardian deity. The shrine is administered by the War Veterans Organization (of the Thai armed forces) and the income is used to support veteran soldiers.

The decision was taken in 1975 to make amulets of the pillar and the deities of the shrine and to sell them to the public to raise money, mainly to make welfare payments to soldiers (and their families) who had suffered injury in fighting "for the security of the country." This phrase refers to the participation by Thai soldiers in the Laotian and Vietnam wars and in action against alleged communist insurgency elements and rebels. This phenomenon being described is yet one more reminder that in Thailand today various kinds of "religious" and "ritual" activities and cults ramify throughout the country's governmental and military, that is, "political," establishment in a supportive manner.

Five medallions of the five guardian deities[2] and one medallion of the pillar itself were made in two colors, gold-dipped and smoky metal (*rom dom*). The gold-dipped were sold for 30 *baht* ($1.50) each and the other for 20 *baht* each. In addition, a silver model of the pillar standing some nine inches high was made and sold for 999 *baht* ($50).

The making and sacralizing of the amulets went through three phases: (1) First, small metal sheets of gold, silver, and red-gold were sent from Bangkok to 108 (an auspicious number) venerable and famous monks throughout the country for each of them to write sacred letters on the sheets (*khīan akkhara*) and to chant sacred words (*pluk sēk*) while writing. We see here how the virtue and potency of the religious virtuosi dispersed and distributed throughout the country are aggregated at the center. (2) Next, the metal sheets were collected, melted, and cast into the medallions and the miniature pillars. (3) Then was staged the final sacralization ceremony.[3] This ceremony was attended by the *Phra Sankharāt* (the supreme patriarch of the *saṅgha*); the government was represented by the deputy prime minister and the minister of defense.

Offerings of meat, crabs, eggs, sweets, and fruits were made to the shrine deities, with the chief court brahman presiding.[4] Thereafter, the most important sequence was staged. While 4 monks at a time, sitting on the side, chanted *paritta* chants (*sūat parit*) continuously, 72 senior monks, divided into three

244

# The process of sacralizing images and amulets

batches of 24, sat for four hours at a time meditating silently and transferring virtue to the pile of amulets by means of a cord (*sāi sin*) that passed through their hands and was attached to the pile. Colloquially, this meditation is called *nang prok*: The monks sit cross-legged, close their eyes, practice concentration (*samādhi*), and say words mentally and silently. The monks are said to achieve the state of "internal sitting" (*nang thāng nai*), which enables them to achieve states of supranormal mystical power, which we have already discussed under the aspect of *iddhi*. The general belief is that by reciting *gāthās* and then sitting in meditation, the monks are able to concentrate power (*saksit*) and transfer it to the amulets. The technique of sacralizing Buddha statues and images is the same: The statue is activated – its eyes are opened – by nine or more monks chanting *paritta* verses and other monks sitting in concentrated meditation and charging the statue.

## The consecration of a Buddha statue (*Phithīkamphutthāphisēk*)[5]

The following account of the procedures for making a metal Buddha statue and sacralizing it was given to me by a monk bearing the *phrakhrū* title. He resided at the central Thammayut sect *wat* in Bangkok, Wat Bovonniwet.

### PHASE I: POURING THE METAL TO CAST THE STATUE

A site has to be selected; it may be a *sālā* (hall) or *bōt* (ordination chapel) in a *wat*, or it may be a central room in a private house. It is enclosed and bounded with a sacred cord (*sāi sin*), which the monks will hold while they chant. An already consecrated Buddha statue should be the presiding entity, and the requisite ritual articles (*khrūeang sakkāra*) must be assembled. They are: flowers; joss sticks and candles (*dāukmai thūpthīan*); puffed rice; a candle called *thīan chai*, which is as tall as the circumference of the head of the sponsor; another two candles called *phra wipatsī*, each of which has a wick made of 28 threads twisted together; and finally "a candle of the consecration chant" (*thīan sūat phutthā-phisēk*), which is a special candle together with four joss sticks.

On a platform, seats are arranged for four monks who will do the chanting in alternation. In front of them and arranged in rows are lit candles, joss sticks, flowers, and puffed rice.

Outside the bounded area of the site is installed an altar for the deities and divine angels (*thēwadā*); offerings are made to them (*būchā lōēk*) before the pouring of the metal and at the end of the ceremony. The deities are integral for ensuring the auspiciousness of the ceremony.

First of all, the *thīan chai* candle is lit, thus marking and highlighting the sponsor of the statue. While it burns, the monks chant until the time of "pouring the gold" (*thē thāūng*); the consecration chants (*sūat phutthāphisēk*) include the

245

familiar victory chant called *sūat chayantō*,[6] which recapitulates the Buddha's famous ten victories over opponents and evildoers. The *thīan chai* candle is put out at an astrologically appointed, auspicious time by the presiding monk.

PHASE 2: THE CONSECRATION

When the statue has been refined, polished, and completed, preparations are made for the consecration proper so that monks will sit in *samādhi* meditation and make the statue have power (*phra khlang*). As described earlier for the consecration of amulets, while one set of monks sits in silent concentration (*nang prok*), another group of monks will sit at the side chanting continuously.

The consecration site must have four entrances and exits. At each corner of the site should be planted flags, umbrellas, banana trees, and sugar cane, which give it a festive appearance. (The same decorations are usually at the site of pouring the metal as well.)

PHASE 3: FEASTING THE MONKS

The final sequence is the celebration on behalf of the participating monks (*chalāūng phra*). Together with the feasting and giving of gifts to the monks may be staged "the opening of the eyes of the statue" (*bōēk phra nēt*). Sometimes a cloth covering the eyes is removed, and sometimes some cotton wool dipped in oil may be used to clean the eyes.[7] While this is being done, the monks chant *sūat thammačak*.

## A public casting of a Buddha statue

There are many Thai living in the United States. In the cities of their heaviest concentration, such as New York, Los Angeles, and Chicago, they have established their *wat* and have invited monks from Thailand to reside in them. In early September 1971, I witnessed the casting of a number of Buddha statues, of which the foremost was a large one that was to be installed in the Los Angeles *wat*. The proceedings show how politicians serve the purpose of the *sangha* and how prominent monks and prominent laity collaborate in the implementation of conspicuous religious projects.

The casting was staged in an ample and a colorful compound of Bangkok's largest *wat*, Wat Mahāthāt, the foremost monastery of the Mahānikāi sect. Its compound was a veritable bazaar, filled with medicine hawkers, amulet and image sellers, food sellers, lecturers on religion, quacks, and *sādhus*. There was a heavy traffic of people walking about, sitting around chatting, transacting a hundred different deals.

The actual "pouring of the gold" into the clay moulds[8] was to take place on

# The process of sacralizing images and amulets

September 6, but two days earlier had begun the first step of collecting contributions of money and metal from the laity – gold ornaments, silver plate, and brass and copper vessels, etc. The organizer and master of ceremonies was the ecclesiastical governor of the province of Chonburī, who previously resided at Wat Mahāthāt: He was an effusive public speaker and kept up a barrage of exhortations and appeals to the public to contribute generously. He was also a much-traveled monk; the highlight of his visit to Europe was, he told me, an audience with the Pope. On the afternoon of the fourth, I saw four women and two monks taking in the contributions and giving receipts to the donors. That same evening at about 8 p.m. nine monks recited the evening chants (*suad mon yen*) at the site; and thereafter, four monks began to chant *paritta* verses, while four others began their meditation. The chanting and meditation terminated at midnight. On the following day, the same solicitation of money and metal, and the exercises of the monks, were repeated.

"The pouring of the gold" took place on the third evening. A large tent had been put up (see Figure 8) and there was an enclosure within it where nine monks sat. (They would be the main chanters at the rite.) At the back of the tent was an elevated platform, on which sat dignitary monks presided over by the ecclesiastical governor of Chonburī. At the right-hand end of the platform was an altar with a Buddha statue. Elsewhere in the tent at ground level sat various lay dignitaries, the foremost of whom on this occasion was the foreign minister, Thanat Khoman.

The figure also shows that in front of the tent was the site of the casting. There was a mould of the chief statue set up; there were other smaller moulds for other statues in a separate group; and there were crucibles with molten metal being fired. A sacred cord (*sāi sin*) had been attached to the Buddha statue at the altar; it was wound around the four extremities of the chanting monks' enclosure and then around the four extremities of the casting shed (within which the moulds were placed). The entire compound was filled with some three thousand people, both men and women. Many monks watched the proceedings from the upper stories of the monastic building.

Matters came to a head when the foreign minister, his wife, and his entourage arrived. The minister lit candles and worshiped at the Buddha altar; the chief officiating monk recited the "three refuges." The minister was handed a bowl of gold coins and jewelry contributed by the faithful; he ostentatiously undid his own golden tie pin and put it in a bowl. Then, while the full assembly of monks chanted, he emptied the gold into a crucible of molten metal brought to him by some six or seven craftsmen in Thai traditional dress.

Then the workmen poured two crucibles of molten metal into the mould and thereafter poured metal into the other molds. When the chanting by the monks stopped, all the lay people broke loose and tried to grab at pieces of the sacred cord, which they then proceeded to tie around their wrists.

The next step would be the polishing of the statues after the moulds were broken and the sacralization of the finished statue (*abhiṣeka*).

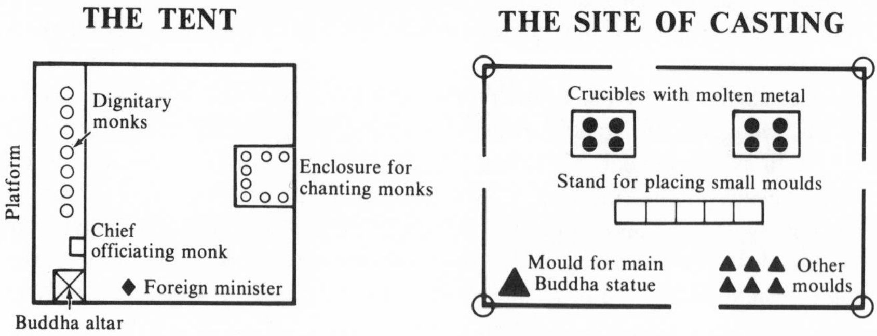

## THE TENT

## THE SITE OF CASTING

*Note:* The sacred cord went from the Buddha altar to the enclosure
for chanting monks, then all round the site for casting.

Figure 8. The casting site for image for Los Angeles *wat*

This piece of ethnography shows that, although the monks are the chief sacralizing officiants, frequently a famous lay sponsor (or sponsors) is integrally involved, not only as the provider of the material assets to make the statues, but also as a ritual participant himself whose "merit" and achievements are also transferred to the statue. This matter can be illustrated in finer detail by the following account of an *abhiṣeka* ceremony provided me by a scholar-monk from a Bangkok *wat*. This account was confirmed by a titled monk in another *wat* in the same city.

### The rite of consecration *Buddhābhiṣeka*

For the consecration of a Buddha statue, my informant said, a special site must be prepared. This site is usually the *bōt* of a *wat*, though this is not a requirement. Taking the *bōt* of a temple as his site, he described the layout as follows (see Figure 9).

A cord unwinds from the main Buddha altar of the *bōt* – the chief statue on the altar is usually a historic one or a reproduction of it – and first surrounds the central space, where well-known and famous monks, who have been specially chosen for the occasion, will sit and chant. These monks themselves enclose the array of statues that are being consecrated. The cord is finally attached to tables, where there are special candles mounted; one terminus is the altar, at which four chanting monks are positioned.

These candles have special names. One of them represents the chief lay sponsor: Its height is the height of the lay sponsor, and its wick is made of the same number of threads as the age of the sponsor. This candle is called *thīan chai*. In Bangkok's famous *abhiṣeka* rites, the chief lay sponsor present, and

# The process of sacralizing images and amulets

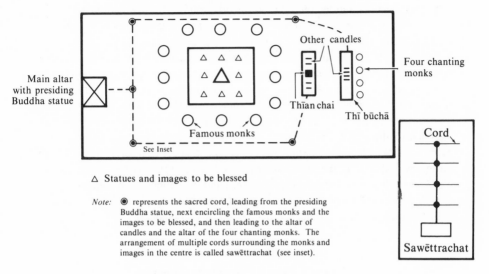

Figure 9. The layout for the *Buddhābhiṣeka* rite.

represented in the *thīan chai*, may be the king or a minister or a leading general. This candle is lit at the appropriate time by a famous, high-ranking monk, the most distinguished of whom is the supreme patriarch himself.

The other candles are: (1) *thīan buddhābhiṣeka*, the candles for consecrating the statue, which are placed at a special altar in front of the four chanting monks; (2) *thīan mahāmongkhon*, which is a large candle used for making holy water; and (3) *thīan nawaharakun*, nine candles.

The main sequences in the sacralization as reported by my informants are as follows:

1. *Būchā Rattanatrī:* Obeisance is made, and candles and joss sticks are lit by the chief presiding monk to the presiding Buddha statue installed at the main altar of the *bōt*.
2. The presiding monks give the precepts to the assembled laity.
3. The monks, encircling the statues, images, and amulets, chant *sūat mon phra paritta*.[9]
4. *Būchā thēwadā* is performed, in which the divine angels are propitiated by the lighting of the small candles; this propitiation is usually done by a layman or a *phrām* ("brahman").
5. The presiding monk lights the *thīan chai*, which represents the lay sponsor. (Sometimes a lay dignitary like the king or a minister may also do this.)
6. The climactic sequence is the chanting by the four monks of the *gāthā buddhābhiṣeka* (verses of consecration); while they chant, the monks sitting in the center make holy water and sprinkle it on the images awaiting sanctification.

The four monks recite a particular cycle of verses, and each recitation takes about thirty-five minutes. They, or four others who may relieve them, will chant these cycles in a chain until about midnight or 1 a.m. In some instances, a *wat* may hold these recitations on three consecutive nights, so that people may bring their own statues and images to be given new or renewed consecration. Recitations held for as long as seven consecutive nights are not unknown.

According to my Bangkok monk informants, the ceremony of "opening the eyes" of the image (*bōēk phra nēt*) is not part of the consecration ceremony, but a separate and less important sequence that is enacted as follows. While some monks chant, the presiding monk will open the eyes by removing the wax daubed over the eyes with a sharp instrument. He will then daub the statue with gold leaf; the back of the paper containing the gold leaf has *paritta* verses written on it. Sometimes two black jewels (*nin dam*) or two pearls may be inserted as eyes in the ceremony, but usually they will already have been inserted by the craftsmen and waxed over. It seems that in North Thailand, and in Cambodia, the opening of the eyes is considered an integral and important part of the *Buddhābhiṣeka* ceremony. I shall comment on this sequence at the end of this chapter.

## A Northern Thai ceremony of consecration

Wells[10] provides us with an informative account of the consecration ceremony, at which the rite of opening the eyes (*suat poek*) preceded the *Buddhābhiṣeka* recitations. The night of Mākha Pūjā is a favored time for dedicating new images and buildings. In 1937, Wat Thā Satori of Chiengmai celebrated the rebuilding of a *vihāra* and conducted rites for the consecration of Buddha images at one grand festival and fair, which began with numerous processions formed by groups representing temples arriving at the host temple with gifts.

After the monks' evening worship, and the Mākha Pūjā service, a chapter of monks and novices seated in a circle began the *suat boek* chants, which were rendered in a melodic and gay form by both treble and bass mixed voices. When the chanting ceased at midnight, the reading of the life of the Buddha began: One monk at a time in succession read a chapter from the palm-leaf manuscript, the orchestra punctuating the intervals between readings.

It is best if we reproduce verbatim Wells's rich account of the remaining sequences and his commentary upon them.[11]

Within the vihāra was an altar with about two dozen bronze images of Buddha, and behind the altar and along the wall were four larger images made of brick and mortar covered with gold leaf. A sincana cord has been wound about from one image to another and one end of the string brought to the monk in the preaching chair. Most of the images were new and many of them had been brought from private homes to be consecrated in this Suat Poek ceremony. The eyes of the new images were sealed with wax and a cloth of white or of yellow was placed over the head and shoulders of each figure. The worshipers, seated on mats, extended from in front of the altar to the door of the vihara and even outside, filling the portico in front. Here before the door was a long low table covered with offerings, each

# The process of sacralizing images and amulets

tray of offerings containing a slip of paper with the name of the donor or of the deceased in whose name the gift had been presented.

As the hours after midnight crept by many of the children in the audience fell asleep. Smoke from the numerous candles rose about the images in a tenuous but continual cloud. The adult auditors continued to sit upright, much of the time with palms of hands together, but they bowed reverently to the floor from time to time to mark the intervals in the reading. The selections were intoned rather than read, and so chosen that the final chapter, recording the death of Buddha and his attainment of Nibbāna, was completed just before dawn. At this point a monk opened a window shutter revealing the first faint streaks of morning light to the group within.

The monks then seated themselves facing the altar and the leader chanted the "Presentation of Incense and Candles" (thvai dhup tien). Then followed the "Consecration of the images of Buddha," or Buddhābhiseka ceremony. In this the Namo and the Saranagamana were chanted, followed by the Dhammacakkappavantana Sutra. Then the Buddha Udāna Gāthā was used and a portion of the Vipassanābhumi Patha. As they chanted:

> Whenever the Dharma is made manifest to a brāhmana who is diligent, such a brāhmana can ward off Mara with all his attendants like the dawn drives away darkness and fills the air with light,[12]

a monk arose and led a few of the laity in the task of unveiling the images and removing the wax from their eyes. As the vihāra faced east the eyes of the images were thus opened upon the first rays of the rising sun. This Buddhābhiseka Ceremony was spoken of as an ordination ceremony whereby the images entered the priesthood. Prior to this service the images were considered to be simply statues, after the service the images were "phra," something worshipful and more than mere metal. They had become sacred and possessed of nāna or spirit of intelligence. At the conclusion of the ceremony[13] the khao madhupāyāsa or celestial food was placed before the newly consecrated images as the handbills had announced. Later in the morning food was presented to the monks and the new vihāra was dedicated to the service of Buddhism. In Bangkok the Suat Poek ceremony is not used, but at a similar service when images are consecrated the Life of Buddha is read.

## A Cambodian consecration of a Buddha statue

The following is a translation of an ample account of a Cambodian consecration ceremony as reported by Adhemard Le Clere in his Cambodge Fêtes Civiles et Religieuses.[14] This account provides us with marvelous sequences that are unknown to my Bangkok informants. The officiant cuts off the hair and shaves the face of the statue, as if it were a candidate for ordination into monkhood, before opening its eyes. (We have already noted that the Northern Thai are explicit that an image is ordained at consecration.) Little children assume the role of divine angels (thēwadā) who witness the proceedings. The monks' recitation includes the recounting of the Buddha's previous births and his victory over Māra: We may therefore underscore the point, which was evident in the descriptions provided earlier as well, that part of the process of animating the statue consists in reciting and injecting into it the biography of the Buddha. As Le Clere remarks elsewhere, "The Cambodians, the Siamese, the Laotians and perhaps other Buddhist peoples recall the interior spiritual event of the Buddha's achieving *bodhi* in miming the literal opening of the statue's eyes with a needle."[15]

The *Achar* repeats three times the invitation to the personification of the Earth, the Blessed Ones (*tévoda*), the heavenly architect Pissanuka (*Visvakarma*), and the supreme Lord (*Bárameysaur*) to come to the ceremony.[16] Then coconut water is poured on the earth. The candles are lit. The stanza is recited to keep evil spirits away from the area where the new statue of the Buddha will be consecrated.

Within the sacred area are hung images of different animals. Then monks recite the *Aphisêk*, which is chanted at the consecration of Buddha statues.

A small chain, called *péât-séma*, made of pure untwisted cotton called *âmbôh*, is led around the room and around each pillar. The cord encloses a space and prevents evil spirits from getting close to the statue.

The *Achar* takes another cotton thread, encircles the Buddha statue on top of the altar, takes one end of the cord from behind this statue on top of the altar, takes one end of the cord from behind this statue to the right and leads it to the unconsecrated statue, circles it, then takes the end to the ground, where monks hold the thread in their clasped hands. The other end is taken from the statue's left side, down the altar, across the sala under the matting or even under the platform to the little raised altar at the east of the sala called *preah řean préah Inṭréa*. The second thread conducts holiness from the old to the new statue by the power of the spoken formulas.

The abbot of the monastery consecrates the statue with lustral water sprinkled from a small leafed branch; he is followed by the *Achar* and the main assistants. This is the *sráñ Préah* ("bathing of the saint"). The water thus used is carefully saved and used by the assistants, whether with their hands or a piece of material, to wash their heads, faces, chests, or shoulders. The *Achar* then recites three times the stanza inviting the supreme Lord to participate in the ceremony.

Then the *Achar* takes scissors and mimes, three times, cutting the statue's hair. Each time he recites a Pali stanza called *pheak kaṇtray* ("face scissors"). He takes a razor and three times mimes shaving the beard and the eyebrows, each time repeating a Pali stanza called *koṁbo et kor* ("the razor blade").

The *Achar* then takes two needles hidden in three or five *méali* flowers, one placed in the left hand and one in the right hand of the statue. All eyes are on him and on the Buddha statue. He salutes the statue three times. Then, taking the needle from the left hand, he pretends to pierce the right eye.

He takes the needle from the right hand and pretends to pierce the left eye. This is repeated three times, and the monks repeat three times in Pali: "We have successfully achieved opening the eyes of the saint." This is called *boek phṇo nét Préah* ("opening the saint's eyes").

252

# The process of sacralizing images and amulets

The gong strikes three times, which signals that the statue is consecrated and that it may now be worshiped.

Two candles are lit. The *Achar* invites the worshipers to say the precepts. This is the *saum soel*. They first recite the five, the eight, and then the ten *silas* of the Patimouk.

Then the worshipers in the *châk saké*, prompted by the *Achar*, pray that the benign gods will hasten there. The deities appear in the form of eight children, who wear crowns of white cotton, four boys called *néak* and four little girls called:

*néaṅ* Peysakkha
*néaṅ* Bonkésey
*néaṅ* srey Krup-lak
*néaṅ* Sobatévi

They sit on cotton-covered mats in front of the altar in two rows, boys in front, girls behind, facing the monks. They are dressed in their best, wearing a white scarf over the right shoulder and under the left armpit. Before them are placed incense sticks stuck in a banana tree trunk with a base of three feet, or a whittled, husked coconut on which are stuck four bamboo rods, one bearing four yellow flowers, another a rolled betel leaf, another an areca nut, and the last a lit stick of incense. This is *chaul-tévoda*, the gateway to the thewada, and the offerings to them.

The monks chant mantras to acquire merit for themselves and the worshipers. This is called *sautr montr*. At this point, the statue is placed on the altar. The monks move from their customary place and sit in front of the altar, their backs to the children representing the thewada, that is, between the altar and the children.

The *sautr thor péahuṅ* follows: It consists of the *Achar*'s aides lighting eight tapers on the altar, the assistants lighting many incense sticks, and monks reciting a prayer recalling the Buddha's fight with the demon Māra.

The *sautr thor Putthéa âphisoek* consists of lighting five more candles and monks saying the formula for consecrating a statue, in which are described the previous existences of the Holy One.

Five more candles are lit and the monks chant the *sautr thor yôk*, which invites the faithful to give alms as a means of acquiring merit.

Five more candles are lit and the monks chant the *sautr thor nômômî*, which is a greeting to the twenty-eight previous Buddhas.

Five more candles are lit and the monks recite the *sautr thor phchaṅ Māra*, which describes the defeat of Māra.

The ceremony customarily ends with offerings to the monks, such as packets of betel, screens, and even ritual clothing.

Later in his book, Le Clere gives another description of a consecration ceremony.[17] The sequences of the rite are similar, except that on this occasion the king, surrounded by the royal family and other notables, attended; and "to his right sat the court, to his left were over 1000 monks of the two Buddhist sects, arranged in four rows." More than 2,000 people were crowded into the temple compound. The presiding Buddha image is referred to as the "emerald Buddha."

Before the actual *abhiṣeka*, which followed the pattern previously described, the following events took place. The *Achar* requested forty-one monks to chant the invitation to the heavenly *devas* and "the faithful, women on the left, men on the right, dignitaries in the middle, prayed and bowed." Next, forty-one new monks appeared, and the *Achar* requested them to perform the aspersion of the outside walls of the temple.

The only new detail in the *abhiṣeka* proper was that after the patriarch of the *saṅgha* had sprinkled lustral water on the statue, the king followed, and after him "princes, ministers, greater and lesser dignitaries"; they kneeled before the statue in turn and sprinkled it with perfumed water. This sequence was called *srâh Pṛéah*, the bathing of the saint.

### The significance of the consecration rite

The consecration rite (*Buddhābhiṣeka*) is one of the components, a central component at that, which cumulatively contribute to the Buddha statue's (and other objects like amulets') possessing efficacy in the eyes of Buddhists. In Chapters 14 through 16, we discussed in what ways the Buddha could be considered to have an "immanent presence" in a statue: the classification of "reminders," the "radiance" and "fiery energy" emanating from the Buddha at the climactic point of achieving enlightenment, the doctrine of the several "bodies" of the Buddha, the iconic construction of the image in the authentic "likeness" of the historical Buddha – all these are germane to the issue.

The final component, discussed in this chapter, is the giving of "life" to the statue through the ritual of consecration. There are many dimensions to this ritual. One is the transmission of some portion of the virtues and powers of an already installed historic statue or a famous statue to the newly fashioned image. As a result, the newly consecrated image is considered to belong to the "lineage" of the presiding image or even as a "reincarnation" of it. A second is the recitations of *paritta* chants, of the Buddha's first sermon, and of the major episodes of his biography by monks; the more famous or the more advanced in the path of liberation these monks, the more efficacious their recitations. A third is the transference of psychic energies to the image by monks sitting in meditation: Here again, the more adept the monks in meditation practice, the more potent the energy transferred. We should note, additionally, that the longer the recitations and meditation sittings by these monks, and the larger the number of them participating, the more efficacious the result. Finally, there is the sequence of "opening the eyes" of the image, which merits further discussion because of certain problems it poses.

## The opening of the eyes of the image

We have observed that, although the consecration rites performed in Bangkok today do not emphasize the sequence of opening the eyes of the statue (which may consist in the insertion of jewels, or the painting of the eyes, or the removing of the layer of wax over the eyes), it is important in the accounts given for North Thailand and Cambodia.

Le Clere gives a quintessentially Buddhist interpretation of this sequence: The statue is first ordained into monkhood, and the final act of opening the eyes signifies and calls to mind the Buddha's attainment of enlightenment and supreme wisdom under the *bodhi* tree. (His eyes of wisdom and radiant presence are attributes that derive from this event.) It is therefore appropriate that in the Thai and Cambodian descriptions the image's eyes are opened either by the presiding monk – who may actually lead a procession of other monks and eminent laity in this act – or by a ritual officiant called an *ācariya* or *brāhm* ("*brahman*") – who is a lay ritual expert, of Buddhist affiliation, who performs auspicious (*mangala*) rituals of allegedly "Brahmanical" origin.

The rite of opening the eyes of Buddha images appears to be a very old one. Buddhaghosa, writing in the fifth century A.D., attributed to the Emperor Aśoka the holding of the festival of *Akkhipūjā* (a Pali term corresponding to the ceremony of opening the eyes). There are references to the ceremony being performed in Sri Lanka in the Mahāvamsa and the Cūḷavamsa chronicles, and they may well refer to historically authentic events. The Cūḷavamsa explicitly states that the great King Parākrama Bāhu I (1153–86) of Polonnaruva used to insert the eyes of the Buddha images himself. Still later, there are copper-plate edicts (*sannasa*) of Kandyan times in the eighteenth century showing that the kings sponsored *netra mangalaya* ceremonies and may have even actually opened the eyes by painting them or by other means.[18] It is recorded of the famous Kandyan King Kīrti Śrī Rājasinha that, on the completion of the Gangārāma Vihāra, "he set the eyes of the image amidst great rejoicing, and the sound of musical instruments."[19]

Although the participation in and the witnessing of eminent and ordinary monks and laity in the opening of the eyes of Buddha images present no special interpretive problems – for after all they are re-enacting the great event of the Buddha's enlightenment and are also animating the image by transferring their virtues to it – the reports by Gombrich of a *nētra pinkama* ("eye ceremony") performed on a Buddha image in the Kandyan hill country of Sri Lanka in 1965 does pose problems. For whereas the ceremony in its other aspects, such as the *paritta* recitation by monks, is similar to the ones already described for Thailand and Cambodia (and Sri Lanka in earlier times), yet the actual sequence of painting the eyes, entrusted to the craftsman (and his assistants) of the smith caste (*navandanno*), who actually made the image, was considered dangerous to onlookers as well as the painter. "The craftsman paints in the eyes at an auspicious moment and is left alone in the closed temple with only his colleagues, while everyone else stands clear even of the outer door. Moreover the craftsman does not dare look the statue in the face, but keeps his back to it and paints sideways or over his shoulder while looking into a mirror, which catches the gaze of the image he is bringing to life. As soon as the painting is done the craftsman himself has a dangerous gaze. He is led out blindfolded and the covering is only removed from his eyes when they will first fall upon something which he then symbolically destroys with a sword stroke." The craftsman, as ritual officiant, after painting the eyes carried a pot, which he smashed on the horns of a bull, and he slashed a milk-exuding tree with a sword or knife. Gombrich interprets the pot as carrying the collected "evil influence" (of what is not stated), and the officiant's acts as signifying that "he 'kills' the tree instead of the bull."[20] In other words, Gombrich chooses to interpret these acts, which the performers regard as "dangerous," as participating in the malevolence associated with "the evil eye," indeed with the "evil" encountered in Siṅhalese healing rituals (which are directed at demons) that "results from making mistakes in ritual, violating taboos, or otherwise arousing the malevolent attention of a supernatural being who conveys the evil by a gaze (*bälma*)."[21] This association is his, not that of the actors. No wonder he is perplexed that a Buddha image's numinous presence should be regarded in this malevolent way and that his interpretation goes nowhere.

A fine point of interpretation *is* at stake. There is a critical difference between the evil power emanating from the eye of a demon or an inauspicious person, which has to be dispelled, and the great power, even omnipotence, emanating from a supreme deity, which has to be muted or cushioned and harnessed so as to benefit the world of lesser beings.[22] These dual conceptions are hierarchical and carry positive versus negative charges. They separate the all-powerful beneficent deities or beings from the less-powerful evil demons and agents, whom the former encompass, command, and dispel. Although the rite reported by Gombrich is a Siṅhala Buddhist enactment, whose integrity and coherence has to be conceded and respected, yet I think that our understanding of its significance can be furthered by reviewing the Hindu notion of *darśan* (seeing) as it relates to the communication between gods and human beings.

In a religious context, *darśan* implies the "auspicious sight" of the divine, and *darśan* relates not only to renowned images of gods and sacred places of pilgrimage, but also to holy persons such as saints and renouncers. In popular terminology, Hindus say that the deity or holy man "gives" *darśan* and the worshiper "takes" *darśan*. "The prominence of the eyes on Hindu divine images

# The process of sacralizing images and amulets

also reminds us that it is not only the worshiper who sees the deity, but the deity sees the worshiper as well. The contact between devotee and deity is exchanged through the eyes. . . . The eyes of Sūrya or Agni or Varuṇa are powerful and all-seeing, and the gods were entreated to look upon men with a kindly eye. . . . The gaze which falls from the newly-opened eyes of the deity is said to be so powerful that it must first fall upon some pleasing offering, such as sweets, or upon a mirror where it may see its own reflection.''[23]

Stella Kramrisch includes the activation of the principal image of a Hindu temple among the rites of consecration at the conclusion of the building of that temple. ''At the beginning, so also on the completion of the building, the rite of auspicious germination . . . is enacted and oblations are given at night. Then at dawn, of another day, the Sthapati, the master architect, and the Sthāpaka, the priest architect, ascend the Vimāna with a golden needle, perform the rite of opening the eyes (netra mokṣa)'' of the image, and thereafter the Sthāpaka installs the image on its pedestal and places in it the seed (bīja) of the temple. It is obvious from this account that the opening of the eyes of a Hindu deity is no inauspicious act.[24]

# 18

# Amulets blessed by contemporary forest saints

The phenomenon of amulets is old in Thailand – perhaps as old as religion itself anywhere and everywhere – yet two things are distinctive about the current situation in Thailand. One is that there is an intensification in the traditional cult of amulets. Evidences of this are that there are many new amulets being produced today; there is an inundation of literature about them and their sacralizers; and the bazaar trade as well as the rituals of sacralization of amulets have multiplied. The second feature is that the most famous sacralizers of amulets are some of the forest monks, the meditation masters and saints (*arahants*) – who have been the focus of the first part of this book. As charismatic persons, some of them are much in the limelight today, and they virtually enjoy a national reputation.

Let me refer the reader back to Chapter 9, "The disciples of the Master," where I listed some thirteen meditation teachers and heads of forest hermitages, who all claimed to be the disciples, or at least associates, of the famous Meditation Master Mun. These derive to some extent their accreditation through their links to the Master. Compared with him, these disciples showed two shifts. One was that whereas the Master remained peripatetic throughout his life, the disciples have tended to found and/or reside in a single hermitage, though at the same time have themselves established branch hermitages or encouraged pupils to do so. But this is not a major deviation from the Master, for he too, we noticed, established a network of cells of disciples, especially in those monasteries he chose for temporary residence during the rains retreat.

The second difference represents a tendency toward polarization among disciples of that which was a coherent duality in the Master. The Master seemed to have a "rationalist" side manifest in his abstract, philosophical, and discursive discourses and in his viewing the meditative technology as a method for developing insight; he also exhibited a tantric, mystical, and ritualistic disposition, evidenced by his visionary and cosmological experiences. Understanding and practice, interior experience and exteriorized cosmology, were dialectically interwoven in him. However, the disciples, and other forest-dwelling, meditating

258

monks unconnected with the Master but rooted in a local forest-monk tradition, have tended either to emphasize the "rationalist" pole of unswerving renunciation and liberation or the tantric, ritualist pole of pursuing trance experience and supranormal powers. It is the latter type of ascetic forest saint, venerated for his loving-kindness (*mettā*) and his willingness to transfer his blessings to humankind while remaining uninterested in the fruits of action, who is implicated in the contemporary cult of amulets. And most of the heads of the famous forest hermitages of today, although themselves dedicated to the ascetic and meditative regime, are not averse to blessing amulets or to devoting some part of their time to blessing, instructing, and relieving the distress of an ardent laity. Moreover, many of them are able to function at different levels and in different modes, according to the context.

But whatever the differences of emphasis among the contemporary forest-monks in Thailand, we have first to comprehend their present-day salience in terms of their position within the larger *saṅgha* as a whole. We have mentioned before that traditionally in the Southeast Asian Buddhist societies there has been a bifurcation of the *saṅgha* into the village- and town-dwelling (*gāmavāsī*) and the forest-dwelling (*āraññavāsī*) monks, but that since the latter part of the nineteenth century the forest dwellers have not played a major role in Thailand, or even been an important part of the mainstream ecclesiastical establishment. Since Mongkut's time it is the *saṅgha* establishment, based in and directed from Bangkok, that has played an active shaping role, conferred legitimacy on the political authorities, and produced exemplary scholar- and administrator-monks who enjoyed great veneration and prestige. The forest-monks of today, only a small component of the *saṅgha* as a whole, do not participate in the monastic examination system, on the basis of which scholar-titles are conferred; forest hermitages (*samnak*) usually have not the requisite consecrated boundaries and stones (*sīmā*) and the sanctified *bōt* in which the ordination of monks can be carried out; indeed, forest-monks, even the most famous ones, are outside the system of administrative and other religious titles, to which the village- and town-monks of the two sects, the Mahānikāi and Thammayut, aspire.

Although situated outside the system of titles and rewards of the ecclesiastical hierarchy, the forest-dwelling and meditating monks enjoy an unusual prominence on the national stage today. The royal family, the ruling generals and politicians, and the largest business and banking houses seek them out and bow down before them, hoping to be edified and strengthened by their visits to them. A few years ago, the king and queen flew from Bangkok to the Northeast to attend the mortuary rites of a famous forest-monk and saint, Acharn Fun. Another famous meditation master flew to Bangkok for the first time in his life – by plane, not under his own propulsion[1] – and camped out under his umbrella on the grounds of the crown prince's palace to enable the crown prince to present in person his daily food and to receive instruction from him.

The intensification since the sixties and seventies of the cult of the amulets, and the radiant glow of charisma attributed to a group of reclusive renouncers who are the sacralizers of the most renowned amulets of recent coinage, are interconnected with other political and economic phenomena that at first sight may seem to have little to do with such exotic happenings. The connection between the seemingly esoteric and mundane can be readily grasped if we appreciate the fact that the amulets in question are frequently the combined efforts of two parties – the monk who is willing to be iconically represented on one side of the amulet-medallion and is also willing to sacralize it and the lay sponsor,[2] who may have his or her insignia imprinted on the back of the same amulet[3] and who collects or contributes the funds for minting the medallions and for staging the rites of sacralization [see Figures 10 (p. 264) and 11 (p. 275)].

The forest-monk's sacralization of amulets and his transfer of power (*saksit*) to them mainly consists of two components, which I have described in the preceding chapter: the chanting of sacred words (*sēk khāthā*), which include the standard *paritta* chants for conferring protection and prosperity; and the sitting in meditation, in particular employing the techniques of concentration (*nang prok*) and of transferring psychic energy. The sacred cord joining the monks to the amulets is an essential part of the process of transference.

### The amulets sacralized by Lūang Pū Wāēn

The most famous of the amulets of recent vintage are those that have been sacralized by an old monk called Lūang Pū (respected grandfather) Wāēn, a Northeasterner by birth, whose early peripatetic, wandering career was much like that of the Master Mun and who in 1979 was residing in a forest hermitage in North Thailand, near Chiengmai. I shall conclude this chapter by reporting a popular biography of him, but let me first concentrate on the numerous batches of amulets blessed by him, which have been sponsored by a variety of famous lay sponsors.

A good sample of the kind of veneration in which Lūang Pū Wāēn is held, and the kind of political and military context in which his "objectified charisma" is employed, is provided by the following news item culled from a Thai-language newspaper called *Matichon* (August 18, 1979): "Yesterday General Kriangsak Chomanan, Prime Minister and Supreme Commander of the Armed Forces, and General Yod Thephasadin, Deputy Army Commander and Deputy Minister of Defence, visited the Third Army Headquarters to bid farewell on the occasion of the former's retirement.

General Kriangsak asserted that Thailand's foremost enemy is the Communist Party of Thailand and its supporters and fellow-travelers. 'Don't think,' he warned, 'that communism in Thailand will be suppressed by the mere fact of our opening diplomatic relations with the Socialist Countries.' He then distributed to the soldiers Lūang Pū Wāēn amulets, and white *phā yan* cloths [cloths imprinted

# Amulets blessed by contemporary forest saints

with mystical *yantra* designs] sanctified by Lūang Phāū Ling Dam;[4] he recommended that the soldiers bind Lūang Phāū Ling Dam's white *phā yan* cloths to the Thai National Flag, and raise them together to the top of the mast, because they will give them protection and safety."

I shall describe two instances of amulet sacralization by Lūang Pū Wāēn that will enable us to see some of the implications of the coming together of saintly monk and lay sponsor in this enterprise.

### THE KING NARĒSŪAN AMULETS

Lūang Pū Wāēn has blessed many batches of amulets, and one such, much publicized in the local press and popular magazines, was sponsored in 1978 by the Fifth Police Headquarters for Special Training, located at Bān Pāng-Kwāng, Amphōē Māētāēng, Chiengmai Province.[5] The organizers, to whom Lūang Pū Wāēn gave his consent, were Police Colonel Phan Chonlasit and Police Major Somnuek Krisanasuwan.

The proceeds from the sale of the medals to the public were to be used for building a shrine (*sān*) to King Narēsūan the Great. The shrine was to be built at the entrance to the police headquarters at Māētāēng District, and a statue of King Narēsūan was to be installed inside. It is because of this dedication that the medals in question were called the batch (*ruon*) commemorating King Narēsūan. The total number of medals minted was 21,000.

The day for the ceremonial making of the medals was April 20, 1978. At 9:29 a.m. Lūang Pū Wāēn "sat" and recited the sacred words (*nang bāurikam*) and charged the medals with potency (*pluk sēk*), while at the same time extending mercy (*phāē mettā*)[6] to all beings. After the recitation, holy water was sprinkled on the medals.

The shape of the medal reproduced that of the very first batch of medals sanctified by Lūang Pū Wāēn: The front of the medal was ox-face shaped and had embossed on it the bust of Lūang Pū Wāēn with his name, "Lūang Pū Wāēn Sučinnō," underneath. On the back of the medal was a shield (*trālō*), under which was written: "the building of the Shrine of King Narēsūan, the Great." Our source reported that it was doubtful whether another batch of medals would be made again by Lūang Pū Wāēn and that "the most recent medals have the combined power of a big elephant (*chāng sān*) and of King Narēsūan." It is also remarked that "the Shrine to King Narēsūan and his statue were constructed in order to give *ming khwan* (auspicious morale) to the Police patrols and to those people who will pass by and pay their respects to him." The building costs were estimated at 5 million *baht* (U.S. $250,000). The laying of the foundation stone was done in late June of 1978, and was presided over by the supreme patriarch, Somdet Phra Ariyawong Sankatayān of Wat Rajbopit.

Three types of medals were made. The first was made of metal given an antique dark finish (*lōha rom*) and cost 30 *baht* each; the second was made of silver and cost 200 *baht* each; the third was of a special "water drop" shape, made of "new metal," and engraved at the bottom with a design of double curves. This last type, 999 in all, cost 99 *baht* each.

King Narēsūan (1555–1605) of Ayudhyā was chosen as the subject of representation on the other side of the amulet because he is known as a great warrior who successfully repulsed Burmese attacks, killed a Burmese crown prince in personal combat, made incursions into Burmese territory (particularly Pegu and some Shan states), successfully attacked Cambodia and made it a vassal, and controlled the northern Chiengmai Kingdom. Narēsūan thus temporarily held a large Thai empire. He died in 1605, having mounted the throne in 1590. As a prince, he was taken as a hostage to Burma when his father was defeated and made a Burmese vassal.[7]

*A commentary.* These amulets, with a relief of the Lūang Pū Wāēn (a contemporary figure following a classical exemplary mode of life) on one side and an inscription on the other side bearing King Narēsūan's markings (a past figure who energizes the present), may be considered to have both diachronic and synchronic roles. They have a "double presence," so to say, which may be elucidated by recourse to the concepts of *indexical symbols* and *indexical icons*. Each face of the amulet has a dual presence. The Narēsūan inscription relates to a past that is a national historical tradition (the reign and acts of King Narēsūan) and it simultaneously evokes this past in a present state of national crisis and warfare. The Lūang Pū Wāēn figure is that of a contemporary and living saint, who is in existential contact today with his followers and disciples, radiating to them his saintly virtues; but what he represents and what mystical powers he possesses derive from the following long-established classical and paradigmatic *arahant*'s ascetic path of meditation and liberation seeking.

Thus the amulets mediate between the past and present in many ways. Their diachronic mission is to carry portions of objectified history into the present; contemporary men and women have these condensed and objectified bits of the past, which they employ for contemporary purposes, dangling from their necks and rattling on their persons. They are also "mnemonic" devices that remind of and invoke past persons and their actions in the present time. The amulets put the wearers in contact with certain events in the past, which were contingent when they occurred and which by a process of collective Thai historical interpretation have been accorded a meaning in a semantic system called "national tradition." And they achieve the feat of keeping alive in the present events that are dead and gone. To adapt Lévi-Strauss for our purposes, the amulets "give a physical existence to history, for in them alone is the contradiction of a completed past and a present in which it survives, surmounted." Amulets, like archives, "are the embodied essence of the event."[8]

To carry the analysis one step further, all those amulets, made and sanctified in different points of time, and commemorating and invoking many disparate and often disconnected events, by surviving into and existing in the present are made to relate to one another through their relative similarities and differences, their virtues and potencies, and the past events to which they point. Of diverse origins, but in being juxtaposed and compared today in the shops where they are sold, or in the catalogues and books in which they are described, or even on the same necklace in which they are strung, they become components of a "paradigmatic" series, in the Saussurean sense. In this manner, their comparative ratings provide a basis for their "stock exchange" values and for their change of hands in market transactions or through more informal transfers.

To complicate matters further, amulets in the possession of individual owners become associated with, indeed partake of, the biographic events of their possessors, especially those incidents of miraculous escape from danger or windfall success in career, which the owners attribute to the efficacy of their amulets. The more prominent the owner, the wider the circulation of the reputation of his own collection of amulets. Thus even among amulets of the same vintage, individual differentiations in reputations occur, though the stories of success or failure of single members in the long run add to or diminish the reputation of the whole class.

The amulets derive another significant synchronic significance by virtue of their existence and circulation in a social and territorial space that is the Thai nation and country of today. In so circulating, they help create a national identity, in that Thai citizens are carrying on their persons pieces of past history that they come to share as a national heritage. Thus some culture hero of the Northern Sukhodaya Kingdom of the thirteenth century, or a warrior king of the Ayudhyā Kingdom of the sixteenth, represented on an amulet becomes the inheritance of, and daily reminder to, a remote townsman in South Thailand; a charismatic Bangkok monk of the mid-nineteenth century similarly becomes part of the religious tradition of a Northeastern villager. Parochial traditions thus become national traditions, and particular traditions are tendentiously propagated from the capital or major centers of rule and religion to the wider peripheries in an attempt to forge a single national identity and an experience of a single unified, common past. The process of nationalization and homogenization of cultural and political traditions has been aided by the better system of communications – by road, by rail, by newspaper and printed materials, by radio and television – which enable the propagation of information to vast numbers of people who only some three decades ago were locked into their regional isolations.

THE CONJUNCTION OF WORLD RULER AND WORLD RENOUNCER

An even more remarkable example of collaboration between forest-monk saint and secular patron is provided by the sponsorship of a batch of amulets by the king of Thailand himself. These amulets had Lūang Pū Wāen's head imprinted on one side and the royal crown (*mongkut*) on the other (see Figure 10). The objective was to collect some 50 million *baht* for the building of hospitals,

Figure 10. A Lūang Pū Wāēn medallion sponsored by the King of Thailand. On the front side is the bust of the monk with the caption "Lūang Pū Wāēn, Wat Doi Māēpang, Chiengmai." At the back is the royal crown (*Mongkut*) with the caption "On the occasion of the Royal founding of the hospital building, 16 March 1978."

especially in the provinces. The prime minister acted as the chairman of a committee composed of both laymen and monks to oversee the venture. The financial drive was successful, and by 1980 several hospitals had been built from the proceeds and ceremoniously opened by members of the royal family.

An important aspect of this meeting of world conqueror and world renouncer was the mobilization of high finance to secure the widest distribution and maximum sale of the amulets. Amulets made of different metals with different price tags were sold through all the major banks and commercial companies in the kingdom, such as the Bangkok Bank of Commerce, Thai Phānit, etc. These institutions displayed advertisements and made amulets available to their customers.

This example illustrates the meeting of ruler and saint for the highest altruistic purpose of charitable donation: Both parties engaged in unalloyed compassionate action. The king of Thailand is not only appreciative of saintly monks, he is also aware of the charisma that has always been traditionally attributed to kings themselves.

Some years ago, the king himself sponsored the making of a batch of Buddha amulets, which were called Lūang Phāu Čittraladā (the name of the present royal palace). Soil from sacred Buddhist sites in India and Thailand (e.g., Nakhon Pathom, which has one of the earliest known *stūpa* in the country); various kinds of metals, including gold and silver; hair from the monarch's head; and other substances were used for the casting of the images. The site at which the amulets were cast and sacralized was Wat Raikhing, whose abbot is famous for making amulets and sacred water and for similar good works. The abbot has a large lay following, and it is significant that the king broke tradition and included this commoner *wat* among the recipients of royal *kathin* presentation at the end of the rains retreat in 1978. This royal act is especially significant because the number of royal *wat* to which the king traditionally personally makes the presentation is small and their choice is a mark of their prestige. The king's decision to honor this *wat* signified, on the one hand, his intention to liberalize and broaden the sphere of his patronage; on the other hand, his choice of this *wat* because of the ritual powers of the incumbent abbot indicates the extent of the royal participation in the current cult of amulets and the reliance of the monarchy, which was traditionally a preeminent source of charisma, on prominent monks to receive additional potency and legitimation.

## A biography of Lūang Pū Wāēn

It is inevitable that a popular saint like Lūang Pū Wāēn should be the subject of a thriving hagiology – in both oral tale and written panegyric. I set down below a free translation of a biography of this monk I came across in a popular Thai-language magazine.[9] There are many such accounts of his life and career to be found in literature of the same genre. The biographer in this instance is a layman who quite unself-consciously reflects popular hagiographical trends and conventions. The tale informs us that Lūang Pū Wāēn showed quite early in his childhood signs of his later renunciatory life – his taking to the life of a vegetarian, meditating, and wandering recluse was foreshadowed by his childhood preferences.

There are two features in this account that are noteworthy. One is that Lūang Pū Wāēn's meeting and association with the Meditation Master, Mun, is underscored as a high point in his career. Secondly, the incidents, which describe Lūang Pū Wāēn's supranormal powers, are largely adduced as examples of the saint's performance of good deeds, such as combating and exposing local demons, on behalf of the ordinary villagers. Thus these stories of extraordinary power bring the Thai popular accounts in line with the popular Burmese accounts of their famous *weikza*; indeed they are not all that distant from the accounts of Tibetan saints who exorcise local demons and eradicate pestilence and disease in impressive episodes that simultaneously exploit the saint's *bodhisattva* compassionate feelings and awesome powers deriving from tantric ritual and "magical arts."[10]

Lūang Pū Wāēn, a native of Lōēi Province, was born in 1888, the same year in which momentous events were taking place in Thailand under the direction of

King Chulalongkorn. In that year Sirirāt Hospital was opened, a treaty with France was signed (involving the cession of Thai territory), and horse-drawn tram service was begun in Bangkok (plying between Lakmūēang and Bāngtāēm).[11]

Two old ladies told the biographer that Lūang Pū when young bore the name of Yān and that on ordination as a novice his name was changed to Wāēn, as is customary in the Northeast, where "ordination for the purpose of studying" (*kān būat rīan*) signifies the beginning of a new life. At the age of twelve, the boy was taken and left under the tutelage of a monk (Phra Uan), who was his father's younger brother (*ā*) in the hope that he would embark on his studies. The temple where he was ordained and resided in was Wat Phō-chai Mongkhon, named thus because in its compound stood five big *bo* trees, believed to be over 500 years old. At the ordination ceremony, Phra Acharn Kammar acted as his principal ordainer (*phra upatchā*), and his uncle acted as his instructor and tutor (*phra phī līang*).

As a child, Wāēn is said to have been well behaved but distinctly quiet, hardly talking to others and playing by himself. It is hinted that his family life was not happy. Wāēn and his younger sister Nāng Beng were born to Nāi Sai (father) and Nāng Kāēo (mother); however, his father took a second wife, to whom was born Nāi Sōphā (who later disappeared after ordination). Wāēn himself was fostered by his paternal grandmother. Wāēn's father was a farmer and a blacksmith, and his house was located on the banks of Hūai River. (It is now lived in by Wāēn's niece and her husband.)

Not long after ordination, Wāēn began to show the first signs of a world renouncer. He gave up eating meat and restricted his food intake to one meal a day. Moreover, as a novice, he behaved with dignity, scarcely talked to anybody, avoided noisy monks and novices, and sought the quiet of a shady *bo* tree or some other spot outside the *wat* where he could recite his lessons. He had a studious mien. Books were scarce in those days, and the only ones available to him were the few *samut khoi* (manuscripts made of long strips of folded paper) in the possession of his uncle. Wāēn was under the good care of his uncle; his grandmother (*yōm yā*) gave him daily almsfood and came to visit him at the *wat* frequently.

### FROM LŌĒI TO UBON

Many relatives apparently informed the biographer that before the first lent was over Wāēn had completed studying the few available books at the *wat*. The village of Na-Poeng was in those days quite remote from "civilization." Even in the town of Lōēi itself (the capital of the province) there was not a single monastic school that could teach Pali and the *Dhamma* to monks and novices.

So it was time to go elsewhere. When lent was over, Wāēn's uncle-monk, having heard of a famous "monastic residence for studying" (*samnak rīan*) in

266

Kasēmsīmā District of Ubon Province, decided to take his young charge there. The principal teacher at the monastic school in question was Phra Acharn Singh Khantayakamo; its abbot was Phra Acharn Lee. The journey was long and had to be done on foot. On the way, a stop was made at a *wat* in Wansapung District of Lōēi Province for a whole lent, and this time was devoted by Wāēn to studies. Before they reached their final destination, the monk and novice had to traverse hamlets, jungles, mountains, rivers, and canals, a journey that took many months. The monk-uncle returned to Lōēi, having left Wāēn at the school in Ubon. Wāēn was then about fourteen years old.

Although the monastic residence was only a *samnak song*,[12] it had a reputation for teaching Pali, the *Dhamma* (Naktham), and Thai language. There were some fifty monks and novices who had come there from various provinces to study. Moreover, Phra Acharn Singh was not only a knowledgeable and able teacher of Buddhist knowledge, he had also specialized in *saiyawēt*, which we may translate here as "magical knowledge and practices." The Thai view this field as being a "science" or "applied knowledge" (*sāt/śāstra*) systematized by "Brahmanical" experts.

The biographer at this point makes an interesting defense of why monks and novices should dabble in this technology. He points out that dwellings and settlements in the forest are subject to illness and to attack by animals and evil spirits. Thus *saiyawēt* is useful for the alleviation of people's suffering and for their enjoyment of happiness. Moreover, he points out that monks of this period played important roles as teachers, doctors, and colonizers and founders of new communities in the frontier areas; they also played a part in the lay administration of villages and towns and acted as "the eyes and ears of the government."[13]

Wāēn made much progress in his studies. A fellow co-resident novice, who is now the abbot of Wat Sangtau and bears the name Phra Acharn Wan, had this to say of Wāēn as novice: "He liked the life of seclusion, and he often sought solitude from the company of others, and sometimes sat alone in the forest all night until dawn. He was at the same time a diligent student, and helpful to friends and villagers." Lūang Pū Wāēn not only studied the *Dhamma* and the Pali and Thai languages from Acharn Singh; he also learned *saiyawēt*[14] because he had a thirst for knowledge and was interested in all "the arts and sciences" (*sinlapa sāt*).

In due course, Wāēn was ordained monk in the Mahānikāi sect together with his fellow novice Wan. Then his monk-uncle, Uan, came to take him back to his home province because his kin and fellow villagers "thought of him." The newly ordained Wāēn duly returned to the temple in his home village and prostrated before the presiding Buddha image in the temple and his ordainer, the local abbot. He then unexpectedly took up residence in the cemetery (*pāchā*) nearby rather than in the living quarters of the *wat*.

# The cult of amulets

## THE BEGINNING OF *THUDONG* (PILGRIMAGE), *ČĀRIK* (WANDERING), AND SEARCH FOR *DHAMMA* (*SAWĀĒNG THAM*)

This subtitle equates the physical aspect of wandering through space with the spiritual conquest of finding the *dhammic* truths. After a return to his home-village *wat* lasting only seven days, Wāēn disappeared without a trace, not even informing his relatives about his departure.

It was many years later, when they learned about his fame from a newspaper account, that his village folk came to know of his whereabouts. When asked by someone why he never returned to his home village again, Lūang Pū Wāēn was to remark that he had no home or relatives; that his affiliation was to a *wat*; that his life was dedicated to Buddhism; and that for him there is no past, present, or future. He could freely go on pilgrimage (*kān dōēn thudong*) because there were no grandparents or parents left in his home village and because all family property had been inherited by his younger sister. He therefore could go wherever he liked to find "contentment" (*khwām sandōt*), to study the *Dhamma*, and in particular to practice meditations (*vipassanā kammaṭṭhāna*).

This very time when Wāēn decided to become a wandering monk was one when Northeast Thailand was awakened by the "truth" (*satča*) and the *Dhamma* being disseminated by the great forest-monk and meditation teacher, Phra Acharn Mun and his disciples. Wāēn had already met some of these disciples and traveled with them, and therefore he was all the more eager to meet the Master.

### MEETING THE MASTER

It was in 1919 that Wāēn was first introduced to Phra Acharn Mun by one of his friends, Phra Acharn Tue, who was a disciple of the Master. At that time Acharn Mun was staying in the forest in Ban Phue District, Udon Province.

Wāēn belonged to the Mahānikāi sect and the Master to the Thammayut sect – a difference normally an obstacle to their practicing the *Dhamma* together. Yet the Master greeted Wāēn with pleasure and allowed him to attend the sermons and discussions. Wāēn benefited from this teaching and appreciated the Master's kindness. At this encounter, Wāēn did not formally become a disciple (*lūksit*) of the Master, which strictly speaking would have entailed his undergoing a new ordination into the Thammayut sect; but he espoused the Master's instructions and decided to put them into practice.

After spending some time with the Master, Wāēn and his companion monk, Tue, left on an extensive wandering. They crossed the Khōng River into Laos and reached "the buffalo mountain" (*phūkhao khwāi*), which the Laotian people considered forbidding and bespelled by jungle spirits. The two monks experienced some difficulties in finding food and in communicating with the local people. Then they had an astonishing encounter with the spirits (*phī*) of the mountain.

When the monks heard from foresters that a malevolent spirit lived up the mountain, and that the local villagers dared not ascend it to gather forest products, they decided to investigate. High up the mountain, they came to a cave in which they could seek shelter. Standing on a cliff, they saw around them nothing but dense jungle. A cold wind made them tremble even inside the cave.

### MEETING THE GHOST

When night fell, the two monks sat in different corners of the cave, abstained from talking, and sat meditating (*nang bhāvanā*). Late at night they heard a cry that, though slight and sharp at first, gradually got louder and louder, until a tall black shadow appeared at the mouth of the cave. It moved about in front without entering. The monk Tue reported later that when he opened his eyes he saw a big monkey twice the size of a human being. Suddenly there appeared two moving green spots of light, the glaring eyes of the animal, which was probably now in a fearsome, angry state.

When the monks saw the spots of light, they began this dialogue:

"Thān Tue, have you seen it?" asked Wāēn.

"Yes, I have seen it," replied Tue.

"What is *Thuk (dukkha* = suffering)?" asked Wāēn.

Tue replied, repeating in Pali the words taught by his Master Mun: "*Jāti pi dukkhā, jarā pi dukkhā, vyādhi dukkho maraṇam pi dukkham.*"

Then Wāēn said slowly, clearly, and deliberately: "Being born, getting old, becoming ill, dying, are all fraught with suffering. The *Winyān* [consciousness] of a dead person, which cannot be reborn, suffers even more. One can bear bodily pain, but insufferable is the suffering of the *winyān*. Only *dhamma* can free one from suffering."

When the animal heard these words it uttered a sorrowful and terrifying scream and disappeared.

At dawn, as the monks descended from the mountain, they discussed the event. They agreed that the recitation of the *Dhamma* had helped the *winyān* they encountered to be reborn, and thus relieved it from its suffering and destructiveness. To the villagers, the monk Tue said these words when they inquired about the mountain ogre:

The demon will not harm you. Every one of you should practice the *dhamma* and practice right livelihood. *Dhamma* protects those who practice *dhamma*. The *winyān* of the jungle demon will not appear again because it has achieved rebirth.[15]

From that time onward the villagers lost their fear of the demon.

### A SECOND ENCOUNTER WITH A WILD BEAST

After wandering about in Laos for a time, the two pilgrims decided to return to Thailand. The waters flowed so fast and strong in the Khōng River at that time that a narrow point had to be searched for in order to cross by boat.

# The cult of amulets

They entered Thailand at the border district of Mukdāhān in Nakhon Phanom Province and came to a rice-farming hamlet situated at the foot of a mountain. Although the monks intended to stay there only a single night, they were prevented from doing so by the entreaties of the villagers, who called upon them to save them from a danger inflicting them. These villagers had heard about the monks' wanderings in the mountains and believed that their survival was due to something meritorious they possessed.

The headman complained that his hamlet was being terrorized by a *phī-kāūngkoi*, a demon that came at night to eat animals, and that it had also claimed a human victim. A dead woman who was discovered with a bite on her body was said to have been killed by the demon.

The two monks agreed to stay and help, and some strange things happened that night. At about 8 or 9 p.m., the monks heard the sound of a monkey crying coming from a treetop; immediately all the other animals stopped making noise, but the birds in the trees started to shriek with fright. Suddenly something heavy fell on the ground; it was an owl, and it quivered and died. On inspection by the monk Tue in the firelight it was found to have a bloody wound on its neck.

Both monks then proceeded to meditate. Around 2 a.m. they heard a cry in the distance. It grew louder as it came closer and stopped behind a big tree. Then something jumped down and the monks saw that it was a large monkey, an extraordinary one for it had red eyes and shining hairs. It bared its teeth, jumped up into a tree, and disappeared as the monks looked on. Shortly afterward the dead body of a squirrel fell down with a thud from the branches of the tree.

When the villagers came to give alms in the morning, the monks showed them the dead owl and squirrel, which bore wounds of the same kind described earlier by the villagers. Wāēn explained to the villagers that what they believed to be a demon was in fact a monkeylike animal that killed and ate other animals.

The villagers discussed ways of catching the animal, but because the catching and killing of animals has nothing to do with the monk's rule of life, the monks did not proffer an opinion on how they should set about it. They however admonished the villagers thus:

Your beliefs should have a basis in reason. Don't believe blindly. What you call *phī kāūngkoi* is most likely a forest monkey. We cannot say what type of monkey it is because we did not see it clearly. But this monkey does have unusual power (*amnāt pralāt*), so be careful in your attempt to destroy it.

Then the monks left the hamlet and headed for Udon in search of the Master Mun.

## "WANDERING LONELY AS A RHINOCEROS"

When the two pilgrims arrived at Udon, they parted, with Tue going north to find his Master Mun and Wāēn setting out alone on a long pilgrimage that lasted a couple of years. Wāēn is said to have walked to the countries of Indochina: He first traversed Laos and arrived at Hanoi. He then turned around and entered Northern Burma, passed through Mandalay, Rangoon, and Moulmein, and then entered North Thailand at the Māēsāut border in Chīangrāi Province.

## THE SECOND MEETING WITH THE MASTER

Wāēn, now about thirty-nine years old, reached Chiengmai and met with his former companion Tue at the historic Wat Čēdī Lūang situated in the equally historic capital, where the Master, Mun, was serving as abbot. This was a Thammayut *wat*, and this time Wāēn decided to become Mun's pupil by seeking ordination into the Thammayut sect.

The Master soon tired of his position as abbot of Čēdī Lūang, because he liked to be peripatetic and live in seclusion. He therefore moved with his disciples to the outlying district of Māērim in the same province and took up residence at Wat Pā Hūai Namrin. Wāēn stayed with the Master there for ten lenten periods (i.e., 10 years). He was now fifty years old.

The Master and his disciples, including Wāēn, moved again. They first went to stay at the landmark cave of Chīangdāo in the district of the same name, and after a while they made for the famous mountain (*doi*) called Māē Pang. At its foot lay the long-established Wat Māē Pang; the Master and his entourage climbed higher and stayed meditating awhile. Then he led some of his party down again, this time southward to San Sāi, with the intention of moving across to Chīangdāo again.

They arrived at the hamlet Ban Poeng in the Māē Tāēng District of Chiengmai. Appreciating its location at the foot of a small mountain, which in turn could serve as a suitable place for meditation for monks, they decided to set up a residence (*samnak song*) there. (Today this institution is called Samnak Song Āranyawiwēk.) For the next few lents, Lūang Pū Wāēn lived here, but went back and forth to another hermitage called Doi Māē Pang,[16] whose founder and abbot was Phra Acharn Nu Sujitto. Upon the urging of this abbot, Lūang Pū Wāēn finally agreed to reside at Doi Māē Pang and has been there continuously up to the present day (1977) for fifteen years.

These two elders, Nu and Wāēn, form a complementary pair. They are both Northeasterners by origin. Abbot Nu, the founder of the *samnak*, has a serious appearance and hardly smiles at anybody, whereas Lūang Pū Wāēn is cheerful and lends warmth to the abbot's life. The abbot, in turn, takes good care of his senior guest. Doi Māē Pang, which began as a lowly monastic residence with a roof thatched with leaves, is today quite extensive and is famous in the North, and indeed throughout the country, as a source of protective amulets (*khrūēang rāng*). It therefore attracts many supplicants and tourists.

Abbot Nu, born in 1915, is now sixty-two years old (1977). He has been a monk for forty-three years. His first *wat* of residence was in a Yasōthon Province; after two years there, he went to Wat Muangkhai in Sakon Nakhon Province,

271

from where, together with two other monks, he went on a pilgrimage to the mountains. He finally went north and founded Doi Māē Pang.

### LŪANG PŪ WĀĒN'S *IDDHI* ENABLES HIM TO FLY

There is a popular belief that Lūang Pū Wāēn has the classical *iddhi* – the power of being airborne that is acquired by meditation adepts. In 1971, precisely at the time that his lay disciples in the royal Thai air force were sponsoring the making of a batch of Lūang Pū Wāēn medallion amulets, a remarkable story was in circulation. A pilot on a practice flight was over the Māē Pang mountain when he saw a monk sitting in meditation upon a cloud, and he had to exercise much skill in swerving away to avoid hitting the apparition. Having grounded the plane, the pilot with his flight map in hand went scouting on the mountain, and there he recognized Lūang Pū Wāēn as the monk he had seen in the clouds. The news of Lūang Pū Wāēn's power of levitation and flying spread quickly – it was broadcast on the radio and splashed in the newspapers. And the public's demand for his medallions soared.

When the biographer questioned abbot Nu in June 1976 as to the veracity of this story, the abbot affirmed its credibility. The abbot himself had once heard a plane flying over the mountain; the noise stopped and started up again. The next day, several air force personnel came to the *wat* in a Jeep and identified Lūang Pū as the person seen serenely sitting in the clouds. On the basis of this evidence, the biographer concluded that Lūang Pū Wāēn has special powers of concentration and of telepathic communication (*samāthi pen ēk, krasāē čit pen yīam*). However, he remarks that Lūang Pū Wāēn has himself neither confirmed nor denied the story; in fact, the saint was himself perplexed by the event that is alleged to have taken place.[17]

This is the end of the story of Lūang Pū Wāēn. His personal property consists, besides his yellow robes, of his spectacles, walking stick, and homemade cigarettes – which would not exceed 500 *baht* (U.S. $25) in value.

This hagiographical sketch, written by a layman in a popular magazine, printed in the "grub streets," and sold in the bazaars of Thai towns, can be read in terms of the framework of this book as signifying two things. Firstly, it authenticates the credentials of Lūang Pū Wāēn to sainthood by showing that he was a disciple of the Master Mun and, like him, wandered fearlessly through forests subduing his impulses and at the same time subduing wild beasts that terrorized villagers as their reified fears. Secondly, it goes further than the Master's biography, by placing the saintly Wāēn squarely in the middle of the cult of amulets and crediting him with the ability to transform his mystical virtues and perfections into tangible good effects for the benefit of worldlings through the techniques of *saiyawēt*. We seem to have reached the borderline here that separates what in Tantric Buddhism is called the altruistic "right-hand path" from the morally dubious "left-hand path,"[18] or what in Burma separates the *weikza* who is a "master of the upper path" (*athelan hsaya*) from one who is "master of the lower path" (*aulan hsaya*). The Burmese *weikza*, as we shall see later, is an adept in alchemy, astrology, and ritual arts, who is at the center of *gaing* associations and is associated with Buddhist millennial promises.

# 19

# Saints on cosmic mountains

## Doing well by doing good

I want to describe now the remarkable circumstances by which the Thai world of commerce, banking, and high society concentrated in the country's metropolis organized a pilgrimage to do homage to and to make gifts to the inmates of Acharn Čūan's hermitage on "the barren mountain." Located on the extreme periphery of the country, the hermitage is in a region that in popular imagination is not only wild and remote, but also infested with insurgency elements and guerrillas threatening the Thai establishment.

Whereas previously I documented how the forest saint's charisma was tapped by the king, the ruling ministers, and the military, a symbiosis that was consonant with tradition, we now face a relatively new situation: *Sāsana* and high finance come together in a direct partnership in which the banks do well by doing good. Modernization theorists should contemplate this new conjunction between religion and commerce in the context of the spread of capitalism in the Third World.

The Bangkok Bank of Commerce, one of the prominent banks in Thailand, with its headquarters in Bangkok and many branches throughout the country, requested that it be allowed to make the *kathin*[1] gift to Acharn Čūan's mountain hermitage at the end of the rains retreat in October 1978. The prime mover in this merit making was a Nongkhāi businessman who was also supervisor of the Bangkok bank's five branches in five Northeastern towns – Nongkhāi, Udon, Nakhon Phanom, Thābāū, and Mukdāhān. Let us call him Mr. Lai. He was already a disciple (*lūksit*) of Acharn Čūan, and he therefore proposed to the bank as a whole that it make its annual *kathin* gift to Acharn Čūan's hermitage. Together with the collection of money and other gifts was undertaken the minting of a large quantity of metal amulets with Acharn Čūan's head on one side and the bank's insignia on the other (see Figure 11). This *kathin* presentation thus affords us a rich opportunity to explore and weave together many themes at once: One is the manner in which powerful, affluent, high-status persons centered in

274

Saints on cosmic mountains

Figure 11. The Acharn Čūan medallion minted by the Bangkok Bank of Commerce. On the front is the seated figure of the monk in a posture of meditation with his name underneath, Phra Acharn Čūan Kulajetthi. On the back is the seal of the bank in the center with the encircling caption "Bangkok Bank of Commerce, Ltd."; and an outer caption describing the occasion as "Kathin, 1976, Wat Phūthaung, Čangwat Naungkhāi."

the capital have their links with provincial wealthy and influential interests, and how both together mobilize their resources to carry out a religious act, traditionally laden with political and social significances as well. Closely linked to this is of course how high finance and business, in patronizing a religious establishment, also by that act enlarge their reputation and receive special grace. Another theme is how, in the troubled political times of today, when the legitimacy and confidence of the ruling elements in the metropolis are weakened, these elements go in search of protective powers and sanctification to the extreme limits and interstices of their country and society – to the world-renouncing forest saints, who coexist in the same ecology with the feared insurgency forces. In this act of communication and exchange, amulets as sedimentations of power and grace play an important role.

THE BANGKOK ELITE CONTROLLING THE BANK

The Bangkok Bank of Commerce has had certain aristocratic connections from the time of its founding. One of the founders of the bank was the husband of the sister of Kukrit Pramoj, who is a descendent of royalty, a newspaper owner and journalist, and more than once a prime minister in recent times. Kukrit's sister's

275

husband (Phra Pinitchonakedee) was a director general of the police force. The general manager of the bank, soon after its founding, was the husband of the sister of Prince Chumpot of Nagara Svarga; and it is said that the prince's surviving spouse, Princess Chumpot, is a major shareholder in the bank and a close friend of Kukrit. (It is not unlikely that the royal family itself may have assets in the bank.)

The network of persons controlling the bank in late 1978 was as follows: The President was Khunying Bunrap,[2] sister of Kukrit Pramoj and surviving wife of the founder, the police general. Seni Pramoj, Kukrit's brother and himself a former prime minister, was a vice-president. His career as a lawyer, diplomat, and politician was as illustrious as his brother's. The general manager was Khun Inthira, who is the stepdaughter of the president.[3] Her husband, Khun Nitiphat,[4] a comember with Kukrit in the Free Thai movement during World War II, was a member of the National Assembly (1978) and a key figure in the Democratic Party, which was headed by Seni Pramoj, under whom he once served as a deputy minister. Anyone who has a close knowledge of Thai politics will realize the importance of this network of persons, who were waiting in the wings to assume a leading role in politics, should popular elections and democratic government come into vogue again. At the time there was no doubt that Kukrit was the most important civilian politician.

This cluster of Bangkok aristocrats, royalists, politicians, and high financiers also had their important connections with the critical centers of Chinese high finance and commerce in Bangkok. (There is no need to underscore here the ruling interests of the Thai-Chinese commercial sector in Thailand's economy.)[5] It is not surprising that one of the directors of the bank board was Khun Thanitpisanbutr, a noted millionaire; he provided the connections with Chinese high finance. Thanitpisanbutr's father, a porcelain-ware merchant in the time of King Chulalongkorn, was given the title of Phraya Pisan by that king, and according to a well-established tradition became an official of the king dealing with the Chinese community. Thanit himself is married into the Wanglee family, known as one of the richest Chinese families in Thailand, with a wide network of banking, industrial, and commercial interests.

Let us now pick up the threads at the provincial end of Nongkhāi and relate how the local organizer of the bank's *kathin* presentation, Mr. Lai, came to establish links with the bank on the one hand and the forest-monk, Acharn Čūan, on the other. Mr. Lai is the son of a Chinese immigrant father and a Thai mother: his father owned a tugboat and plied it on the river from Nakhon Phanom (in the Northeast) transporting rice. Mr. Lai in due course followed him, and during his trips downriver to Nongkhāi met his future wife there. She too is of part-Chinese origins but came from a substantial merchant family with a network of local kinship-*cum*-business connections in Nongkhāi.

Mr. Lai married and settled in Nongkhāi and, while continuing to operate his tugboat, branched into other ventures. He established a couple of ice-making factories, and after World War II he founded a successful motor-transportation company that delivered oil by truck from Bangkok to Laos. He became the owner of some fifty trucks and a couple of gas stations. Although he suffered some business reverses in the past, he is a very substantial businessman today, and his most recent advancement consisted in his connection with the Bangkok Bank of Commerce. He was introduced to the bank's management by a business friend;[6] he soon bought some shares in the bank and was first appointed as guarantor of local credit loans. This "shroff"[7] system lapsed after twelve years, and Mr. Lai was made the regional supervisor of five bank branches. He has been receiving a salary for his bank work for the past four years. He has in due course installed two sons and two sons-in-law in the banking and transport business; the bank at Nongkhāi as well as his transport business were housed in his own three-story building. A joint family of three generations together with a retinue of servants lived in the upper stories. Although Mr. Lai, a self-made man of energy, benevolence, and rectitude, was only educated in Thai up to the lower levels of secondary schooling, his sons have been educated abroad in the United States and Japan and are important links in his web of connections.

A respected personage in the Nongkhāi region, Mr. Lai has himself never entered politics as a parliamentary candidate, nor has he sought public office. But he wields influence at a less obvious level and has indeed been consulted by Bangkok politicians, particularly Kukrit Pramoj, about the names of local notables who might be suitable for nomination to his party as prospective candidates for the National Assembly. In fact, Kukrit has made visits to Nongkhāi, has been a guest of Mr. Lai, and has used his facilities as a base for "politicking."

Now we come to the question of how Mr. Lai came to sponsor the *kathin* ceremony on behalf of Acharn Čūan's hermitage. Mr. Lai, having heard of Acharn Čūan's reputation as a forest-monk, went to see him and offered his services as a prospective disciple (*lūksit*). Acharn Čūan mentioned that he was building a *sālā* on the fifth story of his mountain hermitage (the cosmography of the hermitage is described in the next section), and Mr. Lai volunteered a contribution of 200 pieces of tin sheeting for the roof. This happened some ten years ago, and since then he has been a donor and supporter.

We next come to the matter of making amulets, which is at the heart of our story, for an integral feature of the Bangkok Bank of Commerce's *kathin* sponsorship was the making and sacralization of amulets bearing the Meditation Master's image on one side and the bank's seal and insignia on the other. Mr. Lai once again figures as the prime mover.

Mr. Lai knew that a lay disciple of Acharn Čūan, a retired tax inspector who was a great believer in this monk's mystical powers (*itthirit patihān*), had already made a batch of amulets and had them sacralized by the monk.[8] This medallion had the monk's face on one side and a set of the *dhūtaṅga* monk's *emblems* – umbrella, bowl, and kettle – on the other side. These medallions had acquired a popular reputation for efficacy and strength (*saksit*).

277

# The cult of amulets

Asked what the significance of the three emblems was, Mr. Lai gave a remarkably interesting explanation, which opens a window onto our understanding of how a set of symbols can represent one set of meanings vis-à-vis the ascetic monk and carry another set of meanings for the layman. I have previously mentioned that the forest-monk embraced the *dhūtaṅga* ascetic practices and that the umbrella, bowl, and kettle he carried on his journeys acted as emblems of his vocation. These same objects signified quite another world-affirming prosperity when stamped on the medallion and carried as an amulet by the layman. The begging bowl signified, said our informant, that the amulet owner will acquire material goods and property; the umbrella would afford a peaceful life and provide shade and a cool breeze (*rom yen*); the kettle meant that there will be sufficient water to go with the food. I do not offer this exegesis as one subscribed to generally but as an example of the sort of mundane significance laymen attribute to amulets, thereby transforming the meanings of the amulets' symbols.

Thus it comes as no surprise that Mr. Lai ordered on behalf of the bank the manufacture of 40,000 bronze amulets. For three months during the period of the rains retreat Acharn Čŭan is said to have daily chanted sacred words (*pluk sēk*) over these amulets, which were placed in his hut on the fifth story. A tenth (about 4,000) of these amulets were given to the monk and his hermitage for distribution: Already on the day of the *kathin* ceremony there were notices posted at the hermitage that the medallions could be bought for 20 *baht* (U.S. $1) each. The remaining amulets the bank had reserved for itself, for free distribution to its clients and friends and for purposes of advertisement. (The bank may, I was told, sell some of them at a future date for religious or charitable purposes.) This is the first instance I have come across where "religion" (*sāsana*) and "commerce" have been conjoined in the amulet cult; previously, we have seen the frequent sponsorship of amulet making by political and military interests, a partnership that is not unusual.

### THE *KATHIN* PROCESSION AND PRESENTATION

The bank collected a cash sum of 175,000 *baht* (U.S. $8,750), which it presented to the hermitage in the form of a check, together with a number of material gifts. All the cash was collected from the bank's employees and managers working in the bank's countrywide branches. The check would of course be deposited in an account with the bank in question, and there is every suggestion that by spreading the banking habit in this way, banks will get access to the money assets of rural *wat*.

Three buses, two of them air-conditioned, were hired by the bank, and all employees were invited to join the *kathin* procession to Nongkhāi. About 120 persons, some of them coming specially to Bangkok from branches in South and North Thailand, assembled in Bangkok and traveled overnight to Nongkhāi, where they were accommodated in hotels. The high officials of the bank, such as

278

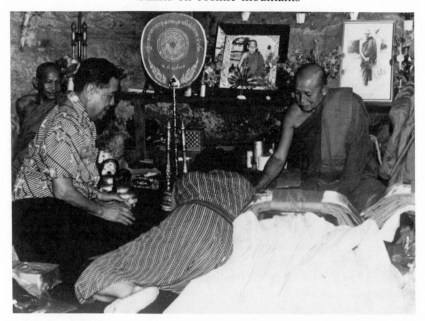

Figure 12. Acharn Čūan receiving *kathin* gifts from representatives of the Bangkok Bank of Commerce.

the general manager and her spouse, Mr. Nithipat, arrived separately by car and were the special guests of Mr. Lai; a director flew in for the day from Bangkok. After breakfast at Nongkhāi at Mr. Lai's residence, the motorcade of buses and cars left for the hermitage on a three-hour journey.

At the hermitage, the donors first feasted the monks and then had lunch themselves. They concluded with the ceremony of first presenting the *kathin* robes to the abbot, then following up with the cash and other gifts (see Figure 12). Many local lay supporters (other than the bank's employees) were also present and had brought gifts of their own.[9] After the presentations, the abbot gave an audience to his lay disciples and distributed amulets to the more illustrious of them. During the proceedings and afterward, many persons climbed the cosmic mountain, curious and awed by its starkness, its steep climb, and its landmarks scattered on the way. New groups of lay devotees could be seen arriving in their specially hired buses to make their own supplementary gifts at the end of the rains retreat. The liberality showered on the hermitage was impressive.

I have hitherto referred to the members of the *kathin* procession as "pilgrims," "devotees," "disciples," and so on. Now I must mention another aspect of the orientations and propensities of Thai Buddhists participating in a merit-making *kathin* presentation: their gaiety, boisterous merry making, and gratification of

279

pleasures both on the way to the *wat* and, more usually and intensely, in the hours after the presentation on their return home.[10]

That night, after merit had been made and piety demonstrated, many of the members of the bank's *kathin* party assembled in Udon to drink, feast, go to nightclubs, and engage in the pleasures of the night, for which Thailand's cities and towns are notorious. After all, the *kathin* festival is a holy day and a holiday.

## The Meditation Master Čŭan's mountain retreat

Phūthok is a "barren mountain"; it is one among several mountains standing stark with eroded irregular profiles in a sparsely wooded region on the Northeastern border between Thailand and Laos. On this mountain, the forest-monk and meditation teacher Acharn Čŭan has built a spectacular hermitage. It stands some 186 kilometers from the town of Nongkhāi in Bung Khat District, Nongkhāi Province. One can reach it by car after a three-hour ride from Nongkhāi town – first along a fast highway, then the last third of the journey on a dirt road, which eventually passes through dusty villages to the bottom of the craggy mountain.

Acharn Čŭan is, like many other forest saints, a disciple of Acharn Mun. His hermitage is therefore Thammayut in affiliation. He first established it some thirty years ago, soon after the conclusion of World War II. At the time of my visit there at the end of the rains retreat in October 1978, the hermitage had seven monks and six novices devoted to meditation practice. There were ten *māēchī* ("nuns"), who lived down below at the base of the mountain in quarters attached to the kitchen.

Acharn Čŭan was fifty-eight years old. Cherub-faced and looking remarkably young, he was like many other forest-monks – taciturn, chewing incessantly a wad of betel leaf and nut that bulged in his right cheek like a swelling.

True to the *dhūtaṅga* tradition, all the monks and novices go on their begging rounds for food to the nearest village, situated about two kilometers away; when eating, they mix all the food in the same bowl; and they eat once a day in the morning. The *māēchī*, however, cook their own food, and they as well as pious laymen may on *wanphra* days and on festival occasions cook food in the hermitage kitchen for a collective offering to the monks.

We are interested in Acharn Čŭan and his hermitage for two reasons. The first is the extraordinary cosmography of the mountain retreat, whose layout is a physical representation of the meditative journey. The second is that this establishment on the far border region of Northeast Thailand was the recipient of lavish *kathin* gifts from worldly sponsors, who came all the way from the capital city of Bangkok, several hundred miles away, to earn merit and receive efficacious grace and mystical power (*saksit*).

# Saints on cosmic mountains

Acharn Čŭan's genius is manifest in his choosing a mountain for a retreat and then in erecting from its base to its summit a number of dispersed structures that transform a strangely beautiful formation of nature into a cosmic mountain that maps the ascent from materiality through spirituality to the infinite void of *nibbāna*. The pilgrim to the hermitage starts at the dusty base. Ascending, he progressively penetrates increasingly wooded slopes and, after a hair-raising scramble at the top, is rewarded with the revelation of a panoramic view of the mundane world below – a view that extends across Thailand and the brown serpentine Mekong River to the vast piled-up mountain range on the other side that is the beginning of Laos. On festival nights the monks, novices, nuns, and lay devotees make the climb, finally circumambulating the summit holding candles and tapers in their hands.

A striking feature of this mountain retreat is that all its structures – halls (*sālā*), meditation huts, cave chambers and mountain niches, and the perpendicular wooden ladders on the upper reaches of the mountain – were constructed by Acharn Čŭan and his ascetic disciples. Lay donors have contributed building materials in the past but did not help build, though today they are urging upon the hermitage installations that would require outside help.[11]

The mountain is a red sandstone outcrop, highly eroded at the top but with woods in the lower reaches. It is an icon of the "path of purification" and of the Buddhist cosmos of graded levels of existence.

At the base of the mountain, built into its rocky side, is a *sālā*, a large wooden hall, to which the meditation monks descend and assemble in order to go on their daily begging rounds, to receive offerings of food from lay donors on special days, and to hold rites associated with them. There is also a kitchen attached for cooking and assembling food. Nearby are the dwellings of the ten nuns who serve the monks in the usual way as cooks.

From the base, there is a path leading up to the summit. This path is punctuated by seven "levels" or "stories" (*chan*), which are rest stations. Midway up the mountain, for the way is steep, wooden ladders and bridges have been built, their slope getting steeper and steeper until level five is reached. On either side of these ladders, dispersed in the woods, are the living huts of the monks and novices. On the brow of the summit, at level five, is a large cave converted into a *sālā*, with abutting roofed extensions, where monks hold their morning and evening chants, *pāṭimokkha* recitations, and *wanphra* services. The *sālā* has the usual altar with Buddha statues and other paraphernalia: A prominent item, however, is a human skeleton serving as an object of meditation on death. Through openings in the cave one can catch glimpses of the valley below.

Now starts the most spectacular and hair-raising part of the ascent. The path circles the mountain's brow, winding upward, and then, at the very top, when no further ascent is possible, a crazy, dizzy bridge is built hugging the summit's

Figure 13. The "heaven–hell bridge" at the summit of Acharn Čūan's cosmic mountain.

side, so that one looks between the boards and from the bamboo sides to an unobstructed drop several hundred yards below, and to a vertiginous expanse extending several miles. This bridge is called the *saphān narok-sawan*, the hell–heaven bridge,'' whose name and significance will be described shortly (see Figure 13).

At the summit, which represents the seventh and final level, as well as at points immediately below, there are natural niches in the caves that have been converted into meditation nooks. These are dotted on all sides at the top, so that meditators, each in his nook, face in all directions. These nooks serve for meditation during day and night, each meditator keeping his vigil according to his rhythm, separated from his fellow seeker, but aware that he is part of a collective enterprise.

The seven levels or stages on the mountain's ascent are in a sense analogous to levels of consciousness and to progressive *jhāna* – victories reached by the meditator. At these stations of achievement, there are posted wooden boards on which are written various slogans, aphorisms, and moral exhortations to the effect that there is no knowledge greater than knowledge of one's self, the greatest conquest is conquest of self, and so on. Let me give a few examples.

Station three displayed these admonitions:[12] "Desire (taṇhā) is unfathomable in depth; precepts, concentration (samādhi), merit are tangible and accessible, but their pursuit is obstructed by self-aggrandizement. The highest achievement of all is enlightenment."

Ascending a little higher, the pilgrim reads: "The three chains that tie people down are children, wife, and property. Non-achievement can be attained only by seeking release from these chains."

The message posted at level four was: "Diligent effort and friendship do not go together; laziness is an intimate friend of poverty." And one of the slogans at level five was: "No happiness is greater than serenity and tranquility."

Now a few words about the hell–heaven bridge. According to an article in a popular Thai magazine, which bears the title "Things that have manifest power"[13] and describes Acharn Čūan's sacred mountain, the steep ladders were built from 1974 onward. The ladder at level four was built so that the nuns could sit and meditate at suitable spots; the ladders leading further up to the summit were built to enable monks and novices to meditate at the higher reaches. Naturally, the most difficult piece of construction was the last bridge hugging the rocky summit. According to the magazine article, it was called the heaven–hell bridge because if a person crossed it with confidence and a sense of enjoyment he would feel as if he was treading the airy heavens, but if he was a careless "show off," and did not concentrate, he would fall to hell to his death. People negotiating this difficult pass have to mindfully chant: "*Buddho, Buddho, Sugato, Sugato.*"

It appears that Acharn Čūan's spectacular enterprise met with a lot of adverse comment at the time it was undertaken; people quipped that if climbers fell to their death the monks would have to spend most of their time reciting the *bangsukūn* mortuary chants. But Acharn Čūan went ahead and accomplished the task with the help of his disciples. The glory of the cosmic mountain is seen on festival occasions, such as: Khaophansā (entering the rains retreat); Mākhabūchā; Visākhabūchā (the day on which the Buddha was born, was enlightened, and passed away); and New Year, when Acharn Čūan and his following monks, novices, nuns, and pious lay devotees climb the mountain from story to story, bearing candlesticks, a luminous procession weaving its way upward to the summit of a transcendental experience.

## The forest hermitage and the amulets of Lūang Phāū Pāng

Acharn Čūan's cosmic mountain is not a freak occurrence. We have earlier noticed at several points that the Thai forest-monks had a penchant for soaring mountains, lush forests, and caves perched on commanding heights, and that they savored encounters with wild animals. I have hinted before that "rationalist" investigators rarely plumb the cosmological layers of popular Buddhism. In my own presentation so far I have attempted to bring into focus the cosmological dimensions of ascetic and meditative forest-monk traditions that were already suggested by the classical *Visuddhimagga*, salient in the biography of Acharn Mun, and now firmly underscored by Acharn Čūan's cosmic mountain. I shall now present another example that helps to confirm the thesis that the cosmological ambience is probably a widespread feature of the indigenous forest-monk tradition.

Lūang Phāū Pāng, a monk of the Thammayut sect and a former disciple of the Meditation Master Acharn Mun, founded his forest hermitage in a wooded, mountainous part of Khon Kāēn Province. It is reached after several miles of travel on a dusty and pitted dirt road.

The hermitage is built on the side of a mountain, and it too has its distinctive cosmography. It is bounded by a canal at the base of the mountain and by a hall (*sālā*) built at the top of the mountain. The hall is used for special rites and collective meditation. In between are laid out the various components of the hermitage.

Figure 14 is a schematic representation of the layout. Somewhere near the base was being built in December 1978 a large *čēdi* (*stūpa*), which stood on a base of 100 square meters and is 28 meters high. The monument was almost finished. When completed, it will have cost 2,500,000 *baht* (U.S. $125,000). This large sum of money was raised from lay donations and by the sale of amulets and charms.

The hermitage, though called Wat Udomkhongkhākhirikhēt, was actually, as is normal with forest-monk establishments, a *samnak song*.[14] Nevertheless, it was quite extensive in its layout. It provides us with a fair picture of how the residence of ascetic forest-monks is linked up with popular lay religiosity through pilgrimage, merit making, and the sale of amulets; and of how the hermitage develops into an elaborate architectural complex with a cosmography that is quite different from that of the usual collection of buildings that comprise the *wat* of the village, town, or city.

We note that at the entrance to the hermitage stand two large stone tigers; they commemorate the tigers Lūang Phāū had withstood in his vigils as an ascetic *thudong* monk. The tiger symbolism, as noted earlier, is central to the hagiology of the forest saints.

Site B, near the entrance, is a complex of buildings consisting of Lūang Phāū's own residence (*kuti*), with a hall attached for receiving visitors. In front of this reception hall is a cemented open space where lay devotees can sit and receive Lūang Phāū's instruction and blessings. Further removed on the right is a *sālā* for selling amulets (*phra khrūēang*) and other religious paraphernalia.

Site A further up is historically and cosmologically more important. On it stands the old *sālā* for receiving guests, and nearby is a small water trough with sacred water (*nammon*) and the sculpture of a snake. The story is told that many

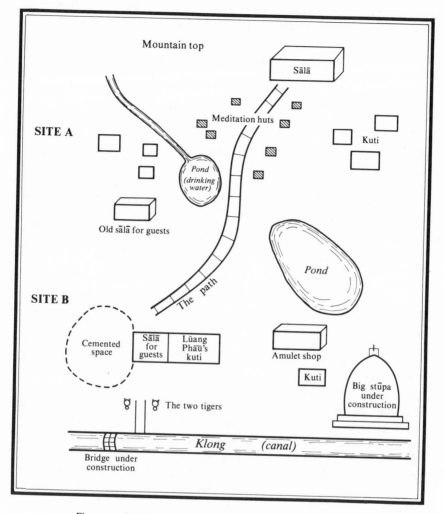

Figure 14. A schematic diagram of Lūang Phāu Pāng's hermitage.

years ago Lūang Phāu was sitting in meditation at this place when a large snake emerged from the ground, opened its mouth, and attempted to swallow the monk's head. The monk sat still, unafraid, and repeated the word *tāi* ("dead"). The snake departed without harming him and the monk had a snake image and a water trough installed there. In the trough is water in which Lūang Phāu has washed his feet. Lay devotees wash their face with it, drink it, and sprinkle it on themselves in the belief that it has curative powers. It is especially efficacious for the cure of headaches.

The figure shows a flight of steps ascending to the mountaintop. On the side of the mountain, in its upper reaches, are placed the residential and meditation huts of the resident monks and novices; they are modest wooden structures dispersed in the woods. At the summit is the *sālā* for recitations, for conducting the acts of the monks as a community (*saṅghakamma*), and for the collective rites.

This religious foundation is practically the achievement of one man. It is therefore informative to know something of his biography.

### THE BIOGRAPHY OF LŪANG PHĀŪ PĀNG

The biography as recorded here was told me in late 1978 by a resident monk. It is, as is to be expected, told with a hagiographical convention that is by now familiar to us.

Lūang Phāū's full name is Pāng Chittakutto. He was born in Khueannai District, Ubon Province (Northeast Thailand). He is now about eighty years old and was ordained when he was forty-two years old. He has completed thirty-eight rains retreats and has resided continuously in the present hermitage for over thirty years.

He was first ordained in the Mahānikāi sect at Wat Bankutkasiyan in Ubon Province, and he traveled as an ascetic (*thudong*) monk in the Northeast and in Cambodia. He then met Acharn Mun, the Meditation Master, and wanted to become his disciple, but was refused on account of his not belonging to the Thammayut sect. So he returned home to be ordained as a Thammayut *bhikkhu*, and he joined Acharn Mun at Wat Pasālwan and studied meditation under him.

He subsequently traveled *thudong* in various parts of the country: He stayed alone for some time in the Thamnamnao cave in Phetchabūn Province (North Thailand), next moved to the forested Plakchong District of Khorāt Province, and finally came to the present site, which was so wild and infested by powerful spirits (*čao thī*) that no previous monk was able to stay for long. It was at this site that once a snake attempted to swallow him and tigers came to devour him. As described earlier, the sculptures of the snake and of the two lean and hungry tigers at the entrance commemorate his victories.

The monk then said that Lūang Phāū had in fact lived out seven of his previous lives in this same location: He had been born in the same place with different identities as a Lao, a Khmer, and a Thai. This is his final birth. In fact, the oral biographer claimed that Prince Vessantara had resided in this same forest.[15]

Lūang Phāū is responsible for converting the virgin forest into the present complex of buildings. The hermitage's name, Udomkhongkhākhirikhēt, literally means "place that has plentiful water bounded by a mountain" (see Figure 14).

For many years after establishing the hermitage, Lūang Phāū traveled *thudong* practically every year after the rains retreat. This year he could not do so on account of his illness. But though sick he never fails to go begging for his food in the morning, true to his ascetic vocation.

The hermitage, affiliated with the Thammayut sect, had at the end of the rains retreat in 1978 fifteen resident monks; during the retreat there were thirty-five monks. In addition, there were two novices and fifteen "nuns" (*māē chī*). All the monks, novices, and nuns learned and practiced meditation.

The monk-hagiographer then went on to extol the supranormal powers of Lūang Phāū. When lay devotees fill his bowl with food, they can gain much merit (*dai bun māk*). Lūang Phāū has given many proofs of his *aphinihān* (supranormal powers), such as the following:

1. As mentioned before, snakes have in vain attempted to swallow him and tigers to devour him in his *thudong* wanderings.
2. When he has accidentally fallen into rivers or swamps, he has not drowned because crocodiles on whose backs he would alight have carried him to safety.
3. He is famous for rendering people invulnerable to physical attack and harm and for making people attractive to others by means of amulets and other articles he has blessed and rites he has conducted.[16]

Thus many soldiers who were being sent to Vietnam came to him for metal medallions (*rīan*) and for Buddha statues, which interestingly were made of clay, herbs, and the betel-chew leavings of Lūang Phāū himself. The biographer claimed that soldiers who had these objects with them cannot be harmed by bombs or penetrated by bullets, even those bullets fired by the modern automatic rapid-fire guns.[17]

It is then no unusual development that Lūang Phāū has attracted a growing lay acclaim and that he is besieged by lay religiosity. This year, for instance (1978), the *kathin* presentation at the end of the rains retreat was made by a layman from Bangkok, Khun Nai Suthee, who gave a personal gift of 50,000 *baht* (U.S. $2,500); in addition, the hermitage received a large number of *phāpā* presentations from visiting parties of devotees.

In some ways, a high point of the saint's career is that the crown prince of Thailand issued an invitation to him through the army to visit him at his Bangkok palace. Lūang Phāū arrived by plane, pitched his umbrella on the palace grounds, and stayed beneath it. Lūang Phāū consented to stay awhile because the crown prince wanted to offer him food (*saibāt*) and converse with him. (Apparently this was Lūang Phāū's first plane ride; he felt dizzy after his return and has not been in good health since.)

## AN AUDIENCE WITH LŪANG PHĀŪ

Two of my research assistants went as members of a *kathin* procession from Bangkok to Khon Kāēn Province in the Northeast; the group, two busloads strong, was going to make a *kathin* presentation to the *wat* in the home village of a monk now residing in a Bangkok *wat*. After the presentation had been made, the Bangkok devotees made a special visit to Lūang Phāū's hermitage to make more merit and acquire amulets.

My assistants gave this account of the audience they had with Lūang Phāū. The group reached the hermitage at 7 a.m. and waited for Lūang Phāū to return from his almsround. They all sat in the open space in front of the *sālā* for receiving guests.

The visitors, about a hundred in number, arranged themselves in two lines, and Lūang Phāū first walked through receiving the balls of sticky rice that some of them had brought as offerings; four "nuns" walked behind Lūang Phāū and their bowls were filled as well.

Lūang Phāū took a seat at a table placed in front of the devotees and a lay helper emptied into Lūang Phāū's bowl of rice two dishes of vegetables and a dish containing pieces of banana and orange; Lūang Phāū, once again following the orthodox *dhūtaṅga* practice that the taste of food is not to be relished, mixed all these together in his bowl and began to eat. I should also note that Lūang Phāū is a vegetarian and, once again following the ascetic code, eats only one meal a day.

While Lūang Phāū was eating, money contributions were collected from the visitors by some of their own ardent members. At the end of Lūang Phāū's meal, because he was himself too weak to chant, another monk gave the five precepts to the congregation, but Lūang Phāū gave advice and blessings. Then many of the visitors who already had amulets hanging around their necks took them off and put them on a tray so that Lūang Phāū would bless and sacralize them (*pluk sēk*). He advised them not to drink liquor. A little child, a boy, began to cry and Lūang Phāū led him to the water trough containing the sacred water (of his feet) and sprinkled some on the boy's head. The child immediately stopped crying, and Lūang Phāū remarked that the water was a good cure for headaches. Then the visitors paid their respects to Lūang Phāū by prostrating themselves before him and trooped off to the shop where Lūang Phāū's amulets and charms were being sold. Having made their purchases, they left the hermitage.

### LŪANG PHĀŪ PĀNG'S AMULETS AND CHARMS

The articles for sale at the hermitage shop had been sacralized by Lūang Phāū. The first batch (*rīan run rāēk*) of amulets were made in B.E. 2512 (1969). They are scarce today and are expensive to purchase.

A second batch was reproduced exactly (the same moulds were used) in 1977 and is displayed for sale at the shop, costing 20 *baht* (U.S. $1) for the smoky metal and 10 *baht* for the copper varieties. These amulets have a relief of Lūang Phāū in a seated position on one side and some sacred letters on the other with the date of manufacture.

The following is an enumeration of the articles in the shop:

1. Pieces of cloth with *yantra* designs (*phā yan*) printed on them. There were four such cloths being sold, one being a flag, another bearing the Buddha's footprint, and two more with *yantra* designs.
2. Color photographs of Lūang Phāū.

3. Five kinds of medallions and coins (*rīan*):
   a. *Rīan Lūang Phāū Sūē Phēn* is the ''Lūang Phāū medallion, leaping-tiger batch'': it is pear-shaped; has Lūang Phāū's bust in front and a leaping tiger at the back; and comes in two sizes, large and small.
   b. *Rīan Rūp Rakhang* is a bell-shaped medallion embossed with Lūang Phāū's bust.
   c. *Rīan Lūang Phāū Pāng run rāēk*: This is the reproduction of the original medallion described earlier; it is oval-shaped.
   d. *Rīan Lūang Phāū Pāng run Čēdī Anusāūn*: A round medallion that has in relief Lūang Phāū's bust in front and a *čēdī* behind, together with the ascetic monk's umbrella, bowl, and water-kettle. The *čēdī* in question is of course the monument that Lūang Phāū is building, and the medallion (which comes in two sizes) was minted specially in order to collect money to finance the building.
   e. The fifth medallion, with Lūang Phāū in a seated posture, is made of ''red gold'' and is quite expensive, 100 *baht* (U.S. $5) for the smaller and 200 *baht* for the larger.
4. An oval-shaped locket of Lūang Phāū, in two sizes, containing a photograph of him.
5. The Lūang Phāū Pāng ring, which costs 20 *baht* and has a picture of him in gold with a blue background and a circular rim of red.
6. A statuette of Lūang Phāū, silver colored, with a *čēdī* representing the one that is being built imprinted on the back.
7. *Phra Kring Rūp mūēan Lūang Phāū Pāng*: I have earlier described the famous Buddha amulets made in the last century by the abbot of Wat Bovonniwet (Pavares), which had a clinking metal piece inside. Here we have such an imitation, but the statue is of Lūang Phāū himself. The small image is made of copper and costs 200 *baht* (U.S. $10).
8. Finally, there is a sticker for a motor vehicle that bears Lūang Phāū's photograph and is in fact referred to as ''Sticker rūp Lūang Phāū Pāng.''

# PART IV

## CONCEPTUAL AND THEORETICAL
## CLARIFICATIONS

# 20

# A commentary on millennial Buddhism in Thailand and Burma

The oral biography of Lūang Phāū Pāng given during a formal conversation by one of his monk disciples is by far more spontaneous than the written biography of Lūang Pū Wāēn in a popular magazine, and this again is more unself-conscious than the classic book-length composition of Acharn Maha Boowa on the Master, Mun. The more spontaneous accounts are less abashed about reporting the supranormal powers of their saintly heroes and of the amulets and lustral water they have sacralized.

Lūang Phāū Pāng's encounters with the snake and tigers are on a superhuman scale; the water in which his feet are washed is, like that of the famous Hindu saints, charged with purity and potency for the worldling devotees; his rebirths at the same location resonate with the legends of the Buddha's rebirth at Kusinārā; indeed, there is the strong suggestion that Lūang Phāū Pāng might be a future Buddha, perhaps one already. Such resonances, reminders, and allusions relating the living saints with the Buddha himself, combined with the reality of the mountain retreats of Čūan and Pāng as *indexical icons* of the Buddhist cosmos itself, inevitably bring to mind phenomena described for Burma under the labels of "messianic and millennial" Buddhism, and thereby suggest a larger presence on the Southeast Asian Buddhist landscape as a whole.

The Thai saints on cosmic mountains and in forest hermitages whom we have dealt with, and who are referred to by their lay devotees as *luang pū, lūang phāū, arahan*, and so on, are prominent members of a bewilderingly larger array of charismatic holy men, who have appeared in the past and continue to appear in the Burmese–Thai–Lao arena. These men of charisma and sanctity have been called by a variety of names, other than the ones mentioned above, such as *phū mī bun, phū wisēt, khrū bā, rūēsī*, and *chīphākhāo*.

Because these holy men have been credited with sacred powers, they have frequently been both the centers around whom cults and associations have formed and the leaders of different kinds of actions seeking to harmonize or transform the world. There is historical evidence to suggest that they might have been importantly implicated in the founding of kingdoms, settlements, and towns. The authors of chronicles frequently describe them as agents in the spread and maintenance of Buddhism. In both these roles they are seen to work on behalf of the "civilizing" mission of state formation and the preservation of Buddhism. But there is a third role that is perhaps even more significant. Some of these holy men have been at the hearts of Buddhist cults and movements that have questioned, and even attacked, the established political and religious systems and their values while championing reformist and millenarian goals.

It is therefore necessary and theoretically important that we address the theme of millennial Buddhism – that we figure out its core constructs and impulsions as well as its manifestations according to the vicissitudes of social, economic, and political circumstances. In other words, the spelling out of its phenomenological and ideological constructs and their logical coherence will constitute its "internal account" (internal history), and the correlating of its phases, magnitudes, and cycles will constitute its "external account" (external history). In fact, both internal and external features dialectically and recursively interact; I shall endeavor to give as complete a picture as possible.

### The variety of holy men: an embarrassment of riches

Before surveying the various expressions of millennial Buddhism in Burma and Thailand,[1] it would be useful to attempt a glossary of the plethora of holy men mentioned earlier. The different names do not designate separate types as such, but they do accent certain characteristics rather than others. It is in this spirit that I attempt the enumeration.

1. *Phū mī bun* literally means "person who has merit," and is a term traditionally used in Thai for the great men of Buddhism. Thus the great Thai cosmological treatise, the *Traiphūm*, lists the Buddha, the *paccekabuddhas*, the *aggasāvakas* (great disciples), the *arahan takhīnāsawas* (saints), *bodhisattvas* (future Buddhas), and *cakravartins* (universal monarchs) as *phū mī bun*.[2] Traditionally, the king of Thailand has been recognized as the man of greatest merit in the kingdom.

It seems, however, that the belief in *phū mī bun* has been a significant basis for millennial expectations and movements,[3] and therefore *phū mī bun* can be taken to be more like religio-political actors and leaders in the *bodhisattva* vein. Thus, in millennial movements, *phū mī bun* might claim to be manifestations or agents of the coming Maitreya Buddha. Thus Ishii states that "the idea of a future king or saviour to come, which is popular among the Buddhists in the Thai Northeast, has found its expression in the vague concept of *phū mī bun*, the claim of a being who appealed to the suffering of Thai-Lao peasants."[4]

2. *Phū wisēt* may be glossed as persons capable of performing supranormal deeds and who possess those kinds of powers denoting *iddhi*. It would seem that

the Burmese term *weikza* more or less parallels the Thai *phū wisēt*. The most frequent candidates who have been called *phū wisēt* have been monks or ex-monks. Some of them have been famous curers, who have written *yantra* designs on the palms or foreheads of persons afflicted with infirmities and diseases; some have been famous alchemists; others have performed purificatory rites and lustrations and distributed amulets credited with supranormal powers.

Keyes has tended to identify the *phū wisēt* as a person typically motivated by "personal" rather than "social" concerns,[5] and as having relations with individual clients. However, under certain conditions of common threat these relations may be transformed into a collective millennial movement led by or participated in by the *phū wisēt*.[6] When this happens the distinction between *phū wisēt* and *phū mī bun* tends to become blurred. Alternatively, the *phū wisēt* and *phū mī bun* appear together as collaborating leaders. I shall later deal with their co-appearance and intersection when I discuss the Thai millennial uprising of 1900–2.

3. *Khrū bā acharn* or *khrū bā*: Speaking of prominent types of religious men in old Siamese society, Charnvit Kasetsiri describes the *khrū bā acharn* as "a teacher to a large number of people" who has undergone religious education and might at one time have been a monk or had "an intense educational life with monks."[7] In more recent times, however, the title is conferred upon monks, usually of advanced age, who are highly venerated for their holiness and personal charisma.[8] The most famous *khrū bā* of the twentieth century was a monk who represented the indigenous Northern Thai or Lān Nā Buddhist traditions; his name was Sīwichai (I shall flesh out his career later in this chapter in the section entitled "*Khrū bā Sīwichai: an activist charismatic monk*").

4. *Arahan* (Pali: *arahant*; Sanskrit: *arhat/arhant*): In its canonical sense (adumbrated in Chapter 2), an *arahan* is the archetypal Buddhist perfected saint, who has traversed the path of salvation, achieved liberation, and is therefore released from the shackles of rebirth. In Thailand this title is not necessarily reserved solely for the ascetic, meditative, reclusive teaching monk like Acharn Mun, for holiness and saintliness can be achieved by town-dwelling monks as well. Examples of other Thai monks who in recent times have been acclaimed by their followers as *arahan* are: the renowned Buddhist thinker, teacher, philosopher, and head of Sūan Mōk (the Park of Liberation) in South Thailand, Buddhadāsa Bhikkhu;[9] and Kittivuḍḍho, a militant anticommunist monk (Phra Kittivuḍḍho), who is under a cloud today and whose claims to the title are more dubious.[10]

5. *Rūēsī* (Thai): This personage appears in the early Thai *tamnān* chronicles and in myths and legends (such as those dealing with the origin of the Sinhala Buddha image, which has been discussed in Chapter 16), though he is not a recognizable figure in contemporary Thailand. The *rūēsī*, it would seem, was a hermit, who dwelt outside established communities, engaged in mystical practices, and therefore denoted the Hindu-type, "individualist" *r̥si, sannyāsin*, or *yogin*. As such, he was in striking contrast to the *bhikkhu*, who belonged to monastic communities and followed a *Vinaya* discipline, which regulated monas-

tic life as well as the monks' relations with the laity. (A parallel term carrying similar associations is *yati*.)[11] But Burmese *yathe*, who are the principal members of the *gaing*, are again similar to *yogin*; at least, they are not ordained Buddhist monks, but their religious practices are Buddhistic.

6. *Chīphākhāo*: The literal meaning of this term is "one who wears a white garment." Kasetsiri glosses the *chīphākhāo* as "usually a man who at one time embraced a strict religious life but could not endure the religious order. However, when he abandoned the full religious life and came out into the lay world, he still observed some religious regulations, and therefore led a life which was different from that of laymen and also from that of strictly religious men."[12] These pious men dressed in white, not ordained *bhikkhu*, appear in legend and even in some local cults[13] as supporters and guardians of Buddhism and the *saṅgha*. It is interesting to note that in the religious cults of Sgaw Karen – influenced by Burmese Buddhist millennial ideas – the priests of Ywa, the high deity, who were called *bu kho*, the term derived from the Mon Buddhist word *pon* meaning merit, were described in 1847 by a missionary as wearing white garments.[14] Another missionary reported that a leader of a cult in 1828 in a village east of Tavoy was a man who was clad as an ascetic, taught abstention from pork and fowl, and instituted the worship of a sacred book that in this instance turned out to be a copy of an English prayer book.

## Holy men in early Thai history

Having enumerated the kinds of holy men who have figured in traditional and modern times, let me draw attention to the remarkable references in the early Thai inscriptions and *tamnān* literature to the creative social activity of three types of holy men, the *rūēsī*, the *chīphākhāo*, and the *khrū bā*. Kasetsiri has asserted that "these three types of religious men were the most active leaders of the old society."[15] The evidence cited from the sources for this assertion is of this sort. A number of *rūēsī* are alleged to have taken a leading role in the foundation of a new settlement at Lamphūn in northern Siam, which was then ruled by a daughter of the Lopburī king, Queen Cāmadevī. The restoration of the southern city of Nagara Śrī Dharmarāja in the thirteenth century, after a period of abandonment, was stimulated by a *chīphākhāo*. This city had been an important Buddhist center and had a shrine in which reposed the Buddha's relics. He founded a new settlement with his kin and followers, with the relic shrine as the settlement's central focus. In the ninth century, four *rūēsī* are credited with the founding of a number of cities in the territory of Chiengmai. The *mūēang* of Sawankalok is alleged to have been founded in the eighth century by two *rūēsī*, who installed a *khrū bā* named Thammarāt as the king because he was an elder credited with special astrological knowledge.

Much later in time than that to which Kasetsiri alludes, the Buddhist monkish chronicle of the sixteenth century, the *Jinakālamālī*, also implicates an ascetic hermit in the legend of origin of the city and kingdom of Haripuñjaya in North Thailand. The chronicle in fact begins its account of Thai events with the following legend, in which the *bhikkhu* chronicler very definitely wants to establish that an ascetic hermit is most productive when he works as an agent of Buddhism:

The account of the founding of Haripuñjaya implicates an ascetic with supranormal powers, a universal monarch (*cakkavatti*), his daughter, and an elephant of dazzling might. We are told that Vāsudeva, who had once been a Buddhist monk and had learned the scriptures, reverted to lay life and finally took to the life of an ascetic. He had gained the powers of higher knowledge. A doe drank Vāsudeva's urine containing his semen, became pregnant, and gave birth to two children, male and female, who married, and for whom Vāsudeva built the city of Migasaṅgara so that they might reign there. A son of this couple turned out to be an evil king who devastated the capital city. Vāsudeva, looking for another location, saw a place that had been visited by the Buddha. He built here on the banks of the Māē Ping River the new city of Haripuñjaya. It was then decided that the appropriate ruler for this city would be "an offspring of the Universal Monarch of the city of Lava." Thus it was that Princess Cāmadevī, already married to the ruler of a vassal state, was chosen; she arrived in the new city with a large retinue of 500 laymen of every class and 500 great monks versed in the Pali canon. So great was the merit that the queen accumulated during her rule that the deities presented her with a majestic white elephant, who frightened away all enemies of the kingdom.

In this founding story, we pass from a first phase – in which an ascetic with supranormal powers founds an unsuccessful, unstable, and unrighteous kingdom with rulers who are the progeny of his union with a forest animal (nature) and who, being brother and sister, make an incestuous marriage and in turn procreate an evil ruler – to a second phase – in which the same ascetic founds the historic kingdom of Haripriñjaya on the basis of impeccable Buddhist credentials: The Buddha had originally visited the location, the first ruler is a child of a universal monarch, she arrives with a complete array of lay subjects and elders of the *saṅgha*, and she is consecrated sitting on a heap of gold. In due course, she receives one of the treasures of a world monarch – the mighty white elephant. Such a Buddhist polity cannot but endure, prosper, and serve as a precedent for other northern Thai kingdoms.

The foregoing discussion has established two points. The first is that the variety of holy men (other than the Buddhist monk) that we have enumerated, whatever their individual features and the longevity of their existence, have in due course, as the Thai, Burmese, and Laotian societies have taken firm shape, been treated as allies or agents of established Buddhism rather than as its antagonists and/or the spearheads of alternative religions. In particular, the famous medieval chronicles have "domesticated" them.

## Conceptual and theoretical clarifications

Some of the holy men have figured in the literature as "pioneers" aiding state formation by working on the frontiers of expanding polities. Whether they antedated the arrival of Buddhism in the region or acted as parallel agents to Buddhist monks in these colonizing activities, we see in Southeast Asia an active collaboration between holy man and political ruler from the very beginning of known dynastic history. Buddhism, with its monastic literary traditions, has in due course provided the best-developed ideological and reflexive statement regarding the union of religion and polity.

But there is another whole dimension to the activities of these holy men, which we can label *millennial Buddhism*; in its most articulated form it may be identified with the messianic hopes surrounding the coming righteous ruler and the coming Maitreya Buddha. In this manifestation, the millennial movements show the holy men frequently as acting subversively against the established political authority and holding out the prospect of a more just order. We have now prepared the ground for the systematic study of millennial Buddhism that follows.

## A Burmese messianic association (*gaing*)

Let us begin by recapitulating some features of "a messianic Buddhist association" in Burma, as documented by E. M. Mendelson.[16] At the outset, let us take note of what seems to be a basic difference between Mendelson's case study and our descriptions: The holy men who are the main actors in the Burmese *gaing* are *yathe*, who are not like ordained monastic *bhikkhu* in the Theravāda sense but more like *yogin* or hermits. We shall therefore later face the issue as to what difference this makes to a general discussion of millennial Buddhism.

1. The leader of the cult was the Bodaw – his full name was Mahagandare Weikzado Apwegyoke – who was thought to be some combination of the coming *setkyamin* (*cakkavatti*/universal king) and the coming Buddha, Metteyya. (For example, Bo Min Guang and Bo Bo Aung were identified with the king of Burma, who precedes the arrival of Metteyya, and the Bodaw in turn was alleged to be a reincarnation of them.) It is not necessary to develop here the well-known "prophecies" in Buddhism concerning the duration of the religion, and the co-appearance of the *cakkavatti* and the next Buddha, but we must remember them as a reiterative theme.

The Bodaw's career is described as compounded of a wandering and reclusive life and the observance of ascetic practices: He is alleged to have spent fifteen years in the legendary Himalaya mountains; subsequently he never went out of his house and ate only rice with lime. His *yogin* appearance was embellished by his long white hair done in a topknot.

2. The Bodaw presided over the Maheikdi *gaing*. The meaning of *gaing* has to be spelled out. Mendelson begins by advancing a narrow definition of the *gaing*,

which is "a group of people – usually a teacher and his disciples – whose manipulation of various magical techniques associated with alchemy, mantras, medicine, and cabbalistic signs leads them to acquire, in step-by-step hierarchical degrees, ever more refined states of material power over animate and inanimate nature and the supernatural."[17] The object of the members was to await the coming Buddha Arimadeya (Metteyya), and before his coming the expectation was that the *weikza* Bo Min Gaung would assume the throne of Burma and "clean up the country."

One would think from the account that the *gaing* is an esoteric and bounded "sect" of master and initiated disciples, but such is not the case; this inner core is embedded in a more open, lay-dominated milieu. Mendelson tells us that the actual membership of the *gaing* was hard to determine. There were first of all some twenty resident *yathes*, who observed the vow of not eating meat and "keep the precepts of the usual Buddhist kind." "Sometimes, they take vows of silence for some months." Besides these *yathes*, "occasionally," reports Mendelson, "a small number of the monks will be found about," thereby implying that the *yathes* are different from the regular *bhikkhu*.[18]

On major ritual occasions staged by the *gaing*, Mendelson has seen 200 or more people participating, the overwhelming number of whom were peasantry and small artisans. But a resident *gaing* official, the Sayagyi, told him that at those major occasions at which the Bodaw himself spoke, persons of middle- and upper-class status were present. Moreover, non-Burmese people from the Shan Hills and Kachin territory attended these occasions. Besides, the *gaing* conducted a variety of charitable activities, "including the feeding of 350 monks every morning."

Now let us consider this additional information: The establishment allowed visitors and residents "to sell their own medicine, sacred objects and mediumic [i.e., mediumistic] powers," and Sayagyi uninterruptedly sold holy water, medicine, beads, and "gifts" from the Bodaw. The result is that the *gaing* with its inner core of master and disciples and penumbra of lay devotees of varying constancy and commitment, and with its ritual acts and sacralized objects, bears a family resemblance to the current cults surrounding many of the forest meditation masters in Thailand.

3. We are now ready to appreciate the cosmological shape of the *gaing*'s headquarters. Mendelson describes the spatial and architectural layout of the *gaing* as occupying three levels, laid out according to the "ascensional" theme of Buddhist cosmology. At the first level were the *pagodas*, the *bodhi* tree, and the underground meditation caves; at the second level were the rooms set out for the visits of Bo Bo Aung and Shin Eizagona, shrines for Bo Ming Aung, and the private room of the Bodaw; and at the third and highest level was the enthroned Buddha statue, surrounded by five standing Buddhas, all faced by kneeling *arahants*. There was also the throne of the coming Buddha Arimadeya. The

entire complex seems on the one hand to reproduce the mythical forest in which the *weikzas* of old practiced their arts, and on the other hand to recreate in Burma the sacred geography in which Arimadeya will appear.

## The Karen Telakhon millennial sect

Much the same three-dimensional contours – millennial expectations centering on the coming *cakkavatti* and Buddha Arimadeya, a cultic movement with an inner core of adepts and a penumbra of lay supporters, and a spatial layout and ritual cycle that enact religio-political cosmology and are recognizably "Buddhist" – characterize a Karen millenarian sect that is described by Theodore Stern.[19] Stern finds the major source of Karen millenarism, which was mounted in reaction to the Burmese domination, in the features of the Buddhist kingdoms that surrounded the Karen – such as the viewing of the ruler as a cosmocrator, the earthly analogue of Indra in the city of the gods; and the prophesy that at the end of 5,000 years of decline the way will be prepared for the arrival of the *cakkavatti*, who will lay the foundation of the new order of the future Buddha.

In the Telakhon movement's ideology, the position of Ariya (the future Buddha) was central. Each of the four previous Buddhas was considered an incarnation of Ariya. Ariya had already appeared in the present era and will again become incarnate from time to time, though perhaps in imperfect form, until he attains his full majesty and glory at the dawn of his proper epoch. (We see how this idea of Ariya, much like the Gotama Buddha of the *Jātaka* tales, progressing through a succession of rebirths to his own enlightenment, allows for several millennial prophets to rise and fall and yet maintain the promise intact.)

Con Yu, the founder of the Phu Chaik ("the fruit of wisdom"), a name for both the movement and its leader, was viewed as an incarnation of a deity who had come down to relieve men of their sins, and also as an embodiment of Ariya. It had also been foretold that in the time of the seventh Phu Chaik – that is, the time of the present incumbent,[20] Con Yu would return to establish his millennium; this prediction was contingent, according to some informants, upon the faithful maintaining the purity of conduct he had ordained.[21]

The organization of the Phu Chaik movement founded by Con Yu in a village, some thirty-five miles north of Moulmein, did not take a "monastic" form as understood in an orthodox Theravāda sense, though it was recognizably "Buddhist" in many of its features. Con Yu and his successors were *yathe* (Stern identifies this term with the Sanskrit *rsi*). They were "hermit monks, clad in yellow robes and with unshorn hair, maintaining celibacy and gaining power through fasting and meditation. Each had a school of disciples from among whom the incumbent chose his successor and with whom during festivals he performed ceremonies in a ritual center, while an assistant, his head of religious affairs (*bu kho* in Sgaw) led lay followers through the same ceremonies at a public festival ground.[22]

After Con Yu's time, the movement divided into two branches that established themselves in Thailand, one based in the southern part of Tāk Province and the other among the Pwo of Kāncanaburī Province in the valley of the Khwāē Noi extending down to the plains. The upper Khwāē Noi movement apparently became an orthodox Buddhist establishment of the Mon-Burmese style when its *yathe* died without a successor in the second decade of this century. The other branch continues under its Phu Chaik, who, while not severing ties with his natal family, "maintains himself often in retreat and cultivates his spiritual powers through meditation and fasting."[23]

The Phu Chaik supports himself by farming and is assisted by his followers during planting and harvest. Though he has special powers conferred upon him by Ariya, he communicates informally with his subordinates. He is assisted in his ritual duties by disciples who either volunteer as youths or are selected by village elders for the honor; "like him, the disciples maintain celibacy until the time when they may desire to return to secular life."[24] Though the Phu Chaik's seat was just across the border in Thailand, the majority of its members, principally Sgaw, dwelt in Burma in the hinterlands of Moulmein.

Stern describes the administrative structure of the Phu Chaik as being "complex," composed of a religious head (*bu kho*) and a secular head (*kaw kho*), each assisted by boards and committees, whose members are inferior *yathes* and lay elders. Together they manage the affairs of the sect; supervise the three major festivals of the year; and oversee corporate business concerns, which derive income principally through a house tax on members and from voluntary gifts. The executive committees also sit as a court enforcing stringent observance of a code controlling sexual conduct, forbidding gambling and the use of intoxicants and narcotics, prohibiting the raising of such animals as might be sacrificed to the spirits, and encouraging the wearing of Karen garb.

Stern's description of the Telakhon has the advantage of charting recent transformations and shifts in the movement in the face of increasing frictions with the Thai and Burmese government officials. He also records the sect's increasingly disenchanted encounters with Christian missionaries who, for purposes of conversion, have tried to engulf it by skillful exploitation of the Karen millennial beliefs in the White Brother of the *Golden Book*.

We see before our eyes how a millennial movement, which was previously manifest in an involuted "ritualistic" existence, moved toward militant action, which we are tempted to call "political" action. There was a tightening of the enforcement of rules of conduct pertaining to sex, liquor, gambling, public entertainment, and the raising of animals suited for spirit sacrifice. More spectacularly, the Phu Chaik, heir to a long line of celibate monks, responded to the overtures of missionaries by taking a wife and making her pregnant. Stern thinks the move fuses the advent of the Ariya Buddha with the advent of the *cakkavatti* and hastens the anticipated reunification of the Karen leading to their political independence. Though some of the Telakhon members left because of these changes, there was an expansion in the scale of the movement, its adherents increasing from 3,000 to 10,000 and being drawn "alike from animists, Buddhists, and from rival sects such as the Leke."

There has also been a new, marked phase of militancy against the Burmese that is compounded of three factors: "an affirmation of the Phu Chaik's *cakkavatti* nature, his attempt to regain the followers he has lost, and a recognition of a common cause with the Free Karen in their struggle for Kawthulay." Two militant engagements with the Burmese authorities took place. In the first, Telakhon members, protected by charms furnished by the Phu Chaik and assisted by some ten Free Karen armed with automatic weapons, prevailed over a force of Burmese soldiers. In the second engagement, the Burmese sent a detachment of Christian Chin Troops, who swiftly defeated the rebel forces.[25]

### *Khrū bā* Sīwichai: an activist charismatic monk

We now come to the celebrated case of a Northern Thai monk of recent times who bore the popular title of *khrū bā* (venerated teacher). He is clearly a follower of an indigenous Northern monastic tradition and exemplifies one modality of the saintly *bhikkhu* as local patriot, activist, cosmocrator, and *nakbun*, that is, "one who is so endowed with merit himself that he can, through compassion toward others, serve as a means for them also to acquire merit."[26]

Sīwichai as a holy man, his activities, and the predominantly lay support he depended on – all provide in some respects an instructive contrast to the current Thai forest meditation masters, their followings, and their activities. I shall concern myself with two questions: In what way does Sīwichai intersect with forest saints such as Acharn Mun? and In what sense can he be included in the general framework of millennial Buddhism?

That *khrū bā* Sīwichai was a local hero is attested by the number of popular biographies recounting his sanctity, charisma, and works.[27] Apart from his monumental building projects, Sīwichai is best remembered for his opposition to the national Thai *saṅgha* as promoted from Bangkok and to some of the ordinances it sought to implement in its policy of unification. Swearer reports: "Everyone in the north, especially in the Chiang Mai valley, knows the story of his life or at least episodes from it, and will probably be wearing a protective amulet or medallion on their amulet chain hanging around their neck. There is a prominent statue of Khrūbā Srīvijaya [Sīwichai] at the foot of the famous Doi Sutep mountain overlooking the city of Chiang Mai, and I once attended an image consecration ceremony in which a statue of the holy monk played a prominent magical role."

## Millennial Buddhism in Thailand and Burma

*Khrū bā* was born in 1878 of poor farming parents in the commune of Bān Pāng situated in the province of Lamphūn, a historic part of North Thailand that has had a long association with Buddhism. He was ordained a novice at the age of eighteen and for a brief period became an apprentice to a well-known meditation teacher. Shortly after his higher ordination at twenty-one, the death of the abbot of his home temple (Wat Bān Pāng) left him and a fellow monk in charge of this temple.

Thereafter, these two monks are reported to have gone into retreat to the forest for another brief period. This, according to one biographer (cited by Keyes), was the turning point in Sīwichai's career: He received an omen in the form of a dream of a full moon among the clouds, which he interpreted as a sign and confirmation of his mission.

Returning to his village, Sīwichai, with the help of lay people he magnetized and led, energetically set about building a complex of dwellings and a meeting hall (*vihāra*) on a hilltop outside the village. This became the new monastery, suited for the practice of meditation and consistent with forest-dwelling traditions. He lived a simple life, ate only one meatless meal a day, and eschewed such habits as smoking and chewing fermented tea (*mīang*) and betel.

Sīwichai's rising reputation was to a significant degree owed to his ascetic mode of life. Keyes reports a respected Thai monk as stating the following in his preface to a recent biography: "He desired very little and was content with what he had. He ordinarily had only three pieces of clothing . . . He subsisted on vegetables and avoided all kinds of meat . . . He said that he behaved according to the model of Mahā Kassapa Thera, the monk who strictly followed the practice of *dhūtaṅga*." (Note that in the received tradition Sīwichai has been assimilated to the forest-monk tradition.)

He soon became the center of public attention and devotion: He attracted followers and converts from tribal peoples like Karen, Meo, and Muser who previously evinced no interest in the *saṅgha*; parents brought their sons to be his novice-disciples; and he was the focus of merit-seeking donations. He was credited with the virtues and supranormal powers of a *bodhisattva* – such as discerning other people's thoughts and intentions and not getting hot or wet by exposure to sun or rain.

*Khrū bā* Sīwichai's local reputation in Lamphūn and Chiengmai provinces escalated when he opposed the growing powers of the national *saṅgha* centered in Bangkok. This opposition must be seen as related to the fact that the Northern Tai Yuan people remained more or less free of Central Thai control until the end of the nineteenth century,[28] when King Chulalongkorn launched his provincial civil, and parallel ecclesiastical, administrative reforms with the aid of Prince Damrong and Prince Wachirayān.[29] The *khrū bā* in particular challenged the ecclesiastical regulation that a monk had to be entitled by the national *saṅgha* before he could instruct and ordain novices as their *upajjhāya*. He was charged with failing to comply with the orders of his ecclesiastical district supervisor and

303

was ordered both to be instructed in the new government regulations and to cooperate in compiling the official census of the religious. Moreover, he was blamed for not discouraging rumors about his supranormal powers and for encouraging schism in the *saṅgha*; these were of course two of the major offenses (*pārājika*) set out in the disciplinary code.

Another reason for the central government's concern with Sīwichai's separation was his extensive campaign to build and restore temples and monasteries in North Thailand. Many of these were historic centers of Northern Thai Buddhism and were associated with the Buddha's alleged visit to the region as recorded in local chronicles.

When called upon to defend himself before the ecclesiastical authorities, first in his local district and later in Bangkok, *khrū bā* Sīwichai held that he was ordaining monks according to the pristine traditions established by the Buddha. *Contra* the authority of the central Thai *saṅgha*, he appealed to the authority of the Buddha's teaching and of his own personal experience as a follower of the Path.

Thompson[30] writes that the Bangkok authorities were fully aware of Sīwichai's popularity in Lamphūn and Chiengmai. Advised by the then-viceroy, Prince Bovaredej, against laying any criminal charges against him, they absolved him and sent him back in honor, declaring that his confinement was sufficient punishment. ''A crowd of ten thousand gave the hero-priest an enthusiastic welcome, all nationalities vying with each other to do him honor. He walked on a carpet made of the silk head-dresses of his Shan advisers, who carried him over the muddiest passages.'' In 1935 he was again brought before the ecclesiastical authorities in Bangkok, for by this time schism was in the air and a certain number of Northern monks had severed connections with their ecclesiastical superiors and declared Sīwichai to be their leader. These monks had pronounced against the new and expanded learning sponsored by Bangkok, and some of their leaders were arrested when they refused to allow ecclesiastical officials to inspect their monasteries. Once again, Sīwichai was treated carefully and was allowed to return to the North after he signed an agreement that he would abide by the *saṅgha* rules and regulations as defined by the central government in the Saṅgha Act of 1902. Thus, schism was avoided. Sīwichai thereafter directed his efforts to raising imposing sums of money and intensifying his building projects of bridges, roads, and temples, activities that were traditionally the quintessential activities of kingship.

As Swearer remarks, Sīwichai was not simply trying to conserve traditional regional monastic practices or to revitalize the glories of Lān Nā Thai Buddhism. He was also attempting to restore the land to its original foundations as a *Buddhadesa* (Buddha-land). In this sense, he was a ''cosmocrator.'' In any event, his manifestation testifies to the persistence of the tradition of the holy man celebrated in the legends, images, and amulets of North Thailand.

*Khrū bā* Sīwichai in actual life was, and was seen by his followers as, a man of many facets and many parts; he defies any simple typing. Keyes rightly notes that, despite his reputation for personal asceticism, Sīwichai's career was not that of a recluse withdrawn from the world; he remained very much in the world, and as a *nakbun* provided a means for others, particularly ordinary folk, to make merit through associating with him; as we have noted, he was credited with the virtues and powers of a *bodhisattva*.

Keyes sees a strong contrast between the activist *khrū bā* Sīwichai, the *nakbun*, and Acharn Mun (the central character in this book), whom he sees primarily as an *arahant*, a recluse who withdrew from the world and sought his own salvation. Keyes therefore has dubbed Sīwichai the "savior saint" and Mun the "mystical saint"; he sees this contrast as echoing a long-standing contrast in the religious traditions that developed in India between those who seek salvation through action in the world and those who do so by rejecting the world. In Buddhist tradition, the contrast is that between the *bodhisattva*, the enlightened being who postpones the final leap to *nibbāna* because of his compassion for human beings, and the *arahant*, who has successfully realized *nibbāna* for himself.

Up to a point, seeing Sīwichai, the people's saint, and Mun, the monks' monk, as "opposed" types makes sense. But I must caution against pushing the contrast too far. For as we have seen in our detailed study of Acharn Mun's career, he was more than a withdrawn recluse – he had a compulsive, peripatetic teaching career and spawned a network of cells of disciples. In addition, he was the focus of popular lay religiosity as an acclaimed saint; and we cannot ignore the cultic beliefs and practices associated with his relics and the amulets minted in his memory. Moreover, we should not lose sight of the general fact that the saintliness of both Sīwichai and Mun rested on their credentials of personal asceticism, meditative contemplation, and detached compassion, though perhaps Mun was the greater proven virtuoso on the first two counts.

Keyes also makes the problematic assertion that the *arahant* model represented by Acharn Mun is a recent phenomenon; its reassertion, he suggests, "appears to have begun first in Burma with the eminent meditation master, the Ledi Sayadaw (1856–1923) and then to have occurred in Sri Lanka and Thailand";[31] moreover, it has only been in the past century, in the wake of radical political-economic changes in societies like Thailand – he has in mind the reforms instituted by Mongkut – that the "mystical saint" has been revived as a significant model for monks.

There is some validity in this thesis, but we should keep in mind these caveats: Firstly, the Thammayut reform sect initiated by Mongkut sponsored certain of the ascetic practices reminiscent of the forest-monk tradition, together with the vocation of Pali learning; the propagation of meditation per se was not one of its main planks. Secondly, whatever the Burmese influence on the Thammayut movement, yet, as I have demonstrated earlier, the Burmese influence with regard to meditation made a great impact in the fifties upon the Mahānikāi sect in Thailand, particularly upon Phra Phimolatham. He did not so much spread the reclusive meditation regime to his fellow monks as recruit urban monasteries to disseminate the technology and benefits of meditation, not only to their member monks and novices, but, more importantly, also to the laity. The search for tranquility for those in the world was the professed objective of this drive. Finally, while not disregarding the new disciplinary "orthodoxy" in line with alleged pristine Buddhist ideals and the rhetoric of purification of religion championed by the Thammayut sect, we should not lose sight of the fact that the forest-monk traditions, within which the vocation of meditation has occupied a prominent part, have a long history in Southeast Asia; not only a long history, but also a long experience of local or regional adaptation and elaboration into distinctive complexes. The line of meditation masters stemming from Acharn Mun has its roots in this earlier regional heritage, as much as it was inflected by the reformed practices latterly initiated by Mongkut and Wachirayān and touched by the religio-political strategies of the Thammayut sect. The latter's more recent impulse impacting on the former worked with its grain. This meeting of streams, this double identity and involvement, is intriguingly revealed by Acharn Mun's biographer, Acharn Maha Boowa, who we have seen can speak with two voices according to context and audience: He can discourse and write doctrine in an impeccable, philosophically and rationally orthodox, manner; he can also entrance his audience with tales of the mystical experiences and supranormal feats of his Master that are plainly cosmological, mystical, and "tantric" in inspiration – that are clearly grounded in an entrenched, esoteric forest-monk tradition long flowering in the forests of the Thai, Burmese, and Laotian border provinces.

Now a few words about situating *khrū bā* Sīwichai. On the one hand his biographers try to assimilate him to forest-monk ascetic and meditational traditions, but on the other hand they also see him as measuring up to the requirements of a *bodhisattva*. The kind of *bodhisattva* he was seen to manifest was integrally related to North Thailand's resistance to Bangkok's unification drive and to the erasure of its own religious heritage. And this situation of resistance dovetails with the restoration of the ideal Buddhist realm studded with pagodas and monuments. Therefore we must in part at least necessarily associate the *khrū bā* with the phenomenon of millennial Buddhism of the kind – widely rooted and sporadically bursting forth in this part of Asia – that looks to the coming universal king (*cakkavatti*), righteous ruler (*dharmarāja*), and coming Buddha (*Maitreya*).

The mortuary rites staged after Sīwichai's decease, and the interpretations put upon the happenings at this crucial time, confirm the messianic and millennial dimensions of his historical appearance.[32] On his deathbed, the saint is alleged to have urged his disciples and followers not to abandon "the work we have done" and to organize further undertakings of construction for merit. The cremation rites, held in March 1946, five years after his death, lasted fifteen days and were staged as a festival. People from all over the North, including many followers among the tribal people, contributed money and labor, and rarely heard or seen

306

traditional Thai music and dancing were performed. The body was burned on a magnificent pyre, and the traditional augury at the rites for a great man – a shower of rain – fell, confirming the dead man as one of merit. There was a division of relics into four parts – in due course one part was enshrined at Sīwichai's village temple at Wat Bān Pāng; another two parts in historic *wat* at two great Northern historic capitals, Wat Cāmadevī at Lamphūn and Wat Sūan Dāūk in Chiengmai; and the last part on the top of a mountain, Doi Ngom, which had a commanding view of all the places in which Sīwichai had constructed his monuments.

The preservation of the memory of the saint and the continued radiation of his virtues and energies via monuments placed at strategic points, and images and amulets distributed as sedimentations of his power, followed a pattern that is familiar to us. Writes Keyes: "Reliquary shrines were not the only monuments constructed to the memory of Khrūbā Sīwichai. As is the tradition in connection with famous monks, medallions bearing his likeness were struck shortly after his death and have continued to be produced to the present day. A number of images of Khrūbā Sīwichai have also been cast, the most famous being one at the foot of Dōi Suthēp and another at the reliquary shrine on top of Dōi Suthēp. These images have been practically covered by gold leaf affixed by pilgrims who come to the mountain." People even today continue to seek contact with these objects "because they have intrinsic power that can be drawn upon for their own needs."

Let me then conclude with this statement of the differences among the *bhikkhu* saints, such as *khrū bā* Sīwichai and Acharn Mun, and among the movements that surround them. Up to a point, it is illuminating to use such dichotomies as "savior saint" versus "mystical saint"; a "rationalistic" mode of speech acts and religious discourse versus a "tantric" mode of mystical and cosmological discourse; and, finally, the engagement in cultic rituals impregnated with religio-political imagery versus the eruption into militant political rebellion. We may do so, provided we are attuned to the complex nature of these phenomena, in which the dichotomies may in fact coexist as strands. In one case, one strand may be more dominant than the other. In another case, each may express itself in different communication contexts. In all cases, each is capable of moving from one dominant phase to the other dominant phase, according to the intensity and salience of contextual circumstances.

## The Saya San rebellion in Burma

The Saya San rebellion in Burma,[33] mounted against the British colonial rulers in the 1930s, took place roughly at the same time as Phra Sīwichai was resisting in North Thailand the encompassing power of the centralizing Thai authorities. The Saya San rebellion enjoys a conspicuous notoriety because, more than any other millennial protest that has occurred in Southeast Asia, it was led by monks (*pongyi*) and ex-monks. I shall tailor my account to demonstrate the point that what seemed like a sudden and violent eruption did in fact portray during its course certain critical features in the ideology and symbolism of millennialism in the Buddhist mode.

A long-term erosion provides the setting for understanding why Buddhist monks led an insurrection against the British in Burma. Factors in this erosion include the "disestablishment" of the Buddhist *sangha* by the colonial authority; the severance of the traditional relation between *sangha* and state; and the withdrawal of both state patronage of the *sangha* and of the guarantees of its authority, entitlements, and property. The erosion of political support for the monasteries also gave rise to an intensified sectarianism and an increasing emergence of radical, militant, "political" monks who could not be disciplined by the *sangha*.[34] By and large, there was a humiliation and loss of national prestige that was keenly felt by the Buddhist monks in particular. The humiliation was intensified by the transfer of the Burmese royal throne to a museum in Calcutta and the British incorporation of Burma into the Indian Rāj – symbolic and administrative acts that to the Burmese denied their existence as a Buddhist polity and a people with an identity and history. These circumstances may be viewed as contributing features of the "long run."

The *immediate* circumstances that sharpened the impulse to rebellion and determined its timing and the place of its occurrence were various economic dislocations caused in the agrarian sphere, especially in the rice bowl in the lower Irrawaddy Basin.[35] The Sayan San insurrection that erupted in 1932 was in this sense primarily a peasant revolt, and it began with a vengeance in the Therrawaddy District with attacks on British authorities and the Indian Chettiyar moneylenders; it then "swept through large portions of the north, central and east central Irrawaddy Delta and extended as far as the Shan States in the northeast . . . Its popular character is beyond doubt; about 9,000 rebels were arrested or captured, 3,000 killed or wounded, and 350 convicted and hanged. The official report remarked on the number of headmen and monks who took leading roles."[36] The rising, once launched, developed into a series of local rebellions that took an independent course of their own in Pegu and Upper Burma.

The economic circumstances that brought previous grievances and resistance to fiscal taxes and levies to a head and caused in 1930 a massive explosion, as sudden as it was widespread (precipitated by the integrating forces of the world market now experienced as the Great Depression), has been well documented by the authorities cited.[37] It is relevant to note that Saya San himself had been the past chairman of a committee sent by the General Council of Buddhist Associations, at the urging of its nationalist faction led by the monk U Sae Thein, to inquire into excesses in the collection of taxes. The association that he formed had as its professed first two purposes the offering of resistance to the forcible collection of the unpopular taxes and the oppressive forest-land ordinances that deprived villagers of the free use of wood for domestic needs.

We can now take up the question of the millennial expression of the revolt.[38]

The British authorities had already noted with some anxiety the appearance of millennial prophets claiming to be *setkyamin* (*cakkavatti*) in 1906, 1910, and 1912, when a large following of 20,000 had formed, and again in 1924–6. Furthermore, as Sarkisyanz has noted, there were many other movements in the late nineteenth century and the twentieth century that never reached the threshold of official notice. So the Saya San eruption, though sudden, was a major explosion in a continuing series of smaller ones. It is of no surprise that its leader, who was seen as striving to restore Burma's political sovereignty and its treasured jewel of religion – indeed, as ushering in the promised Golden Age in which all the pious will achieve salvation – should have assumed, and in turn enthusiastically be invested with, the titles of Setkyamin and Buddha Yaza (future Buddha).[39] Rumors spread that he was of royal descent. In accordance with these claims, he had the Buddha-King's City (Buddha Yaza Myo) pegged out, and erected a palace of bamboo on the jungle mountain of Alauntaung in the Therrawaddy District. At his coronation,[40] as the rebels known as the Galon Army walked past, Saya San is alleged to have called upon – in his capacity as Thupanna Galon Raja undertaking his mission for the advancement of Buddha's religion – the guardian spirits of Buddhism and the various *nats* and *weikza* to help his soldiers on to victory and to protect them from harm.[41] And the oath taken by the rebels contained not so much fulminations against economic grievances as the rhetoric of banding together "to drive out all unbelievers," so that the religion might be saved from them; to gain liberty for themselves; and "to the Galon-King dominion over this land."[42]

We need to know much more than is now provided by the standard sources in English about the meaning and power associated with the signs, symbols, and rituals of initiation and moral rearmament; about the actual organization of the "secret village societies" (Sarkisyanz) or "the associations" (Scott) – the *athin* – that staged the revolts; and about the manner in which the Buddhist monks' Samgha Sametgyi Association, from which came the monk (and former monk) leaders, intersected with and organized the *athin*.

The *galon* is of course the fabulous mythical eagle (known elsewhere as the *garuda*), the intrepid enemy and destroyer of the *nāga* (snake). The interpretive task is to see how the classical symbols were made acutely relevant and employed with deadly potency in the context of the religio-political and economic crisis of the 1930s. The rebels were the *galons*; Saya San, their *galon* king; and the British and their collaborators, the snake to be stamped out. The *galon* was tattooed on the bodies by "village magicians," was a mark of initiation into the *athin*, and signified the protest against the taxes and their nonpayment. An ex-monk named U Yazeinda from the Henzada region who was active in the formation of many village associations "urged non-payment of the capitation tax and said that he had the medicines which would render the villagers proof against the assaults of Government officials. *No member of our athin who has been tattooed will have to pay the capitation tax.*"[43] The tattoo design incised on the body by the charismatic officiant confers upon the recipient some of his mystical powers, in the same way as the blessed amulets earlier analyzed; in this context, the primary power conferred was invulnerability against British arms.[44] A variety of charms, medicines, and amulets also seem to have been employed. Saya San himself was an expert tattoo artist and the author of a work on traditional medicine. Armed with only a few guns, supplemented by crudely manufactured firearms from pipes and bicycle tubing – but fortified with their tattoos and amulets and spurred on by their millennial expectations – the rebels attacked "unflinchingly against rifle and Lewis gun fire of the finest shooting regiments in the Indian army." They "went down in tens and twenties, but still they came on, storming over their lines of dead . . ."[45] A more prosaic official British report said "the rebels were, however, so convinced of their invulnerability that they advanced openly against the police, shouting out that they were going to kill them, and continued to advance in spite of being warned that the police would open fire. This the police were compelled to do, and they continued firing for about an hour and a half before the rebels finally retreated."[46]

If the valor of the rebels was visible to all reporters, the structure of the *athin* that formed "the tenuous organization grid for the revolt" (Scott) has seemed opaque to them. Besides the names of some of the organizing and teaching monks and ex-monks, there is so little known about the pattern of mobilization that we are forced to fall back on the suggestibility of analogy. It seems to me that we have to turn to the organization of *gaings* and the activities of *weikza* and other holy men in Burma, and to our fuller accounts of the cults and followings surrounding contemporary Thai meditation masters, and the network of teacher-pupil cells and of head and branch hermitages, to visualize the techniques and grids that enable the mobilization of peasants at grass-roots level for participation in militant millennial movements. The same analogizing should tell us why in the last resort – even though the British troops were sorely tried and it took some two years to quell the rebellion entirely – the *athin* associations were tenuous, volatile, and fragile, and therefore incapable of establishing the new order. It is also my surmise that similar processes of cell formation are effective for guerilla action in faraway provinces against the rank and file of a solidified administration.

## The millennial uprisings in Northeast Thailand (1899–1902)

Although Burma provides the best examples of millennial cults and rebellions, Thailand has not lacked them, and the revolts at the turn of this century in Northeast Thailand were the most recent, and also the best-documented, example of militant and violent millennialism.[47] As a shorthand expression, I shall refer to them as the 1902 riots.

An earlier-known instance of millennial revolt occurred in 1699, when a Lao named Bun Kwāng, who styled himself a *phū mī bun* (person of merit), managed to establish himself the ruler of the outpost city of Khorāt in the reign of King Nārāi (1656–88). He is alleged to have marshaled over 4,000 men, 84 elephants, and over 100 horses, but was overwhelmed by the Ayudhyan forces sent by the order of King Phetrāchā (1688–1703).

A later occurrence, more an incident than a rebellion, happened in 1924 in Lōēi Province in the Northeast. This time, four men – acclaimed together as *phū mī bun* and hailing from Ban Nong Bankkeo – performed purification rites, distributed various talismanic objects "to hundreds and thousands of Thai-Lao who came to see them from neighboring provinces including Roi-et and Mahasarakham," and attacked a district office. But again, after two months the disturbance was put down by a police reinforcement."[48] Since then, minor incidents have been reported:[49] In 1933, a troubadour singer claimed extraordinary powers and threatened to overthrow Siamese power and establish an independent Lao kingdom; in 1959, a *phū mī bun* claimant bubbled up in Khorāt; in 1973, after the October revolution, Keyes knew of at least two people who claimed to be incarnations of Ariya Maitreya and acquired followings in the Northeastern provinces of Udon and Lōēi; and, at the same time, some scholars have reported coming across pamphlets, mainly circulating in the North and Northeast, describing alleged manifestations, or imminent arrivals, of the messianic Maitreya.

So these sporadic occurrences should warn us against treating the 1899–1902 riots as either unique or inexplicably sudden. Explosive they were, but they exploded out of a smoldering condition of politico-economic frustrations and a widespread attraction to men of extraordinary claims and to millennial promise.

The available descriptions of riots enable us to supplement our preceding account of the Burmese Saya San rebellion in certain ways. When the millennial movement explodes into violence, there is simultaneously an intensification of other appearances – the number of charismatic leaders claiming to be men of special powers multiplies, their capacities are magnified, the actors are carried on a euphoric tide, and finally there occurs a destructive and sacrificial devaluation and negation of the present world in favor of the shining new order.

No doubt the circumstances leading up to the 1902 uprising were many and complex. But most commentators are likely to agree with Tej Bunnag[50] that the time of its occurrence was one when the adverse effects of the territorial integration of the Northeast into a single Thai polity began to be felt by the local privileged sections of the people, who lost many of their traditional bases of both power and wealth.

The Northeast had previously been a region organized as small principalities (*mūēang*) ruled by Lao (and Khmer) nobles (*čao*). In the face of colonial expansionary threats by the French from Indo-China and the British from Burma and Malaya, King Chulalongkorn initiated a system of patrimonial provincial administration through the appointment of Siamese high commissioners, who occupied an intermediate position between the Bangkok court and the Northeastern local elite. In 1892, the position of these elite was even more directly challenged by the appointment of Siamese officials as permanent administrative commissioners; they were invested with critical powers, such as those relating to taxation, that had been previously exercised by the local lords.

In the meantime, there was in 1893 an outbreak of hostilities between the French and the Siamese, and by the treaty of that same year Siam conceded to France all the left-bank territory of the Mekong (and also virtual control of a twenty-five-kilometer zone, which could not be entered by Thai officials or soldiers without French permission). This spurred on Thailand to exercise tighter control over its Northeastern territory and to appoint Prince Sanphasitiprasong as the royal commissioner plenipotentiary of the Northeastern "circle" (Monthon Īsān). From 1894 onward, King Chulalongkorn (with the indispensable services of Prince Damrong) established a centralized provincial administration, which entailed a new territorial mapping of administrative units. The net result was that only a few of the old principalities or domains (mūēang) were given the status of provinces (čangwat), while most of them were accorded the status of districts (amphōē), not an insignificant number even having to settle for the undignified status of the next lower administrative unit, tambon.

The outcome of this revamping was the downgrading of the local nobility and gentry, and even those who retained their lordly status as governors discovered that they were bereft of much power. The most conspicuous evidence of this was the imposition of local taxes by the Siamese commissioners: In 1901–2, they raised the amount of the poll tax. Such impositions, and new limitations on the sale of buffaloes, cattle, and elephants, also coincided with a general deterioration of agriculture, increasingly insecure subsistence farming, and outbreaks of banditry.

It is in these unsettled times that prophecies circulated of the imminent coming of new leaders to alleviate suffering, and a rash of phū mī bun (men of merit) and phū wisēt (men of supranormal powers) broke out. We should note the significant fact that, like the Saya San revolt in Burma, we are witnessing again not a concerted unified and directed Cromwellian rebellion but a number of dispersed mobs coalescing around charismatic men sprouting like wishing trees in various parts of Monthon Udon and Monthon Īsān.

By 1899, Keyes says, Siamese officials were reporting the appearance of phū wisēt distributing to peasants sacralized water (nam mon) and medicine (yā) and performing various rites. Troubador singers and handwritten scripts disseminated the message of the coming phū mī bun, while also making predictions of dreadful disasters and exhorting people to take various remedial actions.[51] Strange occurrences were expected to occur – wax gourds and pumpkins would turn into elephants and horses, water buffaloes into demons (yakkhas).

The "king of righteousness" (thāo thammikarāt, phū mī bun) would appear and perform the alchemical feats of changing laterite lumps (hin hae) into gold and silver. One of these pamphlets claimed of the righteous ruler, Phrayā Thammikarāt, that he had previously ruled over Ayudhyā and the Laotian kingdoms of Lāng Chāng and that his face was again "seen in our time." Here we have a remarkable example of the thesis I have argued before: The notion of rebirth, in the context of Buddhist conceptions of *cakkavatti* and the coming *Buddha*, enables men of personal charisma not only to assume these statuses but also to claim that they are reincarnations of past heroes.

Amid these prophesies, commotions, and awed expectations, there appeared in various localities of the Northeast a number of *phū wisēt* who performed purificatory rites upon the panic-stricken peasants. At least some of these *phū wisēt* were known to be Buddhist monks. An example was Phrakhrū In[52] of the Bang Nong I Tun monastery in Yasothon Province, who performed the rite of "cutting the retributive *karma*" (*tat kam wāng wēn*) on villagers and also urged them to collect laterite lumps for conversion to precious metal. In the same province, Siamese officials reprimanded three ranking monks for performing rites of this nature. The *phū wisēt* performed "miracles" such that the onlookers came to believe that some of them were the awaited *phū mī bun* himself.

We will return to the question of the relation between *phū wisēt* and *phū mī bun* after giving a short sketch of the best-known rebel leader. Ong Man came from a village in Monthon Īsān (actually from the present-day province of Ubon), and he clearly was the leader of peasants several hundred strong. He is reported to have claimed to be Čao Prasāthāūng ["a divine being who had descended from heaven to be reborn as a favor to mankind" (Keyes)] and Phrayā Thammikarāt Phū Mī Bun (the awaited king of righteousness). According to the report of a local official, Man, while he was a *phū wisēt*, had kept the Buddhist eight precepts, had meditated in caves and in the hills, and had performed rites with sacralized water – thereby attracting several local disaffected gentry (Keyes). According to Ishii, with the support of a village doctor, he collected some 200 followers and attempted to attack the town of Ubon to depose the Siamese high commissioner. He gained on the way an initial victory over the governor of Khemarat and soon after was joined by six *phū wisēt*, who served as subleaders. By now the rebel army had grown to about 1,000 men. Another successful operation against a small squad sent by the high commissioner swelled the ranks by an additional 1,500 men. But that was their finest hour; soon afterward, Ong Man and his following were defeated by an army of trained soldiers equipped with modern weapons, sent by the high commissioner. Three hundred casualties were counted and 400 prisoners were taken. This defeat sealed the fate of the uprising.

Although Ong Man's origins seem to be obscure, the evidence seems to indicate that a number of those who claimed to be *phū mī bun* were local officials of minor rank or local nobility. Thāo Bunčan, one of the leaders, was a disaffected noble who came from what is today called Sīsakēt Province. Disappointed that he was not made governor, he left the town and collected local gentry, who all called themselves *phū mī bun*. Similarly, Lek, whose place of origin was today's Mahāsarakham region, together with his followers assumed similar honorific titles.

According to one source (Phaithūn), these *phū mī bun* leaders avowed to establish a separate kingdom that would be under the control of neither the Siamese nor the French. The plan was to have four *phū mī bun* rule at four capitals in Vientiane, Ubon, Thāt Phanom, and Nōng Son (Ayudhyā). Such a polycentric plan accorded with the traditional "galactic" scheme.

Now, from our foregoing discussion, it is evident that no hard and fast distinction can be made between *phū wisēt* and *phū mī bun* (Ong Man himself was apparently both), although there are indications that the *phū wisēt* were more likely to be "holy men" who claimed supranormal powers, perhaps had been committed in some way to ascetic practices and meditation, and quite clearly performed purificatory rites and distributed medicines and amulets. The monks, of whom only a few seemed to have been involved, must have participated as *phū wisēt*,[53] which accords with their professional specialization. The *phū mī bun* – the title sounds in this context as if it meant "man with a righteous political cause" – seem to have been militant rebel leaders, drawn primarily from the ranks of the déclassé nobility and local officials.

Ishii provides this scenario of the unfolding of the millennial uprisings in both 1902 and 1924, which also suggests a particular relation between *phū wisēt* and *phū mī bun*. There is first of all a prediction of an imminent catastrophe, which creates widespread unease and agitation. Then follow prophecies of a savior's descent from above, in the form of *phū mī bun* who would deliver the suffering people and establish the new dispensation. "*Phū wisēt* are heralds to the advent of a messiah. Belief in the latter is generated in the minds of people by the miraculous acts of certain *phū wisēt* of superlative ability." As expected, a *phū mī bun* declares himself and justifies his claim by collecting larger and larger numbers of followers by performing "miracles." Then follow the military adventures with the aim of instituting a new political order. The uprising is defeated by the superior military forces mobilized by the political authorities.

## Some theoretical clarifications

In the light of all these foregoing Burmese, Thai, and Karen examples of mystical cosmographic associations, cults, and finally violent uprisings, all infused with messianic and millennial overtones and expectations, I am tempted to make certain clarifications concerning the current discussion on esoteric-messianic-millennial Buddhism in Buddhist Southeast Asia.

Certain discussions of what has been labeled "esoteric Buddhism" are too narrow. They describe *gaings* as a variety of "quasi-secret sects" (the word "quasi" is usually an escape clause resorted to in insupportable definitions), emphasize too much their devotion to occult doctrines and their closed membership, and leave out as inessential the penumbra of lay devotees and supporters who participate in their ritual activities. The result is that they unduly confine the scale and scope of the movement in question. Spiro is given to this narrowness.[54]

Also, any attempt to delimit the Burmese *weikza* and *yathe* (or Thai *phū wisēt, phū mī bun*, or *khrū bā*) as essentially non-Buddhist in essence or inspiration is liable to mislead. Spiro sees esoteric Buddhism as composed of different strands. One is the belief "in a mythical magician or *weikza* who, supposed to possess enormous supernatural powers, and having overcome death, is the presiding genius or spiritual master of the sect." Another is the belief in the future Buddha and in a universal king, which he recognizes as Buddhist. Now, Spiro insists that "neither *weikza* nor the aspiration to *weikza* are Buddhist in character," indeed they are "anti-Buddhist," and that it is only when the *weikza* belief is combined with the ideas of the future Buddha and *cakkavatti* does the configuration become a distinctive doctrine of esoteric Buddhism.[55] But only two pages later, when Spiro catalogues some of the capacities attributed to *weikza* – "to fly through the air and through the earth, to make oneself invisible, to pass from one place to another in a moment . . ." – he tucks away in a footnote the comment that "these same powers, incidentally, may be achieved by means of *jhānas*, those ecstatic states that sometimes accompany Buddhist meditation."[56] It seems to me that we have to find a more artful way of treating the issue of how the great traditions of Buddhism have developed into particular crystallizations in different local and regional contexts.

Spiro runs into these analytic and interpretive difficulties[57] because, rather than treat Burmese religion as a totality and configuration, he wants to sever it into two opposed religions, Buddhism and animism. (This penchant is not much helped by another axiom – for the most part asserted without adducing historical evidence – that much of what is found in Burma is a deviation from, and vulgarization or distortion of, the canonical purity of early Buddhism, which he too narrowly conceives.) A consequence is that he not only rejects Mendelson's thesis of Burmese religion being a syncretized amalgam of Buddhism and animism, but also – and this is what importantly concerns us here – repudiates Mendelson's view that esoteric Buddhism is a pervasive strand in Burma. This repudiation is upheld by the tendentious pronouncement that "esoteric Buddhism . . . is the Buddhism of the *gaing*" (we have already seen how he defines the *gaing* as some sort of closed secret sect or quasi-sect) and therefore necessarily confined to a minority. Both for Burma and Thailand, this would not be a fair way of representing the attitudes, commitments, and ritual acts of large numbers of people who subscribe in one way or another to what has been labeled esoteric Buddhism.

Spiro breaks down Burmese esoteric Buddhism into "two major ideological systems," eschatological Buddhism and millennial Buddhism. Eschatological Buddhism is based on alchemical practices,[58] which aim at acquiring an extension of life until the appearance of the next Buddha and in order to witness his dispensation. "Since *weikzahood* is a means to the attainment of nirvāṇa, initiation into a sect entails a commitment to the practice of Buddhist discipline. The initiate must agree to observe the moral precepts of Buddhism and to perform Buddhist devotions." In addition, many sect members practice Buddhist meditation as a means of acquiring supranormal powers.[59] It would seem then that the phenomenon identified as eschatological Buddhism accents the sectlike organization and the practice of alchemy for the personalistic aim of prolonging life until the next coming of the Buddha.

By contrast, the system labeled "millennial Buddhism" accents the militant political revolts inspired by the esoteric beliefs. "Millennial Buddhism represents the conjunction of the Buddhist notions of a Universal Emperor and a Future Buddha with the Burmese notions of a Future King, *weikzahood*, and occult power."[60] Thus during the British rule, many peasant revolts were inspired by a configuration of these beliefs, and the future king transferred occult power to followers by alchemic and other means.

In my view, this division of esoteric Buddhism into two systems, demarcated in this manner as eschatological and millennial, obstructs more than it clarifies our understanding. This is true for several reasons: All the actual *gaing* associations or movements we have observed, including the cults surrounding the forest hermits in Thailand, are predicated on a cosmology of *arahants*, Buddhas or coming Buddhas, and *cakkavatti*; the palaces, cosmic mountains, etc., that spatially and architecturally realize the cosmology are *religio-political in expression*; and the ritual actions and disciplinary practices engaged in by adepts and lay followers alike, whether alchemical or meditative or talismanic, are simultaneously of a *personal and collective import*.

Therefore, the more rewarding theoretical issue is the processes by which the *gaings* and cults – which are centered on *weikzas*, saints and men of merit, which mushroom throughout the country, and which ordinarily conduct their religious existence in a primarily *ritualistic and contemplative mode* – are transformed into movements that engage in militant and rebellious millennial action that seems to us more political and activist in character. What are the processes of intensification and expansion of scale by which the small associations, enacting through ascetic practices and in ritual terms their expectations both of the coming universal king and Buddha and of their kingdom on earth, seek to realize those same expectations through large-scale volatile movements, engaging in warlike fighting and rebellious actions that seek to reorder the political order?

We may rephrase Spiro's dichotomy and say: All the forms of esoteric-messianic-millennial Buddhism in Southeast Asia in cultic form embody a cosmological design with religio-political resonances. However, they may move from a principally "ritualistic" mode focused on personal, familial, and local (community) relief of suffering and salvation concerns to a militantly activist mode focused on collective, regional, and ethnic (national) salvation under certain conditions.

## The infrastructure of millennial movements

Many scholars are tempted to seek the underlying basis or infrastructural conditions that give rise to millennial and revivalist movements. One scholar (Worsley) has said that millenarian religions appear in part because they provide integration to stateless societies. Another (Bellah) has pronounced that millenarianism is a product of a "severe social pathology" and is therefore largely ineffective as a vehicle of modernization. A third (Aberle) has attributed millennial movements to conditions of experienced "relative deprivation" combined with "blockage" of attaining relief through normal secular channels. These theses can be multiplied,[61] but such an enumeration does not serve a useful purpose here. What is pertinent is a comment on a recent attempt to delineate a common underlying basis for the millennial uprisings that have taken place in Thailand in the last century, principally the uprisings in Northeast Thailand around 1900–2.[62]

Keyes concludes very plausibly that, while deteriorating economic conditions at the turn of the century among the peasantry may have exacerbated the discontent of the people of Northeast Thailand, it is the radically changed political order instituted by a centralizing Siamese government that took away and threatened the power of local notables (*chao mūēang*) that was a more important cause of the uprising. He asserts that the question is not so much that Theravāda Buddhist beliefs are susceptible to millennial interpretation (they are) but that the millennial uprising of 1902, which was an ideological response formulated in the cultural terms with which the population in question was most familiar, *shows a concern about power*. He thus states a general proposition: "Millennial movements emerge during a crisis centering around conceptions of power."

At a merely substantive level, does this formula adequately cover the millennial movements that have occurred in Thailand and Burma? What appears as a plausible verdict on the Thai 1902 uprising (and even the different kind of confrontation mounted later by *khrū bā* Sīwichai in North Thailand in opposition to the Bangkok-initiated policy of unification and hierarchization of the Thai *saṅgha*) appears not to fit at all the Saya San rebellion in Burma in the 1930s, where the most salient discontent at the time it occurred was agrarian impoverishment and unrest caused by the intrusion of a market and cash economy into the rural areas, increasing loss of land by small holders to large absentee landlords, the change of sharecropping agreements from variable grain payments to fixed cash rents, and so on.[63]

Apart from the uncertainty of the search for an underlying condition or process that may apply to all millennial movements in Buddhist Southeast Asia, too often a weakness of such searches lies in the cut made between infrastructure and superstructure, ideology and practice, and the attempt thereafter to make one level an "expression" of the other. The analytic challenge lies in showing the dialectical and recursive and feedback relations between these levels, such that the dynamic interaction cumulatively produces a total social phenomenon.

If we apply this prescription to the millennial movements in question, we have first of all to begin with the *positive* fact that there is an internal impulse present in popular Buddhism (not a mere minority freakishness but an endemic orientation) to develop millennial expectations around the saint or holy man and to form volatile movements of inner cores of adepts and outer circles of lay followers surrounding the master. In the ordinary lives of villagers and townsmen – victimized by suffering and hopeful of wealth and prosperous lives, although living at the margin of existence – the true renouncer is a hero, extraordinary but accessible, who continually springs from their ranks. Only a few saints are born from the ranks of the high and mighty. Apart from the fact that such exemplars are assimilated to the classical notions of Buddhas and *cakkavatti*, and the classical cosmological blueprints, we have to give full weight to the collective public conviction that men who undergo ascetic practices, control their sensory impulses, and ascend to higher levels of detached contemplation are considered not only worthy of veneration, for they do what ordinary persons cannot and do not wish to do, but also to have access to supranormal powers with which they can fecundate the world like showers of rain.[64]

There is, to borrow a phrase of Troeltsch's, a well-developed ethic of "vicarious offerings and integrations," wherein the saint as a virtuoso offers a "vicarious oblation" for the rest of humankind.[65] He is relied on to transfer his wisdom, purity, and supranormal energies to the laity through his discourses, his blessings, the amulets he has charged with potency, the objects he has touched, and so on. Troeltsch has suggested that wherever asceticism develops as a calling, this kind of vicarious oblation tends to be associated with it. In any case, whereas in the medieval Catholic church asceticism was only one activity (and not a dominant one at that) in the Christian "cosmos of callings," it is at the heart of the Buddhist cosmos of individual attainments; and unlike the Catholic priest, who by the appointment of Christ has in his hands the sacramental impartation of grace, the Buddhist *bhikkhu* (and each of the assortment of holy men we have encountered) ideally transfers merit by virtue of the *kamma* of his own volitional actions.

Given these evaluations and expectations, forest hermitages harboring ordained *arahants* (or *gaings* focused on *weikza*) and analogous occurrences should be expected to occur in popular Buddhism. But the number and frequency of manifestation of these small, volatile communities of lay devotees and adepts, and their liability to intensify their search for power and well-being through vicarious oblation, and/or to transform their ritual acts into militant marches

318

against established authority, armed with bullet-proof amulets, depends on changing political, economic, and social circumstances. These circumstances, acting as a leaven, make millennial movements rise up explosively and pop all too quickly when they confront the armed strength of authority. On the other hand, at times when great power is wielded by centralized or centralizing political authorities, the charisma of holy men, such as that of the forest-monks of contemporary Thailand, may be tapped by such authorities and their elite supporters and used to buttress their supremacy.

What is millennial Buddhism? It is a totality of beliefs, expectations, practices, and actions that have as their object the reconstitution of an existing social order in terms of an ideal order, a future utopia, which at the same time is a return to an ideal and positive beginning.

Millennial Buddhism rests upon conceptions and prophecies concerning the coming righteous ruler and the coming savior Buddha, the two personages co-appearing or being fused in one. Now these very same ideas were an essential part of the ideology of established and institutionalized Buddhist polities of Southeast Asia, whose kings have made claim to be and aspired to be *cakkavatti*, *dharmarāja*, and *bodhisattva*, in different mixes. And capitals and kingdoms have been constructed to represent and enact the cosmology of the realm in which the Buddhist *Dhamma* prevailed.

But millennial Buddhism is the antinomy of the established Buddhist polity wherever it is seen to be corrupt and debased, or to require restoration and resurrection in the face of social decline or alien intrusion. In this sense, it is a counterstatement, dedicated to a substitution and a future replacement, and capable of becoming rebellious. One is tempted to say that if, in the established *Dhamma* realm, the *saṅgha* and kingship are both separated and wedded in reciprocity and mutuality, millennial Buddhism strains toward the fusion of renouncer and ruler in its militant phase.

Now it is true that the Buddhist polities of Southeast Asia have been pulsating, galactic polities, in which "divine kingship" was dogged by "perennial rebellions," and that successive usurping kings have made their claims to legitimacy by invoking the personal charisma of reincarnated and reborn righteous rulers and future buddhas. To this extent, millennial claims have always been part of the regular political process of these galactic polities.

It is, however, meaningful to reserve the term *millennial Buddhism* for the cults centered on the kinds of holy men and saints who have fascinated us in this book. It seems to be these cults' essential feature that – although they periodically, intermittently arise and the ground that gives them birth is a continuing seedbed – as individual formations they rarely, if ever, reach the proportions of a sustained movement. As esoteric cults built around individual masters, they have little staying power after the leader's death, though disciples may reproduce the cells, associations, and networks established by the master.[66] And when they boil up into militant revolts, they are unable to long withstand the organized force deployed by the established political authority, because of their being a peculiar compound of mystical beliefs in invulnerability to guns and bullets, of euphoric moblike indiscipline, and of enthusiastic if fragile attraction to the saint credited with supranormal virtues and powers. Such bubbles form and burst typically in the territorial and social peripheries of established societies and polities, away from the capitals of their ruling political and ecclesiastical elites. In this sense, millennial Buddhism is the counterculture and counterstructure to organized and domesticated Buddhism. *Contra* the treacherous search for an underlying socio-logical condition that generates millennial movements, I have tried to strengthen the line of inquiry and interpretation that sees the place and role of millennial Buddhism, in both its quiescent and militant expressions, as part of a totality, in which "established" Buddhism and polity constitute its dialectical, and fre-quently paramount, counterpart.

# 21

# The sources of charismatic leadership
## Max Weber revisited

Max Weber assigned charismatic leadership and domination a significant role in history because of his belief that charisma is the source of all creative leadership and that no form of political order can work without an element of charisma. As Mommsen remarks: "This is in line with Weber's own personal convictions regarding the role of the individual in history. Weber's charismatic personalities have much in common with Nietzsche's great individuals who set new values for themselves and for their followers, in an attempt to elevate mankind to a high level."[1] Indeed, Weber's view that charismatic leadership was necessary in modern "plebiscitarian democracy" was linked with his lack of conviction in the efficacy of popular sovereignty as such. Great politicians with charismatic quality were essential to keep democracy alive in spite of and in the face of bureaucratic institutions. He saw the need for society to be kept open to enable the rise and recognition of talented politicians with a sense of calling and with the capacity to resist the omnipotence of bureaucracies.

Precisely because charismatic leadership was so important in Weber's sociological theory of the modes of social action, it is both intriguing and puzzling that his discussion of it was plagued by certain dualities and even seemingly antithetical propositions. Weber took the notion of charisma from the Bible. Charisma is referred to in the New Testament, notably in two letters of Saint Paul, namely Romans 12 and I Corinthians 12. The King James Bible renders the Greek word *charisma* as "gift"; the "gifts" referred to in particular are those of wisdom, knowledge, healing, prophecy, ministry, and teaching. All these are seen as gifts of the Spirit, the Holy Spirit who speaks through Christ. "This basic simple meaning of charisma as a gift revealed by divine election became in the course of time the basis of ecclesiastical organization." It originally implied "leadership based upon a transcendental call by a divine being, believed in by both the person called and those with whom he has to deal in exercising his calling."[2]

Weber converted this Christian notion, which was quite precise, into a general concept. In doing so, he was led to locate charismatic experience and inspiration as essentially "affective" (or "affectual") action in comparison with the other modes of orientation in his typology, namely "rational" action and "traditional" action.

Having generalized and made more abstract the original Christian notion, and being forced to identify the charisma that was so productive in history as essentially "affective," "nonreflective," and "irrational" in its source, Weber felt unable to deal adequately with the problem of the sources of charisma, on the ground that their claims were not capable of rational evaluation. Hence he resorted to his "value-free" stance and decided to deal with charisma in terms of its effects on the followers and the conditions for its maintenance and routinization.

It is curious that Weber should have avoided the problem of the source of charisma on the ground that the source as such cannot be "validated" and with the disclaimer that even a pirate genius may exercise a "charismatic domination" in the value-neutral sense he intended. For, in another context, he was able to make a typological distinction between exemplary prophecy and emissary prophecy, which he saw best represented in Buddhism on the one hand and in Christianity and Judaism on the other. This dichotomy was directly relevant to the experience of charisma claimed by the prophet and his substantive message, but Weber used it to contrast two orientations to the world and their effects upon it, rather than as divergent sources of charismatic powers.[3] The burden of this section is that the question of the sources of religious charisma in the Christian and Buddhist cases could be approached in a different way from that adopted by Weber and that the two polar types – emissary and exemplary prophets – additionally imply certain important orientations and consequences other than those singled out by him.

## The Weberian dualities

Weber defined "charisma" as "a certain quality of an individual personality by virtue of which he is set apart from ordinary men and treated as endowed with supernatural, superhuman, or at least specifically exceptional powers or qualities."[4] What is central for Weber is that the exceptional powers or qualities found in the charismatic figure decisively and overpoweringly shape and reorient the dispositions and actions of his or her followers.

Now, as David Little points out, "this inward, immediate 'possession of sacred values' is just the sort of intense emotional and unreflective 'seizure' that exemplifies Weber's description of affectual behavior."[5] The influence of charismatic leadership is experienced as "an uncontrolled reaction" to some "exceptional stimulus," and such "devotion to a personal or ideal" object illustrates *affectual action*, which Weber contrasted with *rational action*.[6]

But of course Weber's typology of three modes of action is not watertight, and there are important overlaps and interconnections between them. It is these dynamic intersections that reveal the strengths and weaknesses of the Weberian sociology of rationalism. But insofar as the charismatic orientation derives from the surrender of the faithful to the extraordinary, it is alien to all laws and regulations and indeed disrupts both rational rule and tradition alike. Such affectual action is therefore *counterrational.*

But Weber also realized that all forms of rationality and tradition are ultimately grounded in subjective values that are irrational or nonrational. It is easy to see this is the case with the traditionalist sacralization of customs and with absolutist rationality, which, being an "ethic of ultimate goals," cares not for pragmatic calculations of either ends or means. But more unexpected is Weber's admission of the same for *Zweckrationalität* as well: "The various great ways of leading a rational and methodical life have been characterized by irrational propositions, which have been accepted simply as 'given' and which have been incorporated into such ways of life."[7] The ends of capitalist economic action or of democratic politics, as indeed of any kind of economic or political action, are ultimately arbitrary, conventional, and irrational.

Charismatic action thus may be affective and counterrational; but the charismatic inspiration often proclaims an authoritative ethic of ultimate ends and thus allows for an opening toward absolutist rationality and a systematization of religious ends and means for achieving those ends. In this regard, we should remember that Weber held "primitive religion" and "magic" to be traditionalist and to consist of ritualized and stereotyped behavior in the form of taboos and proscriptions. Historically, radical, charismatic religious movements have achieved the critical breaks through the cake of tradition and have initiated the development of more systematic "rational" religion with regard to doctrine and practice.[8]

Thus, from Weber's perspective, it is part of the intrinsic disposition of charismatic religious movements, such as Christianity, Buddhism, and Islam – founded in affectional irrationality and originally preaching an ethic of ultimate ends – to progressively "rationalize" in the most general sense of rationality – that is, the elaboration, systematization, and clarification of religious concepts and religious goals and the means to achieve them. But the crux of the Weberian comparative study of religions and of his sociology of rationalism is that only one charismatically inspired religion, Christianity (together with its predecessor Judaism), had the propensity to rationalize in the direction of *Zweckrationalität,* because it alone had a unique *this-worldly posture* that generated an activism integrally linked with formal, relativistic, instrumental, practical, and consequentialist reasoning. We are therefore led back again to consider Weber's division of "affectual action" and of charismatic authority into two polar types, only one of which could lead to and result in rational this-worldly activity, the foundation of Western capitalism, industrialization, and party politics.

Weber, in characteristic fashion, subdivided affectual charismatic action into two types, *ecstatic* and *communal. Ecstasy* is induced by emotional seizures as the result, for example, of orgiastic practices. The ecstatic condition is *asocial* and in institutionalized expressions leads the individual to lose himself in a "euphoria of apathetic ecstasy," as illustrated by the Buddhist theme of the extinction of the self. Buddhist doctrines of compassion, love, and tranquillity are labeled *acosmic love*, that is, general, undifferentiated, and mystical. But *communal* affectual action, rather than repudiating social relations, leads to benevolent and personal attachments between members of the same group; in its quintessential form, it constitutes an *ethic* of brotherly love that is the obverse of the calculating and manipulative strategies of formal, practical rationality.

The celebrated dichotomy on the same lines is Weber's two types of charismatic experience – the *exemplary prophecy* and the *emissary* or *ethical prophecy* – around which he was to group the decisive differences between oriental and occidental salvation religions.[9] Oriental salvation religion is primarily one of "contemplative mysticism," whereas the occidental is primarily "ascetic" in the sense of pursuing virtue with a preference for active conduct in the world.

The *otherworldly asceticism* or *mysticism* of retreat from the world is best expressed by the exemplary prophets, who by their personal example demonstrate to others the way to religious salvation, as in the case of the Buddha. The prophet's preaching refers not to a divine mission, or an ethical duty of obedience, but rather directs itself to the self-interest of those who crave salvation. The exemplary leadership is oriented toward "a contemplative and apathetic-ecstatic life."

The *inner-worldly asceticism* of Christianity, dedicated to a transformation of the world, produces the *ethical* or *emissary* prophet, who regards himself as "an instrument for the proclamation of God and his will." He preaches as "one who has received a commission from God, he demands obedience as an ethical duty." Whereas the Buddhist devotee seeks self-sanctification, the Christian prophet is always an instrument and vessel of his omnipotent God and never his equal.

We may note in passing that Weber's picture of exemplary prophecy oriented to a mystical contemplation and apathetic ecstasy does not do justice to at least two aspects of the Buddhist *bhikkhu*'s vocation: It underplays the highly formalized and systematized technology of meditation and ascetic practices; and it leaves out of account the finely elaborated rules of *Vinaya*, whose objective was the regulation of monastic life and the promotion of "brotherly" conduct among the members of the monastic community.

It is also possible that Weber's tendentious use of the *cognitive–emotional* dichotomy leads to his arguing that the two types of charismatic experience and message lead to two types of religious systems, the other-worldly mystical and the this-worldly ascetic. In the course of the comparison, exemplary prophecy (and Buddhism) becomes tagged to the *emotional* need for an immediate experience of deliverance from suffering, and ethical prophecy (and Christianity) to the *cognitive* need for understanding the sources of suffering and the means for implementing a practical solution. Such a unidimensional typing of an entire religion like Buddhism once again does little justice to Buddhism's onslaught on ignorance (*avijjā*); to its cognitive and intellectual emphasis on the understanding (*paññā*) of the origin and causes of mental formations, attachments, and suffering in the world and its compelling logical and psychological analysis by which their elimination is advocated; and to its ethic of intentional practices accordingly devised to unite knowledge with practice. Buddhism has its own brand of cognitive, emotional, and evaluative inputs; they are different from Christianity's.

## Weber's value-free stance on the sources of charisma

There is another mode in which Weber treated charismatic authority and domination, which shifts the sociological interpretation from considering the charismatic experience of the leader per se to the attitudes and reactions of the followers. This turn that Weber took is also related to his moving away from the classical Christian notion of charisma and his typing it in general as emotional, affective, unreflective, inspirational, and counterrational. By definition, then, an emotional experience and claim cannot in Weberian terms be "rationally" validated; hence his transposing the issue of validation to the level of follower reaction. I shall argue that there is something we can learn by returning to the problem of the *source* of charisma: We can do so by taking the Christian formulation seriously and then contrasting it with the Buddhist formulation of *arahantship* or sainthood as another type of charisma. (In doing so, I by no means wish to belittle the illumination we derive from Weber's discussions of the effect of charismatic leadership and message on followers, the conditions that favor or mitigate against the continuation and success of a charismatic movement, and the signs by which charisma is validated in the eyes of followers.) To make this comparison coherent, I present a general definition of religious charisma[10] that can compass different religious situations.

Religious charisma derives from transcendental claims to authoritative leadership, claims that are made by the leader and accepted by the followers. Transcendental claims are extraworldly and assert the extraworldly to be superior to the world (hence supraworldly) – to encompass it (hence the notion of immanence), to inform and elevate it (hence its ethical centrality), and finally to supersede it (hence its message of salvation). The internal ordering and boundaries of what constitutes the world system differ from religion to religion; this cosmological mapping is an essential comparative task and often holds the answer to different conceptions of charisma and its transmission from leader to follower.

Weber extended and made more general the Christian notion of charisma by using it for all situations, whether they be religious, political, or criminal, and for all heroes – whether they be sorcerers, prophets, or generals – who were seen as having a "personal gift" or "genius." Weber's "value-neutral" stance shifted the discussion of charisma from the claimed *sources* of charisma to the criterion of *recognition* by the leader's followers. The leader had to prove his charisma to his followers by works and deeds; therefore charisma lay in the eyes of the beholder, so to say. In this context of discussion, Weber was interested in showing how personal charisma was volatile and unstable in comparison with institutionalized offices and bureaucracies.

There is another duality and bifurcation in Weber's treatment that emerges from his celebrated notion of "routinization of charisma." Weber is capable of two readings on this matter; it is perhaps more correct, though more untidy, to say that he was simultaneously aware of both possibilities.

One is the view that charisma is essentially personal, unstable, rejects "rational" procedures, relies on inner strength, and is an ideal type opposed to and set apart from institutionalized authority systems, whether traditional or rational, patrimonial or bureaucratic. Charisma's only association with the latter is when it is routinized; but when it is routinized it is weakened and loses its intense experience of grace and its heroic elements. As Eisenstadt comments: "It is not only that charismatic authority is formally contrasted with 'traditional' and 'rational' authorities. Beyond this formal distinction, pure charisma has some inherent antinomian and anti-institutional predispositions."[11] Charismatic leadership in this manifestation can be the stimulus for rebellions, millenarian movements, and visions of new utopias. In this exegetical mode, Weber has written: "Since it is extra-ordinary, charismatic authority is sharply opposed to rational, and particularly bureaucratic, authority – and to traditional authority, whether in its patriarchal, patrimonial, or estate variants, all of which are everyday forms of domination. . . ."[12]

A second exegetical mode takes up the question of how charisma, its orientation and the bonds it sets up, is a constitutive feature of all social action, in that it is not something abnormal but is woven into all concrete situations and is a necessary component of all institutionalized structures. Thus transformed, it manifests itself in structured forms like "lineage charisma," which connotes the transference of charisma through blood ties, and "office charisma," in which charisma becomes "part of an established societal structure" and the belief in revelation and heroism of charismatic personalities is replaced by permanent structures and traditions. Following this line of thought,[13] Shils and Eisenstadt have fruitfully argued that the routinization and objectification of charisma is an aspect of all bureaucratic organizations.[14] The charisma of office was necessarily for Weber a case of the "depersonalization" of charisma; but, as embodying a specific state of grace in a social institution, its occurrence was widespread both in earlier and modern societies. The relation of subjects to the state and its institutions and offices is a good example.[15]

The charisma of office has taken historically important forms: "First of all charisma may be transferred through artificial, magical means, instead of through blood relationship: The apostolic succession secured through episcopal ordination, the indelible charismatic qualification acquired through the priest's ordination, the king's coronation and anointment, and innumerable similar practices among primitive and civilized peoples all derive from this mode of transmission.'' Where we see the linkage of charisma with the holding of an office ''we find that peculiar transformation of charisma into an institution. As permanent structures and traditions replace the belief in the revelation and heroism of charismatic personalities, charisma becomes part of an established social structure.''[16]

Weber makes the brilliant observation that ''the Catholic theory of the priest's *character indelebilis* with its strict distinction between the charisma of office and the worthiness of the person constitutes the polar opposite of the Puritan rejection of office charisma. Here we encounter the most radical form of the depersonalization of charisma and its transfiguration into a qualification that is inherent in everybody who has become a member of the office hierarchy through a magic act, and that sanctifies official acts.''[17]

I interject the complaint, however, that while the disjunction between priestly office and personal grace – and between a (Catholic) narrow specification of saints and a (Puritan) extension of priesthood to all true believers, who are all ''saints'' – may make good sense in a Protestant–Catholic discourse, it fails to catch the spirit of the Buddhist conception of *bhikkhu*. A *bhikkhu*, though necessarily ordained into a status and bound by rules of abstinence, is constantly evaluated by fellow monk and layman alike on his achieved progress on the path of purification and on the charisma of supranormal capacities and sainthood (*arahant*) that derive from individual effort and achievement.

## A digression on Rudolf Sohm

Weber gave credit to Rudolf Sohm for developing ''the sociological character'' of charismatic domination, but at the same time registered this objection: Since Sohm developed ''this category with regard to (only) one historically important case – the rise of the ecclesiastical authority of the early Christian church – his treatment was bound to be one-sided from the viewpoint of historic diversity.''[18] Immediately preceding this appraisal, Weber states his ''value-free'' sociological stance thus: Certain forms of charisma closely associated with ''manic seizure'' and ''constitutional epilepsy'' may not be edifying ''for us,'' ''however, sociology is not concerned with such value judgments''; more important for the discipline is that heroes and magicians ''proved their charisma in the eyes of their adherents.''

It is not clear from Weber's own writings to what extent he actually took into account the Protestant theological debates, particularly the vigorous views of Sohm, in formulating his alleged ''value-free'' view of charismatic leadership.[19] A summary of Sohm's views on charisma is useful for us, both to point to the theoretical relevance of the "source" of charisma and to prove that Weber, despite his alleged value-free stance, did not manage to liberate himself from the dominance of the Christian precedent.

The compatibility between the charismatic authority of the Holy Spirit on the one hand and church law and legal authority in the church on the other hand has been debated by Protestant theologians ever since Luther propounded his conception of the two kingdoms – one of which is the kingdom of God under Christ and the other the kingdom of the world under civil authority. For Luther, these two realms exist under quite different kinds of authority, the one under the love and spirit of Christ, and under the guidance of the Holy Spirit in conjunction with the Word and Sacrament, and the other under legal restraints and under the rule of law of temporal government.

Much of the Protestant theological controversy apparently centered on the role of the Holy Spirit as charismatic inspiration in the establishment of canon law and in the legal authority of the church. A key figure in this controversy was the eminent German jurist and church historian Rudolf Sohm (1841–1917), who viewed "charismatic authority (in conjunction with Scripture and the sacraments) to be altogether incompatible with any 'divine church law.' "[20] Sohm protested against any constitutional legalization of the church, whether of the Roman Catholic or Protestant kinds. The primitive Christian *ecclesia*, under the charismatic authority issued from Christ and the Gospel, necessarily excluded any alien principle of legal direction and restraint, which belongs to the political realm and which if admitted makes the church worldly and leads to the secularization of the church from within. The Christian *ecclesia* was informed by the power of the Holy Spirit; as the Body of Christ, it is constituted by members who are the beneficiaries of gifts of grace (*charismata*), which both call and qualify the individual Christian for different activities. "It is an organization given by God, not a corporation emerging out of human consensus."[21] The efficacy of the Spirit is always connected with Word and Sacrament and not with the obligation to law.

Sohm's reading of church history was that, among other causes, the waning of charismatic leadership led to the development of bureaucratic organization and legal institutions of the Catholic church. The doctrine of apostolic succession, the institution of church offices, the division between clergy and laity, and the "thingification" of piety were outcomes of this process. For Sohm, true Protestantism is based on faith; it constitutes an invisible church or a fellowship of Word and Sacrament.

The Lutheran view, as advocated by Sohm, traced charismatic power to the Holy Spirit *in conjunction* with Word and Sacrament. Weber not only severed charisma and grace from a Christian divine source, but also characterized it as personal, labile, and volatile, ignoring its necessary *conjunction* in Sohm's exposition with Word and Sacrament, that is, with the discipline of received doctrine and ritual practice. Finally, I note that Weber's "routinization" of charisma is less unambiguous and more equivocal than Sohm's denial of the probability of embedding it in bureaucratized institutions. Be that as it may, there is good reason for us to return to the question of sources of "charisma" for comparative purposes, although we need not agree with Sohm's view that charisma as a gift of grace cannot be transmitted to, and embedded in, institutionalized office.

## The flaw in Weber's comparative theory

One of Weber's central theses was that charisma is a phenomenon "in radical contrast to bureaucratic organization" – it knows "no formal and regulated appointment or dismissal, no career, advancement or salary, no supervisory or appeals body, no local or purely technical jurisdiction, and no permanent institutions in the manner of bureaucratic agencies, which are independent of the incumbents and their personal charisma."[22] In this context, Weber was right to emphasize charisma's "highly individual quality" and its rejection of "all methodical rational acquisition, in fact, all rational economic conduct," when the opponent in this contrast was the economic substructure on which bureaucracy depends for deriving its "continuous income" from the money economy and tax money. Charisma is "the strongest anti-economic force, even when it is after material possessions, as in the case of the charismatic warrior. For charisma is by nature not a continuous institution, but in its pure type the very opposite."[23]

But this contrast with bureaucratic organization also impels Weber to see charisma as ruling out all systematic procedures for reaching individual salvation, as in Buddhism, for Weber's "pure type" clings to the Christian type of "prophetic revelation."[24] These pronouncements of Weber decidedly cannot apply to the Buddhist *arahant* as perfected saint: "The specific form of charismatic adjudication is prophetic revelation, the oracle, or the Solomonic award of a charismatic sage . . . genuine charismatic justice does not refer to rules; in its pure type it is the most extreme contrast to formal and traditional prescription and maintains its autonomy toward the sacredness of tradition as much as toward rationalist deductions from abstract norms." All this goes against the Theravāda emphasis on *Dhamma* as scripture and the *Vinaya* rules as the prerequisite for the renouncer's heroic liberation.

## Toward a resolution and a typology

In probing the source of charisma, Edward Shils has widened the conception of charisma from the Christian "gift of grace from God" formula to its close association with "some very central feature of man's existence and the cosmos in which he lives."[25] "Charisma, then, is the quality which is imputed to persons, actions, roles, institutions, symbols, and material objects because of their presumed connection with 'ultimate,' 'fundamental,' 'ritual,' order-determining powers.''[26] The central agents, powers, and conceptions in question could of course vary from society to society, and it is a task of social and cultural analysis to see how the gap between the charismatic as an extraordinary event or quality and as a constituent element of any orderly social life is bridged. I shall exploit this insight and posit two kinds of crystallizations of charisma, one volatile and the other institutionalized. If we then see charismatic leadership in "relationship to transcendental sources" and confine it to a "religious" context only, then we have at least two major types of charisma (see Figure 15).

There is a Judaeo-Christian version of charisma as a gift of grace from God, an elective gift. Quintessentially, this gift is given to the virtuous – the elective are also elect – though one can imagine an extreme formulation of "predestination" being associated with an arbitrary choice of God.

Charisma of this Judaeo-Christian sort further subdivides into two sorts – there is the temporary, unstable, labile, volatile, even rebellious charisma of the inspired biblical prophets and of Christ's warriors like Joan of Arc or the crusading knights. And there is the enduring, routinized, institutionalized charisma of the pope or divine king, both of whom possess, as Kantorowicz[27] has aptly informed us, "two bodies" – the eternal body of the church or state and the mortal body of a human, the former encompassing and infusing the latter. Taking the pope or divine king as our point of reference, we can easily see how indeed charisma is, in some sense, objectified and routinized in every institutionalized office.

It is abundantly clear that the *arahant* of early Buddhism and the forest saint of present-day Thailand present us with a polar opposite, in which charisma is acquired and won in an austere renunciation quest – in which charisma consists in the attainment of detached, discriminating wisdom on the one hand and universal compassion on the other. There are at least two important features that characterize this Buddhist (and Hindu) notion of charisma attained through the ascetic and meditational path.

First of all, the Buddhist orientation is to a "norm" and not a monotheistic God. It is one of the great Buddhist stories that the dying Buddha, during the last moments of his life, when requested to nominate a successor, refused to do so, saying that the *bhikkhu* should be lamps unto themselves, be their own refuges, and that the *Dhamma* that he had brought them should be the guiding norm.

At another level, it is this same orientation to a liberation goal attainable by an ascetic path that encodes a discipline and regime that guides the ascetic forest-monk. This discipline is, as we have seen, set down in the classical texts such as the *Visuddhimagga*, from which are derived the more popular manuals. The discipline is taught and passed on by a spiritual teacher to his disciples, and in theory teacher and pupils can talk about the results and successes of their exercises as objective experiences prescribed in the meditation manuals and repeatedly experienced by the adepts.

# The sources of charismatic leadership

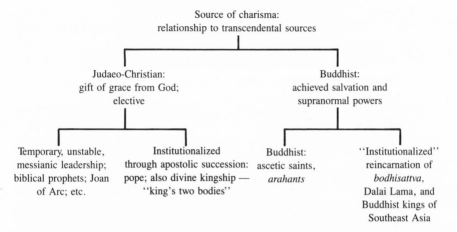

Source of charisma:
relationship to transcendental sources

**Judaeo-Christian:**
gift of grace from God;
elective

**Buddhist:**
achieved salvation and
supranormal powers

Temporary, unstable,
messianic leadership;
biblical prophets; Joan
of Arc; etc.

Institutionalized
through apostolic succession:
pope; also divine kingship —
"king's two bodies"

Buddhist:
ascetic saints,
*arahants*

"Institutionalized"
reincarnation of
*bodhisattva,*
Dalai Lama, and
Buddhist kings of
Southeast Asia

*Comment:* This typology only deals with religious statuses. It is of course clear that in politics, for instance, there can be charismatic-type leadership that springs from other sources. Carl J. Friedrich ("Political Leadership and the Problem of the Charismatic Power," *Journal of Politics,* Vol. 23, No. 1, Feb. 1961, pp. 3–24) distinguished the "ideological" leader, who is a spokesman for a political ideology (exemplified in totalitarian leadership), from the "inspirational" leader, who shows rhetorical skills and personal dynamism (democratic-demagogic leadership). Friedrich preferred these secular forms of political leadership to be kept separate from the charismatic in the strict sense. (See Mommsen, *Age of Bureaucracy,* for a critique of Friedrich.)

The typology excludes the Hindu sources of charisma, because Hinduism combines two modes that are similar to our polar types. Thus the *brahman* is "divinely created" (Code of Manu) and his superior charisma is related to his origin and his observance of a strict code of pure conduct. The *sannyāsi,* on the other hand, like our Buddhist *arahant,* is an individual who achieves *mokṣa* and liberation.

Figure 15. A typology of charismatic sources and statuses of a religious nature.

Thus the Buddhist situation does not fully confirm the extreme comparison and antithesis that Max Weber drew between the charisma incorporated and distributed in a bureaucratic organization of offices and the quintessential expression of charisma as a personal exuberance intransigent toward discipline. Among other things, the charismatic movement, said Weber, knew little of "*the regulated and expert training of the holder of charisma or of his aides,*" and *the charismatic form of settling disputes was typically by prophetic revelation or by Solomonic arbitration.* Whatever the Judaeo-Christian expression of charisma, the Buddhist community of monks (*saṅgha*) has always been subject to an elaborate *Vinaya* code of conduct and set of rules for arbitration of disputes and conduct of affairs by individual residential communities; it is on this base that the ascetic, meditative path consisting of *dhūtaṅga* practices and expert training in meditational exercises was constructed.

Weber's telling statements that "charisma knows only inner determination and inner restraint,'' that the holder of charisma demands obedience by virtue of his mission, and that he is the followers' master ''as long as he knows how to maintain recognition through 'proving' himself'' – these personalistic elements are appropriate in our case only when they are superimposed on the base outlined above. The Buddhist meditation master's personal qualifications are achieved by relating his effort to an institutionalized and formalized vocation.

Just as in the Christian case there are two crystallizations of charisma – one of a volatile, unstable nature in the persons of prophets and saints and their followings and the other in the more institutionalized offices and persons of the pope and divine kings – so in the Buddhist case there are two modal crystallizations. One is exemplified in the persons and followings of the *arahants* and saints, like our Thai meditation masters and forest saints,[28] and the other consists of the enduring ''doctrine of presence'' of the *bodhisattva* in this world, best represented in the office and person of the Tibetan Dalai Lama. The ''priest-king'' of Tibet, the Dalai Lama is regarded as a continuing reincarnation of Bodhisattva *Avalokiteśvara*, a permanent objectification of the Buddhist hero's achievements of understanding wisdom and universal compassion and loving-kindness. To a lesser extent, the institution of Buddhist kingship in the Theravāda polities of Southeast Asia, in Sri Lanka, Burma, Thailand, Laos and so on, which tried to associate the office and person of kings with the charismatic associations of the *dharmarāja* (righteous ruler), *cakravartin* (wheel-rolling universal king), and *bodhisattva* (Buddha-to-be) are also examples of the same institutionalized occurrence of charisma, concordant with Buddhist notions of rebirth, transmigration, and reincarnation.

## The charismatic field of the forest saint and his following

Among these crystallizations, let me comment in detail on the Thai forest saints and their followings, who are our chief interest. There is first of all a certain flexibility in the way each meditation master implements the meditation manual and the specific techniques he advocates, the rigor of the discipline, and the pattern of the instruction he imparts to his disciples. Our previous documentation gives us a lively sense of which of the various meditational subjects stated in the *Visuddhimagga* are advocated by particular masters. It also shows that whether *samādhi* concentration is taken to be a necessary preliminary to *vipassanā* insight meditation or whether the latter is plunged into directly are matters for individual stress allowed within the limits set by the *Visuddhimagga*. How often disciples discuss their meditation experiences with their masters, how often the master gives formal meditational-*cum*-doctrinal-instruction, and the daily timetable with its solitary and communal phases – these again are differently conceived within certain limits in different hermitages and meditation centers.

These flexibilities and latitudes are in accord with the *social field* in which the forest saints act and that they help construct. This social field's contours are best seen when this field is contrasted with two other institutional structures. One is the established *sangha* in Thailand with its hierarchy of royal and commoner temples and its ecclesiastical organization of a hierarchy of titled offices, culminating in that of the "king of the monastic order," the *sangharāja*. The other is the established political system with the king at the apex and below him the ruling political-army elites and the bureaucracies of graded civil officials, petering out at the grass roots with the hamlet headmen and village schoolteachers. Both these ecclesiastical and political establishments radiate from the swollen center of Bangkok outward to the provinces on grids that weaken and die in the rural peripheries. In contrast, the social fields of the forest monks spread and pulsate in those fuzzy frontiers and inaccessible peripheries of the country's frontier provinces.

The forest saints are typically – until they are later lionized by the public – nonestablishment monks. We have noted that their hermitages lack the consecrated *sima*, places in which ordinations into monkhood can take place. They have no Pali degrees and no ecclesiastical titles and formal positions; in fact, because they are *āraññavāsī* – forest dwellers – their membership is excluded from the official *sangha*'s titular system.

But though outside the "establishment" and marginal to the ecclesiastical and governmental centers, they are, by another mode of counting within the doctrinal traditions of Buddhism, the greatest achievers. They have entered the *arahant* path of salvation, which is precisely constituted of that very physical and social exclusion and those austerities and renunciations of worldly power that enable the transcending of desire and suffering, the achieving of liberation, and, seemingly paradoxically but also quite logically, the access to supranatural powers as well.

Now the quintessential forest saint, exemplified by Acharn Mun throughout his life, or the other saints such as Lūang Pū Wāen and Lūang Pū Fun during the greater part of their earlier careers, were *peripatetic* monks: They went into seclusion in the deep forest accompanied by one or more select companions, gained their moral victories, emerged and criss-crossed the country especially in its Northeastern provinces, during the rains retreats took up temporary residences in obscure as well as well-known urban *wats*, and initiated cells of disciples into the discipline of meditation.

Thus over a period of time these recluses did travel, teach, and form highly personalized monastic cells, whose disciple members, devoted and enthralled, were trained by their master. These cells of disciplined meditators were not permanently enduring entities – the disciples followed the master part of the time and went to study with other masters at other times. If they did not derobe, they themselves became peripatetic teachers, attracting their own coteries of disciples as their reputation bloomed.

This propensity, then, of the peripatetic meditation master and forest saint to spawn cells of religious disciples, who would again spawn cells, in the remote areas of the society gained a somewhat firmer structure when meditation masters like Acharn Chā at some stage founded a more or less permanent forest hermitage and from that center founded other branches of subsidiary centers in the vicinity to which disciples are assigned. In this manner, a network of parent and daughter hermitages is established. It is quite easy to see that the networks of cells that forest saints can help establish, cells of devoted and highly motivated disciples focused on their masters, can constitute, if systematically expanded, a formidable system of charismatic influence and presence that is so different from the established ecclesiastical system or the political authority with its patrimonial-bureaucratic attributes and weaknesses. In fact, it can come to be an alternative grid of power and mode of mobilization to the established systems.

But of course nothing so extensive has taken place in the present situation. The networks or hermitages and cells are not vast, not coordinated, and not enduring because they are the creations of a small number of meditation masters who function on their own.

Nevertheless, the potentialities of the forest-monk's "routinized" monastic networks must be recognized. They are ideal dispersed centers for guerrilla-type activity against an established authority or for subterranean activity sponsored by an established authority; they can form a network for mobilizing secretly and for conveying information quietly; they are by their dispersion in rural heartlands suitable for mobilizing the peasantry. Finally, there exists the possibility, as I have demonstrated, that charismatic ascetic monks claiming supranormal powers could become the rallying points for millenarian cults and movements.

In present-day Thailand, the real political significance of the meditation masters is that, although they are themselves not political figures, they have been taken up and assiduously visited by the country's politicians, bureaucrats, and intelligentsia – especially from the metropolis. This is symptomatic of a near political crisis, which will concern us in the concluding pages of this book.

# 22

# The objectification of charisma and the fetishism of objects

What indeed escaped Weber, who was so alive to the routinization and objectification of charisma in institutional structures, was the objectification of charisma in talismans, amulets, charms, regalia, palladia, and so forth – a phenomenon as old as religion, indeed as old as all forms of leadership.

In the Thai case we have examined, people attribute virtues and energies to persons because of their ascetic conduct; these saints are seen as capable of transmitting their charisma to persons directly or, more usually and lastingly, through amulets they have charged and activated. The charisma is concretized and sedimented in objects; these objects are repositories of power.

In this fetishism there are *two social loops* or *cycles* in which *saint* and lay public are implicated. One cycle is the ideologically developed and transparent one; the other is more hidden and manipulative and rides on the former. The first cycle is to be understood in terms of the Buddhist path of salvation: According to its cosmography, the ascetic meditator attains progressively higher spiritual levels of consciousness, leaving the grosser material excrescences behind, and through the control of his sense doors and sensory states attains understanding wisdom and universal compassion. This, then, is a *state of transcendence*, which also generates supranormal powers with which to affect the phenomenal world through detached action. The specifically Buddhist formulation, then, is that detached action is also pragmatically the most effective action – by being removed from the immediacy of desires and entanglements, it is all the more encompassing and creative. Now it is a part of the first cycle that these virtuoso saints are approached by merit-making laymen, to whom the amulets are distributed as part of the saints' dispensation of blessings. At this level of exchange, the conventional Buddhist exegesis has some explanatory value: Amulets (like relics) act as "*reminders*" of the virtues of the saint and the Buddha, and the saints act as "*fields of merit*," in which laymen may plough, sow, and harvest through their donations. Moreover, in this frame the piety of the layman's intentional action is stressed.

335

# Conceptual and theoretical clarifications

At the next remove, we have the cycle of transactions by which laymen possess, accumulate, and secrete on their persons or otherwise employ these amulets to influence, control, seduce, and exploit fellow laymen for worldly purposes – in the corridors of politics, the stratagems of commerce, the intrigues of love, and the sycophancy of clientage. In this arena we perceive two developments: Firstly, the iconic and indexical properties of the amulets are recognized as pragmatically effective. The figures and emblems of the saints, the Buddha, and other beings are indexical icons, which by existential contact with the monk and by virtue of his impregnating them with sacred words, purifying them with sacral water, and other similar acts of transference, embody the monk's virtue and power. This objectification of the virtue of the saint also implies the passage of his spiritual and transcendental powers to lower realms of materiality and the marketplaces of human desire and gratification. They become life affirming and destroying and act as missiles and countermissiles in the transactions of worldlings (see Figure 16). If the ascetic, virtuous path of purification is one of ascent from the states of materiality to the formless states and beyond, the path of gratification is one of descent from the higher realms of spirituality and universality to the lower realms of material desires and limitations of space and time. In simple words, the deep structure of this cosmology that articulates the relation between saint and lay follower is that what goes up must come down.

It is inevitable in the Thai case that this process of vulgar materialization, this law of gravity, should have further consequences. One is that the amulet moves from a context of donation and love (*mettā*) to a context of trade and profit: It is converted into a highly salable good and enters the bazaar and marketplace. When it does so, it also stimulates the production of fakes and becomes a pawn in the usual publicity media of advertisements, catalogues, magazine articles, books, and the mythology of miracles. A second consequence is that the more amulets are produced, the more they are faked, and the more they are purchasable for money, the more they deteriorate in their mystical powers (despite the inflationary spiral of prices for the rare antiques). This means that new amulets come into fashion and many others are condemned to be forgotten or less desired; moreover, the propensity to accumulate amulets increases, in the simple arithmetical calculation that the more you possess, the more clout you have. Thus the comparison of the relative virtues of amulets leads to mystical power itself, which is both limitless and rare, being graduated, weighed in the balance, or quantified in terms of money. Hence the common spectacle of Thai men wearing a necklace on which are hung a number of amulets – the richer and more powerful he is, the better and more numerous the icons protecting his person and helping him to overcome others. To fully comprehend why there is an obsession in contemporary Thailand with amulets possessing power (*saksit*) (especially among urban circles and populations and among men rather than women), one has to bring into view the texture of its social relations, which are woven on the loom of patron–client

336

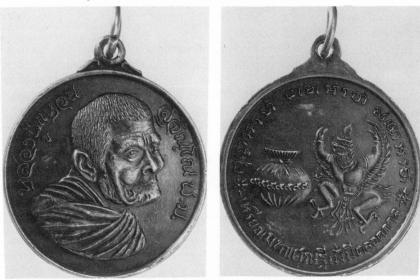

Figure 16. A Lūang Pū Wāēn medallion that promises wealth. On the front side is the bust of Wāēn with his name inscribed. On the back is represented the insignia of the lay sponsor; it consists of a bag of money (with a band of the auspicious number 9 written across it) and the *garuda* bird; the encircling caption says "Medallion of the rich man that [brings] eternal wealth."

relations, and the norms of *bunkhun*, by which leaders and men of rank and power bind in service circles of clients and retainers.

## On charisma and the gift

Wittgenstein, in some remarks he ventured on Frazer's *Golden Bough*,[1] was particularly suspicious of this passage from Frazer:

At a certain stage of early history the king or priest is often thought to be endowed with supernatural powers or to be an incarnation of a deity, and consistently with this belief the course of nature is supposed to be more or less under his control.

Wittgenstein thought neither the people nor their ruler could possibly believe that this was the case. "Rather the notion of his [the ruler's] power," remarked Wittgenstein, "is so adjusted that it can conform to both his and the people's experience. That any hypocrisy plays a part in this is true only so far as it generally does in most of what men do."

The implication of Wittgenstein's comment is to turn our attention away from the reality of the experience of the occult per se as a crucial feature of a religious consciousness, away from the theology of human attitudes and relations to a transcendental or suprahuman presence, and to direct it to the "people's experience'' in their everyday social lives that makes such a theology a plausible projection on their celestial screens.

In fact, this was precisely the kind of explanation sought by Mauss, in his own sociological idiom, for the "primitive" human's conception of *mana*, that sense of force that seemed to pervade the universe, to enter into and be radiated by both people and objects – an "elementary" theory of "causation" of a global scope. So how would we give an answer in Maussian terms for the Thai people's experience that makes the mystical power (*saksit*) and perfections (*bāramī*) of the *lūang phāū*, the saintly ascetic monks of the forest, a plausible entity, a subjective truth as well as an objective reality?

## Mauss on *Mana*

Mauss,[2] taking Codrington's discussion of *mana* in *The Melanesians*[3] as his point of departure, was impressed with the attributes of the conception that seemed to override and surpass normal distinctions: *Mana* was a quality, a thing, an essence; it was a contagious and transmissible force possessed by both objects and spirit beings; it was abstract and general, yet quite concrete. Indeed *mana* – a shorthand concept that included parallel conceptions like *orenda* (Iroquois), *kramat* (Malay), *manitou* (Algonquin) – was "both supernatural and natural, since it spread throughout the tangible world, where it is both heterogeneous and ever immanent";[4] it was impersonal and at the same time clothed in personal forms; it was a power milieu.

Mauss further remarked that this was essentially the same conception embedded in the Hindu notion of *brahman* as the metaphysical principle and power activating the rite, prayer, and formula; moreover, it was the goal of Hindu *yogic* and meditational practices.

"*Brahman* becomes the active, distinct and immanent principle of the whole universe. Only brahman is real, all else is illusion. As a result, anyone who would enter the bosom of brahman through mystical activities (*yoga*: union) becomes a *yogi*, a *yogicvara*, a *siddha*, that is, one who has gained all magical power (*siddhi*: obtaining), and in this way, it is said, has placed himself in the position of creating worlds. Brahman is the prime, total, separate, animate and inert spirit of the universe; it is the quintessence. It is also the triple Veda as well as the fourth."[5] It is the expression of "a fourth spatial dimension."

Although there are real differences in the Hindu and Buddhist ideas of self and salvation, and of the character of the meditational exercises, it is possible to see some affinity between *mokṣa* and *nirvāṇa* as the final state of union with the universal world spirit in the one case or of void and annihilation in the other, in that both are visions of an ultimate cosmic consciousness where all illusions and manifestations terminate as well as begin. It is this ground that enables the *yogi* with his *siddhi* or the *arahant* with his *iddhi* to "create worlds," precisely

# Objectification of charisma, fetishism of objects

because he has transcended the mundane and understands the laws of their formations and because his wisdom and moral virtues can release a truth force that has the power to transform the mundane.

But how does *mana*, or *brahman*, or the charisma of Buddha – to ask Wittgenstein's question – become understandable as a social experience?

Mauss ventured that *mana* is "an unconscious category of understanding," a "category of collective thinking which is the foundation of our judgements and which imposes a classification in things, separating some, bringing together others, establishing lines of influence or boundaries of isolation." From this vantage point, Mauss saw the "magical value of persons or things as (resulting) from the relative position they occupy within society or in isolation to society." We would affirm, says Mauss, that "magic, like religion, is a game involving 'value judgements,' expressive aphorisms which attribute different qualities to different objects entering the system"; it involves social sentiments that surround plants, animals, occupations, sex, heavenly bodies, the elements, and physical phenomena.[6]

In other words, I interpret Mauss as saying that *mana* and *charisma* are "functions" of the social classification and cosmology of a society and that they reflect and stem from the society's differentiated statuses and its hierarchy of persons and objects. If *mana* and *charisma* on the one hand represent the immanent ordering principle of the cosmos pervading its constituents, they are also an expression of the differential potencies and power relations emanating from a society's classified positions.

This perspective thus leads in a somewhat different direction from Weber's focus on the *charismatic* leader and the special qualities attributed to his leadership. In fact, it leads straight back to Mauss's classic, *The Gift*,[7] which focuses on the "power in objects, of exchange." It leads us to the process of the *objectification of power in objects* – of the *sedimentation of charisma* in gifts, valuables, and amulets – that become focal points and vehicles of social exchanges.

Weberian theory leads, as we have seen, to the "routinization of charisma" in social institutions and social positions. But Weber was blind to the symbolism of objectification of charisma in objects and fetishes.

Mauss, on the other hand, was concerned with explaining the "productive capacity" and animate vitality attributed to wealth objects in primitive exchange. He saw that each of these objects was "a sign and surety of life" as well as a "sign and surety of wealth, a magico-religious guarantee of rank and propensity."[8]

A conspicuous feature of Mauss's conception of the "total social fact" was the confusion, perhaps it is better to say conflation, "of objects, values, contracts and men which find expression" in gift exchanges; it is in fact precisely this conflation of property and persons that Sir Henry Maine attributed to societies dominated by "status" as opposed to "contract." In status-bound societies, he said, persons and rights in objects are conflated, rights of persons and rules of property transmission are not kept separate; whereas the institution of contract, distinctive of developed complex societies, made this disjunction.

In a similar vein, Mauss maintained that wealth objects were like "currency," but that the principles expressed in their exchange were different from the circulation of money in modern society in which precious things are "detached" from "groups and individuals" and made permanent and universal statements of value measurement. Mauss's interpretation of the Maori notion of *hau* was that a gift given necessarily evokes a return gift, which is really the "spirit" of the original presentation returning to the point of origin – a "mystical" formulation[9] that, as Marshall Sahlins has revealed, happily rides with a mundane notion of incremental return or turnover that must be returned to the original holder, because "one man's gift should not be another man's capital."[10]

*Hau*, or reciprocity, has multiple meanings. It can figure in the humiliation of rank, as in the agonistic presentations of Kwakiutl potlatch, or it can establish the solidarity of the exchanges, as in the *kula* ring. This is so because when people exchange "things" they are exchanging social relationships, therefore exchanging themselves up to a point. In this sense *hau* is not so much a property of the things exchanged as an organizing principle. It does more than integrate in a material sense; it creates meaning and makes intelligible social relationships. Equality and rank are two possibilities of social relationships, therefore two manifestations of reciprocity. Both dimensions exist not only in a given social moment, but also always within any social relationship and any society. As Mauss said: "The lasting influence of the objects exchanged is a direct expression of the manner in which sub-groups within segmentary societies of an archaic type are constantly embroiled with and feel themselves in debt to each other."[11]

Standing on Mauss's shoulders, we must chart more ideologies of exchange than the simple binary division between primitive and modern, status and contract. We have learned two lessons since the days of *Gemeinschaft* versus *Gesellschaft*: Firstly, probably all societies have their versions of "fetishism" of objects. Secondly, the manner in which objects and persons are intertwined and evaluated differs according to each society's cosmological design and cultural grid, in which social, divine, animal, and object hierarchies are mutually implicated.

Marx, therefore, enters our scene importantly, for in a sense his "fetishism of commodities" did for capitalist society what Mauss's "gift" did for primitive societies. As demonstrated by Marshall Sahlins, their biases are inversions of each other. Marx failed to perceive the cultural design according to which goods are produced,[12] and Mauss was partially color-blind to the margins of material gain that greased the spirit of reciprocity. Perhaps one way to represent the particularities of the Thai case is to sketch in a crude comparison of Marx's description of commodities in capitalist society with the Trobriand passion for the overseas exchange of *kula* valuables and with the Thai preoccupation with the acquisition of amulets – three different examples of the "fetishism of objects," three different codes in the semiotics of exchange. In such an enterprise, it is essential to concede that "alienation" is not solely a deficiency of capitalism and "participation" the sole glue of archaic society. All societies – with the exception of the paradisiacal and affluent pygmies (?) — surely have their own dialectical versions of alienation and participation.

## Three instances of the fetishism of objects

The transference from use value to exchange value, according to Marx, produced in capitalist societies the phenomenon of commodities, whose exchange and circulation vis-à-vis one another, comprising relations between things, obscure – indeed stand for – exchange between social persons. The acquisition and control of goods therefore becomes a ruling passion, to which is linked a market system that continually disgorges goods that must be circulated *and* possessed, *and* exclusively accumulated, *and* speedily consumed in a climate of obsolescence. The possession and consumption of goods is a marked indicator of social-class status. At the same time, the exchange of commodities serves as an ideological screen that hides from direct perception the exploitation of labor and extraction of surplus value upon which the system of production is predicated. In the last resort, the distinctiveness of the capitalist system is that production is the site upon which the fetishism of commodities is launched, commodities that are not representative so much of pragmatic rationality as of cultural design and cultural obsession.

The *kula* valuables are counters in another game of exchange. The official ideology of *kula* is that a valuable goes around and around in circulation, each possessor in the ring only keeping it temporarily and being forced to give it away in order to keep the exchange going. Not to possess but to give away: That is the mark of the Trobriand valuable. The grimier it is from handling, the greater its value and historicity. The players in the game are alleged to be "individuals" who are thought to win or lose according to their personal magnetism and renown (*butura*), best represented in the tenuous and elaborate practice of beauty magic and the seduction of male partners as if they were women (an elaborate game, from which women are excluded but in which women furnish the imagery for the sailors' fears of shipwreck and their hopes for overcoming their adversaries). Ultimately, the implication of this ideology is that by seducing one's exchange partner overseas to part with valuables by means of one's beauty, one keeps *confirming* and validating one's youth and beauty, and one's power to entice, and thereby gains possession of the immortality of youth. But of course one knows that this cultural screen of exchange predicated on personal beauty magic and personal dynamism also masks another form of control and "exploitation." The winners in the *kula* in fact are the chiefs, *guyau* aristocrats and *dala* headmen – men who mobilize labor to build the canoes and select the *kula* crews, men who

341

receive *urigubu* or *pokala* yams as prescriptive gifts and distribute *kula* valuables as personal favors, men whose own canoes lead the flotilla of canoes on the *uvalaku* expeditions, and men who enjoy precedence over junior crew members in the exchanges with overseas partners.

The possession and circulation of amulets in Thailand represents still another semiotic code. The ascetic saint of the forest distributes his charisma as a donation inspired by compassion and loving-kindness (*mettā*). He himself does not expect a return from his gift to the worldlings at large. The amulet is indexically or metonymically related to the ascetic monk and represents a materialization of his virtue, achieved by means of a rite of transfer. Amulets are made in plenty and distributed to many, for the saint's *mettā* is inexhaustible and does not diminish by sharing, provided he continues to cleave to his ascetic and meditative life and to experience the bliss of tranquil joy and detachment.[13]

But of course we also know that, in the Thai instance, amulets are comparable on the basis of the differential charisma of the saints and ascetics; though donated to the public at large, they in practice become scarce and assume a commercial value. They become, at a second less obvious round of social relations, private and hidden possessions of laymen who expect to use the amulets' potency to manipulate, overpower, seduce, and control their fellow men and women in an ongoing drama of social transactions. Thus there is a two-level discourse — the charisma of the saint, who in transcending the world is able to shower upon it his virtue, and the gratification of desires on the part of the laymen, for whom prosperity and fortune approach the logic of a zero-sum game. The hidden dimension of the Thai ideology of amulets consists in the differential power distribution and social control vested in its lay social hierarchy – of kings, generals and bureaucrats, urban workers and rural farmers. The more historic, more famous, more potent amulets are in the hands of the rulers and the wealthy, for they are the sponsors of the ascetic saint as an amulet maker; these amulets confirm them in their power and act as sureties of wealth; in the words of Mauss, they are a ''magico-religious guarantee of rank and prosperity.'' They reflect and legitimate, to put it in a Thai idiom, the hierarchy of *merit*.

Thai society is dramatically different from, on the one hand, a full-blown ''capitalist economy'' and, on the other, the Trobriand Islands of Malinowski's time, which produced yams and valuables for a limited circulation (see Table 22.1). Until a couple of decades ago, it would have been accurate to label Thailand a ''neo-colonial'' dependent economy, which produced rice, teak and tin, and certain other primary articles for the international capitalist-controlled markets and which in turn was a market for capitalist-manufactured goods. Such a country was administered by an authoritative military regime; and in such a society politics and economics were interrelated in such a way that political and military power enabled access to wealth and to material goods by various channels and devices – by siphoning off income from government-run monopo-

Table 22.1. *The semiotics of fetishism of objects*

| | Commodity type and velocity of exchange | Basis of control | Kind of fetishism | Source of charisma | Dominant value orientation |
|---|---|---|---|---|---|
| Western capitalist: commodity exchange | High velocity of exchange; high commodity accumulation/high consumption: production according to a planned obsolescence. | Exchange rides on exploitation of producers and labor. | Highly impersonal society where the relations between objects stand for relations between men and act as indexes of social class/wealth/power. | Alleged spirit of entrepreneurship and capitalist ethic; highly individualized conception, open to all. | Centrality of conspicuous consumption for society at large; the centrality of "ethic of work" for entrepreneurs as justification of success. |
| Trobriand: *kula* exchange | High velocity of circulation; durable valuables: historic objects. | Exchange ultimately rides on exploitation of kin. | Highly personalized society where exchange of valuables objectifies seduction/control over stranger-partners. | Control of "beauty magic"; highly individualized conception, open to all. | Centrality of achieving "renown" (*butura*): dynamic volatile action on high seas; quest for "immortality." |
| Thailand: amulet trade | Fairly high velocity after conversion to trade objects; personal accumulation; historic objects. | Exchange rides on differential rank, power and wealth of owners/sponsors. | Highly personalized but stratified society where objects as sedimentations of virtue index merit hierarchy and enable control of others. | Disinterested ascetics who transcend society; highly individualized; open to all. | Centrality to Buddhist monk of asceticism as path to liberation, wisdom, and compassionate "detached action." Centrality of "merit making" for laymen, whose power enables access to consumption of goods and affirms their merit. |

lies and industries, by milking local Chinese business, and by appropriating part of the foreign aid, principally military aid, provided by the United States.

Pretty much the same principles and tendencies prevail today and affirm that the amulets radiating various powers are really "political" prizes providing access to and control of good things of this world.

Thailand's economic development may have been progressively changing in recent decades to what is perhaps more accurately called "associated-dependent development,"[14] in that multinational corporations, both Western and Japanese, have been establishing certain kinds of factories and plants to take advantage of cheap labor and other advantages in a narrow sector of the country, principally in the Bangkok region. These corporations and business interests make their deals with the ruling generals and ministers in exchange for favorable contracts and taxation terms. Thus to some extent the interests of these foreign corporations become compatible with the internal prosperity of the dependent country. But this same linkage enables the military rulers, even in the face of external constraints and growing internal contradictions and tensions, to impose their own development model on Thailand. And it also allows the stimulation of manufacturing and other activities around Bangkok to perpetuate a stagnation in the rural provinces, whose rice production is becoming increasingly irrelevant to Thailand's national revenue. By and large, then, the rural provinces represent an "underdeveloped peripheral economy." This asymmetry allows the military and bureaucratic elites and urban merchant interests to have a conspicuous-consumption style of life while condemning the peasants to poverty. Such a domination cannot remain self-assured for long, and a crisis of legitimacy is besetting Thailand today.

### The crisis of legitimacy and the obsession with amulets

A component of the first reading of Weber's discussion of charisma is that, together with charisma's unstable, volatile, rebellious nature, goes its coming into prominence "in times of psychic, physical, economic, ethical, religious, political distress."[15] This particular hypothesis of Weber's connecting the emergence of charismatic movements with conditions of stress has been a central point in many studies;[16] more than one study of political processes in Third World countries has surmised that they resort to charismatic leaders and symbols as panaceas for the disturbed situations in which they find themselves.

As I have said many times earlier, although the tradition of amulets and votive tablets is an ancient one in Thailand (and elsewhere in Southeast Asia), there has been an *intensification* in their manufacture and in people's resorting to them in recent years. There are two striking aspects to this intensification.

Firstly, although in the past many of the sacralizers of amulets were capital-based, prestigious monks within the established *saṅgha* and political personages like royalty, in recent years the ascetic forest-monks, burrowed away at the margins of

# Objectification of charisma, fetishism of objects

Thai society, have been singled out as the shining, disinterested possessors of mystical power and as the dispensers of the loving-kindness that the country badly needs and lacks, especially when the *sangha*'s ecclesiastical establishment is itself seen as tainted or lacking vigor.[17]

Secondly, the most ardent pursuers and collectors of amulets sanctified by the meditation masters and forest *arahants* are the urban ruling elements, the intelligentsia, and the wielders of force, the military. The political center is losing its self-confidence, but it has not lost its might; it searches for and latches onto the merit of the holy men who are the center of religion but peripheral to its established forms.

Thus a sociological answer must be given as to why the propensity to seek contact with transcendent powers possessed by the world renouncers, and to resort to the fetishism of amulets, has shown greater force and conspicuousness in recent years. The answer to the intensification may lie in the internal and external political circumstances confronting Thailand today – circumstances that have eroded and put into question the *legitimacy* of the ruling elements and privileged sectors of the society.[18]

Externally, the collapse of the established governments in Vietnam, Cambodia, and Laos, in which both outside communist elements and internal dissident insurgents played roles, have naturally placed the instituted, conservative, and undemocratic government of Thailand in peril. The sweeping aside of the monarchy and the Buddhist *sangha* in both Cambodia and Laos has assailed fundamental principles on which the Thai polity and society have been erected and maintained. Perhaps even more corrosive of legitimacy and stability have been internal crises: the student insurrections of 1973 and 1976; the fateful involvement of the monarchy and the court in active politics, which appears to have progressively driven them fatefully into alliance with the rightist elements; and the determined policy of a reactionary but powerful military not to liberalize. This drove the opposition into a greater radicalism than it had intended. With the 1976 coup, the military regained power, which they have continued to hold.

No more is it possible for the Thai rulers or Western observers to dismiss the insurgents of the Northeast and the South as disaffected extremists, as creatures of communist intrigue and parasites living off the local populations. For the truth is that the traditionally quiescent, passive, nonparticipatory rural peasantry are beginning to express their outrage at increasing landlessness and at the benign neglect by the rulers.[19] In the urban areas, equally neglected and unprotected laborers are unionizing and engaging in sporadic strikes. It may well be that the time when the state apparatus is weakened is the time when mass peasant protest also builds up to produce an upheaval of "revolutionary" proportions. A principal argument in a recent book on revolutions is that certain historic and massive revolutions have occurred when traditional relations between the state apparatus and the underlying, largely peasant, populations were profoundly upset. Because of both internal and international developments, the state was no longer able to

345

exercise its own hegemony, and that of the dominant classes, in the face of revolts from below.[20] But these are reflections on the imminent and possible in Thailand, and a wise man should eschew prophecy.

## The Path of Purification and the stream of history

As a final reflection, I return to the tradition of Buddhist ascetic meditation and place it in the stream of history.

The system of meditation in all its variants practiced by the forest saints of today finds its legitimation in such classical texts as the *Visuddhimagga*, written in the fifth century A.D. In fact, all the variant "paths" practiced are contained within the scope of the original text. In one sense there has been a continuity in the tradition over the centuries – continuity not necessarily as an unbroken pursuit in time, for we know that the monastic orders periodically declined and re-formed at different periods, but as a vocation for monks that can be periodically reactivated because of the existence of the authoritative classical texts as points of reference and as precedents. In this sense, the meditative quest has a "regressive," retrospective dimension.

It is certain that ascetic forest-monks have had different positional significances at different historical times, within then-existing religio-political fields. In the late 1970s, the forest saints in Thailand had a prominence that can be understood only in relation to the wider religious and political scene. In this sense, the "progressive" or "becoming" aspects of the meditative tradition are best appreciated in the context of the present political crisis and the declining legitimacy of the established *sangha* and rulers. But the classical forms – whether of meditation techniques, ascetic practices, traditions of dress, or ritual procedures and votive tablets – persist more or less intact; it is the intensity and breadth of the public acclamation, and the participation of lay sponsors and merit-makers of elite status, that has changed quantitatively. But from the earliest times – even going back to the time of the Buddha – we know that the *bhikkhu* were peripatetic mendicants, some of whom were espousers of the ascetic meditational path, and all of whom, time and again, engaged with kings, merchants, and other lay devotees.

The Buddha has for too long been *exclusively* interpreted in some circles as an "individualized" world renouncer, who signified a self-absorbed withdrawal from the world and preached a message of world rejection and world negation. I believe that the larger truth of Buddhism can be comprehended only if *other* features of it are taken integrally into account at the same time – that a saint, prophet, or *guru* takes a stand vis-à-vis his society and his world, that his quest and his message were meant to reform and transform them, and that in this sense he has a "civilizing" mission. Early Buddhism, let alone later Buddhism, does not make sense unless we give full weight to the fact that the Buddha founded a

346

monastic community (or communities), the *saṅgha*, and that this was a disciplined social order. On the one hand, the *saṅgha* marked itself off from the lay householders' way of life. But on the other hand, it lived symbiotically upon that way, requiring it not for material sustenance alone, but also as a witness to an exemplary life, to be touched by it, and to guarantee its morality.

When the saint renounces his home, wife, and children, and passes into the world as a homeless wanderer, he does two things. He founds another social order, which as a fraternity (or sorority) of openly recruited celibates, following an ascetic life, is the opposite of particularized kin bonds and the mundane involvements of the family and household life. In transcending particular bonds, he also thereby takes humanity as a whole as his family and his community and warms them with his cosmic compassion and wisdom. This is one of the main lessons of our study of the Buddhist *arahant*. I think many religious traditions hold that he who would be father, or she who would be mother, of us all cannot carry out his or her ministry if he or she is the exclusive conceiver and parent of a few.

# Notes

*1. Introduction and manifesto*

1　Cambridge: Cambridge University Press, 1976.
2　Arthur Burks, "Icon, Index, and Symbol," *Philosophy and Phenomenological Research*, Vol. IX, No. 4, pp. 673–89; and Roman Jakobson, *Selected Writings*, Vol. 2, *Word and Language,* "Shifters, Verbal Categories and the Russian Verb" (The Hague: Mouton, 1971), pp. 130–47. I have developed and used the concepts of indexical symbol and iconic symbol in "A Performative Approach to Ritual," Radcliffe-Brown Lecture 1979, *Proceedings of the British Academy*, Vol. LXV, 1979 (London: Oxford University Press, 1981).
3　Indexical icons similarly encode dual meanings: On the one hand the icon represents the likeness of an original object or person, and on the other it transfers values to its users.
4　Wilfred Cantwell Smith, *The Meaning and End of Religion: A New Approach to the Religious Traditions of Mankind* (New York: Macmillan, 1962–63).
5　Chicago: University of Chicago Press, 1981.

*2. The Buddhist conception of the* arahant

1　T. W. Rhys Davids, *Buddhism* (London: Society for Promoting Christian Knowledge, 1877).
2　Padmanabh S. Jaini, *The Jaina Path of Purification* (Berkeley: University of California Press, 1979).
3　R. Spence Hardy, *A Manual of Buddhism, In Its Modern Development* (London: Partridge and Oakey, 1853).
4　E. Conze, *Buddhist Meditation* (London: Unwin Books, 1972).
5　Etienne Lamotte, *Histoire du Buddhisme Indien* (Louvain: Publications Universitaires, 1958).
6　See *The Minor Readings (Khuddakapātha), The First Book of the Minor Collection (Khuddakanikāya),* trans. Bhikkhu Ñāṇamoli, Pali Text Society, Translation Series, No. 32 (London: Luzac, 1960). The jewel discourse is to be found at Ch. 6, pp. 170–8.
7　Asserting that the wheel or gem jewel of the wheel-turning monarch (*cakkavatti*) is

never the equal of the Buddha jewel, and recapitulating the contents of the *Mahāsudassana Sutta*, it glosses "jewel" (*ratanam*) as something "much admired," of "great value," "rarely seen," and so on. The *Mahāsudassana Sutta* lists these as the seven jewels of the *cakkavatti*: the wheel, the elephant, the horse, the gem, the woman, the treasurer, and the counselor.

8 This list is cited by Ria Kloppenborg, *The Paccekabuddha, A Buddhist Ascetic: A Study of the Concept of Paccekabuddha in Pali Canonical and Commentarial Literature* (Leiden: Brill, 1974), p. 22.

9 Cited in Wilhelm Geiger, *Culture of Ceylon in Medieval Times*, ed. Heinz Bechert (Weisbaden: Otto Harrassowitz, 1960), p. 17.

10 B. Horner, trans. and ed., *The Middle Length Sayings (Majjhima Nikāya)*, 3 vols., Pali Text Society Translation Series, Nos. 29–31 (London: Luzac, 1954–9), Vol. I, pp. 181–2.

11 Horner glosses the expression "cannot be discerned" as their having made the ultimate achievement of "going beyond" (*paraṅgata*).

12 *The Questions of King Milinda*, trans. from the Pali by T. W. Rhys Davids (New York: Dover, 1963), Parts I and II. The original text appears to have been translated into Pali at an early date, and its Siṅhalese translation, possibly made in the eighteenth century, was published for the first time in 1877.

13 *Mahāvagga* I, 23–4. See T. W. Rhys Davids and H. Oldenberg, trans., *Vinaya Texts* (Delhi: Motilal Banarsidass, repr. 1968), Part I, pp. 144–50.

14 For earlier discussions by me of these dichotomies in Buddhism, see my *Buddhism and the Spirit Cults* (Cambridge: Cambridge University Press, 1976), Chs. 9, 12.

15 Michael Carrithers, "The Modern Ascetics of Sri Lanka and the Pattern of Change in Buddhism," *Man*, Vol. 14, No. 2, 1979, pp. 294–310.

16 John P. Ferguson, "The Arahat Ideal in Modern Burmese Buddhism," unpub. paper delivered at the annual meeting of Association for Asian Studies, 1977.

17 Bhikkhu Teliwatte Rahula's *A Critical Study of the Mahavastu* (Delhi: Motilal Banarsidass, 1978) has a long section III (pp. 120–53), in which he gives the lives of the Buddha's early disciples, culled from many Pali and Sanskrit sources, canonical and noncanonical.

18 On the half-days of the lunar month, i.e., full moon and no moon, monks convene and recite the *pāṭimokkha*, the confessional that enumerates the 227 rules.

19 See Rhys Davids and Oldenberg, *Vinaya Texts*, Part I, p. 94. (The original text is *Mahavagga*, Ch. 1, verses 16, 17.)

20 See T. W. Rhys Davids, *Dialogues of the Buddha, Sacred Books of the Buddhists*, Vol. II (London: Henry Frowde, 1879), pp. 226–32.

21 Rhys Davids and Oldenberg, *Vinaya Texts*, Part I, pp. 172–4.

22 As we shall see, these are some of the 13 ascetic practices enumerated by the *Vissuddhimagga* as those recommended, though optional, for the monk dedicated to meditation.

23 Rhys Davids and Oldenberg, *Vinaya Texts*, Part III, pp. 238–63.

24 Note that dwelling under trees is expressly forbidden during the season of the rains in *Mahāvagga* III, 12, 5.

25 Kloppenborg, *Paccekabuddha*, pp. 18–20.

26 *Questions of King Milinda*, pp. 174–5.

27 This rule is enshrined in the *Pāṭimokkha.*

28 The Buddha's stricture is to be found in the *Kevaddha Suttanta* (see T. W. Rhys Davids, *Dialogues of the Buddha*, Vol. II).

29 H. C. Norman, ed., *The Commentary of the Dhammapada* (London: Pali Text Society, 1912), Vol. 3, p. 204.

30 See T. W. Rhys Davids, *Buddhist Suttas, The Sacred Books of the East*, Vol. XI (Oxford: Oxford University Press, 1900).

31 See Andre Bareau, "The Superhuman Personality of the Buddha and its Symbolism in the *Mahāparinirvāṇasūtra* of the Dharmagupta," in *Myth and Symbols*, ed. J. M. Kitagawa and C. H. Long (Chicago: University of Chicago Press, 1971).

32 See Lamotte, *Histoire du Buddhisme Indien*, pp. 765–70. Also see pp. 683–6, where he discusses the stage of the *arahant.* I shall only cite some of the numerous sources he cites. My citations from Lamotte in quotation marks are somewhat free translations from the French.

33 I shall comment later on the literary genre called *avadāna.*

34 Lamotte indicates that these poems in Pali had their corresponding poems in the Buddhist Sanskrit literature; however, *Sthavira-Sthaviri-gatha*, which are often mentioned in the Sanskrit Agama, have not survived.

35 Lamotte cites here J. Przyluski, *Le Conseil de Rājagṛha* (Paris: Paul Guethner 1926–8).

36 Nirodhasamāpatti apparently signifies the ability to enter the bliss of *nibbāna* for a brief period, such as seven days, before returning to normal existence.

37 The Pali tradition, however, has it that he died before his father and his Master Śāriputra.

38 The Caturmahārājikadeva.

39 Lamotte here cites, among others, S. Lévi and E. Chavannes, "Les Seize Arhat Protecteurs de la Loi," *Journal Asiatique*, Vol. 8, 1916, pp. 5–50, 189–304.

40 Charles Duroiselle, *Report of the Superintendent, Archaeological Survey, Burma, for the Year Ending 31st March 1923* (Rangoon: Superintendent, Government Printing, 1923), pp. 22–7.

41 Upagutta is said to have been the fourth patriarch of the *saṇgha*, the preceptor of Aśoka, the chief actor in the Third Buddhist Council, and the composer of the *Kathavatthu.*

42 Tambiah, *Buddhism and the Spirit Cults*, Ch. 10. Also see Charles Duroiselle, "Upagutta et Mara," *Bulletin de l'Ecole Française d'Extrême Orient*, Vol. 4, 1904, pp. 414–28; Shway Yoe, *The Burman, His Life and Notions* (London: Macmillan, 1896); R. Grant Brown, "Rain Making in Burma," *Man*, No. 80, 1908, pp. 145–6.

43 The story is found in the Asātarūpa Jātaka.

44 Richard F. Gombrich, *Precept and Practice* (Oxford: Clarendon Press, 1971), pp. 185–6.

45 I myself think that, in certain contexts, especially relating to ascetic forest-monks, claims of *arahant*ship have been made even in present times and that Gombrich ignores this segment of popular religious attitudes. I shall later cite Carrithers's study of recent forest-monks in Sri Lanka (see Chapter 5).

46 John P. Ferguson, "The Arahat Ideal in Modern Burmese Buddhism," unpub. paper delivered at annual meeting of Association for Asian Studies, 1977.

47 This description echoes the classification of the 7 classes of minds in *Questions of King Milinda.*

48 The quotations are taken from pp. 190, 191, and 218 of Phra Acharn Maha Boowa Nyanasampanno, *The Venerable Phra Acharn Mun Bhuridatta Thera, Meditation Master*, trans. Siri Buddhasukh (Bangkok: Mahāmakut Rajavidyalaya Press, 1976). See Chapter 6 of this book for details.

### 3. The Path of Purification: the ascetic practices

1 Bhikkhu Ñāṇamoli, *The Path of Purification (Visuddhimagga)* (Colombo: Semage, 1956).

2 The *Mahāvihāra*, the "great monastery" in Anurādhapura, committed the *Tipiṭaka* to writing in the first century B.C., and it is surmised that this writing was done at a time when Sanskritic Buddhist literature and sectarianism were threatening the Theravāda establishment. But this early Sinhalese literary activity was apparently followed by a lean period until the fourth century A.D.

3 Ñāṇamoli cites as his source *Mahāvaṃsa*, Ch. 37, verses 215–47. This portion of the text is, in translation, included in the first chapter of the *Cūlavamsa*. See: *Cūlavamsa, Being the More Recent Part of the Mahāvaṃsa*, trans. Wilhelm Geiger and from the German into English by C. M. Rickmers (Colombo: Ceylon Government, 1953), Part I, Ch. 37, pp. 215–47.

4 Ñāṇamoli, *Path of Purification*, pp. xxiv–xxvi.

5 I shall use both of these as interchangeable terms.

6 Note, however, that certain portions, such as the discussion of *sīla*, relate to the laity also.

7 *Saṃyutta Nikāya*, 1.13.

8 The elements in the Eightfold Path as listed in the sermon are: (1) right understanding, (2) right thought, (3) right speech, (4) right action, (5) right livelihood, (6) right effort, (7) right mindfulness, and (8) right concentration. There is no suggestion of hierarchy or sequence in this enumeration. Buddhaghosa grouped in three sequential groups elements 3–5 as *sīla*, 6–8 as *samādhi*, and 1–2 as *paññā*.

9 Ñāṇamoli, *Path of Purification*, p. 6.

10 Ñāṇamoli, *Path of Purification*, p. xxxi.

11 The canonical source cited for this is *Majjhima Nikāya* i, 33.

12 Ñāṇamoli, *Path of Purification*, p. 19. We are also told: Walking, the *bhikkhu* "goes with downcast eyes, seeing the length of a plough yoke, restrained, not looking . . . at a pedestrian, a woman, not looking up, not looking down, not staring this way and that" (pp. 19–20).

13 It is not necessary to elaborate the point that sexuality of all kinds is disallowed. The temptations arising from intercourse with women are the focus of special elaboration: A *bhikkhu* is warned against letting women massage him, joking and amusing himself with women, listening to the sound of women through a wall or fence, recalling jokes he had shared or games he formerly had played with women.

14 *Dhuta* is glossed as "ascetic"; ascetic because he has shaken off defilement. *Anga* is glossed as "practice."

15 Predictably, this vow is infrequently taken in Thailand. A meditation master may spend the occasional night or successive nights engaged in sitting and walking meditation, but he cannot be expected never to sleep lying down. The vow thus seems to go with intensified periods of meditation.

### 4. The states and rewards of Buddhist meditation

1 Edward Conze, *Buddhist Meditation* (London: Unwin, 1972), p. 1. There are many modern expositions of Buddhist meditation as developed by the Theravāda School. Good guides, for example, are the Conze work cited here [also his *Buddhism: Its Essence and Development* (Oxford: Cassirer, 1953)], and Nayanaponika Thera, *The Heart of Buddhist Meditation* (New York: Citadel Press, 1969). A number of books and tracts have been published in recent years in Thai, mainly written by monks (and translated by others into English), which attest to the increasing interest on the part of monks, laity, and foreigners in the practice of meditation. Examples of these works with English titles are: the extensive writings of Buddhadasa, which are documented and discussed in Donald K. Swearer, *Towards the Truth* (Philadelphia: Westminster Press, 1971); Phra Maha Narasabho, *Buddhism, a Guide to a Happy Life* (Bangkok: Kurusapha Press, 1971); and S. Dhammasuddhi, *Insight Meditation* (London: n.p., 1968). In addition, there are numerous pamphlets on meditation written by meditation teachers such as Tepsiddhimuni Mahathera and Phra Acharn Thate Desaransi. A final example is Acharn Maha Boowa, whose writings will be discussed in Chapter 6.

2 See P. V. Bapat, *Vimuttimagga*, (Poona: n.p., 1937).

3 F. L. Woodward, *Manual of a Mystic, Being a Translation from the Pali and Sinhalese Work Entitled The Yogavachara's Manual* (London: Pali Text Society, 1916).

4 Conze, *Buddhist Meditation*, p. 1.

5 Caroline A. Rhys Davids, *Psalms of the Brethren* (London: Pali Text Society, 1909–13), and I. B. Horner, *Women Under Primitive Buddhism* (London: George Routledge, 1930).

6 *Samādhi* means literally "collective or continual fitting together" (synthesis); exegetically, it is explained as "right placing of consciousness on object." See Woodward, *Manual of a Mystic*, p. xiii.

7 See Bhikkhu Ñāṇamoli, *Path of Purification (Visuddhimagga)* (Colombo: Semage, 1956), pp. 117–18.

8 Ibid., p. 119.

9 We shall take up later the Path of Insight, but in less detail, because the major points I wish to discuss can be presented with respect to the methods of concentration.

10 Of course, this is not the only position recommended; meditating while standing, walking, or reclining is permissible. Meditators usually alternate between these positions in preferred combinations.

11 Conze suggests (*Buddhist Meditation*, p. 21) that the effect of gazing intently at the chosen device is probably similar to that of hypnosis, where, entranced by the uniform stimulus of a shining light, or suchlike, the disciple drops the objects altogether. "As the initial object is subjected to the influence of transic mentality, it gradually changes its character. At its later stages, it is called the "mental image, and its transformations have been described with great subtlety."

12 Ibid., p. 144.

13 At their highest levels, the path of *samādhi* and the path of *paññā* can meet. One who has attained to sufficient one-pointedness of mind can steer himself to *nibbāna* by contemplating his own mind, and the master of insight can choose to focus on a single object of awareness and traverse the *jhānic* levels.

14  Daniel Goldman, *The Buddha on Meditation and Higher States of Consciousness* (Kandy, Sri Lanka: Buddhist Publication Society, 1973), gives a useful summary of the Path of Insight as set out in the *Visuddhimagga*.

15  It is surmised that the setting of this limit may be linked to the limits of endurance of the human body, for various physiological processes accompany the cessation of consciousness: The heartbeat slows down and metabolic processes are at a residual level, and the meditator's body cannot, it is said, be distinguished from a corpse.

16  There are 10 kinds of success referred to. "Success born by *kamma* result" is exemplified by the natural capacity of birds to fly, and also of deities to do the same. Examples of "success due to right exertion" are on the one hand the mastery of arts and crafts such as is evidenced in trade, medicine, or learning the Vedas and on the other hand the abandonment of defilements by following the *arahant* path; again, there is "success through the sciences," which label refers to creating magical effects through spells and charms. The other types mentioned, such as "success in mind-made body," "success by intervention of concentration," and "success by resolve," could well be results associated with meditation.

17  The source cited is *Dīgha Nikāya* i, 77.

18  "It is only in Buddhas, Pacceka Buddhas, Chief Disciples . . . who have vast previous endeavor behind them, that this transformation by supernormal power and other such special qualities as the Discriminations are brought to success simply with the attainment of Arahantship and without the progressive course of development of the kind just described" (p. 412).

19  The canonical source cited is *Dīgha Nikāya* i, 79.

20  The *Visuddhimagga* does not recount a famous incident recorded in the canon that is relevant to this discussion. In the course of his last journey, during his stop at the Cāpāla shrine near the city of Vaiśāli, the Buddha converses with Ānanda about the beauty of that city and remarks that the man who is master of the four parts of the supranormal power (*ṛddhipāda*) is able to prolong his life until the end of the world epoch. In spite of a threefold repetition, Ananda does not understand the hint and remains silent. Māra, the tempter, then intervenes and invites the Buddha to enter *nibbāna*, now that his teaching mission is finished. The Buddha declares that he will enter *nibbāna* in three months' time. A terrible earthquake accompanies this incident. Later, Ānanda, on being told by the Buddha the eight reasons for the occurrence of an earthquake – one of which is the moment a buddha decides to enter *parinibbāna* – realizes his terrible mistake and, in vain, begs the Buddha to prolong his life.

21  The details of the Buddhist cosmology are to be found, for example, in R. Spence Hardy, *A Manual of Buddhism in its Modern Development* (London: Partridge and Oakey, 1853), especially pp. 24–6. Also see the Siamese version, as portrayed in *Chulakantha-mangala*, trans. G. E. Gerini (1893) (Bangkok: Siam Society, 1976). There are of course many other sources for the cosmology and many versions of it. A recent English translation of the *Traiphūm* is Frank and Mani Reynolds, *The Three Worlds of King Ruang*, Berkeley Buddhist Studies, Series 4 (Berkeley: Asian Humanities Press/Motilal Banarsidass, 1982).

22  *World Conqueror and World Renouncer; A Study of Buddhism and Polity in Thailand against a Historical Background* (Cambridge: Cambridge University Press, 1976), Ch. 1.

*5. The forest-monk tradition in Southeast Asia: a historical backdrop*

1  K. Malalgoda, *Buddhism in Sinhalese Society 1750–1900, A Study of Religious Revival and Change* (Berkeley: University of California Press, 1976), identifies "practice" as the primary goal of a *bhikkhu* and "learning" as a "secondary goal" for him and cites in support the *Dhammapada* (1: 19–20), which says that a person of realization, even though he has only a little learning, is superior to one who has great learning but no realization.

2  W. Rahula, *History of Buddhism in Ceylon* (Colombo: M. D. Gunasena, 1956), p. 158.

3  Ibid., pp. 194, 214, 260. Malalgoda, *Buddhism*, also confirms that there was a fundamental conflict between "practice" and "learning," and that the latter came to be recognized as the basis of the *sāsana*. Out of this debate between the "ascetics" (*paṁsukūlikas*) and the "preachers" arose the vocational differentiation between the vocation of books and the vocation of meditation.

4  R. A. L. H. Gunawardana, *Robe and Plough, Monasticism and Economic Interest in Medieval Sri Lanka* (Tucson, Ariz.: University of Arizona Press, 1979).

5  There are good reasons for thinking that the *Vimuttimagga* might have been a text of the *Abhayagirinikāya*, whereas the *Visuddhimagga* was certainly the work of Buddhaghosa, who was associated with the *Mahāvihāra* sect.

6  Gunawardana, *Robe and Plough*, p. 42, cites the *Cūlavamsa* 51.52 as his source. See *The Cūlavamsa*, Part 1, tr. W. Geiger and M. Rickmers (Colombo: Ceylon Government, n.d.), p. 152.

7  Ibid., p. 45.

8  Ibid., p. 46.

9  This would be so if the Siṅhalese name of Dimbulāgala is taken to be the same as Udumbaragiri/Udumbarapabbata (Pali); they are exact translations of each other.

10  This reform and subsequent ones such as are recorded in the *Dambadēni Katikāvata* are described and discussed by N. Ratnapala, *The Katikāvatas, Laws of the Buddhist Order of Ceylon from the 12th Century to the 18th Century* (Munich: Mikrokopie, 1971); Gunawardana, *Robe and Plough*; Heinz Bechert, *Buddhismus Staat und Gesellschaft in den Laendern des Theravāda-Buddhismus*, 3 vols. (Frankfurt am Main: Metzner, 1966–73). See also my *World Conqueror and World Renouncer: A Study of Buddhism and Polity in Thailand against a Historical Background* (Cambridge: Cambridge University Press, 1976), Ch. 9.

11  It is also interesting that most of the monk-dignitaries who took part in the synod came from monasteries located in the provinces. Thus this historic example of "purification" and unification of the *saṅgha* was one which the center relied on the periphery to achieve.

12  The first *mahāsāmi* appointed after the reform under Parākrama Bāhu I was Sāriputta, who was a scholar and is not identified as a forest dweller. Whether or not a forest-dwelling monk actually held the post of *mahāsāmi*, it is clear that dignitaries from the Dimbulāgala monasteries participated in the purifying synods. Medhaṅkara, who as *mahāsthavira* of the forest-dwelling fraternity assisted a synod held during the reign of Vijayabahu III (A.D. 1232–6), might have served as *mahāsāmi* during the reign of Pārakrama Bahu II (see Gunawardana, *Robe and Plough*, p. 332).

13    See Malalgoda, *Buddhism*, Ch. 1, for information on Valvita Saranamkara and his reform fraternity, called the Silvat Ramāgama. Born in 1698, Saranamkara became a novice at 16. He spent his early years in the order living reclusively and studying Pali, and he collected a few followers who formed the nucleus of "the fraternity of the pious." They aspired to return to the practices set down in the *Vinaya* texts and to observe the ideal of poverty. They revived the practice of mendicancy. This reform movement made a strong impression when in Kandy the *upasampadā* ceremonies were no more being held and the tradition of worldly *ganinānse* (not monks but laymen in white or saffron cloth who observed the 10 precepts and maintained wives and children) had developed. Without training or without undergoing higher ordination, the *ganinānse* controlled temples and their lands and passed them on to their relatives.

Saranamkara and his pious fraternity gained royal patronage; he reestablished the higher ordination with Siamese help in the reign of Kīrti Śrī Rājasinha (1747–82); the visiting Siamese monks stayed on for some time conducting further ordinations and teaching the *Dhamma* and the *Vinaya*.

14    Michael Carrithers, "The Forest Monks of Lanka, An Historical and Anthropological Study," D. Phil. thesis, Oxford University, 1977. To be published by Oxford University Press.

15    Bechert, *Buddhismus*, Vol. 1.; Richard F. Gombrich, *Precept and Practice: Traditional Buddhism in the Rural Highlands of Ceylon* (Oxford: Oxford University Press, 1971), repeats Bechert's view (pp. 283–4) and opines that the "entire behavior" of Sri Lanka's forest-dwelling monks "is intended as a revival (though to some extent it may be a pseudo-revival) of ancient practices which have long lapsed."

16    The segmentation of the *sangha* and the formation of new fraternities in Sri Lanka throughout the nineteenth century, and thereafter, is a complex issue, resulting from numerous factors, from internal reasons of "reform" and alleged return to the stricter standards of early Buddhism to "contextual" factors of caste, regional particularism, social mobility, lay pressures, and clashes of leading monks. Moreover, the discourse framed in terms of reform is inflected by context, and the dialectic between them is recursive and intertwined. Apart from Malalgoda, *Buddhism*, see Steven Kemper's informative and original essay, "Reform and Segmentation in Monastic Fraternities in Low Country Sri Lanka," *Journal of Asian Studies*, Vol. 40, No. 1, 1980, pp. 27–41. This essay explores the larger social context within which reform and segmentation are situated. The founding of forest-monk hermitages is only a small aspect of the larger issue of monastic segmentation in the nineteenth century.

17    The biography was by Kodagoda Upasena and its title is *Śrī Paññānanda Mahā Thera Caritaya* (Colombo: n.p., n.d.); it was based on an earlier *caritaya* by Matara Nānindāsabha.

18    Samsthāva means eremetical establishment.

19    Carrithers, "Forest Monks."

20    Michael Carrithers, "The Modern Ascetics of Lanka and the Pattern of Change in Buddhism," *Man*, new series, Vol. 14, No. 2, 1979, pp. 294–310; for an account of the earlier phase of the movement, see Nur Yalman, "The Ascetic Buddhist Monks of Ceylon," *Ethnology*, Vol. 1, No. 3, 1962, pp. 315–28.

21    Carrithers, "Modern Ascetics," pp. 306–7, reports that the majority of lay supporters came from the *navandanna, vahumpara,* and *batgama* castes.

# Notes to pp. 62–7

22   E. Michael Mendelson, *Sangha and State in Burma: A Study of Monastic Sectarianism and Leadership*, ed. John P. Ferguson (Ithaca, N.Y.: Cornell University Press, 1975), p. 46. This section is primarily based on the information and interpretation contained in this work.

23   Mendelson, *Sangha and State*, pp. 47–8; he quotes from U. Pannasami, *The History of the Buddhist Sangha (Sasanavamsa)*, trans. B. C. Law (London: Luzac, 1952).

24   In passing, I note that the alleged "lone" forest dwellers in turn founded new or enlarged existing monasteries and that the names of the groupings that are "established" and that are "reformist" may change from time to time and from context to context.

25   Than Tun, who embraces Luce's view on this matter, is reported as seeing the events of the thirteenth century in these terms: The Burmese forest-monks were the Ari monks, representing the Upper Burma *arahanta* traditions; they were the opponents of the Sri Lanka components of the *sangha*. The Ari monks acquired great power and royal patronage through the process of acquiring and developing land in relatively unpopulated areas and thus helped the territorial expansion of the kingdom. Their leader was Mahākāssapa, who was the rival of the monks sent to Sri Lanka in 1237 and 1248, perhaps for the purpose of stemming the growth of the forest-monks. See Than Tun, "Mahā Kāssapa and His Tradition," *Journal of the Burma Research Society*, Vol. 42, 1959, pp. 99–118.

26   Ibid., p. 50.

27   Michael Aung Thwin, "The Role of Sasana Reform in Burmese History: Economic Dimensions of a Religious Purification," *Journal of Asian Studies*, Vol. 38, No. 4, 1979, pp. 671–88; and "Kingship, the *Sangha*, and Society in Pagan," in *Explorations in Early Southeast Asian History: The Origins of Southeast Asian Statecraft*, ed. Kenneth R. Hall and John Whitmore, Michigan Papers on South and Southeast Asia, 11 (Ann Arbor: Center for South and Southeast Asian Studies, University of Michigan, 1976), has documented the scale and frequency of such royal seizure of monastic lands in Pagan. It is interesting that in medieval Sri Lanka (or later) monastic lands by and large came to enjoy immunity from such royal intrusion, although disputes with royal officials did occur. See Gunawardana, *Robe and Plough*, pp. 181–211.

28   A recent informative essay is my source here: John P. Ferguson, "The Quest for Legitimation by Burmese Monks and Kings: The Case of the Shwegyin Sect, 19th–20th Centuries," in *Religion and Legitimation of Power in Thailand, Laos, and Burma*, ed. Bardwell Smith (Chambersburg, Pa.: Anima Books, 1978).

29   Ibid.

30   Ibid.

31   See Donald K. Swearer and Sommai Premchit, "The Relation between the Religious and Political Orders in Northern Thailand (14th–16th Centuries)" in Smith, *Religion and Legitimation of Power*, pp. 20–33.

32   Ibid., p. 25.

33   Ibid., pp. 22–30.

34   Swearer and Premchit, "Relation between Religious," comment that this new Sinhala order is "presumably of the Mahāvihāra tradition," and, in contrast to their rivals, they "did not cover their alms bowls with their robes, nor did they carry staffs." But from Gunawardana, *Robe and Plough*, one infers that the Sumana order, because of its Udumbaragiri links, is also of the Mahāvihāra parentage. That both orders could be

branches within the Mahāvihāra order is not contradictory, in the light of my previous comments.

35  H.R.H. Prince Damrong Rajanubhab, *A History of Buddhist Monuments in Siam* (Bangkok: Siam Society, 1962), p. 7.

36  Prince Dhani Nivat, *Monarchical Protection of the Buddhist Church in Siam* (Bangkok: World Fellowship of Buddhists, 1964), pp. 5–8.

37  See Charnvit Kasetsiri, *The Rise of Ayudhya, A History of Siam in the Fourteenth and Fifteenth Centuries* (Kuala Lumpur: Oxford University Press, 1976), for hints of the active leadership provided by a variety of holy men in North Thailand in early times, as could be gleaned from inscriptions and from the *Tamnān* chronicles (legends and myths that were primarily concerned with the history of the spread of Buddhism in the region). We shall return to these holy men in the next chapter, but let me note here that if they are to be seen as separate from the *bhikkhu*, they nevertheless worked with the grain of Buddhism and in the same direction as forest-monk establishments. They were agents promoting the cause of Buddhist polities.

38  Ibid., p. 43.

39  F. L. Woodward, *Manual of a Mystic, Being a Translation from the Pali and Sinhalese Work Entitled The Yogavachara's Manual* (London: Pali Text Society, 1916). T. W. Rhys Davids, who analyzed the text, which was copied from the original palm-leaf manuscript, found both the copy and the source deficient. Nevertheless, the text is considered important because Rhys Davids claimed that no other work in Buddhist literature, either Pali or Sanskrit, devoted itself to the details of *samādhi* concentration meditation.

40  Ibid., p. xiv.

41  Ibid., pp. v–viii.

42  See earlier reference to him in this chapter.

43  See Craig Reynolds, "The Buddhist Monkhood in Nineteenth Century Thailand," Ph.D. thesis, Cornell University, 1972, for a full and informative discussion. This issue is also treated in my *World Conqueror and World Renouncer*, Chs. 10 and 11.

44  Richard Allan O'Connor, "Urbanism and Religion: Community, Hierarchy, and Sanctity in Urban Thai Buddhist Temples," Ph.D. thesis, Cornell University, 1978. See especially pp. 141–51.

45  In Bangkok, many royal cremations were held at Wat Rātchāthirāt, situated along the river to the north of the city; Wat Sangwēt, at the northern edge, was a major crematorium, as was Wat Sakēt, at the eastern edge. It is not being suggested that every *wat* that specialized in cremations was dedicated to the vocation of meditation.

46  I have developed at length the notion of the "galactic polity" in Southeast Asia in my *World Conqueror and World Renouncer*, and in my essay "The Galactic Polity: The Structure of Traditional Kingdoms in Southeast Asia" in *Anthropology and the Climate of Opinion*, ed. Stanley Freed, *Annals of the New York Academy of Sciences*, Vol. 293, 1977, pp. 69–97.

47  See Samuel Beal, *Travels of Fah-Hian and Sung-Yun, Buddhist Pilgrims from China to India* (400 A.D. and 518 A.D.), trans. from the Chinese (London: Trubner, 1869), p. 47; and Gunawardana, *Robe and Plough*, p. 228. Also: Wilhelm Geiger, *Culture of Ceylon in Medieval Times* (Wiesbaden: Harrassowitz, 1960), pp. 213–15, documents the history of the tooth relic and its travels in the medieval period.

48 When the tooth relic first arrived in Sri Lanka during the reign of Sirimeghavanna (A.D. 301–28), it was placed in a shrine next to the palace. Geiger, *Culture of Ceylon*, documents a number of kings who successively possessed the relic and always kept it in a temple near the royal palace.

49 *Cūlavaṁsa*, trans. W. Geiger and C. M. Rickmers, 2 vols. (Colombo: Government of Ceylon, 1953), Vol. 2, Ch. 74, p. 43 (verses 239–40), speaks of the rain-inducing powers of the relic when it was taken in procession.

50 See H. L. Seneviratne, *Rituals of the Kandyan State* (Cambridge: Cambridge University Press, 1978), for an authoritative and illuminating description and interpretation of the *perahera* festivities.

51 Ibid., pp. 85–7.

52 A. B. Griswold, *Towards a History of Sukhodaya Art* (Bangkok: Fine Arts Department, 1967), pp. 36–7.

53 See Robert Lingat, "Le Culte du Bouddha d'Emeraude," *Journal of the Siam Society*, Vol. 27, No. 1, 1934, pp. 9–38; Camille Notton, *The Cult of the Emerald Buddha* (Bangkok: Bangkok Times Press, 1933); Frank Reynolds, "The Holy Emerald Jewel; Some Aspects of Buddhist Symbolism and Political Legitimation in Thailand" in Smith, *Religion and Legitimation of Power*, pp. 175–93.

## 6. The biography of a modern saint

1 The Thai word *acharn* (*āčān*) derives from the Sanskrit word *ācārya*, teacher. Because in the most important sources I cite the transcription *acharn* is used, I shall also use it throughout.

2 Charles F. Keyes, "Death of Two Buddhist Saints in Thailand," *Journal of the American Academy of Religion, Thematic Studies*, Vol. 48, Nos. 3 and 4, pp. 149–80, makes the plausible suggestion that Maha Boowa first related the biography in a series of oral sermons.

3 Phra Acharn Maha Boowa Hyanasampanno, *The Venerable Phra Acharn Mun Bhuridatta Thera, Meditation Master,* trans. Siri Buddhasukh (Bangkok: Mahāmakut Rajavidyalaya Press, 1976).

While this work is my chief source for the summary and all page references are to this translation, I also use on occasion information provided in this article: Parādāun Rattanakun, "Life and Religious Practice of Lūang Pu Wāēn," *Lan Phō*, Feb. 1977. This source is a Thai-language journal. As a matter of fact, Maha Boowa's biography in Thai has also been translated into English by Ruth-Inge Heinze, *The Biography of Ahjan Man (1871–1949)*, Asian Folklore and Social Life Monographs, Vol. 89 (Taipei: Chinese Association for Folklore, 1976). This translation is both incomplete and in places unsatisfactory.

The appropriate transliteration of the names of our modern saint and his biographer are Man and Būa, but the published English translation by Buddasukh that is my text renders these names as Mun and Boowa. I have therefore chosen to follow my text.

4 It is very likely that Acharn Mun was giving voice to the conventional view that the scholarly study of books – *ganthadhura* – was a specialized avocation that is differently structured from the pursuit of *vipassanādhura*, meditative practice, which leads to the knowledge of liberation.

358

5   We are of course reminded here of the *Mālaya Sutta*, which holds an important place in Thai Buddhism: Phra Mālai enjoyed the mystical powers by which he descended to the hells and ascended to the heavens; in Tāvatiṁsa heaven he met the Buddha to come, Metteyya.

6   We shall keep track of this most interesting fact – that the famous "wandering ascetics" did occasionally visit the large towns, in this case the capital, where they did have links with titled abbots who had achieved fame by climbing the orthodox *saṅgha* hierarchy. The implications of these periodic returns and links with the city monks and materially supportive urban laymen need to be worked out.

7   The biographer glosses that the nonreturner is one in whom the five lower spiritual fetters are destroyed, namely, holding the wrong idea concerning self, the subjection to doubt or hesitation, the clinging to the efficacy of rites and rituals, subjection to sensual desire, and irritation. If the supreme final Path of the *arahant* is not attained within that lifetime, he will pass on to any one of the five subtle higher realms of *Brahma* heavens (p. 31). This gloss is orthodox (see Chapter 2).

8   Every Buddha and *arahants* of some categories have made use of this universal language in helping others, especially invisible beings. This language is therefore a great help in facilitating the communication between minds (p. 191).

9   The biographer says at another place: "There seems to be an inexplicable bond of friendship between a *dhūtaṅga bhikkhu* and animals . . ." (p. 41).

10   As we shall see later, in Part III (which is on the cult of amulets), the saintly monk who peacefully subdues and communicates with wild animals and transcends fear of them is able to transfer his powers to amulets, which enable the laity who wear them to be protected from attack and injury by these "aggressive" beasts.

11   Michael Carrithers, "The Forest Monks of Lanka, An Historical and Anthropological Study," D.Phil. thesis, Oxford University, 1977. To be published by Oxford University Press.

12   F. L. Woodward, *Manual of a Mystic, Being a Translation from the Pali and Sinhalese Work Entitled the Yogavachara's Manual* (London: Pali Text Society, 1916).

13   One place where he spent a rains retreat, the village of Pone Sawang in Sawang Dandin, is mountainous, wild, and frequented by *dhūtaṅga bhikkhu* to this day.

14   It is therefore interesting and instructive to contemplate the activities of these "natural" missionaries and to compare their style and success with those of the recent government-sponsored *Thammathūt (dhammadūta*, meaning emissary of the *dhamma*) programs. [See S. J. Tambiah, *World Conqueror and World Renouncer* (Cambridge: Cambridge University Press, 1976); Somboon Suksamran, *Political Buddhism in Southeast Asia, The Role of the Sangha in the Modernization of Thailand* (New York: St. Martin's Press, 1977).]

15   There are no ordained nuns in the canonical orthodox sense today in Thailand (or Burma or Sri Lanka). However, women may shave their heads, wear white robes, take 8 or 10 precepts, and live on the "edge of the religious community, practicing meditation and cooking food for the monks or novices."

The Acharn's attitude toward women as the feeble sex, which has to be protected and also comprises a danger to the chastity of monks, has once again a basis in early Buddhism. The *Cullavagga* has a vivid account of how the Buddha reluctantly allowed himself to be persuaded by his foster mother, Mahāprajāpatī (the first nun), and his favorite pupil, Ānanda, to allow women to become nuns. The Buddha laid down rules by which the female order would be subordinate to the male order and would depend on monks to conduct various ceremonies. The Buddha is reported to have said with grave misgivings that the life of the Buddhist religion would be cut in half to 500 years because of the admission of women into the *saṅgha*. Hermann Oldenberg [*Buddha, His Life and his Doctrine* (London: Williams and Norgate, 1882), p. 165] asserts: "Women are to the Buddhist of all the snares which the tempter has spread for men, the most dangerous; in women are embodied all the powers of infatuation, which bind them to the world." However, for a sympathetic discussion of early Buddhist attitudes toward women, see I. B. Horner, *Women under Primitive Buddhism: Lay Women and Almswomen* (London: Routledge, 1930).

16 One is also reminded of the "lion roar" of the Buddha.

17 It is noteworthy that not only Acharn Mun but also at least one other noted Thai forest hermit and meditation master – the biographer himself – have this special relationship with their mothers. Their mothers become nuns, live in the forest hermitage and receive instruction, and in turn attend to the food needs of the monk and his disciples.

One cannot help but recall in this context that the Buddha also had a special relationship with his mother, Māyā, who died 10 days after giving him birth, and whom he visited in Dāwadueng heaven during one rains retreat to give her moral instruction. He returned in glory from the heavens attended by deities.

18 This name, given to the sermon preached, was later to be the title of a small book containing his biography and teachings, which was distributed at the cremation rites of Acharn Mun.

19 This is the doctrine of the conditionality of all physical and psychical phenomena, the cause of suffering (based upon ignorance and the *karma*-formations it leads to), and, in reverse form, it reveals the mode of cessation of suffering. It encompasses the second and fourth of the Four Noble Truths.

20 Readers of this account of Acharn Mun's reaching enlightenment will no doubt spontaneously compare it with the description of the Buddha's contemplative breakthrough under the *bodhi* tree and the legendary events associated with it. Also, there is a parallel between the Buddha's compassionate decision to postpone his extinction (*parinibbāna*) so as to teach the way to humans and Acharn Mun's similar dedication of the rest of his life to spread the message.

21 This dialogue asserts things concerning the different bodies of the *Dhamma*, and the nature of the Buddha's presence in the world, that will be discussed in Chapters 15 and 17, and the conception of *nibbāna* as the "signless state," as propounded by Buddhaghosa, which has been discussed in Chapter 4.

22 This vow made in a previous existence to become a buddha (or an *arahant*) follows a classical precedent. As we shall see, the biography of the historical Buddha himself begins with this resolution, which is embedded in a stream of rebirths; so do the biographies of the previous buddhas, and of the Buddha's disciples – Sāriputta, Mahākāśyapa, Ānanda, and so on – who attained enlightenment.

23 It is possible that Germany figures in this vision because there have been some famous German Buddhist monks in recent times, who have lived exemplary lives in Southeast Asia and made important scholarly contributions.

24 *Wanphra*, days devoted to the Buddha's commemoration, fall on full moon, half

moon, and the day before the new moon, and are somewhat analogous to the biblical "sabbath" in that there is worship, a sermon, the taking of precepts, etc.

25  Later, the biographer documents the following under the caption "food restraint": An aspirant who finds that his mind is unruly with regard to food and always overcome by its taste will reduce the intake of food or sometimes go without food for a day or two if his body is able to stand it.

If his mind is still disobedient, a *dhūtaṅga bhikkhu* should do this: "When offered food that he likes, he stops to scrutinize the condition of his mind first. If it is enslaved by desire and shows uncontrollable delight in it, he refuses that kind of food and accepts that which the mind refuses . . . . Some kinds of food are pleasant to taste or beneficial to the health of the body but can be disagreeable to the health of the mind. This kind of food is also to be avoided" (p. 240).

26  The first discourse given by the Buddha after his enlightenment to his former five disciples.

27  This is sometime later than 1941.

28  We note that the Buddha died in his eightieth year, and that it is after a similar span that this *arahant*, as well as many other Buddhist saints in Sri Lanka and elsewhere, are alleged to have died. As far as I can see, the dates in some historically known cases are accurate, and the classical mould is repeated in real life. See also Carrithers, "Forrest Monks," Ch. 5, on Bhikkhu Niyonatilaka.

29  The posture in which the Buddha dies, which was also adopted by dying *arahants*.

30  This distribution reminds me of the distribution of ashes that took place after the Buddha's cremation as related in the *Mahāparinibbāna Sutta*.

### 7. The Buddha's life as paradigm

1  Two well-known works in English, which are based on Burmese and Thai accounts of the Buddha's life, are P. Bigandet, *The Life or Legend of Gaudama, the Buddha of the Burmese*, 2 vols., 4th ed. (London: Kegan Paul, Trench, Trubner, 1911); Henry Alabaster, *The Wheel of the Law; Buddhism Illustrated from Siamese Sources* (London: Trubner, 1871). For Sri Lanka, see R. Spence Hardy, *A Manual of Buddhism in its Modern Development* (London: Partridge and Oakey, 1853).

2  John P. Ferguson, in his essay "The Arahant Ideal in Modern Burmese Buddhism," unpublished paper delivered at annual meeting of Assoc. for Asian Studies, 1977, refers to popular Burmese biographies of saints. The Burmese accounts affirm the special supramundane powers of popular *arahants*, classical and modern. Especially impressive are the encounters between German pilots and Burmese flying *arahants* in World War II.

3  I have earlier cited from the work of Carrithers biographies of forest-monks such as Paññānanda (see Chapter 5).

4  Carolis de Silva, *The Life of Dhammaratana of Miripanne* (Galle, Sri Lanka: n.p., 1888).

5  The works in question are Saṅgharāja Sadhucariyāva (1779) and Sangarajavata (ca. 1780). The former was edited and published in book form in 1947. A biography in English, D. B. Jayatilaka's *Saranankara: The Last Sangha-raja of Ceylon* (Colombo: n.p., 1934) relies heavily on these two works.

6  Charles F. Keyes, "Death of Two Buddhist Saints in Thailand," *Journal of the*

*American Academy of Religion, Thematic Studies*, Vol. 48, Nos. 3 and 4, pp. 149–80.

7  Ibid., p. 151.

8  The existence of these palm-leaf texts suggests that (*contra* Keyes) written biographies may well have been composed before the advent of printing as such in this century. A search for such palm-leaf texts and their proper dating may lead to a revision of present views.

9  See T. W. Rhys Davids and Hermann Oldenberg, trans., *Vinaya Texts*, parts 1, 2, 3 (Oxford: Oxford University Press, 1882).

10  See E. H. Johnston, ed., *The Buddhacarita: Or, the Acts of the Buddha*, Part 1, Sanskrit Text, Punjab University Oriental Publications, No. 31 (Calcutta: Baptist Mission Press, 1935–6).

11  Strictly speaking, he cannot be referred to as the Buddha until his enlightenment.

12  A. K. Warder, *An Introduction to Indian Historiography* (Bombay: Prakashan, 1972), p. 29.

13  Bhikkhu Telivatte Rahula, *A Critical Study of the Mahāvastu* (Delhi: Motilal Banarsidass, 1978), p. 3.

14  See J. Przyluski, *La Legende d'Empereur* (Paris: AMG, 1923).

15  Frank Reynolds [in his essay "The Many Lives of the Buddha," in *The Biographical Process, Studies in the History of the Psychology of Religion*, ed. Frank E. Reynolds and Donald Capps (The Hague: Mouton, 1976)] provides a useful survey of writings dealing with the Buddha's life in the works of several modern buddhologists.

16  Reynolds and Capps, *Biographical Process*, p. 3.

17  Warder, *Introduction to Indian Historiography*, p. 30. See also his *Indian Buddhism* (Delhi: Motilal Banarsidass, 1980), pp. 333–40.

18  Hermann Oldenberg, *Buddha: His Life and His Doctrine*, trans. from the German by William Hoey (London: Williams and Norgate, 1882). There are other standard biographies of the Buddha: examples are E. J. Thomas, *The Life of the Buddha as Legend and History* (London: Routledge & Kegan Paul, 1927), W. W. Rockhill, *The Life of Gotama the Buddha* (London: Routledge & Kegan Paul, 1926). See Reynolds and Capps, *Biographical Process*, for a fuller list.

19  Oldenberg, *Buddha*, p. 78.

20  The *Vinayas* of these six schools are the subject matter of Erich Frauwallner's discussion in *The Earliest Vinaya and the Beginnings of Buddhist Literature* (Serie Orientale Roma) (Rome: Instituto per il Medio ed Estremo Oriente): Sarvāstivādin, Dharmaguptaka, Mahīśāsaka, the Pali school, Mūlasarvāstivādin, and Mahāsāṁghika.

21  Frauwallner, *Earliest Vinaya*, p. 43.

22  Ibid., p. 49.

23  The Pali and the Kāśyapa schools coupled the early biography with the Jātaka collection of birth stories. The Mūlasarvāstivādin school apparently went its own way and attached to the end of the *Skandhaka* all that it gathered concerning the biography of the Buddha.

The *Mahāvastu* [see *Mahāvastu*, trans. into English from E. Senart's 3 vols. (1882–97) by J. J. Jones (London: Luzac, 1949–56)] is interestingly considered by the Lokottaravādins, a branch of the Mahāsāṁghika school, as the first book in their *Vinaya Pitaka*. *Mahāvastu*, the "great story" or "great subject," refers to the life of the Buddha, and, as I have mentioned before, is a collection of all the *avadāna*-type legends and narratives of heroic deeds. The contents of the *Mahāvastu* were – as E. J. Thomas also affirms in support of Finot and Frauwallner – preliminary to the *Vinaya* proper, and consisted of the following: (1) biographical accounts pertaining to the Buddha's career; (2) stories relating to his former existences (*jātaka*); (3) stories about his disciples and devotees (*avadāna*); and (4) discourses and expositions (*sūtra, vyākaraṇa*).

The *Mahāvastu* uses the oldest forms of genuine tradition as well as exegetical elaborations of later origin: "In the earlier strata of this development, the Buddha is spoken of, and presented as, human, whereas in the successive stages of the growth of the so-called legend the human figure of Gautama Śākyamuni is seen gradually being replaced by mythical imagery" (Rahula, *A Critical Study*, pp. 181–2). The *Mahāvastu* does not differ from many other sources with regard to the theme that the Buddha's career in this world was the culmination of an earnest resolve made aeons ago and backed by numerous deeds of virtue and piety. The Buddha's life, seen as an infinite series of births and rebirths, fits well into the "supramundanist" view of the Lokottaravādins, that there exists an Ādi-Buddha, an eternal Buddha, who never becomes extinct and sends manifestations or incarnations of himself whenever the world needs a Buddha (Rahula, Ibid., pp. 184–90).

One more example: The *Divyāvadāna* [see *Divyāvadāna, A Collection of Early Buddhist Legends*, ed. E. B. Cowell and A. A. Neil (Cambridge: Cambridge University Press, 1886)] also belongs to the *avadāna* class of Buddhist literature. The editors use as their text a collection of early Buddhist legends, written in Sanskrit, which was discovered in Nepal. The editors comment: "Many of our legends belong to the *Vinaya pitaka*, as they continually bring in some reference to a point of discipline; but they do not seem to be translated from any Pali original; we would rather regard them, like the others which relate to Asoka's history, as coming down from an independent source. They have all suffered from the careless ignorance which characterizes Northern as opposed to Southern Buddhism; they are the isolated fragments which alone survive from what was once a large literature" (p. viii).

24 Finot's thesis has, it seems, found approval with E. Obermiller, de La Vallée Poussin, and Etienne Lamotte, but has been criticized by Paul Demiéville and J. Filliozat. Concerning Frauwallner's stimulating elaboration Lamotte in his *Histoire du Bouddhisme Indien* (Louvain: Publications Universitaires, 1958) says that in the *Vinayas* of the Sarvāstivādin the account of the two councils does not form part of the original edition. He thinks that the *Vinaya* of the Mūlasarvāstivādin, which has an ample biography of the Buddha, did not arise in the early Buddhist community settled in Mathura, but is a much later work.

In any case, Lamotte doubts that the initial biography of the Buddha, which served as an introduction to the *Vinaya*, had been the point of departure and the model for the separate biographies of the Buddha written later. These latter volumes do not end with the conversion of Śāriputra and Maudgalyayana and are more developed than the fragments of biography in the *Vinaya*. There is, for instance, no comparison between the bulky *Nidānakathā* of the *Jātaka* and the brief, fragmentary accounts at the beginning of the *Khandhaka* of the Pali school. Furthermore, the later biographies could have drawn their subject matter from the *Sūtrapiṭaka*, which contains many detailed biographical pieces. Lamotte also cites Demiéville as indicating that the accounts of the councils may have been attached to the *Vinaya* by editors who were different from the composers of the ancient *Vinaya* of Upali.

Lamotte's position is that the *Vinayapiṭaka* is developed directly from the rulings made during the very origins for the Buddhist community and that the hypothesis of an Old

Skandhaka that is distinct from the ancient *Vinaya* of Upali complicates further an already complicated problem.

25 *Vaṁsa*, referring to the line or "genealogy" of kings, or of patriarchs of the Buddhist *saṅgha*, or of an ordination "lineage" of monks, later expands into stories or historical accounts of the Buddhist *saṅgha* and religion, whose fortunes and changes, whose decay and renewal, and whose maintenance of the canonically "pure" tradition and line of succession are the central themes. Some famous examples are the Siṅhalese chronicles – *Dīpavaṁsa, Mahāvaṁsa, Cūlavaṁsa* – and the Burmese *Sāsanavaṁsa*. The Thai word *tamnān* is an equivalent concept, and a quintessential example of *tamnān* literature is the *Jinakālamāli* chronicle.

In the Hindu literary tradition, the labels *itihāsa, purāna, kāvya,* and *vaṁśa* refer to oral and written traditions, stories, proto-histories and legends, chronicles of royal genealogies, and divine manifestations. Concerning these concepts and their connotations, see V. S. Pathak, *Ancient Historians of India, A Study of Historical Biographies* (London: Asia Publishing House, 1966); Warder, *Introduction to Indian Historiography.*

26 The *Mahāvaṁsa or The Great Chronicle of Ceylon*, trans. Wilhelm Geiger (Colombo: Government of Ceylon, 1950).

27 Incidentally, we are told of the Buddha's intimate relationship with King Bimbisāra of Magadha in these terms: "Bimbisāra and the prince Siddhattha were friends, and friends likewise were the fathers of both. The Bodhisatta was five years older than Bimbisāra . . . when he had striven six years and thereafter had attained to wisdom, he being thirty-five years old, visited Bimbisāra" (p. 12).

28 Charnvit Kasetsiri, *The Rise of Ayudhya* (Kuala Lumpur: Oxford University Press, 1976), p. 1. Kasetsiri gives a useful account of "ancient Thai historiography" and contrasts the *tamnān* with the genre labeled *phongsāwadān*, derived from the Sanskrit words *vaṁsa* and *avatāra*, meaning "history or annals of members of a line, dynasty or kingdom," i.e., dynastic histories that portray history "from the point of view of kingship and the state." He asserts that the latter dynastic chronicles appeared in Thailand for the first time in the seventeenth century, whereas the *tamnān* tradition is older, a large number appearing in the fifteenth century in the area of Chiengmai. He admits that there are many Thai texts that reflect a blend of both these kinds. See David K. Wyatt and Constance M. Wilson, "Thai Historical Materials in Bangkok," *Journal of Asian Studies*, Vol. 25, No. 1, 1965, pp. 105-22, for a listing of Thai sources and traditional Thai historical writing.

29 Ibid., p. 3.

30 In fact, in some respects the *Jinakāla*'s account of the Buddha's life is closer, as regards contents and length, to what is to be found in the Siṅhalese *Dīpavaṁsa* (which is older than the *Mahāvaṁsa*), especially in such matters as the story of the Buddha's reaching enlightenment, his peripatetic teaching career (including his miraculous feats), his royal genealogy stemming from Mahāsammata, and so on. Naturally, the *Dīpavaṁsa* gives more lengthy accounts of the Buddha's visits to and sanctification of the island of Lanka, and of Mahinda's missionary visit to and conversion of that island to Buddhism. See Hermann Oldenberg, *The Dipavamsa: An Ancient Buddhist Historical Record* (London: Williams and Norgate, 1879).

31 These and other episodes we have already read about in Chapter 4, which gives the contents of the *Visuddhimagga*.

### 8. The ordering principles behind Buddhist saintly biography

1  Donald A. Stauffer, *English Biography before* 1700 (New York: Russell and Russell, 1964), p. 5.
2  Ibid.
3  Ibid., p. 7.
4  Helen C. White, *Tudor Books of Saints and Martyrs* (Madison: University of Wisconsin Press, 1963).
5  Ibid., p. 6.
6  Peter Brown, *Religion and Society in the Age of Saint Augustine* (London: Faber and Faber, 1972), p. 31.
7  Peter Brown, *The Cult of the Saints: Its Rise and Function in Latin Christianity* (Chicago: University of Chicago Press, 1981), pp. 5–6.
8  W. Y. Evans-Wentz, ed., *Tibet's Great Yogi – Milarepa, a Biography, from the Tibetan, being the Jetsün-Kahbum (or Biographical History of Jetsum-Milarepa, according to the late Lama Kazi Dawa-Samdup's English rendering)* (Oxford: Oxford University Press, 1969). Another well-known Tibetan masterpiece is the life and teachings of the great Guru Padma-Sambhava; see *The Tibetan Book of the Great Liberation*, ed. W. Y. Evans-Wentz (Oxford: Oxford University Press, 1954).
9  Emmanuel Le Roy Ladurie, *Montaillou, the Promised Land of Error,* trans. Barbara Bray (New York: Vintage Books, 1979).
10  P. Bigandet, *The Life or Legend of Gaudama, the Buddha of the Burmese*, 2 vols., 4th ed. (London: Kegan Paul, Trench, Trubner, 1911). It is clear that Bigandet's chief sources were Burmese literary compositions.

It has recently come to my notice that there is an important Thai work that can be used effectively along the same lines. Frank Reynolds, "The Many Lives of Buddha" [in *The Biographical Process, Studies in the History of the Psychology of Religion*, ed. Frank E. Reynolds and Donald Capps (The Hague: Mouton, 1976)] informs us of a major biography of the Buddha, titled *Paṭhamasambodhikathā*, written by H. R. H. Paramanuchitchinorot, who served as the *saṅgharāja* of the Thai *saṅgha* in the mid-nineteenth century. This biography, considered a classic of Thai literature, is based on the sacred biographies of the classical *Nidānakathā* type, but contains other additional materials: For example, it includes an account, drawn from the *Buddhavaṁsa* commentary, of the places where the Buddha spent the rainy season retreats during the second half of his ministry; and an account of the final phase of the Buddha's life, which has been preserved in the *Mahāparinibbāna Sutta*. These episodes are clearly relevant to the biography of Acharn Mun, but at present I have no way of knowing whether the *Paṭhamasambodhikathā* consciously or unconsciously served as a model for Maha Boowa's composition. I hope to investigate this matter in the future.

11  Earlier on, Māra flings this accusation at the Buddha, which the latter disproves: Māra approached the meditating Buddha and said: "Thesadat Siddartha, this throne is not made for you; vacate it forthwith; it is my property." The Buddha calmly answered: "You have not as yet practiced the two great virtues, nor gone through the five acts of self-denial; you have never devoted your life to help others to acquire merits; . . . This throne, therefore, cannot be yours." This again affirms the Buddha's compassionate and meritorious acts in this world (Bigandet, *Life or Legend of Gaudama*, Vol. 1., pp. 88–9).

12  In Bigandet, ibid., Vol. 1, pp. 99–100.

13  Ibid., Vol. 2. Chs. 3, 4.

14  Let me illustrate this: As Bigandet has perceptively recorded (ibid., Vol. 2, Ch. 3), the Burmese conduct their cremation rites in the style of a "festival," with music, dancing, feasting, and so on. In the translated text, the Malla princes are described, on hearing the news of the passing of the Buddha, as directing one of their family "to go throughout the city and collect all the richest and rarest perfumes, to keep in readiness the drums, harps, flutes, and all other musical instruments, and have them carried to the place where the remains of the Buddha were lying. Having reached the spot, the princes began to make offerings of flowers and perfumes with the greatest profusion, in the midst of dancings, rejoicings, and the uninterrupted sounds of all the musical instruments" (Vol. 2, p. 77). In fact, Sāriputta's mortuary rites, which took place before the Buddha's, are described as if they were a Burmese ritual.

15  "Adzatathat [Ajātasattu] ordered the soil to be dug very deep. With the earth bricks were made, and eight *dzedis* (*cetiya*) were built. . . . The depth of the hole was eighty cubits. Its bottom was lined with iron bars. To that bottom was lowered a chapel monastery made of brass, similar in shape and proportions to the great *wihara* (*vihāra*) of Ceylon. Six gold boxes containing the precious relics were placed in this chapter monastery. Each box was enclosed in one of silver, the latter in one adorned with precious stones; and so on, until eight boxes were placed one within the other. There were also arrayed 550 statues, representing Buddha in 550 preceding existences . . . and the statues of the eighty great disciples. . . . There were also arranged 500 lamps of gold and 500 lamps of silver, filled with the most fragrant oil, with wicks made of the richest cloth" (Bigandet, ibid., Vol 2., pp. 97–8).

## 9. The disciples of the Master

1  Douglas M. Burns, *The Ahjahns (Meditation Teachers) of Northeast Thailand* (Bangkok: Thaikasem Press, 1970). This document is a 19-page guide.

2  Sunno Bhikkhu, *A Brief Guide to Meditation Temples of Thailand*, World Federation of Buddhists Book Series No. 44 (Bangkok: Chuang Printing Press, 1978).

3  Acharn Fun died in 1978.

4  Acharn Sing Tong is more accurately a disciple of Acharn Maha Boowa.

5  Lūang Pū Wāēn is exceptional in establishing his hermitage in the North; he is, however, Northeastern in origin.

6  From Max Weber, *Max Weber: Essays in Sociology*, trans. and ed. H. H. Gerth and C. Wright Mills (London: Routledge & Kegan Paul, 1948), p. 358.

7  It is, however, necessary to record that something of a cult has developed around Acharn Mun's relics, medallions bearing his likeness have been made since his death and distributed to people, and a memorial exhibit of his robes and almsbowl have been installed at Wat Suthawat in Sakon Nakhon (Charles F. Keyes, "Death of Two Buddhist Saints in Thailand," *Journal of the American Academy of Religion, Thematic Studies*, Vol. 48, Nos. 3 and 4, p. 167).

8  Jack Kornfield, *Living Buddhist Masters* (Santa Cruz, Calif.: Unity Press, 1977), is confirmed by Burns, *The Ahjahns*, who remarks that Chā "is the only disciple of Ahjahn Mahn I know who is of the *Mahanikaya* sect."

9  The numbers could have been more accurately reported by Burns: Let us suppose that the higher totals relate to the *Vassa* season and the lower to the period afterward.

10  Kornfield, *Living Buddhist Masters.*

11  As usual, the nuns' accommodation is more crowded; they eat their meals after the monks have finished.

12  We may note that Acharn Chā continues with the Mahānikāi sect's emphasis on morning and evening chanting.

13  Burns, *The Ahjahns*, reports that a decade earlier (in 1969) Acharn Chā had 8 branch monasteries. In December 1978 an official of the World Fellowship of Buddhists in Bangkok told me that Acharn Chā was the biggest attraction among all the present-day forest teachers and that he had established some 14 branch hermitages. Most recently, in 1981 Chaokhun Rajavaramuni, the scholar-monk, confirmed this reputation enjoyed by Acharn Chā.

14  We shall later comment on the structural features of such networks.

15  Burns, *The Ahjahns*, gives the number of inmates as about 7 in 1970, while Sunno Bhikkhu, *A Brief Guide*, gives the number as around 20 when he visited it in 1978. The latter's estimates tend to be inflated.

16  Burns, *The Ahjahns.*

17  For example, *World Federation of Buddhists Review*, Vol. 15, Nos. 3, 4, 1978.

18  Kornfield, *Living Buddhist Masters*, Ch. 9.

### 10. The biographer as exemplary forest-monk, meditator, and teacher

1  Jack Kornfield, *Living Buddhist Masters* (Santa Cruz, Calif.: Unity Press, 1977).

2  Like most other forest hermitages, Pā Bān Tāt is a "residence" (*samnak*) and has no consecrated *bōt* where ordination of monks and novices can take place. The closest Thammayut sect *wat* where ordination can take place is in the town of Udon.

3  One informant gave as an example the seeing of a spot of light during meditation; the meditator must not follow the light but must bring it inside himself. A teacher instructs the pupil how to recognize such *nimitta* – internal and external – and how to control them.

4  This is of course in line with the *Vinaya* prescription, which makes it a *pārājika* offense to falsely boast about one's supranormal powers (*iddhi*).

5  These were Acharn Singtong and Lūang Phāū Būa (who is illiterate and was for a while associated with Maha Boowa).

6  As I have stated before, the path of the *bhikkhu* is conventionally divided into three parts: *pariyatti* (study), *paṭipatti* (practice), and *paṭivedha* (realization, enlightenment). The three parts relate to a monk's career, culminating in enlightenment. In Thailand during the course of conversation, monks frequently refer to the first two when speaking of what a monk concentrates upon. "Study" is usually associated with the vocation of books (*ganthadhura*) and is said to be the preoccupation of most monks and novices attending monastic schools. "Practice" comes to be associated with meditation (*vipassanādhura*) and is associated with a minority who devote themselves to this difficult discipline.

7  A series of short essays titled "Manners of Practice of the Dhutanga Kammatthana Bhikkhus in the Lineage of the Late Venerable Meditation-Master, Phra Acharn Mun Bhuridatto" are printed in *World Federation of Buddhists Review: Vesakha number*, Vol. 15, No. 3, May – June 1978, supplement pp. 1–13; and Sangha number, Vol. 15, No. 4,

July–Aug. 1978, pp. 17–33. These essays report and recall the teachings of Acharn Mun, though they do not reproduce the mystical and "tantric" episodes in the biography of the Master.

8 Kornfield, *Living Buddhist Masters*, pp. 164–83, reports Maha Boowa's views under the caption "Wisdom Develops Samadhi."

9 For a more extended discussion of monastic networks in Christian Europe and Thailand, see my *World Conqueror and World Renouncer: A Study of Buddhism and Polity in Thailand against a Historical Background* (Cambridge: Cambridge University Press, 1976), pp. 360–4.

10 Kornfield, *Living Buddhist Masters*.

## 11. Sectarianism and the sponsorship of meditation

1 The foundation is a financial institution in its own right in which member monasteries invest their monies and earn interest. The fund is administered by a committee of laymen and monks, whose chairman is the abbot of Wat Bovonniwet. The lay members manage the funds' financial operations, the "manager" of the fund being a layman.

2 Rāma III thus conferred the title of "deputy king" (*uparāt*) on his royal brother, whom he had preceded to the throne and whose claims to succeed him were tacitly recognized.

3 Prince Chulalongkorn, ordained as novice in 1866, resided in the *wat* for 6 months. But when he was ordained monk for 15 days just before his coronation, he resided in a small chapel within the royal palace. However, Pavares, the abbot of Wat Bovonniwet, presided over the ordination ceremony as his *upajjhāya* (preceptor).

4 I must take the opportunity of correcting a mistake I made in my *World Conqueror and World Renouncer: A Study of Buddhism and Polity in Thailand against a Historical Background* (Cambridge: Cambridge University Press, 1976), in which on p. 215 I said that all the sons of King Mongkut were ordained at Wat Bovonniwet. Actually, all ordinations of princes take place in the royal chapel, Wat Phra Kāēo, and the princes and monarchs I have mentioned here resided afterward at Wat Bovonniwet. According to the Thai-language newspaper *Matichon* (Nov. 6, 1978), four princely sons of Mongkut and four sons of King Chulalongkorn, all of *Čaofā* or *Phraongčao* status, resided at Wat Bovonniwet as ordained princes.

5 The present crown prince's ordination ceremony was performed at the royal chapel, Wat Phra Kāēo, with monks from both sects presiding. The officiating monk of *upajjhāya* status was the supreme patriarch, who happened at that time to be of the Mahānikai sect; two *achāriyas* were chosen from the two sects.

But since the crown prince was later to reside at Wat Bovonniwet as a Thammayut monk, a second ordination had to be performed. For, according to the sect's rules, established by Mongkut himself, a valid ordination can be conducted only by Thammayut monks according to a set procedure. So the crown prince underwent a second ordination ceremony at Wat Bovonniwet after his official ceremony, before taking up his residence. This of course was resented by the Mahānikai monks.

6 Thus the present king and crown prince each spent the first night in Tamnak Panyā.

7 I have already referred to his essays in *World Federation of Buddhists Review*. I have also earlier stated in Chapter 6 the facts concerning the publication and free distribution of the biography of Acharn Mun.

8   The World Federation of Buddhists Center in 1978 sponsored meditation classes both in its own building and at Wat Bovonniwet. It was reported to me that about 20–30 regulars attended the classes held at the center. Both class instructors were monks.

9   See my *World Conqueror and World Renouncer*, Ch. 14.

10  Relevant sources are D. K. Wyatt, *The Politics of Reform in Thailand: Education in the Reign of King Chulalongkorn* (New Haven, Conn.: Yale University Press, 1969); A. L. Moffat, *Mongkut and the King of Siam* (Ithaca, N.Y.: Cornell University Press, 1961); R. Lingat, "La vie religieuse du Roi Mongkut," *Journal of the Siam Society*, Vol. 20, pp. 129–48; C. J. Reynolds "The Buddhist Monkhood in Nineteenth Century Thailand" Ph.D. thesis, Cornell University 1972; A. B. Griswold, "King Mongkut in Perspective," *Journal of the Siam Society*, Vol. 45, 1957, pp. 1–41; and V. Thompson, *Thailand: The New Siam* (New York: Macmillan, 1941). They have all been cited in my *World Conqueror and World Renouncer*, Chs. 10–12. Two relevant essays have been recently published: John W. Butt, "Thai Kingship and Religious Reforms 18th–19th Centuries," and A. T. Kirsch, "Modernizing Implications of Nineteenth Century Reforms in the Thai Sangha," both in Bardwell Smith, ed., *Religion and Legitimation of Power in Thailand, Laos, and Burma* (Chambersburg, Pa: Anima Books, 1978).

11  That Mongkut was influnced by the *dhūtaṅga* practices as discussed in the *Visuddhimagga* is given an enduring affirmation at Wat Bovonniwet, at which Mongkut presided as abbot from 1837 until he became king in 1851. The Wihan Phra Sasada houses in one of its rooms the famous Buddha image that gives the *wihan* its name, and on the walls of its other rooms are beautiful murals illustrating the 13 ascetic practices. Mongkut sponsored these murals.

12  As I have argued elsewhere, one should not overrate Mongkut's rationalist, demythologizing stance, for as an innovator he initiated a new orthodoxy that was allegedly grounded in the past. Mongkut introduced certain new Buddhist festivals, wrote new *paritta* chants, and when he was king interpolated new Buddhist sequences into the traditional "Brahmanical" royal rites. Kingship with its trappings, including the cosmic rites magnifying it, were never as splendid in Thailand as in the nineteenth century. Incidentally, the very epoch of Buddhist revival was also one in which elaborate tonsure ceremonies were held during the reigns of King Chulalongkorn and King Mongkut before him; these ceremonies were loaded with traditional cosmological and "Brahmanical" symbolism.

13  The monk in question is Čaokhun Rājavinayabara, who enjoys the unique privilege of being the deputy abbot of Wat Čēdi Lūang in Chiengmai as well as of the prestigious Wat Bovonniwet in Bangkok. See C. F. Keyes, "Buddhism in a Secular City," in *Viasakha Puja* (Bangkok: Buddhist Association of Thailand, 1976), pp. 64–5; and David L. Gosling, "Redefining the Sangha's Role in Northern Thailand: An Investigation of Monastic Careers of Five Chiang Mai Wats," to be published in the *Southeastern Journal of Social Science*.

14  John P. Ferguson and Shalardchai Ramitanondh, "Monks and Hierarchy in Northern Thailand," *Journal of the Siam Society*, Vol. 64, pt. 1, pp. 138–40.

15  Kirsch, "Modernizing Implications," p. 52.

16  Wat Samorai, where Mongkut once resided, became part of the Thammayut. Others newly founded were Wat Paramanivāsa, Vijaynati, Pupphārāma, and Khruavan – the first by Mongkut and the others by members of the nobility who held high official positions.

17  In his first years as king, Mongkut founded four new Thammayut monasteries: Wat Somanassa (1853), Padumavana (1857), Rajpratistha (1864), and Makutaksatriya. The next king, Chulalongkorn, in turn founded two more Thammayut monasteries at the beginning of his reign, namely Rajapavitra (1870) and Devacireinda (1878).

18  Once upon the throne, Mongkut chose as his first patriarch his uncle, Prince Pramunuchit, the abbot of Wat Chetuphon and of the Mahānikai sect, as the supreme patriarch. Pramunuchit died after two years of service, and King Mongkut appointed no other for the rest of his reign.

King Chulalongkorn made Prince Pavaret (abbot of Wat Bovonniwet and head of the Thammayut sect) head of the *sangha* without the full status of supreme patriarch in 1874, and gave him the full title only in 1891. On Pavaret's death the next year, another Thammayut monk, Phra Ariyawongsakhatayan, was appointed patriarch. When he died in 1900, once again King Chulalongkorn kept the position vacant, presumably because the candidate who would be most acceptable, Prince Wachirayān, was too junior to be appointed yet. See Craig Reynolds, "The Buddhist Monkhood in Nineteenth-Century Thailand," Ph.D. thesis, Cornell University, 1972, for a detailed discussion concerning the appointments to the patriarchship from 1851–93.

19  The *sangha* by the act of 1902 was divided into four parts, three of which were the geographical divisions of the Mahānikai sect (north, south, and central regions), and the fourth the Thammayut sect.

20  In 1937, there were only 272 Thammayut monasteries in the country with about 3,000 monks; in 1959 the numbers were 819 monasteries and 9,892 monks; in 1966, 1,023 monasteries and 8,807 monks; in 1969, 1,094 monasteries and 9,703 monks.

By comparison, in 1966 there were 23,000 monasteries and about 166,000 monks, and in 1969 24,000 *wat* and 180,000 monks, of Mahānikai affiliation. (These figures apply to residents during the rains retreat seasons.) Though throughout the years the rate of increase of Thammayut *wat* and monks is greater than that of their Mahānikai counterparts, the Thammayut still remains a distinct minority. For example, in 1969 there were 24 times more temples and 18 times more monks belonging to the Mahānikai.

21  Tambiah, *World Conqueror and World Renouncer*, pp. 257–61.

22  Let me reproduce here a statement by an informant made in 1978, which can be added to the "versions" of this clerical struggle I have already recorded in my *World Conqueror and World Renouncer*. The present informant is an ex-Thammayut monk who is now a university teacher, and he gives us some insights into the manner in which monks and rulers strike up a symbiotic relationship:

"In the early years of the sectarian rivalry when the 1941 Act was in force, Phra Phimolatham of Wat Mahāthāt seemed to be winning. He and the abbot of Wat Makut first competed for the position in the Interior Ministry (Pokkhrāūng) which was in charge of monastic education and propagation of the Dhamma. Phra Phimolatham got the post, because he enjoyed the favors of the then Prime Minister, Phibunsongkhrām. When Phibunsongkhrām emerged unscathed from the *coup d'etat* attempted by the Navy in 1951, a number of Mahānikai monks sent him a letter expressing their 'gladness.' The Thammayut monks did not participate in this show of loyalty and were critical of Mahānikai's 'political' activity. Under Phibunsongkhrām the Mahānikai was in favor and won more of the ecclesiastical cabinet posts.

"But in the subsequent regime of Prime Minister Sarit, the Thammayut engaged in more successful politics. They were in favor with Sarit, who sacked Phimolatham, and who was the patron of the abbot of Wat Makut. Colonel Pin Mutukan, ex-Thammayut monk, Director General of the Religious Affairs Department, was the willing bureaucratic agent through whom Sarit effected the so-called reform of the *saṅgha*. Subsequently, Sarit became in the fifties the special patron of two Thammayut *wat* – Wat Rajabopit and Wat Rajapradit. The abbot of the latter (Čaokhun Mettāthammarot) was a famous astrologer, and Sarit consulted him often, and used his wife's mother as his emissary. Sarit's timing of the *coup d'etat* of 1957, and of his takeover in 1959, was done in consultation with the abbot. The same abbot has been consulted on several occasions by the king and queen, who sent their horoscopes through palace emissaries for monthly readings. In fact, the auspicious times for the crown prince's monthly engagement and wedding ceremonies were 'officially' computed by this abbot.

"Sarit's successor as Prime Minister, Thanom Kittikachorn, had his own favorite astrologer elsewhere. But the abbot-astrologer of Wat Rajapradit has an influential clientele that includes Army and Navy top brass, merchants, and bureaucrats."

23 Tambiah, *World Conqueror and World Renouncer*, pp. 260–1.

### 12. The Mahānikāi sect's propagation of lay meditation

1 As reported by the Department of Religious Affairs, *Annual Report* (Bangkok: Department of Religious Affairs, 1969).

2 See Sunno Bhikkhu, *A Brief Guide to Meditation Temples of Thailand* (Bangkok: Chiang Printing Press, 1978), for accounts of the meditation program at Wat Pāknām and Wat Pleng.

3 The details regarding the institution are given in my *World Conqueror and World Renouncer: A Study of Buddhism and Polity in Thailand against a Historical Background* (Cambridge: Cambridge University Press, 1976), pp. 464–72.

4 There were also said to be various other *wat* in the Northeast in Chaināt, Chaiyaphūm, and elsewhere, which continued the old program.

5 In that year, eight new monks had been ordained before the rains retreat and two had already disrobed by this date.

6 In the countries of Theravāda Buddhism, there is no order of nuns (*bhikkhunī*) left, the order having died out in Sri Lanka many centuries ago. As one can see, *māē chī* are pious women who have become reclusive and taken shelter in the *wat*, tending to monks' needs and devoting themselves to pious activities.

7 Sometimes women may temporarily assume white clothes in fulfillment of a vow taken before the Buddha (i.e., a Buddha statue), usually concerning the cure of an illness or relief of a problem. Women in this condition may temporarily join the *māē chī* population of a *wat*. In any case, *māē chī* come and go freely and visit different *wat*. Their special status allows them a mobility that is not as easily available to ordinary women.

8 See Chapter 20 for details of this monk who many Northern Thai view as having reached *arahant* status.

9 When asked how the monks came to be associated with rockets (*bāūk fai*) and balloons (*kom loi/wāo*) in North Thailand, he gave me an interesting Buddhist interpretation of the symbolism. Rockets have a hidden meaning: The rocket is made up of ingredients like gunpowder, saltpeter, etc., and if it lacks one it cannot ascend; in the same way, the human

body must engage in the three practices of *dāna, sīla,* and *bhāvanā* if it is to achieve liberation.

There are eight conditions of the world (*loka dhamma*) that affect our lives: gain and loss of gain, honor and loss of honor, praise and blame, happiness and suffering. A human being is like a balloon. If he is praised for his conduct, he is elevated and goes up high like an inflated balloon; but if he is not worthy of honor and praise, he is deflated and falls down. The ascent and descent of balloons is like the arising and dissolution of mental formations and illustrates the conditioned nature of all phenomena.

10  As usual, there are exceptions to general patterns and tendencies. That the *ārāma* (hermitage) tradition is not foreign to the movement initiated by Phra Phimolatham is illustrated by Wat Phrabāttakphā, situated in Pāsāng, in Lamphūn Province. It is a famous monastery and a place of pilgrimage.

This large and well-maintained monastery is situated at the edge of a small village and has the layout and architectural patterns associated with a hermitage, principally individual *kuti* dwellings dispersed among the trees and orchards. However, this monastery has – unlike the hermitages of the *dhūtaṅga* tradition but like other established *wat* – numerous novices together with monks and has concentrated on study (*pariyatti*) just as much as on meditation (*paṭipatti*).

In October 1971, when I visited this *wat*, there were 23 monks (11 "temporary" monks ordained before lent had already left), 60 novices, 2 nuns, and 5 temple boys.

Monks and novices have to declare their interest either in "study" or in "practice" and thereafter concentrate on one or the other. The scholars engage in Pali studies and sit the ecclesiastical *prayōk* examinations. I was told that practically all the novices are engaged in "study" rather than meditation and that only 10 of the 23 monks are engaged in the path of meditation. And just like Wat Mūēang Man, here too a number of monks from other *wat* have come to practice meditation for variable periods of time.

The principal meditation teacher was the abbot, Phrakhrū Phrommawaksangwāūn, 74 years of age, whose brother, also a monk, founded another well-known meditation center at Wat Nāūbāūluang in Sanpātāūng District. Both came to be associated with the Phra Phimolatham movement.

Phrakhrū Phrommawak was ordained a novice as a boy, subsequently as a monk in a *wat* in Pāsāng District and, after two lents, decided to become a *dhūtaṅga* monk. He walked on foot in the forest tradition and even went to Burma. It was much later that he was enrolled into Phra Phimolatham's program. He made a trip to Bangkok and stayed at Wat Mahāthāt for three months. Thus, in this meditation teacher's case, we have an old man who was already steeped in the Old Northeastern and Northern *dhūtaṅga* tradition and later was incorporated into the Wat Mahāthāt dissemination program. He has trained two assistants, who help him in teaching the pupils.

Wat Buddhabāttākphā has, like the usual Mahānikāi sect's commoner *wat* (*wat rāt*), a committee to administer its affairs. A fund (*mūnnithi*), whose money has been contributed by lay donors, is operated by the abbot with the assistance of a lay accountant. A principal use of this money is the running of a kitchen to feed the monks and novices. Each day, five monks and five novices go on an almsround to the village, which is quite far and cannot donate sufficient food. The village households, in traditional Northern fashion, are divided into groups, each being responsible for the offerings on a day according to a system of rotation.

11  S. J. Tambiah, *World Conqueror and World Renouncer, A Study of Buddhism and Polity in Thailand against a Historical Background* (Cambridge: Cambridge University Press, 1970), Chs. 14 and 15.

12  Phra Sobhuna Dhammasudhi published a book, *Insight Meditation* (London: n.p., 1965). He subsequently left the *saṅgha*.

13  The Pali grades in the ecclesiastical examinations extend from *prayōk* 3 to 9.

14  This cult is described in my essay, "The Cosmological and Performative Significance of a Thai Cult of Healing through Meditation," *Culture, Medicine and Psychiatry*, 1, 1977, pp. 97–132.

15  It is significant that this informant invokes hierarchical canons and considers the use of meditation for "practical" uses to be the way of a "lower" path. He is also, however, crudely, aware of the psychosomatic possibilities of *samādhi* meditation.

### 13. The center–periphery dialectic: the Mahāthāt and Bovonniwet sponsorship of meditation compared

1  S. J. Tambiah, *World Conqueror and World Renouncer: A Study of Buddhism and Polity in Thailand against a Historical Background* (Cambridge: Cambridge University Press, 1976), Ch. 18; and Somboon Suksamran, *Political Buddhism in Southeast Asia: The Role of Modernization in Thailand* (New York: St. Martin's Press, 1976).

2  Recent work by David Gosling in Northern Thailand has shown that while the Thammathūt movement promoted from Bangkok has declined, there is a vigorous effort being launched by the provincial monks. An essay by Gosling is in press, and provides the latest information on that subject: its title is "Redefining the Sangha's Role in Northern Thailand" and it will appear in the *Southeast Asian Journal of Social Science*.

3  See *World Conqueror and World Renouncer*, pp. 441–50.

4  Somboon Suksamran, *Political Buddhism*, argues that the presupposition that the monks are the best agents for national development and integration, with consequent political modernization, seems unjustified. On the contrary, the use of Buddhism and the *saṅgha* to serve political ends may in fact bring undesirable consequences for the *saṅgha*'s position and for Buddhism.

5  I discovered in 1978 that since 1976 Mahāčulālongkāūn and Mahāmakut universities' joint special *Dhamma patana* project to train provincial monks for missionary work had been dropped for lack of financial support. However, graduates from the universities were still being sent to the provinces as *Dhamma* teachers and "moral supervisors." The *Annual Report of the Religious Affairs Department for 1977* says that 50 such supervisors were appointed in the previous year and about $13,000 spent on them. It also reports the contemplation of other projects such as "The Program for Teaching Villages," which entails sending the monks into villages to start Sunday schools, inculcate in villagers "love of Nation, Religion, and King," loyalty to a "democratic government with the King as head," and an "identification with Thai Culture," etc. Twenty "units" of monks were reported as engaged in 22 provinces in this work in the previous year, and the work was planned with the cooperation of provincial ecclesiastical governors and their assistants.

6  A perceptive government official remarked that this problem of succession to the headship was further compounded by the poor quality of the staff of the religious affairs department. Most of the staff are ex-monks who, though recruited as civil servants, are

considered inferior to the regular civil servants and cannot transfer to other branches and departments of the national civil service. Moreover, the department is considered inferior by other member departments of the Ministry of Education. On the recruitment to the Department of Religious Affairs, see my *World Conqueror and World Renouncer*, pp. 303–8.

7 On the student revolt of 1973, see Frank Reynolds, "Legitimation and Rebellion: Thailand's Civil Religion and the Student Uprising of October, 1973," in Bardwell Smith, ed., *Religion and Legitimation of Power in Thailand, Laos, and Burma* (Chambersburg, Pa.: Anima Books, 1978); and Narong Sinsawadi, *Thailand: Student Activism and Political Change* (Bangkok: Allied Printers, 1974). Other sources are cited in notes below.

8 Throughout 1974, villagers, particularly in North Thailand in the Chiengmai region, expressed their agrarian and political grievances, and many thousands came in procession to protest at the capital. In the same year was formed the Peasant Federation, which petitioned the government for the implementation of the Land Rent Control Act, for the formulation of land-reform legislation, for the release of villagers arrested for trespassing on government land, for the issuance of title deeds to squatters on forest-reserve land, etc. The federation went underground after a series of assassinations of its leaders. I am indebted to Katherine A. Bowie for this information.

9 This secular university should not be confused with Mahāčulālongkāūn, which is the monks' university.

10 Halls (*sālā*) in the *wat* are rented to keep the corpse for the three or seven days during which chanting is done before cremation or before storing the corpse (for which a fee is charged) for later cremation. Another fee is charged for the actual use of the crematorium to burn the corpse. Many Bangkok *wat* have an organization of lay helpers to provide funerary services, which are paid for and range from providing the coffin, flowers, and wreaths to collecting and storing the ashes. The long cremation rites are punctuated by numerous chantings by monks who are on each occasion given packets of personal gifts.

11 A case cited by informants is that of Somdet Mahāwirong of Wat Si Mahāthāt, who came from Ubon Province, and who was not confirmed in the position of *Sangharāja*, although he was twice called to be acting head.

12 See C. F. Keyes, "Political Crisis and Militant Buddhism in Contemporary Thailand," in Smith, ed., *Religion and Legitimation of Power*, pp. 147–64. Kittivuḍḍho founded Cittabhavana College to train novices and monks to play an active role in propagating the *Dhamma*. His activist Buddhism took after the 1973 student insurrection a strong anticommunist stance, and he supported an ultraright nationalist movement called Nawaphon. He also accused the young monks of being communists. In due course, Kittivuḍḍho, previously acclaimed by some as a saint (*arahant*), was accused of behavior improper for a monk, and since then his reputation has suffered.

## *14. The cult of images and amulets*

1 A. B. Griswold, "What Is a Buddha Image?" *Thai Culture, New Series*, Fine Arts Department, Bangkok, No. 19, B. E. 2511 (1968), p. 3.

2 There is a range of other objects and vehicles that in principle are similar to amulets with regard to the power attributed to them. Square pieces of white cloth bearing sacred

*yantra* [designs that are composed of animal or human representations, geometrical shapes, and sacred letters usually in *khāūm (khmer)* language] are a case in point. In Thai, they are called *phā yan* (cloth with *yantra* designs). Another related variant are body tattoo designs. In this discussion, I shall leave these *phā yan* and tattoo designs out of account.

3   My research assistant invoked the example of the invisible effect of waves of electric current to help me understand.

4   I am not sure that this is an invariant rule. There are other famous lay personages whose images are to be seen in amulets. A good example is Komlūang Chumphon, the patron saint of the navy. I am uncertain whether monks did the *pluk sēk* for his amulets.

5   A famous occasion, when silver medallions bearing the images of the king and queen and of royal insignia were sacralized by a large number of famous and titled Bangkok monks, and distributed to the public, was the return of the king and queen home after traveling abroad on a goodwill mission. It was the then–prime minister, Sarit, a skilled propagandist of the theme that kingship was indissolubly linked with Buddhism, national consciousness, and anticommunism, who sponsored the making of the medallions. The medallions were not "sold" so much as "exchanged" for donations of money, and the sum collected was then presented to the king as a fund that he could use to sponsor a charitable or benevolent activity (*sadet phrarātcha kuson*). This is a characteristic manner in which money is collected today from the public in the name of or under the sponsorship of royalty.

6   See Andre Bareau, "The Superhuman Personality of the Buddha and Its Symbolism in the Mahaparinirvanasutra of the Dharmagupta," in J. M. Kitagawa and C. H. Long, eds., *Myth and Symbols* (Chicago: University of Chicago Press, 1971).

7   *The Questions of King Milinda*, trans. from the Pali by T. W. Rhys Davids, 2 parts (New York: Dover, 1963), Part 1, pp. 144–54.

8   Ananda K. Coomaraswamy, "The Origin of the Buddha Image," *Art Bulletin*, College Art Association of America, Vol. 9, No. 4, 1927, pp. 287–329.

9   See Camille Notton, trans., *P'ra Buddha Sihinga* (Bangkok: Bangkok Times Press, 1933).

10   Griswold, "What Is a Buddha Image?" p. 14.

11   Much more amplification than is provided by the simpleminded proposition that lay Buddhists "cognitively" know the Buddha is extinct, but "affectively" or "psychologically" desire and feel his presence. This dichotomy is arbitrarily imposed and theoretically untenable, as Gregory Bateson has demonstrated [see J. R. Ruesch and G. Bateson, *Communication* (New York: Norton, 1968)], and is of little help in understanding the orientations of Buddhists toward relics and images. Richard F. Gombrich [*Precept and Practice* (Oxford: Clarendon Press, 1971), p. 105] employs this dichotomy; he borrowed it from G. Obeyesekere, "The Buddhist Pantheon in Ceylon and Its Extensions," in Manning Nash, ed., *Anthropological Studies in Theravada Buddhism* (New Haven, Conn.: Yale University Southeast Asia Studies, 1966), pp. 1–26.

12   *The Vinayapiṭaka* (The book of discipline), 5 vols. (*Sacred Books of the Buddhists*, vols. 10–14, 20) (London: Oxford University Press, 1879–83), Vol. 1, Ch. 7.

13   For details, see Ananda Coomaraswamy, *Elements of Buddhist Iconography* (Cambridge, Mass.: Harvard University Press, 1935); also see his "Origin of the Buddha Image."

14   Coomaraswamy, *Elements of Buddhist Iconography*, p. 18.

15 Ibid., p. 24.

16 Ibid.

17 Paul Mus, *Barabudur* (Hanoi: Imprimerie d'Extreme Orient, 1935).

18 See, e.g.: (1) Louis de la Vallée Poussin, "Studies in Buddhist Dogma: The Three Bodies of a Buddha (*Trikaya*)," *Journal of the Royal Asiatic Society*, 1906, pp. 943–77; see also his "Notes sur les corps du Buddha," *Le Museon*, 1913, pp. 251–90. (2) Paul Mus, "Buddha Paré," *Bulletin de l'École Francaise D'Extrême-Orient*, Tome 28, Nos. 1–2, 1928, pp. 153–278. (3) Nagao Gadjin, "On the Theory of Buddha-Body," *Eastern Buddhist* (n.s.), No. 1, 1973, pp. 25–53.

19 D. L. Snellgrove, *Four Lamas of Dolpo, Tibetan Biographies* (Cambridge, Mass.: Harvard University Press, 1967), Vol. 1, p. 21. Snellgrove also describes another conception of buddhahood oriented in space: one for each of the four directions; one from the center; and a sixth, the *Powerbolt-Holder*, being sometimes added to represent "the supreme and essential unity of the more usual set of five" (ibid., p. 21).

20 See Frank Reynolds, "The Several Bodies of Buddha: Reflections on a Neglected Aspect of Theravāda Tradition," *History of Religions*, Vol. 16, No. 4 (The Mythic Imagination), May 1977, pp. 374–406, for a most helpful discussion and documentation of sources.

21 *Samyutta Nikāya* 3, 120; *Majjhima Nikāya* 3, 29.

22 See Chapter 4.

23 Reynolds discusses the fifteenth-century Sinhalese compendium called *Saddhar-maratna-karaya*, and a text associated with the "Yoga vacara clansmen" of Northern Thailand and Laos [a tradition also possibly represented in Sri Lanka, as evidenced by F. L. Woodward, *Manual of a Mystic, Being a Translation from the Pali and Sinhalese Work Entitled The Yogavachara's Manual* (London: Pali Text Society, 1916)].

## 15. An enumeration of historic and popular amulets

1 The primary source for this discussion is a Thai book: Thanakāūn Khongsat, *Kittikhun Phra Thēra Phra Khanāčān* (Bangkok: Suvanna Press, n.d.). There are literally dozens of similar works that can be purchased in Bangkok and elsewhere.

2 *Pārāmi*, in Pali, refers to the 10 virtues that a saint must develop on his way to buddhahood.

3 It is noteworthy that in this Thai book (and in similar literature, as well as in ordinary speech) the prefix *Lūang Phāū* (respected–honored–great father) is attached to the names of statues. This same prefix is attached to the names of famous elderly monks who figure as famous makers and/or sacralizers of amulets; it is also used to refer to certain guardian deities. Thus in certain contexts Buddha statues, guardian deities, and monks credited with sacred powers are brought together under one rubric.

4 This peculiar iconographic feature is alleged to be the result of King Līthai's misreading of the scriptures in his attempt to glean from them the true likeness of the Buddha. Some centuries later, another greater Buddhist revivalist and advocate of "pristine" Buddhism – King Mongkut – is reported to have searched the Pali canon for the true physical features of the Buddha and concluded that the Buddha had no hair. The Phra Sam Buddha Banni, now to be found on the front altar of the chapel royal, was cast in accordance with this reading.

For us, perhaps, the interesting point is that just as the Buddhists periodically search for the most correct form of the Pali canon, so are they motivated to produce images in the true likeness of the historical Buddha. Both searches are motivated by the underlying belief that the most authentic likeness is the "purest" and the most efficacious, for Theravāda Buddhism's true source and fountainhead of religion is the Buddha himself. In this the Buddhists present a striking contrast to the Hindus, whose myths and legends of origin and creation are attributed to acts of divinities. The Hindu theory of a cosmos of divine origin cannot logically generate a search for the true facts relating to the creator as a historical personage.

5  Their names were Bā In, Bā Phrom, Bā Phitsanu, Bā Rātchasang, and Bā Rātchakuson. "Bā" means teacher, as in "khrū bā." See Chapter 20 for a discussion of khrūbā as a type of holy man.

6  Quoted from *Wat Bovoranives Vihara* (Bangkok: Siva Phorn, 1972), pp. 27–8, the "official" history of the *wat* published in English.

7  See A. B. Griswold, *Towards a History of Sukhodaya Art* (Bangkok: Fine Arts Department, 1967), for a discussion of this king's contributions.

8  *Uparāt* is variously translated as "deputy king," "second king," "viceroy," etc. This office is part of the dual arrangement characteristic of the traditional polity, which had queens of the right and left, minister of the north and minister of the south, front palace and back palace, etc.

9  The former presiding image, now sitting at the back of Buddha Jinasīha, is also a famous image called Lūang Phāū Tō (the Great Royal Father). It is large and was brought to Bangkok from Phetchaburī Province (south of Bangkok), where it had been the principal image of Wat Sra Tapan. It too was floated down to Bangkok, but in several small sections on account of its size.

10  This flanking of Buddha Jinasīha by three princely abbots is paralleled by the flanking of the Emerald Buddha, the palladium of the country, by statues of the first two kings of the Čakkrī dynasty represented as *bodhisattva* figures.

11  See Charnvit Kasetsiri, *The Rise of Ayudhya* (Oxford: Oxford University Press, 1976), for a trenchant statement of this view. In any case, from my point of view, such acts are magnificent illustrations of the appropriation of past glories by succeeding kings.

12  This precedent was followed again by the present king and queen when they returned from a similar trip abroad. See Chapter 14.

13  Such as Somdet Phra Buddhaghosācārya (Māūm Rātchawong Carōēn, an aristocrat) of Wat Rakhang of Bangkok, Phrakhrū Wimon Kunakāūn (Suk) of Wat Pakklongmakkamtao, and Phrakhrū Niwattammakhan (Lūang Phāū Dōēm) of Wat Nong Po.

14  S. J. Tambiah, *World Conqueror and World Renouncer: A Study of Buddhism and Polity in Thailand against a Historical Background* (Cambridge: Cambridge University Press, 1976), pp. 97–8.

15  Rāma III, who ruled in the first half of the nineteenth century, introduced a third royal outfit for the dry season, to be in conformity with the idea of three seasons. Because this outfit is royal as opposed to monastic, the basic comparison still holds. On the Sinhalese tooth relic's symbolism and powers, see H. L. Seneviratne, whose imaginative and authoritative work [*Rituals of the Kandyan State* (Cambridge: Cambridge University Press, 1978)] surveys previous writings on the relic, including Hocart's, and carries the story to modern times.

16  The crowned Buddha in Mahāyāna conception is the Buddha-Cakravartin, about

whom Mus has written, especially with regard to the cult of Bodhgaya (see Paul Mus, "Le Buddha pare," *Bulletin de l'École Francaise Extrême-Orient*, Vol. 28, 1928, pp. 153–278). In a sense, then, the Emerald Buddha jewel itself oscillated in its Buddha manifestations as renouncer and as *cakkavattī*. I shall refer in this chapter to King Tilok of Chiengmai's alleged association with the Bodhgaya tradition.

The oscillation in the existence of the Emerald Buddha between renunciation and rulership is further attested by the fact that the *Vessantara Jātaka*, called in Thailand the *Mahāchāt*, the great story now elaborated into 13 chapters, is recited at the end of the rains retreat, actually at the time of changing the Emerald Buddha's clothes from a monk's garb to the full regalia of kingship. See G. E. Gerini, *The Thet Maha Chat Ceremony*, 2d ed. (orig. pub. 1892) (Bangkok: Siam Society, 1976).

17  See my *Buddhism and the Spirit Cults in Northeast Thailand* (Cambridge: Cambridge University Press, 1970), Ch. 10; also see Frank Reynolds, "The Holy Emerald Jewel," in Bardwell L. Smith, ed., *Religion and Legitimation of Power in Thailand, Laos, and Burma* (Chambersburg, Pa.: Anima Books, 1978), p. 184.

18  See N. A. Jayawickrama, *The Sheaf of Garlands of the Epochs of the Conqueror, Being a Translation of Jinākalamālipakaranam of the Ratanapanna Thera of Thailand* (London: Pali Text Society, 1968).

19  See Camille Notton, trans., *The Chronicle of the Emerald Buddha* (Bangkok: Bangkok Times Press, 1933). I shall hereafter for convenience call this the *Amarakaṭa*.

20  Robert Lingat's "Le Culte du Bouddha d'Emeraude," *Journal of the Siam Society*, Vol. 27, No. 1, 1934, pp. 9–38, has long been a classic on the sources and "history" of the image. Reynolds, "Holy Emerald Jewel," published recently, is the most comprehensive extant essay on sources and on the symbolism associated with the image.

21  An account of the *Phra Sihinga* statue will follow this.

22  The *Jinakālamāli* describes the emerald jewel as lying "within the same walled enclosure where the treasured jewel of the luminant gem is, amidst over 5,000 gems of the sevenfold varieties . . ." (Jayawickrama, *Sheaf of Garlands*, p. 141).

23  The gem in question is, of course, one of the 7 treasures of the *cakkavattī* as described in the famous Pali canonical *Mahāsudassana Sutta*.

24  In this context, it is relevant to note that King Aśoka was called in this same sense a *bala cakravartirāja* in the *Divyāvadāna*. The notion of lesser manifestations or incarnations of a higher celestial enduring entity is, as we have noted before, with respect to the many bodies of the Buddha, a quintessential Mahāyāna formulation. It is this logic that categorizes *cakkavatti* into four ranked types according to the material of their wheel (gold, silver, copper, iron), the number of the continents they rule over, and their manner of conquest. Aśoka is rated as belonging to the last type. [I owe this reference to Prof. John Strong, whose source is L. de la Vallée Poussin, trans., *L'Abhidharmakoça de Vasubandhu* 6 vols. (Paris: P. Guethner, 1923–31), Vol. 3, pp. 197–202.] See also Thomas Watters, *On Yuan Chwang's Travels in India 629–645 A.D.* (London: Royal Asiatic Society, 1904): Hiuen Tsiang reports the same fourfold classification of the wheel.

25  These other associations are documented and developed in Reynolds, "Holy Emerald Jewel," pp. 181–8.

26  According to Buddhist tradition, the Buddha is alleged to have prophesied that the religion would last for 5,000 years.

27  There is evidence of a holy jewel being venerated in Angkor as part of the *devarāja*

cult. Lingat, "Culte," is of the view that the Angkor jewel of King Sūryavarman's time in the early eleventh century is the same as the Emerald Buddha, which was in later times fashioned from the jewel. Reynolds, "Holy Emerald Jewel," is skeptical of this thesis; but he says that in any case the Emerald Buddha cult took the Angkor cult as its model and incorporated similar ideas of sacredness, guardianship, and divine kingship.

It would take us too far afield if we discussed here the character of the *devarāja* cult in Angkor. Some recent essays have questioned former views of "divine kingship" as practiced in Angkor. Hermann Kulke (*Devaraja Cult*, Data Paper No. 108, Southeast Asia Program, Cornell University, 1978) has argued from inscriptional evidence that it was the God Siva, before whom the king was consecrated, who was the god king, and the palladium of the kingdom was the movable image of the *linga* consecrated as *devarāja*. Again, I. W. Mabbett ("Devarāja," *Journal of Southeast Asian History*, Vol. 10, No. 2, 1969, pp. 202–23) argues that the *devarāja* cult in its earlier form was a cult for installing the god, who then moved with the king, giving legitimacy for his rule via the rituals performed by a *Brahmanical* priesthood.

28 Chiengmai and other Lānnā kingdoms, as I have stated before (Chapter 5), were chiefly influenced by the Mon-Lāva and Thai traditions. Siṅhala forest-monk influences were transmitted via Sokhodaya and Ayudhyā. Burmese influences became important after the conquest in 1578. See Donald K. Swearer and Sommai Premchit, "The Relationship between the Religious and Political Orders in Northern Thailand," in Bardwell Smith, ed., *Religion and Legitimation of Power in Thailand, Laos, and Burma* (Chambersburg, Pa.: Anima Books, 1978). Ratanapañña is of course writing in the sixteenth century.

29 In fact, the *Amarakaṭa* concludes by saying that "three images of the omniscient Lord are at the present time to be found" at Vientiane, the third being the historic Laotian image P'ra Bang. It is interesting that although the P'ra Bang was also brought to Bangkok by Rāma I, it was sent back to its Laotian home on account of the antipathy existing between it and the Emerald Buddha.

30 It is the same personage, Lūang Phāū Tō, who is today a central source of sacred power in a healing cult centered at Samnak Pū Sawan ("the center of heavenly grandfathers"). The cult center is at Thonburī, on the outskirts of the capital.

31 *Wat Bovoranives* (Bangkok: Siva Phorn, 1972).

32 See Richard A. O'Connor, "Urbanism and Religion: Community, Hierarchy and Sanctity in Urban Thai Buddhist Temples," Ph.D. dissertation, Cornell University, 1978, for a discussion of the events by which the capital became the predominant locus of sanctity. O'Connor provides information on the differentiation between monasteries of the center (*nai mūēng*) and monasteries outside the city (*nok mūēng*).

33 Wat In's concentration on the teaching and practice of meditation extends at least to the reign of Rāma I, when a meditation master, Čaokhun Āranyik, served as its abbot. (While čaokhun suggests an ecclesiastical title, āranyik indicates his forest-dweller affiliation.) In the reign of Rāma II, a resident monk, Phra Acharn Duang of the Order of Forest Monks, received a royal appointment as meditation teacher; he is also listed as having received candles from the king in the next reign (ibid.). Somdet Tō was a distinguished pupil of Čaokhun Āranyik. Thus we see here that the forest order at the edge of the city was recognized and incorporated into the overall *saṅgha* hierarchy, a pattern of domestication and distance being characteristic of the order's relation with the capital.

34 In this expression, two meanings are fused. *Rak* means "love" and also is the name

of the black lac tree (*ton rak*); similarly, *yom* is the name of the lord of death, Phra Yom (Yama) and is also the name of the Indian mahogany tree (*ton yom*). Thai ritual frequently exploits the metaphorical and metonymical properties of homonyms.

35 See Tambiah, *Buddhism and the Spirit Cults*, Ch. 18, for a description of Thai exorcism.

36 For confirmation of this observation, see Elizabeth Wray, Clare Rosenfeld, and Dorothy Bailey, *Ten Lives of the Buddha, Siamese Temple Paintings and Jātaka Tales* (New York and Tokyo: Weatherhill, 1972), pp. 135–7.

### 16. The "likeness" of the image to the original Buddha: the case of the Siṅhala Buddha

1 A. B. Griswold, *Dated Buddha Images of Northern Siam, Artibus Asiae*, Supplementum 16, Basel, 1957, p. 47.

2 Ibid., p. 46.

3 See N. A. Jayawickrama, *The Sheaf of Garlands of the Epochs of the Conqueror, Being a Translation of Jinākalamālipakaranam of the Ratanapanna Thera of Thailand* (London: Pali Text Society, 1968).

4 See Camille Notton, trans., *P'ra Buddha Sihinga* (Bangkok: Bangkok Times Press, 1933).

5 See Jayawickrama, *Sheaf of Garlands*, p. 122.

6 Notton, *P'ra Buddha Sihinga*.

7 In all probability, the same Mahābrahma who, according to the *Jinakālamāli*, also controlled Chīangrāi.

8 Jayawickrama, *Sheaf of Garlands*, p. 126.

9 Ibid., p. 120.

10 The dragon (*nāga*), who transforms himself into an apparition of the Buddha in the attitude of meditation, invites exegesis, which however I cannot undertake here. Note that *nāgas* play in certain Buddhist legends a benign and protective role and that they are associated with the watery elements. Further interpretive clues can be gleaned by considering in this context C. Duroiselle, "Upagutta et Māra," *Bulletin de l'École Francaise d'Extrême-Orient*, 1904, pp. 414–28. This essay deals with the famous legend of Māra (*Divyāvadāna*, ch. 36), the archenemy of the Buddha, who assumes the shape of the Buddha in a similar incident. The Burmese text *Lokapaññati* also reports the same story of the encounter between Māra and Upagutta, the monk.

11 Jayawickrama, *Sheaf of Garlands*, p. 127. Siridhamma is Nagara Śrī Dharmarāja, Jayanāda is Chaināt, Ayojjhā is Ayudhyā, Vajirapākāra is Kamphāēngphet, Nabbisi is Chiengmai, Jaṁrāya is Chīangrāi, and the islet is in Chīangsāēn.

12 S. J. Tambiah, "The Galactic Polity: The Structure of Traditional Kingdoms in Southeast Asia," in *Anthropology and the Climate of Opinion*, ed. Stanley Freed, *Annals of the New York Academy of Sciences*, vol. 293, 1977.

### 17. The process of sacralizing images and amulets: the transfer of power by monks

1 The *lak mūēang* is not unique to Bangkok. Many of the provincial cities of Thailand have city pillars and shrines associated with them. It is surmised that the pillar, which is

ideally, and usually, found in the center of each city's old city walls, was closely associated with the political authority of the *mūēang* (principality, satellite province), which in earlier times, especially before King Chulalongkorn's centralization program in the late nineteenth century, enjoyed greater autonomy than do the provinces of today. The guardian spirit associated with the pillar is believed to protect the locality or territory that constitutes the *mūēang*. Today the pillar shrine at Bangkok is considered to be the foremost in the country. For further information on the cult, see B. J. Terwiel, "The Origins and Meaning of the Thai 'City Pillar,'" *Journal of the Siam Society*, Vol. 66, Pt. 2, July 1976, pp. 159–71.

2 The five are Phra Sūēa Mūēang, Phra Song Mūēang, Phra Kanchaisī, Čao Phāū Phaukrong, and Čao Phāū Čethakup. Their statues are placed on an altar behind the pillar, and they are credited with power of protection, guardianship, and punishment.

3 It was called *phithī pluksēk rīan phra Lak Mūēang lae Phra Lak Mūēang Čamlāūng* (ceremony for sacralizing the medallions of the Lak Mūēang deities and the miniature Lak Mūēang).

4 The deities are given strong foods, and the court *brahman* (*rājaguru*) makes the offerings, as he does at the Siva and Vishnu temples; the relation between "Brahmanical" rites, spirit cults and Buddhist rites cannot be taken up here; however, it should be noted that they form an interrelated set, with different values being attached to them in a single religious field.

5 Aphisēk, equals Sanskrit *Abhiṣeka*, the rite of consecration; *phuthāphisēk*, equals Sanskrit *buddhābhiṣeka*.

6 This victory chant is an important component of *paritta* recitations, which confer protection and blessing [see K. E. Wells, *Thai Buddhism: Its Rites and Activities* (Bangkok: Police Printing Press, 1960)].

7 It is interesting that in Bangkok the chief feature in the activation of the Buddha statue is the transferring of vitality through chanting and meditation by monks, whereas in other places the actual opening of the eyes is given more prominence. I shall comment on this later in this chapter.

8 The casting of statues is done by the "lost wax" process, which has been long followed in South and Southeast Asia. The metal poured into the mould is an alloy that may include different proportions of gold, silver, bronze, brass, copper, lead, iron, etc., according to the affluence of the sponsors and donors.

9 The *paritta* chants are, as all students of Buddhism know, standardized, and their recitation is believed to give protection and blessing. An exegesis of the main *paritta* verses and the ritual employment of them has been given in my *Buddhism and the Spirit Cults in Northeast Thailand* (Cambridge: Cambridge University Press, 1970), Ch. 12. Since the contents of these verses, and the efficacy attributed to them and to the chanting itself as a performative utterance, have been dealt with in that book, and amplified in my essay "The Cosmological and Performative Significance of Healing through Meditation," in *Culture, Medicine and Psychiatry*, Vol. 1, 1977, pp. 97–132, I shall not deal with these issues here.

10 *Thai Buddhism*, pp. 122–30. I shall reproduce Wells's spellings of Thai and Pali words.

11 Ibid., pp. 126–9.

12 Buddha Udana Gatha.

13 The origin of this ceremony is found in India. There, when a man has purchased an

image, "it is his invariable practice to perform certain ceremonies called 'Pran Partishta' or the endowment of animation, by which he believes that its nature is changed from that of the mere materials of which it is formed and that it acquires not only life but supernatural powers." L. S. S. O'Malley, *Popular Hinduism* (New York: Macmillan, 1935), p. 26.

14 Adhemard Le Clere, *Cambodge Fêtes Civiles et Religieuses* (Paris: Imprimerie Nationale, 1916), pp. 144–50.

15 Ibid., p. 383.

16 I reproduce Le Clere's spelling of all Khmer and Pali terms.

17 Le Clere, *Cambodge Fêtes*, pp. 374–85.

18 The precise sources are cited in Ananda K. Coomaraswamy, *Medieval Sinhalese Art*, (New York: Pantheon, 1956; orig. pub. 1908), pp. 70–5, and in Richard Gombrich, "The Consecration of a Buddhist Image," *Journal of Asian Studies*, Vol. 26, No. 1, 1966, pp. 23–36.

19 Coomaraswamy, *Medieval Sinhalese Art*, p. 73.

20 Gombrich, "Consecration of a Buddhist Image," p. 36.

21 Ibid., p. 24.

22 So the officiant in the Sinhalese rite did not "kill" the bull and "tree," as Gombrich sees it, but "mute" and helped release the encompassing presence of the Buddha. The act of cutting a tree so that its milk flows is an eminently auspicious act, signifying the flow of plenty. The bull on whose horns the pot is smashed is also an auspicious host and insulator.

23 Diana L. Eck, *Darsan: Seeing the Divine Image in India* (Chambersburg, Pa.: Anima Books, 1981), pp. 5–6.

24 Stella Kramrisch, *The Hindu Temple*, 2 vols. (Calcutta: University of Calcutta Press, 1946), Vol. 2, p. 359.

### 18. Amulets blessed by contemporary forest saints

1 The point of the remark is made clear by this story from Burma. A German fighter pilot cruising over Mandalay during World War II gave chase to a flying *arahant*, but because his plane could not go fast enough, he lost him in the clouds. It is told in Sri Lanka that in olden times there were so many *arahants* cruising about in the sky that they darkened the sun and farmers had trouble growing their rice.

2 Sometimes a *wat* may sponsor the making and sacralizing of an amulet to elaborate the reputation and achievements of one of its own monks, especially its abbot.

3 If the lay sponsor does not have his or her insignia imprinted, they may substitute the *dhūtaṅga* monks' emblems, such as the umbrella, water kettle, begging bowl, etc.

4 Lūang Phāü Ling Dam (Honored Father Black Monkey) is a monk who is popular with the elite and powerful Bangkok circles today. He is an abbot of a *wat* outside Bangkok in Central Thailand; he teaches meditation to laymen and acts as counselor to them. It is rumored that the meditation rooms are connected to a loudspeaker system, over which this monk gives homilies and advice to his disciples, and that the *wat* owns a fleet of Mercedes-Benz cars, presumably donated by lay well-wishers.

5 My main source for this account is an article in the Thai magazine *Chumthāng Phra Khrūēang*, No. 14, June 1978, pp. 14–16. This article begins with the assertion that the source of the confidence and decision making, indeed bravery, of a Thai Buddhist is the protection he enjoys from *sing-saksit* ("power"). This power, which is a hidden force

(*amnāt ren-lap*) brings tasks undertaken to a successful conclusion. As all Thai Buddhists know, it is not connected with ghosts and corpses, but derives from people's taking refuge in monks and fastening their minds to them. The amulets (*rīan*) of Lūang Pū Wāēn are an example.

6  Note this double aspect of the Buddhist saints: They charge objects with mystic power because of their *iddhi*; they also radiate compassion and mercy (*mettā*) like the Bodhisattva.

7  W. A. R. Wood, *A History of Siam* (Bangkok: Chalermnit Bookshop, 1959).

8  Claude Lévi-Strauss, *The Savage Mind* (London: Wiedenfeld and Nicolson, 1966), p. 242. Levi-Strauss's discussion relates to the roles of the Australian *churinga* and the *Archives Nationales*.

9  Parādāūn Rattanakun, "The Life and Religious Career of Lūang Pū Wāēn," *Lān Phō*, Bangkok, Feb. 1977.

10  I have in mind here D. L. Snellgrove, *Four Lamas of Dolpo, Tibetan Biographies* (Cambridge, Mass.: Harvard University Press, 1967), Vol. 1, Introduction and Translations. For instance, the Lama Merit intellect resolves in the face of a smallpox epidemic: "I must now bring my strict seclusion to an end and do all that I can to succour these people." He then describes the blessings he gave, the purification rites he performed, and the "potent amulets" he distributed to the people who came for succour (pp. 115–16). The Lama Religious Protector Glorious and Good shows his prowess at "suppressing demons, performing oblations, hurling spells and other good methods" (p. 131).

11  Lūang Pū means "great or respected grandfather" and is a prefix by which all well-known and honored elderly monks are addressed by the public.

12  A *samnak song* is a monastic residence that has not the status of a *wat*. A *wat*, properly speaking, has a *bōt* in which ordination ceremonies can take place and which is marked off by *sīmā* stones.

13  There are two comments that can be made about the biographer's commentary. Firstly, it is noteworthy that he defines *saiyawēt* as a useful and positive applied knowledge for curing and alleviating suffering. It is not considered "magic" in the deprecatory sense of false technology and dubious traffic with the supernatural, as it was by seventeenth-century English orthodox theologians and rationalists [Keith Thomas, *Religion and the Decline of Magic* (New York: Scribner's, 1971)]. Secondly, the writer attributes to monks of the past positive service roles to the lay society at large. He cites as an "example" of a colonizer a famous monk (Phrakrū Khīhāūm), of whom I shall write in Ch. 20.

14  The Thai word *wēt* derives from the Sanskrit word *vedá*.

15  I note here that the monks not only accept the *phī* as phenomenal reality, just as the fifth-century text *Visuddhimagga* does, but also place them within the Buddhist cosmos in terms of the concepts of *karma*, rebirth, and so on. The demon in question, like the hungry ghosts (*preta*) who suffer from unrequited desires and limbo existence, is enabled by the monks' volition and good offices to be reborn.

16  Doi Māē Pang is a more recently established residence (*samnak song*) and is not to be confused with the older Wat Māē Pang, which is located at the foot of the mountain.

17  The mystery thus remains exquisitely ambiguous; Lūang Pū Wāēn himself has remained orthodox in not claiming *iddhi*.

18  As expounded by W. Y. Evans-Wenz, *The Tibetan Book of the Dead* (Oxford: Oxford University Press, 1960).

### 19. Saints on cosmic mountains

1 The *kathin* (*kaṭhina*) ceremony, whose canonical authority is found in the *Mahāvagga* (VII, 1), is a classical presentation of robes and other necessities by the laity to monks at the end of the rains retreat (*vassa*).

2 Kukrit Pramoj is said to be close to this sister and has his home in her compound in Bangkok. She is said to assist him financially, because his expenses incurred by various activities have not left him a rich man.

3 Khun Inthira is a daughter of the police general by a previous marriage.

4 Khun Nitiphat was trained as an engineer in England, where he joined the Free Thai movement. His wife, Inthira, also studied in England.

5 See William Skinner, *Leadership and Power in the Chinese Community of Thailand* (Ithaca, N.Y.: Cornell University Press, 1958); and R. J. Coughlin, *Double Identity: The Chinese in Modern Thailand* (Hong Kong: Hong Kong University Press, 1960).

6 This friend was a Chinese businessman (Mr. Yip Insol) involved in tin mining near Nakhon Phanom, and Mr. Lai transported the ore for him to Bangkok. Mr. Yip was already an agent for the bank in South Thailand, and when the bank wanted to open branches in the Northeast he acted as mediator between the bank and Mr. Lai.

7 In India and Ceylon, such a local official working for British mercantile banks used to be called a ''shroff.'' In Mr. Lai's case, if he guaranteed loans, he received 50% of the bank's interest profits.

8 This disciple, like a true devotee and retainer, accompanied the monk on his various visits to other parts of Thailand and has invited the monk to go with him to India to visit the holy sites.

9 These would be *phāpā* gifts, usually hung on a small tree or branch, to simulate the pristine monks' taking shreds of cloth hanging form trees in the forest or discarded in cemeteries to make them into robes.

10 See S. J. Tambiah, *World Conqueror and World Renouncer: A Study of Buddhism and Polity in Thailand against a Historical Background* (Cambridge: Cambridge University Press, 1976), pp. 456–7, for another description and comment.

11 The hermitage's development into a famous pilgrimage site has also resulted in plans for bringing electricity to it, and no doubt soon there will be donations of buildings of an urban design.

12 I give free translations from the Thai language.

13 This article, whose Thai title is ''Singsaksit lae Aphinihān,'' appeared in *Khwan Ruen*, Vol. 166, No. 10, 1978, pp. 124–9. The magazine is a very popular women's journal.

14 A monastic residence without the consecrated boundary stones (*sima*) and without the *bōt* (chapel) in which ordination rites into monkhood are held.

15 The informant is not actually claiming Lūang Phāu was himself in a previous incarnation Prince Vessantara (the Buddha's incarnation before his last). But true to Buddhist legendary traditions, the geography of sacred places in India (*Jambudīpa*) is transferred to the Southeast Asian Buddhist countries.

The biographer is also following an important hagiological tradition. The Buddha, for instance, claimed in the *Mahāsudassana Sutta* that he had been born seven times in succession, the last time as Cakkavatti Mahasudassana, in the city of Kusinārā. (In the *Mahāparinibbāna*

*Sutta*, the Buddha stated the wish that he be cremated at Kusinārā with all the honors due a cakkavatti, because it was at Kusinārā that he had ruled as Mahāsudassana.) Apart from the Buddha's legendary career, the careers of other famous disciples and saints of course contain similar episodes.

16 The actual Thai expressions used by our monk informant were: *aphinihān* (supranormal power), *yū yong khongkaphan* (invulnerability), and *mettā niyom* (make attractive).

17 While the monk was telling us this, an old woman who was listening interposed that a *rīan* of Lūang Phāū had protected her from injury when she fell from a bus in Samut Prakān, a suburb of Bangkok.

### 20. A commentary on millennial Buddhism in Thailand and Burma

1 I shall limit myself to these two countries because, apart from the fact that they form an arena of shared experience, they – or rather, the writings about them – provide the ample information I require for a sustained analysis. For millennial Buddhism in Sri Lanka, see K. Malalgoda, "Millennialism in Relation to Buddhism," *Comparative Studies in Society and History*, Vol. 12, No. 4, Oct. 1970, pp. 424–41.

2 See Yoneo Ishii, "A Note on Buddhist Millenarian Revolts in Northeastern Siam," *Journal of Southeast Asian Studies*, Vol. 6, No. 2, 1975, pp. 121–6.

3 Besides Ishii above, see C. F. Keyes, "Millennialism, Theravāda Buddhism, and Thai Society," *Journal of Asian Studies*, Vol. 36, No. 2, Feb. 1977, pp. 283–302.

4 Ishii, "Note on Buddhist Millenarian Revolts," p. 126.

5 Ibid.

6 I would not go so far as Keyes does to separate "personal" concerns, whether they relate to individual suffering or salvation, from "social" concerns. For one thing, individual "sufferings" are also the concerns of families, neighbors, and village communities (as attested by curing rites, mortuary rites, and collective-merit transfers). Even more importantly, it is my central thesis that these holy men are always foci of cults, clients, and congregations. The men of charisma are surrounded by an inner core of disciples and an outer penumbra of lay followers for whom they conduct rites and moral discourses.

7 Charnvit Kasetsiri, *The Rise of Ayudhya, A History of Siam in the Fourteenth and Fifteenth Centuries* (Oxford: Oxford University Press, 1976), p. 5.

8 I take this gloss from Donald K. Swearer, "The Monk as Prophet and Priest," unpublished essay.

9 On Buddhadasa, see D. K. Swearer, *Buddhism in Transition* (Philadelphia: Westminster Press, 1970); B. Buddhadasa, *Toward the Truth*, ed. Donald K. Swearer (Philadelphia: Westminster Press, 1971).

10 See C. F. Keyes, "Political Crisis and Militant Buddhism in Contemporary Thailand," in Bardwell Smith, ed., *Religion and Legitimation of Power in Thailand, Laos and Burma* (Chambersburg, Pa.: Anima Books, 1978).

11 According to W. Geiger [*Culture of Ceylon in Medieval Times* (Wiesbaden: Otto Harrassowitz, 1960), p. 184] *yati*, meaning ascetic, was "an honorific name" for a *bhikkhu* in medieval Sri Lanka.

12 Kasetsiri, *Rise of Ayudhya*, p. 5.

13 In Northeast Thailand, as for instance in a village studied by me in the early sixties, there was a cult of *čao phāū phākhāo*, an "ancestor" dressed in white, who was treated as

the guardian of the *wat*. The *čao phāū phākhāo* was said to be the spirit (*phī*) of a pious man who had observed the 10 precepts of the novice and ministered to the needs of the monks. In Buddhist terms, the white clothes are the insignia of a pious layman (*upāsaka*). See my *Buddhism and the Spirit Cults in Northeast Thailand* (Cambridge: Cambridge University Press, 1970), Ch. 15.

14 See Theodore Stern, "Ariya and the Golden Book: A Millenarian Buddhist Sect Among the Karen," *Journal of Asian Studies*, Vol. 27, No. 1, Nov. 1967, pp. 297–327. The *bu kho*, like some of the other holy men described earlier, seem to be no definable unitary types. Thus Stern writes: ". . . *Bu khos* differ in condition: they may be single or wedded, young or old, in solitary office or with female associate. They are limited by their character of priesthood and by knowledge of the ancient chants; they are often described as sorcerers as well as prophets . . . and they are often clad in ascetic garments and are set well apart from their followers. . . . Pagodas appear repeatedly as a focus of worship, sometimes with *zayats* (open buildings for the congregation) oriented to them. As early as 1832 and repeatedly in sects after 1860, the name of Metteya is associated with the chief object of worship" (p. 305).

15 Kasetsiri, *Rise of Ayudhya*, p. 5.

16 E. Michael Mendelson, "A Messianic Buddhist Association in Upper Burma," *Bulletin of the School of Oriental and African Studies*, University of London, Vol. 24, 1961, pp. 560–80. See also his "The King of the Weaving Mountain," *Royal Central Asian Journal*, Vol. 48, 1961, pp. 229–37; and "Observations on a Tour in a region of Mount Popa, Central Burma," *France-Asie*, Vol. 19, No. 179, 1963, pp. 780–807.

17 Mendelson, "Messianic Buddhist Association," p. 566.

18 Ibid., p. 569.

19 Stern, "Ariya and the Golden Book," pp. 297–327. Stern principally examines two millennial movements among the Karen of the Burma — Thailand borders: the Leke sect, which came into being around 1860; and the Telakhon sect, which formed a little later. Both movements appeared in circumstances where the external advocates of change were the missionaries of the American Protestant denominations, and which involved "religious syncretism of different degrees between native Karen and Theravāda Buddhist faiths" (p. 297). The reactions of the two movements to the antagonistic Baptist missionaries were different, one favorable, the other antagonistic. I shall only describe features of the Telakhon sect, which Stern describes more amply than the Leke.

20 The time of Stern's research and writing the essay is the late 1960s.

21 The Telakhon fused the Buddhist Ariya with the "white brother" of the Karen myth and maintained they were in possession of the Golden Book, which contained the knowledge that gave power and prosperity to Europeans today.

22 Stern, "Ariya and the Golden Book," p. 314. The Karen *buk kho* here appears analogous to the Sayagyi, the resident official, referred to by Mendelson earlier.

23 Ibid., p. 315.

24 Ibid.

25 Ibid., p. 325.

26 C. F. Keyes, "Death of Two Buddhist Saints in Thailand," *Journal of the American Academy of Religion, Thematic Studies*, Vol. 48, Nos. 3 and 4, p. 149. The Northern Thai word *nakbun* for Sīwichai can be glossed as "one experienced in merit," i.e., one especially capable of performing meritorious acts. It also brings to mind the word *nābun*,

"field of merit," which is of course a classical Buddhist concept, the Pali word being *puññakkhetta* and the Sanskrit being *puṇyakṣetra*.

27 My main source for the account of Sīwichai is Swearer, "Monk as Prophet and Priest." It is supplemented by Keyes, "Death of Two Buddhist Saints," and "Millennialism"; and Virginia Thompson, *Thailand and the New Siam* (New York: Macmillan, 1941), pp. 642–3.

Both Swearer and Keyes refer to the biographies devoted to this saint. Keyes uses a major biography of Sīwichai published in 1956 by Saṅghā Suphūpā, an editor of a religious magazine in North Thailand; another very brief biography he refers to is a 1963 pamphlet by the Northern Thai historian, folklorist, and publisher, Sangūan Chōtisukharat. Swearer has drawn attention to a biography of Sīwichai by Fā Wongmahā, serialized in the journal *Thān Tawan* (Weekly alms) and also to at least two biographies written in Yuan (Northern Thai). (*Thān Tawan* usually means "royal sunshade" or "sunflower.")

28 The Northern Thai polities of Lamphūn, Lampāng, Chiengmai, etc., have a long history going back to times coeval with Sukhodaya. The Burmese exercised control over the Chiengmai region from the mid-sixteenth to the end of the eighteenth centuries as their satellite principalities. See Chapter 5.

29 See Tej Bunnag, *The Provincial Administration of Siam from 1892 to 1915: The Ministry of the Interior under Prince Damrong Rajanubhab* (London: Oxford University Press, 1977); for the implications of extending the *saṅgha* hierarchy, see C. F. Keyes, "Buddhism and National Integration," *Journal of Asian Studies*, Vol. 30, No. 3, 1971, pp. 551–68.

30 Thompson, *Thailand*, p. 642.

31 Keyes, "Death of Two Buddhist Saints," p. 150.

32 See ibid., pp. 169–71. Keyes compares the rites held for Sīwichai to those held for Acharn Mun, which we have described earlier (Chapter 6). Although there were discernible differences in the tones of the two sets of rites, we cannot overlook the common link they bear to the classical Buddhist mortuary rites surrounding the deaths of both the Buddha and the Cakkavatti, including the distribution of relics and the subsequent production of shrines, amulets, and other "reminders."

33 For the implications of this disestablishment, see, in particular, D. E. Smith, *Religion and Politics in Burma* (Princeton, N.J.: Princeton University Press, 1965).

34 In these circumstances, with the British forbidding local officials and headmen from engaging in politics, the monastery that freely recruited monks provided a sanctuary from which to attack the colonial authorities. Rural monks could lead associations that were simultaneously "religious" and "political" in their objectives.

35 For information on, and interpretation of, the economic circumstances – such as the break-up of the tenets of the traditional "moral economy"; and the increasing number of absentee landlords; peasant indebtedness to Chettiyar moneylenders and foreclosures on mortgages; the increasingly commercialized landlord–tenant relations; and the forcible collection of capitation and *thathameda* taxes by the British, especially when there was a general depression of the international paddy market – that contributed to the "subsistence crisis" of the peasantry, see James C. Scott, *The Moral Economy of the Peasant, Rebellion and Subsistence in Southeast Asia* (New Haven, Conn.: Yale University Press, 1976); and Albert D. Moscotti, *British Policy and the Nationalist Movement in Burma: 1917–1937*, Asian Studies at Hawaii, No. 12 (Honolulu: University Press of Hawaii, 1974). The

British official inquiry into grievances and the course of the rebellion is to be found in India Office, Great Britain, *Report on the Rebellion in Burma up to 3 May 1931 and Communique Issued by the Government of Burma 19 May 1931*, Cmd 3900, 1931. See also *The Origin and Causes of the Burma Rebellion 1930–1932* (Rangoon: Government of Burma, 1934).

36 Scott, *Moral Economy*, p. 149.

37 Moscotti, *British Policy*, has interesting information on the vagaries of the pricing policy. There was a fall in rice prices during the world depression. The British were able to hold down the domestic price of rice by maintaining a sizable control over the processing plants. Earlier in 1918 the government of India had established a Rice Control Board to stabilize prices in the face of soaring world market prices. The differential between prices paid by the millers and the money received from foreign markets went to diminish India's floating debt and to benefit India as a whole; later, the profits were diverted to Burma to support various projects, particularly road building. In other words, the peasant rice sector shouldered a major part of the colonial expenditure on the country as a whole.

38 Aside from the sources already cited, see, in particular, E. Sarkisyanz, *Buddhist Backgrounds of the Burmese Revolution* (The Hague: Martinus Nijhoff, 1965), and R. L. Solomon, "Saya San and the Burmese Rebellion," *Modern Asian Studies*, Vol. 3, No. 3, 1969, pp. 209–23.

39 Sarkisyanz (*Buddhist Backgrounds*, pp. 160–1) has this to say: "Yet this Burmese 'Peasant War' was not motivated by economic grievances (confined to Lower Burma) alone: It was also propelled by militant folk Buddhism . . . with strong ingredients of pre-Buddhist Animist Lore. . . . It was a phenomenon of what anthropologists call 'nativistic' response against overwhelming impacts of an alien civilization that has been dissolving traditional society up to its economic foundations and challenging the world conception of Burmese folk Buddhism." Sarkisyanz, following through in this vein, sees the revolt as a "desperate attempt to restore the old symbols of cosmic 'social harmony.'" Solomon ("Saya San") remarks that to call the rebellion "nativistic" is inappropriate because it was an authentic expression of traditional values that continued into colonial times.

40 He donned the royal rainments prescribed by ancient usage: They included ruby earrings ("crown of victory"), gem-studded slippers, gem encrusted "sword of victory," royal whisk, and the white umbrella.

41 See Smith, *Religion and Politics*, p. 108; Sarkisyanz, *Buddhist Backgrounds*, p. 162.

42 See Moscotti, *British Policy*, p. 207.

43 Cited from *Origin and Causes of the Burma Rebellion* by Scott, *Moral Economy*, p. 153.

44 Just as the *garuda* sign was an antidote to snake poison, so would it neutralize the "poison" of bullets and spears (Solomon, "Saya San").

45 An eyewitness account by C. V. Warren, *Burmese Interlude* (London: n.p., 1937), cited by Sarkisyanz, *Buddhist Backgrounds*, p. 162.

46 I am indebted to Jamey Rosenfield for providing me with this excerpt from India Office, *Report on the Rebellion*.

47 I rely on certain authoritative essays by authors who have done their homework and consulted relevant sources in the Thai language. The following two essays in English cite

the relevant sources, the second being more ample: Ishii, "Note on Buddhist Millenarian Revolts"; and Keyes, "Millennialism."

48   Both incidents are in Ishii, "Note on Buddhist Millenarian Revolts," pp. 121, 123.

49   See Keyes, "Millennialism."

50   Bunnag, *Provincial Administration of Siam.*

51   For instance, in Roiet there circulated a prediction of a terrible wind that would rage for seven days and nights; the remedial actions recommended were the burning of a certain type of wood and the planting of lemon grass at the stairways to houses. Unmarried women were urged to consummate their unions. Special efficacy was attributed to the sprinkling of sacralized water by monks.

52   This is a low-level ecclesiastical title.

53   Of the 400 rebels captured at the critical engagement, which took place soon after the attack of Khemmarat, only one of the major leaders taken was a monk. This monk, together with the three ranking monks previously reprimanded by the Siamese officials, was ordered to remain in monkhood for life on pain of being jailed. The official Thai *sangha*, whose highest-ranking monk in Monthon Īsān was Phra Yānarakkhit, was subsequently called upon to investigate the causes of the uprising, and submitted the finding that the poverty of the region served to stimulate unrest among the population.

54   My comments relate to Chapter 7, "Esoteric Buddhism: A Religion of Chiliastic Expectations," in Melford Spiro, *Buddhism and Society: A Great Tradition and its Burmese Vicissitudes* (New York: Harper & Row, 1970).

55   Ibid., p. 164.

56   Ibid., p. 166. Also, in a preceding discussion on meditation on pp. 48–51, Spiro refers to the five supranormal powers (*abhiññā*), such as clairvoyance, clairaudience, remembrance of one's past and knowledge of one's future rebirths, the power to know the thoughts of others, and the powers of levitation. He however declares with a certainty that is lacking in the canonical writings – we have surveyed earlier the canonical equivocations and disputations, and the problematic treatment in the *Visuddhimagga* – that the *jhāna* states "are not to be cathected."

After much ado about the un-Buddhist character of the *weikza*, Spiro treats us to this glorious piece of psychological reductionism (psychologists apparently have the license to unite what anthropologists divide): Although doctrinally the state of *nibbāna* and *weikzahood* are poles apart, yet psychologically these beliefs are all but identical, for after all absence of desire is analogous to the instant satisfaction of all desire!

57   Once again, I am mystified by Spiro's assertion that "peasant beliefs in a monarch to come relate more to the Burmese notion of a Future King than to the Buddhist notion of a Universal Emperor" (p. 173). Spiro spins another quandary when he goes out of his way to say that alchemical practices in Burma "in the first instance have no relationship to Buddhism."

58   Ibid., pp. 169–70.

59   On Spiro's evidence, two of the total of four monks in Yeighi, the location of his intensive fieldwork, indulged in this form of meditation, and many layman of all categories – the educated, elite, and less-educated urban and rural folk – dabbled in alchemy.

60   Ibid., p. 172.

61   Some standard treatments are the works of Norman Cohn, e.g., *The Pursuit of the*

*Millennium* (New York: Harper & Row, Torchbooks, 1961); Sylvia Thrupp, ed., *Millennial Dreams in Action, Comparative Studies in Society and History*, Supplement II (The Hague: Mouton, 1962); Bryan Wilson, "Millennialism in Comparative Perspective," *Comparative Studies in Society and History*, Vol. 6, 1963–4, pp. 94–114. The rich literature on the cargo cults of New Guinea by Worsley, Lawrence, Burridge, and others is well known. See Kenelm Burridge, *Mambu, A Melanesian Millennium* (London: Methuen, 1960); Peter Lawrence, *Road Belong Cargo* (Melbourne: Melbourne University Press, 1967); Peter Worsley, *The Trumpet Shall Sound* (London: McGibbon and Kee, 1957); Robert N. Bellah, *Beyond Belief* (New York: Harper & Row, 1970), pp. 279–87; and David Aberle, "A Note on Deprivation Theory as Applied to Millenarian and Other Cult Movements," in Thrupp, *Millennial Dreams*, pp. 109–14.

62 Keyes, "Millennialism."

63 Although the notion of "power" can be stretched to all relations of dominance, inequality, etc., I am following here Keyes's own distinction between what he considers to be "political" and "economic."

64 I note, in passing, that the holy men of Syria in the fifth and sixth centuries also "achieved" their saintly powers by deliberately placing themselves on the mountains, beating out their virtues "like cold metal work, from a lifetime of asceticism," and played their role as mediators in rural communities by virtue of their status as noncommitted "strangers." See Peter Brown, "The Rise and Function of the Holy Man in Late Antiquity," *Journal of Roman Studies*, Vol. 61, 1971, pp. 80–101.

65 See E. Troeltsch, *The Social Teachings of the Christian Churches* (New York: Free Press, 1949), Vol. 1, pp. 239–40. I am indebted to Ilana Silber for drawing my attention to this discussion.

66 See Chapter 9, in which the organization features of forest hermitages and their networks were scrutinized.

### 21. The sources of charismatic leadership: Max Weber revisited

1 Wolfgang J. Mommsen, *The Age of Bureaucracy: Perspectives on the Political Sociology of Max Weber* (New York: Harper & Row, Torchbooks, 1974), p. 79. Of course, Weber crucially differed from Nietzsche's excessive conviction about the historic mission of great men irrespective of the interests of the masses.

2 Carl J. Friedrich, "Political Leadership and the Problem of the Charismatic Power," *Journal of Politics*, Vol. 23, No. 1, Feb. 1961, pp. 3–24.

3 This point comes through in this commentary by two Weberian scholars: "Ethical prophecy applies politically transcendent standards to the powers-that-be, which thus appear sinful and depraved and destined to ultimate destruction, while exemplary prophecy endeavors to achieve its impact not by preaching but by exemplary conduct. Exemplary prophets try to win adherents and followers by elevating their own conduct above the ordinary." Guenther Roth and Wolfgang Schluchter, *Max Weber's Vision of History, Ethics and Methods* (Berkeley: University of California Press, 1979).

4 Max Weber, *Economy and Society*, 3 vols., ed. Guenther Roth and Claus Wittich (New York: Bedminster Press, 1968), Vol. 1, p. 241.

5 David Little, "Max Weber and the Comparative Study of Religious Ethics," *Journal of Religious Ethics*, Vol. 2, No. 2, 1974, pp. 5–41.

6 The Weberian typology of action orientations into rational, traditional, and affectual

modes is well known, and no detailed commentary is required here. Weber subdivided rational action into two types: *Zweckrationalität*, usually translated "formal (or instrumental) rationality," is translated by Little as "this-worldly relativistic form of consequentialist reasoning." *"Wertrationalität,"* usually translated as "substantive rationality," is translated by Little as "absolutist rationality." Traditional action (besides the type that is automatic reaction to habitual stimuli) implies as normative orientation "the belief in the everyday routine as an inviolable norm of conduct." Little, in his essay "Max Weber," gives a fine-grained analysis of this typology, and brings out the multiple meanings, ambiguities, and dualities embodied in Weber's discussion.

7  See *From Max Weber*, trans. H. H. Gerth and C. W. Mills (New York: Oxford University Press, 1958), p. 281.

8  "A new charismatic annunciation and promise, such as is found in the Kerygma of Jesus or Buddha, apparently wrenches the established patterns and opens the way for the rationalization process to take place." Little, "Max Weber," p. 24.

9  See Weber, *Economy and Society*, Vol. 1, Pt. 2, Ch. 6.

10  The words "religious charisma" may sound redundant; but this wording is intended to demarcate the phenomena under consideration from secular charisma, such as that purported to attach to political and economic leadership and success in societies that define politics and economics as secular activities divorced from religion.

11  Max Weber, *On Charisma and Institution Building, Selected Papers*, ed. with an introduction by S. N. Eisenstadt (Chicago: University of Chicago Press, 1968). See Eisenstadt's illuminating introduction, p. xxx.

12  Weber, *Economy and Society*, Vol. 1, p. 244. Elsewhere, he has stated that it is a fate of charisma "to recede with the development of permanent institutional structures" (ibid., Vol. 3, p. 1133).

13  Besides sources already cited, see Max Weber, "The Sociology of Charismatic Authority," in *From Max Weber: Essays in Sociology*, trans. and ed. H. H. Gerth and C. Wright Mills (New York: Oxford University Press, 1946). Also see Weber, "The Social Psychology of Religion," in *From Max Weber*.

14  This central insight has, however, opened itself to such objections as the one voiced by Mommsen that Weber's "functionalist value-neutral approach" would tend to conflate the stable maintenance of power or domination with consent and legitimation and that in any case it could not deal with "illegitimate" domination. See Mommsen, *Age of Bureaucracy*, Ch. 4, for a good critique of this value-free stance.

15  See Weber, *Economy and Society*, Vol. 2, pp. 1139–41, for a discussion of office charisma.

16  See Weber, *Economy and Society*, Vol. 2, p. 1139.

17  Ibid., p. 1114.

18  Ibid., p. 1112.

19  In a footnote to his judgment I have reported above, Weber cites references to Sohm's works, *Kirchenrecht*, I and II (1892) and *Outlines of Church History* (1887).

20  James Luther Adams, *On Being Religiously: Selected Essays in Religion and Society* (Boston: Beacon Press, 1976); see especially Ch. 13, "Law and the Religious Spirit: Rudolf Sohm."

21  Ibid., p. 195.

22  Weber, *Economy and Society*, Vol. 2, p. 1112.

23 Ibid., p. 1113.

24 The bias stemming from the Christian precedent shows unabashedly in this sentence: "Instead of reverence for customs that are ancient and hence sacred, it (charisma) enforces the inner subjection to the unprecedented and absolutely unique and therefore Divine" (ibid., p. 1117).

25 Edward Shils, "Charisma," in *International Encyclopaedia of the Social Sciences*, Vol. 2, p. 386.

26 Shils, "Charisma, Order and Status," *American Sociological Review*, Vol. 30, 1965, pp. 199–213, points out that this central power has been conceived as God, the ruling power or creator of the universe, and it might be a "fundamental principle or principles, a law or laws governing the universe, the underlying driving force of the universe. . .''

27 E. H. Kantorowicz, *The King's Two Bodies: A Study in Medieval Political Theory* (Princeton, N.J.: Princeton University Press, 1957).

28 What is meant by this is that the charismatic Buddhist saints come and go sporadically, their followings dissipate after their deaths, and they are not the basis of an enduring institutionalized cult.

### 22. The objectification of charisma and the fetishism of objects

1 I am referring to Ludwig Wittgenstein, "Remarks on Frazer's *Golden Bough*," trans. A. C. Miles and Rush Rhees, *Human World*, No. 3 (May 1971), pp. 28–41.

2 Marcel Mauss, *A General Theory of Magic*, trans. Robert Brain (London: Routledge & Kegan Paul, 1972).

3 R. H. Codrington, *The Melanesians: Studies in their Anthropology and Folklore* (Oxford: Clarendon Press, 1891).

4 Mauss, *General Theory*, p. 111.

5 Ibid., p. 117.

6 Ibid., pp. 120–1.

7 Marcel Mauss, *The Gift* (New York: Norton, 1976).

8 Ibid., p. 43.

9 The immortal formulation by the Maori of the "spirit of the thing given" is worth repeated citation: "Now this *taonga* I received from him is the spirit (*hau*) of the *taonga* I received from you and which I passed on to him. The *taonga* which I receive on account of the *taonga* that came from you, I must return to you" (ibid., p. 9).

10 Marshall Sahlins, "The Spirit of the Gift," in his *Stone Age Economics* (Chicago: Aldine, 1972), Ch. 4, pp. 149–83.

11 Ibid., p. 31.

12 Marshall Sahlins, *Culture and Practical Reason* (Chicago: University of Chicago Press, 1976). On this issue, also see Jean Baudrillard, *The Mirror of Production* (St. Louis: Telos Press, 1975).

13 In Hindu theory, an ascetic who observes *tapas* husbands his sexual energy and transmutes it into *siddhi* (supranormal spiritual powers) can dissipate the latter, for they are ultimately constrained by the physical capacity to produce semen. Thus there is a preoccupation with controlled use. In the Buddhist case, as elucidated in the *Visuddhimagga*, the path of meditation and purification is not predicated on such an emphatic

and obsessive chemistry of transforming sexual energy. The control of the senses and fewness of wishes, which include celibacy, allows for progress upward from gross materiality to transcendent states. However, in Tibetan Vajrayāna Buddhist meditation, *yogic* ideas of seminal fluid are found. See David L. Snellgrove, *Four Lamas of Dolpo, Tibetan Biographies*, Vol. 1 (Cambridge, Mass.: Harvard University Press, 1967), pp. 25–7.

14 I borrow this phrase from Fernando H. Cardoso, "Associated-Dependent Development: Theoretical and Practical Implications," in Alfred Stepan, ed., *Authoritarian Brazil, Origins, Policies and Future* (New Haven, Conn.: Yale University Press, 1973).

15 *From Max Weber*, p. 245.

16 For instance, T. W. Adorno et al., *The Authoritarian Personality* (New York: Harper, 1950); Norman Cohn, *The Pursuit of the Millennium*, 2d ed. (New York: Harper & Row, Torchbooks, 1961); Leon Festinger, Henry W. Riecken, and Stanley Schachter, *When Prophecy Fails* (Minneapolis: University of Minnesota Press, 1956); and Anthony F. Wallace, "Revitalization Movements," *American Anthropologist*, Vol. 58, No. 2, 1956, pp. 264–81.

17 The established *sangha* of titled monks, with its seats in the historic, prosperous *wat*, has long cooperated with the government; the Council of Elders (*mahāthērasamākhom*) has been moribund and inactive. The missionary programs (*thammathūt*), by which monks sought to participate in national development, active in the sixties and seventies, are virtually dead today. And some monks have even discredited themselves by charges of corruption and of associating with violence.

For relevant details, see S. Suksamran, *Political Buddhism in Southeast Asia* (New York: St. Martin's Press, 1977); C. F. Keyes, "Political Crisis and Militant Buddhism in Contemporary Thailand," in Bardwell L. Smith, ed., *Religion and Legitimation of Power in Thailand, Laos and Burma* (Chambersburg, Pa.: Anima Books, 1978); and S. J. Tambiah, *World Conqueror and World Renouncer: A Study of Buddhism and Polity in Thailand against a Historical Background* (Cambridge: Cambridge University Press, 1976).

18 The following books in English should give the reader a fair idea of the contemporary political and economic situation in Thailand. The list is not exhaustive. David Morell and Chai-anan Samudavanija, *Political Conflict in Thailand, Reform, Reaction, and Revolution* (Cambridge, Mass.: Oelgeschlager, Gunn and Hain, 1981); E. T. Flood, *The United States and the Military Coup in Thailand: A Background Study* (Washington, D.C.: Indochina Resource Center, 1976); Norman Jacobs, *Modernization Without Development: Thailand as an Asian Case Study* (New York: Praeger, 1971); Clark Neher, ed., *Modern Thai Politics: From Village to Nation* (Cambridge, Mass.: Schenkman, 1976); and Ross Prizzia and Narong Sinsawasdi, *Thailand: Student Activism and Political Change* (Bangkok: Allied Printers, 1974).

19 I am here referring to the farmers' federations and the protests staged in Bangkok by disaffected farmers from the North.

20 This is a principal argument in Theda Skocpol, *State and Social Revolutions, A Comparative Analysis of France, Russia and China* (New York: Cambridge University Press, 1979).

# Index

# Index

# Index

phenomenon, 7–8; *see also* Mahāyāna Buddhism; millennial Buddhism; Theravāda Buddhism
Buddhist schools, 116–18
Bunčan, Thāo, 313–14
*bunkhun,* 337
Bunnag, Tej, 311
Bunrap, Khunying, 276
bureaucratic organizations, 326, 328, 329, 331
Burks, Arthur, 4
Burma, 3, 26, 118; biographies of monks in, 111–12; division of *saṅgha* in, 165; forest-monk tradition in, 3, 4, 61–6; millennial Buddhism in, 6, 293–320; popular saints in, 24–5; reform sects in, 53, 54
Burns, Douglas M., 137–8, 139

*cakkavatti* (king of kings; universal monarch), 11, 77, 297, 300, 302, 306, 313, 315, 316, 318, 319, 387n32; four ranked types of, 378n24; lineage of, 117; seven jewels of, 349n7 *see also cakravartin*
*cakkavatti*-Buddha relationship, 130
Čakkrī dynasty, 71, 75, 212, 213, 214, 215, 239, 244, 377n10
*cakravartin* (wheel-rolling universal king), 294, 332, *see also cakkavatti*
Cāmadevī, princess, 123, 297; queen, 296
*Cāmadevīvaṁsa* (chronicle), 121, 232
Cambodia, 345
Campaka Monastery, 62
canonical *suttas,* 130
canonical texts, 2, 15; relation to life of Buddha, 115
Čao Phāū (personification of shrine of the pillar), 244
Čao Phāū Čethakup (deity), 381n2
*čao phāū phākhāo* (cult), 385–6n13
Čao Phāū Phaukrong (deity), 381n2
Čao Prasātthāūng, king, 313
Čao Sām Phrayā National Museum, 222
capital city(ies): triadic structure in, 72–5
capitalism, 340, 341
Capps, Donald, 115
Carrithers, Michael, 58, 59, 60, 89–90
Cathar heresy, 129
Catholic Church, 129, 318, 327, 328
Caturmahārājikadeva (deities), 350n38
Čēdī Lūang (*wat*), 162
celebration(s): in consecration of Buddha statue (*chalāūng phra*), 246; *see also* festivals
celibacy, 393n13
center-periphery relations, 3, 221, 222, 240–1, 333
*cetiya:* mound erected over ashes, 20; (reminders), 201–3

Chā, Acharn, 136–8, 154, 334
Chandaka, 113
chants, chanting, 146, 243; at consecration of Buddha statue, 245–6, 247, 248, 249–51, 254, 260; sacred words (*sēk khāthā*) over amulets, 199–200
characterology, 39
charisma, 3, 6, 27, 76, 136, 265, 335, 344; defined, 322, 329–30; of forest saints, 77, 185, 260; and the gift, 337–8; objectification of, 5, 335–47; routinization of, 326, 328–9, 330, 332, 339; as source of leadership, 16, 321–2 (*see also* charismatic leaders, leadership); sources of, 325–7, 328, 329–30; typology of, 329–32; understandable as social experience, 338, 339
charismatic leaders, leadership, 311, 312, 313, 319, 339; sources of, 321–34
charms, 139
charnel grounds, 71
charnel-ground-dweller's practice, 34, 36, 37
Charnvit Kasetsiri, 69–70, 121, 295, 296
Chīangdāo, cave, 271
Chiengmai (Lān Nā), 66, 67, 70, 172, 218; Acharn Mun in, 90, 91, 96–101
Chomanan, Gen. Kriangsak, 260–1
Chonlasit, Police Col. Phan, 261
Chōtisukharat, Sangūan, 387n27
Christian missionaries, 112, 301, 386n19
Christian monasteries, 150
Christianity, 126, 322, 323, 325, 327, 328, 332; asceticism in, 324
Chulalongkorn, king, 71, 157, 158, 160, 161–2, 166, 212, 219, 221, 222, 232, 266, 276, 303; centralization program, 381n1; distribution of amulets, 213; made Prince Pavaret head of *saṅgha,* 370n18; monasteries founded by, 370n17; ordained sons of, 368n4; ordination of, 368n3; patrimonial provincial administration, 311–12
Chulalongkorn University, 188
Chumphon, Kromlūang, 375n4
Chumpot, prince, 276
Chumpot, princess, 276
Chuvanon, Mrs. Noon, 108
Cittabhavana College, 374n12
Cittagutta, elder, 32
clairaudience, 26, 100, 389n56
clairvoyance, 26, 94, 100, 389n56
Codrington, R. H.: *Melanesians, The,* 338
commerce and religion, 274–5, 278
commodities, fetishism of, 6, 341
communications system, 263
Communist Party, 260
communists, 190, 345
community-development projects, 96, 185

398

# Index

comparison (mental state), 41
compassion for humanity (*mettā*), 45, 88, 89,
124, 324, 342; Acharn Mun, 135–6; as basis
of saintliness, 305; universal, 128, 330, 335,
347; *see also* cosmic love; loving-kindness
concentration (*samādhi*), 29, 30, 38, 41, 70,
139, 160, 179, 181–2, 332, 351n8; access
and absorption, 42; developing, 152–3; *iddhi*
powers deriving from, 45, 46, 47; levels of,
42, 50, 93; methods of, 149; path of, 39–42,
44; psychosomatic possibilities of, 373n15; in
sacralization process, 245, 246, 260; wisdom
and, 151–2
consciousness (*sati*), 181
consciousness (*viññāṇa*), 11–12, 152; cosmic,
338; levels of, 50; map of, parallels map of
cosmos, 30–1, 38, 48, 49–52, 140
consecration rite, 254–5, 381n5; of Buddha
statue (*Buddhābhiṣeka*), 245–54
contemplation, 44, 136–8, 149, 151; as basis
of saintliness, 305; of death, 39–41; *see also*
concentration (*samādhi*); meditation (*vipassanādhura*) (vocation)
Conze, Edward, 38, 352n11
coolness (*sītala*), 31
Coomaraswamy, Ananda K., 201
cosmic love (*mettā*), 77
cosmography: Wat Phūthok, 280, 218–3
cosmology, 299–300, 316, 318, 336;
meditative states and, 49–52
cosmos: map of mental consciousness parallels,
38, 48, 49–52, 140; mythology re, 161
Council of Rajagṛha, 22
Council of Sarvāstivādin elders, 113
councils, 118, 119
creation stories, 51, 119, 120, 377n4
cremation, crematoriums, 71, 165
cremation rites, 131, 188–9, 199, 366n14
crisis, collective, 128–9
Čüan, Acharn: hermitage of, 274–5, 276,
277–83, 284, 293
*Cūlavaṁsa* chronicle, 57, 255, 364n25
*Cullavagga*, 18–19, 113, 116, 359n15
Cūlodara (*nāga*–king), 122
cult of amulets, 76, 139, 154, 169, 185,
195–207; forest saints in, 258–73;
intensification of, 164, 258, 259–60
cult of images, 195–207
cult of saints, 21, 24–5, 45, 126–7, 155, 187
*Cult of the Saints, The* (Brown), 8
cultic ritual, 307
cults, 63, 294, 296, 298–300, 310, 314, 316,
385–6n13; centered on holy men, 319–20,
transformed into militant movements, 316–17

*dāgaba*, 200

Dalai Lama, 332
Dambadēni Katikāvata, 57
Damrong, prince, 68–9, 162, 212, 232, 303,
312
*daṇḍābhiñña*, 110
*darśan* (seeing), 149, 256–7
"dawn of deliverance" (*muttodaya*), 97
"day procession" (*Daval Perahera*), 74
death, contemplation of, 39–41
decaying corpses (*asubbhas*), 39
deities, 138, 245
deliverance (goal), 84, 85, 129, absolute, 99;
of Acharn Mun, 98
delusion (*moha*), 51
Demiéville, Paul, 363n24
Democratic Party (Thailand), 276
detached action, 335
detachment, 39–41, 43, 128
*deva loka*, 50
Devadatta, 19
Devānampiya Tissa, king, 122
*devarāja* cult, 378–9n27
devices (*kasiṇas*), 39, 41–2, 46
*Dhamma(s)* (morality/duty), 2, 11, 41, 77, 86,
87, 89, 94, 98, 101, 102, 151, 200;
biography of Buddha integral part of, 113,
119; brought into conformity with empirical
science, 161; codification of, 120; custodianship of, 206; different bodies of,
360n21; employed in sacralization of
amulets, 199; instruction in, 104; Kāśyapa
codifier of, 17; mental, 152–3; not found
in books, 138; reminders of, 202; as
scripture, 329; teaching of, 169, 185
*Dhammapatana* project, 373n5
*Dhammacakka* (Wheel of *Dhamma*) level, 97
*Dhammacakkappavattana–sutta* (setting in mo-
tion the wheel of truth), 30, 104
Dhamacedi, Chaokhun, 102, 108
Dhammacetiya, Chao Khun, 101
*Dhamma-dāna*, 54
*dhammadīpa* of Lanka, 118
*Dhamma-Kāya* (Body of Law), 205, 206
*Dhammapada Commentary*, 20
Dhammarakkhita (guru), 215
Dhammaratana, Miripanna, 111
Dhammasudhi, Phra Sobhuna: *Insight
Meditation*, 373n12
Dharma of mind (*nāma*), 152
Dharmaguptakas: *Vinaya* of, 116
Dharmaraksa, 22
Dharmapāla, Anagārika, 59
*dhūtaṅga* monks, 54, 84–5, 96, 128, 135;
as Buddhist missionaries, 94; communities
of, 91–3; Nong Phue forest hermitage
center for, 105–6; tantric association, 138;

# Index

wild beasts and, 86–7, 88–90
*dhūtaṅga* practices, 131, 137, 212, 331; forest hermitages, 147, 288; Thammayut sect, 160, 161, 163; Wat Phūthok, 280
*dhūtaṅga* tradition: of meditation, 175–6
*Dīghanikāya*, 116
Dīpaṁkara, 121
*Dīpavaṁsa* chronicle, 54, 364n25, n30
"direct knowledge," 48, 49
disciples of Buddha, 15–16, 21–2, 113, 117, 122, 360n22; hierarchy of, 99; *iddhi* powers of, 48–9
disciplinary code (*vinaya*): offenses in, 303
disciplinary practices: personal and collective import of, 316–17; Thammayut sect, 160, 161
disciplinary rules, 18–19, 73, 99, 119, 150, 174–5; codification of, 118; forest hermitage of Maha Boowa, 144, 148; Mahānikāi and Thammayut sects, 164
discipline, 3, 330; *arahant* and, 15
divine abidings, 39
"divine ear element," 47
*Divyāvadāna*, 363n23
Diyawadana Nilame (the), 74
doctrinal reminders (*dhammacetiya*), 202, 203; *see also* reminders doctrine of presence, 204–5
*dōēn thudong*, 32; *see also* pilgrimage (*kān dōēn thudong*)
Doi Māē Pang, 271, 272
domination, 391n14; charismatic, 325, 327
Duang, Phra Acharn, 379n33
Dumont, Louis, 7
Duroiselle, Charles, 24, 25
*Duṭṭhagāmaṇī (Dutugamunu) (king)*, 25, 123
Dwaya (sect), 63
dwelling (resource of monastic life), 18, 34, 36–7

Earth-Lotus, 203
ecclesiastical hierarchy, 2, 189; *see also saṅgha* (order of monks)
ecclesiastical positions, titled, 163
ecstasy, 323–4
education, 168, 190, 329; role of monks in elementary, 161–2, 185 *see also* monastic education
effort (*viriya*), 148–9, 181
eight precepts (the), 31
Eightfold Path, 351n8
Eisenstadt, S. N., 6, 326
*Ekottarāgama*, 21
Emerald Buddha, 5, 75, 210, 214–19, 233, 377n10, 378n16; cult, 379n27; palladium of Thailand, 214, 239; travels of, 217–19, 241

energy, vigor, 31, 41; kinds of, 181–2
enlightenment, 38, 41, 207, 367n6; Buddha's achievement of, 116, 119, 203, 205, 231, 237, 254, 255, 360n20; paths to, 30
equanimity, 44, 45, 46, 50, 51
eschatological Buddhism, 315–16
esoteric Buddhism, 63, 314–17
*Etadaggavagga*, 21
Eusebius Pamphili: *Ecclesiastical History*, 126
evil action: modes of, 15
evil eye, 256
exchange, 339–44
eye faculty, 31, 49
eyes, kinds of, 182

Fa-Hian, 73
faith (*saddhā*), 41, 182
Fān, Lūang Pū, 333
Fan, Phra Acharn, 197
Fāng, Phra Čao, 212
feelings (*vedanā*), 152
Ferguson, J. P., 16, 26, 163
festivals, 146, 164, 174–5, 250, 283; *kathin*, 279–80
fetishism, 6; of objects, 335–47
"field of merit": (*nābun*, 386–7n26) (*puññakkhetta*), 16, 54, 386–7n26
Fifth Buddhist Council, 63, 65
Filliozat, J., 363n24
Finot, Louis, 116, 117, 363n23, n24
First Council, 15, 16, 17
"fluency of discernment," 26–7
folk asceticism, 59, 60, 90
followers: and sources of charisma, 225–7
food (resource of monastic life), 18, 39, 92–3; forest monks, 85, 103–4
food-restraint (practice), 104
footprints (*pāduka*) (symbol), 201, 202
foreign disciples, 173; *see also* Western disciples
forest hermitages, 27, 185, 259, 333; administrative organization, 145; branch, 134, 137, 334; and cult of amulets, 258, 259; daily routine, 103–4, 137, 138, 146–8; different from urban, 175–6; discipline in, 138; established by disciples of Acharn Mun, 133, 134; evolving into establishment organizations, 163–4, 165; of Maha Boowa, 142, 143–50, 172; represent Thammayut sect in Northeast, 189–90; sponsored by *saṅgha*, 163–4; supported by Bangkok, 155; system of, 310, 334; in tradition of Acharn Mun, 142; transformed into militant movements, 318–19
forest saints, 164, 274–89; amulets blessed by, 258–73; charismatic field of, 332–4; meditation system, 346–7; potential for

# Index

exploitation by political authorities, 334;
transfer of power through amulets, 335, 336,
342, 359n10; *see also arahant(s);*
forest-dwelling monks (*araññavāsin*)
forest teachers, 133, 139; acclaimed as
*arahant*, 154–5; in periphery-center dialectic,
184–5; propagation of lay meditation,
168–82; in service of political authorities,
167; supported by highest circles, 189; *see
also* meditation masters
forest-dweller's monasteries, at city's edge, 71
forest-dweller's practice, 34, 36; sanctioned
by Buddha, 17
forest-dwelling monks (*araññavāsin*), 2–4, 6,
16, 17, 27, 57–8, 168, 278; ascetic practice
hallmark of, 33; cells of disciples, 333–4;
civilizing role of, 69–70, 77, 141, 185,
393n17; contact with *saṅgha* hierarchy,
359n6; as countervailing agent to religious
establishment, 77; duality; meditation
path/teaching, 137, 139–41, 149, 258–9;
in hermitage of Maha Boowa, 145;
institutionalized networks created by, 60, 65,
71; lay adulation of, 3, 168–9, 344–5;
mystical power of, 338; national prominence
of, 259–60; open to political manipulation,
190; politicization of, 96, 163–4; position
relative to *saṅgha*, 163–4, 259–60;
relationship with kings, 64, 65; relationship
with society, 77; relationship with Thai
dynastic politics, 66–9; sacralization of
amulets, 209, 221, 258; Siṅhala sect, 233;
Sri Lanka, 57, 58–61; tradition developed
by, 131; triadic relation with king and
establishment *saṅgha*, 72–5; vocation of
(*araññavāsī/vanavāsī*), 53, 54, 57–8, 72,
136–9, 165
forest-monk tradition, 53–77, 131, 306;
cosmological dimensions of, 284; paradigms
for, 72–7
founding stories, 297
Four Great Events, 201
Four Noble Truths, 30, 41, 102, 130, 139,
203, 360n19
Fourth Council, 123
Francis of Assisi, St., 89
Frauwallner, Erich, 116–18, 363n23, n24
Frazer, Sir James: *Golden Bough,* 337
Fun, Acharn, 138–9, 155, 259
funerary rites: for laity, 145; *see also* cremation
rites; mortuary rites

*gaing(s)* (volatile movements and cults), 63,
273, 296, 314–15, 316, 318; in Burma,
298–300; organization of, 310
Galvihāra inscription, 57
Ganavipāla, Phrakhrū Phiphat, 172–6

*ganinānse,* 355n13
"gapless wanderer" (*sapadāna-cārin*), 33, 37
Gedigē Vihāre (shrine), 74
General Council of Buddhist Associations, 308
ghosts (*preta*), 100, 138, 180, 269; *see also*
spirit world
gift, 340
gift giving (*dāna*), 169, 178
gifts to monasteries, 62–3
*Golden Book,* 301, 386n21
Gombrich, Richard F., 25–6, 255, 256,
375n11, 382n22
Good Law, 23
Gosling, David, 373n2
gratification: path of, 336
Great Man (*mahā-puruṣa*), 17
greed (*rāga*), 51
Griswold, A. B., 75, 195–6, 202, 203–4,
230, 238, 239
guerilla action, 310, 334; *see also* insurgency
forces
Gunawardana, R. A. L. H., 55
Gunupamacariya, Phra Upali, 87, 96–7

hagiographical tradition, 21, 112, 113, 128,
140; *see also* biographical traditions,
Buddhist
hagiography, 3, 4, 5; Christian, 114; common
elements in, 124, 125, 127; stereotyped
themes in, 23–4, 132, 190; *see also*
biography
hagiological tradition, 384n15
hagiology, 265; of forest saints, 85, 86, 284
Hardy, Spence: *Manual of Buddhism, A,* 20
Haripuñjaya (city and kingdom), 123
hate (*dosa*), 51
Haṭhayoga, 39
*hau* (reciprocity), 340
"having been one, he becomes many," 46–7
healing, 179, 256, 295
healing cult, 379n30
heart (*čai*), 151, 153
"heaven-hell bridge" (Wat Phūthok), 282, 283
hermitages, 6; Sri Lanka, 58, 59; *see also* forest
hermitages; *wat*
Himi, Tāpasa, 60–1
Hīnayāna Buddhism, 21
Hindu concepts, 338–9; ascetic in, 392n13
Hindu literature, 364n25
Hindus, 377n4
historiography, Buddhist, 114, 115–16,
117–18, 119
Hnyetwin (sect), 63
holy men (*chīphākhāo; khrū-bā-āčān*), 60–70,
295, 296, 302; agents of Buddhist polities,
357n37; cities, kingdoms founded by, 294,
296–8; as civilizing agents, 293–4, 297–8;

401

# Index

cults centered on, 319–20; millennial expectations around, 318–19; as political insurgents, 294, 298; variety of, 294–6; *see also* forest saints
homeless (*anagārika*) man, 12
house-dwelling (*agārika*) man, 12
house-to-house-seeker's practice, 33, 35, 37
human beings (*manussa*), 12; differential capacities and efforts of, 181–2
hypnosis, 352n11

iconography, 201, 203
*iddhi* powers, 44, 85, 104, 245, 338–9; acquisition of, 45–9, 50; Lūang Pū Wāēn, 272–3; of *phū wisēt* 294–5
Ignatius of Antioch, 126
image(s), 5, 152; line of authenticated, 230, 254
immaterial and formless states, 39
impermanence, 139, 152
In, Bā, 377n5
In, Phrakhrū, 313
indexical icons, 5, 293, 336, 348n3; amulets as, 262–3
indexical symbol, 4–5, 132; biography of Acharn Mun as, 190–1; Buddha image as, 204
India, 7, 18, 118, 129; Rice Control Board, 388n37
indicative or prescribed reminders (*uddesika; uddesikacetiya*), 201, 202–3; *see also* reminders
individual: role of, in history, 321
Indology, 6, 7
Indra, 50, 51, 215, 216, 217
Indrakhila (cult), 216
initiate(s) (*sekkha*), 12
insight (*prajñā: paññā*), 12, 17, 26, 29, 30; methods of, 149; path of, 47; *see also* wisdom
insight (*vipassanā*), 90; path of, 42–4
insight, higher (*pattapatisambhidā*), 14
insight (*vipassanā*) meditation, 41, 160
"insight practice," 139
insurgency forces, 275, 345
intentionality, 181, 200
"internal sitting" (*nang thāng nai*), 245
Inthira, Khun, 276
Ishii, Yoneo, 294, 313, 314
Islam, 323
Island Hermitage (Sri Lanka), 58–9

Jakobson, Roman, 4
Jambudvīpa, 129, 131
*Jātaka*, 104, 114; accounts, 113; collection, Pali school, 117; tales, 60, 300, 362n23; tradition, 59

Jayatilaka, D. B., 70
Jespersen, J. O. H., 4
Jetavana fraternity, 73
Jetavana Grove, 122
Jetavana Nikāya, 55, 56
Jethādhirāja, king, 219
jewel(s) (*ratanam*), 11–12; wheel or gem, 348n7
"jewel discourse" (*Ratanasuttam*), 11–12
*jhāna* concentration, 42
*jhāna* consciousness, 39
*jhāna* levels, 46, 47, 50, 51, 70, 315, 389n56; mastery of, 42; in Wat Phūthok cosmography, 281, 282–3
*Jinakālamālī* (chronicle), 68, 75, 114, 119, 120–3, 214–15, 218, 231–2, 233, 235, 236–7, 240, 297, 364n25
Jinavaṁsa, Kadavādduve, 59–60
Judaeo-Christian charisma (type), 330
Judaism, 322, 323
*Jūjaka* amulets, 226
Juvanon, Khun Mae Noom, 103

Kālidāsa: *Raghuvaṁśa*, 113
*Kaliṅgabodhi Jātaka*, 201–2
*Kalyāṇamitta* ("the good friend"), 41
*kāma loka*, 50, 51
Kammar, Phra Acharn, 266
Kandyan Kingdom, 57, 58, 73–4
*Kanhājāli* amulets, 226
Kaniṣka (ruler), 113
Kankaw, Nai Kamduang, 82
Kantorowicz, E. H., 330
Kapilavathu (monk), 142–3
Kapilavatthu (place), 122
Karen Telakhon millennial sect, 300–2
*karma*, 11, 148
Kassapa, 121, 130–1
Kāśyapa school, 362n23
*kathin*: gift to Wat Phūthok, 274–5, 276, 277–80; merit-making presentation, 279–80; *see also* merit-making ceremonies
Kauśāmbi (place), 23, 117
Kautanya, 16
Keyes, Charles F., 112, 295, 303, 305, 307, 311, 312, 313, 316, 387n32, 390n63
Khamanāmool, Mrs., 109
Khambong, monastery, 83
*Khandhaka*, 363n24
*khandhas*, 41
Khane, Lūang Phāū, 228
Khantayakamo, Phra Acharn Singh, 267
Khao, Phra, 98
Khao Yai (Great Mountains), 87
Khaophansā (festival), 283
*khattiyas* (warriors), 19
*Khīao mū thūēan* amulets, 227

402

# Index

# Index

magical practices (*saiyawēt*), 267, 272–3
Maha Boowa, Acharn, 4, 138, 158; Bangkok
connections, 155–9, 184, 189; biography of
Mun, 81, 104, 111, 112, 128, 143–4,
154–5, 189, 293, 365n10; as disciple and
biographer, 133, 139–41; as exemplary
forest-monk, 142–53; forest hermitage of,
142, 143–50, 172; rational/tantric strains in,
306; teaching, instruction, 147–9, 150–3
Mahā Dhammarāja, Somdet Phra, 211
Mahābrahma, king, 235, 236
Mahāčulālongkāūn (monks' university), 170,
184, 186, 373n5
Mahāčulālongkāūn Monks' University Fund,
178
Mahākassapa (Mahā Kāśyapa), 16–17, 21, 22,
57, 356n25, 360n22
Mahā-Kātyāyana, 22
Mahāmakut Monks' University, 81, 156, 159,
373n5
Mahāmakut Press, 158, 189
Mahāmakuṭa Rājavidyālaya Foundation, 156,
189
Mahāmakuṭarājavidyālaya, 161
Mahā-Maudgalyāyana, 22
Mahāmāyā, queen, 121
Mahā-mitta, elder, 32–3
Mahāmoggallāna, 21, 48–9, 122
*mahā-nāyaka* (monk leader), 57
Mahānikāi (Mahānikāya) sect, 5, 71, 73–4,
138, 158, 174, 183, 268, 368n5, n6;
geographical divisions of, 370n19; monasteries of, 370n20; Pramunuchit abbot of,
370n18; propagation of lay meditation by,
168–82; rivalry with Thammayut sect, 154,
160, 163, 164, 165, 166–7, 186–91;
village- and town-dwelling, 259; Wat Mahāthāt
foremost monastery of, 246
*mahāpaññā* (great wisdom), 104; *see also*
wisdom (*paññā*)
*Mahāparinibbāna Sutta*, 20, 116, 130, 200,
206, 361n30, 365n10, 384–5n15
Mahāprajāpati (foster mother of Buddha),
359n15
*Mahāsamaya Sutta*, 104
*mahāsāmi* (head of *saṅgha*), 57
Mahāsāmi (monk), 75
Mahāsammata, 117, 120, 121
*mahāsati* (great-mindfulness), 104
*mahā-sthavira* (monk), 57
*Mahāsudassana Sutta*, 11, 216, 378n23,
384n15
*Mahāvagga*, 18, 113, 116
*Mahāvaṁsa* (chronicle), 12, 25, 28–9, 54,
114, 119–20, 121, 123, 255, 364n25, n30
*Mahāvastu*, 115, 117, 362n23
Mahāvihāra fraternity, 38, 73

Mahāvihāra (Great Monastery) Nikāya, 28–9,
55, 56, 57, 351n2
Mahāvihāra tradition, 356n34
Mahāwirong, Somdet, 374n11
Mahawithudarama Taik (monastery), 64
Mahāyāna Buddhism, 17, 19, 21, 23, 24, 206;
Buddha image in, 203, 231; doctrine of
presence in, 204–5
Maheikdi *gaing*, 298–9
Mahinda, 122
Mahinda IV, 56
Mahīśāsaka: *Vinaya* of, 116
Mahiyangana (place), 120
Mahodara (*nāga*-king), 122
Maine, Sir Henry, 339
Maitreya Buddha, 17, 22, 23, 50, 298, 299,
306
*Majjhima Nikāya*, 12–13
Mākhabūchā (festival), 146, 250, 283
Mālai, Phra, 359n5
Malalgoda, K., 111–12
malaria, 92, 105, 106
*Mālaya Sutta*, 359n5
Malaysia, 156
Maliyadeva, 25
Malwatta fraternity, 74
Malwatta monastery, 57–8, 74
man (*purisa*), 12
Man, Ācān, 112; *see also* Mun, Phra Acharn
Man, Ong, 313–14; *see also* Mun, Phra
Acharn
*mana*, 338–41
*maṇḍala*, 207
Mandalay, 64
Maṅgaladebamuni, Čaokhun, 170
Mangalapabitra image, 196
*Maṅgalatthadīpanī* (commentary), 66
Mangalyayana, 363n24
Mango Grove, 74–5
Mango Grove Monastery, 66, 69
Mangrāi, king, 67
Mani Mekhala (goddess), 216
*Maṇijoti* (resplendent jewel), 215
Mañjuśrī, 23
*Manorathapūraṇī*, 21
*mantra*, 139, 199
*Manual of a Mystic, The*, 38, 70, 90
*Manual of Buddhism, A* (Hardy), 20
Māra, 24, 130, 380n10
Maramma (Upper Burma) Saṅgha, 62
Martaban, 66
martyr(s), martyrology, 125–7
Marx, Karl, 6, 340–1
mass media, 170
*Matichon* (newspaper), 260
Maudgalyāyana, 116, *see also* Moggallāna
Mauss, Marcel, 6, 338–41; *The Gift*, 339

# Index

# Index

159–60, 163, 165, 305, 368n5; monasteries founded by, 370n17; ordained sons of, 368n4; presided at Wat Bovonniwet, 369n11
monkeys, 89
monks: collaboration with government, 161–3, 184–5, 186, 190, 393n17; degenerate, 227; education of, 112 (*see also* monastic education); place of origin, 188; political power/threat of, 167, 186–7; radical, political, 308; ranking of spiritual achievement, 12–13; relation with laity, 37, 54; relation with rulers, 370n22; religious specialization, 135–9, 160, 221, 358n4, 372n10; role in enlightening people, 161–2; sacralization of amulets, 208, 213, 219–23; temporary, 173, 181; traditional, 25–6; transfer of power through sacralization, 243–57, 359n10; vocations, 16, 53–4; *see also dhūtaṅga* monks; forest-dwelling monks (*āraññavāsin*); village- and town-dwelling monks (*gāmavāsī/nagaravāsī*)
Mon-Lāva tradition, 379n28
monuments, 127
moral causality (doctrine), 115
morality (*sīla*), 101, 102–3, 124, 150–1, 351n8
More, Sir Thomas, 124
mortification of the flesh (*tapas*), 17–18
mortuary rites, 71, 131, 387n32
Mount Meru, 50
Mount Sineru, 48, 49
Mount Yugandhara, 48
Muchalinda (serpent), 201
*mūēang* (principality), 381n1
Mūlasarvāstivādin: *Vinaya* of, 116, 117
Mūlasarvāstivādin school, 362n23, 363n24
*Mūlasāsana* (chronicle), 75
Mun, Phra Acharn, 81–110, 112, 149, 162, 163, 175, 184, 189, 222, 260, 295, 306–7; Acharn Čūan disciple of, 280; achievement of *arahantship*, 96–100; biography of, 128–31, 132, 154–5, 159, 190–1, 284, 293, 365n10; contrasted with Sīwachai, 305; created cells of disciples at nodal points, 134–5, 258; cult around relics of, 366n7; death of, 90, 91; deeds credited to, 100–1; disciples of, 86, 88, 90–3, 94–5, 98, 100, 101, 102, 103–4, 105–8, 110, 129, 132–41, 148, 258–9; duality: meditation/teaching, 137, 149, 258–9; fatal illness and mortuary rites, 107–10; individual guidance of disciples by 93, 98, 106; interpretation of biography of, in Buddha paradigm, 114–15, 120–1, 131, 132; and Lūang Phāū Pāng discipleship, 286; Lūang Pū Waēn's association with, 265, 268–9, 271, 272; Maha Boowa as disciple and biographer, 139–41,

143; as model, 98; peripatetic wanderings, 85, 90–107, 128–9, 133–4, 258; queried Buddha re images, 204; quintessential forest saint, 333; relationship with mother, 95–6; rites for, 387n32; teaching, instruction, 101–3, 104, 105, 106, 107, 128, 133
*munimuni*, 12
*munis*, 12
Mus, Paul, 7, 205, 378n16
*mutta-muttaka*, 54
Mutukan, Co. Pin, 186, 371n22
mystic powers (*iddhi*), 16, 32–3; available through meditation, 38; available to *arahants*, 20–1; (*saksit*), 338; *see also iddhi* powers; supranormal (supramundane) powers (*abhiññā*)
mystical visions, 139
mysticism, 324
myths, 7

*nāga*–kings, 94, 122
Nagara order, 68
Nagara Śrī Dharmarāja, 233, 235, 236
*nāgas*, 380n10
Nāgasena (monk), 14–15, 201, 215, 216, 217
Nāi Sai, 266
Nāi Sōphā, 266
Nakhon Phanom (province), 190
Namone (village), 103, 104, 105
Ñāṇagambhīra (monk), 68
Ñāṇamoli, Bhikkhu, 28, 31, 45
Ñāṇārāma (monk), 59–60
Nandopananda (royal *Nāga*), 49
Nāng Beng, 266
Nāng Chan, 82
Nāng Kāēo, 266
*Nāng Kwak* amulets, 225
Nārāi, king, 211, 311
Nārēsūan, king, 211; amulets, 261–3
National Museum of Bangkok, 239
nationalism, 374n12
*navandanna* caste, 355n21
Nawaphon (nationalist movement), 347n12
*nāyakas* (chief monk), 58
"neither-perception-nor-nonperception," 44, 50
New Year (festival), 283
*nibbāna*, 13, 22, 23, 29, 45, 153, 206, 389n56; attaining, 42, 43, 44; goal of meditation, 151; as signless state, 360n21; *see also nirvāṇa*
*Nidāna Bra Buddhasihiṅga*, 121
*Nidānakathā*, 115, 117, 363n24, 365n10
*Niddesa*, 12
Nietzsche, F., 321
*nikāyas* (sects, fraternities), 17, 55
*Nirmāṇa-Kāya* (buddhas as humans), 205
*nirodha* (cessation), 44, 45

# Index

# Index

# Index

346-7; Wat Phūthok as icon of, 281
puritanical sects, 63
Pūrṇa-Maitrāyanīputra, 22
Putlawithinayok (Bun), Phra, 213

*Questions of King Milinda, The*, 13-14, 20, 30, 201

*Raghuvaṃśa* (Kālidāsa), 113
Rahula, W., 54
Rāhula (son of Buddha), 22, 23, 113
rain making, 24, 214
rains-retreat (*vassa*), 74
Rājagaha (Rājagṛha), 19, 117
*Rājavaṃsa*, 120
Rajavaramuni, Chaokhun, 367n13
Rājavinayabara, Čaokhun, 369n13
*Rak yom* amulets, 223, 228
Rāma I, king, 75, 214, 239, 379n29, n33
Rāma II, king, 157, 212, 379n33
Rāma III, king, 158, 368n2, 377n15
Rāma IV (Mongkut), king, 212; *see also* Mongkut, king
Rāma V, king, 209, 212-13
Rāma IX, king, 239-40
Rāmañña Nikāya (sect), 59, 60
Rāmēsūan, king, 211, 212
Ramitanondh, Shalardchai, 163
Rāmkhamhāēng, king, 66, 233, 235
Rammaṇa, 70
Rammaṇadesa (place), 75
*Ratanabimbavaṃsa* (chronicle), 214
Ratanapaññā (monk), 218
Rātchakuson, Bā, 377n5
Rātchasang, Bā, 377n5
rational action, 42, 322-5, 391n6
rationalist path, 135, 139-41, 161, 258-9, 307
rationality: formal (instrumental), 45, 391n6; substantive (absolutist), 391n6
Rattanakosin celebrations, 239-40
rebellions: charisma as stimulus for, 326
rebirth, 26, 119, 121, 313, 384n15
"recollection of past lives," 26, 47-8, 49
recollections: ten kinds of, 39
reflection, 14
refuse-rag-wearer's practice, 33, 34
regalia, 6, 241, 335
relic basket (*karanduva*), 74
relic shrine (Mahādhātu), 72
relics, 5, 6, 127, 130-1, 200-5, 387n32; Acharn Mun's ashes, 109-10; *see also* Buddha relics
religion (*sāsana*), 5, 7, 54, 56, 112, 118, 119; Burmese, 315-16; cognitive-emotional dichotomy in, 324-5; learning as basis of,

354n3; organizational structure of, 57; primitive, 323; propagation of, 159, 162, 170, 237
religiosity, popular, 140-1, 168-82, 185, 196, 305; and forest monks, 284, 287
religious authorities: propagation of religion by, 159
religious change, 8
religious charisma, 325-7, 330-2; *see also* charisma
religious specialization, 221, 358n4; polarization in, 135-9, 160
remembrance of past, 389n56
reminders, 231, 254, 335, 387n32
reminders by association (*paribhogika, paribhogacetiya*), 201, 202
renouncer(s), 125, 318; authenticity of, 128-9
renouncer saint (*arahant*), 126, 127; see also *arahant(s)*
renunciation quest, 330
"reserved points" (*avyākṛtavastu*), 21
"restraint of the faculties," 31, 32
Revata, 16
Reynolds, Frank E., 115, 206, 365n10
Rhys Davids, Mrs. C. A. F., 70
Rhys Davids, T. W., 13, 115, 357n39
right livelihood, 31
righteous ruler (*dharmarāja*), 306, 319, 332
ritual acts, 119, 139, 273, 316, 346; transformed into militancy, 318-19
ritual articles (*khrūēang sakkāra*), 245
robe (resource of monastic life), 18
royal ordinations, 157-8, 159-60, 368n4
royal sponsorship: of monks, hermitages, 155, 157-8, 163, 184, 189, 265; of religion, 162, 165-6; of Thammayut sect, 187-8, 189
"royal vocabulary" (*rājāśabda*), 196
Rūang, Phra, 223
*rūēsī* (*ṛṣi*) (holy men), 69, 119, 295-6
ruler(s): *brahman* and *kṣatriya*, 2; lack of stable dynasties, 241; *see also* kings
*rūpa brahma loka*, 50, 51
rūpakāya, 206

*Sā Sapdā* (Glorious Week) (journal), 81
sacralization, 203, 230; of amulets, 154, 200, 258, 260-5; process of, 243-57
sacralized water, 138, 196
sacred cord, 245, 247, 248, 260
sacred formula (*gāthā*), 196
sacred knowledge, 119, 129-31
sacred objects, 196, 203-4; fetishism of, 335-47
sacred words (*sēk khāthā*), 243
sacrifice, 119

409

# Index

Saddharmaratna-karaya (compendium), 376n23
Sahlins, Marshall, 340
Sai amulets, 226
saintliness: savior/mystical traditions, 305–6, 307
saints, see arahant(s)
sakadāgāmins, 13
Sakka (Indra) (deity), 29, 50, 100, 122
Sakon Nakhon (town), 91
Śākyamunibuddhacarita, 115
sālā, 144, 145
Sālikā khū amulets, 226
salvation, 20, 27
salvation Path, 207, 335
salvation quest, 15
salvation religions, 324
Sām Fāng Kāen, king, 67
Sambhoga-Kāya (beatific body), 205, 206
Samgha Sametgyi Association, 309
Sammana-Phala Sutta, 20
sammasāmbuddha (complete Buddha), 12, 14
Samnak Pū Sawan (place), 379n30
Samnak Song Āranyawiwēk, 271
saṃvega, 88, 97
Sangarajavata, 361n5
saṅgha (order of monks), 1, 16, 41, 99, 120, 190, 355n16, 370n19; administrative organization of, 57–8, 70–1, 166–7, 186–7; Burmese, 62, 63, 64, 65; Council of Elders (Mahāthērasamākhom), 157, 167, 186, 187, 189, 393n17; custodian of Buddhist doctrine, 118, 119, 206; declining legitimacy of, 345, 346; disciplined social relations, 347; "disestablishment" of by British in Burma, 308; duality of vocations in, 2–3, 53–4, 72, 73, 160, 165, 259; Ecclesiastical Assembly, 187; Ecclesiastical Cabinet (Khana Sangkhamontrī), 170; exploited by government, 186–7; internal differentiation, 191; as "merit field" (puññakkhetta), 54; missionary efforts by, 156, 184; national, 70, 160, 162–3; opposition to, by Sīwichai, 302, 303–4; politics of, 155; predominantly Northeastern monks, 177, 183, 188; Prince Pavaret head of, 370n18; reform of, 161, 162 (see also monastic reform); reformist orthodoxy radiated out from Bangkok, 221; relation with forest monks, 163–4, 259–60; relation with kingship, 2; relation with laity, 76–7; relation with political authority, 185; restraint by rules of (Pāṭimokkha), 31; royal patronage of, 165–6; sacralization by, 344; sectarian rivalry within, 155 (see also sectarianism); unified, hierarchization, 317
saṅgha, establishment, 17, 20; Acharn Chā and, 138; activities of, 169; contrasted with social field of forest saint, 333–4; cooperation with

government, 393n17; crisis of, 128; triadic relation with king and forest monks, 72–5
Saṅgha Act of 1902, 71, 162
Saṅgha Act of 1941, 186, 187, 370n22
Saṅgha Act of 1963, 186, 187
saṅgha hierarchy, 99, 379n33; and dhūtaṅga monks, 129; forest-order communities in, 71
saṅgharāja, 333
Saṅgharāja Sadhucariyāva, 361n5
Sankatayān, Somdet Phra Ariyawong, 261
sannyāsi, 32
Sanphasitiprasong, prince, 312
Sao, Phra Acharn, 85–6, 105
Sao Kaṇtasilo, Phra Acharn, 83
Saraṇaṃkara, Vālvita, 53, 58, 70, 111–12
Sarika Cave, 87–90, 91
Śāriputra (disciple of Buddha), 15, 16, 19, 21, 22, 101, 116, 122, 354n12, 360n22, 363n24; mortuary rites, 366n14
Sāriputta, Thera, 120
Sarit, prime minister, 166–7, 183, 187, 370–1n22, 375n5
Sarkisyanz, E., 309
Sarn, Phra, 98
Sarvāstivadin school, 363n24
Sāsanāsobhana, Phra (Phra Cham), 213
Sāsanavaṃsa (Paññasāmi), 62, 364n25
Śāsta, Phra Srī, 212
Sathimmajotika (monk), 172
Satipaṭṭhānasutta, 38, 175
Savage Mind, The (Lévi-Strauss), 118
Saya San rebellion (Burma), 307–10, 311, 312, 317
Sayadaw, Mahasi, 172, 175, 177
Sayadaw, Sankin, 65
Sayadaw, Shangalegyun, 64
Sayadaw, Shwegyin, 64–5
Sayadaw, Taungdaw, 65
schisms, 117, 118, 119, 120, 304
scholar monks, scholarship (ganthadhura) (vocation), 7, 8, 70; see also study (pariyatti) (vocation)
Scott, James C., 309, 310
sectarianism, 5, 67, 308; Burma, 63; resurgence of, 187–91; and sponsorship of meditation, 154–67; weakened Thammathūt program, 186–7
sekhamuni, 12
self-mortification, 17–18
self-ordination, 60–1
Sena II, 56
Seng, Lūang Phāū, 228
sexual energy: transmitted into siddhi, 382–3n14
sexuality, 351n13
Sgaw Karen, 296
shifter (concept), 4

410

# Index

# Index

Tambiah, Stanley Jeyaraja: *World Conqueror and World Renouncer*, 1, 2, 57

*tamnān* (literary genre), 119, 121, 364n25, n28

*Tamnān* chronicle, 357n37

*Tamnān Mūlasānā Wat Sūan Dāūk* (chronicle), 67

*Tamnān Mūnlasātsanā (Mūlasāsanā)*, 121

tantric pole (path), 135–6, 138, 139–41, 258–9, 265, 272–3, 307

Tāpasa Movement, 60–1

*tapassi* (hermit or ascetic), 54

Tathāgata, 14, 98

*Tāvatimsa* (celestial realm), 50, 100

teachers, 119; *arahants* as, 27; importance of, in meditation, 41, 43, 85, 86, 102; *see also* meditation masters

Telakhon sect, 386n19

telepathic communication, 272

temperament: and meditation, 39, 41, 151

Temple of the Tooth, 61

temple slaves (*khā-phra*), 69, 70

temples, 69–70, 304

"Ten Corruptions of Insight, The," 43, 44

"ten great disciples," 22

ten precepts (the), 31

"ten signs" (*nimitta*), 43, 44

Tertullian, 125–6

Thai civilization: continuity of, 212

Thai dynasty: forest monks participation in, 66–9

Thailand, 1, 2, 53, 118, 121; *arahant* ideal in, 26; biographies of monks in, 111–12; Buddhism in, 120, 123; center-periphery dialectic in, 155, 183–91; centralization, 381n1; crisis of legitimacy in, 128–9, 344–6; democratization of, 166; Department of Religious Affairs, 184, 186, 373n6; division of *sangha*, 165; Emerald Buddha palladium of, 214, 239; forest-monk tradition in, 3, 4, 54, 66–77; government exploitation of *sangha*, 186–7; government patronage of established *sangha*, 128; millennial Buddhism in, 6, 293–320; millennial uprisings in, 310–14; Ministry of Education, 374n6; national identity, 233, 263; nationalization, 162, 311–12; revolution of 1932, 162, 187, 295; socioeconomic conditions in, 342–4

*Thammačarik* program, 184

Thammarāt (holy man), 296

Thammasat University, 188

*Thammathūt* programs, 184, 185–6, 359n14

Thammayut (Thammayutika) sect, 5, 53, 70, 71, 81–2, 157, 159, 177, 221, 268, 271, 280, 368n5, 370n18, n19; administrative organization of, 156; central committee, 187; discipline in, 138; elitist, 188; internal differentiation, 164–6; monasteries of, 370n20; politics of, 370–1n22; press, 158, 161, 189; promotion of cult of forest saints, 187; reform efforts, 305, 306; rivalry with Mahānikāi sect, 154, 156, 159–67, 186–7, 187–91; sponsorship of provincial "saints," 155; village- and town-dwelling monks in, 259; Wat Bovonniwet central *wat* of, 220

Thamnamnao cave, 286

Thanitpisanbutr, Khun, 276

Thatanadara (monk), 62

*Thathana Linkara Sadan*, 62

Thein, U. Sae, 308

Theosophists, 7, 59

Thephasadin, Gen. Yod, 260

Thepsiddhimuni, Phra, 169, 170, 171, 176–81, 183–4

*Thera-gāthā*, 21, 22, 39

*theras* (elders), 118

Theravāda Buddhism, 1, 2, 17, 19, 24, 26, 28, 200, 231; Buddha's bodies, 206; Buddha's image in, 203; doctrine of presence in, 204, 205; revival of, 66

Theravāda School, 38, 115

*Therī-gāthā*, 21, 22, 39

Thet, Phra, 98

*theyyasamvāsaka*, 60

Thibaw, king, 65

Third Council, 57, 118, 206

Third World, 344

Thirty-three (the), 51

Thīwali (Sīvali thera), Shin, 24–5

Thomas, E. J., 115, 363n23

Thompson, Virginia, 304

Thonburī (city), 71

Three Councils (the), 120, 122

Three Jewels (the), 49; *see also* Triple Gem

Thudhamma (sect), 63, 65

Thudhamma Council, 64

tiger symbolism, 284

Tilakapanattu, king, 232

Tilok (Tilokarāja), king, 216, 218, 232, 238, 378n16

Tipañña, king, 235

*Tipiṭaka* (Pali) ("three baskets"), 28, 29, 54, 67, 115; codification of, 120

Tissa, Mogalliputta, 57, 118, 120

Tō, Somdet, 71–2, 219–20, 221–2, 379n33

tooth relic festival, 73–4

Touen-houang, caves of, 22

tradition, 323, 346, 347

Trailōkanāt, King Borom, 211

*Traiphūm* (treatise), 161, 294

Traipidok, Somdet Phra Sītham, 210–11

tranquility (mental state), 41, 324

transcendence, state of, 335

transcendental claims, 325

412

# Index

# Index

# CAMBRIDGE STUDIES IN SOCIAL ANTHROPOLOGY

*Editor*: Jack Goody

416

* Also available as a paperback

417

## DATE DUE

| | | | |
|---|---|---|---|
| | | | |
| | | | |
| | | | |
| | | | |
| | | | |
| | | | |
| | | | |
| | | | |
| | | | |
| | | | |
| | | | |
| | | | |
| | | | |
| | | | |
| | | | |
| | | | |
| | | | |
| | | | |